LEADERSHIP

Richard L. Daft
Owen Graduate School of Management
Vanderbilt University

With the assistance of
Patricia G. Lane

SOUTH-WESTERN
CENGAGE Learning™

Australia • Brazil • Japan • Korea • Mexico • Singapore • Spain • United Kingdom • United States

SOUTH-WESTERN
CENGAGE Learning™

Leadership, Fifth Edition
Richard L. Daft
With the assistance of Patricia G. Lane

Vice President of Editorial, Business:
  Jack W. Calhoun

Vice President/Editor-in-Chief:
  Melissa Acuña

Executive Editor: Scott Person

Developmental Editor: Erin Guendelsberger

Marketing Manager: Clinton Kernen

Marketing Coordinator: Julia Tucker

Senior Content Project Manager:
  Colleen A. Farmer

Media Editor: Rob Ellington

Frontlist Buyer, Manufacturing:
  Arethea Thomas

Production Service and Compositor:
  S4Carlisle Publishing Services

Copyeditor: Rebecca Roby

Senior Art Director: Tippy McIntosh

Internal and Cover Designer:
  Kim Torbeck, Patti Hudepohl

Photo Credits:

Cover Image: Shutterstock

B/W Image: Comstock Images

Sr. Text Rights Acquisitions Account Manager:
  Mardell Glinski Schultz

Text Permissions Researcher:
  Karyn Morrison

© 2011, 2008 South-Western, Cengage Learning

ALL RIGHTS RESERVED. No part of this work covered by the copyright herein may be reproduced, transmitted, stored, or used in any form or by any means graphic, electronic, or mechanical, including but not limited to photocopying, recording, scanning, digitizing, taping, web distribution, information networks, or information storage and retrieval systems, except as permitted under Section 107 or 108 of the 1976 United States Copyright Act, without the prior written permission of the publisher.

For product information and technology assistance, contact us at **Cengage Learning Customer & Sales Support, 1-800-354-9706**

For permission to use material from this text or product, submit all requests online at **www.cengage.com/permissions** Further permissions questions can be emailed to **permissionrequest@cengage.com**

Exam*View*® is a registered trademark of eInstruction Corp. Windows is a registered trademark of the Microsoft Corporation used herein under license. Macintosh and Power Macintosh are registered trademarks of Apple Computer, Inc. used herein under license.

© 2008 Cengage Learning. All Rights Reserved.

Cengage Learning WebTutor™ is a trademark of Cengage Learning.

Library of Congress Control Number: 2009942042

International Student Edition ISBN-13: 978-0-538-46828-2
International Student Edition ISBN-10: 0-538-46828-9

Cengage Learning International Offices

Asia
cengageasia.com
tel: (65) 6410 1200

Australia/New Zealand
cengage.com.au
tel: (61) 3 9685 4111

Brazil
cengage.com.br
tel: (011) 3665 9900

India
cengage.co.in
tel: (91) 11 30484837/38

Latin America
cengage.com.mx
tel: +52 (55) 1500 6000

UK/Europe/Middle East/Africa
cengage.co.uk
tel: (44) 207 067 2500

Represented in Canada by Nelson Education, Ltd.
nelson.com
tel: (416) 752 9100 / (800) 668 0671

For product information: **www.cengage.com/international**
Visit your local office: **www.cengage.com/global**
Visit our corporate website: **www.cengage.com**

Availability of resources may differ by region. Check with your local Cengage Learning representative for details.

Printed in China by China Translation & Printing Services Limited
2 3 4 5 6 7 13 12 11 10

*To the spiritual leaders who shaped my growth
and development as a leader and as a human being.*

BRIEF CONTENTS

CONTENTS

Part 3: The Personal Side of Leadership   85

Part 4: The Leader as a Relationship Builder 197

Part 5: The Leader as Social Architect   347

Richard L. Daft, Ph.D., is the Brownlee O. Currey, Jr., Professor of Management in the Owen Graduate School of Management at Vanderbilt University. Professor Daft specializes in the study of leadership and organization theory. Dr. Daft is a Fellow of the Academy of Management and has served on the editorial boards of *Academy of Management Journal, Administrative Science Quarterly,* and *Journal of Management Education.* He was the Associate Editor-in-Chief of *Organization Science* and served for three years as Associate Editor of *Administrative Science Quarterly.*

Professor Daft has authored or coauthored 13 books, including *Organization Theory and Design* (South-Western, 2010), *Management* (South-Western, 2010), and *What to Study: Generating and Developing Research Questions* (Sage, 1982). He coauthored, with Robert Lengel, *Fusion Leadership: Unlocking the Subtle Forces That Change People and Organizations* (Berrett-Koehler, 2000). His most recent book, *The Executive and the Elephant,* will be available in 2010 (Jossey-Bass). He has also authored dozens of scholarly articles, papers, and chapters. His work has been published in *Administrative Science Quarterly, Academy of Management Journal, Academy of Management Review, Strategic Management Journal, Journal of Management, Accounting Organizations and Society, Management Science, MIS Quarterly, California Management Review,* and *Organizational Behavior Teaching Review.* Professor Daft has been awarded several government research grants to pursue studies of organization design, organizational innovation and change, strategy implementation, and organizational information processing.

Dr. Daft also is an active teacher and consultant. He has taught management, leadership, organizational change, organizational theory, and organizational behavior. He has served as associate dean, produced for-profit theatrical productions, and helped manage a start-up enterprise. He has been involved in management development and consulting for many companies and government organizations including the American Banking Association, AutoZone, Bell Canada, Nortel, Bridgestone, TVA, Pratt & Whitney, Allstate Insurance, State Farm Insurance, the United States Air Force, the U.S. Army, J. C. Bradford & Co., Central Parking System, USAA, Bristol-Myers Squibb, First American National Bank, and the Vanderbilt University Medical Center.

Many leaders have recently had their assumptions challenged about how organizations work. The crisis in the housing, mortgage, and finance industries and resulting recession, the failures of several large long-standing organizations and the government bailout of others, volatile oil prices, ethical scandals, political turmoil, and other events have dramatically shifted the organizational and economic landscape. Leaders are struggling to make sense of the shifting environment and learn how to lead effectively and successfully in the midst of turmoil. This edition of *Leadership* addresses themes and issues that are directly relevant to the current turbulent environment. My vision for the fifth edition is to give students an exciting, applied, and comprehensive view of what leadership is like in today's world. *Leadership* integrates recent ideas and applications with established scholarly research in a way that makes the topic of leadership come alive. Organizations are undergoing major changes, and this textbook addresses the qualities and skills leaders need in this rapidly evolving world.

Recent chaotic events, combined with factors such as a growing need for creativity and innovation in organizations, the emergence of e-business, the use of virtual teams, globalization, and other ongoing transformations, place new demands on leaders that go far beyond the topics traditionally taught in courses on management or organizational behavior. My experiences teaching leadership to students and managers, and working with leaders to change their organizations, have affirmed for me the value of traditional leadership concepts, while highlighting the importance of including new ideas and applications.

Leadership thoroughly covers the history of leadership studies and the traditional theories, but goes beyond that to incorporate valuable ideas such as leadership vision, shaping culture and values, leadership courage, and the importance of moral leadership. The book expands the treatment of leadership to capture the excitement of the subject in a way that motivates students and challenges them to develop their leadership potential.

New to the Fifth Edition

A primary focus for revising *Leadership*, fifth edition, has been to relate leadership concepts and theories to events in today's turbulent environment. Each chapter has been thoroughly revised and updated to bring in current issues that leaders face. Sections that are particularly relevant to fast-shifting current events have been marked with a "Turbulent Times" icon.

Topics that have been added or expanded in the fifth edition include the Wall Street meltdown; developing leadership courage as a skill; appreciative

Availability of resources may differ by region. Check with your local Cengage Learning representative for details.

inquiry; soft versus hard power; leadership coaching; operational, collaborative, and advisory leadership roles; coalitional leadership; understanding one's leadership strengths; entrepreneurial leadership; leading diverse people and people with varied personalities; enhancing emotional intelligence; the Johari Window framework; nonverbal communication; the dilemma of teamwork; the team leader's role in shaping norms; leading virtual teams; leader frames of reference; open innovation; and building ethical corporate cultures. The book also includes several new cases for analysis that are related to current issues.

   Leadership continues to offer students great opportunities for self-assessment and leadership development. An important aspect of learning to be a leader involves looking inward for greater self-understanding, and the fifth edition provides numerous opportunities for this reflection. Each chapter includes multiple questionnaires or exercises that enable students to learn about their own leadership beliefs, values, competencies, and skills. These exercises help students gauge their current standing and connect the chapter concepts and examples to ideas for expanding their own leadership abilities. A few of the self-assessment topics are innovation, networking, personality traits, leading diverse people, developing a personal vision, spiritual leadership, leadership courage, and leading with love versus leading with fear. Self-assessments related to basic leadership abilities such as listening skills, emotional intelligence, motivating others, and using power and influence are also included.

Organization

The organization of the book is based on first understanding basic ways in which leaders differ from managers, and the ways leaders set direction, seek alignment between organizations and followers, build relationships, and create change. Thus the organization of this book is in five parts:

1. Introduction to Leadership
2. Research Perspectives on Leadership
3. The Personal Side of Leadership
4. The Leader as a Relationship Builder
5. The Leader as Social Architect

The book integrates materials from both micro and macro approaches to leadership, from both academia and the real world, and from traditional ideas and recent thinking.

Distinguishing Features

This book has a number of special features that are designed to make the material accessible and valuable to students.

Turbulent Times This new feature calls attention to examples, book reviews, or topics that are related to current issues leaders face in today's fast-shifting and uncertain world.

In the Lead *Leadership* is loaded with new examples of leaders inboth traditional and contemporary organizations. Each chapter opens with a real-life example that relates to the chapter content, and several additional examples are highlighted within each chapter. These spotlight examples are drawn from a wide variety of organizations including education, the military, government agencies, businesses, and nonprofit organizations.

Consider This! Each chapter contains a Consider This! box that is personal, compelling, and inspiring. This box may be a saying from a famous leader, or wisdom from the ages. These Consider This! boxes provide novel and interesting material to expand the reader's thinking about the leadership experience.

Leader's Bookshelf Each chapter also includes a review of a recent book relevant to the chapter's content. The Leader's Bookshelf connects students to issues and topics being read and discussed in the worlds of academia, business, military, education, and nonprofit organizations.

Action Memo This margin feature helps students apply the chapter concepts in their own lives and leadership activities, as well as directs students to self-assessments related to various chapter topics.

Leader's Self-Insight boxes provide self-assessments for learners and an opportunity to experience leadership issues in a personal way. These exercises take the form of questionnaires, scenarios, and activities.

Student Development Each chapter ends with Discussion Questions and then activities for student development. **Leadership at Work**, is a practical, skill-building activity that engages the student in applying chapter concepts to real-life leadership. These exercises are designed so students can complete them on their own outside of class or in class as part of a group activity. Instructor tips are given for maximizing in-class learning with the Leadership at Work exercises. At the end of the book are **Leadership Development—Cases for Analysis**, which provides two short, problem-oriented cases for analysis. These cases test the student's ability to apply concepts when dealing with real-life leadership issues. The cases challenge the student's cognitive understanding of leadership ideas while the Leadership at Work exercises and the feedback questionnaires assess the student's progress as a leader.

Ancillaries

This edition offers a wider range than previous editions of instructor ancillaries to fully enable instructors to bring the leadership experience into the classroom. These ancillaries include:

Instructor's Manual with Test Bank

A comprehensive Instructor's Manual and Test Bank is available to assist in lecture preparation. Included in the Instructor's Manual are the chapter outlines, suggested answers to end-of-chapter materials, and suggestions for further study. The Test Bank includes approximately 60 questions per chapter to assist in writing examinations. Types of questions include true/false, multiple choice, completion, short-answer, and essay. For this edition, we've doubled the number of multiple-choice questions.

ExamView

The ExamView contains all of the questions in the printed test bank. This program is an easy-to-use test creation software compatible with Windows or Macintosh. Instructors can add or edit questions, instructions, and answers, and select questions (randomly or numerically) by previewing them on the screen.

PowerPoint Lecture Presentation

An asset to any instructor, the lectures provide outlines for every chapter, graphics of the illustrations from the text, and additional examples providing instructors with a number of learning opportunities for students.

Videos

Videos compiled specifically to accompany *Leadership,* fifth edition, use real-world companies to illustrate international business concepts as outlined in the text. Focusing on both small and large businesses, the videos give students an inside perspective on the situations and issues that global corporations face.

Companion Web site (www.cengage.com/international)

Leadership's Web site provides a multitude of resources for both instructors and students.

Premium Web site (www.cengage.com/login)

This new optional Premium Web site features text-specific resources that enhance student learning by bringing concepts to life. Dynamic interactive learning tools include online quizzes, flashcards, PowerPoint slides, learning games, and more.

Acknowledgments

Textbook writing is a team enterprise. This book has integrated ideas and support from many people whom I want to acknowledge. I want to extend special thanks to my editorial associate, Pat Lane. I could not have undertaken this revision without Pat's help. She skillfully drafted materials for the chapters, found original sources, and did an outstanding job with last-minute changes, the copyedited manuscript, art, and galley proofs. Pat's talent and personal enthusiasm for this text added greatly to its excellence.

Here at Vanderbilt I want to thank my assistant, Barbara Haselton, for the tremendous volume and quality of work she accomplished on my behalf that gave me time to write. Jim Bradford, the Dean at Owen, and Dawn Iacobucci, the Senior Associate Dean, have maintained a positive scholarly atmosphere and supported me with the time and resources to complete the revision of this book. I also appreciate the intellectual stimulation and support from friends and colleagues at the Owen School—Bruce Barry, Ray Friedman, Neta Moye, Rich Oliver, David Owens, Ranga Ramanujam, Bart Victor, and Tim Vogus.

I want to acknowledge the reviewers who provided feedback. Their ideas helped me improve the book in many areas:

Thomas H. Arcy
University of Houston—Central Campus

Janey Ayres
Purdue University

Kristin Backhaus
SUNY New Paltz

William Russell Brown
Navarro College

Glenn K. Cunningham
Duquesne University

Delia J. Haak
John Brown University

Ann Horn-Jeddy
Medaille College

Gregory Manora
Auburn University–Montgomery

Richard T. Martin
Washburn University

Ranjna Patel
Bethune Cookman College

Gordon Riggles
University of Colorado

Dan Sherman
University of Alabama at Huntsville

Shane Spiller
University of Montevallo

Ahmad Tootonchi
Frostburg State University

Joseph W. Weiss
Bentley University

Donald D. White
University of Arkansas

George A. Wynn
University of Tampa

Bill Bommer
Georgia State University

Jared Caughron
University of Oklahoma

Ron Franzen
Saint Luke's Hospital

Nell Hartley
Robert Morris College

Ellen Jordan
Mount Olive College

Joseph Martelli
The University of Findlay

Mark Nagel
Normandale Community College

Chad Peterson
Baylor University

Bill Service
Samford University

Bret Simmons
North Dakota State University

Shand H. Stringham
Duquesne University

Mary L. Tucker
Ohio University

Xavier Whitaker
Baylor University

Jean Wilson
The College of William and Mary

The editors at South-Western also deserve special mention. Scott Person and Joe Sabatino, Executive Editors, supported the concept for this book and obtained the resources necessary for its completion. Erin Guendelsberger, Developmental Editor, provided terrific support for the book's writing, reviews, and production. Colleen Farmer, Senior Content Project Manager, smoothly took the book through the production process. Tippy McIntosh, Art Director, created the design for the fifth edition. Clinton Kernen, Marketing Manager, led the marketing efforts for the book.

I also thank Bob Lengel, at the University of Texas at San Antonio. Bob's enthusiasm for leadership many years ago stimulated me to begin reading, teaching, and training in the area of leadership development. His enthusiasm also led to our collaboration on the book *Fusion Leadership: Unlocking the Subtle Forces That Change People and Organizations*. I thank Bob for keeping our shared leadership dream alive, which in time enabled me to pursue my dream of writing this leadership textbook.

Finally, I want to acknowledge my loving family. I received much love and support from my wife, Dorothy Marcic, and daughters Danielle, Amy, Roxanne, Solange, and Elizabeth. Although everyone is now pursuing their own lives and careers, I appreciate the good feelings and connections with my children and grandchildren. On occasion, we have been able to travel, ski, watch a play, or just be together—all of which reconnect me to the things that really count.

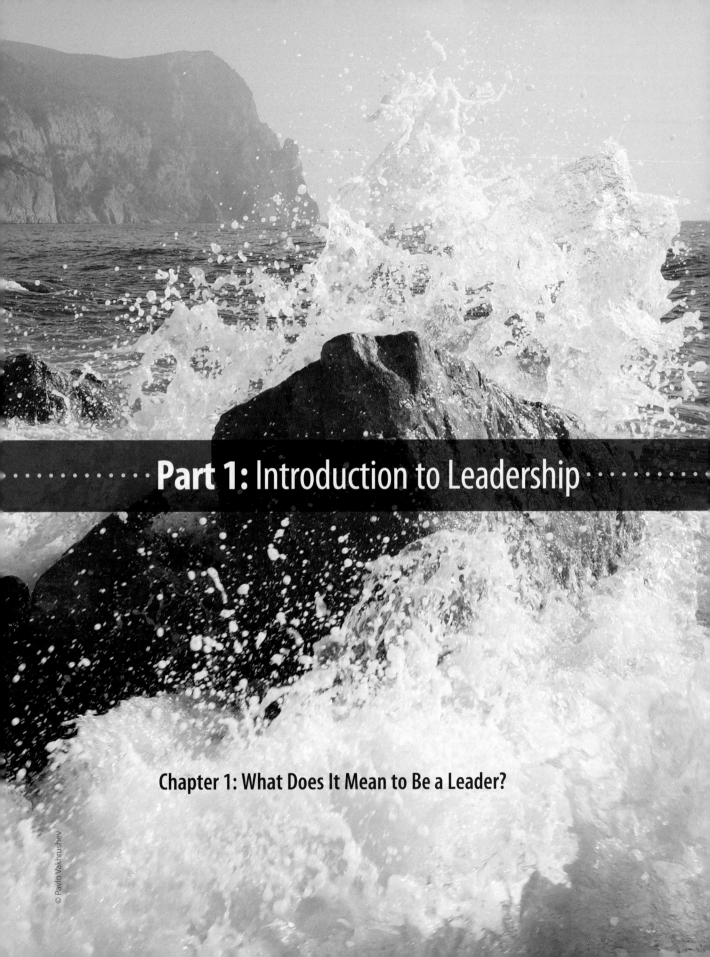

Part 1: Introduction to Leadership

Chapter 1: What Does It Mean to Be a Leader?

© Pavlo Vakhrushev

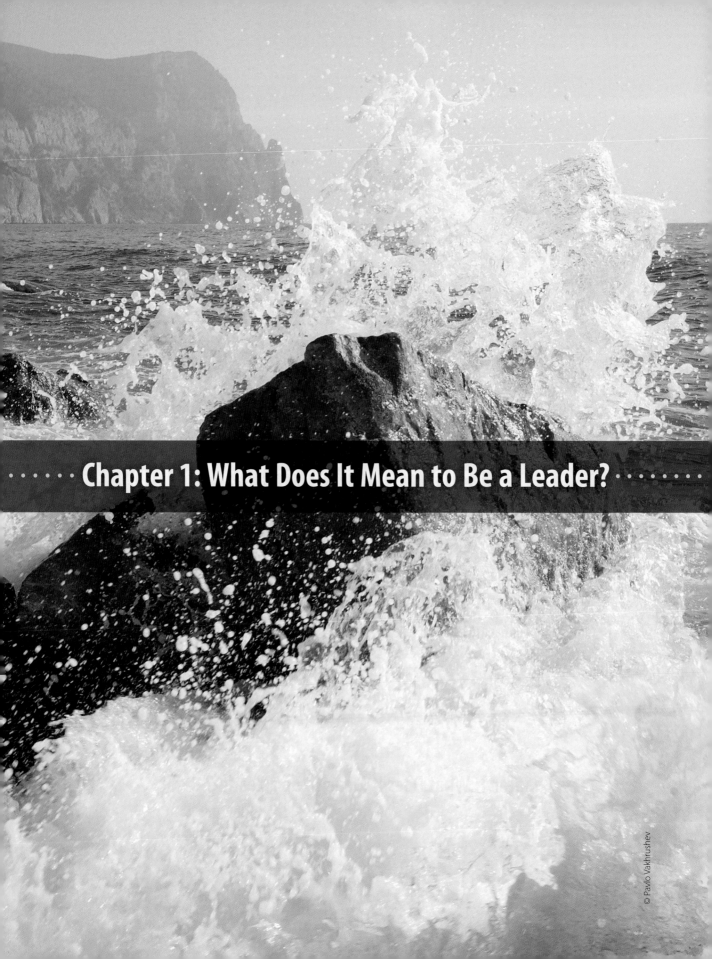

Chapter 1: What Does It Mean to Be a Leader?

© Pavlo Vakhrushev

Your Leadership Challenge

After studying this chapter, you should be able to:

- Understand the full meaning of leadership and see the leadership potential in yourself and others.

- Recognize and facilitate the six fundamental transformations in today's organizations and leaders.

- Identify the primary reasons for leadership derailment and the new paradigm skills that can help you avoid it.

- Recognize the traditional functions of management and the fundamental differences between leadership and management.

- Appreciate the crucial importance of providing direction, alignment, relationships, personal qualities, and outcomes.

- Explain how leadership has evolved and how historical approaches apply to the practice of leadership today.

Chapter Outline

The first thing Charles O. Holliday did when he landed in the United States after meeting with a major customer in Japan was call his top leadership team to an emergency meeting. It was early October 2008, and the DuPont Company CEO had a bad feeling. The Japanese executive Holliday had met with said he ordered all his managers to start conserving cash in case the spreading financial crisis affected his company's ability to raise capital. Holliday heard the wake-up call—the financial industry's problems were going to pervade every business in every industry and dramatically hurt DuPont's sales. Holliday took immediate steps to make sure everyone throughout DuPont got the message as well. Within a few weeks, every single employee had had a face-to-face meeting with a manager who explained the gathering financial storm, how it was affecting DuPont's business, what leaders were doing to cushion the company and its people, and what employees needed to be doing to help. After the meetings, leaders conducted polls to see how people were feeling. Were they scared? Energized? Confused? Were they ready to meet the challenges facing them?[1] Thanks to Holliday's ability to face reality and energize his leadership team and the entire organization, DuPont has weathered the recent global economic maelstrom better than many other companies.

Referring to the economic situation in March 2009, David Rothkopf wrote in *The Washington Post*, "This is not just a global economic crisis. It is a global leadership crisis."[2] Yet, as the example of Charles Holliday illustrates, there are leaders who have risen to the challenge. Holliday was set to retire at the end of

2008. He could have coasted through his last few months and left the problem for his successor, Ellen Kullman, to cope with on her own. But Holliday has long been recognized as a leader who understands the importance of doing the right thing rather than the easiest thing. "Just saying you're ethical isn't very useful," Holliday once stated. "You have to earn trust by what you do every day."[3] In addition to group meetings, Holliday took the time to meet individually with each of the company's top 14 executives to discuss the crisis and how to make sure DuPont would survive it and come out stronger on the other side.

Do you have the capacity and commitment required for taking a leadership role in your school, community, or workplace? What does it mean to be a leader? For many people, leadership stems from a desire to make a difference in the lives of others and the world. It means believing in yourself and those you work with, loving what you do, and infusing others with energy and enthusiasm to accomplish a vision for a better future. There are leaders making a difference every day, not only in businesses like DuPont but in nonprofit organizations, the military, educational systems and governmental agencies, sports teams and volunteer committees, big cities and small rural communities, as well.

When many people think of leaders, they recall great historical figures such as Abraham Lincoln, Napoleon, and Alexander the Great, or they think of "big names" in the news, such as U.S. President Barack Obama or former General Electric CEO Jack Welch, who still commands a spotlight years after his retirement. Yet there are leaders working in every organization, large and small. In fact, leadership is all around us every day, in all facets of our lives—our families, schools, communities, churches, social clubs, and volunteer organizations, as well as in the world of business, sports, and the military.

For example, Captain Chesley B. "Sully" Sullenberger made the news in January 2009 by successfully landing U.S. Airways flight 1549 on the Hudson River. He was called a hero for his leadership of the flight crew that saved the lives of 155 passengers and crew. But the 58-year-old Sullenberger had been quietly acting as a leader in anonymity for most of his adult life, first as an Air Force fighter pilot, where he attained the rank of captain, and later as a commercial pilot, flight instructor, safety consultant, volunteer committee officer, and accident investigator. His first public comment after the accident? "I know I can speak for the entire crew when I tell you we were simply doing the job we were trained to do." One police officer on the scene of the accident said, "That guy is one cool customer. He... was behaving like it was just another day at the office."[4] The primary qualities that make a good leader are similar whether one is leading a flight crew, a military unit, a basketball team, a volunteer group, a small company, or a huge international corporation.

The Nature of Leadership

Before we can examine what makes an effective leader, we need to know what leadership means. Leadership has been a topic of interest to historians and philosophers since ancient times, but scientific studies began only in the twentieth century. Scholars and other writers have offered hundreds of definitions of the term *leadership,* and one authority on the subject has concluded that leadership "is one of the most observed and least understood phenomena on earth."[5] Defining leadership has been a complex and elusive problem largely because the nature of leadership itself is complex. Some have even suggested that leadership is nothing more than a romantic myth, perhaps based on the false hope that someone will come along and solve our problems by sheer force of will.[6]

There is some evidence that people do pin their hopes on leaders in ways that are not always realistic. Think about how some struggling companies recruit well-known, charismatic CEOs and invest tremendous hopes in them, only to find that their problems actually get worse.[7] For example, Robert Nardelli was hailed as a brilliant leader when he took over as CEO of The Home Depot, and expectations were great. Nardelli's years as an executive working under Jack Welch at General Electric and his assertive, outgoing personality had given him celebrity status in the business world. Unfortunately, although Nardelli's leadership brought some quick gains, implementing many of his plans turned out to cause even more problems for the company. Unhappy shareholders, concerns over Nardelli's exorbitant pay package, and other issues led Nardelli and the board to mutually agree to his resignation.[8] Whether Nardelli got more or less blame than he deserved for Home Depot's problems is debatable, but the example serves to illustrate the unrealistic expectations people often have of "larger-than-life" leaders.

Particularly when times are tough, people often look to a grand, heroic type of leader to alleviate fear and uncertainty. As Bill George, a professor at Harvard Business School and former chair and CEO of Medtronic, put it, people "fall into the trap of choosing leaders for their style rather than their substance, for their image instead of their integrity."[9] In recent years, the romantic or heroic view of leadership has been challenged.[10] Much progress has been made in understanding the essential nature of leadership as a real and powerful influence in organizations and societies.

Definition of Leadership

Leadership studies are an evolving discipline and the concept of leadership will continue to develop. For the purpose of this book, we will focus on a single definition that delineates the essential elements of the leadership process: **Leadership is an influence relationship among leaders and followers who intend real changes and outcomes that reflect their shared purposes.**[11]

Exhibit 1.1 summarizes the key elements in this definition. Leadership involves influence, it occurs among people, those people intentionally desire significant changes, and the changes reflect purposes shared by leaders and followers. *Influence* means that the relationship among people is not passive;

Leadership
an influence relationship among leaders and followers who intend real changes and outcomes that reflect their shared purposes

---

Exhibit 1.1 What Leadership Involves

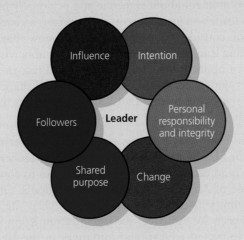

however, also inherent in this definition is the concept that influence is multidi-rectional and noncoercive. The basic cultural values in North America make it easiest to think of leadership as something a leader does to a follower.[12] However, leadership is reciprocal. In most organizations, superiors influence subordinates, but subordinates also influence superiors. The people involved in the relationship want substantive *changes*—leadership involves creating change, not maintaining the status quo. In addition, the changes sought are not dictated by leaders, but reflect *purposes* that leaders and followers share. Moreover, change is toward an outcome that leader and followers both want, a desired future or shared purpose that motivates them toward this more preferable outcome. An important aspect of leadership is influencing others to come together around a common vision. Thus, leadership involves the influence of people to bring about change toward a desirable future.

Also, leadership is a *people* activity and is distinct from administrative paper-work or planning activities. Leadership occurs *among* people; it is not something done *to* people. Since leadership involves people, there must be *followers*. An individual performer who achieves excellence as a scientist, musician, athlete, or woodcarver may be a leader in her field of expertise but is not a leader as defined in this book unless followers are involved. Followers are an important part of the leadership process, and all leaders are sometimes followers as well. Good leaders know how to follow, and they set an example for others. The issue of *intention* or will means that people—leader and followers—are actively involved in the pursuit of change. Each person takes personal responsibility to achieve the desired future.

One stereotype is that leaders are somehow different, that they are above others; however, in reality, the qualities needed for effective leadership are the same as those needed to be an effective follower.[13] Effective followers think for themselves and carry out assignments with energy and enthusiasm. They are committed to something outside their own self-interest, and they have the cour-age to stand up for what they believe. Good followers are not "yes people" who blindly follow a leader. Effective leaders and effective followers may sometimes be the same people, playing different roles at different times. At its best, leader-ship is shared among leaders and followers, with everyone fully engaged and accepting higher levels of responsibility.

Leadership and the Business of Living

Think for a moment about someone you personally have known that you would consider a leader—a grandparent, a supervisor, a coach, or even a fellow student. Perhaps you consider yourself a leader, or know that you want to be one. If we stop equating leadership with greatness and public visibility, it becomes easier to see our own opportunities for leadership and recognize the leadership of people we interact with every day. Leaders come in all shapes and sizes, and many true leaders are working behind the scenes. Leadership that has big outcomes often starts small.

- Wendy Kopp was a senior at Princeton University when she first came up with the idea of a sort of "Peace Corps for teachers," a national organization that would recruit recent college graduates to commit to teach for two years at some of America's toughest public schools. One of her Princeton profes-sors admits he called her "deranged" when she proposed the idea to him. Yet, Teach for America, the organization Kopp started, became one of the most respected educational initiatives in the United States. In 2006, fully

10 percent of the graduating class of Yale University applied to participate in the program.[14]

- After Hurricane Katrina wiped out communities along the Gulf Coast in August 2005, official rescue and relief agencies were woefully slow to respond. In contrast, informal leaders in the community of Villa Platte quickly organized rescue and relief efforts around the slogan, *If not us, then who?* The community, made up of about 11,000 people with an average yearly income of only $5,300, served 5,000 traumatized Katrina victims—rescuing people from rooftops, picking up the dead, transporting the injured to trauma centers, and inviting displaced people to stay in their homes.[15]

- Greg Mortenson had a vision that the best way to fight terrorism was by building secular schools and promoting education, especially for girls, in northern Pakistan and neighboring Afghanistan. He wrote nearly 600 letters and submitted 16 grant applications, but received only one favorable reply—a $100 check from Tom Brokaw. Undeterred, Mortenson sold all his possessions and began appealing to everyday people. Schoolchildren donated hundreds of dollars in pennies, inspiring adults to donate as well. With the $12,000 he eventually raised, Mortenson built his first school in Korphe in 1996. Today, he runs the Central Asia Institute (CAI), which as of 2008 had built 78 schools serving 33,000 students, as well as completed a number of other projects focused on providing potable water, vocational centers for women, and rural health camps. CAI has continued its "Pennies for Peace" project (http://www.penniesforpeace.org) to educate American children about the larger world and show them they can have a positive impact.[16]

- During his five years working as a car salesman, Robert Chambers was disgusted by how some dealers and finance institutions preyed on low-income customers. After he retired from a varied career, the 62-year-old electrical engineer decided to do something about it. He founded Bonnie CLAC (Car Loans and Counseling), which steers low-income people toward buying new, base-model cars at low prices and on good loan terms. With branches in New Hampshire, Vermont, and Maine, Bonnie CLAC has negotiated price and extended warranty deals with a dozen or so auto dealers and worked with banks to provide low interest rates. Bonnie CLAC guarantees the loan, and then works with clients to help them manage their finances.[17]

There are opportunities for leadership all around us that involve influence and change toward a desired goal or outcome. Without leadership, our families and communities, as well as our organizations, would fall apart. The leaders of tomorrow's organizations will come from anywhere and everywhere, just as they always have. You can start now, wherever you are, to practice leadership in your own life. Leadership is an everyday way of acting and thinking that has little to do with a title or formal position in an organization. As we will discuss in the following section, business leaders need to understand this tenet more than ever in the world of the twenty-first century.

Action Memo

As a leader, you can recognize opportunities for leadership and act to influence others and bring about changes for a better future.

The New Reality for Today's Organizations

Globalization. Outsourcing. Shifting geopolitical forces. Advancing technologies. Virtual teams. E-business. People in organizations around the world are feeling the impact of these and other trends and are forced to adapt to new ways of

Exhibit 1.2 The New Reality for Leadership

OLD Paradigm	NEW Paradigm
Stability	Change and crisis management
Control	Empowerment
Competition	Collaboration
Uniformity	Diversity
Self-centered	Higher ethical purpose
Hero	Humble

working. Add to this the recent economic crisis, widespread ethical scandals, global health scares such as the "swine flu" outbreak, and the insecurity associated with war and terrorism, and leaders are facing challenges they couldn't even imagine just a few years ago. In a survey by the Center for Creative Leadership, 84 percent of leaders surveyed say the definition of effective leadership changed significantly within the first few years of the twenty-first century.[18]

Some historians and other scholars believe our world is undergoing a transformation more profound and far-reaching than any experienced since the dawn of the modern age and the Industrial Revolution some 500 years ago. Rapid environmental changes are causing fundamental shifts that have a dramatic impact on organizations and present new challenges for leaders. These shifts represent a transition from a traditional to a new paradigm, as outlined in Exhibit 1.2.[19] A **paradigm** is a shared mindset that represents a fundamental way of thinking about, perceiving, and understanding the world.

Although many leaders are still operating from an old-paradigm mindset, as outlined in the first column of Exhibit 1.2, they are increasingly ineffective. Successful leaders in the twenty-first century will respond to the new reality outlined in the second column of the exhibit.

From Stability to Change and Crisis Management

In the past, many leaders assumed that if they could just keep things running on a steady, even keel, the organization would be successful. Yet today's world is in constant motion, and nothing seems certain anymore. If leaders still had an illusion of stability at the dawn of the twenty-first century, it is surely shattered by now. Consider the following recent events:

- The mortgage and finance industries in the United States suffered a meltdown of historic proportions. After surviving every crisis of the twentieth century, 85-year-old Bear Stearns crashed and disappeared almost overnight early in the twenty-first. Another Wall Street icon, Lehman Brothers, filed for Chapter 11 bankruptcy soon afterward. American International Group (AIG) had to be bailed out by the U.S. government, and Merrill Lynch was saved by becoming part of Bank of America.[20] In the year following these events, almost every firm in the financial services industry was shaken to its core.

- The price of oil skyrocketed in the spring and summer of 2008, catching most businesses as well as consumers by surprise. People altered their buying habits, travel routes, and vacation plans, creating even bigger headaches for organizations already struggling with higher costs. Retailers, airlines, auto makers, food processors, trucking companies, restaurants, school systems, car rental firms, and every other type of organization felt the pinch.

Paradigm
a shared mindset that represents a fundamental way of thinking about, perceiving, and understanding the world

- Following years of declining sales, slipping market share, and mounting costs, General Motors, one of the world's largest companies and long considered central to the U.S. economy, teetered on the brink of collapse and became the second-largest industrial bankruptcy in history.[21]
- China and India emerged from dismal poverty to become the "dragon and the tiger" of global commerce. In the first decade of the twenty-first century, Chinese companies spent around $115 billion on foreign acquisitions, including purchasing Canada's PetroKazakhstan, a 10 percent stake in U.S. based Morgan Stanley, and a 20 percent stake in South Africa's Standard Bank.[22]

Most leaders, whether in business, politics, the military, education, social services, the arts, or the world of sports, recognize that trying to maintain stability in a world of such unexpected and far-reaching change is a losing battle. Today's best leaders accept the inevitability of change and crisis and recognize them as potential sources of energy and self-renewal. Rather than being laid low, they develop effective *crisis management* skills that help their organizations weather the storm and move toward something better. Leaders have to "wake up every morning, go to work, and pave a path to the other side—and a better future."[23] Every company is subject to periods of instability and crisis, and leaders are responsible for helping their organizations renew themselves. Even large successful organizations are subject to decline, and recent events have verified that they can fall hard and fast if leaders make mistakes. This chapter's Leader's Bookshelf on page 10 describes how leaders can help companies avoid the fate that has befallen icons such as Bear Stearns, Lehman Brothers, and General Motors.

From Control to Empowerment

Leaders in powerful positions once thought workers should be told what to do and how to do it. They believed strict control was needed for the organization to function efficiently and effectively. Rigid organizational hierarchies, structured jobs and work processes, and detailed, inviolate procedures let everyone know that those at the top had power and those at the bottom had none.

Today, the old assumptions about the distribution of power are no longer valid. An emphasis on control and rigidity serves to squelch motivation, innovation, and morale rather than produce desired results. Effective leaders share power rather than hoard it and find ways to increase an organization's brainpower by getting everyone in the organization involved and committed.

One reason for this is that the financial basis of today's economy is becoming *information* rather than the tangible assets of land, buildings, and machines. This means human capital is becoming more important than financial capital, which increases the power of employees.[24] When all the organization needed was workers to run machines eight hours a day, traditional command-and-control systems generally worked quite well, but the organization received no benefit from employees' minds. Now, success depends on the intellectual capacity of all employees. One of the leader's most challenging jobs is to enable people to embrace and use their power effectively.[25]

From Competition to Collaboration

Although some companies still encourage internal competition and aggressiveness, most successful organizations stress teamwork, compromise, and cooperation so that all employees can become the best they can be. Self-directed teams and other forms of horizontal collaboration are breaking down boundaries between

Leader's Bookshelf

How the Mighty Fall—and Why Some Companies Never Give In
By Jim Collins

TURBULENT TIMES

In late 2008, as Jim Collins watched one venerable company after another slide toward doom, he had already been thinking about how and why organizations tumble "from iconic to irrelevant." The result of his thinking is *How the Mighty Fall*, based on substantial research that had begun years before the recent troubled times. *"Every institution is vulnerable, no matter how great,"* Collins writes.

The Silent Creep of Impending Doom

As this title of Collins' first chapter makes clear, it is easy for leaders to miss the signals that an organization is going downhill. By understanding five stages of decline, leaders can detect the seeds of decline before they take root, or increase their chances of avoiding a fall if decline has already begun.

- *Stage 1: Hubris Born of Success.* Leaders can become arrogant about their company's success, viewing it almost as an entitlement. "Luck and chance play a role in many success-

ful outcomes, and those who fail to acknowledge [that]—and thereby overestimate their own merit and capabilities—have succumbed to hubris."

- *Stage 2: Undisciplined Pursuit of More.* Unchecked, hubris causes leaders to think they can accomplish anything, so they go for more growth, more power, more acclaim. They may leap into new areas where they truly *cannot* achieve success. *Overreaching* often describes how the mighty fall.
- *Stage 3: Denial of Risk and Peril.* At this stage, there are plenty of internal warning signs, but the company still looks good on the outside. Leaders discount negative data and amplify positive data. They refer to problems as temporary setbacks.
- *Stage 4: Grasping for Salvation.* Risks that go bad have now thrown the company into Stage 4, where decline becomes visible to everyone inside and outside the organization. Rather than "lurching for a quick salvation," such as recruiting a charismatic new

CEO, wise leaders take the company back to the focus and discipline that led to success in the first place.

- *Stage 5: Capitulation to Irrelevance or Death.* Companies that linger in Stage 4, "repeatedly grasping for silver bullets," continue to spiral downward. At Stage 5, leaders have abandoned all hope for saving the company.

Never Give In

Xerox, IBM, Merck, Texas Instruments, Nordstrom, Disney, and Nucor are examples of companies that have at some point taken a tremendous fall, yet recovered and grown stronger. In every case, Collins points out, "leaders emerged who broke the trajectory of decline and simply refused to give up. . . ." *How the Mighty Fall* describes each of the five stages and offers ideas for how leaders can take the right steps at each stage.

How the Mighty Fall, by Jim Collins, is published by HarperCollins.

marble: © Ioannis Drimilis   library: www.istockphoto.com/nikada

departments and helping to spread knowledge and information throughout the organization.

There is also a growing trend toward increasing collaboration with other organizations so that companies think of themselves as teams that create value jointly rather than as autonomous entities in competition with all others.[26]

A new form of global business is made up of networks of independent companies that share financial risks and leadership talents and provide access to one another's technologies and markets.[27]

Collaboration presents greater leadership challenges than did the old concept of competition. It is often more difficult to create an environment of teamwork and community that fosters collaboration and mutual support. Yet the call for empowerment, combined with an understanding of organizations as fluid, dynamic, interactive systems, makes the use of intimidation and manipulation obsolete as a means of motivating people toward goals.

Action Memo

Go to Leader's Self-Insight 1.1 to learn about your own "intelligence" for dealing with collaboration and with the other new realities facing organizations.

Leader's Self-Insight 1.1
Your Learning Style: Using Multiple Intelligences

Multiple Intelligence theory suggests that there are several different ways of learning about things; hence there are multiple "intelligences," of which five are interpersonal (learn via interactions with others); intrapersonal (own inner states); logical-mathematical (rationality and logic); verbal-linguistic (words and language); and musical (sounds, tonal patterns, and rhythms). Most people prefer one or two of the intelligences as a way of learning, yet each person has the potential to develop skills in each of the intelligences.

The items below will help you identify the forms of intelligence that you tend to use or enjoy most, as well as the forms that you use less. Please check each item below as Mostly False or Mostly True for you.

	Mostly False	Mostly True
1. I like to work with and solve complex problems.	_____	_____
2. I recently wrote something that I am especially proud of.	_____	_____
3. I have three or more friends.	_____	_____
4. I like to learn about myself through personality tests.	_____	_____
5. I frequently listen to music on the radio or iPod-type player.	_____	_____
6. Math and science were among my favorite subjects.	_____	_____
7. Language and social studies were among my favorite subjects.	_____	_____
8. I am frequently involved in social activities.	_____	_____
9. I have or would like to attend personal growth seminars.	_____	_____
10. I notice if a melody is out of tune or off key.	_____	_____
11. I am good at problem-solving that requires logical thinking.	_____	_____
12. My conversations frequently include things I've read or heard about.	_____	_____

	Mostly False	Mostly True
13. When among strangers, I easily find someone to talk to.	_____	_____
14. I spend time alone meditating, reflecting, or thinking.	_____	_____
15. After hearing a tune once or twice, I am able to sing it back with some accuracy.	_____	_____

Scoring and Interpretation

Count the number of items checked Mostly True that represent each of the five intelligences as indicated below.

Questions 1, 6, 11, Logical-mathematical intelligence.
Mostly True = _____.
Questions 2, 7, 12, Verbal-linguistic intelligence.
Mostly True = _____.
Questions 3, 8, 13, Interpersonal intelligence.
Mostly True = _____.
Questions 4, 9, 14, Intrapersonal intelligence.
Mostly True = _____.
Questions 5, 10, 15, Musical intelligence.
Mostly True = _____.

Educational institutions tend to stress the logical-mathematical and verbal-linguistic forms of learning. How do your intelligences align with the changes taking place in the world? Would you rather rely on using one intelligence in-depth or develop multiple intelligences? Any intelligence above for which you received a score of three is a major source of learning for you, and a score of zero means you may not use it at all. How do your intelligences fit your career plans and your aspirations for the type of leader you want to be?

Source: Based on Kirsi Tirri, Petri Nokelainen, and Martin Ubani, "Conceptual Definition and Empirical Validation of the Spiritual Sensitivity Scale," *Journal of Empirical Theology* 19 (2006), pp. 37–62; and David Lazear, *Seven Ways of Knowing: Teaching for Multiple Intelligences* (Palatine, IL: IRI/Skylight Publishing, 1991).

marble: © Kirill Matkov   sunset: © Marco Regalia

From Uniformity to Diversity

Many of today's organizations were built on assumptions of uniformity, separation, and specialization. People who think alike, act alike, and have similar job skills are grouped into a department, such as accounting or manufacturing, separate from other departments. Homogenous groups find it easy to get along, communicate, and understand one another. The uniform thinking that arises, however, can be a disaster in a world becoming more multinational and diverse.

Bringing diversity into the organization is the way to attract the best human talent and develop an organizational mindset broad enough to thrive in a multinational world. Two business school graduates in their twenties discovered the importance of diversity when they started a specialized advertising firm. They worked hard, and as the firm grew, they hired more people just like themselves—bright, young, intense college graduates who were committed and hard working. The firm grew to about 20 employees over two and a half years, but the expected profits never materialized. The two entrepreneurs could never get a handle on what was wrong, and the firm slid into bankruptcy. Convinced the idea was still valid, they started over, but with a new philosophy. They sought employees with different ages, ethnic backgrounds, and work experience. People had different styles, yet the organization seemed to work better. People played different roles, and the diverse experiences of the group enabled the firm to respond to unique situations and handle a variety of organizational and personal needs. The advertising firm is growing again, and this time it is also making a profit.

From Self-Centered to Higher Ethical Purpose

A seemingly endless series of corporate scandals and the shock of the Wall Street crisis have prompted a determined and conscious shift in leader mindset from a self-centered focus to emphasis on a higher ethical purpose. Public confidence in business leaders in particular is at an all-time low, but politics, sports, and nonprofit organizations have also been affected.

Unfortunately, the old-paradigm emphasis on individual ability, success, and prosperity sometimes pushed people to cross the line, culminating in organizational corruption on a broad scale and ugly headlines exposing many organization leaders as unethical and self-serving rogues. More than half of Americans say they are not proud of the country's leaders in business, government, education, and other fields, according to a poll conducted for *U.S. News & World Report* and Harvard University's Center for Public Leadership. Only 39 percent believe most leaders have high ethical standards.[28]

In the new paradigm, leaders emphasize accountability, integrity, and responsibility to something larger than individual self-interest, including employees, customers, the organization, and all stakeholders.[29] This chapter's *Consider This* box presents 10 commandments based on 1950s western film star Gene Autry's Cowboy Code that can be regarded as applicable to new paradigm leaders.

Marilyn Nelson, CEO of the Carlson Companies (Radisson Hotels, TGI Fridays, Regent Seven Seas Cruises), says being a true leader means you "have to subordinate your own emotions, your own desires, even make decisions on behalf of the whole that might conflict with what you would do on an individual basis."[30] A stunning example of this occurred in the spring of 2009 when a United States–flagged cargo ship, the *Maersk Alabama*, was seized and raided by Somali pirates. Captain Richard Phillips ordered crew members of the unarmed ship not to fight and gave himself up as a hostage to free the ship and crew.[31]

Consider **This!**

Should Leaders Live by the Cowboy Code?

1. A cowboy never takes unfair advantage—even of an enemy.
2. A cowboy never goes back on his word or betrays a trust.
3. A cowboy always tells the truth.
4. A cowboy is kind and gentle with children, the elderly, and animals.
5. A cowboy is free from racial or religious prejudice.
6. A cowboy is always helpful and lends a hand when anyone's in trouble.
7. A cowboy is a good worker.
8. A cowboy stays clean in thought, speech, action, and personal habits.
9. A cowboy respects womanhood, parents, and the laws of his nation.
10. A cowboy is a patriot to his country.

Source: Gene Autry's Cowboy Commandments are reported, with some variations in wording, in multiple sources.

© majaiva

From Hero to Humble

A related shift is the move from the celebrity "leader-as-hero" to the hard-working behind-the-scenes leader who quietly builds a strong enduring company by supporting and developing others rather than touting his or her own abilities and successes.[32]

Jim Collins, author of *Good to Great* and *How the Mighty Fall*, calls this new breed "Level 5 leaders."[33] In contrast to the view of great leaders as larger-than-life personalities with strong egos and big ambitions, Level 5 leaders often seem shy and unpretentious and have no need to be in the limelight. They are more concerned with the success of the team or company than with their own success. For example, the coach of the University of Maryland soccer team discovered that the best team captains are typically the guys who don't call attention to themselves.

IN THE LEAD

Scotty Buete, University of Maryland Terrapins

As head coach of the University of Maryland Terrapins, or "Terps," as they are known to fans, Sasho Cirovski led a bottom-ranked soccer team to six straight NCAA tournament showings. But then, something went wrong. Cirovski realized he was doing a good job of recruiting high-caliber talent, but he wasn't doing so well picking good team leaders.

Soccer is a game with no time-outs, so leadership on the field is crucial. Cirovski called on his brother, a human resources vice president for Cardinal Health Inc., for advice. His brother helped him administer a survey and analyze the results to identify "off the radar leaders." His recommendation for team captain? Scotty Buete, a quiet sophomore that Cirovski had never even considered for a leadership role. Why? Buete seemed too shy, too unassuming, somehow too *small* to be a leader. "This was the same kid I had to . . . convince he was good enough to play at Maryland," Cirovski recalls.

But it turned out that Buete was the player that other players turned to. The survey showed that Buete had the respect of almost everyone and exerted a tremendous influence on his teammates. Rather than calling attention to himself, Buete did whatever was needed for the good of the team. "Scotty was the glue, and I didn't see it," Cirovski says.[34]

Scotty Buete, who remained an effective team leader of the Terps until graduation, reflects the humility of a Level 5 leader. These leaders are characterized by an almost complete lack of ego, coupled with a fierce resolve to do what is best for the organization. They accept full responsibility for mistakes, poor results, or failures, but they typically give credit for successes to other people. A corporate example is Reuben Mark, CEO of Colgate-Palmolive. Mark shuns personal publicity and turns down requests for media profiles because he believes a personal profile takes credit for the efforts of his employees. At annual meetings, Mark pays tribute to employees around the world who make even seemingly minor contributions to innovation, market increases, or business operations.[35] Although most research regarding the new type of leader has been on corporate CEOs, it is important to remember that new-paradigm or Level 5 leaders are in all positions in all types of organizations.

Action Memo

As a leader, you can respond to the reality of change and crisis, the need for empowerment, collaboration, and diversity, and the importance of a higher, ethical purpose. You can channel your ambition toward achieving larger organizational goals rather than feeding your own ego.

Leadership and the Wall Street Meltdown

Unfortunately, humility and emphasis on a higher ethical purpose are qualities that some executives find difficult to attain and uphold. It wasn't so many years ago that a number of high-flying companies, including Enron, WorldCom, Tyco, and Arthur Andersen, came crashing down due to the unbridled greed, arrogance, irresponsibility, and deceptiveness of top executives. Did corporate leaders learn anything? Apparently some did not. The impact of those failures pales in comparison to what has occurred as a result of the recent Wall Street meltdown.

The mess started partly with loan originators like Washington Mutual, New Century Financial, and Countrywide that aggressively pushed subprime and low- or no-documentation loans to borrowers with low incomes and low credit scores. Companies such as Bear Stearns, Lehman Brothers, and Merrill Lynch got themselves into serious trouble by borrowing heavily to invest in these risky real estate assets, then packaged them into bond-like securities and sold them to investors as investments rated very safe. Leaders at these companies prided themselves on finding new and clever ways to package mortgage-related assets and earn lucrative fees. The business media and investment rating companies contributed to the calamity by blessing the investments, praising these companies and their leaders for their ingenuity and ambitious, aggressive business models.

Legal experts and government watchdogs are trying to sort out how much of the mess can be attributed to activities that were actually illegal but, the question of legality aside, the whole episode reflects a failure of responsible leadership. The media praise and the lure of big salaries and bigger bonuses caused executives in these companies to, at the least, suspend their judgment, and in many cases to make decisions and take action based on what best served their own self-interest rather than what was good for clients or the company. For instance, loan originators frequently made loans to people who obviously could not afford the home they were purchasing, or the payments on the loan, simply for the purpose of generating loan volume—thus grabbing as much of the pie as they could, with little concern for who might be hurt in the process. Similarly, executives at companies that securitized and packaged the loans continued to pay themselves huge salaries and bonuses even as losses mounted into the billions. AIG, for instance, paid out around $165 million in bonuses—with one executive receiving $6.4 million and six others receiving more than $4 million each—even after the company reported the largest quarterly loss in history and had accepted a $170 billion bailout from the U.S. government.[36] Although a number of AIG executives who received bonuses later returned the money, the incident shed light on an organization where judgment and values were horribly out of whack.

"The current crisis was not caused by subprime mortgages, credit default swaps, or failed economic policies," said Harvard's Bill George. "The root cause is failed leadership."[37] The Wall Street crisis has vaporized trillions of dollars in investment capital, ripped another trillion or so from taxpayers' pockets, devastated trust funds and endowments, led to massive layoffs, and contributed to numerous small business failures. Yet despite the turmoil and confusion of these trying times, there are sensible, responsible, ethical leaders doing good things, and some of them will be profiled throughout this text. In addition, new leaders will emerge from the crisis who can look beyond the current situation and help people move to something new and better.

Comparing Management and Leadership

Management can be defined as the attainment of organizational goals in an effective and efficient manner through planning, organizing, staffing, directing, and controlling organizational resources. So, what is it that distinguishes the process of leadership from that of management? Managers and leaders are not inherently different types of people. There are managers at all hierarchical levels in today's organizations who are also good leaders, and most people can develop the qualities needed for effective leadership. Both management and leadership are essential in organizations and must be integrated effectively to lead to high performance.[38] That is, leadership cannot replace management; it should be in addition to management.

Exhibit 1.3 compares management to leadership in five areas crucial to organizational performance—providing direction, aligning followers, building relationships, developing personal qualities, and creating leader outcomes.[39]

Action Memo

You can evaluate your own leadership potential by completing the quiz in Leader's Self-Insight 1.2.

Providing Direction

Both leadership and management are concerned with providing direction for the organization, but there are differences. Management focuses on establishing detailed plans and schedules for achieving specific results, then allocating resources to accomplish the plan. Leadership calls for creating a compelling vision of the future and developing farsighted strategies for producing the changes needed to achieve that vision. Whereas management calls for keeping an eye on the bottom line and short-term results, leadership means keeping an eye on the horizon and the long-term future.

A **vision** is a picture of an ambitious, desirable future for the organization or team.[40] It can be as lofty as Motorola's aim to "become the premier company in the world" or as down-to-earth as the Swedish company IKEA's simple vision "to provide affordable furniture for people with limited budgets."

To be compelling for followers, the vision has to be one they can relate to and share. Consider that in *Fortune* magazine's study of the "100 Best Companies to

Management
the attainment of organizational goals in an effective and efficient manner through planning, organizing, staffing, directing, and controlling organizational resources

Vision
a picture of an ambitious, desirable future for the organization or team

Exhibit 1.3 Comparing Management and Leadership

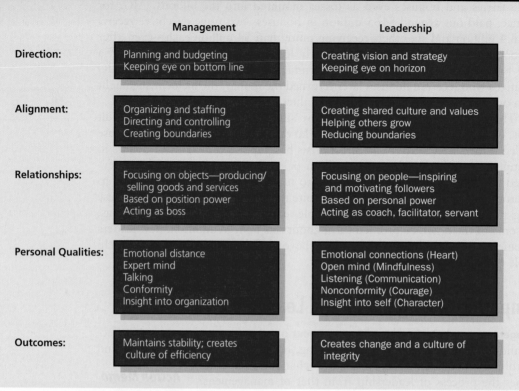

	Management	Leadership
Direction:	Planning and budgeting Keeping eye on bottom line	Creating vision and strategy Keeping eye on horizon
Alignment:	Organizing and staffing Directing and controlling Creating boundaries	Creating shared culture and values Helping others grow Reducing boundaries

Relationships:	Focusing on objects—producing/
	  selling goods and services
	Based on position power
	Acting as boss
		Focusing on people—inspiring
		  and motivating followers
		Based on personal power
		Acting as coach, facilitator, servant

Personal Qualities:	Emotional distance Expert mind Talking Conformity Insight into organization	Emotional connections (Heart) Open mind (Mindfulness) Listening (Communication) Nonconformity (Courage) Insight into self (Character)

Outcomes:	Maintains stability; creates
	  culture of efficiency
		Creates change and a culture of
		  integrity

Source: Based on John P. Kotter, *A Force for Change: How Leadership Differs from Management* (New York: The Free Press, 1990).

Work for in America," two of the recurring traits of great companies are a powerful, visionary leader and a sense of purpose beyond increasing shareholder value.[41]

Aligning Followers

Management entails organizing a structure to accomplish the plan; staffing the structure with employees; and developing policies, procedures, and systems to direct employees and monitor implementation of the plan. Leadership is concerned instead with communicating the vision and developing a shared culture and set of core values that can lead to the desired future state. Whereas the vision describes the destination, the culture and values help define the journey toward it. Leadership focuses on getting everyone lined up in the same direction.

Rather than simply directing and controlling employees to achieve specific results, leaders "align [people] with broader ideas of what the company should be and why."[42] Leaders encourage people to expand their minds and abilities and to assume responsibility for their own actions. Think about classes you have taken at your college or university. In some classes, the professor tells students exactly what to do and how to do it, and many students expect this kind of direction and control. Have you ever had a class where the instructor instead inspired and encouraged you and your classmates to find innovative ways to meet goals? The difference reflects a rational management versus a leadership approach.

Building Relationships

In terms of relationships, management focuses on objects such as machines and reports, on taking the steps needed to produce the organization's goods and services. Leadership, on the other hand, focuses on motivating and inspiring people.

Leader's Self-Insight 1.2
Your Leadership Potential

Questions 1–6 below are about you right now. Questions 7–14 are about how you would like to be if you were the head of a major department at a corporation. Answer Mostly False or Mostly True to indicate whether the item describes you accurately, or whether you would strive to perform each activity as a department head.

Now

	Mostly False	Mostly True
1. When I have a number of tasks or homework assignments to do, I set priorities and organize the work to meet the deadlines.	_____	_____
2. When I am involved in a serious disagreement, I hang in there and talk it out until it is completely resolved.	_____	_____
3. I would rather sit in front of my computer than spend a lot of time with people.	_____	_____
4. I reach out to include other people in activities or when there are discussions.	_____	_____
5. I know my long-term vision for career, family, and other activities.	_____	_____
6. When solving problems, I prefer analyzing things myself to working through them with a group of people.	_____	_____

Head Of Major Department

	Mostly False	Mostly True
7. I would help subordinates clarify goals and how to reach them.	_____	_____
8. I would give people a sense of long-term mission and higher purpose.	_____	_____
9. I would make sure jobs get out on time.	_____	_____
10. I would scout for new product or service opportunities.	_____	_____
11. I would give credit to people who do their jobs well.	_____	_____
12. I would promote unconventional beliefs and values.	_____	_____
13. I would establish procedures to help the department operate smoothly.	_____	_____
14. I would verbalize the higher values that I and the organization stand for.	_____	_____

Scoring and Interpretation

Count the number of Mostly True answers to even-numbered questions: _____. Count the number of Mostly True answers to odd-numbered questions: _____. Compare the two scores.

The even-numbered items represent behaviors and activities typical of leadership. Leaders are personally involved in shaping ideas, values, vision, and change. They often use an intuitive approach to develop fresh ideas and seek new directions for the department or organization. The odd-numbered items are considered more traditional management activities. Managers respond to organizational problems in an impersonal way, make rational decisions, and work for stability and efficiency.

If you answered yes to more even-numbered than odd-numbered items, you may have potential leadership qualities. If you answered yes to more odd-numbered items, you may have management qualities. Management qualities are an important foundation for new leaders because the organization first has to operate efficiently. Then leadership qualities can enhance performance. Both sets of qualities can be developed or improved with awareness and experience.

Sources: John P. Kotter, *Leading Change* (Boston, MA: Harvard Business School Press, 1996), p. 26; Joseph C. Rost, *Leadership for the Twenty-first Century* (Westport, CT: Praeger, 1993), p. 149; and Brian Dumaine, "The New Non-Manager Managers," *Fortune* (February 22, 1993), pp. 80–84.

marble: © Kirill Matkov   sunset: © Marco Regalia

Whereas the management relationship is based on position and formal authority, leadership is a relationship based on personal influence. For example, in an authority relationship, both people accept that a manager can tell a subordinate to be at work at 7:30 A.M. or her pay will be docked. Leadership, on the other hand, relies on influence, which is less likely to use coercion. The role of leadership is to attract and energize people, motivating them through personal identification with challenging jobs rather than rewards or punishments.[43] The differing source of power is one of the key distinctions between management and leadership. Take away a manager's formal position and will people choose to follow her? That is the mark of a leader.

Developing Personal Leadership Qualities

Leadership is more than a set of skills; it relies on a number of subtle personal qualities that are hard to see, but are very powerful. These include things like enthusiasm, integrity, courage, and humility. First of all, good leadership springs from a genuine caring for the work and a genuine concern for other people. The process of management generally encourages emotional distance, but leadership means being emotionally connected to others. Where there is leadership, people become part of a community and feel that they are contributing to something worthwhile. Whereas management means providing answers and solving problems, leadership requires the courage to admit mistakes and doubts, to listen, and to trust and learn from others.

Action Memo

As a leader, you can awaken your leadership qualities of enthusiasm, integrity, courage, and moral commitment. You can make emotional connections with followers to increase your leadership effectiveness.

Developing leadership qualities takes work. For leadership to happen, leaders may have to undergo a journey of self-discovery and personal understanding.[44] Leadership experts agree that a top characteristic of effective leaders is that they know who they are and what they stand for. In addition, leaders have the courage to act on their beliefs.

True leaders tend to have open minds that welcome new ideas rather than closed minds that criticize new ideas. Leaders listen and discern what people want and need more than they talk to give advice and orders. Leaders are willing to be nonconformists, to disagree and say no when it serves the larger good, and to accept nonconformity from others rather than try to squeeze everyone into the same mindset. Consider the following example.

IN THE LEAD

Jamie Dimon, JPMorgan Chase

Jamie Dimon, chairman and CEO of JPMorgan Chase, has been widely applauded for steering JPMorgan Chase away from the business of securitizing subprime mortgages, even as that business was booming, and for avoiding more exotic—and lucrative— financial instruments that eventually brought down companies such as Lehman Brothers and Merrill Lynch.

But Dimon is the first to admit that he has plenty of flaws and has made plenty of mistakes. He gives credit for the company's successes to his leadership team. "By its nature, business is a risk," says Dimon, "but risks have to be taken in the best interest of clients." When Dimon first became CEO of Bank One (later bought by JPMorgan), he realized the company was in trouble. The management team knew there were problems, but no one had taken action. Dimon cut perks like company cars and club memberships, and then asked managers how much they should get for their annual bonuses.

> Most thought a cut of 10 to 15 percent was reasonable. Dimon, though, suggested a bonus of $0 and set an example by not accepting his own guaranteed bonus.
>
> Dimon is aware that being a leader in a huge, prestigious organization can breed arrogance and greed, so he is continually on guard against that trend. He sees his job as finding the right people and creating an environment in which the right decisions get made. He encourages people to speak up, to say what they think even if it isn't popular, to admit their mistakes, and to say *no*–even to the CEO—when no is the right answer. One new manager was shocked to see people openly debating and challenging Dimon, questioning his decisions, and telling him he was wrong. "The best thing I can do for JPM is leave the place with high integrity, high-powered people who are always learning, always changing," says Dimon. "That DNA will set the company forward for a hundred years."[45]

Even though JPMorgan Chase was not one of the companies devastated by the subprime mess, in a symbolic gesture, Dimon reportedly refused his 2008 bonus. "One of the truths," he said about the crisis, "is that a lot of people were paid a lot of money at companies that blew up or failed."[46]

Creating Outcomes

The differences between management and leadership create two differing outcomes, as illustrated at the bottom of Exhibit 1.3. Management maintains a degree of stability, predictability, and order through a *culture of efficiency*. Leadership, on the other hand, creates change, often radical change, within a *culture of integrity* that helps the organization thrive over the long haul by promoting openness and honesty, positive relationships, and long-term innovation. Leadership facilitates the courage needed to make difficult and unconventional decisions that may sometimes hurt short-term results.

Evolving Theories of Leadership

To understand leadership as it is viewed and practiced today, it is important to recognize that the concept of leadership has changed over time. Leadership typically reflects the larger society, and theories have evolved as norms, attitudes, and understandings in the larger world have changed.

Historical Overview of Major Approaches

The various leadership theories can be categorized into six basic approaches, each of which is briefly described in this section. Many of these ideas are still applicable to leadership studies today and are discussed in various chapters of this text.

Great Man Theories This is the granddaddy of leadership concepts. The earliest studies of leadership adopted the belief that leaders (who were always thought of as male) were born with certain heroic leadership traits and natural abilities of power and influence. In organizations, social movements, religions, governments, and the military, leadership was conceptualized as a single "Great Man" who put everything together and influenced others to follow along based on the strength of inherited traits, qualities, and abilities.

Trait Theories Studies of these larger-than-life leaders spurred research into the various traits that defined a leader. Beginning in the 1920s, researchers looked to see if leaders had particular traits or characteristics, such as intelligence or energy, that distinguished them from non-leaders and contributed to success. It was thought that if traits could be identified, leaders could be predicted, or perhaps even trained. Although research failed to produce a list of traits that would always guarantee leadership success, the interest in leadership characteristics has continued to the present day.

Behavior Theories The failure to identify a universal set of leadership traits led researchers in the early 1950s to begin looking at what a leader does, rather than who he or she is.[47] One line of research focused on what leaders actually do on the job, such as various management activities, roles, and responsibilities. These studies were soon expanded to try to determine how effective leaders differ in their behavior from ineffective ones. Researchers looked at how a leader behaved toward followers and how this correlated with leadership effectiveness or ineffectiveness. Chapter 2 discusses trait and behavior theories.

Contingency Theories Researchers next began to consider the contextual and situational variables that influence what leadership behaviors will be effective. The idea behind contingency theories is that leaders can analyze their situation and tailor their behavior to improve leadership effectiveness. Major situational variables are the characteristics of followers, characteristics of the work environment and follower tasks, and the external environment. Contingency theories, sometimes called *situational theories*, emphasize that leadership cannot be understood in a vacuum separate from various elements of the group or organizational situation. Chapter 3 covers contingency theories.

Influence Theories These theories examine influence processes between leaders and followers. One primary topic of study is *charismatic leadership* (Chapter 12), which refers to leadership influence based not on position or formal authority but, rather, on the qualities and charismatic personality of the leader. Related areas of study are *leadership vision* (Chapter 13) and *organizational culture* (Chapter 14). Leaders influence people to change by providing an inspiring vision of the future and shaping the culture and values needed to attain it. Several chapters of this text relate to the topic of influence because it is essential to understanding leadership.

Relational Theories Since the late 1970s, many ideas of leadership have focused on the relational aspect, that is, how leaders and followers interact and influence one another. Rather than being seen as something a leader does to a follower, leadership is viewed as a relational process that meaningfully engages all participants and enables each person to contribute to achieving the vision. Interpersonal relationships are seen as the most important facet of leadership effectiveness.[48] Two significant relational theories are *transformational leadership* (Chapter 12) and *servant leadership* (Chapter 6).

Other important relational topics covered in various chapters of the text include the personal qualities that leaders need to build effective relationships, such as emotional intelligence, a leader's mind, integrity and high moral standards, and personal courage. In addition, leaders build relationships through motivation and empowerment, leadership communication, team leadership, and embracing diversity.

A Model of Leadership Evolution

Exhibit 1.4 provides a framework for examining the evolution of leadership from the early Great Man theories to today's relational theories. Each cell in the model

Exhibit 1.4 Leadership Evolution

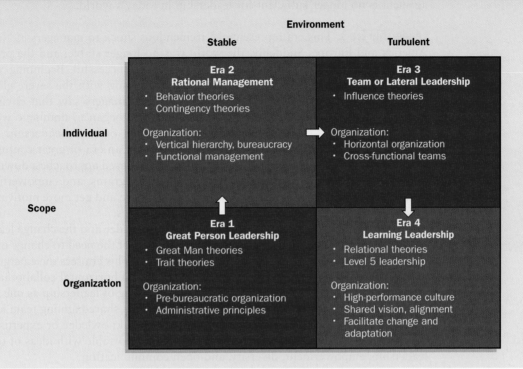

summarizes an era of leadership thinking that was dominant in its time but may be less appropriate for today's world.

Leadership Era 1 This era may be conceptualized as pre-industrial and pre-bureaucratic. Most organizations were small and were run by a single individual who many times hired workers because they were friends or relatives, not necessarily because of their skills or qualifications. The size and simplicity of organizations and the stable nature of the environment made it easy for a single person to understand the big picture, coordinate and control all activities, and keep things on track. This is the era of Great Man leadership and the emphasis on personal traits of leaders. A leader was conceptualized as a single hero who saw the big picture and how everything fit into a whole.

Leadership Era 2 In Era 2, we see the emergence of hierarchy and bureaucracy. Although the world remains stable, organizations have begun to grow so large that they require rules and standard procedures to ensure that activities are performed efficiently and effectively. Hierarchy of authority provides a sensible mechanism for supervision and control of workers, and decisions once based on rules of thumb or tradition are replaced with precise procedures. This era sees the rise of the "rational manager" who directs and controls others using an impersonal approach. Employees aren't expected to think for themselves; they are expected to do as they're told, follow rules and procedures, and accomplish specific tasks. The focus is on details rather than the big picture.

The rational manager was well-suited to a stable environment. The behavior and contingency theories worked here because leaders could analyze their situation, develop careful plans, and control what happened. But rational management is no longer sufficient for leadership in today's world.

Leadership Era 3 This era represented a tremendous shock to managers in North America and Europe. Suddenly, the world was no longer stable, and the prized techniques of rational management were no longer successful. Beginning with the OPEC oil embargo of 1972 to 1973 and continuing with the severe global competition of the 1980s and early 1990s, many managers saw that environmental conditions had become chaotic. The Japanese began to dominate world commerce with their ideas of team leadership and superb quality. This became an era of great confusion for leaders. They tried team-based approaches, downsizing, reengineering, quality programs, and empowerment as ways to improve performance and get more motivation and commitment from employees.

Action Memo

As a leader, you can use the leadership skills that fit the correct era for your organization. You can use influence and relational aspects as appropriate for your organization.

This is the era of the team leader and the change leader. Influence was important because of the need to change organizational structures and cultures. This era sees the emergence of knowledge work, an emphasis on horizontal collaboration, and a shift to influence theories. Rather than conceiving of leadership as one person always being firmly "in charge," leadership is often shared among team leaders and members, shifting to the person with the most knowledge or expertise in the matter at hand.[49] Many leaders have become comfortable with ideas of team leadership, empowerment, diversity, and open communication.

Leadership Era 4 Enter the digital information age. It seems that everything is changing, and changing fast. Era 4 represents the **learning leader** who has made the leap to giving up control in the traditional sense. Leaders emphasize relationships and networks, and they influence others through vision and values rather than power and control. They are constantly experimenting, learning, and changing, in both their personal and professional lives, and they encourage the development and growth of others. Era 4 requires the full scope of leadership that goes far beyond rational management or even team leadership.

Implications The flow from Great Man leadership to rational management to team leadership to learning leadership illustrates trends in the larger world. The implication is that leadership reflects the era or context of the organization and society. Most of today's organizations and leaders are still struggling with the transition from a stable to a chaotic environment and the new skills and qualities needed in this circumstance. Thus, Era 3 issues of diversity, team leadership, empowerment, and horizontal relationships are increasingly relevant. In addition, many leaders are rapidly shifting into Era 4 leadership by focusing on change management and facilitating a vision and values to encourage high performance and continuous adaptation. Era 3 and Era 4 leadership is what much of this book is about.

Leadership Is Intentional

Learning leader
a leader who is open to learning and change and encourages the growth and development of others

Many leaders are caught in the transition between the practices and principles that defined the industrial era and the new reality of the twenty-first century. Attempts to achieve collaboration, empowerment, and diversity in organizations may fail because the beliefs and thought processes of leaders as well as employees are stuck in an old paradigm that values control, stability, and homogeneity. It is difficult for many leaders to let go of methods and practices that have made them and their organizations successful in the past. Yet leaders can make the leap to a new paradigm by intentionally practicing and applying new paradigm principles.

Action Memo

Leader's Self-Insight 1.3 gives you a chance to test your people skills and see if there are areas you need to work on.

One of the most important aspects of shifting to the new paradigm of leadership is intentionally using human skills to build a culture of performance, trust, and collaboration. A few clues about the importance of acquiring new leadership skills were brought to light by the Center for Creative Leadership in Greensboro, North Carolina.[50] The study compared 21 derailed executives with 20 executives who successfully arrived at the top of a company. The derailed managers were successful people who were expected to go far, but they reached a plateau, were fired, or were forced to retire early. They were all bright, worked hard, and excelled in a technical area such as accounting or engineering.

The striking difference between the two groups was the ability to use human skills. Only 25 percent of the derailed group were described as being good with people, whereas 75 percent of those who arrived at the top had people skills. Exhibit 1.5 lists the top seven reasons for failure. Unsuccessful managers were insensitive to others, abrasive, cold, arrogant, untrustworthy, overly ambitious and selfish, unable to delegate or build teams, and unable to acquire appropriate staff to work for them.

Selena Lo learned the importance of human skills when she started her own company, Ruckus Wireless. Formerly, as a vice president at Alteon Web Systems, Lo's colleagues described her leadership style as "drive-by shootings." Her insensitive approach didn't derail her career only because her boss came along behind her and mopped up the damage. When she started her own company, however, Lo had a hard time getting good people to work for her. She intentionally embarked on the process of developing stronger human skills. She started listening to others, asking for their input and explaining her decisions, and giving people more autonomy to make their own choices. Although Lo hasn't lost her aggressive personality, she has tempered it with concern and respect for the people around her, helping her recruit talented employees.[51]

Exhibit 1.5 Top Seven Reasons for Executive Derailment

1. Acting with an insensitive, abrasive, intimidating, bullying style
2. Being cold, aloof, arrogant
3. Betraying personal trust
4. Being overly ambitious, self-centered, thinking of next job, playing politics
5. Having specific performance problems with the business
6. Overmanaging, being unable to delegate or build a team
7. Being unable to select good subordinates

Sources: Based on Morgan W. McCall, Jr., and Michael M. Lombardo, "Off the Track: Why and How Successful Executives Get Derailed" (Technical Report No. 21), (Greensboro, NC: Center for Creative Leadership, January 1983); and Carol Hymowitz, "Five Main Reasons Why Managers Fail," *The Wall Street Journal* (May 2, 1988).

Leader's Self-Insight 1.3

Are You on a Fast Track to Nowhere?

Many fast-trackers find themselves suddenly derailed and don't know why. Many times, a lack of people skills is to blame. To help you determine whether you need to work on your people skills, take the following quiz, answering each item as Mostly False or Mostly True. Think about a job or volunteer position you have now or have held in the past as you answer the following items.

People Skills

	Mostly False	Mostly True
1. Other people describe me as a real "people person."	_____	_____
2. I spend a part of each day making small talk with coworkers (or teammates or classmates).	_____	_____
3. I see some of my coworkers (or teammates or classmates) outside of work, and I know many of them socially.	_____	_____
4. Because I have good work relationships, I often succeed where others fail.	_____	_____

Working with Authority

	Mostly False	Mostly True
5. When I have a good reason for doing so, I will express a view that differs from that of leaders in the organization.	_____	_____
6. If I see a leader making a decision that seems harmful to the organization, I speak up.	_____	_____
7. People see me as someone who can independently assess an executive decision and, when appropriate, offer an alternative perspective.	_____	_____

	Mostly False	Mostly True
8. When senior people ask for my opinion, they know that I'll respond with candor.	_____	_____

Networking

	Mostly False	Mostly True
9. I spend at least part of each week networking with colleagues.	_____	_____
10. I belong to organizations where I can make professional contacts.	_____	_____
11. A few times each month, I am invited to join key members of my team or organization for lunch.	_____	_____
12. I regularly interact with peers at other organizations.	_____	_____

Scoring and Interpretation

Tally the number of "Mostly Trues" checked for each set of questions.

People Skills:_____; Working with Authority: _____; Networking: _____

If you scored 4 in an area, you're right on track. Continue to act in the same way.

If your score is 2–3, you can fine-tune your skills in that area. Review the questions where you said Mostly False and work to add those abilities to your leadership skill set.

A score of 0–1 indicates that you're dangerously close to derailment. You should take the time to do an in-depth self-assessment and find ways to expand your interpersonal skills.

Source: Adapted from "Are You Knocking Out Your Own Career?" *Fast Company* (May 1999), p. 230, a quiz based on the research of Dr. Lois P. Frankel (see http://www.drloisfrankel.com/).

The inability to surround oneself with good people and help them learn and contribute can doom a top leader. The best leaders, at all levels, are those who are genuinely interested in other people and find ways to bring out the best in them.[52] In addition, today's successful leaders intentionally value change over stability, empowerment over control, collaboration over competition, diversity over uniformity, and integrity over self-interest, as discussed earlier.

The industry of *executive coaching* emerged partly to help people through the transition to a new paradigm of leadership. Executive coaches encourage leaders to confront their own flaws and hang-ups that inhibit effective leadership, and then help them develop stronger emotional and interpersonal skills.

> **Action Memo**
>
> As a leader, you can cultivate your people skills to avoid executive derailment. You can treat others with kindness, interest, and respect and avoid overmanaging by selecting good followers and delegating effectively.

This brings up an interesting question: How do people become good leaders? As Kembrel Jones, associate dean of full-time MBA programs at Emory University's Goizueta Business School, said, "If the elements of leadership were easy . . . we wouldn't be seeing the problems we see today."[53] But can leadership be taught? Many people don't think so, because so much of leadership depends on self-discovery. But it can be learned.

Learning the Art and Science of Leadership

As we have discussed in this chapter, the concept of leadership has evolved through many perspectives and continues to change. Today's reality is that the old ways no longer work, but the new ways are just emerging. Everywhere, we hear the cry for leadership as the world around us is rocked by massive and often painful events.

How can a book or a course on leadership help you to be a better leader? It is important to remember that leadership is both an art and a science. It is an art because many leadership skills and qualities cannot be learned from a textbook. Leadership takes practice and hands-on experience, as well as intense personal exploration and development. However, leadership is also a science because a growing body of knowledge and objective facts describes the leadership process and how to use leadership skills to attain organizational goals.

Knowing about leadership research helps people analyze situations from a variety of perspectives and learn how to be more effective as leaders. By exploring leadership in both business and society, students gain an understanding of the importance of leadership to an organization's success, as well as the difficulties and challenges involved in being a leader. Studying leadership can also lead to the discovery of abilities you never knew you had. When students in a leadership seminar at Wharton were asked to pick one leader to represent the class, one woman was surprised when she outpolled all other students. Her leadership was drawn out not in the practice of leadership in student government, volunteer activities, or athletics, but in a classroom setting.[54]

Studying leadership gives you skills you can apply in the practice of leadership in your everyday life. Many people have never tried to be a leader because they have no understanding of what leaders actually do. The chapters in this book are designed to help you gain a firm knowledge of what leadership means and some of the skills and qualities that make a good leader. You can build competence in both the art and the science of leadership by completing the Self-Insight exercises throughout the book, by working on the activities and cases at the end of each chapter, and by applying the concepts you learn in class, in your relationships with others, in student groups, at work, and in voluntary organizations. Although this book and your instructors can guide you in your development, only you can apply the concepts and principles of leadership in your daily life. Kenneth Chenault, CEO of American Express, has a favorite saying: "Everyone can make a conscious choice to be a leader."[55] Learning to be a leader starts now, with you. Are you up to the challenge?

Organization of the Rest of the Book

The plan for this book reflects the shift to a new paradigm summarized in Exhibit 1.2 and the discussion of management versus leadership summarized in Exhibit 1.3. The framework in Exhibit 1.6 illustrates the organization of the book. Part 1 introduces leadership, its importance, and the transition to a new leadership paradigm. Part 2 explores basic research perspectives that evolved during a more stable time when rational management approaches were effective. These basic perspectives, including the Great Man and trait theories, behavior theories, and contingency theories, are relevant to dealing with specific tasks and individuals and are based on a premise that leaders can predict and control various aspects of the environment to keep the organization running smoothly.

Parts 3, 4, and 5 switch to leadership perspectives that reflect the paradigm shift to the turbulent, unpredictable nature of the environment and the need for fresh leader approaches. Part 3 focuses on the personal side of leadership and looks at some of the qualities and forces that are required to be effective in the new reality. These chapters emphasize the importance of self-awareness and self-understanding, the development of one's own leadership mind and heart, moral leadership and courage, and appreciating the role of followership. Part 4 is about

Exhibit 1.6 Framework for the Book

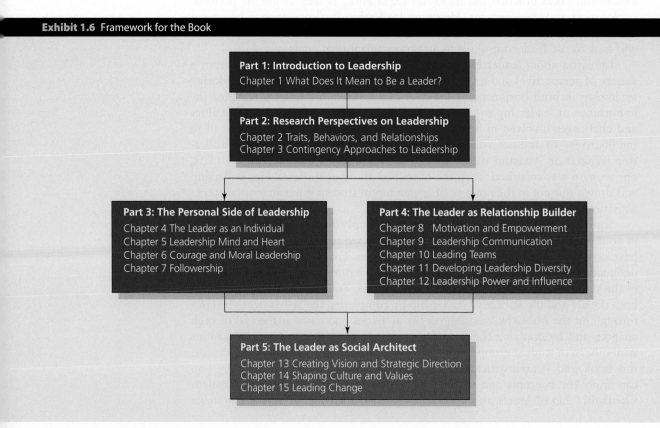

building effective relationships, including motivating and empowering others, communicating as a leader, leading teams, embracing the diversity of today's world, and using power and influence.

Part 5 brings together all of these ideas to examine the leader as builder of a social architecture that can help an organization create a brighter future. These chapters deal with creating vision and strategic direction, aligning culture and values to achieve the vision, and leading change.

Taken together, the sections and chapters paint a complete portrait of the leadership experience as it has evolved to the present day and emphasize the new paradigm skills and qualities that are relevant from today and into the future. This book blends systematic research evidence with real-world experiences and impact.

Leadership Essentials

- This chapter introduced the concept of leadership and explained how individuals can grow as leaders. Leadership is defined as an influence relationship among leaders and followers who intend real changes and outcomes that reflect their shared purposes. Thus leadership involves people in a relationship, influence, change, a shared purpose, and taking personal responsibility to make things happen. Most of us are aware of famous leaders, but most leadership that changes the world starts small and may begin with personal frustrations about events that prompt people to initiate change and inspire others to follow them. Your leadership may be expressed in the classroom, at work, or in your neighborhood, religious community, or volunteer organizations.

- Concepts of leadership have evolved over time. Major research approaches include Great Man theories, trait theories, behavior theories, contingency theories, influence theories, and relational theories. Elements of all these approaches are still applicable to the study of leadership.

- The biggest challenge facing leaders today is the changing world that wants a new paradigm of leadership. The new reality involves the shift from stability to change and crisis management, from control to empowerment, from competition to collaboration, from uniformity to diversity, and from a self-centered focus to a higher ethical purpose. In addition, the concept of leader as hero is giving way to that of the humble leader who develops others and shares credit for accomplishments. These dramatic changes suggest that a philosophy based on control and personal ambition will probably fail in the new era. The challenge for leaders is to evolve to a new mindset that relies on human skills, integrity, and teamwork.

- The "soft" skills of leadership complement the "hard" skills of management, and both are needed to effectively guide organizations. Although leadership is often equated with good management, leadership and management are different processes. Management strives to maintain stability and improve efficiency. Leadership, on the other hand, is about creating a vision for the future, designing social architecture that shapes culture and values, inspiring and motivating followers, developing personal qualities, and creating change within a culture of integrity. Leadership can be integrated with management to achieve the greatest possible outcomes. Organizations need to be both managed and led, particularly in today's turbulent environment. Many managers already have the qualities needed to be effective leaders, but they may not have gone through the process needed to bring these qualities to life. Leadership is an intentional act. It is important to remember that most people are not born with natural leadership skills and qualities, but leadership can be learned and developed.

Discussion Questions

1. Look through recent magazines and newspapers and identify one leader who seems to illustrate the "leader-as-hero" mindset and one who seems more typical of the humble Level 5 leader described in the text. Describe their differing characteristics. Which was easier to find?

2. What do you consider your own strengths and weaknesses for leadership? Discuss your answer with another student.

3. Of the elements in the leadership definition as illustrated in Exhibit 1.1, which is the easiest for you? Which is hardest? Explain.

4. How might the paradigm shift from competition to collaboration make the job of a leader more difficult? Could it also make the leader's job easier? Discuss.

5. Describe the best leader you have known. How did this leader acquire his or her capability?

6. Why do you think there are so few people who succeed at both management and leadership? Is it reasonable to believe someone can be good at both? Discuss.

7. Discuss some recent events and societal changes that might have contributed to a shift "from hero to humble." Do you agree or disagree that humility is important for good leadership?

8. "Leadership is more concerned with people than is management." Do you agree? Discuss.

9. What personal capacities should a person develop to be a good leader versus those developed to be a good manager?

10. Why is leadership considered both an art and a science?

Leadership at Work

LEADERSHIP RIGHT–WRONG

Leader Wrong: Think of a specific situation in which you were working with someone who was in a leadership position over you, and that person was doing something that was wrong for you. This person might have been a coach, teacher, team leader, employer, immediate boss, family member, or anyone who had a leadership position over you. "Wrong for you" means that person's behavior reduced your effectiveness, made you or your coworkers less productive, and was de-motivating to you or your colleagues. *Write a few words below that describe what the leader was doing that was wrong for you.*

_____

_____

_____

Think of a second situation in which someone in a leadership position did something wrong for you. *Write a few words below that describe what the leader was doing that was wrong for you.*

_____

_____

_____

Leader Right: Think of a specific situation in which you were working with someone who was in a leadership position over you, and that person was doing something that was *right* for you. This person might have been a coach, teacher, team leader, employer, immediate boss, family member, or anyone who had a leadership position over you. "Right for you" means that person's behavior made you or your coworkers more productive, highly motivated you or others, and removed barriers to make you more successful. *Write a few words below that describe what the leader was doing that was right for you.*

_____

_____

_____

Think of a second situation in which someone in a leadership position did something right for you. *Write a few words below that describe what the leader was doing that was right for you.*

_____

_____

_____

The previous answers are data points that can help you understand the impact of leader behaviors. Analyze your four incidents—what are the underlying qualities of leadership that enable you to be an effective performer? Discuss your answers with another student. What leadership themes are present in the eight combined incidents? What do these responses tell you about the qualities you both want and don't want in your leaders?

In Class: An interesting way to use this exercise in class is to have students write (five words maximum) their leader "rights" on one board and their leader "wrongs" on another board. The instructor can ask small groups to identify underlying themes in the collective set of leader data points on the boards to specify what makes an effective leader. After students establish four or five key themes, they can be challenged to identify the one key theme that distinguishes leaders who are effective from those who are not.

Source: Based on Melvin R. McKnight, "Organizational Behavior as a Phenomenological, Free-Will Centered Science," Working Paper, College of Business Administration, Northern Arizona University, 1997.

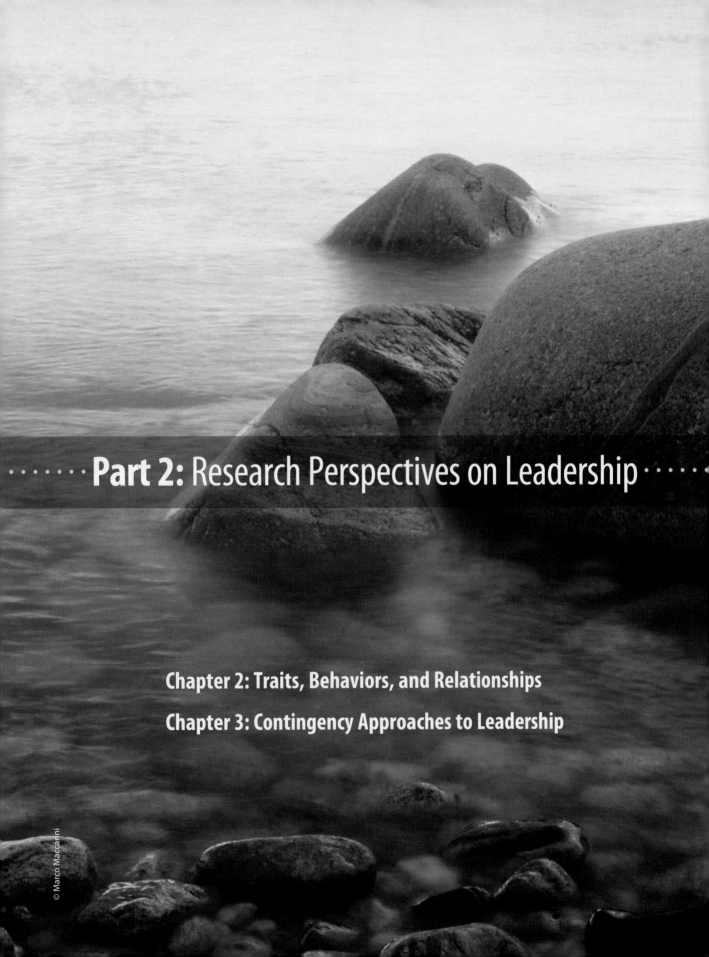

Part 2: Research Perspectives on Leadership

© Marco Maccarini

Chapter 2: Traits, Behaviors, and Relationships

© Marco Maccarini

Your Leadership Challenge

After reading this chapter, you should be able to:

- Identify the strengths you can bring to a leadership role.

- Outline some personal traits and characteristics that are associated with effective leaders.

- Recognize autocratic versus democratic leadership behavior and the impact of each.

- Know the distinction between people-oriented and task-oriented leadership behavior and when each should be used.

- Understand how the theory of individualized leadership has broadened the understanding of relationships between leaders and followers.

- Distinguish among various roles leaders play in organizations, including operations roles, collaborative roles, and advisory roles, and where your strengths might best fit.

Chapter Outline

Julia Stewart's first job as a 16-year-old was serving food at International House of Pancakes (IHOP) in San Diego. A few decades later, Stewart landed in the CEO's chair at IHOP headquarters. Some of the personal characteristics that helped get her there include ambition, persistence, conscientiousness, persuasiveness, and enthusiasm.[1] It is likely that those traits define a number of leaders who have attained higher levels in organizations. Personal traits are what captured the imagination of the earliest leadership researchers. However, look at any two successful and effective leaders and they will likely share some traits but have others that are quite dissimilar. Each individual has a unique set of qualities, characteristics, and strengths to bring to a leadership role.

Leaders display traits through patterns in their behavior. Consequently, many researchers have examined the behavior of leaders to determine what behavioral features comprise leadership style and how particular behaviors relate to effective leadership. Later research specified behavior between a leader and each distinct follower, differentiating one-on-one behavior from leader-to-group behavior.

This chapter first considers the importance of leaders understanding their own unique leadership strengths, and then provides an overview of the initial leadership research in the twentieth century. We examine the evolution of the trait approach and the behavior approach, and introduce the theory of individualized leadership. The path illuminated by the research into leader traits and behaviors is a foundation for the field of leadership studies and still enjoys remarkable dynamism for explaining leader success or failure. The final section of the chapter looks at how various traits and behaviors are suited to three different roles leaders play in organizations.

Know Your Strengths

The idea of *leader as hero* discussed in Chapter 1 has caused many people to think a leader has to be "all things to all people"—to have a complete set of skills, characteristics, and abilities to handle any problem, challenge, or opportunity that comes along. However, the leader who tries to be and do it all will surely fail. The myth of the complete leader can cause stress and frustration for leaders and followers, as well as damage to the organization.[2] *Interdependence* is the key to effective leadership. Sixty percent of leaders in one survey acknowledge that leaders face challenges that go beyond any individual's capabilities.[3] Therefore, the best leaders recognize and hone their strengths, while trusting and collaborating with others to make up for their weak points, as further discussed in this chapter's Leader's Bookshelf.

Becoming an effective leader requires discovering your own unique strengths and capabilities and learning how to make the most of them.[4] Every leader has a limited capacity; good leaders are those who tap into their key strengths that can make a difference. One leader might be particularly good at analyzing complex situations and making good decisions under time pressure. Another might struggle with managing her time effectively but be a whiz at getting a grasp on big problems. Some leaders don't do very well giving public speeches but are experts at building good one-on-one relationships with followers. Everyone has strengths, but many leaders fail to recognize and apply them, often because they are hampered by the idea that they should be good at everything. Benjamin Franklin referred to wasted strengths as "sundials in the shade."[5] Only when leaders understand their strengths can they use these abilities effectively to make their best contribution.

As you read about the traits, behaviors, and qualities associated with effective leadership in the remainder of this chapter, look for how you fit. Remember that it is not about having all the "right" characteristics, but rather about finding the strengths that you can best exemplify and apply as a leader.

The Trait Approach

Early efforts to understand leadership success focused on the leader's personal traits. **Traits** are the distinguishing personal characteristics of a leader, such as intelligence, honesty, self-confidence, and appearance. Research early in the twentieth century examined leaders who had achieved a level of greatness, and hence became known as the Great Man approach. Fundamental to this theory was the idea that some people are born with traits that make them natural leaders. The **Great Man approach** sought to identify the traits leaders possessed that distinguished them from people who were not leaders. Generally, research found only a weak relationship between personal traits and leader success.[6] Indeed, the diversity of traits that effective leaders possess indicates that leadership ability is not a genetic endowment.

Nevertheless, with the advancement of the field of psychology during the 1940s and 1950s, trait approach researchers expanded their examination of personal attributes by using aptitude and psychological tests. These early studies looked at personality traits such as creativity and self-confidence, physical traits

Traits
the distinguishing personal characteristics of a leader, such as intelligence, honesty, self-confidence, and appearance

Great Man approach
a leadership perspective that sought to identify the inherited traits leaders possessed that distinguished them from people who were not leaders

Leader's Bookshelf

Strengths Based Leadership—Great Leaders, Teams, and Why People Follow

by Tom Rath and Barry Conchie

Strengths Based Leadership is the most recent contribution in the Gallup Organization's series of books looking at how good leaders apply their unique strengths in a way to connect with followers and build teams that fortify the leader's weak spots.

Three Lessons for Influential Leadership

"If you look at great historical leaders such as Winston Churchill or Mahatma Gandhi, you might notice more differences than similarities—and it is the differences that defined them and led to their success," write authors Tom Rath and Barry Conchie. They offer three lessons, based on a review of decades of Gallup data on leadership, along with a new survey of more than 10,000 followers around the world. Here's what the most influential leaders do:

- *Continually invest in strengths*. Great leaders resist the temptation to try to excel at everything. What great leaders have in common is that they know their strengths and can call upon the right strength at the right time. In addition, good leaders focus on and develop the strengths of their followers, which builds follower confidence and motivation.
- *Maximize the team*. "Effective leaders surround themselves with the right people and build on each person's strengths." The best leadership teams have people with a combination of strengths in four areas: executing, influencing, relationship building, and strategic thinking.
- *Understand followers' needs*. When 10,000 people were asked what they want and need from a leader, four basic needs stood out: trust,

compassion, stability, and hope. No matter what an individual leader's strengths are, he or she can apply them in a way to build trust, show compassion, provide a sense of stability and confidence, and inspire hope.

Applying Strengths Based Leadership

No one can be good at everything, but leaders can learn to make the most of their unique capabilities. This book is packed with resources to help people identify their strengths and apply the lessons of influential leadership in real-life situations.

Strengths Based Leadership, by Tom Rath and Barry Conchie, is published by Gallup Press.

such as age and energy level, abilities such as knowledge and fluency of speech, social characteristics such as popularity and sociability, and work-related characteristics such as the desire to excel and persistence against obstacles. Effective leaders were often identified by exceptional follower performance, or by a high status position within an organization and a salary that exceeded that of peers.[7]

In a 1948 literature review,[8] Stogdill examined more than 100 studies based on the trait approach. He uncovered several traits that appeared consistent with effective leadership, including general intelligence, initiative, interpersonal skills, self-confidence, drive for responsibility, and personal integrity. Stogdill's findings also indicated, however, that the importance of a particular trait was often relative to the situation. Initiative, for example, may contribute to the success of a leader in one situation, but it may be irrelevant to a leader in another situation. Thus, possessing certain personal characteristics is no guarantee of success.

Many researchers discontinued their efforts to identify leadership traits in light of Stogdill's 1948 findings and turned their attention to examining leader behavior and leadership situations. However, others continued with expanded trait lists and research projects. Stogdill's subsequent review of 163 trait studies conducted between 1948 and 1970 concluded that some personal traits do indeed seem to contribute to effective leadership.[9] The study identified many of the same traits found in the 1948 survey, along with several additional characteristics, including aggressiveness, independence, and tolerance for stress. However,

marble: © Kirill Matkov   sunset: © Marco Regalia

Stogdill again cautioned that the value of a particular trait or set of traits varies with the organizational situation.

In recent years, there has been a resurgence of interest in examining leadership traits. A review by Kirkpatrick and Locke identified a number of personal traits that distinguish leaders from non-leaders, including some pinpointed by Stogdill.[10] Other studies have focused on followers' perceptions and indicate that certain traits are associated with people's perceptions of who is a leader. For example, one study found that the traits of intelligence, masculinity, and dominance were strongly related to how individuals perceived leaders.[11] Others have found that charismatic CEOs are perceived to be more effective than other leaders, even though there is no evidence showing they actually are.[12] In summary, trait research has been an important part of leadership studies throughout the twentieth century and continues into the twenty-first.

Exhibit 2.1 presents some of the traits and their respective categories that have been identified through trait research over the years. Many researchers still contend that some traits are essential to effective leadership, but only in combination with other factors.[13] For example, charisma, like other traits outlined in Exhibit 2.1, can certainly be associated with effective leadership, but not every effective leader has charisma, and many good leaders don't have any charisma at all. A few traits typically considered highly important for leadership are optimism and self-confidence, honesty and integrity, and drive.

Optimism and Self-Confidence Emerging research points to a positive outlook as one key to effective leadership.[14] **Optimism** refers to a tendency to see the positive side of things and expect that things will turn out well. Numerous surveys indicate that an optimistic attitude is the single characteristic most common to top executives. People rise to the top because they have the ability to see opportunities where others see problems and can instill in others a sense of hope for the future. Leaders at all levels need some degree of optimism to see possibilities even through the thickest fog and rally people around a vision for a better tomorrow. One leadership researcher has

Exhibit 2.1 Personal Characteristics of Leaders

Personal Characteristics	**Social Characteristics**
Energy	Sociability, interpersonal skills
Passion	Cooperativeness
Physical stamina	Ability to enlist cooperation
Intelligence and Ability	Tact, diplomacy
Intelligence, cognitive ability	**Work-Related Characteristics**
Knowledge	Drive, desire to excel
Judgment, decisiveness	Responsibility in pursuit of goals
Personality	Persistence against obstacles, tenacity
Optimism	**Social Background**
Self-confidence	Education
Honesty and integrity	Mobility
Enthusiasm	
Charisma	
Desire to lead	
Independence	

Optimism
a tendency to see the positive side of things and expect that things will turn out well

Sources: *Bass and Stogdill's Handbook of Leadership: Theory, Research, and Management Applications*, 3rd ed. (New York: The Free Press, 1990), pp. 80–81; and S. A. Kirkpatrick and E. A. Locke, "Leadership: Do Traits Matter?" *Academy of Management Executive* 5, no. 2 (1991), pp. 48–60.

Leader's Self-Insight 2.1
Rate Your Self-Confidence

This questionnaire is designed to assess your level of self-confidence as reflected in a belief in your ability to accomplish a desired outcome. There are no right or wrong answers. Please indicate your personal feelings about whether each statement is Mostly False or Mostly True by checking the answer that best describes your attitude or feeling.

	Mostly False	Mostly True
1. When I make plans, I am certain I can make them work.	_____	_____
2. One of my problems is that I often cannot get down to work when I should.	_____	_____
3. When I set important goals for myself, I rarely achieve them.	_____	_____
4. I often give up on things before completing them.	_____	_____
5. I typically put off facing difficult situations.	_____	_____
6. If something looks too complicated, I may not even bother to try it.	_____	_____
7. When I decide to do something, I go right to work on it.	_____	_____

	Mostly False	Mostly True
8. When an unexpected problem occurs, I often don't respond well.	_____	_____
9. Failure just makes me try harder.	_____	_____
10. I consider myself a self-reliant person.	_____	_____

Scoring and Interpretation

Give yourself one point for checking Mostly True for items 1, 7, 9, and 10. Also give yourself one point for checking Mostly False for items 2, 3, 4, 5, 6, and 8. Enter your score here: _____. If your score is 8 or higher, it may mean that you are high on self-confidence. If your score is 3 or less, your self-confidence may be low. If your score is low, what can you do to increase your self-confidence?

Source: This is part of the general self-efficacy subscale of the self-efficacy scale published in M. Sherer, J. E. Maddux, B. Mercadante, S. Prentice-Dunn, B. Jacobs, and R. W. Rogers, "The Self-Efficacy Scale: Construction and Validation," *Psychological Reports* 51 (1982), pp. 663–671. Used with permission.

marble: © Kirill Matkov   sunset: © Marco Regalia

gone so far as to say that "The opposite of a leader isn't a follower. The opposite of a leader is a pessimist."[15]

A related characteristic is having a positive attitude about oneself. Leaders who know themselves develop **self-confidence**, which is assurance in one's own judgments, decision making, ideas, and capabilities. Self-confidence doesn't mean being arrogant and prideful, but rather knowing and trusting in oneself. Pittsburgh Steelers Coach Mike Tomlin, who at the age of 36 became the youngest Super Bowl head coach in league history, provides an illustration. "Shocked is not a word that I would use," Tomlin said, referring to his confidence in his ability to succeed and achieve goals. When he quit law school to take his first $12,000 a year coaching job, his mother was appalled, but Tomlin assured her calmly that he knew what he was doing.[16] A leader who has a positive self-image and displays certainty about his or her own ability fosters confidence among followers, gains respect and admiration, and meets challenges. The confidence a leader displays and develops creates motivation and commitment among followers for the mission at hand.

Active leaders need self-confidence and optimism. How many of us willingly follow someone who is jaded and pessimistic, or someone who obviously doesn't believe in himself or herself? Leaders initiate change and they often must make decisions without adequate information. Problems are solved continuously. Without

Action Memo

Do you believe you have the self-confidence to be a strong and effective leader? Complete the questionnaire in Leader's Self-Insight 2.1 to assess your level of self-confidence.

Self-confidence
assurance in one's own judgments, decision making, ideas, and capabilities

Action Memo

As a leader, you can develop the personal traits of self-confidence, integrity, and drive, which are important for successful leadership in every organization and situation. You can work to keep an optimistic attitude and be ethical in your decisions and actions.

the confidence to move forward and believe things will be okay, even if an occasional decision is wrong, leaders could be paralyzed into inaction. Setbacks have to be overcome. Risks have to be taken. Competing points of view have to be managed, with some people left unsatisfied. The characteristics of optimism and self-confidence enable a leader to face all these challenges.[17]

Honesty and Integrity Positive attitudes have to be tempered by strong ethics or leaders can get into trouble. Consider Bernard Madoff, who masterminded the largest financial fraud in history and was sent to jail on 11 criminal charges including securities fraud and perjury. As a leader, Madoff displayed strong self-confidence and optimism, which is one reason he was able to attract so many investors. The problem was that he didn't have a strong ethical grounding to match. Thanks to Madoff's scam, thousands of people were swindled out of their life's savings, charities and foundations were ruined, and pension funds were wiped out, while Madoff and his wife lived in luxury.[18]

Effective leaders are ethical leaders. One aspect of being an ethical leader is being honest with followers, customers, shareholders and the public, and maintaining one's integrity. **Honesty** refers to truthfulness and nondeception. It implies an openness that followers welcome. **Integrity** means that a leader's character is whole, integrated, and grounded in solid ethical principles, and he or she acts in keeping with those principles. Leaders who model their ethical convictions through their daily actions command admiration, respect, and loyalty. Honesty and integrity are the foundation of trust between leaders and followers.

Sadly, trust is sorely lacking in many organizations following years of corporate scandals and rampant Wall Street greed. Leaders need the traits of honesty and integrity to rebuild trusting and productive relationships. People today are wary of authority and the deceptive use of power, and they are hungry for leaders who hold high moral standards. Successful leaders have also been found to be highly consistent, doing exactly what they say they will do when they say they will do it. Successful leaders prove themselves trustworthy. They adhere to basic ethical principles and consistently apply them in their leadership. One survey of 1,500 managers asked the values most desired in leaders. Honesty and integrity topped the list. The authors concluded:

> *Honesty is absolutely essential to leadership. After all, if we are willing to follow someone, whether it be into battle or into the boardroom, we first want to assure ourselves that the person is worthy of our trust. We want to know that he or she is being truthful, ethical, and principled. We want to be fully confident in the integrity of our leaders.*[19]

Honesty
truthfulness and nondeception

Integrity
the quality of being whole, integrated, and acting in accordance with solid moral principles

Drive
high motivation that creates a high effort level by a leader

Drive Another characteristic considered essential for effective leadership is drive. Leaders often are responsible for initiating new projects as well as guiding projects to successful completion. **Drive** refers to high motivation that creates a high effort level by a leader. Leaders with drive seek achievement, have energy and tenacity, and are frequently perceived as ambitious. If people don't strive to achieve something, they rarely do. Ambition can enable leaders to set challenging goals and take initiative to reach them.[20] Stephen Schwarzman, cofounder, chairman, and CEO of Blackstone Group, provides a good example of drive.

IN THE LEAD

Stephen Schwarzman, Blackstone Group

He stands just 5'6" tall, but Stephen Schwarzman is a giant in the investment industry. When Schwarzman pursues deals, he's out to win, no holds barred. And more often than not, he does. "I didn't get to be successful by letting people hurt Blackstone or me. I never choose to go into battle first," Schwarzman says. "But I won't back down."

Schwarzman made a financial killing when he took Blackstone public, but he says money isn't really the goal for him. Money is just the "measuring stick," a reflection of accomplishment. Schwarzman displayed strong drive at an early age. Working weekends at his family's Philadelphia retail store at the age of 15, he urged his father to open more stores and grew frustrated when his dad refused. He couldn't understand why a person wouldn't want to reach for more.

Schwarzman has been reaching for more ever since. He proudly says he was president of his junior high and high school classes, was on the podium on Class Day at Yale University, and was president of the prestigious Century Club at Harvard Business School. After graduate school, he went to work at Lehman Brothers and quickly rose through the ranks. In 1985, he and a colleague, Peter G. Peterson, decided to start a buyout firm. To start Blackstone, Peterson suggested they try to raise $50 million. Schwarzman's drive kicked in once again. He decided $1 billion, a huge amount at the time, was a better goal. They didn't quite make it, but the pair raised $830 million for their first fund, and Blackstone has been dependably successful ever since. Of his leadership style Schwarzman says, "I'm a consistent little person."[21]

Like most companies in the world of finance, Blackstone has been through some tough times recently. Schwarzman and Peterson, although generously paid, cut their base salary and gave up their bonuses when the company lost money in 2008.[22]

A strong drive is also associated with high energy. Leaders work long hours over many years. They have stamina and are vigorous and full of life in order to handle the pace, the demands, and the challenges of leadership. Jeff Immelt, CEO of General Electric, provides another example of strong drive. "There are 24 hours in a day, and you can use them all," says Immelt. He claims he's been working 100 hours a week for a quarter of a century, long before he took over the top job at General Electric. "You have to have real stamina," he says.[23]

Working 100-hour weeks certainly isn't necessary for effective leadership, but all leaders have to display drive and energy to be successful. Clearly, various traits such as drive, self-confidence, optimism, and honesty have great value for leaders. One study of 600 executives by Hay Group, a global organizational and human resources consulting firm, found that 75 percent of the successful executives studied possessed the characteristics of self-confidence and drive.[24] This chapter's *Consider This* box presents the notion that personal characteristics of the leader are ultimately responsible for leadership outcomes.

In Chapter 4, we will further consider individual characteristics and qualities that play a role in leadership effectiveness. However, as indicated earlier, traits alone cannot define effective leadership. The inability of researchers to define effective leadership based solely on personal traits led to an interest in looking at the behavior of leaders and how it might contribute to leadership success or failure.

Behavior Approaches

Rather than looking at an individual's personal traits, diverse research programs on leadership behavior have sought to uncover the behaviors that effective leaders

Consider **This!**

Leader Qualities

The quality of the leader determines the quality of the organization.

A leader who lacks intelligence, virtue, and experience cannot hope for success.

In any conflict, the circumstances affect the outcome.

Good leaders can succeed in adverse conditions.

Bad leaders can lose in favorable conditions.

Therefore, good leaders constantly strive to perfect themselves, lest their shortcomings mar their endeavors.

When all other factors are equal, it is the character of the leader that determines the outcome.

Source: Excerpt from page 66 ["Leader Qualities"] from *Everyday Tao: Living with Balance and Harmony* by Deng Ming-Dao. Copyright © 1996 by Deng Ming-Dao. Reprinted by permission of HarperCollins Publishers, Inc.

© majaiva

engage in. Behaviors can be learned more readily than traits, enabling leadership to be accessible to all.

Autocratic versus Democratic Leadership

One study that served as a precursor to the behavior approach recognized autocratic and democratic leadership styles. An **autocratic** leader is one who tends to centralize authority and derive power from position, control of rewards, and coercion. A **democratic** leader delegates authority to others, encourages participation, relies on subordinates' knowledge for completion of tasks, and depends on subordinate respect for influence.

The first studies on these leadership behaviors were conducted at the University of Iowa by Kurt Lewin and his associates.[25] The research included groups of children, each with its own designated adult leader who was instructed to act in either an autocratic or democratic style. These experiments produced some interesting findings. The groups with autocratic leaders performed highly so long as the leader was present to supervise them. However, group members were displeased with the close, autocratic style of leadership, and feelings of hostility frequently arose. The performance of groups who were assigned democratic leaders was almost as good, and these groups were characterized by positive feelings rather than hostility. In addition, under the democratic style of leadership, group members performed well even when the leader was absent. The participative techniques and majority-rule decision making used by the democratic leader trained and involved the group members so that they performed well with or without the leader present. These characteristics of democratic leadership may partly explain why the empowerment of employees is a popular trend in companies today.

This early work implied that leaders were either autocratic or democratic in their approach. However, further work by Tannenbaum and Schmidt indicated that leadership behavior could exist on a continuum reflecting different amounts of employee participation.[26] Thus, one leader might be autocratic (boss-centered), another democratic (subordinate-centered), and a third a mix of the two styles. Exhibit 2.2 illustrates the leadership continuum.

Autocratic
a leader who tends to centralize authority and derive power from position, control of rewards, and coercion

Democratic
a leader who delegates authority to others, encourages participation, relies on subordinates' knowledge for completion of tasks, and depends on subordinate respect for influence

Exhibit 2.2 Leadership Continuum

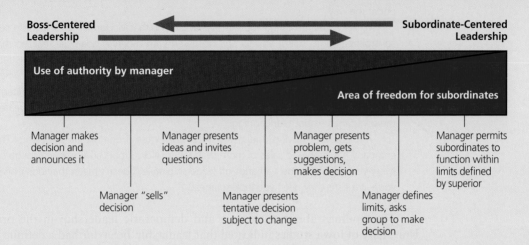

Source: *Harvard Business Review*. An exhibit from Robert Tannenbaum and Warren Schmidt, "How to Choose a Leadership Pattern" (May–June 1973). Copyright 1973 by the president and Fellows of Harvard College.

Tannenbaum and Schmidt also suggested that the extent to which leaders should be boss-centered or subordinate-centered depended on organizational circumstances, and that leaders might adjust their behaviors to fit the circumstances. For example, if there is time pressure on a leader, or if it takes too long for subordinates to learn how to make decisions, the leader will tend to use an autocratic style. When subordinates are able to learn decision-making skills readily, a democratic style can be used. Also, the greater the skill difference, the more autocratic the leader approach, because it is difficult to bring subordinates up to the leader's expertise level.[27]

Jack Hartnett, president of D. L. Rogers Corporation and franchise owner of 54 Sonic drive-in restaurants, provides an example of the autocratic leadership style. He tells workers to "do it the way we tell you to do it," rather than asking for their input or suggestions.[28] The style works well in the fast-food restaurant business where turnover is typically high and many employees are young and low skilled. In contrast, the CEO of Applegate Farms, a purveyor of organic and natural meats, is an extreme example of a democratic leader.

> **Action Memo**
>
> *As a leader, you can use a democratic leadership style to help followers develop decision-making skills and perform well without close supervision. An autocratic style might be appropriate when there is time pressure or followers have low skill levels.*

IN THE LEAD

Stephen McDonnell, Applegate Farms

For most of Applegate Farms' history, its CEO hasn't even been in the office. When Stephen McDonnell bought a struggling meat products company (then called Jugtown Mountain Smokehouse) nearly 20 years ago, he spent the first six months working full-time on-site, but since then he's been working mostly from home.

From his experience at other companies, McDonnell had observed that most organizational problems were more easily diagnosed, and more effectively solved, within specific teams or work groups rather than by top managers. He decided that the best way to get a company running smoothly was to give everyone access to relevant information, empower them with the freedom and responsibility to act on it, and then stay out of the way.

What's most interesting about the whole story is that McDonnell is a self-confessed control-freak boss, full of anxiety and obsessed with meeting goals. He realized that working mostly from home was the best way to protect the company from his tendency to micromanage. McDonnell goes into the office only on Wednesdays, when he performs a variety of tasks, such as taste testing new products, discussing strategic issues with senior managers, and dealing with any staff problems that might threaten the company's smooth functioning.

Applegate is thriving under this system of extreme democratic leadership. The company has grown to sales of more than $35 million. Profits and productivity go up every year. To McDonnell, a hands-off leadership style "doesn't mean they don't need you—it means they need you looking ahead."[29]

The findings about autocratic and democratic leadership in the original University of Iowa studies indicated that leadership behavior had a definite effect on outcomes such as follower performance and satisfaction. Equally important was the recognition that effective leadership was reflected in behavior, not simply by what personality traits a leader possessed. The Stephen McDonnell example indicates that leaders can adopt behaviors that are almost in direct opposition to their natural traits when it is necessary. Jay Vogt, a consultant to Applegate, says of McDonnell: "If he's at the company on some days he might do more harm than good, and he knows that. How many CEOs have that self-awareness?"[30]

Ohio State Studies

The idea that leadership is reflected in behavior and not just personal traits provided a focus for subsequent research. One early series of studies on leadership behavior was conducted at the Ohio State University. Researchers conducted surveys to identify specific dimensions of leader behavior. Narrowing a list of nearly 2,000 leader behaviors into a questionnaire containing 150 examples of definitive leader behaviors, they developed the Leader Behavior Description Questionnaire (LBDQ) and administered it to employees.[31] Hundreds of employees responded to various examples according to the degree to which their leaders engaged in the behaviors. The analysis of ratings resulted in two wide-ranging categories of leader behavior, later called *consideration* and *initiating structure*.

Action Memo

Discover your leadership orientation related to consideration and initiating structure by completing the self-assessment exercise in Leader's Self-Insight 2.2.

Consideration describes the extent to which a leader cares about subordinates, respects their ideas and feelings, and establishes mutual trust. Showing appreciation, listening carefully to problems, and seeking input from subordinates regarding important decisions are all examples of consideration behaviors.

Initiating structure describes the extent to which a leader is task oriented and directs subordinates' work activities toward goal achievement. This type of leader behavior includes directing tasks, getting people to work hard, planning, providing explicit schedules for work activities, and ruling with an iron hand.

Although many leaders fall along a continuum that includes both consideration and initiating structure behaviors, these behavior categories are independent of one another. In other words, a leader can display a high degree of both behavior types, or a low degree of both behavior types. Additionally, a leader might demonstrate high consideration and low initiating structure, or low consideration and high initiating structure behavior. Research indicates that all four of these leader style

Consideration
the extent to which a leader is sensitive to subordinates, respects their ideas and feelings, and establishes mutual trust

Initiating structure
the extent to which a leader is task oriented and directs subordinates' work activities toward goal achievement

Leader's Self-Insight 2.2
What's Your Leadership Orientation?

The following questions ask about your personal leadership orientation. Each item describes a specific kind of behavior but does not ask you to judge whether the behavior is desirable or undesirable.

Read each item carefully. Think about how frequently you engage in the behavior described by the item in a work or school group. Please indicate whether each statement is Mostly False or Mostly True by checking the answer that best describes your behavior.

	Mostly False	Mostly True
1. I put into operation suggestions agreed to by the group.	_____	_____
2. I treat everyone in the group with respect as my equal.	_____	_____
3. I back up what other people in the group do.	_____	_____
4. I help others with their personal problems.	_____	_____
5. I bring up how much work should be accomplished.	_____	_____
6. I help assign people to specific tasks.	_____	_____
7. I frequently suggest ways to fix problems.	_____	_____
8. I emphasize deadlines and how to meet them.	_____	_____

Scoring and Interpretation

Consideration behavior score—count the number of checks for Mostly True for items 1–4. Enter your consideration score here: _____.

A higher score (3 or 4) suggests a relatively strong orientation toward consideration behavior by you as a leader. A low score (2 or less) suggests a relatively weak consideration orientation.

Initiating structure behavior score—count the number of checks for Mostly True for items 5–8. Enter your initiating structure score here: _____.

A higher score (3 or 4) suggests a relatively strong orientation toward initiating structure behavior by you as a leader. A low score (2 or less) suggests a relatively weak orientation toward initiating structure behavior.

Source: Sample items adapted from: Edwin A Fleishman's *Leadership Opinion Questionnaire.* (Copyright 1960, Science Research Associates, Inc., Chicago, IL.) This version is based on Jon L. Pierce and John W. Newstrom, *Leaders and the Leadership Process: Readings, Self-Assessments & Applications*, 2nd ed. (Boston: Irwin McGraw-Hill, 2000).

marble: © Kirill Matkov   sunset: © Marco Regalia

combinations can be effective.[32] The following examples describe two U.S. Marine leaders who display different types of leadership behavior that correlate to the *consideration* and *initiating structure* styles. Sometimes these styles clash.

IN THE LEAD

Col. Joe D. Dowdy and Maj. Gen. James Mattis, U.S. Marine Corps

Only a few weeks into the war in Iraq, Marine Col. Joe D. Dowdy had both accomplished a grueling military mission and been removed from his command by Maj. Gen. James Mattis. The complicated and conflicting tales of why Col. Dowdy was dismissed are beyond the scope of this text, but one issue that came under examination was the differing styles of Col. Dowdy and Gen. Mattis, as well as the difficult, age-old wartime tension of "men versus mission."

Gen. Mattis has been referred to as a "warrior monk," consumed with the study of battle tactics and whose own battle plans in Iraq were considered brilliant. Gen. Mattis saw speed as integral to success in the early days of the Iraqi war, pushing for regiments to move quickly to accomplish a mission despite significant risks. For Col. Dowdy, some risks seemed too high, and he made decisions that delayed his mission, but better

TURBULENT TIMES

protected his Marines. Col. Dowdy was beloved by his followers because he was deeply concerned about their welfare, paid attention to them as individuals, and treated them as equals, going so far as to decline certain privileges that were available only to officers.

Despite their different styles, both leaders were highly respected by followers. When asked about Gen. Mattis, Gunnery Sgt. Robert Kane, who has served under both leaders, says he would certainly "follow him again." However, when he learned that Col. Dowdy had been dismissed, Sgt. Kane says he "wanted to go with him. If [he] had said 'Get your gear, you're coming with me,' I would've gone, even if it meant the end of my career."[33]

Gen. Mattis might be considered highly task-oriented, reflecting an initiating structure approach, while Col. Dowdy seems more people-oriented, reflecting a consideration behavioral style. Whereas Gen. Mattis typically put the mission first, combined with a concern for the Marines under his command, Col. Dowdy typically put Marines first, even though he also gave his all to accomplish the mission.

Additional studies that correlated these two leader behavior types and impact on subordinates initially demonstrated that "considerate" supervisors had a more positive impact on subordinate satisfaction than did "structuring" supervisors.[34] For example, when leader effectiveness was defined by voluntary turnover or amount of grievances filed by subordinates, considerate leaders generated less turnover and grievances. But research that utilized performance criteria, such as group output and productivity, showed initiating structure behavior was rated more effective. Other studies involving aircraft commanders and university department heads revealed that leaders rated effective by subordinates exhibited a high level of both consideration and initiating structure behaviors, whereas leaders rated less effective displayed low levels of both behavior styles.[35]

University of Michigan Studies

Studies at the University of Michigan took a different approach by directly comparing the behavior of effective and ineffective supervisors.[36] The effectiveness of leaders was determined by productivity of the subordinate group. Initial field studies and interviews at various job sites gave way to a questionnaire not unlike the LBDQ, called the Survey of Organizations.[37]

Over time, the Michigan researchers established two types of leadership behavior, each type consisting of two dimensions.[38] First, **employee-centered** leaders display a focus on the human needs of their subordinates. Leader support and interaction facilitation are the two underlying dimensions of employee-centered behavior. This means that in addition to demonstrating support for their subordinates, employee-centered leaders facilitate positive interaction among followers and seek to minimize conflict. The employee-centered style of leadership roughly corresponds to the Ohio State concept of consideration.

In contrast to the employee-centered leader, the **job-centered** leader directs activities toward scheduling, accomplishing tasks, and achieving efficiency. Goal emphasis and work facilitation are dimensions of this leadership behavior. By focusing on reaching task goals and facilitating the structure of tasks, job-centered behavior approximates that of initiating structure.

However, unlike the consideration and initiating structure styles defined by the Ohio State studies, Michigan researchers considered employee-centered leadership and job-centered leadership to be distinct styles in opposition to one another. A leader is identifiable by behavior characteristic of one or the other style, but not both. Another hallmark of later Michigan studies is the acknowledgment that often the behaviors of goal emphasis, work facilitation,

Employee-centered
a leadership behavior that displays a focus on the human needs of subordinates

Job-centered
leadership behavior in which leaders direct activities toward efficiency, cost-cutting, and scheduling, with an emphasis on goals and work facilitation

support, and interaction facilitation can be meaningfully performed by a subordinate's peers, rather than only by the designated leader. Other people in the group could supply these behaviors, which enhanced performance.[39]

In addition, while leadership behavior was demonstrated to affect the performance and satisfaction of subordinates, performance was also influenced by other factors related to the situation within which leaders and subordinates worked. The importance of situation will be explored in the next chapter.

The Leadership Grid

Blake and Mouton of the University of Texas proposed a two-dimensional leadership theory called **The Leadership Grid** that builds on the work of the Ohio State and Michigan studies.[40] Based on a week-long seminar, researchers rated leaders on a scale of one to nine according to two criteria: the concern for people and the concern for production. The scores for these criteria are plotted on a grid with an axis corresponding to each concern. Exhibit 2.3 depicts the two-dimensional model and five of the seven major leadership styles.

Team management (9,9) often is considered the most effective style and is recommended because organization members work together to accomplish tasks. *Country club management* (1,9) occurs when primary emphasis is given to people rather than to work outputs. *Authority-compliance management* (9,1) occurs when efficiency in operations is the dominant orientation. *Middle-of-the-road management* (5,5) reflects a moderate amount of concern for both people and production. *Impoverished management* (1,1) means the absence of a leadership

The Leadership Grid
a two-dimensional leadership model that describes major leadership styles based on measuring both concern for people and concern for production

Exhibit 2.3 The Leadership Grid Figure

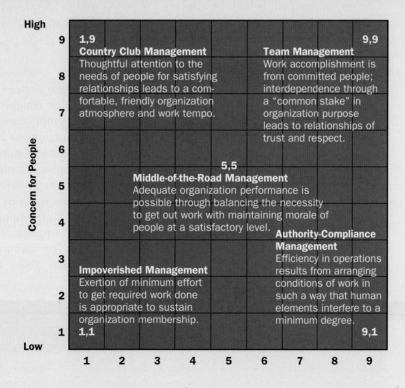

Source: The Leadership Grid figure from *Leadership Dilemma—Grid Solutions* by Robert R. Blake and Anne Adams McCanse (formerly the Managerial Grid by Robert R. Blake and Jane S. Mouton). Houston: Gulf Publishing Company, p. 29. Copyright 1991 by Scientific Methods, Inc. Reproduced by permission of the owners.

philosophy; leaders exert little effort toward interpersonal relationships or work accomplishment. Consider these examples:

IN THE LEAD

Pamela Forbes Lieberman, TruServ, and Douglas R. Conant, Campbell Soup Company

When Pamela Forbes Lieberman learned that her subordinates called her *the dragon lady*, she embraced the moniker and hung a watercolor of a dragon in her office. Lieberman makes no apologies for her hard-driving management style. Her emphasis on tough goals and bottom-line results has restored the health of hardware cooperative TruServ, which supplies inventory to True Value hardware stores. As soon as Lieberman became CEO, she began slashing costs and setting tough performance targets. "If [people] succeed, they will be rewarded, but if they don't, then we're going to have to look for new people sitting in their chairs," Lieberman said.

Compare Lieberman's approach to that of Douglas R. Conant, CEO of Campbell Soup. Conant has turned a lackluster company into one of the most innovative and profitable firms in the food industry by using a different approach. Conant doesn't shy away from making tough operational decisions, but his primary emphasis has been on reinvigorating morale. Conant has sent more than 16,000 handwritten thank-you notes to employees at all levels of the company. Rather than looking for what is wrong, Conant says, he tries to "celebrate what's right." Every six months, he has lunch with a dozen or so employees to get feedback, ask about their problems, and see ways he can help them do their jobs better.[41]

The leadership of Pamela Forbes Lieberman is characterized by high concern for tasks and production and low-to-moderate concern for people. Douglas Conant, in contrast, is high on concern for people and moderate on concern for production. In each case, both concerns shown in The Leadership Grid are present, but they are integrated at different levels.

Theories of a "High-High" Leader

The leadership styles described by the researchers at Ohio State, University of Michigan, and University of Texas pertain to variables that roughly correspond to one another: consideration and initiating structure; employee-centered and job-centered; concern for people and concern for production, as illustrated in Exhibit 2.4. The research into the behavior approach culminated in two predominate types of leadership behaviors—people-oriented and task-oriented.

The findings about two underlying dimensions and the possibility of leaders rated high on both dimensions raise three questions to think about. The first question is whether these two dimensions are the most important behaviors of leadership. Certainly, these two behaviors are important. They capture fundamental, underlying aspects of human behavior that must be considered for organizations to succeed. One reason why these two dimen-

Exhibit 2.4 Themes of Leader Behavior Research

	People-Oriented	Task-Oriented
Ohio State University	Consideration	Initiating Structure
University of Michigan	Employee-Centered	Job-Centered
University of Texas	Concern for People	Concern for Production

sions are compelling is that the findings are based on empirical research, which means that researchers went into the field to study real leaders across a variety of settings. When independent streams of field research reach similar conclusions, they probably represent a fundamental theme in leadership behavior. A review of 50 years of leadership research, for example, identified task-oriented behavior and people-oriented behavior as primary categories related to effective leadership in numerous studies.[42] Concern for tasks and concern for people must be shown toward followers at some reasonable level, either by the leader or by other people in the system. Although these are not the only important behaviors, as we will see throughout this book, they certainly require attention.

The second question is whether people orientation and task orientation exist together in the same leader, and how. The Grid theory argues that yes, both are present when people work with or through others to accomplish an activity. Although leaders may be high on either style, there is considerable belief that the best leaders are high on both behaviors. John Fryer, superintendent of Florida's Duvall County Schools, provides an example of a leader who succeeds on both dimensions. A former U.S. Air Force officer, Fryer developed a strategic plan for the school system, set high performance standards for both teachers and students, and directed everyone toward the accomplishment of specific tasks and goals. At first skeptical of the new superintendent, teachers were won over by his genuine concern for their ideas and their anxieties. He gained commitment by involving teachers in the planning process and learning what they needed to succeed. "We finally got a superintendent who will listen," said Terrie Brady, president of the teachers' union.[43]

Action Memo

As a leader, you can succeed in a variety of situations by showing concern for both tasks and people. People-oriented behavior is related to higher follower satisfaction, and task-oriented behavior is typically associated with higher productivity.

The third question concerns whether people can actually change themselves into leaders high on people- or task-orientation. In the 1950s and 1960s, when the Ohio State and Michigan studies were underway, the assumption of researchers was that the behaviors of effective leaders could be emulated by anyone wishing to become an effective leader. In general it seems that people can indeed learn new leader behaviors. There is a belief that "high-high" leadership is a desirable quality, because the leader will meet both needs simultaneously. Although "high-high" leadership is not the only effective style, researchers have looked to this kind of leader as a candidate for success in a wide variety of situations. However, as we will see in Chapter 3, the next generation of leadership studies refined the understanding of situations to pinpoint more precisely when each type of leadership behavior is most effective.

Individualized Leadership

Traditional trait and behavior theories assume that a leader adopts a general leadership style that is used with all group members. A more recent approach to leadership behavior research, *individualized leadership,* looks instead at the specific relationship between a leader and each individual follower.[44] **Individualized leadership** is based on the notion that a leader develops a unique relationship with each subordinate or group member, which determines how the leader behaves toward the member and how the member responds to the leader. In this view, leadership is a series of *dyads,* or a series of two-person interactions. The dyadic view focuses on the concept of *exchange,* what each party gives to and receives from the other.[45]

The first individualized leadership theory was introduced nearly 40 years ago and has been steadily revised ever since. Exhibit 2.5 illustrates the development

Individualized leadership
a theory based on the notion that a leader develops a unique relationship with each subordinate or group member, which determines how the leader behaves toward the member and how the member responds to the leader

Exhibit 2.5 Stages of Development of Individualized Leadership

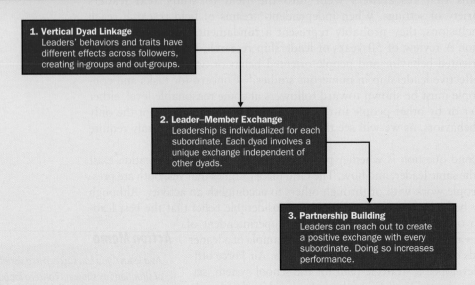

1. Vertical Dyad Linkage
Leaders' behaviors and traits have different effects across followers, creating in-groups and out-groups.

2. Leader–Member Exchange
Leadership is individualized for each subordinate. Each dyad involves a unique exchange independent of other dyads.

3. Partnership Building
Leaders can reach out to create a positive exchange with every subordinate. Doing so increases performance.

Sources: Based on Fred Danereau, "A Dyadic Approach to Leadership: Creating and Nurturing This Approach Under Fire," *Leadership Quarterly* 6, no. 4 (1995), pp. 479–490, and George B. Graen and Mary Uhl-Bien, "Relationship-Based Approach to Leadership: Development of Leader–Member Exchange (LMX) Theory of Leadership over 25 Years: Applying a Multi-Level, Multi-Domain Approach," *Leadership Quarterly* 6, no. 2 (1995), pp. 219–247.

of research in this area. The first stage was the awareness of a relationship between a leader and each individual, rather than between a leader and a group of followers. The second stage examined specific attributes of the exchange relationship. The third stage explored whether leaders could intentionally develop partnerships with each group member.

Vertical Dyad Linkage Model

The **Vertical Dyad Linkage (VDL) model** argues for the importance of the dyad formed by a leader with each member of the group. Initial findings indicated that followers provided very different descriptions of the same leader. For example, some reported a leader, and their relationship with the leader, as having a high degree of mutual trust, respect, and obligation. These high-quality relationships might be characterized as high on both people and task orientation. Other followers reported a low-quality relationship with the same leader, such as having a low degree of trust, respect, and obligation. These followers perceived the leader as being low on important leadership behaviors.

Based on these two extreme behavior patterns, subordinates were found to exist in either an in-group or an out-group in relation to the leader. Exhibit 2.6 delineates the differences in leader behavior toward in-group versus out-group members. Most of us who have had experience with any kind of group, whether it be a college class, an athletic team, or a work group, recognize that some leaders may spend a disproportionate amount of time with certain people, and that these "insiders" are often highly trusted and may obtain special privileges. In the terminology of the VDL model, these people would be considered to participate in an *in-group relationship* with the leader, whereas other members of the group who did not experience a sense of trust and extra consideration would participate in an *out-group relationship*. In-group members, those who rated the leader

Vertical Dyad Linkage (VDL) model
a model of individualized leadership that argues for the importance of the dyad formed by a leader with each member of the group

Exhibit 2.6 Leader Behavior Toward In-Group Versus Out-Group Members

In-Group	Out-Group
• Discusses objectives; gives employee freedom to use his or her own approach in solving problems and reaching goals	• Gives employee specific directives for how to accomplish tasks and attain goals
• Listens to employee's suggestions and ideas about how work is done	• Shows little interest in employee's comments and suggestions
• Treats mistakes as learning opportunities	• Criticizes or punishes mistakes
• Gives employee interesting assignments; may allow employee to choose assignment	• Assigns primarily routine jobs and monitors employee closely
• Sometimes defers to subordinate's opinion	• Usually imposes own views
• Praises accomplishments	• Focuses on areas of poor performance

Source: Based on Jean-François Manzoni and Jean-Louis Barsoux, "The Set-Up-to-Fail Syndrome," *Harvard Business Review* (March–April, 1988), pp. 101–113.

highly, had developed close relationships with the leader and often became assistants who played key roles in the functioning of the work unit. Out-group members were not key players in the work unit.

Thus, by focusing on the relationship between a leader and each individual, the Vertical Dyad Linkage research found great variance of leader style and impact within a group of followers.

Leader–Member Exchange

Stage two in the development of the individualized leadership theory explored the **leader–member exchange (LMX)** in more detail, discovering that the impact on outcomes depends on how the leader–member exchange process develops over time. Studies evaluating characteristics of the LMX relationship explored such things as communication frequency, value agreement, characteristics of followers, job satisfaction, performance, job climate, and commitment. Leaders typically tend to establish in-group exchange relationships with individuals who have characteristics similar to those of the leader, such as similarity in background, interests, and values, and with those who demonstrate a high level of competence and interest in the job. Overall, studies have found that the quality of the leader–member exchange relationship is substantially higher for in-group members. LMX theory proposes that this higher-quality relationship will lead to higher performance and greater job satisfaction for in-group members, and research in general supports this idea.[46] High-quality LMX relationships have been found to lead to very positive outcomes for leaders, followers, work units, and the organization. For followers, a high-quality exchange relationship may mean more interesting assignments, greater responsibility and authority, and tangible rewards such as pay increases and promotions. Leaders and organizations clearly benefit from the increased effort and initiative of in-group participants to carry out assignments and tasks successfully.

Partnership Building

In this third phase of research, the focus was on whether leaders could develop positive relationships with a large number of subordinates. Critics of early LMX theory pointed out the dangers of leaders establishing sharply differentiated

Action Memo

Answer the questions in Leader's Self-Insight 2.3 to understand how LMX theory applies to your own work experience.

Leader–member exchange (LMX)
individualized leadership model that explores how leader–member relationships develop over time and how the quality of exchange relationships affects outcomes

What was the quality of your leader's relationship with you? Think back to a job you held and recall your feelings toward your leader, or if currently employed use your supervisor. Please answer whether each item below was Mostly False or Mostly True for you.

	Mostly False	Mostly True
1. I very much liked my supervisor as a person.	___	___
2. My supervisor defended my work to people above him if I made a mistake.	___	___
3. The work I did for my supervisor went well beyond what was required.	___	___
4. I admired my supervisor's professional knowledge and ability.	___	___
5. My supervisor was enjoyable to work with.	___	___
6. I applied extra effort to further the interests of my work group.	___	___
7. My supervisor championed my case to others in the organization.	___	___
8. I respected my supervisor's management competence.	___	___

Scoring and Interpretation

LMX theory is about the quality of a leader's relationship with subordinates. If you scored 6 or more Mostly True, your supervisor clearly had an excellent relationship with you, which is stage two in Exhibit 2.5. You had a successful dyad. If your supervisor had an equally good relationship with every subordinate, that is a stage three level of development (partnership building). If you scored 3 or fewer Mostly True, then your supervisor was probably at level one, perhaps with different relationships with subordinates, some or all of which were unsuccessful. What do you think accounted for the quality of your and other subordinates' relationships (positive or negative) with your supervisor? Discuss with other students to learn why some supervisors have good LMX relationships.

Source: Based on Robert C. Liden and John M. Maslyn, "Multidimensionality of Leader–Member Exchange: An Empirical Assessment Through Scale Development," *Journal of Management* 24 (1998), pp. 43–72.

Action Memo

As a leader, you can build a positive, individualized relationship with each follower to create an equitable work environment and provide greater benefits to yourself, followers, and the organization.

in-group and out-group relationships, in that this may lead to feelings of resentment or even hostility among out-group participants.[47] If leaders are perceived to be granting excessive benefits and advantages to in-group members, members of the out-group may rebel, which can damage the entire organization. Moreover, some studies have found that leaders tend to categorize employees into in-groups and out-groups as early as five days into their relationship.[48]

Thus, the third phase of research in this area focused on whether leaders could develop positive relationships with *all* followers. In this approach, the leader views each person independently, and may treat each individual in a different but positive way. That is, leaders strive to develop a positive relationship with each subordinate, but the positive relationship will have a different form for each person. For example, one person might be treated with "consideration," another with "initiating structure," depending on what followers need to feel involved and to succeed.

In the LMX research study, leaders were trained to offer the opportunity for a high-quality relationship to all group members, and the followers who responded to the offer dramatically improved their performance. As these relationships matured, the entire work group became more productive, and the payoffs were tremendous. Leaders could count on followers to provide the assistance needed for high performance, and followers participated in and influenced decisions. The implications of this finding are that true performance and productivity gains can be achieved by having the leader develop positive relationships one-on-one with each subordinate.

Entrepreneurial Leadership

Another topic of special concern in today's fast-changing world is entrepreneurial leadership. *Entrepreneurship* is the process of initiating a business venture, organizing the necessary resources, and assuming the associated risks and rewards.[49] Entrepreneurs are leaders of innovation and change. An entrepreneur recognizes a viable idea for a business product or service and carries it out by finding and assembling the necessary resources—money, people, machinery, location—to undertake the business venture. Entrepreneurs assume the risks and reap the rewards or profits of the business.

A good example of an entrepreneur is Jeff Fluhr, who dropped out of Stanford University graduate school to launch StubHub, which resells event tickets. Fluhr saw the opportunity and then struggled to raise money and develop the business. His tenacity paid off as he convinced executives from Viacom Inc., Home Box Office, and Madison Square Garden to invest in his plan to reinvent the online ticket resale industry. StubHub allows sellers to list tickets free of charge and sell them either by auction or at a fixed price.[50]

Entrepreneurial leaders also exist within established organizations. These leaders take risks to create novel solutions to competitive challenges confronting a business, especially the development or enhancement of products and services. Entrepreneurial leadership is a source of innovation and change for established companies. Entrepreneurial leaders proactively pursue new opportunities and translate new ideas into practice. Entrepreneurial leaders display creativity, drive, enthusiasm, and future vision. They tend to be persistent and independent. They are drawn to new opportunities, are action oriented, and try to influence their teams toward creativity, higher performance, and higher profits. Entrepreneurial leaders are more concerned with innovation and creating new processes than with maintaining the status quo. They are willing to stretch themselves and take risks for improvement.[51]

Matching Leaders with Roles

As we've discussed in this chapter, although there are a number of characteristics associated with effective leadership, each individual leader has different strengths and a different combination of traits and behaviors. Recent research suggests that different personal characteristics and behavioral styles might be better suited to different types of leadership roles.[52] Exhibit 2.7 illustrates three types of leadership roles identified in today's organizations by a team of experts at Hay Group. The researchers found that, although there is a core set of competencies that all leaders need, there is significant variation in the personal characteristics, behaviors, and skills that correlate with success in the different roles.

The **operational role** is the closest to a traditional, vertically oriented management role, where an executive has direct control over people and

Operational role
a vertically oriented leadership role in which an executive has direct control over people and resources and the position power to accomplish results

Exhibit 2.7 Three Types of Leadership Roles

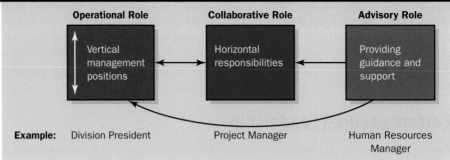

Operational Role	Collaborative Role	Advisory Role
Vertical management positions	Horizontal responsibilities	Providing guidance and support

Example: Division President   Project Manager   Human Resources Manager

Action Memo

As a leader, you can understand the type of leadership role in which your personality traits and behavioral style would be most effective and satisfying. You can pursue an operational, collaborative, or advisory leadership role depending on your natural tendencies.

resources to accomplish results. Operational leaders fill traditional line and general management positions in a business, for example. They set goals, establish plans, and get things done primarily through the vertical hierarchy and the use of position power. Operational leaders are doggedly focused on delivering results. They need high self-confidence and tend to be assertive, always pushing forward and raising the bar. Successful operational leaders are typically analytical and knowledgeable, yet they also have the ability to translate their knowledge into a vision that others can become passionate about.

The **collaborative role** is a horizontal role and includes people such as project managers, matrix managers, and team leaders in today's more horizontally-organized companies. This role, which has grown tremendously in importance in recent years, is quite challenging. Leaders in collaborative roles typically don't have the strong position power of the operational role. They often work behind the scenes, using their personal power to influence others and get things done. Collaborative leaders need excellent people skills in order to network, build relationships, and obtain agreement through personal influence. They also are highly proactive and tenacious, and they exhibit extreme flexibility to cope with the ambiguity and uncertainty associated with the collaborative role.

Leaders in an **advisory role** provide guidance and support to other people and departments in the organization. Advisory leadership roles are found, for example, in departments such as legal, finance, and human resources. These leaders are responsible for developing broad organizational capabilities rather than accomplishing specific business results. Advisory leaders need great people skills and the ability to influence others through communication, knowledge, and personal persuasion. In addition, leaders in advisory roles need exceptionally high levels of honesty and integrity to build trust and keep the organization on solid ethical ground.

The Hay Group research findings shed new light on the types of roles leaders fill in today's organizations and emphasize that individual traits and behaviors can influence how effective a leader might be in a particular role. Leadership success partly depends on matching leaders with roles where their personal traits and natural behavioral styles can be most effective.

Collaborative role
a horizontal leadership role (such as team leader) in which the leader often works behind the scenes and uses personal power to influence others and get things done.

Advisory role
a leadership role that provides advice, guidance, and support to other people and departments in the organization

Leadership Essentials

■ The point of this chapter is to understand the importance of traits and behaviors in the development of leadership theory and research. Some traits associated with effective leadership include optimism, self-confidence, honesty, and drive. It is important for leaders to recognize their strengths and acknowledge the interdependence that is key to effective leadership. A large number of personal traits and abilities have been associated with successful leaders, but traits themselves are not sufficient to guarantee effective leadership.

■ The behavior approach explored autocratic versus democratic leadership, consideration versus initiating structure, employee-centered versus job-centered leadership, and concern for people versus concern for production. The theme of people versus tasks runs through this research, suggesting these are fundamental behaviors through which leaders meet followers' needs. There has been some disagreement in the research about whether a specific leader is either people- or task-oriented or whether one can be both. Today, the consensus is that leaders can achieve a "high-high" leadership style.

■ Another approach is the dyad between a leader and each follower. Followers have different relationships with the leader, and the ability of the leader to develop a positive relationship with each follower contributes to team performance. The leader–member exchange theory says that high-quality relationships have a positive outcome for leaders, followers, work units, and the organization. Leaders can attempt to build individualized relationships with each individual as a way to meet needs for both consideration and structure.

■ The historical development of leadership theory presented in this chapter introduces some important ideas about leadership. Although certain personal traits and abilities indicate a greater likelihood for success in a leadership role, they are not in themselves sufficient to guarantee effective leadership. Rather, behaviors are equally significant. Therefore, the style of leadership demonstrated by an individual greatly determines the outcome of the leadership endeavor. Often, a combination of behavioral styles is most effective. To understand the effects of leadership on outcomes, the specific relationship behavior between a leader and each follower is also an important consideration.

■ Entrepreneurial leadership is of great concern in today's turbulent environment because entrepreneurial leadership is an important source of innovation and change. Entrepreneurial leaders take risks to bring new organizations into being or create novel solutions to competitive challenges confronting existing organizations.

■ Finally, the chapter examined three types of leadership roles: operational roles, collaborative roles, and advisory roles. Recent studies suggest that different traits and behavioral styles are better suited to different types of leadership roles, and leaders can be more effective when they are in positions that best match their natural tendencies.

Discussion Questions

1. Why is it important for leaders to know their strengths? Do you think leaders should spend equal time learning about their weak points?

2. Suggest some personal traits of leaders you have known. What traits do you believe are most valuable? Why?

3. The chapter suggests that optimism is an important trait for a leader, yet some employees complain that optimistic leaders create significant stress because they don't anticipate problems and expect their subordinates to meet unreasonable goals. Do you agree? Why?

4. What is the difference between trait theories and behavioral theories of leadership?

5. Would you feel most comfortable using a "consideration" or an "initiating-structure" leadership style? Discuss the reasons for your answer.

6. The Vertical Dyad Linkage model suggests that followers respond individually to the leader. If this is so, what advice would you give leaders about displaying people-oriented versus task-oriented behavior?

7. Does it make sense to you that a leader should develop an individualized relationship with each follower? Explain advantages and disadvantages to this approach.

8. Why would subordinates under a democratic leader perform better in the leader's absence than would subordinates under an autocratic leader?

9. Why is an entrepreneurial leader important to an organization? How is this role different from other leader roles?

10. Pick three traits from the list in Exhibit 2.1 that you think would be most valuable for a leader in an operational role. Pick three that you think would be most valuable for a leader in a collaborative role. Explain your choices.

Leadership at Work

YOUR IDEAL LEADER TRAITS

Spend some time thinking about someone you believe is an ideal leader. For the first part of the exercise, select an ideal leader you have heard about whom you don't personally know. It could be someone like Mother Teresa, Martin Luther King, Abraham Lincoln, or any national or international figure that you admire. Write the person's name here: _____. Now, in the space below, write down three things you admire about the person, such as what he or she did or the qualities that person possesses.

_____

_____

_____

For the second part of the exercise, select an ideal leader whom you know personally. This can be anyone from your life experiences. Write the person's name here: _____. Now, in the space below, write down three things you admire about the person, such as what he or she did or the qualities that person possesses.

_____

_____

_____

The first leader you chose represents something of a projective test based on what you've heard or read. You imagine the leader has the qualities you listed. The deeds and qualities you listed say more about what you admire than about the actual traits of the leader you chose. This is something like an inkblot test, and it is important because the traits you assign to the leader are traits you are aware of, have the potential to develop, and indeed can develop as a leader. The qualities or achievements you listed are an indicator of the traits you likely will express as you develop into the leader you want to become.

The second leader you chose is someone you know, so it is less of a projective test and represents traits you have had direct experience with. You know these traits work for you and likely will become the traits you develop and express as a leader.

What is similar about the traits you listed for the two leaders? Different? Interview another student in class about traits he or she admires. What do the traits tell you about the person you are interviewing? What are the common themes in your list and the other student's list of traits? To what extent do you display the same traits as the ones on your list? Will you develop those traits even more in the future?

_____

_____

_____

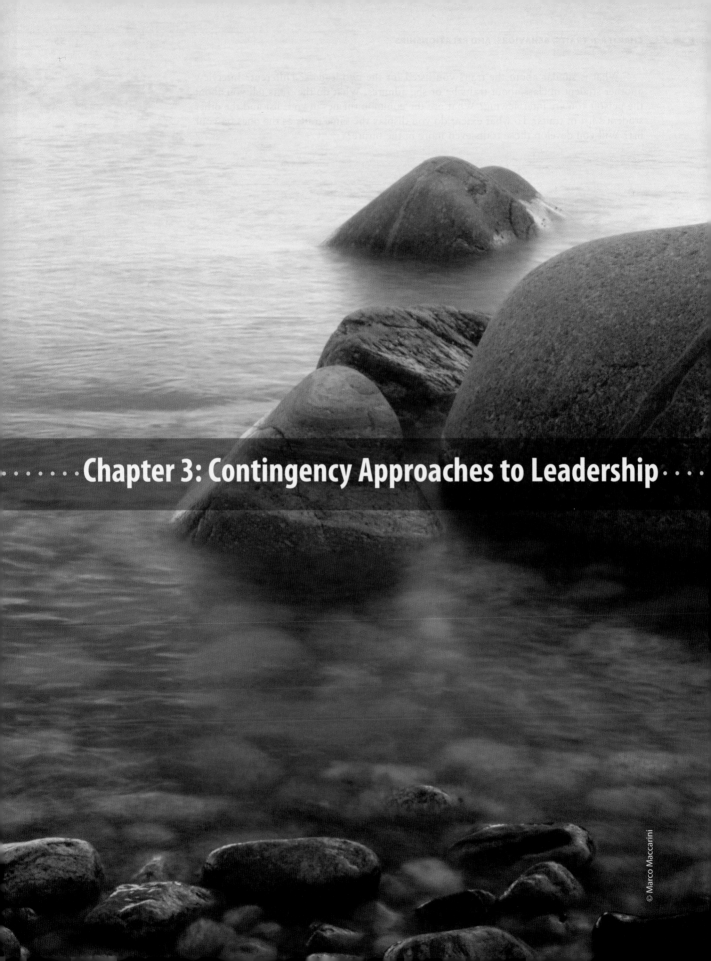

Chapter 3: Contingency Approaches to Leadership

© Marco Maccarini

Your Leadership Challenge

After studying this chapter, you should be able to:

- Understand how leadership is often contingent on people and situations.

- Apply Fiedler's contingency model to key relationships among leader style, situational favorability, and group task performance.

- Apply Hersey and Blanchard's situational theory of leader style to the level of follower readiness.

- Explain the path–goal theory of leadership.

- Use the Vroom–Jago model to identify the correct amount of follower participation in specific decision situations.

- Know how to use the power of situational variables to substitute for or neutralize the need for leadership.

Chapter Outline

Steven Sinofsky leads a team of Microsoft software engineers working on the next generation of Windows operating system software. Over at Apple, Bertrand Serlet is leading a team to try to make sure the new Macintosh operating system is better. Although they hold the same type of job, Sinofsky and Serlet are widely different in their leadership styles. Sinofsky is a meticulous planner and likes to run a tight ship. "Under Sinofsky," one engineer said, "you plan and you stick to the plan." Serlet, on the other hand, prefers things to be a little chaotic. He isn't a stickler for rules and procedures, emphasizing a more flexible, laid-back style. A programmer who has worked under both leaders compared Sinofsky's style to that of a martial marching band, while Serlet's was compared to an improvisational jazz group.[1]

Two leaders, both considered among the technological elite, both highly successful, but with two very different approaches to leading. This difference points to what researchers of leader traits and behaviors eventually discovered: Many different leadership styles can be effective. What, then, determines the success of a leadership style?

This chapter explores the relationship between leadership effectiveness and the situation in which leadership activities occur. Over the years, researchers have observed that leaders frequently behave situationally—that is, they adjust their leadership style depending on a variety of factors in the situations they face. In this chapter, we discuss the elements of leader, followers, and the situation, and the impact each has upon the others. We examine several theories that define how leadership styles, follower attributes, and organizational characteristics fit together to enable successful leadership. The important point of this chapter is that the most effective leadership approach depends on many factors. Understanding the contingency approaches can help a leader adapt his or her approach, although it is important to recognize that leaders also develop their ability to adapt through experience and practice.

The Contingency Approach

The failure to find universal leader traits or behaviors that would always determine effective leadership led researchers in a new direction. Although leader behavior was still examined, the central focus of the new research was the situation in which leadership occurred. The basic tenet of this focus was that behavior effective in some circumstances might be ineffective under different conditions. Thus, the effectiveness of leader behavior is *contingent* upon organizational situations. Aptly called *contingency approaches*, these theories explain the relationship between leadership styles and effectiveness in specific situations.

The universalistic approach as described in Chapter 2 is compared to the contingency approach used in this chapter in Exhibit 3.1. In the previous chapter, researchers were investigating traits or behaviors that could improve performance and satisfaction in any or all situations. They sought universal leadership traits and behaviors. **Contingency** means that one thing depends on other things, and for a leader to be effective there must be an appropriate fit between the leader's behavior and style and the conditions in the situation. A leadership style that works in one situation might not work in another situation. There is no one best way of leadership. Contingency means "it depends." This chapter's Leader's Bookshelf talks about a new approach to leadership for a new kind of contingency facing organizations today.

Contingency
a theory meaning one thing depends on other things

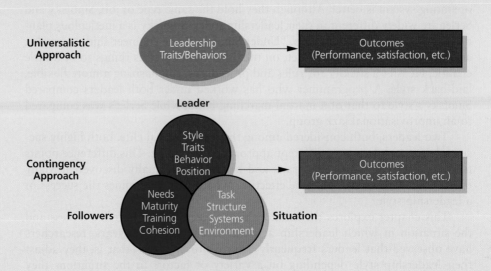

Exhibit 3.1 Comparing the Universalistic and Contingency Approaches to Leadership

Universalistic Approach

Leadership Traits/Behaviors → Outcomes (Performance, satisfaction, etc.)

Leader

Contingency Approach

Style
Traits
Behavior
Position

Needs
Maturity
Training
Cohesion

Task
Structure
Systems
Environment

→ Outcomes (Performance, satisfaction, etc.)

Followers   **Situation**

Leader's Bookshelf

Leadership and the New Science
by Margaret J. Wheatley

TURBULENT TIMES

One lesson learned from the Wall Street meltdown and the recent economic crisis is that being a leader in today's world means dealing with dramatic and unexpected change. Leaders have to think about the organization in a new way.

In searching for a better understanding of organizations and leadership, Margaret Wheatley looked to science for answers. In the world of Newtonian physics, every atom moves in a unique predictable trajectory determined by the forces exerted on it. Prediction and control are accomplished by reducing wholes into discrete parts and carefully regulating the forces that act on those parts. Applied to organizations, this view of the world led to rigid vertical hierarchies, division of labor, task description, and strict operating procedures designed to obtain predictable, controlled results.

Just as Newton's law broke down as physics explored ever-smaller elements of matter and ever-wider expanses of the universe, rigid, control-oriented leadership doesn't work well in a world of instant information, constant change, global competition, and far-reaching crises. The physical sciences responded to the failure of Newtonian physics with a new paradigm called quantum mechanics. In *Leadership and the New Science,* Wheatley explores how leaders

are redesigning organizations to survive in a quantum world.

Chaos, Relationships, and Fields

From quantum mechanics and chaos theory emerge new understandings of order, disorder, and change. Individual actions, whether by atoms or people, cannot be easily predicted and controlled. Here's why:

- Nothing exists except in relationship to everything else. It is not things, but the relationships among them, that are the key determinants of a well-ordered system we perceive. Order emerges through a web of relationships that make up the whole, not as a result of controls on individual parts.
- The empty space between things is filled with *fields,* invisible material that connects elements together. In organizations, the fields that bind people include vision, shared values, culture, and information.
- Organizations, like all open systems, grow and change in reaction to disequilibrium, and disorder can be a source of new order.

Implications for Leadership

These new understandings provide a new way to see, understand, and lead today's organizations. The new sciences can influence leaders to:

- Nurture relationships and the fields between people with a clear vision, statements of values, expressions of caring, the sharing of information, and freedom from strict rules and controls.
- Focus on the whole, not on the parts in isolation.
- Reduce boundaries between departments and organizations to allow new patterns of relationships.
- Become comfortable with uncertainty and recognize that any solutions are only temporary, specific to the immediate context, and developed through the relationship of people and circumstances.
- Recognize that healthy growth of people and organizations is found in disequilibrium, not in stability.

Wheatley believes leaders can learn from the new sciences how to lead in today's fast-paced, chaotic world, suggesting that "we can forgo the despair created by such common organization events as change, chaos, information overload, and cyclical behaviors if we recognize that organizations are conscious entities, possessing many of the properties of living systems."

Leadership and the New Science, by Margaret J. Wheatley, is published by Berrett-Koehler Publishers.

marble: © Ioannis Drimilis   library: www.istockphoto.com/nikada

The contingencies most important to leadership as shown in Exhibit 3.1 are the situation and followers. Research implies that situational variables such as task, structure, context, and environment are important to leadership style. The nature of followers has also been identified as a key contingency. Thus, the needs, maturity, and cohesiveness of followers make a significant difference to the best style of leadership.

Several models of situational leadership have been developed. The contingency model developed by Fiedler and his associates, the situational theory of

Exhibit 3.2 Meta-Categories of Leader Behavior and Four Leader Styles

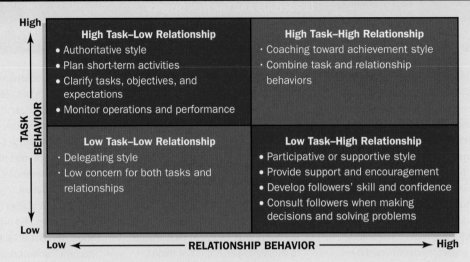

Source: Based on Gary Yukl, Angela Gordon, and Tom Taber, "A Hierarchical Taxonomy of Leadership Behavior: Integrating a Half Century of Behavior Research," *Journal of Leadership and Organizational Studies* 9, no. 1 (2002), pp. 15–32.

Hersey and Blanchard, path–goal theory, the Vroom–Jago model of decision participation, and the substitutes for leadership concept will all be described in this chapter. These **contingency approaches** seek to delineate the characteristics of situations and followers and examine the leadership styles that can be used effectively. Assuming that a leader can properly diagnose a situation and muster the flexibility to behave according to the appropriate style, successful outcomes are highly likely.

Two basic leadership behaviors that can be adjusted to address various contingencies are *task behavior* and *relationship behavior*, introduced in the previous chapter. Research has identified these two *meta-categories*, or broadly defined behavior categories, as applicable to leadership in a variety of situations and time periods.[2] A leader can adapt his or her style to be high or low on both task and relationship behavior. Exhibit 3.2 illustrates the four possible behavior approaches—high task–low relationship, high task–high relationship, low task–high relationship, and low task–low relationship. The exhibit describes typical task and relationship behaviors. High task behaviors include planning short-term activities, clarifying tasks, objectives, and role expectations, and monitoring operations and performance. High relationship behaviors include providing support and recognition, developing followers' skills and confidence, and consulting and empowering followers when making decisions and solving problems.

Both Fiedler's contingency model and Hersey and Blanchard's situational theory, discussed in the following sections, use these meta-categories of leadership behavior but apply them based on different sets of contingencies.

Action Memo

Complete the questionnaire in Leader's Self-Insight 3.1 to assess your relative emphasis on two important categories of leadership behavior.

Contingency approaches
approaches that seek to delineate the characteristics of situations and followers and examine the leadership styles that can be used effectively

Fiedler's Contingency Model

An early extensive effort to link leadership style with organizational situation was made by Fiedler and his associates.[3] The basic idea is simple: Match the leader's style with the situation most favorable for his or her success.

Leader's Self-Insight 3.1

T–P Leadership Questionnaire: An Assessment of Style

The following items describe aspects of leadership behavior. *Assume you are under great pressure for performance improvements as the leader of a manufacturing work group of six machine operators. Respond to each item according to the way you would most likely act in this pressure situation.* Indicate whether each item below is Mostly False or Mostly True for you as a work-group leader.

	Mostly False	Mostly True
1. I would take charge of what should be done and when to do it.	____	____
2. I would stress getting ahead of competing groups.	____	____
3. I would ask the members to work harder.	____	____
4. I would speak for the group if there were visitors present.	____	____
5. I would keep the work moving at a rapid pace.	____	____
6. I would permit members to use their own judgment in solving problems.	____	____
7. I would ask for group feedback on my ideas.	____	____
8. I would let members do their work the way they think best.	____	____
9. I would turn the members loose on a job and let them go for it.	____	____
10. I would permit the group to set its own pace.	____	____
T____ P____	____	____

Scoring and Interpretation

The T–P Leadership Questionnaire is scored as follows: Your "T" score is the number of Mostly True answers for questions 1–5. Your "P" score is the number of Mostly True answers for questions 6–10. A score of 4 or 5 would be considered high for either T or P.

Some leaders deal with people needs, leaving task details to followers. Other leaders focus on specific details with the expectation that followers will carry out orders. Depending on the situation, both approaches may be effective. The important issue is the ability to identify relevant dimensions of the situation and behave accordingly. Through this questionnaire, you can identify your relative emphasis on two dimensions of leadership: task orientation (T) and people orientation (P). These are not opposite approaches, and an individual can rate high or low on either or both.

What is your leadership orientation? Compare your results from this assignment to your result from the quiz in Leader's Self-Insight 2.2 in the previous chapter. What would you consider an ideal leader situation for your style?

Source: Based on the T–P Leadership Questionnaire as published in "Toward a Particularistic Approach to Leadership Style: Some Findings," by T. J. Sergiovanni, R. Metzcus, and L. Burden, *American Educational Research Journal* 6, no. 1 (1969), pp. 62–79.

marble: © Kirill Matkov   sunset: © Marco Regalia

Fiedler's contingency model was designed to enable leaders to diagnose both leadership style and organizational situation.

Leadership Style

The cornerstone of Fiedler's theory is the extent to which the leader's style is relationship-oriented or task-oriented. A *relationship-oriented leader* is concerned with people. As with the consideration style described in Chapter 2, a relationship-oriented leader establishes mutual trust and respect and listens to employees' needs. A *task-oriented leader* is primarily motivated by task accomplishment. Similar to the initiating structure style described earlier, a task-oriented leader provides clear directions and sets performance standards.

Leadership style was measured with a questionnaire known as the least preferred coworker (LPC) scale. The LPC scale has a set of 16 bipolar adjectives

Fiedler's contingency model
a model designed to diagnose whether a leader is task-oriented or relationship-oriented and match leader style to the situation

along an eight-point scale. Examples of the bipolar adjectives used by Fiedler on the LPC scale follow:

open	guarded
quarrelsome	harmonious
efficient	inefficient
self-assured	hesitant
gloomy	cheerful

If the leader describes the least preferred coworker using positive concepts, he or she is considered relationship-oriented, that is, a leader who cares about and is sensitive to other people's feelings. Conversely, if a leader uses negative concepts to describe the least preferred coworker, he or she is considered task-oriented, that is, a leader who sees other people in negative terms and places greater value on task activities than on people.

Situation

Fiedler's model presents the leadership situation in terms of three key elements that can be either favorable or unfavorable to a leader: the quality of leader–member relations, task structure, and position power.

Leader–member relations refers to group atmosphere and members' attitudes toward and acceptance of the leader. When subordinates trust, respect, and have confidence in the leader, leader–member relations are considered good. When subordinates distrust, do not respect, and have little confidence in the leader, leader–member relations are poor.

Task structure refers to the extent to which tasks performed by the group are defined, involve specific procedures, and have clear, explicit goals. Routine, well-defined tasks, such as those of assembly-line workers, have a high degree of structure. Creative, ill-defined tasks, such as research and development or strategic planning, have a low degree of task structure. When task structure is high, the situation is considered favorable to the leader; when low, the situation is less favorable.

Position power is the extent to which the leader has formal authority over subordinates. Position power is high when the leader has the power to plan and direct the work of subordinates, evaluate it, and reward or punish them. Position power is low when the leader has little authority over subordinates and cannot evaluate their work or reward them. When position power is high, the situation is considered favorable for the leader; when low, the situation is unfavorable.

Combining the three situational characteristics yields a list of eight leadership situations, which are illustrated in Exhibit 3.3. Situation I is most favorable to the leader because leader–member relations are good, task structure is high, and leader position power is strong. Situation VIII is most unfavorable to the leader because leader–member relations are poor, task structure is low, and leader position power is weak. Other octants represent intermediate degrees of favorableness for the leader.

Contingency Theory

When Fiedler examined the relationships among leadership style, situational favorability, and group task performance, he found the pattern shown at the top of Exhibit 3.3. Task-oriented leaders are more effective when the situation is

Exhibit 3.3 Fiedler's Classification: How Leader Style Fits the Situation

	Very Favorable		Intermediate				Very Unfavorable	
Leader–Member Relations	Good	Good	Good	Good	Poor	Poor	Poor	Poor
Task Structure	Structured		Unstructured		Structured		Unstructured	
Leader Position Power	Strong	Weak	Strong	Weak	Strong	Weak	Strong	Weak
Situations	I	II	III	IV	V	VI	VII	VIII

Source: Based on Fred E. Fiedler, "The Effects of Leadership Training and Experience: A Contingency Model Interpretation," *Administrative Science Quarterly* 17 (1972), p. 455.

either highly favorable or highly unfavorable. Relationship-oriented leaders are more effective in situations of moderate favorability.

The task-oriented leader excels in the favorable situation because everyone gets along, the task is clear, and the leader has power; all that is needed is for someone to take charge and provide direction. Similarly, if the situation is highly unfavorable to the leader, a great deal of structure and task direction is needed. A strong leader defines task structure and can establish authority over subordinates. Because leader–member relations are poor anyway, a strong task orientation will make no difference to the leader's popularity. Researchers at the University of Chicago looked at CEOs of companies in turnaround situations—where companies typically have high debt loads and a need to improve results in a hurry—and found that tough-minded, task-focused characteristics such as analytical skills, a focus on efficiency, and setting high standards were more valuable leader qualities than were relationship skills such as good communication, listening, and teamwork.[4]

The relationship-oriented leader performs better in situations of intermediate favorability because human relations skills are important in achieving high group performance. In these situations, the leader may be moderately well liked, have some power, and supervise jobs that contain some ambiguity. A leader with good interpersonal skills can create a positive group atmosphere that will improve relationships, clarify task structure, and establish position power.

A leader, then, needs to know two things in order to use Fiedler's contingency theory. First, the leader should know whether he or she has a relationship- or task-oriented style. Second, the leader should diagnose the situation and determine whether leader–member relations, task structure, and position power are favorable or unfavorable. Consider how Mark Hurd's leadership style fit the situation he found at Hewlett-Packard.

IN THE LEAD

Mark Hurd, Hewlett-Packard

In a spring 2009 article, *Fortune* magazine said Mark Hurd was the kind of guy you wanted running your company during the economic downturn. Since taking over as CEO of Hewlett-Packard (HP) in 2005, Hurd has shown himself to be a leader who thrives in unfavorable circumstances. All computer companies have struggled in recent years due to the changing environment and global competition, but when Hurd became CEO of HP, the company was the "computer industry doormat." Four years later, it was the world's biggest technology company and ranked number 30 on *Fortune's* list of the world's most admired companies.

Hurd, known as a "peerless control freak" who keeps a spreadsheet to track and analyze his daily tasks, brought a strong task-oriented style to the struggling HP. One of his first moves was to slash 10 percent of the workforce and institute rigorous standards for operational efficiency. He admits he'd rather talk in numbers than words, and his leadership style reflects that he'd rather deal with reports and analysis than with people.

"Mark's a rack-and-stack guy, and I am, too," says A. G. Lafley, CEO of Procter & Gamble. "When we meet, there's no chitchat or warm-up. It's right to business." Hurd uses the same approach with managers and staffers at HP, where he stresses discipline and accountability and openly complains if he is unhappy with someone's performance. He sets tough goals and standards for managers, but also gives them the autonomy to solve problems and meet targets their own way.

When Hurd was appointed as CEO, some observers were questioning whether anyone could restore HP to glory, much less the unknown and unproven Hurd. Yet by 2009, the company was one of the best performers in the industry, and Hurd was being called one of the best managers in corporate America. Although HP and its employees have felt some pain due to the recession, the moves Hurd made early in his tenure put the company in a position to weather the crisis better than most.[5]

Mark Hurd might be characterized as using a task-oriented style in an unfavorable situation. The morale of HP employees was at an all-time low, contributing to poor leader–member relations, and the nature of many tasks in the industry is unstructured. Hurd had strong position power, but employees had little faith in his ability to make things better. Overall, HP's circumstances created a very unfavorable situation, as illustrated in Exhibit 3.3, making Hurd's task-oriented style just right.

Action Memo

As a leader, you can effectively use a task-oriented style when the organizational situation is either highly unfavorable or highly favorable to you as a leader. Use a relationship-oriented style in situations of intermediate favorability because human relations skills can create a positive atmosphere.

An important contribution of Fiedler's research is that it goes beyond the notion of leadership styles to try to show how styles fit the situation. Many studies have been conducted to test Fiedler's model, and the research in general provides some support for the model.[6] However, Fiedler's model has also been criticized.[7] Using the LPC score as a measure of relationship- or task-oriented behavior seems simplistic to some researchers, and the weights used to determine situation favorability seem to have been determined in an arbitrary manner. In addition, some observers argue that the empirical support for the model is weak because it is based on correlational results that fail to achieve statistical significance in the majority of cases. The model also isn't clear about how the model works over time. For instance, if a task-oriented leader such as Mark Hurd is matched with an unfavorable situation and is successful, the organizational situation is likely to improve, as it did at Hewlett-Packard, thus becoming a situation more appropriate for a relationship-oriented leader. Will Hurd's task-oriented style continue to be effective since he contributed to the more favorable circumstances? Can or should he try to shift to a more relationship-oriented leader style? Fiedler's model doesn't address this issue.

Finally, Fiedler's model and much of the subsequent research fail to consider *medium* LPC leaders, who some studies indicate are more effective than either high or low LPC leaders in a majority of situations.[8] Leaders who score in the mid-range on the LPC scale presumably balance the concern for relationships with a concern for task achievement more effectively than high or low LPC leaders, making them more adaptable to a variety of situations.

New research has continued to improve Fiedler's model,[9] and it is still considered an important contribution to leadership studies. However, its major impact may have been to stir other researchers to consider situational factors more seriously. A number of other situational theories have been developed in the years since Fiedler's original research.

Hersey and Blanchard's Situational Theory

The **situational theory** developed by Hersey and Blanchard is an interesting extension of the leadership grid outlined in Chapter 2. This approach focuses on the characteristics of followers as the most important element of the situation, and consequently of determining effective leader behavior. The point of Hersey and Blanchard's theory is that subordinates vary in readiness level. People low in task readiness, because of little ability or training, or insecurity, need a different leadership style than those who are high in readiness and have good ability, skills, confidence, and willingness to work.[10]

Leader Style

According to the situational theory, a leader can adopt one of four leadership styles, based on a combination of relationship (concern for people) and task (concern for production) behavior. The appropriate style depends on the readiness level of followers.

Exhibit 3.4 summarizes the relationship between leader style and follower readiness. The upper part of the exhibit indicates the four leader styles: telling, selling, participating, and delegating. The *telling style* reflects a high concern for tasks and a low concern for people and relationships. This is a very directive style. The leader gives explicit directions about how tasks should be accomplished. The *selling style* is based on a high concern for both relationships and tasks. With this approach, the leader explains decisions and gives followers a chance to ask questions and gain clarity about work tasks. The *participating style* is characterized by high relationship and low task behavior. The leader shares ideas with followers, encourages participation, and facilitates decision making. The fourth style, the *delegating style*, reflects a low concern for both tasks and relationships. This leader provides little direction or support because responsibility for decisions and their implementation is turned over to followers.

Follower Readiness

The bell-shaped curve in Exhibit 3.4 is called a prescriptive curve because it indicates when each leader style should be used. The readiness level of followers is indicated in the lower part of the exhibit. R1 is low readiness and R4 represents

Situational theory
Hersey and Blanchard's extension of the Leadership Grid focusing on the characteristics of followers as the important element of the situation, and consequently, of determining effective leader behavior

Exhibit 3.4 Hersey and Blanchard's Situational Theory of Leadership

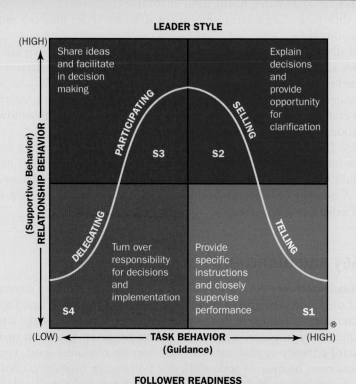

LEADER STYLE

(HIGH)

S3 — Share ideas and facilitate in decision making — PARTICIPATING

S2 — Explain decisions and provide opportunity for clarification — SELLING

S4 — Turn over responsibility for decisions and implementation — DELEGATING

S1 — Provide specific instructions and closely supervise performance — TELLING

(Supportive Behavior)
RELATIONSHIP BEHAVIOR

(LOW) ◄──── TASK BEHAVIOR ────► (HIGH)
(Guidance)

FOLLOWER READINESS

HIGH	MODERATE		LOW
R4	R3	R2	R1
Able and Willing or Confident	Able but Unwilling or Insecure	Unable but Willing or Confident	Unable and Unwilling or Insecure

FOLLOWER DIRECTED   LEADER DIRECTED

Source: Paul Hersey, Kenneth Blanchard, and Dewey Johnson, *Management of Organizational Behavior: Utilizing Human Resources,* 7th ed. (Upper Saddle River, NJ: Prentice Hall, 1996), p. 200. Used with permission.

very high readiness. The essence of Hersey and Blanchard's situational theory is for the leader to diagnose a follower's readiness and select a style that is appropriate for the readiness level, such as the follower's degree of education and skills, experience, self-confidence, and work attitudes.

Low Readiness Level When one or more followers exhibit very low levels of readiness, the leader has to be very specific, "telling" followers exactly what to do, how to do it, and when. For example, Phil Hagans owns two McDonald's franchises in northeast Houston and gives many young workers their first job. He uses a telling style regarding everything from how to dress to the correct way to clean the grill, giving young workers the strong direction they need to develop to higher levels of skill and self-confidence.[11]

Moderate Readiness Level A selling leadership style works well when followers lack some education and experience for the job but demonstrate confidence, ability, interest, and willingness to learn. With a selling style, the leader gives some direction but also seeks input from and clarifies tasks for followers rather than merely instructing how tasks should be performed. Sheryl Sandberg uses a selling style in her new job as chief operating officer at Facebook. Many Facebook employees are fresh out of college with little experience, but they are energetic, enthusiastic, and committed. Sandberg's style combines decisive leadership with persuasion and consensus building. She uses logic and data to explain her decisions, but she also seeks input and feedback from employees. She describes herself as a leader who tends to "mentor and demand at the same time."[12]

Action Memo

As a leader, you can tell followers how to perform their tasks if they have few skills, little experience, or low self-confidence. If followers have a moderate degree of skill and show enthusiasm and willingness to learn, provide direction but seek followers' input and explain your decisions.

High Readiness Level A participating style can be effective when followers have the necessary education, skills, and experience, but they might be insecure in their abilities and need some direction from the leader. The leader can guide followers' development and act as a resource for advice and assistance. An example of the participating style is Eric Brevig, a visual-effects supervisor with Industrial Light and Magic, who maximizes the creativity of artists and animators by encouraging participation. Rather than telling people how to do their jobs, Brevig presents them with a challenge and works with them to figure out the best way to meet it.[13]

Very High Readiness Level The delegating style of leadership can be effectively used when followers have very high levels of education, experience, and readiness to accept responsibility for their own task behavior. The leader provides a general goal and sufficient authority to do the tasks as followers see fit. Highly educated professionals such as lawyers, college professors, and social workers would typically fall into this category. There are followers in almost every organization who demonstrate high readiness. For example, many fast-food outlets have had great success hiring retirees for part-time jobs. These older employees often have high levels of readiness because of their vast experience and positive attitudes, and leaders can effectively use a delegating style.

Action Memo

As a leader, you can act as a resource to provide advice and assistance when followers have a high level of skill, experience, and responsibility. Delegate responsibility for decisions and their implementation to followers who have very high levels of skill and positive attitudes.

In summary, the telling style works best for followers who demonstrate very low levels of readiness to take responsibility for their own task behavior, the selling and participating styles are effective for followers with moderate-to-high readiness, and the delegating style is appropriate for employees with very high readiness. In today's multigenerational workplace, with people of widely different ages and readiness levels working side-by-side, many leaders find that they have to use multiple styles. Aaron Brown supervises a team at IBM that includes employees who span four decades in age, have work experience of between three and 30 years, and have varied attitudes, expectations, and ways of working.[14] For Brown, getting the best performance out of employees who differ so widely is as challenging—and as energizing—as coping with today's faster, more competitive business landscape.

Hersey and Blanchard's contingency model is easier to understand than Fiedler's model because it focuses only on the characteristics of followers,

Leader's Self-Insight 3.2

Are You Ready?

A leader's style can be contingent upon the readiness level of followers. Think of yourself working in your current or former job. Answer the questions below based on how you are on that job. Please answer whether each item is Mostly False or Mostly True for you in that job.

	Mostly False	Mostly True
1. I typically do the exact work required of me, nothing more or less.	___	___
2. I am often bored and uninterested in the tasks I have to perform.	___	___
3. I take extended breaks whenever I can.	___	___
4. I have great interest and enthusiasm for the job.	___	___
5. I am recognized as an expert by colleagues and coworkers.	___	___
6. I have a need to perform to the best of my ability.	___	___
7. I have a great deal of relevant education and experience for this type of work.	___	___
8. I am involved in "extra-work" activities such as committees.	___	___
9. I prioritize my work and manage my time well.	___	___

Scoring and Interpretation

In the Situational Theory of Leadership, the higher the follower's readiness, the more participative and delegating the leader can be. Give yourself one point for each Mostly False answer to items 1–3 and one point for each Mostly True answer to items 4–9. A score of 8–9 points would suggest a "very high" readiness level. A score of 7–8 points would indicate a "high" readiness level. A score of 4–6 points would suggest "moderate" readiness, and 0–3 points would indicate "low" readiness. What is the appropriate leadership style for your readiness level? What leadership style did your supervisor use with you? What do you think accounted for your supervisor's style? Discuss your results with other students to explore which leadership styles are actually used with subordinates who are at different readiness levels.

marble: © Kirill Matkov   sunset: © Marco Regalia

Action Memo

Answer the questions in Leader's Self-Insight 3.2 to determine your own readiness level and the style of leadership that would be most appropriate for you as a follower.

not those of the larger situation. The leader should evaluate subordinates and adopt whichever style is needed. The leader's style can be tailored to individual subordinates similar to the leader–member exchange theory described in Chapter 2. If one follower is at a low level of readiness, the leader must be very specific, telling exactly what to do, how to do it, and when. For a follower high in readiness, the leader provides a general goal and sufficient authority to do the task as the follower sees fit. Leaders can carefully diagnose the readiness level of followers and then tell, sell, participate, or delegate.

Classroom teachers face one of the toughest leadership challenges around because they usually deal with students who are at widely different levels of readiness. Consider how Carole McGraw of the Detroit, Michigan, school system met the challenge.

IN THE LEAD

Carole McGraw, Detroit Public Schools

Carole McGraw describes what she sees when she walks into a classroom for the first time: "A ubiquitous sea of easily recognizable faces. There's Jamie, whose eyes glow with enthusiasm for learning. And Terrell, who just came from the crib after having no breakfast, no supervision of his inadequate homework, and a chip on his shoulder because he needed to flip hamburgers 'til 10 o'clock at night. . . . And Matt, who slumps over his desk, fast asleep from the Ritalin he took for a learning disorder that was probably misdiagnosed to correct a behavior problem. . . ." And on and on.

McGraw diagnosed what teenagers have in common to find the best way to help students of such varying degrees of readiness learn. She realized that teenagers are exposed to countless hours of social networking Web sites, television programs, iPods and disc jockeys. They spend a lot of time playing sports, eating junk food, text messaging, talking on the phone, playing computer games, going to the movies, reading pop magazines, hanging out with peers, and avoiding adults. After considering this, McGraw developed her teaching method focused on three concepts: painless, interesting, and enjoyable. Students in McGraw's biology class now do almost all of their work in labs or teamwork sessions. During the labs, a captain is selected to act as team leader. In teams, students select a viable problem to investigate and then split up the work and conduct research in books, on the Internet, and in laboratory experiments. Teams also spend a lot of time engaged in dialogue and brainstorming. McGraw will throw out an idea and let the students take off with it.

McGraw's teaching method combines telling and participating. Students are provided with direction about certain concepts, vocabulary words, and so forth that they must master, along with guidelines for doing so. This provides the structure and discipline some of her low-readiness level students need to succeed. However, most of her leadership focuses on supporting students as they learn and grow on their own. Does McGraw's innovative approach work? Sixty percent of the students get a grade of A and all score fairly well on objective tests McGraw gives after the teamwork is complete. Students from her classes score great on standardized tests like the SAT because they not only accumulate a lot of knowledge but also gain self-confidence and learn how to think on their feet. "All the stress my kids lived with for years disappears," McGraw says. "My classroom buzzes with new ideas and individual approaches."[15]

Path–Goal Theory

Another contingency approach to leadership is called the path–goal theory.[16] According to the **path–goal theory**, the leader's responsibility is to increase subordinates' motivation to attain personal and organizational goals. As illustrated in Exhibit 3.5, the leader increases follower motivation by either (1) clarifying the follower's path to the rewards that are available or (2) increasing the rewards that the follower values and desires. Path clarification means that the leader works with subordinates to help them identify and learn the behaviors that will lead to successful task accomplishment and organizational rewards. Increasing rewards means that the leader talks with subordinates to learn which rewards are important to them—that is, whether they desire intrinsic rewards from the work itself or extrinsic rewards such as raises or promotions. The leader's job is to increase personal payoffs to subordinates for goal attainment and to make the paths to these payoffs clear and easy to travel.[17]

Path–goal theory
a contingency approach to leadership in which the leader's responsibility is to increase subordinates' motivation by clarifying the behaviors necessary for task accomplishment and rewards

Exhibit 3.5 Leader Roles in the Path–Goal Model

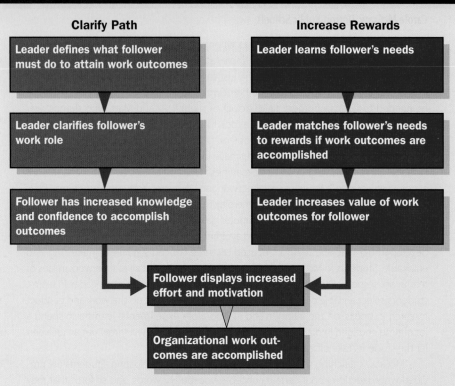

Source: Based on and reprinted from Bernard M. Bass, "Leadership: Good, Better, Best," *Organizational Dynamics* 13 (Winter 1985), pp. 26–40. Copyright 1985, with permission from Elsevier.

This model is called a contingency theory because it consists of three sets of contingencies—leader style, followers and situation, and the rewards to meet followers' needs.[18] Whereas the Fiedler theory made the assumption that new leaders could take over as situations change, in the path–goal theory, leaders change their behaviors to match the situation.

Action Memo

As a leader, you can increase follower motivation, satisfaction, and performance by adopting a leadership behavior that will clarify the follower's path to receiving available rewards or increase the availability of rewards the follower desires.

Leader Behavior

The path–goal theory suggests a fourfold classification of leader behaviors.[19] These classifications are the types of behavior the leader can adopt and include supportive, directive, achievement-oriented, and participative styles.

Supportive leadership shows concern for subordinates' well-being and personal needs. Leadership behavior is open, friendly, and approachable, and the leader creates a team climate and treats subordinates as equals. Supportive leadership is similar to the consideration or people-oriented leadership described earlier.

Directive leadership tells subordinates exactly what they are supposed to do. Leader behavior includes planning, making schedules, setting performance goals and behavior standards, and stressing adherence to rules and regulations. Directive leadership behavior is similar to the initiating structure or task-oriented leadership style described earlier.

Participative leadership consults with subordinates about decisions. Leader behavior includes asking for opinions and suggestions, encouraging participation in decision making, and meeting with subordinates in their workplaces. The participative leader encourages group discussion and written suggestions, similar to the selling or participating style in the Hersey and Blanchard model.

Achievement-oriented leadership sets clear and challenging goals for subordinates. Leader behavior stresses high-quality performance and improvement over current performance. Achievement-oriented leaders also show confidence in subordinates and assist them in learning how to achieve high goals.

To illustrate achievement-oriented leadership, consider the training of army officers in the Reserve Officers' Training Corps (ROTC). This training goes far beyond how to command a platoon. It involves the concepts of motivation, responsibility, and the creation of a team in which decision making is expected of everyone. Fundamentally, this training will enable officers to respond to any situation, not just those outlined in the manual. Thus achievement-oriented leadership is demonstrated: The set goals are challenging, require improvement, and demonstrate confidence in the abilities of subordinates.[20]

The four types of leader behavior are not considered ingrained personality traits as in the earlier trait theories; rather, they reflect types of behavior that every leader is able to adopt, depending on the situation. Here's how Alan Robbins, founder of Plastic Lumber Company, shifted from a participative to a directive style and got better results from his employees.

IN THE LEAD

Alan Robbins, Plastic Lumber Company

Alan Robbins started Plastic Lumber Company because he saw a way to both help the planet and make money by converting plastic milk and soda bottles into fake lumber. He also had definite ideas about how to run a company. Robbins wanted to be both a boss and a friend to his employees. His leadership style stressed teamwork and participation, and Robbins spent a lot of time running ideas by workers on the factory floor. However, he soon learned that most of his low-skilled workers didn't really want a chance to participate; they just wanted clear direction and consistent standards so that people knew what was expected of them.

The degree of freedom Robbins allowed with his participative style actually led to some serious problems. Some workers were frequently absent or late without calling, showed up under the influence of alcohol or drugs, and started fights on the factory floor. Letting employees participate in decision making weakened Robbins's authority in many employees' eyes. Those who genuinely wanted to do a good job were frustrated by the lack of order and the fact that some employees seemed to get away with anything.

Even though Robbins had a natural tendency to be a participative leader, he shifted to a directive leadership style to try to restore some order. With a comprehensive rules and policy manual, drug testing for all workers, and clear standards of behavior, the work environment and employee performance at Plastic Lumber improved significantly.[21]

Alan Robbins had believed his participative style would be appreciated by employees. However, employee satisfaction increased when he began using a directive style and specifying what was expected and what behaviors would not be tolerated. This style enabled people to focus on meeting performance standards by following clear procedures and guidelines. Thus, although Robbins would prefer to be participative, he realized it was not the best approach for the situation. The *Consider This* box provides an interesting perspective on the disadvantages of persisting in a behavior style despite the processes of change.

Consider **This!**

The phrase "too much of a good thing" is relevant in leadership. Behavior that becomes overbearing can be a disadvantage by ultimately resulting in the opposite of what the individual is hoping to achieve.

Polarities

All behavior consists of opposites or polarities. If I do anything more and more, over and over, its polarity will appear. For example, striving to be beautiful makes a person ugly, and trying too hard to be kind is a form of selfishness.

Any over-determined behavior produces its opposite:

- An obsession with living suggests worry about dying.
- True simplicity is not easy.
- Is it a long time or a short time since we last met?
- The braggart probably feels small and insecure.
- Who would be first ends up last.

Knowing how polarities work, the wise leader does not push to make things happen, but allows process to unfold on its own.

Source: John Heider, *The Tao of Leadership: Leadership Strategies for a New Age* (New York: Bantam Books, 1986), p. 3. Copyright 1985 Humanic Ltd., Atlanta, GA. Used with permission.

© majaiva

Situational Contingencies

The two important situational contingencies in the path–goal theory are (1) the personal characteristics of group members and (2) the work environment. Personal characteristics of followers are similar to Hersey and Blanchard's readiness level and include such factors as ability, skills, needs, and motivations. For example, if an employee has a low level of ability or skill, the leader may need to provide additional training or coaching in order for the worker to improve performance. If a subordinate is self-centered, the leader may use monetary rewards to motivate him or her. Subordinates who want or need clear direction and authority require a directive leader to tell them exactly what to do. Craft workers and professionals, however, may want more freedom and autonomy and work best under a participative leadership style.

The work environment contingencies include the degree of task structure, the nature of the formal authority system, and the work group itself. The task structure is similar to the same concept described in Fiedler's contingency theory; it includes the extent to which tasks are defined and have explicit job descriptions and work procedures. The formal authority system includes the amount of legitimate power used by leaders and the extent to which policies and rules constrain employees' behavior. Work-group characteristics consist of the educational level of subordinates and the quality of relationships among them.

Use of Rewards

Recall that the leader's responsibility is to clarify *the path to rewards* for followers or to increase *the amount of rewards* to enhance satisfaction and job performance. In some situations, the leader works with subordinates to help them acquire the skills and confidence needed to perform tasks and achieve rewards already available. In others, the leader may develop new rewards to meet the specific needs of subordinates.

Exhibit 3.6 illustrates four examples of how leadership behavior is tailored to the situation. In the first situation, the subordinate lacks confidence; thus, the supportive leadership style provides the social support with which to encourage the subordinate to undertake the behavior needed to do the work and receive the rewards. In the second situation, the job is ambiguous, and the employee is not performing effectively. Directive leadership behavior is used to give instructions and clarify the task so that the follower will know how to accomplish it and receive rewards. In the third situation, the subordinate is unchallenged by the task; thus, an achievement-oriented behavior is used to set higher goals. This clarifies the path to rewards for the employee. In the fourth situation, an incorrect reward is given to a subordinate, and the participative leadership style is used to change this. By discussing the subordinate's needs, the leader is able to identify the correct reward for task accomplishment. In all four cases, the outcome of fitting the leadership behavior to the situation produces greater employee effort by either clarifying how subordinates can receive rewards or changing the rewards to fit their needs.

Path–goal theorizing can be complex, but much of the research on it has been encouraging.[22] Using the model to specify precise relationships and make exact predictions about employee outcomes may be difficult, but the four types of

Exhibit 3.6 Path–Goal Situations and Preferred Leader Behaviors

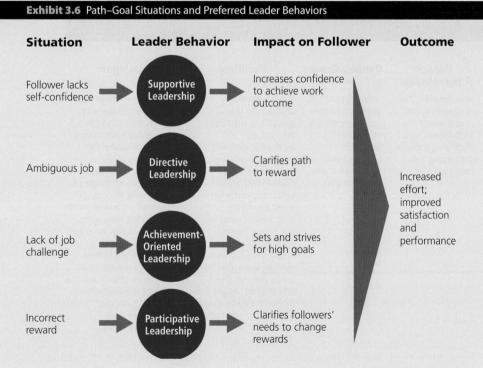

leader behavior and the ideas for fitting them to situational contingencies provide a useful way for leaders to think about motivating subordinates.

The Vroom–Jago Contingency Model

The **Vroom–Jago contingency model** shares some basic principles with the previous models, yet it differs in significant ways as well. This model focuses specifically on varying degrees of participative leadership, and how each level of participation influences quality and accountability of decisions. A number of situational factors shape the likelihood that either a participative or autocratic approach will produce the best outcome.

This model starts with the idea that a leader faces a problem that requires a solution. Decisions to solve the problem might be made by a leader alone, or through inclusion of a number of followers.

The Vroom–Jago model is very applied, which means that it tells the leader precisely the correct amount of participation by subordinates to use in making a particular decision.[23] The model has three major components: leader participation styles, a set of diagnostic questions with which to analyze a decision situation, and a series of decision rules.

Vroom–Jago contingency model
a contingency model that focuses on varying degrees of participative leadership, and how each level of participation influences quality and accountability of decisions

Leader Participation Styles

The model employs five levels of subordinate participation in decision making, ranging from highly autocratic (leader decides alone) to highly democratic (leader delegates to group), as illustrated in Exhibit 3.7.[24] The exhibit shows five decision

Exhibit 3.7 Five Leader Decision Styles

Area of Influence by Leader				Area of Freedom for Group
Decide	**Consult Individually**	**Consult Group**	**Facilitate**	**Delegate**
You make the decision alone and either announce or "sell" it to the group. You may use your expertise in collecting information that you deem relevant to the problem from the group or others.	You present the problem to the group members individually, get their suggestions, and make the decision.	You present the problem to the group members in a meeting, get their suggestions, and then make the decision.	You present the problem to the group in a meeting. You act as facilitator, defining the problem to be solved and the boundaries within which the decision must be made. Your objective is to get concurrence on a decision. Above all, you take care to show that your ideas are not given any greater weight than those of others simply because of your position.	You permit the group to make the decision within prescribed limits. The group undertakes the identification and diagnosis of the problem, develops alternative procedures for solving it, and decides on one or more alternative solutions. While you play no direct role in the group's deliberations unless explicitly asked, your role is an important one behind the scenes, providing needed resources and encouragement.

Source: Victor H. Vroom, "Leadership and the Decision-Making Process," *Organizational Dynamics* 28, no. 4 (Spring 2000), pp. 82–94. This is Vroom's adaptation of Tannenbaum and Schmidt's Taxonomy.

styles, starting with the leader making the decision alone (Decide), presenting the problem to subordinates individually for their suggestions and then making the decision (Consult Individually), presenting the problem to subordinates as a group, collectively obtaining their ideas and suggestions, then making the decision (Consult Group), sharing the problem with subordinates as a group and acting as a facilitator to help the group arrive at a decision (Facilitate), or delegating the problem and permitting the group to make the decision within prescribed limits (Delegate). The five styles fall along a continuum, and the leader should select one depending on the situation.

Diagnostic Questions

How does a leader decide which of the five decision styles to use? The appropriate degree of decision participation depends on a number of situational factors, such as the required level of decision quality, the level of leader or subordinate expertise, and the importance of having subordinates commit to the decision. Leaders can analyze the appropriate degree of participation by answering seven diagnostic questions.

1. **Decision significance:** *How significant is this decision for the project or organization?* If the decision is highly important and a high-quality decision is needed for the success of the project or organization, the leader has to be actively involved.

2. **Importance of commitment:** *How important is subordinate commitment to carrying out the decision?* If implementation requires a high level of commitment to the decision, leaders should involve subordinates in the decision process.

3. **Leader expertise:** *What is the level of the leader's expertise in relation to the problem?* If the leader does not have a high amount of information, knowledge, or expertise, the leader should involve subordinates to obtain it.

4. **Likelihood of commitment:** *If the leader were to make the decision alone, would subordinates have high or low commitment to the decision?* If subordinates typically go along with whatever the leader decides, their involvement in the decision-making process will be less important.

5. **Group support for goals:** *What is the degree of subordinate support for the team's or organization's objectives at stake in this decision?* If subordinates have low support for the goals of the organization, the leader should not allow the group to make the decision alone.

6. **Goal expertise:** *What is the level of group members' knowledge and expertise in relation to the problem?* If subordinates have a high level of expertise in relation to the problem, more responsibility for the decision can be delegated to them.

7. **Team competence:** *How skilled and committed are group members to working together as a team to solve problems?* When subordinates have high skills and high desire to work together cooperatively to solve problems, more responsibility for the decision making can be delegated to them.

These questions seem detailed, but considering these seven situational factors can quickly narrow the options and point to the appropriate level of group participation in decision making.

Selecting a Decision Style

Further development of the Vroom–Jago model added concern for time constraints and concern for follower development as explicit criteria for determining the level of participation. That is, a leader considers the relative importance of time versus follower development in selecting a decision style. This led to the development of two decision matrixes, *a time-based model,* to be used if time is critical, for example, if the organization is facing a crisis and a decision must be made immediately, and a *development-based model,* to be used if time and efficiency are less important criteria than the opportunity to develop the thinking and decision-making skills of followers.

Action Memo

As a leader, you can use the Vroom–Jago model to determine the appropriate amount of follower participation to use in making a decision. You can follow the time-based guidelines when time is of the essence, but use development-based guidelines when cultivating followers' decision-making skills is also important.

Consider the example of a small auto parts manufacturer, which owns only one machine for performing welds on mufflers. If the machine has broken down and production has come to a standstill, a decision concerning the purchase of a new machine is critical and has to be made immediately to get the production line moving again. In this case, a leader would follow the time-based model for selecting the decision style. However, if the machine is scheduled for routine replacement in three months, time is not a critical factor. The leader is then free to consider the importance of involving production workers in the decision making to develop their skills. Thus, the leader may follow the development-based model because time is not a critical concern.

Exhibits 3.8 and 3.9 illustrate the two decision matrixes—a timesaving-based model and an employee development-based model—that enable leaders to adopt a participation style by answering the diagnostic questions in sequence. Returning to the example of the welding machine, if the machine has broken down and must be replaced immediately, the leader would follow the timesaving-based model in Exhibit 3.8. The leader enters the matrix at the left side, at Problem Statement. The matrix acts as a funnel as you move left to right, responding to the situational questions across the top, answering high (H) or low (L) to each one and avoiding crossing any horizontal lines.

The first question (decision significance) would be: *How significant is this decision for the project or organization?* If the answer is High, the leader proceeds to importance of commitment: *How important is subordinate commitment to carrying out the decision?* If the answer is High, the next question pertains to leader expertise: *What is the level of the leader's expertise in relation to the problem?* If the leader's knowledge and expertise is High, the leader next considers likelihood of commitment: *If the leader were to make the decision alone, how likely is it that subordinates would be committed to the decision?* If there is a high likelihood that subordinates would be committed, the decision matrix leads directly to the Decide style of decision making, in which the leader makes the decision alone and presents it to the group.

As noted earlier, this matrix assumes that time and efficiency are the most important criteria. However, consider how the selection of a decision style would differ if the leader had several months to replace the welding machine and considered follower development of high importance and time of little concern. In this case, the leader would follow the employee development-driven decision matrix in Exhibit 3.9. Beginning again at the left side of the matrix: *How significant is this decision for the project or organization?* If the answer is High, proceed to importance of commitment: *How important is subordinate commitment?* If high, the next question concerns likelihood of commitment (leader expertise is not

Exhibit 3.8 Timesaving-Based Model for Determining an Appropriate Decision-Making Style—Group Problems

1. Decision Significance?	2. Importance of Commitment?	3. Leader Expertise?	4. Likelihood of Commitment?	5. Group Support?	6. Group Expertise?	7. Team Competence?	
H	H	H	H	–	–	–	Decide
H	H	H	L	H	H	H	Delegate
H	H	H	L	H	H	L	Consult (Group)
H	H	H	L	H	L	–	Consult (Group)
H	H	H	L	L	–	–	
H	H	L	H	H	H	H	Facilitate
H	H	L	H	H	H	L	Consult (Individually)
H	H	L	H	H	L	–	Consult (Individually)
H	H	L	H	L	–	–	
H	H	L	L	H	H	H	Facilitate
H	H	L	L	H	H	L	Consult (Group)
H	H	L	L	H	L	–	Consult (Group)
H	H	L	L	L	–	–	
H	L	H	–	–	–	–	Decide
H	L	L	–	H	H	H	Facilitate
H	L	L	–	H	H	L	Consult (Individually)
H	L	L	–	H	L	–	Consult (Individually)
H	L	L	–	L	–	–	
L	H	–	H	–	–	–	Decide
L	H	–	L	–	–	H	Delegate
L	H	–	L	–	–	L	Facilitate
L	L	–	–	–	–	–	Decide

Source: Victor H. Vroom, "Leadership and the Decision-Making Process," *Organizational Dynamics* 28, no. 4 (Spring 2000), pp. 82–94.

considered because the development model is focused on involving subordinates, even if the leader has knowledge and expertise): *If the leader were to make the decision alone, how likely is it that subordinates would be committed to the decision?* If there is a high likelihood, the leader next considers group support: *What is the degree of subordinate support for the team's or organization's objectives at stake in this decision?* If the degree of support for goals is low, the leader would proceed directly to the Group Consult decision style. However, if the degree of support for goals is high, the leader would then ask: *What is the level of group members' knowledge and expertise in relation to the problem?* An answer of

Exhibit 3.9 Employee Development–Based Model for Determining an Appropriate Decision-Making Style—Group Problems

1. Decision Significance?	2. Importance of Commitment?	3. Leader Expertise?	4. Likelihood of Commitment?	5. Group Support?	6. Group Expertise?	7. Team Competence?	
H	H	H	–	H	H	H	Delegate
				H	H	L	Facilitate
				H	L	–	Consult (Group)
				L	–	–	Consult (Group)
H	H	L	–	H	H	H	Delegate
				H	H	L	Facilitate
				H	L	–	Facilitate
				L	–	–	Consult (Group)
H	L	–	–	H	H	H	Delegate
				H	H	L	Facilitate
				H	L	–	Consult (Group)
				L	–	–	Consult (Group)
L	H	–	H	–	–	–	Decide
	H	–	L	–	–	–	Delegate
	L	–	–	–	–	–	Decide

(Left axis label: PROBLEM STATEMENT)

Source: Victor H. Vroom, "Leadership and the Decision-Making Process," *Organizational Dynamics* 28, no. 4 (Spring 2000), pp. 82–94.

High would take the leader to the question: *How skilled and committed are group members to working together as a team to solve problems?* An answer of High would lead to the Delegate style, in which the leader allows the group to make the decision within certain limits.

Note that the timesaving-driven model takes the leader to the first decision style that preserves decision quality and follower acceptance, whereas the employee development-driven model takes other considerations into account. It takes less time to make an autocratic decision (Decide) than to involve subordinates by using a Facilitate or Delegate style. However, in many cases, time and efficiency are less important than the opportunity to further subordinate development. In many of today's organizations, where knowledge sharing and widespread participation are considered critical to organizational success, leaders are placing greater emphasis on follower development when time is not a critical issue.

Leaders can quickly learn to use the model to adapt their styles to fit the situation. However, researchers have also developed a computer-based program that allows for greater complexity and precision in the Vroom–Jago model and incorporates the value of time and value of follower development as situational factors rather than portraying them in separate decision matrixes.

The Vroom–Jago model has been criticized as being less than perfect,[25] but it is useful to decision makers, and the model is supported by research.[26] Leaders can learn to use the model to make timely, high-quality decisions. Let's try applying the model to the following problem.

IN THE LEAD

Art Weinstein, Whitlock Manufacturing

When Whitlock Manufacturing won a contract from a large auto manufacturer to produce an engine to power its flagship sports car, Art Weinstein was thrilled to be selected as project manager. The engine, of Japanese design and extremely complex, has gotten rave reviews in the automotive press. This project has dramatically enhanced the reputation of Whitlock Manufacturing, which was previously known primarily as a producer of outboard engines for marine use.

Weinstein and his team of engineers have taken great pride in their work on the project, but their excitement was dashed by a recent report of serious engine problems in cars delivered to customers. Fourteen owners of cars produced during the first month had experienced engine seizures. Taking quick action, the auto manufacturer suspended sales of the sports car, halted current production, and notified owners of the current model not to drive the car. Everyone involved knows this is a disaster. Unless the engine problem is solved quickly, Whitlock Manufacturing could be exposed to extended litigation. In addition, Whitlock's valued relationship with one of the world's largest auto manufacturers would probably be lost forever.

As the person most knowledgeable about the engine, Weinstein has spent two weeks in the field inspecting the seized engines and the auto plant where they were installed. In addition, he has carefully examined the operations and practices in Whitlock's plant where the engine is manufactured. Based on this extensive research, Weinstein is convinced that he knows what the problem is and the best way to solve it. However, his natural inclination is to involve other team members as much as possible in making decisions and solving problems. He not only values their input, but he also thinks that by encouraging greater participation he strengthens the thinking skills of team members, helping them grow and contribute more to the team and the organization. Therefore, Weinstein chooses to consult with his team before making his final decision.

The group meets for several hours that afternoon, discussing the problem in detail and sharing their varied perspectives, including the information Weinstein has gathered during his research. Following the group session, Weinstein makes his decision. He will present the decision at the team meeting the following morning, after which testing and correction of the engine problem will begin.[27]

In the Whitlock Manufacturing case, either a timesaving-based or an employee development–based model can be used to select a decision style. Although time is of importance, the leader's desire to involve subordinates can be considered equally important. Do you think Weinstein used the correct leader decision style? Let's examine the problem using the employee development-based decision tree, since Weinstein is concerned about involving other team members. Moving from left to right in Exhibit 3.9, the questions and answers are as follows: *How significant is this decision for the organization?* Definitely high. Quality of the decision is of critical importance. The company's future may be at stake. *How important is subordinate commitment to carrying out the decision?* Also high. The team members must support and implement Weinstein's solution. Question #3 (leader expertise) is not considered in the employee development-driven model, as shown in Exhibit 3.9. The next question would be *If Weinstein makes the decision on his own, will team members have high or low commitment to it?* The answer to this question is probably also high. Team members respect Weinstein, and they are likely to accept his analysis of the problem. This leads to the question *What is the degree of subordinate support for the team's or organization's objectives at stake in this decision?* The answer, definitely high, leads to the question, *What is the level of group members' knowledge and expertise in relation to the problem?* The answer to this question is probably Low, which leads to the Consult Group decision style. Thus, Weinstein used the style that would be recommended by the Vroom–Jago model.

Now, assume that Weinstein chose to place more emphasis on efficient use of time than on employee involvement and development. Using the timesaving-based decision matrix in Exhibit 3.8, answer the questions across the top of the matrix based on the information just provided (rate Weinstein's level of expertise in Question 3 as high). Remember to avoid crossing any horizontal lines. What decision style is recommended? Is it the same or different from that recommended by the employee development-based tree?

Substitutes for Leadership

The contingency leadership approaches considered so far have focused on the leader's style, the follower's nature, and the situation's characteristics. The final contingency approach suggests that situational variables can be so powerful that they actually substitute for or neutralize the need for leadership.[28] This approach outlines those organizational settings in which task-oriented and people-oriented leadership styles are unimportant or unnecessary.

Exhibit 3.10 shows the situational variables that tend to substitute for or neutralize leadership characteristics. A **substitute** for leadership makes the

Substitute
a situational variable that makes leadership unnecessary or redundant

Exhibit 3.10 Substitutes and Neutralizers for Leadership

Variable		Task-Oriented Leadership	People-Oriented Leadership
Organizational variables	Group cohesiveness	Substitutes for	Substitutes for
	Formalization	Substitutes for	No effect on
	Inflexibility	Neutralizes	No effect on
	Low position power	Neutralizes	Neutralizes
Task characteristics	Highly structured task	Substitutes for	No effect on
	Automatic feedback	Substitutes for	No effect on
	Intrinsic satisfaction	No effect on	Substitutes for
Follower characteristics	Professionalism	Substitutes for	Substitutes for
	Training/experience	Substitutes for	No effect on
	Low value of rewards	Neutralizes	Neutralizes

leadership style unnecessary or redundant. For example, highly educated, professional subordinates who know how to do their tasks do not need a leader who initiates structure for them and tells them what to do. In addition, long-term education often develops autonomous, self-motivated individuals. Thus, task-oriented and people-oriented leadership is substituted by professional education and socialization.[29]

A **neutralizer** counteracts the leadership style and prevents the leader from displaying certain behaviors. For example, if a leader is physically removed from subordinates, the leader's ability to give directions to subordinates is greatly reduced. Kinko's, a nationwide copy center, provides an example. With numerous locations widely scattered across regions, regional managers have very limited personal interaction with store managers and employees. Thus, their ability to both support and direct is neutralized.

Situational variables in Exhibit 3.10 include characteristics of the followers, the task, and the organization itself. For example, when subordinates are highly professional, such as research scientists in companies like Merck or Monsanto, both leadership styles are less important. The employees do not need either direction or support. With respect to task characteristics, highly structured tasks substitute for a task-oriented style, and a satisfying task substitutes for a people-oriented style.

When a task is highly structured and routine, like auditing cash, the leader should provide personal consideration and support that is not provided by the task. Satisfied people don't need as much consideration. Likewise, with respect to the organization itself, group cohesiveness substitutes for both leader styles. For example, the relationship that develops among air traffic controllers and jet fighter pilots is characterized by high-stress interactions and continuous peer training. This cohesiveness provides support and direction that substitute for formal leadership.[30] Formalized rules and procedures substitute for leader task orientation because the rules tell people what to do. Physical separation of leader and subordinate neutralizes both leadership styles.

The value of the situations described in Exhibit 3.10 is that they help leaders avoid leadership overkill. Leaders should adopt a style with which to complement the organizational situation. For example, the work situation for bank tellers provides a high level of formalization, little flexibility, and a highly structured task. The head teller should not adopt a task-oriented style because the organization already provides structure and direction. The head teller should concentrate on a people-oriented style. In other organizations, if group cohesiveness or previous training meets employee social needs, the leader is free to concentrate on task-oriented behaviors. The leader can adopt a style complementary to the organizational situation to ensure that both task needs and people needs of followers are met.

Recent studies have examined how substitutes (the situation) can be designed to have more impact than leader behaviors on outcomes such as subordinate satisfaction.[31] The impetus behind this research is the idea that substitutes for leadership can be designed into organizations in ways to complement existing leadership, act in the absence of leadership, and otherwise provide more comprehensive leadership alternatives. For

Action Memo

As a leader, you can avoid leadership overkill. Adopt a style that is complementary to the organizational situation to ensure that both task needs and people needs are met.

Action Memo

Measure how the task characteristics of your job or a job you've held in the past might act as substitutes for leadership by answering the questions in Leader's Self-Insight 3.3.

Action Memo

As a leader, you can use a people-oriented style when tasks are highly structured and followers are bound by formal rules and procedures. You can adopt a task-oriented style if group cohesiveness and followers' intrinsic job satisfaction meet their social and emotional needs.

Neutralizer
a situational characteristic that counteracts the leadership style and prevents the leader from displaying certain behaviors

Leader's Self-Insight 3.3

Measuring Substitutes for Leadership

Think about your current job, or a job you have held in the past. Please answer whether each item below is Mostly False or Mostly True for you in that job.

	Mostly False	Mostly True
1. Because of the nature of the tasks I perform, there is little doubt about the best way to do them.	____	____
2. My job duties are so simple that almost anyone could perform them well after a little instruction.	____	____
3. It is difficult to figure out the best way to do many of my tasks and activities.	____	____
4. There is really only one correct way to perform most of the tasks I do.	____	____
5. After I've completed a task, I can tell right away from the results I get whether I have performed it correctly.	____	____
6. My job is the kind where you can finish a task and not know if you've made a mistake or error.	____	____
7. Because of the nature of the tasks I do, it is easy for me to see when I have done something exceptionally well.	____	____
8. I get lots of satisfaction from the work I do.	____	____
9. It is hard to imagine that anyone could enjoy performing the tasks I have performed on my job.	____	____
10. My job satisfaction depends primarily on the nature of the tasks and activities I perform.	____	____

Scoring and Interpretation

For your task structure score, give yourself one point for Mostly True answers to items 1, 2, and 4, and for a Mostly False answer to item 3. This is your score for Task Structure: _____

For your task feedback score, give yourself one point for Mostly True answers to items 5 and 7, and for a Mostly False answer to item 6. This is your score for Task Feedback: _____

For your intrinsic satisfaction score, score one point for Mostly True answers to items 8 and 10, and for a Mostly False answer to item 9. This is your score for Intrinsic Satisfaction: _____

A high score (3 or 4) for Task Structure or Task Feedback indicates a high potential for those elements to act as a substitute for *task-oriented leadership*. A high score (3) for Intrinsic Satisfaction indicates the potential to be a substitute for *people-oriented leadership*. Does your leader adopt a style that is complementary to the task situation, or is the leader guilty of *leadership overkill*? How can you apply this understanding to your own actions as a leader?

Source: Based on "Questionnaire Items for the Measurement of Substitutes for Leadership," Table 2 in Steven Kerr and John M. Jermier, "Substitutes for Leadership: Their Meaning and Measurement," *Organizational Behavior and Human Performance* 22 (1978), pp. 375–403.

Action Memo

As a leader, you can provide minimal task direction and personal support to highly-trained employees; followers' professionalism and intrinsic satisfaction substitute for both task- and people-oriented leadership.

example, Paul Reeves, a foreman at Harmon Auto Parts, shared half-days with his subordinates during which they helped him perform his leader tasks. After Reeves' promotion to middle management, his group no longer required a foreman. Followers were trained to act on their own.[32] Thus, a situation in which follower ability and training were highly developed created a substitute for leadership.

The ability to use substitutes to fill leadership "gaps" is often advantageous to organizations. Indeed, the fundamental assumption of substitutes-for-leadership researchers is that effective leadership is the ability to recognize and provide the support and direction not already provided by task, group, and organization.

Leadership Essentials

▪ The most important point in this chapter is that situational variables affect leadership outcomes. The contingency approaches were developed to systematically address the relationship between a leader and the organization. The contingency approaches focus on how the components of leadership style, subordinate characteristics, and situational elements impact one another. Fiedler's contingency model, Hersey and Blanchard's situational theory, the path–goal theory, the Vroom–Jago model, and the substitutes-for-leadership concept each examine how different situations call for different styles of leadership behavior.

▪ According to Fiedler, leaders can determine whether their leadership style is suitable for the situation. Task-oriented leaders tend to do better in very favorable or very unfavorable situations, whereas relationship-oriented leaders do best in situations of intermediate favorability. Hersey and Blanchard contend that leaders can adjust their task or relationship style to accommodate the readiness level of their subordinates. The path–goal theory states that leaders can use a style that appropriately clarifies the path to desired rewards. The Vroom–Jago model indicates that leaders can choose a participative decision style based on contingencies such as quality requirement, commitment requirement, or the leader's knowledge and expertise. In addition, concern for time (the need for a fast decision) versus concern for follower development is taken into account. Finally, the substitutes-for-leadership concept recommends that leaders adjust their style to provide resources not otherwise provided in the organizational situation.

▪ By discerning the characteristics of tasks, subordinates, and organizations, leaders can determine the style that increases the likelihood of successful leadership outcomes. Therefore, effective leadership depends partly on developing diagnostic skills and being flexible in your leadership behavior.

Discussion Questions

1. Consider Fiedler's theory as illustrated in Exhibit 3.3. How often do you think very favorable, intermediate, or very unfavorable situations occur to leaders in real life? Discuss.

2. Do you think leadership style is fixed and unchangeable or can leaders be flexible and adaptable with respect to style? Why?

3. Consider the leadership position of the managing partner in a law firm. What task, subordinate, and organizational factors might serve as substitutes for leadership in this situation?

4. Compare Fiedler's contingency model with the path–goal theory. What are the similarities and differences? Which do you prefer?

5. If you were a first-level supervisor of a team of telemarketers, how would you go about assessing the readiness level of your subordinates? Do you think most leaders are able to easily shift their leadership style to suit the readiness level of followers?

6. Think back to teachers you have had, and identify one each who fits a supportive style, directive style, participative style, and achievement-oriented style according to the path–goal theory. Which style did you find most effective? Why?

7. Do you think leaders should decide on a participative style based on the most efficient way to reach the decision? Should leaders sometimes let people participate for other reasons?

8. Consider the situational characteristics of group cohesiveness, organizational formalization, and physical separation. How might each of these substitute for or neutralize task-oriented or people-oriented leadership? Explain.

Leadership at Work

TASK VERSUS RELATIONSHIP ROLE PLAY

You are the new distribution manager for French Grains Bakery. Five drivers who deliver French Grains baked goods to grocery stores in the metropolitan area report to you. The drivers are expected to complete the Delivery Report to keep track of actual deliveries and any changes that occur. The Delivery Report is a key element in inventory control and provides the data for French Grains invoicing of grocery stores. Errors become excessive when drivers fail to complete the report each day, especially when store managers request different inventory when the driver arrives. As a result, French Grains may not be paid for several loaves of bread a day for each mistake in the Delivery Report. The result is lost revenue and poor inventory control.

One of the drivers accounts for about 60 percent of the errors in the Delivery Reports. This driver is a nice person and generally reliable, although he is occasionally late for work. His major problem is that he falls behind in his paperwork. A second driver accounts for about 30 percent of the errors, and a third driver for about 10 percent of the errors. The other two drivers turn in virtually error-free Delivery Reports.

You are a high task-oriented (and low relationship-oriented) leader, and have decided to talk to the drivers about doing a more complete and accurate job with the Delivery Reports. Write below exactly how you will go about correcting this problem as a task-oriented leader. Will you meet with drivers individually or in a group? When and where will you meet with them? Exactly what will you say and how will you get them to listen?

_____

_____

_____

Now adopt the role of a high relationship-oriented (and low task-oriented) leader. Write below exactly what you will do and say as a relationship-oriented distribution manager. Will you meet with the drivers individually or in a group? What will you say and how will you get them to listen?

_____

_____

_____

In Class: The instructor can ask students to volunteer to play the role of the Distribution Manager and the drivers. A few students can take turns role-playing the Distribution Manager in front of the class to show how they would handle the drivers as task- and relationship-oriented leaders. The instructor can ask other students for feedback on the leader's effectiveness and on which approach seems more effective for this situation, and why.

Source: Based on K. J. Keleman, J. E. Garcia, and K. J. Lovelace, *Management Incidents: Role Plays for Management Development* (Dubuque, IA: Kendall Hunt Publishing Company, 1990), pp. 69–72.

Part 3: The Personal Side of Leadership

istockphoto.com/AVTG

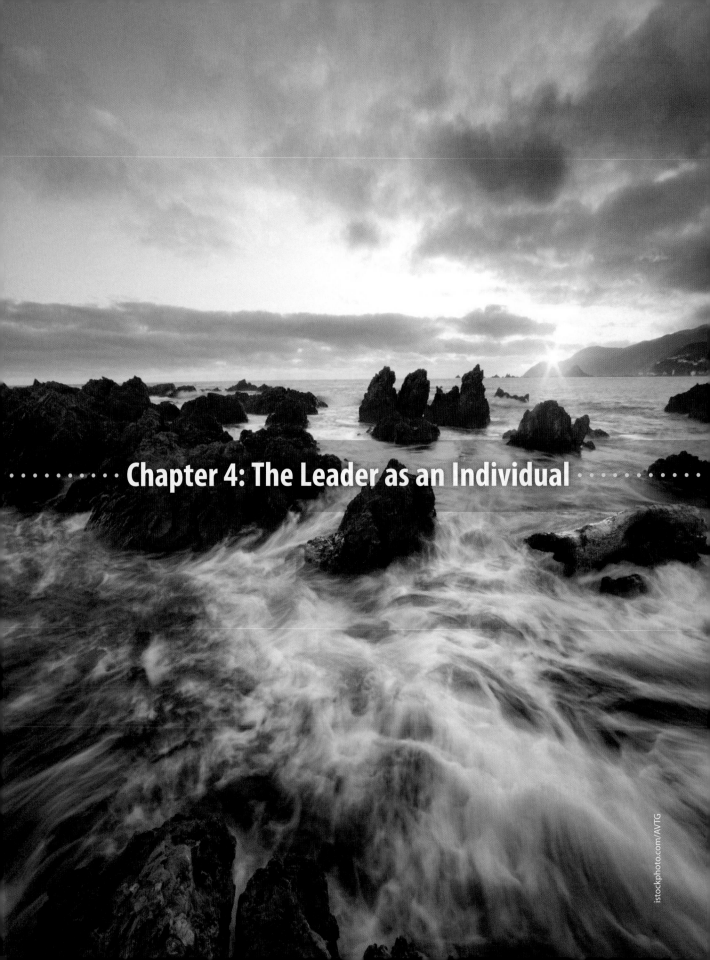

Chapter 4: The Leader as an Individual

istockphoto.com/AVTG

Your Leadership Challenge

After reading this chapter, you should be able to:

- Identify major personality dimensions and understand how personality influences leadership and relationships within organizations.

- Clarify your instrumental and end values, and recognize how values guide thoughts and behavior.

- Define *attitudes* and explain their relationship to leader behavior.

- Explain attribution theory and recognize how perception affects the leader–follower relationship.

- Recognize individual differences in cognitive style and broaden your

own thinking style to expand leadership potential.

- Understand how to lead and work with people with varied personality traits.

Chapter Outline

When people describe Sander A. Flaum, former CEO of health-care advertising agency Robert A. Becker Euro RSCG, they use words like *tough*, *diligent*, *competitive*, and *ambitious*. For most of his life, Flaum has put work first. His son, Jonathon Flaum, on the other hand, is described as spiritual, self-reliant, and determined to lead a balanced life. Their differing values and personality traits have long caused tension between the two, who recently collaborated on a book, *The 100 Mile Walk: A Father and Son on a Quest to Find the Essence of Leadership*.[1]

We all know that people differ in many ways. Some, like Sander Flaum, put a high value on work and achievement whereas others, like his son Jonathon, place greater value on family and personal relationships. Some are competitive and hard-charging; others are laid-back and easygoing. Some are thoughtful and serious while others are impulsive and fun-loving. Individual differences affect the leader–follower interaction just as they affect the father–son relationship of Sander and Jonathon Flaum and indeed all human relationships. Differences in personality, attitudes, values, and so forth influence how people interpret an assignment, whether they like to be told what to do, how they handle challenges, and how they interact with others. Leaders' personalities and attitudes, as well as their ability to understand individual differences among employees, can profoundly affect leadership effectiveness. Many of today's organizations are using personality and other psychometric tests as a way to help people better understand and relate to one another.

In Chapter 2, we examined studies of some personality traits, individual qualities, and behaviors that are thought to be consistent with effective leadership. Chapter 3 examined contingency theories of leadership, which consider the relationship between leader activities and the situation in which they occur, including followers and the environment. Clearly, organizational leadership is both an individual and an organizational phenomenon. This chapter explores the individual in more depth, looking at some individual differences that can influence leadership abilities and success. We begin by looking at personality and some leader-related personality dimensions. Then, the chapter considers how values affect leadership and the ways in which a leader's attitudes toward self and others influence behavior. We also explore the role of perception, discuss attribution theory, and look at cognitive differences, including a discussion of thinking and decision-making styles and the concept of brain dominance. Finally, the chapter considers a few techniques for working with different personality types.

Personality and Leadership

Personality is the set of unseen characteristics and processes that underlie a relatively stable pattern of behavior in response to ideas, objects, or people in the environment. Leaders who have an understanding of how individuals' personalities differ can use this understanding to improve their leadership effectiveness.

A Model of Personality

Most people think of personality in terms of traits. As we discussed in Chapter 2, researchers have investigated whether any traits stand up to scientific scrutiny, and we looked at some traits associated with effective leadership. Although investigators have examined thousands of traits over the years, their findings have been distilled into five general dimensions that describe personality. These often are called the **Big Five personality dimensions**, which describe an individual's extraversion, agreeableness, conscientiousness, emotional stability, and openness to experience.[2] Each dimension contains a wide range of specific traits—for example, all of the personality traits that you would use to describe a teacher, friend, or boss could be categorized into one of the Big Five dimensions. These factors represent a continuum, in that a person may have a low, moderate, or high degree of each of the dimensions.

Extraversion is made up of traits and characteristics that influence behavior in group settings. Extraversion refers to the degree to which a person is outgoing, sociable, talkative, and comfortable meeting and talking to new people. Someone low on extraversion may come across as quiet, withdrawn, and socially unassertive. This dimension also includes the characteristic of *dominance*. A person with a high degree of dominance likes to be in control and have influence over others. These people often are quite self-confident, seek out positions of authority, and are competitive and assertive. They like to be in charge of others or have responsibility for others. It is obvious that both dominance and extraversion could be valuable for a leader. However, not all effective leaders necessarily have a high degree of these characteristics.

Personality
the set of unseen characteristics and processes that underlie a relatively stable pattern of behavior in response to ideas, objects, and people in the environment

Big Five personality dimensions
five general dimensions that describe personality: extraversion, agreeableness, conscientiousness, emotional stability, and openness to experience

Extraversion
the degree to which a person is outgoing, sociable, talkative, and comfortable meeting and talking to new people

Leader's Self-Insight 4.1
The Big Five Personality Dimensions

Each individual's collection of personality traits is different; it is what makes us unique. But, although each *collection* of traits varies, we all share many common traits. The following phrases describe various traits and behaviors. Rate how accurately each statement describes you, based on a scale of 1 to 5, with 1 being very inaccurate and 5 very accurate. Describe yourself as you are now, not as you wish to be. There are no right or wrong answers.

	1	2	3	4	5	
	Very Inaccurate			Very Accurate		

Extraversion

I am usually the life of the party.	1 2 3 4 5
I feel comfortable around people.	1 2 3 4 5
I am talkative.	1 2 3 4 5

Neuroticism (Low Emotional Stability)

I often feel critical of myself.	1 2 3 4 5
I often envy others.	1 2 3 4 5
I am temperamental.	1 2 3 4 5

Agreeableness

I am kind and sympathetic.	1 2 3 4 5
I have a good word for everyone.	1 2 3 4 5
I never insult people.	1 2 3 4 5

Openness to New Experiences

I am imaginative.	1 2 3 4 5
I prefer to vote for liberal political candidates.	1 2 3 4 5
I really like art.	1 2 3 4 5

Conscientiousness

I am systematic and efficient.	1 2 3 4 5
I pay attention to details.	1 2 3 4 5
I am always prepared for class.	1 2 3 4 5

Which are your most prominent traits? For fun and discussion, compare your responses with those of classmates.

Source: These questions were adapted from a variety of sources.

marble: © Kirill Matkov   sunset: © Marco Regalia

For example, many successful top leaders, including Bill Gates of Microsoft, Warren Buffett of Berkshire Hathaway, Brenda Barnes, CEO of Sara Lee, and Markus Frind, who started the online dating site Plenty of Fish, are introverts, people who become drained by social encounters and need time alone to reflect and recharge their batteries. One study found that 4 in 10 top executives test out to be introverts.[3] Thus, the quality of extraversion is not as significant as is often presumed. In addition, a high degree of dominance could even be detrimental to effective leadership if not tempered by other qualities, such as agreeableness or emotional stability.

Agreeableness refers to the degree to which a person is able to get along with others by being good-natured, cooperative, forgiving, compassionate, understanding, and trusting. A leader who scores high on agreeableness seems warm and approachable, whereas one who is low on this dimension may seem cold, distant, and insensitive.

Action Memo

See where you fall on the Big Five scale for extraversion, agreeableness, conscientiousness, emotional stability, and openness to experience by answering the questions in Leader's Self-Insight 4.1.

Agreeableness
the degree to which a person is able to get along with others by being good-natured, cooperative, forgiving, compassionate, understanding, and trusting

Traits of agreeableness seem to be particularly important for leaders in today's collaborative organizations. The days are over when a hard-driving manager can run roughshod over others to earn a promotion. Today's successful leaders are not the tough guys of the past but those men and women who know how to get people to like and trust them.[4] Lloyd C. Blankfein, CEO of Goldman Sachs, points out that the recent financial crisis brought this to light for him and other top leaders. During the worst of the crisis, Blankfein says communication, teamwork, and driving a sense of collaboration and partnership became crucial leadership skills. Blankfein began sending a daily voicemail to the entire firm, as well as walking around to talk to people, answer questions, seek out opinions, and build confidence among employees. Leaders are also making a concerted effort to present a friendlier face to the public and shareholders after years of headlines exposing white-collar crime, CEO arrogance, and complaints over exorbitant pay. Lee Raymond, the former CEO of ExxonMobil, made plenty of money for investors but was described by some shareholders as "stubborn, self-important, [and] rude." In contrast, Raymond's successor, Rex Tillerson, was publicly thanked at one annual meeting for his "friendliness, humor, and candor."[5]

One recent book argues that the secret to success in work and in life is *likability*. We all know we're more willing to do something for someone we like than for someone we don't, whether it be a teammate, a neighbor, a professor, or a supervisor. Leaders can increase their likability by developing characteristics of agreeableness, including being friendly and cooperative, understanding other people in a genuine way, and striving to make people feel positive about themselves.[6]

The next personality dimension, **conscientiousness**, refers to the degree to which a person is responsible, dependable, persistent, and achievement-oriented. A conscientious person is focused on a few goals, which he or she pursues in a purposeful way, whereas a less conscientious person tends to be easily distracted and impulsive. This dimension of personality relates to the work itself rather than to relationships with other people. Many entrepreneurs show a high level of conscientiousness. For example, Marc Ecko, founder of Marc Ecko Enterprises, a manufacturer of urban street-inspired apparel, started making and selling airbrushed T-shirts when he was in the 8th grade. Although his high school guidance counselor convinced him to go to college, Ecko dropped out in his third year to pursue his dream. He started his business by carefully painting T-shirts, sweatshirts, and jackets and personally selling them to shops and at street fairs. There were some tough times in the beginning, but Ecko stayed focused on his goals. Within 15 years, Marc Ecko Enterprises had a staff of 1,500 and global sales of $1.5 billion.[7]

The dimension of **emotional stability** refers to the degree to which a person is well adjusted, calm, and secure. A leader who is emotionally stable handles stress well, is able to handle criticism, and generally doesn't take mistakes or failures personally. Leaders with emotional stability typically develop positive relationships and can also improve relationships among others. For example, Bob Iger's emotional stability could be one reason the "snake pit of warring egos" at Walt Disney Company has been transformed into a peaceful, profitable organization.

Conscientiousness
the degree to which a person is responsible, dependable, persistent, and achievement-oriented

Emotional stability
the degree to which a person is well adjusted, calm, and secure

IN THE LEAD

Bob Iger, Walt Disney Company

Bob Iger once thought he was going to be CEO of Capital Cities/ABC. Instead, the company he expected to lead was sold to the Walt Disney Company. Iger ended up working for 10 years under the leadership of Disney CEO Michael Eisner before taking the top job himself a few years ago. Rather than let the disappointment get him down, Iger set about absorbing all he could at Disney and today says he feels grateful for all he learned working with the former CEO.

However, despite all the good things Michael Eisner did when he was CEO, by the time Iger took over relationships both within the company and with outsiders were strained. Eisner was known as a micromanaging, imperious, and aggressive leader. Iger, a quiet, behind-the-scenes guy, seemed to many an odd choice to get Disney back on track. "There were many naysayers," recalls one investor. "People would call him 'mini-Eisner,' his yes man." Again, Iger didn't let the criticism bother him. He simply began the hard work of revitalizing the company. One of his first moves was to mend the fractured relationship with Steve Jobs and Pixar Films. Now, Disney owns Pixar and Jobs is a committed board member. About Iger, Jobs says, "He's a really solid guy."

Smoothing internal working relationships was just as important. Although he could have tossed Eisner's loyal people out, Iger instead got them on board with his own plans and goals for the company. He gave executives running the various divisions more autonomy to make their own decisions, helping to rebuild a can-do attitude. Iger believes in ruling by consensus, not fiat, and he prefers to stay in the background and let the limelight of success shine on others. His easy manner, good nature, and humility enabled Iger to transform Disney's troubled culture in a surprisingly short time period. That, in turn, has contributed to both a creative and a financial revival at the company. "It's the happiest place on earth," says Iger of Disney. And he plans to keep it that way.[8]

In contrast to a leader like Bob Iger with a high degree of emotional stability, leaders who have a low degree of emotional stability are likely to become tense, anxious, or depressed. They generally have lower self-confidence and may explode in emotional outbursts when stressed or criticized. The related topic of *emotional intelligence* will be discussed in detail in the next chapter.

The final Big Five dimension, **openness to experience**, is the degree to which a person has a broad range of interests and is imaginative, creative, and willing to consider new ideas. These people are intellectually curious and often seek out new experiences through travel, the arts, movies, reading widely, or other activities. People lower in this dimension tend to have narrower interests and stick to the tried-and-true ways of doing things. Open-mindedness is important to leaders because, as we learned in Chapter 1, leadership is about change rather than stability. In an interesting study of three nineteenth-century leaders—John Quincy Adams, Frederick Douglass, and Jane Addams—one researcher found that early travel experiences and exposure to different ideas and cultures were critical elements in developing open-minded qualities in these leaders.[9] Travel during the formative years helped these leaders develop a greater degree of openness to experience because it put them in situations that required adaptability.

Few studies have carefully examined the connection between the Big Five and leadership success. One summary of more than 70 years of personality and leadership research did find evidence that four of the five dimensions were consistently related to successful leadership.[10] The researchers found considerable evidence that people who score high on the dimensions of extraversion, agreeableness, conscientiousness, and emotional stability are more successful leaders. Results for openness to experience were less consistent; that is, in some cases, higher scores on this dimension related to better performance, but they did not seem to make a difference in other cases. Yet, in a study by a team of psychologists of the personality traits of the greatest U.S. presidents (as determined by historians), openness to

Action Memo

As a leader, you can learn about your own basic personality dimensions and how to emphasize the positive aspects of your personality in dealing with followers.

Openness to experience
the degree to which a person has a broad range of interests and is imaginative, creative, and willing to consider new ideas

experience produced the highest correlation with historians' ratings of greatness. The study noted that presidents such as Abraham Lincoln and Thomas Jefferson were high on this personality dimension. Other personality dimensions the team found to be associated with great presidents were extraversion and conscientiousness, including traits such as assertiveness, setting ambitious goals, and striving for achievement. Although agreeableness did not correlate with greatness, the ability to empathize with others and being concerned for others, which could be considered elements of emotional stability, did.[11]

The value of the Big Five for leaders is primarily to help them understand their own basic personality dimensions, and then learn to emphasize the positive and mitigate the negative aspects of their own natural style. For example, people who are introverts often stagnate, especially in large organizations, because they have a difficult time getting noticed and are therefore less likely to be rewarded for their hard work.[12] One experiment found that people who spoke up more often were rated as better leaders, even if they were less competent than their quieter colleagues.[13] Exhibit 4.1 gives some tips for both introverts and extraverts to help them be more effective and successful.

Many factors contribute to effective leadership. As we learned in the previous two chapters, situational factors play a role in determining which traits may be most important. In addition, a leader's intelligence, knowledge of the business, values and attitudes, and problem-solving styles, which are not measured by the Big Five, also play a role in leadership effectiveness. Later in this chapter, we will discuss values and attitudes, as well as examine some cognitive differences that affect leadership. First, let's look more closely at two personality attributes that have significant implications for leaders.

Personality Traits and Leader Behavior

Two specific personality attributes that have a significant impact on behavior and are thus of particular interest for leadership studies are locus of control and authoritarianism.

Locus of Control Some people believe that their actions can strongly affect what happens to them. In other words, they believe they are "masters of their own fate." Others feel that whatever happens to them in life is a result of luck, chance, or outside people and events; they believe they have little control over their fate.

Exhibit 4.1 Maximizing Leadership Effectiveness

Tips for Extraverts	Tips for Introverts
• *Don't bask in the glow of your own personality.* Learn to hold back and let others sometimes have the limelight.	• *Get out and about.* Resist the urge to hibernate.
• *Try to underwhelm.* Your natural exuberance can be intimidating and cause you to miss important facts and ideas.	• *Practice bteing friendly and outgoing in settings outside of work.* Take your new skills to the office.
• *Talk less; listen more.* Develop the discipline to let others speak first on an issue to avoid the appearance of arrogance.	• *Give yourself a script.* Come up with a few talking points you can rely on to cover silences in conversations.
• *Don't be Mr. or Ms. Personality.* Extraverts tend to agree too quickly just to be liked. These casual agreements can come back to haunt you.	• *Smile.* A frown or a soberly introspective expression can be misinterpreted. A bright countenance reflects confidence that you know where you're going and want others to follow.

Source: Based on Patricia Wallington, "The Ins and Outs of Personality," *CIO* (January 15, 2003), pp. 42, 44.

A person's **locus of control** defines whether he or she places the primary responsibility within the self or on outside forces.[14] People who believe their actions determine what happens to them have a high *internal* locus of control (internals), whereas those who believe outside forces determine what happens to them have a high *external* locus of control (externals). One leader who reflects a strong internal locus of control is Chris Hughes, cofounder of Facebook.

IN THE LEAD

Chris Hughes, Facebook and MyBarackObama.com

Chris Hughes grew up in Hickory, North Carolina, as the only child of older parents. His father was a paper salesman and his mother a former public school teacher. When Hughes entered high school, he decided he wanted something different than graduating from the local school and getting a job in town. In fact, what he wanted was to attend a prestigious prep school and go on to an Ivy League university.

With his family's background and modest means, it was definitely an ambitious goal, but Hughes believed his fate was in his own hands. Without telling his parents, he began researching and applying to various boarding schools. Eventually he was offered a generous financial aid package from Phillips Academy in Andover, Massachusetts. A few years later, he left there with a scholarship to Harvard.

Hughes met Mark Zuckerberg and Dustin Moskovitz during his freshman year at Harvard and the three founded Facebook. Then, during the 2008 presidential campaign, Hughes became attracted to the idea of using new media to get Barack Obama elected. Volunteers flooded the site he built, MyBarackObama.com, from the day it launched. Hughes was later featured on the cover of *Fast Company* magazine as "The Kid Who Made Obama President."[15]

Chris Hughes exhibits many characteristics associated with internal locus of control. Research has shown real differences in behavior between internals and externals across a wide range of settings.[16] Internals in general are more self-motivated, are in better control of their own behavior, participate more in social and political activities, and more actively seek information. There is also evidence that internals are better able to handle complex information and problem solving, and that they are more achievement-oriented than externals. In addition, people with a high internal locus of control are more likely than externals to try to influence others, and thus more likely to assume or seek leadership opportunities. People with a high external locus of control typically prefer to have structured, directed work situations. They are better able than internals to handle work that requires compliance and conformity, but they are generally not as effective in situations that require initiative, creativity, and independent action. Therefore, since externals do best in situations where success depends on complying with the direction or guidance of others, they are less likely to enjoy or succeed in leadership positions.

> ### Action Memo
>
> *Do you believe luck, chance, or the actions of other people play a major role in your life, or do you feel in control of your own fate? Learn more about your locus of control by completing the questionnaire in Leader's Self-Insight 4.2.*

Authoritarianism The belief that power and status differences *should* exist in an organization is called **authoritarianism**.[17] Individuals who have a high degree of this personality trait tend to adhere to conventional rules and values, obey established authority, respect power and toughness, judge others critically, and disapprove of the expression of personal feelings. A leader's degree of authoritarianism will affect how the leader wields and shares power. A highly authoritarian leader is likely to rely heavily on formal authority and unlikely

Locus of control
defines whether a person places the primary responsibility for what happens to him or her within himself/herself or on outside forces

Authoritarianism
the belief that power and status differences should exist in an organization

For each of these 10 questions, indicate the extent to which you agree or disagree using the following scale:

1 = Strongly disagree   5 = Slightly agree
2 = Disagree   6 = Agree
3 = Slightly disagree   7 = Strongly agree
4 = Neither agree nor disagree

	Strongly Disagree						Strongly Agree
1. When I get what I want, it's usually because I worked hard for it.	1	2	3	4	5	6	7
2. When I make plans, I am almost certain to make them work.	1	2	3	4	5	6	7
3. I prefer games involving some luck over games requiring pure skill.	1	2	3	4	5	6	7
4. I can learn almost anything if I set my mind to it.	1	2	3	4	5	6	7
5. My major accomplishments are entirely due to my hard work and ability.	1	2	3	4	5	6	7
6. I usually don't set goals, because I have a hard time following through on them.	1	2	3	4	5	6	7
7. Competition discourages excellence.	1	2	3	4	5	6	7
8. Often people get ahead just by being lucky.	1	2	3	4	5	6	7
9. On any sort of exam or competition, I like to know how well I do relative to everyone else.	1	2	3	4	5	6	7
10. It's pointless to keep working on something that's too difficult for me.	1	2	3	4	5	6	7

Scoring and Interpretation

To determine your score, reverse the values you selected for questions 3, 6, 7, 8, and 10 (1 = 7, 2 = 6, 3 = 5, 4 = 4, 5 = 3, 6 = 2, 7 = 1). For example, if you strongly disagreed with the statement in question 3, you would have given it a value of 1. Change this value to a 7. Reverse the scores in a similar manner for questions 6, 7, 8, and 10. Now add the point values from all 10 questions together.

Your score:_____

This questionnaire is designed to measure locus of control beliefs. Researchers using this questionnaire in a study of college students found a mean of 51.8 for men and 52.2 for women, with a standard deviation of 6 for each. The higher your score on this questionnaire, the more you tend to believe that you are generally responsible for what happens to you; in other words, high scores are associated with internal locus of control. Low scores are associated with external locus of control. Scoring low indicates that you tend to believe that forces beyond your control, such as powerful other people, fate, or chance, are responsible for what happens to you.

Sources: Adapted from J. M. Burger, *Personality: Theory and Research* (Belmont, CA: Wadsworth, 1986), pp. 400–401, cited in D. Hellriegel, J. W. Slocum, Jr., and R. W. Woodman, *Organizational Behavior,* 6th ed. (St. Paul, MN: West Publishing Co., 1992), pp. 97–100. Original

Source: D. L. Paulhus, "Sphere-Specific Measures of Perceived Control," *Journal of Personality and Social Psychology* 44 (1983), pp. 1253–1265.

marble: © Kirill Matkov sunset: © Marco Regalia

to want to share power with subordinates. High authoritarianism is associated with the traditional, rational approach to management described in Chapter 1. The new leadership paradigm requires that leaders be less authoritarian, although people who rate high on this personality trait can be effective leaders as well. Leaders should also understand that the degree to which followers possess authoritarianism influences how they react to the leader's use of power and authority. When leaders and followers differ in their degree of authoritarianism, effective leadership may be more difficult to achieve.

A trait that is closely related to authoritarianism is *dogmatism*, which refers to a person's receptiveness to others' ideas and opinions. A highly dogmatic person is closed-minded and not receptive to others' ideas. When in a leadership position, dogmatic individuals often make decisions quickly based on limited information, and they are unreceptive to ideas that conflict with their opinions and decisions. Effective leaders, on the other hand, generally have a lower degree of dogmatism, which means they are open-minded and receptive to others' ideas.

Understanding how personality traits and dimensions affect behavior can be a valuable asset for leaders. Knowledge of individual differences gives leaders valuable insights into their own behavior as well as that of followers. It also offers a framework that leaders can use to diagnose situations and make changes to benefit the organization.

> **Action Memo**
>
> As a leader, you can improve your effectiveness by recognizing how traits such as authoritarianism and locus of control affect your relationships with followers. You can tone down a strong authoritarian or dogmatic personality to motivate others.

Values and Attitudes

In addition to personality differences, people differ in the values and attitudes they hold. These differences affect the behavior of leaders and followers.

Instrumental and End Values

Values are fundamental beliefs that an individual considers to be important, that are relatively stable over time, and that have an impact on attitudes, perception, and behavior.[18] Values are what cause a person to prefer that things be done one way rather than another way. Whether we recognize it or not, we are constantly valuing things, people, or ideas as good or bad, pleasant or unpleasant, ethical or unethical, and so forth.[19] When a person has strong values in certain areas, these can have a powerful influence on behavior. For example, a person who highly values honesty and integrity might lose respect and lessen his commitment and performance for a leader who tells "little white lies."

One way to think about values is in terms of instrumental and end values.[20] Social scientist Milton Rokeach developed a list of 18 instrumental values and 18 end values that have been found to be more or less universal across cultures. **End values**, sometimes called *terminal values,* are beliefs about the kind of goals or outcomes that are worth trying to pursue. For example, some people value security, a comfortable life, and good health above everything else as the important goals to strive for in life. Others may place greater value on social recognition, pleasure, and an exciting life. **Instrumental values** are beliefs about the types of behavior that are appropriate for reaching goals. Instrumental values include such things as being helpful to others, being honest, or exhibiting courage.

Although everyone has both instrumental and end values, individuals differ in how they order the values into priorities, which accounts for tremendous variation among people. Part of this difference relates to culture. In the United States, independence is highly valued and is reinforced by many institutions, including schools, religious organizations, and businesses. Other cultures place less value on independence and more value on being part of a tightly knit community. A person's family background also influences his or her values. Values are learned, not inherited, but some values become incorporated into a person's thinking very early in life. Some leaders cite their parents as a primary source of their leadership abilities because they helped to shape their values.[21] Bill Farmer, president of the Jackson-Monroe (Mississippi) division of Time Warner Cable, says his mother instilled in him the importance of giving back to the community. Farmer volunteers as a guest reader at Jackson State University's Learning Center, has served on the boards of numerous nonprofit organizations, and is actively involved in

Values
fundamental beliefs that an individual considers to be important, that are relatively stable over time, and that have an impact on attitudes and behavior

End values
sometimes called terminal values, these are beliefs about the kind of goals or outcomes that are worth trying to pursue

Instrumental values
beliefs about the types of behavior that are appropriate for reaching goals

Leader's Self-Insight 4.3
Instrumental and End Values

In each column below, place a check mark by the five values that are most important to you. After you have checked five values in each column, rank-order the checked values in each column from 1 to 5, with 1 = most important and 5 = least important.

Rokeach's Instrumental and End Values

End Values		Instrumental Values	
A comfortable life	_____	Ambition	_____
Equality	_____	Broad-mindedness	_____
An exciting life	_____	Capability	_____
Family security	_____	Cheerfulness	_____
Freedom	_____	Cleanliness	_____
Health	_____	Courage	_____
Inner harmony	_____	Forgiveness	_____
Mature love	_____	Helpfulness	_____
National security	_____	Honesty	_____
Pleasure	_____	Imagination	_____
Salvation	_____	Intellectualism	_____
Self-respect	_____	Logic	_____
A sense of accomplishment	_____	Ability to love	_____
Social recognition	_____	Loyalty	_____
True friendship	_____	Obedience	_____
Wisdom	_____	Politeness	_____
A world at peace	_____	Responsibility	_____
A world of beauty	_____	Self-control	_____

NOTE: The values are listed in alphabetical order and there is no one-to-one relationship between the end and instrumental values.

Scoring and Interpretation

End values, according to Rokeach, tend to fall into two categories—personal and social. For example, mature love is a personal end value and equality is a social end value. Analyze the five end values you selected and their rank order, and determine whether your primary end values tend to be personal or social. What do your five selections together mean to you? What do they mean for how you make life decisions? Compare your end value selections with another person, with each of you explaining what you learned about your end values from this exercise.

Instrumental values also tend to fall into two categories—morality and competence. The means people use to achieve their goals might violate moral values (e.g., be dishonest) or violate one's personal sense of competence and capability (e.g., be illogical). Analyze the five instrumental values you selected, and their rank order, and determine whether your primary instrumental values tend to focus on morality or competence. What do the five selected values together mean to you? What do they mean for how you will pursue your life goals? Compare your instrumental value selections with another person and describe what you learned from this exercise.

Warning: The two columns shown to the left do *not* represent the full range of instrumental and end values. Your findings would change if a different list of values were provided. This exercise is for discussion and learning purposes only and is not intended to be an accurate assessment of your actual end and instrumental values.

Sources: Robert C. Benfari, *Understanding and Changing Your Management Style* (San Francisco: Jossey-Bass, 1999), pp. 178–183; and M. Rokeach, *Understanding Human Values* (New York: The Free Press, 1979).

Action Memo

Complete the exercise in Leader's Self-Insight 4.3 to see what you can learn about your own values and how they affect your decisions and actions. Were you surprised by any of your instrumental or end values?

local Chamber of Commerce initiatives designed to create a positive community environment.[22]

Our values are generally fairly well established by early adulthood, but a person's values can also change throughout life. This chapter's *Consider This* reflects on how the values that shape a leader's actions in a moment of crisis have been developed over time. Values may affect leaders and leadership in a number of ways.[23] For one thing, values influence how leaders relate to others. A leader who values obedience, conformity, and politeness may have a difficult time understanding and appreciating a follower who is self-reliant, independent, creative, and a bit rebellious. Recognizing value differences can help

Consider **This!**

Developing Character

"The character that takes command in moments of critical choices has already been determined. It has been determined by a thousand other choices made earlier in seemingly unimportant moments. It has been determined by all those 'little' choices of years past—by all those times when the voice of conscience was at war with the voice of temptation—whispering a lie that 'it doesn't really matter.' It has been determined by all the day-to-day decisions made when life seemed easy and crises seemed far away, the decisions that piece by piece, bit by bit, developed habits of discipline or of laziness; habits of self-sacrifice or self-indulgence; habits of duty and honor and integrity—or dishonor and shame."

Source: President Ronald Reagan, quoted in Norman R. Augustine, "Seven Fundamentals of Effective Leadership," an original essay written for the Center for the Study of American Business, Washington University in St. Louis, *CEO Series*, no. 27 (October 1998).

leaders find compatible job situations, as well as help them better understand and work with varied followers. Personal values affect how leaders perceive opportunities, situations, and problems, as well as the decisions they make in response to them. Consider the differing values illustrated in the following example.

IN THE LEAD

Craig Newmark and Jim Buckmaster, Craigslist

The classified advertising Web site Craigslist is used by tens of millions of people a day all over the world, but founder Craig Newmark and CEO Jim Buckmaster continue to confound much of the business world. Why? Because making money is not one of their values. When investment bank UBS analyst Ben Schachter asked the Craigslist CEO at a global media conference how the company planned to maximize revenue, Buckmaster replied that it "wasn't part of the goal." Schachter was momentarily stunned speechless.

Buckmaster and Newmark have consistently emphasized community over cash. Craigslist doesn't charge a fee for posting on most types of listings, nor does it take a cut of successful transactions, such as eBay does. Wall Street analysts have suggested that the company could easily earn half a billion dollars a year simply by running banner advertising and charging for a few more types of listings. No way, say Newmark and Buckmaster. They'd rather keep things just the way they are, thank you very much.

The "nerd values" that guide Craigslist are reflected in the leaders' personal lives. They both admit they live comfortably, but Newmark drives an aging Toyota and Buckmaster doesn't even own a car. "We know a lot of these really rich guys and they are no happier than anyone else," says Newmark. "Money has become a burden to them. That reinforces the values that Jim and I share, about living simply." How simply? When Buckmaster needed a BlackBerry, he bought a discontinued model from—where else—Craigslist.[24]

To many businesspeople, the values that guide Craigslist seem eccentric, if not downright senseless. However, the crisis that has hit Wall Street in recent years clearly shows the danger of placing too much emphasis on maximizing revenues and profits. The investment banking unit of UBS, for instance, like many other banks, is now suffering due to heavy losses related to risky mortgage-based securities and charges from investors that they were misled by bank leaders. In early 2009, UBS reported the largest annual loss ever by a Swiss company.[25]

Values guide a leader's choices and actions. A leader who places high value on being courageous and standing up for what one believes in, for example, is much more likely to make decisions that may not be popular but that he believes are right. Values determine how leaders acquire and use power, how they handle conflict, and how they make decisions. A leader who values competitiveness and ambition will behave differently from one who places a high value on cooperativeness and forgiveness. Ethical values help guide choices concerning what is morally right or wrong. Values concerning end goals also help determine a leader's actions and choices in the workplace. Leaders can be more effective when they clarify their own values and understand how values guide their actions and affect their organizations. In addition, for many organizations today, clarifying and stating their corporate values, including ethical values, has become an important part of defining how the organization operates.

How Attitudes Affect Leadership

Values help determine the attitudes leaders have about themselves and about their followers. An **attitude** is an evaluation—either positive or negative—about people, events, or things. As we discussed in Chapter 2, an optimistic attitude or positive outlook on life is often considered a key to successful and effective leadership.

Behavioral scientists consider attitudes to have three components: cognitions (thoughts), affect (feelings), and behavior.[26] The cognitive component includes the ideas and knowledge a person has about the object of an attitude, such as a leader's knowledge and ideas about a specific employee's performance and abilities. The affective component concerns how an individual feels about the object of an attitude. Perhaps the leader resents having to routinely answer questions or help the employee perform certain tasks. The behavioral component of an attitude predisposes a person to act in a certain way. For example, the leader might avoid the employee or fail to include him or her in certain activities of the group. Although attitudes change more easily than values, they typically reflect a person's fundamental values as well as a person's background and life experiences. A leader who highly values forgiveness, compassion toward others, and helping others would have different attitudes and behave very differently toward the previously mentioned subordinate than one who highly values personal ambition and capability.

One consideration is a leader's attitudes about himself or herself. **Self-concept** refers to the collection of attitudes we have about ourselves and includes the element of self-esteem, whether a person generally has positive or negative feelings about himself. A person with an overall positive self-concept has high self-esteem, whereas one with a negative self-concept has low self-esteem. In general, leaders with positive self-concepts are more effective in all situations. Leaders who have a negative self-concept, who are insecure and have low self-esteem, often create environments that limit other people's growth and development.[27] They may also sabotage their own careers. The Leader's Bookshelf further discusses how certain attitudes and behavior patterns can limit a leader's effectiveness and career development.

The way in which the leader relates to followers also depends significantly on his or her attitudes about others.[28] A leader's style is based largely on attitudes about human nature in general—ideas and feelings about what motivates people, whether people are basically honest and trustworthy, and about the extent to which people can grow and change. One theory

Attitude
an evaluation (either positive or negative) about people, events, or things

Self-concept
the collection of attitudes we have about ourselves; includes self-esteem and whether a person generally has a positive or negative feeling about himself/herself

Action Memo

As a leader, you can clarify your values so you know what you stand for and how your values may conflict with others in the organization. You can cultivate positive attitudes toward yourself and others, and learn to expect the best from followers.

marble: © Ioannis Drimilis   library: www.istockphoto.com/nikada

Leader's Bookshelf
What Got You Here Won't Get You There
by Marshall Goldsmith and Mark Reiter

Success, says executive coach Marshall Goldsmith, makes many people believe they must be doing everything right. Therefore, they sabotage their continued effectiveness and career advancement by failing to recognize and correct the mistakes they make in interpersonal relationships. "All other things being equal, your people skills (or lack of them) become more pronounced the higher up you go," he writes in *What Got You Here Won't Get You There*. Goldsmith and his collaborator, Mark Reiter, identify 20 behavioral habits that damage organizational relationships and hold leaders back.

NOBODY'S PERFECT

Every leader has some habits or negative behaviors that can limit his or her effectiveness. Following are a few of the behavioral flaws Goldsmith and Reiter describe. Do you recognize any of these in your own behaviors?

- **Winning at all costs and in all situations.** We all know them—those people who feel like they have to win every argument and always be right. They want to win the big points, the small points, and everything in between. If they go along with another's idea that doesn't work out, they adopt an "I told you so" attitude. In the workplace, a leader's need to be right and to point out that he or she is right damages relationships and destroys teamwork.

- **Clinging to the past.** There's nothing wrong with looking at and understanding the past as a way to come to terms with it or learn from it. Too often, though, people cling to the past as a way to blame others for things that have gone wrong in their lives, using the past as a weapon to control others or punish them for not doing exactly what the leader wants.

- **Never being able to say you're sorry.** It's not true that "love means never having to say you're sorry." Apologizing is love in action. Refusing to apologize probably causes more ill will—whether it be in a romance, a family, or a work relationship—than any other interpersonal flaw. "People who can't apologize at work may as well be wearing a T-shirt that says: 'I don't care about you,'" Goldsmith writes.

CHANGE IS POSSIBLE

As an executive coach, Goldsmith has spent his career helping leaders find and fix their behavioral blind spots. His prescription for success can benefit any leader who genuinely wants to improve his or her interpersonal relationships. The first step is to gather feedback that helps you identify the specific behaviors you need to change. Next, focus on fixing the problem by apologizing for your behavioral flaws, advertising your efforts to change, listening to the input of others, showing gratitude for others' contributions to your change process, and following up on your progress. When you acknowledge your dependence on others, Goldsmith points out, they typically not only agree to help you be a better person, they also try to become better people themselves.

What Got You Here Won't Get You There, by Marshall Goldsmith and Mark Reiter, is published by Hyperion Books.

---

developed to explain differences in style was developed by Douglas McGregor, based on his experiences as a manager and consultant and his training as a psychologist.[29] McGregor identified two sets of assumptions about human nature, called **Theory X** and **Theory Y**, which represent two very different sets of attitudes about how to interact with and influence subordinates. Exhibit 4.2 explains the fundamental assumptions of Theory X and Theory Y.

In general, Theory X reflects the assumption that people are basically lazy and not motivated to work and that they have a natural tendency to avoid responsibility. Thus, a supervisor who subscribes to the assumptions of Theory X believes people must be coerced, controlled, directed, or threatened to get them to put forth their best effort. In some circumstances, the supervisor may come across as bossy or overbearing, impatient with others, and unconcerned

Theory X
the assumption that people are basically lazy and not motivated to work and that they have a natural tendency to avoid responsibility

Theory Y
the assumption that people do not inherently dislike work and will commit themselves willingly to work that they care about

Exhibit 4.2 Attitudes and Assumptions of Theory X and Theory Y

Assumptions of Theory X	Assumptions of Theory Y
• The average human being has an inherent dislike of work and will avoid it if possible.	• The expenditure of physical and mental effort in work is as natural as play or rest. The average human being does not inherently dislike work.
• Because of the human characteristic of dislike for work, most people must be coerced, controlled, directed, or threatened with punishment to get them to put forth adequate effort toward the achievement of organizational objectives.	• External control and the threat of punishment are not the only means for bringing about effort toward organizational objectives. A person will exercise self-direction and self-control in the service of objectives to which he or she is committed.
• The average human being prefers to be directed, wishes to avoid responsibility, has relatively little ambition, and wants security above all.	• The average human being learns, under proper conditions, not only to accept but also to seek responsibility.
	• The capacity to exercise a relatively high degree of imagination, ingenuity, and creativity in the solution of organizational problems is widely, not narrowly, distributed in the population.
	• Under the conditions of modern industrial life, the intellectual potentialities of the average human being are only partially utilized.

Source: Douglas McGregor, *The Human Side of Enterprise* (New York: McGraw-Hill, 1960), pp. 33–48.

with people's feelings and problems. Referring back to Chapter 2, the Theory X leader would likely be task-oriented and highly concerned with production rather than people. Theory Y, on the other hand, is based on assumptions that people do not inherently dislike work and will commit themselves willingly to work that they care about. Theory Y also assumes that, under the right conditions, people will seek out greater responsibility and will exercise imagination and creativity in the pursuit of solutions to organizational problems. A leader who subscribes to the assumptions of Theory Y does not believe people have to be coerced and controlled in order to perform effectively. These leaders are more often people-oriented and concerned with relationships, although some Theory Y leaders can also be task- or production-oriented. McGregor believed Theory Y to be a more realistic and productive approach for viewing subordinates and shaping leaders' attitudes. Studies exploring the relationship between leader attitudes and leadership success in general support his idea, although this relationship has not been carefully explored.[30]

Social Perception and Attribution Theory

By **perception**, we mean the process people use to make sense out of their surroundings by selecting, organizing, and interpreting information. Values and attitudes affect perceptions, and vice versa. For example, a person might have developed the attitude that managers are insensitive and arrogant, based on a pattern of perceiving arrogant and insensitive behavior from managers over a period of time. If the person moves to a new job, this attitude will continue to affect the way he or she perceives superiors in the new environment, even though managers in the new workplace might take great pains to understand and respond to employees' needs. As another example, a leader who greatly values

Perception
the process people use to make sense out of the environment by selecting, organizing, and interpreting information

ambition and career success may perceive a problem or a subordinate's mistake as an impediment to her own success, whereas a leader who values helpfulness and obedience might see it as a chance to help a subordinate improve or grow.

Because of individual differences in attitudes, personality, values, interests, and experiences, people often "see" the same thing in different ways. Consider that one survey of nearly 2,000 workers in the United States found that 92 percent of managers think they are doing an "excellent" or "good" job managing employees, but only 67 percent of workers agree. As another example, in a survey of finance professionals, 40 percent of women said they perceive that women face a "glass ceiling" that keeps them from reaching top management levels, whereas only 10 percent of men share that perception.[31]

Perceptual Distortions

Of particular concern for leaders are **perceptual distortions**, errors in perceptual judgment that arise from inaccuracies in any part of the perceptual process. Some types of errors are so common that leaders should become familiar with them. These include stereotyping, the halo effect, projection, and perceptual defense. Leaders who recognize these perceptual distortions can better adjust their perceptions to more closely match objective reality.

Stereotyping is the tendency to assign an individual to a group or broad category (e.g., female, black, elderly or male, white, disabled) and then to attribute widely held generalizations about the group to the individual. Thus, someone meets a new colleague, sees he is in a wheelchair, assigns him to the category "physically disabled," and attributes to this colleague generalizations she believes about people with disabilities, which may include a belief that he is less able than other coworkers. However, the person's inability to walk should not be seen as indicative of lesser abilities in other areas. Indeed, the assumption of limitations may not only offend him, but it also prevents the person making the stereotypical judgment from benefiting from the many ways in which this person can contribute. Stereotyping prevents people from truly knowing those they classify in this way. In addition, negative stereotypes prevent talented people from advancing in an organization and fully contributing their talents to the organization's success.

The **halo effect** occurs when the perceiver develops an overall impression of a person or situation based on one characteristic, either favorable or unfavorable. In other words, a halo blinds the perceiver to other characteristics that should be used in generating a more complete assessment. The halo effect can play a significant role in performance appraisal. For example, a person with an outstanding attendance record may be assessed as responsible, industrious, and highly productive; another person with less-than-average attendance may be assessed as a poor performer. Either assessment may be true, but it is the leader's job to be sure the assessment is based on complete information about all job-related characteristics and not just his or her preferences for good attendance.

Projection is the tendency of perceivers to see their own personal traits in other people; that is, they project their own needs, feelings, values, and attitudes into their judgment of others. A leader who is achievement oriented might assume that subordinates are as well. This might cause the manager to restructure jobs to be less routine and more challenging, without regard for employees' actual satisfaction. The best safeguards against errors based on projection are self-awareness and empathy.

Perceptual defense is the tendency of perceivers to protect themselves against ideas, objects, or people that are threatening. People perceive things that are satisfying and pleasant, but tend to disregard things that are disturbing and unpleasant.

Perceptual distortions
errors in judgment that arise from inaccuracies in the perceptual process

Stereotyping
the tendency to assign an individual to a broad category and then attribute generalizations about the group to the individual

Halo effect
an overall impression of a person or situation based on one characteristic, either favorable or unfavorable

Projection
the tendency to see one's own personal traits in other people

Perceptual defense
the tendency to protect oneself by disregarding ideas, situations, or people that are unpleasant

In essence, people develop blind spots in the perceptual process so that negative sensory data do not hurt them. For example, the director of a nonprofit educational organization in Tennessee hated dealing with conflict because he had grown up with parents who constantly argued and often put him in the middle of their arguments. The director consistently overlooked discord among staff members until things would reach a boiling point. When the blow-up occurred, the director would be shocked and dismayed, because he had truly perceived that everything was going smoothly among the staff. Recognizing perceptual blind spots can help people develop a clearer picture of reality.

Attribution Theory

As people organize what they perceive, they often draw conclusions, such as about an object, event, or person. **Attribution theory** refers to how people explain the causes of events or behaviors. For example, many people attribute the success or failure of an organization to the top leader, when in reality there may be many factors that contribute to organizational performance. People also make attributions or judgments about what caused a person's behavior—something about the person or something about the situation. An *internal attribution* says characteristics of the person led to the behavior ("My subordinate missed the deadline because he's lazy and incompetent"). An *external attribution* says something about the situation caused the person's behavior ("My subordinate missed the deadline because he didn't have the team support and resources he needed"). Attributions are important because they help people decide how to handle a situation. In the case of a subordinate missing a deadline, a leader who blames the mistake on the employee's personal characteristics might reprimand the person or, more effectively, provide additional training and direction. A leader who blames the mistake on external factors will try to help prevent such situations in the future, such as making sure team members have the resources they need, providing support to remove obstacles, and insuring that deadlines are realistic.

Social scientists have studied the attributions people make and identified three factors that influence whether an attribution will be external or internal.[32] Exhibit 4.3 illustrates these three factors.

1. *Distinctiveness*. Whether the behavior is unusual for that person (in contrast to a person displaying the same kind of behavior in many situations). If the behavior is distinctive, the perceiver probably will make an *external* attribution.

2. *Consistency*. Whether the person being observed has a history of behaving in the same way. People generally make *internal* attributions about consistent behavior.

3. *Consensus*. Whether other people tend to respond to similar situations in the same way. A person who has observed others handle similar situations in the same way will likely make an *external* attribution; that is, it will seem that the situation produces the type of behavior observed.

In addition to these general rules, people tend to have biases that they apply when making attributions. When evaluating others, we tend to underestimate the influence of external factors and overestimate the influence of internal factors. This tendency is called the **fundamental attribution error**. Consider the case of someone being promoted to CEO. Employees, outsiders, and the media generally focus on the characteristics of the person that allowed him or her to achieve the promotion. In reality, however, the selection of that person might have been

Attribution theory
how people draw conclusions about what caused certain behaviors or events

Fundamental attribution error
the tendency to underestimate the influence of external factors on another's behavior and overestimate the influence of internal factors

Exhibit 4.3 Factors Influencing Whether Attributions Are Internal or External

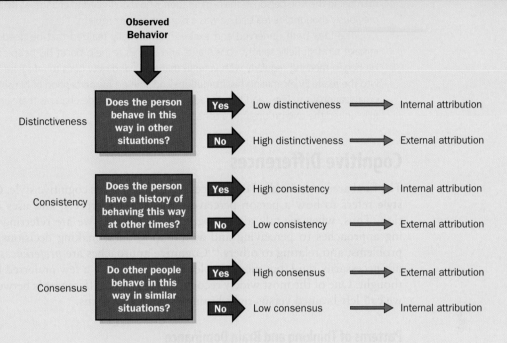

heavily influenced by external factors, such as business conditions creating a need for someone with a strong financial or marketing background at that particular time.

Another bias that distorts attributions involves attributions we make about our own behavior. People tend to overestimate the contribution of internal factors to their successes and overestimate the contribution of external factors to their failures. This tendency, called the **self-serving bias**, means people give themselves too much credit for what they do well and give external forces too much blame when they fail. Thus, if a leader's subordinates say she doesn't listen well enough, and the leader thinks subordinates don't communicate well enough, the truth may actually lie somewhere in between. At Emerald Packaging, Kevin Kelly examined his attributions and improved his leadership effectiveness by overcoming the self-serving bias, as described in the following example.

IN THE LEAD

Kevin Kelly, Emerald Packaging

As the top leader of his family's California company, Emerald Packaging—a maker of plastic bags for the food industry—Kevin Kelly thought of himself as on top of his game, chief architect of the company's growing sales and profits. When Emerald began to falter, Kelly blamed it on his managers' resistance to new ideas that could keep the business thriving. He thought everyone needed to change except him.

For some time, Kelly's leadership approach was to reprimand and complain. Then, he decided to look at things in a different way. Was it really all his managers' fault? Realizing that everyone was under stress from several years of rapid growth, Kelly decided to hire a pack of new managers to reinforce his exhausted troops. Surprisingly, though, things just seemed to get worse, with the new managers feeling adrift and the

Self-serving bias
the tendency to overestimate the influence of internal factors on one's successes and the influence of external factors on one's failures

old-timers seeming even less focused than before. Kelly had to face a hard truth: Rather than being the one person in the organization who didn't need to change, as Kelly had previously thought, he realized he was a big part of the problem.

The idea both unnerved and excited him as Kelly realized that he needed to remake himself. Kelly sought consultants and classes to help boost his people skills. He began meeting regularly with veteran managers and new hires to integrate them into the team. By examining his attributions and shifting his perception of himself, the organizational situation, and his managers' abilities, Kelly made changes that successfully united the two groups into a cohesive team.[33]

Cognitive Differences

The final area of individual differences we will explore is cognitive style. **Cognitive style** refers to how a person perceives, processes, interprets, and uses information. Thus, when we talk about cognitive differences, we are referring to varying approaches to perceiving and assimilating data, making decisions, solving problems, and relating to others.[34] Cognitive approaches are *preferences* that are not necessarily rigid, but most people tend to have only a few preferred habits of thought. One of the most widely recognized cognitive differences is between what we call left-brained versus right-brained thinking patterns.

Patterns of Thinking and Brain Dominance

Neurologists and psychologists have long known that the brain has two distinct hemispheres. Furthermore, science has shown that the left hemisphere controls movement on the body's right side and the right hemisphere controls movement on the left. In the 1960s and 1970s, scientists also discovered that the distinct hemispheres influence thinking, which led to an interest in what has been called left-brained versus right-brained thinking patterns. The left hemisphere is associated with logical, analytical thinking and a linear approach to problem solving, whereas the right hemisphere is associated with creative, intuitive, values-based thought processes.[35] A JC Penney television commercial provides a simple illustration. The commercial shows a woman whose right brain is telling her to go out and spend money to buy fun clothes, while the left brain is telling her to be logical and save money. As another simplified example, people who are very good at verbal and written language (which involves a linear thinking process) are using the left brain, whereas those who prefer to interpret information through visual images are more right-brained.

Although the concept of left-brained versus right-brained thinking is not entirely accurate physiologically (not all processes associated with left-brained thinking are located in the left hemisphere and vice versa), this concept provides a powerful metaphor for two very different ways of thinking and decision making. It is also important to remember that everyone uses both left-brained and right-brained thinking, but to varying degrees.

More recently, these ideas have been broadened to what is called the **whole brain concept**.[36] Ned Herrmann began developing his concept of whole brain thinking while he was a manager at General Electric in the late 1970s and has expanded it through many years of research with thousands of individuals and organizations. The whole brain approach considers not only a person's preference for right-brained versus left-brained thinking, but also for conceptual versus experiential thinking. Herrmann's whole brain model thus identifies four quadrants of the brain that are related to different thinking styles. Again, while not entirely accurate physiologically, the whole brain model is an excellent metaphor for understanding differences in thinking patterns. Some people strongly lean toward using one quadrant in most

Cognitive style
how a person perceives, processes, interprets, and uses information

Whole brain concept
an approach that considers not only a person's preference for right-brained versus left-brained thinking, but also conceptual versus experiential thinking; identifies four quadrants of the brain related to different thinking styles

Leader's Self-Insight 4.4
What's Your Thinking Style?

The following characteristics are associated with the four quadrants identified by Herrmann's whole brain model. Think for a moment about how you approach problems and make decisions. In addition, consider how you typically approach your work or class assignments and how you interact with others. Circle 10 of the terms below that you believe best describe your own cognitive style. Try to be honest and select terms that apply to you as you are, not how you might like to be. There are no right or wrong answers.

A	B	C	D
Analytical	Organized	Friendly	Holistic
Factual	Planned	Receptive	Imaginative
Directive	Controlled	Enthusiastic	Intuitive
Rigorous	Detailed	Understanding	Synthesizing
Realistic	Conservative	Expressive	Curious
Intellectual	Disciplined	Empathetic	Spontaneous
Objective	Practical	Trusting	Flexible
Knowledgeable	Industrious	Sensitive	Open-Minded
Bright	Persistent	Passionate	Conceptual
Clear	Implementer	Humanistic	Adventurous

The terms in Column A are associated with logical, analytical thinking (Quadrant A); those in Column B with organized, detail-oriented thinking (Quadrant B); those in Column C with empathetic and emotionally based thinking (Quadrant C); and those in Column D with integrative and imaginative thinking (Quadrant D). Do your preferences fall primarily in one of the four columns, or do you have a more balanced set of preferences across all four? If you have a strong preference in one particular quadrant, were you surprised by which one?

situations, whereas others rely on two, three, or even all four styles of thinking. An individual's preference for each of the four styles is determined through a survey called the *Herrmann Brain Dominance Instrument (HBDI)*, which has been administered to hundreds of thousands of individuals.

The whole brain model provides a useful overview of an individual's mental preferences, which in turn affect patterns of communication, behavior, and leadership.

Quadrant A is associated with logical thinking, analysis of facts, and processing numbers. A person who has a quadrant-A dominance is rational and realistic, thinks critically, and likes to deal with numbers and technical matters. These people like to know how things work and to follow logical procedures. A leader with a predominantly A-quadrant thinking style tends to be directive and authoritative. This leader focuses on tasks and activities and likes to deal with concrete information and facts. Opinions and feelings are generally not considered as important as facts.

Quadrant B deals with planning, organizing facts, and careful detailed review. A person who relies heavily on quadrant-B thinking is well-organized, reliable, and neat. These people like to establish plans and procedures and get things done on time. Quadrant-B leaders are typically conservative and highly traditional. They tend to avoid risks and strive for stability. Thus, they may insist on following rules and procedures, no matter what the circumstances are.

Quadrant C is associated with interpersonal relationships and affects intuitive and emotional thought processes. C-quadrant individuals are sensitive to others and enjoy interacting with and teaching others. They are typically emotional and

Action Memo

A simplified exercise to help you think about your own preferences appears in Leader's Self-Insight 4.4. Before reading further, follow the instructions and complete the exercise to get an idea about your dominant thinking style according to Herrmann's whole brain model. Then, read the following descriptions of each quadrant.

Quadrant A
the part of the brain associated in the whole brain model with logical thinking, analysis of facts, and processing numbers

Quadrant B
the part of the brain associated in the whole brain model with planning, organizing facts, and careful detailed review

Quadrant C
the part of the brain associated in the whole brain model with interpersonal relationships and intuitive and emotional thought processes

expressive, outgoing, and supportive of others. Leaders with a predominantly quadrant-C style are friendly, trusting, and empathetic. They are concerned with people's feelings more than with tasks and procedures and may put emphasis on employee development and training.

Quadrant D is associated with conceptualizing, synthesizing, and integrating facts and patterns, with seeing the big picture rather than the details. A person with a quadrant-D preference is visionary and imaginative, likes to speculate, break the rules, take risks, and may be impetuous. These people are curious and enjoy experimentation and playfulness. The D-quadrant leader is holistic, imaginative, and adventurous. This leader enjoys change, experimentation, and risk-taking, and generally allows followers a great deal of freedom and flexibility.

Exhibit 4.4 illustrates the model with its four quadrants and some of the mental processes associated with each. There is no style that is necessarily better or worse, though any of the styles carried to an extreme can be detrimental. Each style can have both positive and negative results for leaders and followers. It is important to remember that every individual, even those with a strong preference in one quadrant, actually has a coalition of preferences from each of the four quadrants.[37]

Therefore, leaders with a predominantly quadrant-A style may also have elements from one or more of the other styles, which affects their leadership effectiveness. For example, a leader with a strong A-quadrant preference might also have preferences from quadrant C, the interpersonal area, which would cause her to have concern for people's feelings even though she is primarily concerned with tasks, facts, and figures.

In addition, Herrmann believes people can learn to use their "whole brain," rather than relying only on one or two quadrants. His research indicates that very few, if any, individuals can be wholly balanced among the four quadrants, but people can be aware of their preferences and engage in activities and experiences that help develop the other quadrants. Leaders who reach the top of organizations often have well-balanced brains, according to Herrmann's research. In fact, the typical CEO has at least two, usually three, and often four strong preferences and thus has a wide range of thinking options available to choose from. A broad range of thinking styles is particularly important at higher levels of organizations because leaders deal with a greater variety and complexity of people and issues.[38]

Quadrant D
the part of the brain associated in the whole brain model with conceptualizing, synthesizing, and integrating facts and patterns

Exhibit 4.4 Herrmann's Whole Brain Model

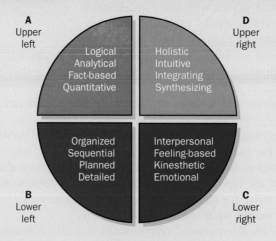

Source: Ned Herrmann, *The Whole Brain Business Book* (New York: McGraw-Hill, 1996), p. 15.

Understanding that individuals have different thinking styles can also help leaders be more effective in interacting with followers. Some leaders act as if everyone responds to the same material and behavior in the same way, but this isn't true. Some people prefer facts and figures, whereas others want to know about relationships and patterns. Some followers prefer freedom and flexibility, whereas others crave structure and order. Jeff Koeze, who left a career as a law professor to take over his family's business selling nuts and candies, used an understanding of cognitive differences to help him make the tough transition from teacher to business leader.

IN THE LEAD

Jeff Koeze, Koeze Company

Jeff Koeze never saw himself running Koeze Company, the 86-year-old family nut and candy business based in Michigan. But when his father Scott Koeze told Jeff he was sick of the business, Jeff agreed to take over. Boy, did he have a lot to learn. One of the biggest challenges was finding a way to communicate with employees.

Jeff's thinking and communication style tended strongly toward Quadrant A— hyperrational, rigorous, and data-driven—with some elements of Quadrant D—an interest in learning, experimentation, and synthesis. His approach to communication was to present lots of facts and data and expect the best argument to win. He sometimes had trouble making a decision because of a tendency to overanalyze. Workers were confused. They expected Koeze, as the boss, to tell them what to do, not try to engage them in a debate.

Gradually, through extensive reading and working with consultants, Koeze shifted his style. Rather than relying on facts and arguments, Koeze started building personal relationships. He shared his thoughts and concerns with employees, which helped put them at ease. He worked on developing patience and started trying to meet employees on their own terms rather than his. For example, he assigned one employee with a near-compulsive tendency to plan and organize the job of setting up new processes and procedures. He learned that sometimes he had to stop researching and just make a decision and that for some workers, direct orders were appreciated much more than discussion and debate.

Koeze is still logical and numbers-obsessed, but he's also much more compassionate and understanding of individual differences in thinking styles. Employees are happier, and Koeze has noticed that many of them have learned and grown right along with him.[39]

Jeff Koeze learned that being a CEO meant he needed a more balanced thinking style, especially more quadrant C, than that he once used as a law professor. As this example illustrates, leaders can shift their styles and behaviors to more effectively communicate with followers and help them perform up to their full potential. Leaders can also recruit people with varied cognitive styles to help achieve goals.

Action Memo

As a leader, you can strive for "whole brain" thinking to deal effectively with a wide variety of people and complex issues. You can be aware of your natural thinking patterns and include other perspectives that help you develop a broader understanding.

Problem-Solving Styles: The Myers–Briggs Type Indicator

Another approach to cognitive differences grew out of the work of psychologist Carl Jung. Jung believed that differences in individual behavior resulted from preferences in how we go about gathering and evaluating information for solving problems and making decisions.[40] One of the most widely used tests in the United States, the **Myers–Briggs Type Indicator (MBTI)™** assessment, is one way of measuring how individuals differ in these areas.[41] The MBTI™ assessment has been taken by millions of people around the world and can help individuals better understand themselves and others. Nearly 90 percent of *Fortune* 100 companies report using the MBTI™ instrument to help leaders make hiring and promotion decisions.[42]

Myers–Briggs Type Indicator (MBTI)™
test that measures how individuals differ in gathering and evaluating information for solving problems and making decisions

The MBTI™ instrument uses four different pairs of attributes to classify people in 1 of 16 different personality types:

1. **Introversion versus extraversion:** This dimension focuses on where people gain interpersonal strength and mental energy. Extraverts (E) gain energy from being around others and interacting with others, whereas introverts (I) gain energy by focusing on personal thoughts and feelings.

2. **Sensing versus intuition:** This identifies how a person absorbs information. Those with a sensing preference (S) gather and absorb information through the five senses, whereas intuitive people (N) rely on less direct perceptions. Intuitives, for example, focus more on patterns, relationships, and hunches than on direct perception of facts and details.

3. **Thinking versus feeling:** This dimension relates to how much consideration a person gives to emotions in making a decision. Feeling types (F) tend to rely more on their values and sense of what is right and wrong, and they consider how a decision will affect other people's feelings. Thinking types (T) tend to rely more on logic and be very objective in decision making.

4. **Judging versus perceiving:** The judging versus perceiving dimension concerns an individual's attitudes toward ambiguity and how quickly a person makes a decision. People with a judging preference like certainty and closure. They enjoy having goals and deadlines and tend to make decisions quickly based on available data. Perceiving people, on the other hand, enjoy ambiguity, dislike deadlines, and may change their minds several times before making a final decision. Perceiving types like to gather a large amount of data and information before making a decision.

The various combinations of these preferences result in 16 unique MBTI™ types. There are a number of exercises available in print and on the Internet that can help people determine their preferences according to the MBTI™ assessment. Individuals develop unique strengths and weaknesses as a result of their preferences for introversion versus extraversion, sensing versus intuition, thinking versus feeling, and judging versus perceiving. As with the whole brain approach, MBTI™ types should not be considered ingrained or unalterable. People's awareness of their preferences, training, and life experiences can cause them to change their preferences over time.

Leaders should remember that each type can have positive and negative consequences for behavior. By understanding their MBTI™ type, leaders can learn to maximize their strengths and minimize their weaknesses. John Bearden, chief executive of GMAC Home Services, took the MBTI™ assessment and learned that he was an ENTJ (extraverted, intuitive, thinking, and judging). ENTJ types can be dynamic, inspiring, and self-confident in making tough decisions. However, they can also be overbearing, insensitive, and hasty in their judgments. Bearden said learning his type was a "quantum leap" in his understanding of his strengths and weaknesses. He began consciously refining his leadership style, making a determined effort to give more consideration to hard data and listen more carefully to colleagues' opinions. Bearden put himself to the test at a recent national convention. "In the past, I would have gotten very much involved interjecting my own position very early on and probably biasing the process," he said. "But here I found myself quite content to allow their positions to be articulated and argued with creative tension. All I did was sit and absorb. It was a very satisfying process."[43]

Action Memo

Go to Leader's Self-Insight 4.5, on page 122 at the end of this chapter, to complete an exercise that will identify your preferences for the four pairs of attributes identified by the MBTI™ assessment.

There has been an increasing application of the MBTI™ assessment in leadership studies.[44] These studies confirm that there is no "leader type," and all 16 of the MBTI™ types can function effectively as leaders. As with the four quadrants of the whole brain model, leaders can learn to use their preferences and balance their approaches to best suit followers and the situation. However, research reveals some interesting, although tentative, findings. For example, although extraversion is often considered an important trait for a leader, leaders in the real world are about equally divided between extraverts and introverts. In regard to the sensing versus intuition dimension, data reveal that sensing types are in the majority in fields where the focus is on the immediate and tangible (e.g., construction, banking, manufacturing). However, in areas that involve breaking new ground or long-range planning, intuitive leaders are in the majority. Thinking (as opposed to feeling) types are more common among leaders in business and industry as well as in the realm of science. In addition, thinking types appear to be chosen more often as managers even in organizations that value "feeling," such as counseling centers. Finally, one of the most consistent findings is that judging types are in the majority among the leaders studied.

Thus, based on the limited research, the two preferences that seem to be most strongly associated with successful leadership are thinking and judging. However, this doesn't mean that people with other preferences cannot be effective leaders. Much more research needs to be done before any conclusions can be reached about the relationship between MBTI™ types and leadership.

Working with Different Personality Types

As this chapter has shown, leaders have to work with individuals who differ in many ways. Personality differences, in particular, can make the life of a leader interesting and sometimes exasperating. These differences can create an innovative environment but also lead to stress, conflict, and negative feelings.

Leaders can learn to work more effectively with different personality types by following some simple guidelines.[45]

- Understand your own personality and how you react to others. Avoid judging people based on limited knowledge, and realize that everyone has different facets to their personality. Learn to control your frustration to help you keep different personality types focused on the goal and the tasks needed to reach it.
- Treat everyone with respect. People like to be accepted and appreciated for who they are. Even if you find someone's personality grating, remain professional and keep your irritation to yourself. Don't gossip or joke about others.
- Everyone wants to be recognized for their unique talents, so be sure to acknowledge and make use of people's useful personality characteristics. For instance, a pessimistic person can be difficult to be around, but these gloomy folks can sometimes be helpful by calling attention to legitimate problems with an idea or plan.
- A good approach to take with a personality type widely different from yours is to clarify questions every time there's a potential for miscommunication. Follow up each question or request with a statement explaining why you asked and how it will benefit the organization as well as the individual.
- Remember that everyone wants to fit in. No matter their personalities, people typically take on behavior patterns that are the norm for their environment. Leaders can create norms that keep everyone focused on positive interactions and high performance.

Occasional personality conflicts are probably inevitable in any group or organization, but by using these techniques, leaders can generally keep the work environment positive and productive.

Leader's Self-Insight 4.5

Personality Assessment: Jung's Typology

For each item below, circle either "a" or "b." In some cases, both "a" and "b" may apply to you. You should decide which is *more* like you, even if it is only slightly more true.

1. I would rather
   a. Solve a new and complicated problem
   b. Work on something that I have done before
2. I like to
   a. Work alone in a quiet place
   b. Be where "the action" is
3. I want a boss who
   a. Establishes and applies criteria in decisions
   b. Considers individual needs and makes exceptions
4. When I work on a project, I
   a. Like to finish it and get some closure
   b. Often leave it open for possible change
5. When making a decision, the most important considerations are
   a. Rational thoughts, ideas, and data
   b. People's feelings and values
6. On a project, I tend to
   a. Think it over and over before deciding how to proceed
   b. Start working on it right away, thinking about it as I go along
7. When working on a project, I prefer to
   a. Maintain as much control as possible
   b. Explore various options
8. In my work, I prefer to
   a. Work on several projects at a time, and learn as much as possible about each one
   b. Have one project that is challenging and keeps me busy
9. I often
   a. Make lists and plans whenever I start something and may hate to seriously alter my plans
   b. Avoid plans and just let things progress as I work on them
10. When discussing a problem with colleagues, it is easy for me
    a. To see "the big picture"
    b. To grasp the specifics of the situation
11. When the phone rings in my office or at home, I usually
    a. Consider it an interruption
    b. Don't mind answering it

12. The word that describes me better is
    a. Analytical
    b. Empathetic
13. When I am working on an assignment, I tend to
    a. Work steadily and consistently
    b. Work in bursts of energy with "down time" in between
14. When I listen to someone talk on a subject, I usually try to
    a. Relate it to my own experience and see if it fits
    b. Assess and analyze the message
15. When I come up with new ideas, I generally
    a. "Go for it"
    b. Like to contemplate the ideas some more
16. When working on a project, I prefer to
    a. Narrow the scope so it is clearly defined
    b. Broaden the scope to include related aspects
17. When I read something, I usually
    a. Confine my thoughts to what is written there
    b. Read between the lines and relate the words to other ideas
18. When I have to make a decision in a hurry, I often
    a. Feel uncomfortable and wish I had more information
    b. Am able to do so with available data
19. In a meeting, I tend to
    a. Continue formulating my ideas as I talk about them
    b. Only speak out after I have carefully thought the issue through
20. In work, I prefer spending a great deal of time on issues of
    a. Ideas
    b. People
21. In meetings, I am most often annoyed with people who
    a. Come up with many sketchy ideas
    b. Lengthen the meeting with many practical details
22. I tend to be
    a. A morning person
    b. A night owl
23. My style in preparing for a meeting is
    a. To be willing to go in and be responsive
    b. To be fully prepared and sketch out an outline of the meeting

Personality Assessment: Jung's Typology (*continued*)

24. In meetings, I would prefer for people to
    a. Display a fuller range of emotions
    b. Be more task-oriented
25. I would rather work for an organization where
    a. My job was intellectually stimulating
    b. I was committed to its goals and mission
26. On weekends, I tend to
    a. Plan what I will do
    b. Just see what happens and decide as I go along
27. I am more
    a. Outgoing
    b. Contemplative

28. I would rather work for a boss who is
    a. Full of new ideas
    b. Practical

In the following, choose the word in each pair that appeals to you more:

29. a. Social
    b. Theoretical
30. a. Ingenuity
    b. Practicality
31. a. Organized
    b. Adaptable
32. a. Activity
    b. Concentration

Scoring

Count one point for each item listed below that you circled in the inventory.

Score for I (Introversion)	Score for E (Extraversion)	Score for S (Sensing)	Score for N (Intuition)
2a	2b	1b	1a
6a	6b	10b	10a
11a	11b	13a	13b
15b	15a	16a	16b
19b	19a	17a	17b
22a	22b	21a	21b
27b	27a	28b	28a
32b	32a	30b	30a

Totals ____ ____   ____ ____

Circle the one with more points:

I or E   (If tied on I/E, don't count #11)

S or N   (If tied on S/N, don't count #16)

Score for T (Thinking)	Score for F (Feeling)	Score for J (Judging)	Score for P (Perceiving)
3a	3b	4a	4b
5a	5b	7a	7b
12a	12b	8b	8a
14b	14a	9a	9b
20a	20b	18b	18a
24b	24a	23b	23a
25a	25b	26a	26b
29b	29a	31a	31b

Totals ____ ____   ____ ____

Circle the one with more points:

T or F   (If tied on T/F, don't count #24)

J or P   (If tied on J/P, don't count #23)

Your Score Is: I or E _____ S or N _____ T or F _____ J or P _____

Your type is: _____ (example: INTJ; ESFP; etc.)

(continued)

Personality Assessment: Jung's Typology (*continued*)

Scoring and Interpretation

The scores above measure variables similar to the Myers-Briggs Type Indicator (MBTI™), assessment based on the work of psychologist Carl Jung. The MBTI™ assessment, which was described in the chapter text, identifies four dimensions and 16 different "types." The dominant characteristics associated with each dimension and each type are shown below. Remember that no one is a pure type; however, each individual has preferences for introversion versus extraversion, sensing versus intuition, thinking versus feeling, and judging versus perceiving. Based on your scores on the survey, read the description of your dimension and type in the chart. Do you believe the description fits your personality?

Characteristics associated with each dimension

Extraversion: Energized by outer world of people and objects, broad interests, thinks while speaking

Introversion: Energized by inner world of thoughts and ideas, deep interests, thinks before speaking

Sensing: Likes facts, details, and practical solutions.

Intuition: Likes meanings, theory, associations among data, and possibilities.

Thinking: Makes decisions by analysis, logic, and impersonal criteria.

Feeling: Makes decisions based on values, beliefs, and concern for others.

Judging: Lives life organized, stable, systematic, and under control.

Perceiving: Lets life happen, spontaneous, open-ended, last minute.

Characteristics associated with each type

ISTJ: Organizer, trustworthy, responsible, good trustee or inspector.	**ISFJ**: Quiet, conscientious, devoted, handles detail, good conservator.	**INFJ**: Perseveres, inspirational, quiet caring for others, good counselor.	**INTJ**: Independent thinker, skeptical, theory, competence, good scientist.
ISTP: Cool, observant, easy-going, good craftsperson.	**ISFP**: Warm, sensitive, team player, avoids conflict, good artist.	**INFP**: Idealistic, strong values, likes learning, good at noble service.	**INTP**: Designer, logical, conceptual, likes challenges, good architect.
ESTP: Spontaneous, gregarious, good at problem solving and promoting.	**ESFP**: Sociable, generous, makes things fun, good as entertainer.	**ENFP**: Imaginative, enthusiastic, starts projects, good champion.	**ENTP**: Resourceful, stimulating, dislikes routine, tests limits, good inventor.
ESTJ: Order, structure, practical, good administrator or supervisor.	**ESFJ**: People skills, harmonizer, popular, does things for people, good host.	**ENFJ**: Charismatic, persuasive, fluent presenter, sociable, active, good teacher.	**ENTJ**: Visionary planner, takes charge, hearty speaker, natural leader.

Source: From *Organizational Behavior: Experience and Cases*, 4th ed., by Dorothy Marcic. © 1995. Reprinted with permission of South-Western, a part of Cengage Learning: www.cengage.com/permissions.

Leadership Essentials

▨ This chapter explored some of the individual differences that affect leaders and the leadership process. Individuals differ in many ways, including personality, values and attitudes, and styles of thinking and decision making.

▨ One model of personality, the Big Five personality dimensions, examines whether individuals score high or low on the dimensions of extraversion, agreeableness, conscientiousness, emotional stability, and openness to experience. Although there is some indication that a high degree of each of the personality dimensions is associated with successful leadership, individuals who score low on various dimensions may also be effective leaders. Two specific personality traits that have a significant impact on leader behavior are locus of control and authoritarianism.

▨ Values are fundamental beliefs that cause a person to prefer that things be done one way rather than another. One way to think about values is in terms of instrumental and end values. End values are beliefs about the kinds of goals that are worth pursuing, whereas instrumental values are beliefs about the types of behavior that are appropriate for reaching goals. Values also affect an individual's attitudes. A leader's attitudes about self and others influence how the leader behaves toward and interacts with followers. Two sets of assumptions called Theory X and Theory Y represent two very different sets of attitudes leaders may hold about people in general.

▨ Differences in personality, values, and attitudes influence perception, which is the process people use to select, organize, and interpret information. Perceptual distortions include stereotyping, the halo effect, projection, and perceptual defense. Attribution theory refers to how people explain the causes of events or behaviors. Based on their perception, people may make either internal or external attributions.

▨ Another area of individual differences is cognitive style. The whole brain concept explores a person's preferences for right-brained versus left-brained thinking and for conceptual versus experiential thinking. The model provides a powerful metaphor for understanding differences in thinking styles. Individuals can learn to use their "whole brain" rather than relying on one thinking style. Another way of looking at cognitive differences is the Myers–Briggs Type Indicator, which measures an individual's preferences for introversion versus extraversion, sensing versus intuition, thinking versus feeling, and judging versus perceiving.

▨ Finally, the chapter offered some tips for how leaders can work more effectively with varied personality types. By understanding their own personalities, treating everyone with respect, recognizing people's unique abilities, circumventing communication breakdowns, and creating a positive environment, leaders can better keep diverse people productive and focused on goals instead of personality differences.

Discussion Questions

1. Extraversion is often considered a "good" quality for a leader to have. Why might introversion be considered an equally positive quality?

2. A survey found that 79 percent of CEOs surveyed fall into the category of being "highly optimistic," whereas a much lower percentage of chief financial officers

were rated as highly optimistic. Do you think these differences reflect personality characteristics or the different requirements of the two jobs? Discuss.

3. The chapter suggests that one way to work effectively with different personalities is to treat everyone with respect. How might a leader deal with a subordinate who is perpetually rude, insensitive, and disrespectful to others?

4. What might be some reasons the dimension of "openness to experience" correlates so strongly with historians' ratings of the greatest U.S. presidents but has been less strongly associated with business leader success? Do you think this personality dimension might be more important for business leaders of today than it was in the past? Discuss.

5. Leaders in many of today's organizations use the results of personality testing to make hiring and promotion decisions. Discuss some of the pros and cons of this approach.

6. From Leader's Self-Insight 4.3, identify four or five values (instrumental or end values) that could be a source of conflict between leaders and followers. Explain.

7. Do you believe understanding your preferences according to the whole brain model can help you be a better leader? Discuss.

8. How can a leader use an understanding of brain dominance to improve the functioning of the organization?

9. Why do you think *thinking* and *judging* are the two characteristics from the Myers–Briggs Type Indicator that seem to be most strongly associated with effective leadership?

10. One social critic suggests that leaders' overly-optimistic attitudes are partly to blame for the recent financial crisis. Do you think this is the case? How can leaders prevent optimism from creating a threat to their organizations?

Leadership at Work

PAST AND FUTURE

Draw a life line below that marks high and low experiences during your life. Think of key decisions, defining moments, peak experiences, and major disappointments that shaped who you are today. Draw the line from left to right, and identify each high and low point with a word or two.

Birth Year: _____   Today's Date: _____

What made these valued experiences? How did they shape who you are today?

_____

_____

Now take the long view of your life. In 10-year increments, write below the leader experiences you want to have. Provide a brief past-tense description of each decade (e.g., next 10 years—big starting salary, bored in first job, promoted to middle management).

Next 10 years: _____

_____

Following 10 years: _____

_____

Following 10 years: _____

_____

Following 10 years: _____

_____

What personal skills and strengths will you use to achieve the future?

_____

_____

What is your core life purpose or theme as expressed in the life line and answers above?

_____

_____

What would your desired future self say to your present self?

_____

_____

How do your answers above relate to your scores on the Leader Self-Insight questionnaires you completed in this chapter?

_____

_____

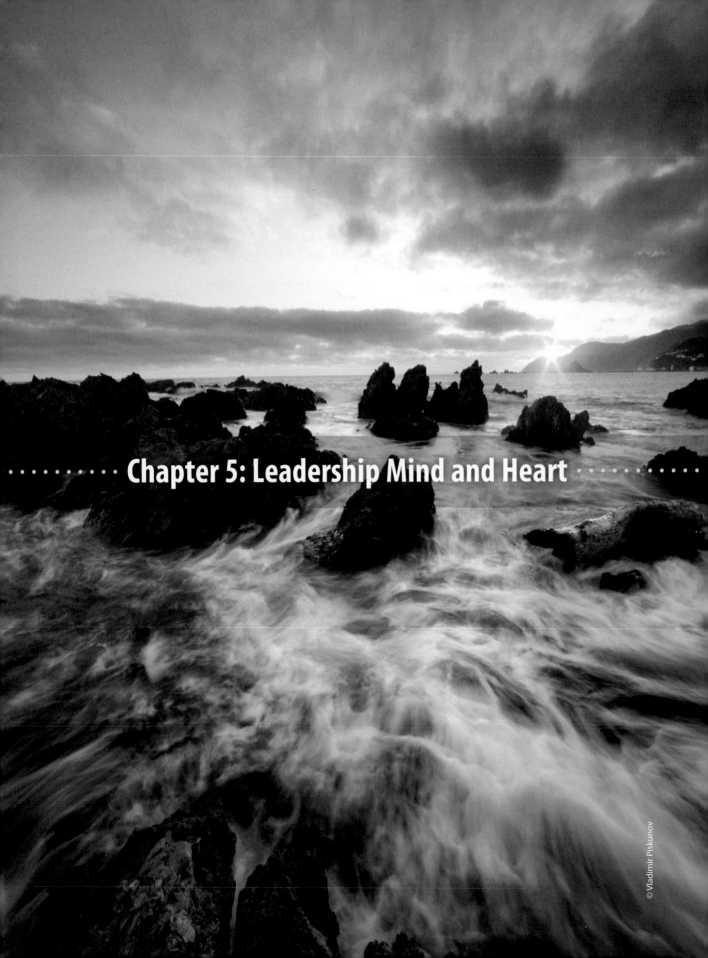

Chapter 5: Leadership Mind and Heart

© Vladimir Piskunov

Your Leadership Challenge

After reading this chapter, you should be able to:

- Recognize how mental models guide your behavior and relationships.

- Engage in independent thinking by staying mentally alert, thinking critically, and being mindful rather than mindless.

- Break out of categorized thinking patterns and open your mind to new ideas and multiple perspectives.

- Begin to apply systems thinking and personal mastery to your activities at school or work.

- Exercise emotional intelligence, including being self-aware, managing your emotions, motivating yourself, displaying empathy, and managing relationships.

- Apply the difference between motivating others based on fear and motivating others based on love.

Chapter Outline

As Lieutenant Colonel Howard Olson surveys the crowd before him, he knows that most of the people in the room outrank him. Still, Olson opens his talk with the following statement: "Each and every one of you has something that makes you a jerk. . . . Some of you have more than one. I know. I've talked to you."

The lecture is part of what the United States Army informally calls "charm school," a week-long course held annually for the select few who are promoted to brigadier general. Everyone knows about the Army's skill at getting new recruits in boot camp to think and act in a new way, but few people have seen firsthand the training it uses to get high-ranking officers to make a mental and emotional leap. At charm school, new generals are advised to get in touch with their inner jerk and work on overcoming that aspect of their personality.

Other recurring themes during the training include avoiding even the appearance of ethical violations, leading with moral courage, and overcoming arrogance, the "first deadly sin of the general officer." Lieutenant General John Keane, a long-time infantry commander, reminds officers that they must "lead from the front: You've got to put yourself in harm's way. . . . You must feel the horror they feel, the loneliness and despair. . . ." It's a reminder that the great officers are those who genuinely care about their soldiers.[1]

There's no equivalent training in corporate America, but the lessons taught at the Army's charm school are also being taken to heart at many of today's business organizations, where leaders are learning to build work relationships based on trust, humility, caring, and respect.

People cannot be separated from their emotions, and it is through emotion that leaders generate a commitment to shared vision and mission, values and culture, and caring for the work and each other. Noted leadership author and scholar Warren Bennis has said that "there's no difference between being a really effective leader and becoming a fully integrated person."[2] This chapter and the next examine current thinking about the importance of leaders becoming fully integrated people by exploring the full capacities of their minds and spirits. By doing so, they help others reach their full potential and contribute fully to the organization. We first define what we mean by leader capacity. Then we expand on some of the ideas introduced in the previous chapter to consider how the capacity to shift our thinking and feeling can help leaders alter their behavior, influence others, and be more effective. We discuss the concept of mental models, and look at how qualities such as independent thinking, an open mind, and systems thinking are important for leaders. Then we take a closer look at human emotion as illustrated in the concept of emotional intelligence and the emotions of love versus fear in leader–follower relationships. The next chapter will turn to spirit as reflected in moral leadership and courage.

Leader Capacity versus Competence

Traditionally, effective leadership, like good management, has been thought of as competence in a set of skills; once these specific skills are acquired, all one has to do to succeed is put them into action. However, as we all know from personal experience, working effectively with other people requires much more than practicing specific, rational skills; it often means drawing on subtle aspects of ourselves—our thoughts, beliefs, or feelings—and appealing to those aspects in others. Anyone who has participated on an athletic team knows how powerfully thoughts and emotions can affect performance. Some players are not as highly skilled from a technical standpoint but put forth amazing performances by playing with heart. Players who can help others draw on these positive emotions and thoughts often emerge as team leaders.

In organizations, just like on the playing field, skills competence is important, but it is not enough. Although leaders have to attend to organizational issues such as production schedules, structure, finances, costs, profits, and so forth, they also tend to human issues, particularly in times of uncertainty and rapid change. Current issues that require leaders to use more than rational skills include how to give people a sense of meaning and purpose when major changes occur almost daily; how to make employees feel valued and respected in an age of massive layoffs and job uncertainty; and how to keep morale and motivation high in the face of corporate bankruptcies and dissolutions, ethical scandals, and economic crises.

Capacity
the potential each of us has to do more and be more than we are now

Action Memo

As a leader, you can expand the capacity of your mind, heart, and spirit by consciously engaging in activities that use aspects of the whole self. You can reflect on your experiences to learn and grow from them.

In this chapter, rather than discussing *competence*, we explore a person's *capacity* for mind and heart. Whereas competence is limited and quantifiable, capacity is unlimited and defined by the potential for expansion and growth.[3] **Capacity** means the potential each of us has to be more than we are now. The U.S. Army's leadership expression "Be, Know, Do," puts *Be* first because who a leader is as a person—his or her character, values, spirit, and moral center— colors everything else.

Developing leadership capacity goes beyond learning the skills for organizing, planning, or controlling others. It also involves something deeper and more subtle than the leadership traits and styles we discussed in

Chapters 2 and 3. Living, working, and leading based on our capacity means using our whole selves, including intellectual, emotional, and spiritual abilities and understandings. A broad literature has emphasized that being a whole person means operating from mind, heart, spirit, and body.[4] Although we can't "learn" capacity the way we learn a set of skills, we can expand and develop leadership capacity. Just as the physical capacity of our lungs is increased through regular aerobic exercise, the capacities of the mind, heart, and spirit can be expanded through conscious development and regular use. In the previous chapter, we introduced some ideas about how individuals think, make decisions, and solve problems based on values, attitudes, and patterns of thinking. This chapter builds on some of those ideas to provide a broader view of the leadership capacities of mind and heart.

Mental Models

A mental model can be thought of as an internal picture that affects a leader's actions and relationships with others. **Mental models** are theories people hold about specific systems in the world and their expected behavior.[5] A system means any set of elements that interact to form a whole and produce a specified outcome. An organization is a system, as is a football team, a sorority pledge drive, a marriage, the registration system at a university, or the claims process at an insurance company.

Leaders have many mental models that tend to govern how they interpret experiences and how they act in response to people and situations. For example, one mental model about what makes an effective team is that members share a sense of team ownership and feel that they have authority and responsibility for team actions and outcomes.[6] A leader with this mental model would likely push power, authority, and decision making down to the team level and strive to build norms that create a strong group identity and trust among members. However, a leader with a mental model that every group needs a strong leader to take control and make the decisions is less likely to encourage norms that lead to effective teamwork. Exhibit 5.1 shows the mental model that Google's top leaders use to keep the company on the cutting edge as its core business of search matures. At Google, risk-taking, a little craziness, and making mistakes is encouraged for the sake of innovation. Too much structure and control is considered death to the company.[7]

Leaders at Google, as well as other organizations, strive to create mental models that are aligned with organizational

Mental models
theories people hold about specific systems in the world and their expected behavior

Action Memo

As a leader, you can become aware of your mental models and how they affect your thinking and behavior. You can learn to regard your assumptions as temporary ideas and strive to expand your mindset.

Exhibit 5.1 Google Leaders' Mental Model

- Stay uncomfortable
- Let failure coexist with triumph
- Use a little less "management" than you need
- Defy convention
- Move fast and figure things out as you go

Source: Based on Adam Lashinsky, "Chaos by Design," *Fortune* (October 2, 2006). pp. 86–98.

needs, goals, and values. However, personal values, attitudes, beliefs, biases, and prejudices can all affect one's mental model. A leader's assumptions play an important role in shaping his or her mental model, but leaders can examine their assumptions and shift mental models when needed to keep their organizations healthy.[8]

Assumptions

In the previous chapter, we discussed two very different sets of attitudes and assumptions that leaders may have about subordinates, called Theory X and Theory Y, and how these assumptions affect leader behavior. A leader's assumptions naturally are part of his or her mental model. Someone who assumes that people can't be trusted will act very differently in a situation than someone who has the assumption that people are basically trustworthy. Leaders have assumptions about events, situations, and circumstances as well as about people. Assumptions can be dangerous because people tend to accept them as "truth." For example, the author of a recent book about the U.S. involvement in Iraq suggests that the original decision to go to war was based on a set of faulty assumptions (such as that Iraq possessed weapons of mass destruction). Bush administration leaders were so sure their assumptions were right that they looked for intelligence to support their views and ignored any counsel of military leaders and intelligence professionals that contradicted those beliefs.[9]

U.S. auto manufacturers provide an example from the business world. Leaders at these companies for too long assumed that their way of doing business, which kept the companies profitable for decades, would continue to be successful even as the environment changed dramatically. At General Motors, Rick Wagoner was asked by the Obama administration to resign as chairman and CEO because the government's auto task force believed a new set of assumptions was needed at the flailing company.

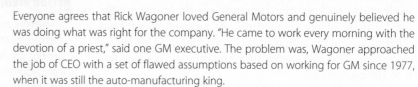

IN THE LEAD

General Motors

Everyone agrees that Rick Wagoner loved General Motors and genuinely believed he was doing what was right for the company. "He came to work every morning with the devotion of a priest," said one GM executive. The problem was, Wagoner approached the job of CEO with a set of flawed assumptions based on working for GM since 1977, when it was still the auto-manufacturing king.

GM was already in trouble when Wagoner took over. Indeed, the company had been losing market share since the 1960s and had been in "perpetual turnaround" since the 1980s. One problem at GM is that the corporate culture emphasized conformity and consistency, and leaders, including Wagoner, had a tough time breaking out of that mindset. During his nine years as CEO—even as thousands of people were laid off, market share tanked, and the stock price fell from $70 to less than $4—Wagoner maintained a belief in the basic strength and solidity of the company's business model. He couldn't accept, for instance, that in a changed environment, GM was spreading itself way too thin with too many car and truck models. Considering the multitude of GM's brands, each requiring expensive technical and marketing support, Wagoner decided to cut only one brand, Oldsmobile, from the lineup. He resisted a 2006 drive to forge a partnership with Nissan/Renault because he believed GM could and should stand on its own. Similarly, he never took any drastic measures to change the company's costly labor and benefits structure. In other words, Wagoner ran the company pretty much the way it had been run in the 1970s and 1980s. Only shortly before he was asked to step down in 2009 did Wagoner acknowledge the need for a new approach to doing business.

It remains to be seen whether new CEO Fritz Henderson, also a GM insider, has the right mental model needed to save the company. However, Henderson and Ed Whitacre Jr., who took over as chairman after GM emerged from Chapter 11 bankruptcy, say they are committed to making radical changes. In connection with a government-led restructuring, the two have significantly thinned the bloated management ranks, asking hundreds of executives to step down, replaced more than half the board with new members who aren't mired in the old way of thinking and doing things, appointed an executive specifically in charge of leading the overhaul of GM's corporate culture, and formed a small cross-functional leadership team to speed up decision making.[10]

Everyone who cares about the U.S. auto industry is hoping new leaders can bring more realistic assumptions to the challenge of reinventing GM. Whitacre, a highly skilled leader who took Southwestern Bell from the smallest regional Bell company to the largest and renamed it AT&T, has made it clear that he won't tolerate the "seemingly endless patience" the old board had with Rick Wagoner. He says the board will evaluate Henderson and his management team on a daily basis to see if they have the right mental model to lead GM over the long term. "He's there to make a success of GM, or he'll die trying," said a former colleague of Whitacre.[11]

As the example of General Motors illustrates, it is important for leaders to regard their assumptions as temporary ideas rather than fixed truths. The more aware a leader is of his or her assumptions, the more the leader understands how assumptions guide behavior and decisions. In addition, the leader can question whether long-held assumptions fit the reality of the current situation. Questioning assumptions can help leaders understand and shift their mental models.

Changing Mental Models

The mindset of the top leader has always played a key role in organizational success. A Harvard University study ranking the top 100 business leaders of the twentieth century found that they all shared what the researchers refer to as "contextual intelligence," the ability to sense the social, political, technological, and economic context of the times and adopt a mental model that helped their organizations best respond.[12] In a world of rapid and discontinuous change, the greatest factor determining the success of leaders and organizations may be the ability to change one's mental model.[13]

For business leaders, the uncertainty and volatility of today's environment is hard to ignore. As one reflection, consider the free fall in the stock market in 2008 and early 2009. Stock analysts' research reports began using the word *decremental* to describe the widespread decline in corporate profitability and loss of earning power.[14] Words from a 2006 *Fortune* article by Geoff Colvin seem even more fitting for today's environment: "The forecast for most companies is continued chaos with a chance of disaster."[15] Coping with this volatility requires a tremendous shift in mental models for most leaders. Yet many leaders become prisoners of their own assumptions and mindsets. They find themselves simply going along with the traditional way of doing things—whether it be running a manufacturing company such as General Motors, managing a foundation, handling insurance claims, selling cosmetics, or coaching a basketball team—without even realizing they are making decisions and acting within the limited frame of their own mental model.[16]

A study by Stephan Lewandowsky, a psychology professor at the University of Western Australia, Crawley, demonstrates the tremendous power mental

TURBULENT TIMES

models can have on our thinking. Researchers showed more than 860 people in Australia, Germany, and the United States a list of events associated with the United States–led invasion of Iraq. Some were true, some were originally reported as fact by the media but later retracted, and some were completely invented for the study. After interpreting the results, researchers determined that people tended to believe the "facts" that fit with their mindset about the Iraqi war, even if those facts were clearly not true. People who accepted as valid the official U.S. justification for the war continued to believe reports that cast the United States in a good light and the Iraqi forces in a bad light, even if they knew the reports had been retracted. Those who were suspicious of U.S. motives easily discounted the misinformation. Lewandowsky says supporters of the war held fast to believing what they originally heard, even though they knew it had been retracted, "because it fits with their mental model, which people seek to retain whatever it takes." This is an important point: People tend to believe what they want to believe because doing otherwise "would leave their world view a shambles."[17]

Despite the mental discomfort and sense of disorientation it might cause, leaders must allow their mental models to be challenged and even demolished.[18] Becoming aware of assumptions and understanding how they influence emotions and actions is the first step toward being able to shift mental models and see the world in a new way. Leaders can break free from outdated mental models. They can recognize that what worked yesterday may not work today. Following conventional wisdom about how to do things may be the surest route to failure. Effective leaders learn to continually question their own beliefs, assumptions, and perceptions in order to see things in unconventional ways and meet the challenge of the future head on.[19] Leaders also encourage others to question the status quo and look for new ideas. Getting others to shift their mental models is perhaps even more difficult than changing one's own, but leaders can use a variety of techniques to bring about a shift in thinking, as described in the Leader's Bookshelf.

Developing a Leader's Mind

How do leaders make the shift to a new mental model? The leader's mind can be developed beyond the non-leader's in four critical areas: independent thinking, open-mindedness, systems thinking, and personal mastery. Taken together, these four disciplines provide a foundation that can help leaders examine their mental models and overcome blind spots that may limit their leadership effectiveness and the success of their organizations.

Independent Thinking

Independent thinking means questioning assumptions and interpreting data and events according to one's own beliefs, ideas, and thinking, not according to pre-established rules, routines, or categories defined by others. People who think independently are willing to stand apart, to have opinions, to say what they think, and to determine a course of action based on what they personally believe rather than on what other people think or say. Good leadership isn't about following the rules of others, but standing up for what you believe is best for the organization.

To think independently means staying mentally alert and thinking critically. Independent thinking is one part of what is called leader mindfulness.[20]

Independent thinking
questioning assumptions and interpreting data and events according to one's own beliefs, ideas, and thinking, rather than pre-established rules or categories defined by others

marble: © Ioannis Drimilis   library: www.istockphoto.com/nikada

Leader's Bookshelf

Changing Minds: The Art and Science of Changing Our Own and Other People's Minds
by Howard Gardner

After about the age of 10, psychologist Howard Gardner asserts, people tend to retreat to old ideas rather than open up to new possibilities. "I'm not stating on small matters it's difficult to change people's minds," Gardner writes. "But on fundamental ideas of how the world works, about what your enterprise is about, about what your life goals are, about what it takes to survive—it's on these topics that it's very difficult . . . ."

Why? Because, over time, as people gain more formal and informal knowledge, patterns of thought become engraved in our minds, making it tough to shift to fresh ways of thinking. Yet lasting change in mindset is achievable, Gardner believes, if leaders use specific mind-changing tools.

GETTING OTHERS TO SEE THINGS DIFFERENTLY

Based on decades of extensive psychological research and observation, Gardner details seven "levers of change" that can be used to shift people's mindsets. He advises leaders to "think of them as arrows in a quiver" that can be used in different combinations for different circumstances. Here are some of Gardner's lessons:

- *Take your time, and approach change from many vantage points.* To shift people's way of thinking, leaders get the message out many different times in many different ways, using a variety of approaches and symbols. Gardner calls this *representational redescription,* which means finding diverse ways to get the same desired mind change across to people. "Give your message in more than one way, arranging things so the [listener] has a different experience." For example, simply talking about something in a different setting, such as over coffee or a drink after work, can sometimes be effective because the usual assumptions and resistances may be diminished.

- *Don't rely on reason alone.* Using a rational approach complemented by research and statistical data can shore up your argument. But effective leaders know they have to touch people's emotions as well, which Gardner calls *resonance.* Using stories, imagery, and real-world events can be a highly effective way to bring about change. Gardner uses the example of former British Prime Minister Margaret Thatcher. Thatcher effectively shifted the mindset of her constituency toward the idea that Britain could reemerge as a leading global power because her message resonated with people.

As the daughter of a poor grocer, Thatcher worked her way through school and raised a family before she entered politics.

- *Don't underestimate how powerful resistances can be.* As head of Monsanto, Robert Shapiro strongly believed in the benefits of genetically altered foods, and he assumed that the rest of the world would gladly embrace them. He was wrong, and his company suffered greatly because of his failure to understand and effectively address the resistances he encountered. Gardner identifies several specific types of barriers and advises leaders to arm themselves as if for battle when trying to change minds.

LASTING CHANGE IS VOLUNTARY CHANGE

Some people tend to think secrecy and manipulation is the quickest way to bring about change, and Gardner admits that in the short run, deception is effective. However, he emphasizes that change doesn't stick unless people change voluntarily. Manipulation backfires. Leaders who want to effect lasting changes in mindset wage their change campaigns openly and ethically.

Changing Minds, by Howard Gardner, is published by Harvard Business School Press.

Mindfulness can be defined as continuously reevaluating previously learned ways of doing things in the context of evolving information and shifting circumstances. Mindfulness involves independent thinking, and it requires leader curiosity and learning. Mindful leaders are open minded and stimulate the thinking of others through their curiosity and questions. Mindfulness is the opposite of *mindlessness,* which means blindly accepting rules and labels created by others. Mindless people let others do the thinking for them, but mindful leaders are always looking for new ideas and approaches.

Mindfulness
the process of continuously reevaluating previously learned ways of doing things in the context of evolving information and shifting circumstances

In the world of organizations, circumstances are constantly changing. What worked in one situation may not work the next time. In these conditions, mental laziness and accepting others' answers can hurt the organization and all its members. Leaders apply critical thinking to explore a situation, problem, or question from multiple perspectives and integrate all the available information into a possible solution. When leaders think critically, they question all assumptions, vigorously seek divergent opinions, and try to give balanced consideration to all alternatives.[21]

Leaders at today's best-performing organizations deliberately seek board members who can think independently and are willing to challenge senior management or other board members. Consider the board member at Medtronic who stood his ground against the CEO and 11 other members concerning an acquisition. The board approved the acquisition, but then-CEO Bill George was so persuaded by the dissenter's concerns that he reconvened the board by conference call. After hearing the dissenting board member's cogent argument that the deal would take Medtronic into an area it knew nothing about and divert attention from its core business, the board reconsidered and decided against the deal.[22]

Thinking independently and critically is hard work, and most of us can easily relax into temporary mindlessness, accepting black-and-white answers and relying on standard ways of doing things. Companies that have gotten into trouble in recent years often had executives and board members who failed to question enough or to challenge the status quo. For example, bank directors have been faulted for the deepening financial troubles at some of the Federal Home Loan Banks, a group of 12 regional cooperative banks created by Congress in 1932 to support the housing market. Analysts at Federal Financial Analytics, a research firm in Washington, D.C., say directors mindlessly went along with bank executives' decisions to buy large amounts of private-label mortgage securities packaged by Wall Street, rather than asking tough questions about the risks involved.[23]

Action Memo

Evaluate your skill in three dimensions of mindfulness, including intellectual stimulation, by completing the exercise in Leader's Self-Insight 5.1

Good leaders also encourage followers to be mindful rather than mindless. Bernard Bass, who has studied charismatic and transformational leadership, talks about the value of *intellectual stimulation*—arousing followers' thoughts and imaginations as well as stimulating their ability to identify and solve problems creatively.[24] People admire leaders who awaken their curiosity, challenge them to think and learn, and encourage openness to new, inspiring ideas and alternatives.

Open-Mindedness

One approach to independent thinking is to break out of the mental boxes, the categorized thinking patterns we have been conditioned to accept as correct. Leaders have to "keep their mental muscle loose."[25]

The power of the conditioning that guides our thinking and behavior is illustrated by what has been called the *Pike Syndrome*. In an experiment, a northern pike is placed in one half of a large glass-divided aquarium, with numerous minnows placed in the other half. The hungry pike makes repeated attempts to get the minnows, but succeeds only in battering itself against the glass, finally learning that trying to reach the minnows is futile. The glass divider is then removed, but the pike makes no attempt to attack the minnows because it has been

Leader's Self-Insight 5.1
Mindfulness

Think back to how you behaved toward others at work or in a group when you were in a formal or informal leadership position. Please respond to the following items based on how frequently you did each behavior. Indicate whether each item is Mostly False or Mostly True for you.

		Mostly False	Mostly True
1.	Enjoyed hearing new ideas.	_____	_____
2.	Challenged someone to think about an old problem in a new way.	_____	_____
3.	Tried to integrate conversation points at a higher level.	_____	_____
4.	Felt appreciation for the viewpoints of others.	_____	_____
5.	Would ask someone about the assumptions underlying his or her suggestions.	_____	_____
6.	Came to my own conclusion despite what others thought.	_____	_____
7.	Was open about myself to others.	_____	_____
8.	Encouraged others to express opposing ideas and arguments.	_____	_____
9.	Fought for my own ideas.	_____	_____
10.	Asked "dumb" questions.	_____	_____
11.	Offered insightful comments on the meaning of data or issues.	_____	_____
12.	Asked questions to prompt others to think more about an issue.	_____	_____
13.	Expressed a controversial opinion.	_____	_____
14.	Encouraged opposite points of view.	_____	_____
15.	Suggested ways of improving my and others' ways of doing things.	_____	_____

Scoring and Interpretation

Give yourself one point for each Mostly True checked for items 1–8 and 10–15. Give yourself one point for checking Mostly False for item 9. A total score of 12 or higher would be considered a high level of overall mindfulness. There are three subscale scores that represent three dimensions of leader mindfulness. For the dimension of open or beginner's mind, sum your responses to questions 1, 4, 7, 9, and 14. For the dimension of independent thinking, sum your scores for questions 3, 6, 11, 13, and 15. For the dimension of intellectual stimulation, sum your scores for questions 2, 5, 8, 10, and 12.

My scores are:
Open or Beginner's Mind: _____
Independent Thinking: _____
Intellectual Stimulation: _____

These scores represent three aspects of leader mindfulness—what is called open mind or beginner's mind, independent thinking, and intellectual stimulation.

A score of 4.0 or higher on any of these dimensions is considered high because many people do not practice mindfulness in their leadership or group work. A score of 3 is about average, and 2 or less would be below average. Compare your three subscale scores to understand the way you use mindfulness. Analyze the specific questions for which you did not get credit to see more deeply into your pattern of mindfulness strengths or weaknesses. Open mind, independent thinking, and intellectual stimulation are valuable qualities to develop for effective leadership.

Sources: The questions above are based on ideas from R. L. Daft and R. M. Lengel, *Fusion Leadership*, Chapter 4 (San Francisco: Berrett-Koehler, 2000); B. Bass and B. Avolio, *Multifactor Leadership Questionnaire*, 2nd ed. (Menlo Park, CA: Mind Garden, Inc.); and P. M. Podsakoff, S. B. MacKenzie, R. H. Moorman, and R. Fetter, "Transformational Leader Behaviors and Their Effects on Followers' Trust in Leader, Satisfaction, and Organizational Citizenship Behaviors," *Leadership Quarterly* 1, no. 2 (1990), pp. 107–42.

marble: © Kirill Matkov   sunset: © Marco Regalia

conditioned to believe that reaching them is impossible. When people assume they have complete knowledge of a situation because of past experiences, they exhibit the Pike Syndrome, a trained incapacity that comes from rigid commitment to what was true in the past and an inability to consider alternatives and different perspectives.[26]

Leaders have to forget many of their conditioned ideas to be open to new ones. This openness—putting aside preconceptions and suspending beliefs and opinions—can be referred to as "beginner's mind." Whereas the expert's mind rejects new ideas based on past experience and knowledge, the beginner's

Consider **This!**
An Empty Sort of Mind

Reflecting on How Winnie the Pooh Found Eeyore's Missing Tail:

"An Empty sort of mind is valuable for finding pearls and tails and things because it can see what's in front of it. An Overstuffed mind is unable to. While the clear mind listens to a bird singing, the Stuffed-Full-of-Knowledge-and-Cleverness mind wonders what *kind* of bird is singing. The more Stuffed Up it is, the less it can hear through its own ears and see through its own eyes. Knowledge and Cleverness tend to concern themselves with the wrong sorts of things, and a mind confused by Knowledge, Cleverness, and Abstract Ideas tends to go chasing off after things that don't matter, or that don't even exist, instead of seeing, appreciating, and making use of what is right in front of it."

Source: Benjamin Hoff, *The Tao of Pooh* (New York: E. P. Dutton, 1982), pp. 146–147.

mind reflects the openness and innocence of a young child just learning about the world. The value of a beginner's mind is captured in the story told in this chapter's *Consider This.*

One leader who illustrates the importance of keeping an open mind is Lisa Drakeman, who went from teaching religion at Princeton to being CEO of a biotechnology company. Drakeman found that being a business leader meant she needed to think and act in a new way. She had to learn how to delegate and how to get employees to share their ideas and opinions rather than acting as a teacher with all the answers. One of the most important lessons she learned? "Don't be afraid to look stupid by asking basic questions," Drakeman says.[27]

Action Memo

As a leader, you can train yourself to think independently. You can be curious, keep an open mind, and look at a problem or situation from multiple perspectives before reaching your conclusions.

Effective leaders strive to keep open minds and cultivate an organizational environment that encourages curiosity and learning. They understand the limitations of past experience and reach out for diverse perspectives. Rather than seeing any questioning of their ideas as a threat, these leaders encourage everyone throughout the organization to openly debate assumptions, confront paradoxes, question perceptions, and express feelings.[28]

Leaders can use a variety of approaches to help themselves and others keep an open mind. At McKinsey & Co., worldwide managing director Rajat Gupta reads poetry at the end of the partners' regular meetings. Poetry and literature, he says, "help us recognize that we face tough questions and that we seldom have perfect answers."[29]

Systems Thinking

Systems thinking
the ability to see the synergy of the whole rather than just the separate elements of a system and to learn to reinforce or change whole system patterns

Systems thinking means the ability to see the synergy of the whole rather than just the separate elements of a system and to learn to reinforce or change whole system patterns.[30] Many people have been trained to solve problems by breaking a complex system, such as an organization, into discrete parts and working to make each part perform as well as possible. However, the success of each piece does not add up to the success of the whole. In fact, sometimes changing one part to make it better actually makes the whole system function less effectively. Consider that, in recent years, new drugs have been a lifesaver for people living with HIV, but the drop in mortality rates has led to a reduction in perceived risk and therefore more incidences of risky behavior. After years of decline, HIV infection rates began rising again, indicating that the system of HIV treatment is not well understood. As another example, a small city embarked on a road-building program to solve traffic congestion without whole-systems thinking. With new roads available, more people began moving to the suburbs. The solution actually increased traffic congestion, delays, and pollution by enabling suburban sprawl.[31]

It is the *relationship* among the parts that form a whole system—whether it be a community, an automobile, a nonprofit agency, a human being, or a business organization—that matters. Systems thinking enables leaders to look for patterns of movement over time and focus on the qualities of rhythm, flow, direction, shape, and networks of relationships that accomplish the performance of the whole. Systems thinking is a mental discipline and framework for seeing patterns and interrelationships.

It is important to see organizational systems as a whole because of their complexity. Complexity can overwhelm leaders, undermining confidence. When leaders see the structures that underlie complex situations, they can facilitate improvement. But it requires a focus on the big picture. Leaders can develop what David McCamus, former chairman and CEO of Xerox Canada, calls "peripheral vision"—the ability to view the organization through a wide-angle lens, rather than a telephoto lens—so that they perceive how their decisions and actions affect the whole.[32]

An important element of systems thinking is to discern circles of causality. Peter Senge, author of *The Fifth Discipline,* argues that reality is made up of circles rather than straight lines. For example, Exhibit 5.2 shows circles of influence for producing new products. In the circle on the left, a high-tech firm grows rapidly by pumping out new products quickly. New products increase revenues, which enable the further increase of the R&D budget to add more new products.

Exhibit 5.2 Two Circles of Causality in an Organization

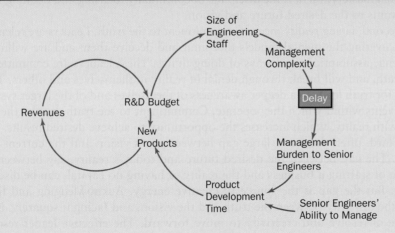

Source: From *The Fifth Discipline: The Art and Practice of the Learning Organization* by Peter M. Senge, p. 97. Copyright © 1990 by Peter M. Senge. Used by permission of Doubleday, a division of Bantam Doubleday Dell Publishing Group, Inc.

Action Memo

As a leader, you can cultivate an ability to analyze and understand the relationships among parts of a team, organization, family, or other system to avoid making changes that have unintended negative consequences.

But another circle of causality is being influenced as well. As the R&D budget grows, the engineering and research staff increases. The burgeoning technical staff becomes increasingly hard to manage. The management burden falls on senior engineers, who provide less of their time for developing new products, which slows product development time. The slowing of product development time has a negative impact on new products, the very thing that created organizational success. Maintaining product development time in the face of increasing management complexity depends upon senior engineers' management ability. Thus, understanding the circle of causality enables leaders to allocate resources to the training and development of engineering leadership as well as directly to new products. Without an understanding of the system, top leaders would fail to understand why increasing R&D budgets can actually increase product development time and reduce the number of new products coming to market.

The other element of systems thinking is learning to influence the system with reinforcing feedback as an engine for growth or decline. In the example of new products, after managers see how the system works, they can allocate revenues to speed new products to market, either by hiring more engineers, or by training senior engineers in management and leadership skills. They can guide the system when they understand it conceptually. Without this kind of understanding, managers will hit blockages in the form of seeming limits to growth and resistance to change because the large complex system will appear impossible to manage. Systems thinking is a significant solution.

Personal Mastery

Another concept introduced by Senge is *personal mastery,* a term he uses to describe the discipline of personal growth and learning, of mastering yourself in a way that facilitates your leadership and achieves desired results.[33]

Personal mastery embodies three qualities—personal vision, facing reality, and holding creative tension. First, leaders engaged in personal mastery know and clarify what is important to them. They focus on the end result, the vision or dream that motivates them and their organization. They have a clear vision of a desired future, and their purpose is to achieve that future. One element of personal mastery, then, is the discipline of continually focusing and defining what one wants as the desired future and vision.

Second, facing reality means a commitment to the truth. Leaders are relentless in uncovering the mental models that limit and deceive them and are willing to challenge assumptions and ways of doing things. These leaders are committed to the truth, and will break through denial of reality in themselves and others. Their quest for truth leads to a deeper awareness of themselves and of the larger systems and events within which they operate. Commitment to the truth enables them to deal with reality, which increases the opportunity to achieve desired results.

Third, often there is a large gap between one's vision and the current situation. The gap between the desired future and today's reality, say between the dream of starting a business and the reality of having no capital, can be discouraging. But the gap is the source of creative energy. Acknowledging and living with the disparity between the truth and the vision, and facing it squarely, is the source of resolve and creativity to move forward. The effective leader resolves the tension by letting the vision pull reality toward it, in other words, by reorganizing current activities to work toward the vision. The leader works in a way that moves things toward the vision. The less effective way is to let reality pull

Personal mastery
the discipline of personal growth and learning and of mastering yourself; it embodies personal visions, facing reality, and holding creative tension

the vision downward toward it. This means lowering the vision, such as walking away from a problem or settling for less than desired. Settling for less releases the tension, but it also engenders mediocrity. Leaders with personal mastery learn to accept both the dream and the reality simultaneously, and to close the gap by moving toward the dream.

All five elements of mind are interrelated. Independent thinking and open-mindedness improve systems thinking and enable personal mastery, helping leaders shift and expand their mental models. Since they are all interdependent, leaders working to improve even one element of their mental approach can move forward in a significant way toward mastering their minds and becoming more effective.

Emotional Intelligence—Leading with Heart and Mind

Psychologists and other researchers, as well as people in all walks of life, have long recognized the importance of cognitive intelligence, or IQ, in determining a person's success and effectiveness. In general, research shows that leaders score higher than most people on tests of cognitive ability, such as IQ tests, and that cognitive ability is positively associated with effective leadership.[34] Increasingly, leaders and researchers are recognizing the critical importance of emotional intelligence, or EQ, as well. Some have suggested that emotion, more than cognitive ability, drives our thinking and decision making, as well as our interpersonal relationships.[35] **Emotional intelligence** refers to a person's abilities to perceive, identify, understand, and successfully manage emotions in self and others. Being emotionally intelligent means being able to effectively manage ourselves and our relationships.[36]

Emotional understanding and skills impact our success and happiness in our work as well as our personal lives. Leaders can harness and direct the power of emotions to improve follower satisfaction, morale, and motivation, as well as to enhance overall organizational effectiveness. The U.S. Air Force started using EQ to select recruiters after learning that the best recruiters scored higher in EQ competencies. Leaders who score high in EQ are typically more effective and rated as more effective by peers and subordinates.[37] Moreover, in a study of entrepreneurs, researchers at Rensselaer Polytechnic Institute found that those who are more expressive of their own emotions and more in tune with the emotions of others make more money, as illustrated in Exhibit 5.3.

Emotional intelligence
a person's abilities to perceive, identify, understand, and successfully manage emotions in self and others

Exhibit 5.3 Emotional Intelligence and Earning Power

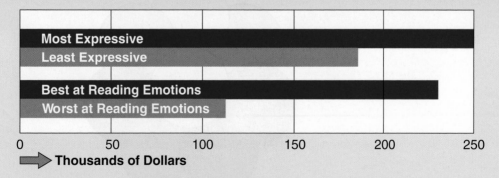

Entrepreneurs who scored in the top 10 percent in these two categories earn more money than those in the bottom 10 percent.

Source: Rensselaer Polytechnic Institute, Lally School of Management and Technology, as reported in *BusinessWeek Frontier* (February 5, 2001), p. F4.

Some leaders act as if people leave their emotions at home when they come to work, but we all know this isn't true. Indeed, a key component of leadership is being emotionally connected to others and understanding how emotions affect working relationships and performance.

What Are Emotions?

There are hundreds of emotions and more subtleties of emotion than there are words to explain them. One important ability for leaders is to understand the range of emotions people have and how these emotions may manifest themselves. Many researchers accept eight categories or "families" of emotions, as illustrated in Exhibit 5.4.[38] These categories do not resolve every question about how to categorize emotions, and scientific debate continues. The argument for there being a set of core emotions is based partly on the discovery that specific facial expressions for four of them (fear, anger, sadness, and enjoyment) are universally recognized. People in cultures around the world have been found to recognize these same basic emotions when shown photographs of facial expressions. The primary emotions and some of their variations follow.

- *Anger:* fury, outrage, resentment, exasperation, indignation, animosity, annoyance, irritability, hostility, violence
- *Sadness:* grief, sorrow, gloom, melancholy, self-pity, loneliness, dejection, despair, depression
- *Fear:* anxiety, apprehension, nervousness, concern, consternation, wariness, edginess, dread, fright, terror, panic
- *Enjoyment:* happiness, joy, relief, contentment, delight, amusement, pride, sensual pleasure, thrill, rapture, gratification, satisfaction, euphoria
- *Love:* acceptance, respect, friendliness, trust, kindness, affinity, devotion, adoration, infatuation
- *Surprise:* shock, astonishment, amazement, wonder
- *Disgust:* contempt, disdain, scorn, abhorrence, aversion, distaste, revulsion
- *Shame:* guilt, embarrassment, chagrin, remorse, humiliation, regret, mortification, contrition

Exhibit 5.4 Eight Families of Emotions

Leaders who are attuned to their own feelings and the feelings of others can use their understanding to enhance the organization. For example, studies of happiness in the workplace find that employee happiness can play a major role in organizational success. And a *Gallup Management Journal* survey emphasizes that leaders, especially frontline supervisors, have a lot to do with whether employees have positive or negative feelings about their work lives.[39]

The Components of Emotional Intelligence

The competencies and abilities of emotional intelligence are grouped into four fundamental categories, as illustrated in Exhibit 5.5.[40] It is important to remember that emotional intelligence can be learned and developed. Anyone can strengthen his or her abilities in these four categories.

Self-awareness might be considered the basis of all the other competencies. It includes the ability to recognize and understand your own emotions and how they affect your life and work. People who are in touch with their emotions are better able to guide their own lives. Leaders with a high level of self-awareness learn to trust their "gut feelings" and realize that these feelings can provide useful information about difficult decisions. Answers are not always clear as to whether to propose a major deal, let an employee go, reorganize a business, or revise job responsibilities. When the answers are not available from external sources, leaders have to rely on their own feelings. This component also includes the ability to accurately assess your own strengths and limitations, along with a healthy sense of self-confidence.

Self-management, the second key component, includes the ability to control disruptive, unproductive, or harmful emotions and desires. An interesting experiment from the 1960s sheds some light on the power of self-management. A group of four-year-olds and five-year-olds were offered a marshmallow, which the researcher placed in front of each child on the desk. Then, the children were told that if they could wait a few minutes while the researcher ran an errand, they would be given two marshmallows. Some children were unable to resist the temptation of a marshmallow "right now" and ate theirs immediately. Others employed all sorts

Self-awareness
the ability to recognize and understand your own emotions and how they affect your life and work

Self-management
the ability to control disruptive or harmful emotions

Exhibit 5.5 The Components of Emotional Intelligence

	SELF	OTHERS
AWARENESS	**Self-Awareness** • Emotional self-awareness • Accurate self-assessment • Self-confidence	**Social Awareness** • Empathy • Organizational awareness • Service orientation
BEHAVIOR	**Self-Management** • Emotional self-control • Trustworthiness • Conscientiousness • Adaptability • Optimism • Achievement-orientation • Initiative	**Relationship Management** • Development of others • Inspirational leadership • Influence • Communication • Change catalyst • Conflict management • Bond building • Teamwork and collaboration

Source: Adapted from Richard E. Boyatzis and Daniel Goleman, *The Emotional Competence Inventory—University Edition* (Boston, MA: The Hay Group, 2001).

Action Memo

As a leader, you can recognize and manage your own emotions so that negative feelings don't cloud your mind, distort your judgment, or cripple your ability to lead.

of techniques, from singing or talking to themselves to hiding under the desk, to resist their impulses and earn the reward of two marshmallows instead of one. Researchers then followed the children over a period of 20 years and found some interesting results. As young men and women, the ones who had resisted the desire to eat the marshmallow revealed a much higher ability to handle stress and embrace difficult challenges. They also were more self-confident, trustworthy, dependable, and tenacious in pursuing goals.[41] The children who developed techniques for self-management early in life carried these with them into adulthood.

It is never too late for people to learn how to manage their emotions and impulses. Leaders learn to balance their own emotions so that worry, desire, anxiety, fear, or anger do not get in the way, thus enabling them to think clearly and be more effective. Managing emotions does not mean suppressing or denying them but understanding them and using that understanding to deal with situations productively.[42]

Other characteristics in this category include *trustworthiness*, which means consistently displaying honesty and integrity, *conscientiousness*, which means managing and honoring your responsibilities, and *adaptability*, which refers to the ability to adjust to changing situations and overcome obstacles. Showing initiative to seize opportunities and achieve high internal standards is also a part of self-management. Leaders skilled at self-management remain hopeful and optimistic despite obstacles, setbacks, or even outright failures. Martin Seligman, a professor of psychology at the University of Pennsylvania, once advised the MetLife insurance company to hire a special group of job applicants who tested high on optimism but failed the normal sales aptitude test. Compared to salespeople who passed the regular aptitude test but scored high on pessimism, the "optimistic" group made 21 percent more sales in their first year and 57 percent more in the second.[43]

Social awareness relates to one's ability to understand others. Socially aware leaders practice **empathy**, which means being able to put yourself in other people's shoes, sense their emotions, and understand their perspective. These leaders understand that effective leadership sometimes means pushing people beyond their comfort zone, and they are sensitive to the fear or frustration this can engender in followers. They learn to engage in "professional intimacy," which means they can display compassion and concern for others without becoming so wrapped up in others' emotions that it clouds their judgment.[44] Socially aware leaders are also capable of understanding divergent points of view and interacting effectively with many different types of people and emotions. The related characteristic of *organizational awareness* refers to the ability to navigate the currents of organizational life, build networks, and effectively use political behavior to accomplish positive results. This component also includes a *service orientation,* which refers to the ability to recognize and serve the needs of employees, customers, or clients.

Relationship management refers to the ability to connect with others and build positive relationships. Leaders with high emotional intelligence treat others with compassion, sensitivity, and kindness.[45] This aspect of EQ encompasses developing others, inspiring others with a powerful vision, learning to listen and communicate clearly and convincingly, and using emotional understanding to influence others in positive ways. Leaders use their understanding of emotions to inspire change and lead people toward something better, to build teamwork and collaboration, and to resolve conflicts that inevitably arise. These leaders cultivate and maintain a web of relationships both within and outside the organization.

Social awareness
one's ability to understand and empathize with others

Empathy
being able to put yourself in someone else's shoes

Relationship management
the ability to connect with others and build positive relationships

For example, Jim McNerney has reinvigorated Boeing by using his relationship management abilities. McNerney is known as a good listener, a motivator, and a team-builder who inspires people with his vision and his integrity. He spent much of his first six months as CEO talking with employees around the company to understand Boeing's strengths and challenges and emphasize the need for cooperation and teamwork.[46]

Taken together, the four components shown in Exhibit 5.5 build a strong base of emotional intelligence that leaders can use to more effectively guide teams and organizations. One research project suggests that all effective leadership styles arise from different components of emotional intelligence.[47] The best leaders combine styles or vary their styles, depending on the situation or problem at hand, by using all of the components. By being sensitive to their own and others' emotions, these leaders can recognize what effect they are having on followers and seamlessly adjust their approach to create a positive result. Consider how Mike Krzyzewski, coach of the Duke University Blue Devils, uses emotional intelligence to bring out the best in his players.

Action Memo

As a leader, you can empathize with others, treat people with compassion and sensitivity, build teamwork, and learn to listen, interpret emotions, and resolve interpersonal conflicts.

IN THE LEAD

Mike Krzyzewski, Duke University Blue Devils

Mike Krzyzewski doesn't think of himself as a basketball coach. He considers himself a leader who just happens to coach basketball. And for Krzyzewski, almost everything in leadership depends on one element: personal relationships.

Although he's a tough man with tough standards, Krzyzewski has been accused of "coaching like a girl" because of his interactive, emotionally charged style. When the legendary coach of Duke University's Blue Devils recruits a player, for example, he tells him, "We're developing a relationship here, and if you're not interested, tell me sooner rather than later." The emphasis on relationships comes partly from Krzyzewski's years playing, and later coaching, at the U.S. Military Academy at West Point, which he calls the greatest leadership school in the world because it teaches officers how to bond soldiers together. As a coach, Krzyzewski emphasizes teamwork rather than individual performers, fosters a family feeling among players, and says he coaches "by feel." That is, he gets to know his players as individuals and learns how they can best interact to succeed. He builds such strong positive relationships among players that they communicate constantly and effortlessly on the court, sometimes without saying a word.

Leading a basketball team, Krzyzewski believes, is just like leading a business, a military unit, a school, a volunteer group, or anything else: "You gotta get through all their layers and get right into their hearts."[48]

Mike Krzyzewski has created the kind of workplace that many of today's organizations need—one in which leaders are more interactive than "command-and-control," where leadership and decision making is spread across all levels, and where individual goals are met through teamwork and collaboration. In an environment where relationships with employees and customers are becoming more important than technology and material resources, interest in developing leaders' emotional intelligence continues to grow. All leaders have to pay attention to the emotional climate in their organization. Recent events

Action Memo

Evaluate your level of emotional intelligence by completing the questionnaire in Leader's Self-Insight 5.2.

Leader's Self-Insight 5.2
Emotional Intelligence

For each of the following items, rate how well you display the behavior described. Before responding, try to think of actual situations in which you have had the opportunity to use the behavior. Indicate whether each item below is Mostly False or Mostly True for you.

	Mostly False	Mostly True
1. Associate different internal physiological cues with different emotions.	___	___
2. Relax when under pressure in situations.	___	___
3. Know the impact that your behavior has on others.	___	___
4. Initiate successful resolution of conflict with others.	___	___
5. Know when you are becoming angry.	___	___
6. Recognize when others are distressed.	___	___
7. Build consensus with others.	___	___
8. Produce motivation when doing uninteresting work.	___	___
9. Help others manage their emotions.	___	___
10. Make others feel good.	___	___
11. Identify when you experience mood shifts.	___	___
12. Stay calm when you are the target of anger from others.	___	___
13. Know when you become defensive.	___	___
14. Follow your words with actions.	___	___
15. Engage in intimate conversations with others.	___	___
16. Accurately reflect people's feelings back to them.	___	___

Scoring and Interpretation

Sum your Mostly True responses to the 16 questions to obtain your overall emotional intelligence score. Your score for self-awareness is the total of questions 1, 5, 11, and 13. Your score for self-management is the total of questions 2, 8, 12, and 14. Your score for social awareness is the sum of questions 3, 6, 9, and 15. Your score for relationship management is the sum of questions 4, 7, 10, and 16. This questionnaire provides some indication of your emotional intelligence. If you received a total score of 14 or more, you are certainly considered a person with high emotional intelligence. A score from 10 to 13 means you have a good platform of emotional intelligence from which to develop your leadership capability. A score of 7 to 9 would be moderate emotional intelligence. A score below 7 indicates that you realize that you are probably below average in emotional intelligence.

For each of the four components of emotional intelligence—self-awareness, self-management, social awareness, and relationship management—a score of 4 is considered high, whereas a score of 2 or fewer would be considered low. Review the discussion in this chapter about the four components of emotional intelligence and think about what you might do to develop those areas where you scored low. Compare your scores to those of other students. What can you do to improve your scores?

Source: Adapted from Hendrie Weisinger, *Emotional Intelligence at Work* (San Francisco: Jossey-Bass, 1998), pp. 214–215.

marble: © Kirill Matkov   sunset: © Marco Regalia

and challenges have thrust emotions to the forefront for both individuals and organizations.

The Emotionally Competent Leader

In discussing Abraham Lincoln's leadership, noted historian Doris Kearns Goodwin attributes the 16th U.S. President's almost magical touch not to charisma or political astuteness, but to emotional intelligence.[49] How is emotional intelligence related to effective leadership? A high level of self-awareness and an ability to manage one's own emotions enable a leader to display self-confidence, earn respect and trust, and consider the needs of others. Emotionally competent leaders are more resilient, more adaptable to ever-changing circumstances, more willing to step outside their comfort zone, and more open to the opinions and ideas of others.[50]

Emotional intelligence is also important for leaders because the emotional state of the leader impacts the entire team, department, or organization. Most of us recognize that we can "catch" emotions from others. If we're around someone who is smiling and enthusiastic, the positive emotions rub off on us. Conversely, someone in a bad mood can bring us down. At Mesa Airlines, CEO Jonathan Ornstein's former administrative assistant says she was in charge of tracking the unpredictable and frequently short-tempered leader's moods and warning other executives when they needed to stay away. "Sometimes he would come into the office in a bad mood . . . and it would set the tone for the whole office," she says.[51] This *emotional contagion*[52] means that leaders who are able to maintain balance and keep themselves motivated can serve as positive role models to help motivate and inspire those around them. The energy level of the entire organization increases when leaders are optimistic and hopeful rather than angry or depressed. The ability to empathize with others and to manage interpersonal relationships also contributes to motivation and inspiration because it helps leaders create feelings of unity and team spirit.

Action Memo

As a leader, you can develop emotional intelligence and act as a positive role model by being optimistic and enthusiastic.

Perhaps most importantly, emotional intelligence enables leaders to recognize and respect followers as whole human beings with feelings, opinions, and ideas of their own. They can use their emotional intelligence to help followers grow and develop, see and enhance their self-image and feelings of self-worth, and help meet their needs and achieve their personal goals.

In one study, two-thirds of the difference between average and top performing leaders was found to be due to emotional competence, with only one-third due to technical skills.[53] There are many training programs for developing one's emotional intelligence, but people can also take some simple steps on their own. Here are a few ideas that have been suggested as ways to enhance emotional intelligence:[54]

- *Take responsibility for your life.* Some people are always looking for someone to blame when things go wrong. Taking responsibility means assuming ownership for the situations and the condition of your own life, which provides a foundation for emotional intelligence. It is natural to want to blame someone or something else for problems, but taking responsibility gives you power and control over your own emotions and engenders respect from others.
- *Take a course in public speaking.* Many people have a fear of public speaking, so this is a good way to practice self-management, such as learning to control nervousness and self-consciousness. In addition, being a good public speaker means understanding the audience. The best speakers make it more about the audience and less about themselves. Thus, practicing public speaking can help you learn to empathize with others and take their needs and interests into account.
- *Practice meditation or yoga.* The disciplines of meditation and yoga promote mindfulness, as described earlier, and enable the individual to attain a state of relaxed awareness. Meditation and yoga can help you learn to manage your emotions so that stress, depression, and negative thoughts and feelings don't cloud your judgment and control your actions.

The Emotional Intelligence of Teams

Much of the work in today's organizations, even at top management levels, is done in teams rather than by individuals. Although most studies of emotional intelligence have focused on individuals, research is beginning to emerge concerning how emotional intelligence relates to teams. For example, one study found that untrained teams made up of members with high emotional intelligence performed as well as trained teams made up of members who rated low on emotional intelligence.[55] The high emotional intelligence of the untrained team members enabled them to assess and adapt to the requirements of teamwork and the tasks at hand.

Moreover, research has suggested that emotional intelligence can be developed as a *team* competency and not just an individual competency.[56] That is, teams themselves—not just their individual members—can become emotionally intelligent. Leaders build the emotional intelligence of teams by creating norms that support emotional development and influence emotions in constructive ways. Emotionally intelligent team norms are those that (1) create a strong group identity, (2) build trust among members, and (3) instill a belief among members that they can be effective and succeed as a team.

Leaders "tune in" to the team's emotional state and look for unhealthy or unproductive norms that inhibit cooperation and team harmony.[57] Building the emotional intelligence of the team means exploring unhealthy norms, deliberately bringing emotions to the surface, and understanding how they affect the team's work. Raising these issues can be uncomfortable, and a leader needs both courage and individual emotional intelligence to guide a team through the process. Only by getting emotions into the open can the team build new norms and move to a higher level of group satisfaction and performance. Leaders continue to build emotional intelligence by encouraging and enabling the team to explore and use emotion in its everyday work.

Leading with Love versus Leading with Fear

Traditionally, leadership has been based on inspiring fear in employees. An unspoken notion among many senior-level executives is that fear is a good thing and benefits the organization.[58] Indeed, fear can be a powerful motivator, but many of today's leaders are learning that an environment that reflects care and respect for people is much more effective than one in which people are fearful. When organizational success depended primarily on people mindlessly following orders, leading with fear often met the organization's needs. Today, though, success in most organizations depends on the knowledge, mindpower, commitment, and enthusiasm of everyone in the organization. A fear-based organization loses its best people, and the knowledge they take with them, to other firms. In addition, even if people stay with the organization, they typically don't perform up to their real capabilities. There is evidence that people who experience positive emotions at work perform better.[59]

Action Memo

To learn about your own motivations concerning love versus fear, complete the exercise in Leader's Self-Insight 5.3.

One major drawback of leading with fear is that it creates avoidance behavior, because no one wants to make a mistake, and this inhibits growth and change. Leaders can learn to bind people together for a shared purpose through more positive forces such as caring and compassion, listening, and connecting to others on a personal level. The emotion that attracts people to take risks, learn, grow, and move the organization forward comes from love, not fear. Douglas Conant, CEO of Campbell Soup, profiled in Chapter 2, says true leaders get employees to "fall in love with your company's agenda" by engaging with them personally and treating them with respect.[60]

The following items describe reasons why you work. *Answer the questions twice,* the first time for doing work (or homework) that is not your favorite, and the second time for doing a hobby or sports activity that you enjoy. *Consider each item thoughtfully and respond according to your inner motivation and experience.* Indicate whether each item below is Mostly False or Mostly True for you.

	Mostly False	Mostly True
1. I feel it is important to perform well so I don't look bad.	___	___
2. I have to force myself to complete the task.	___	___
3. I don't want to have a poor outcome or get a poor grade.	___	___
4. I don't want to embarrass myself or do less well than others.	___	___
5. The experience leaves me feeling relieved that it is over.	___	___
6. My attention is absorbed entirely in what I am doing.	___	___
7. I really enjoy the experience.	___	___
8. Time seems to pass more quickly than normal.	___	___
9. I am completely focused on the task at hand.	___	___
10. The experience leaves me feeling great.	___	___

Scoring and Interpretation

These items reflect motivation shaped by either love or fear. Your "fear of failure" score is the number of Mostly True answers for questions 1–5. Your "love of task" score is the number of Mostly True answers for questions 6–10. A score of 4 or 5 would be considered high for either love or fear, and a score of 0–2 would be considered low. You would probably score more points for "love of task" for your hobby or sports activity than for homework.

Some people are motivated by high internal standards and fear of not meeting those standards. This may be called fear of failure, which often spurs people to great accomplishment. Love of task provides a great intrinsic pleasure but won't always lead to high achievement. Love of task is related to the idea of "flow" wherein people become fully engaged and derive great satisfaction from their activity. Would love or fear influence your choice to become a leader or how you try to motivate others? Discuss with other students the relative importance of love or fear motivation in your lives.

Love in the workplace means genuinely caring for others and sharing one's knowledge, understanding, and compassion to enable others to grow and succeed.

Showing respect and trust not only enables people to perform better, but it also allows them to feel emotionally connected with their work so that their lives are richer and more balanced. Leaders can rely on negative emotions such as fear to fuel productive work, but by doing so they may slowly destroy people's spirits, which ultimately is bad for employees and the organization.[61]

Fear in Organizations

The workplace can hold many kinds of fear, including fear of failure, fear of change, fear of personal loss, and fear of the boss. All of these fears can prevent people from doing their best, from taking risks, and from challenging and changing the status quo. Fear gets in the way of people feeling good about their work, themselves, and the organization. It creates an atmosphere in which people feel powerless, so that their confidence, commitment, enthusiasm, imagination, and motivation are diminished.[62]

Action Memo

As a leader, you can choose to lead with love, not with fear. You can show respect and trust toward followers and help people learn, grow, and contribute their best to achieve the organization's vision.

Aspects of Fear A particularly damaging aspect of fear in the workplace is that it can weaken trust and communication. Employees feel threatened by repercussions if they speak up about work-related concerns. A survey of employees in 22 organizations around the country found that 70 percent of them "bit their tongues" at work because they feared repercussions. Twenty-seven percent reported that they feared losing their credibility or reputation if they spoke up. Other fears reported were lack of career advancement, possible damage to the relationship with their supervisor, demotion or losing their job, and being embarrassed or humiliated in front of others.[63] When people are afraid to speak up, important issues are suppressed and problems hidden. Employees are afraid to talk about a wide range of issues, but by far the largest category of "undiscussables" is the behavior of executives, particularly their interpersonal and relationship skills. When leaders inspire fear, they destroy the opportunity for feedback, blinding them to reality and denying them the chance to correct damaging decisions and behaviors.

Relationship with Leaders Leaders control the fear level in the organization. Exhibit 5.6 outlines some indicators of love-based versus fear-based leadership in organizations. Organizations driven by love are marked by openness and authenticity, a respect for diverse viewpoints, and emphasis on positive interpersonal relationships. Organizations driven by fear, on the other hand, are characterized by cautiousness and secrecy, blaming others, excessive control, and emotional distance among people. The relationship between an employee and his or her direct supervisor is the primary factor determining the level of fear experienced at work. Unfortunately, the legacy of fear and mistrust associated with traditional hierarchies in which bosses gave orders and employees jumped to obey "or else" still colors life in many organizations. Leaders can create a new environment that enables people to feel safe speaking their minds. Leaders can act from love rather than fear to free employees and the organization from the chains of the past.

Bringing Love to Work

Organizations have traditionally rewarded people for strong qualities such as rational thinking, ambition, and competitiveness. These qualities are important,

Exhibit 5.6 Indicators of Love versus Fear in Organizations

Fear-Driven Indicators	Love-Driven Indicators
Caution and secrecy	Openness and authenticity, even when it's difficult
Blaming and attacking	Understanding diverse viewpoints
Excessive control	Expecting others to do great things
Sidelines criticalness	Involvement and discernment
Coming unglued	Keeping perspective
Aloofness and distance	Interpersonal connection
Resistance hidden	Resistance out in open, explored
Separate and competing interests	Alignment and common ground sought

Source: Daniel Holden, "Team Development: A Search for Elegance," *Industrial Management* (September–October 2007), pp. 20–25.

but their overemphasis has left many organizational leaders out of touch with their softer, caring, creative capabilities, unable to make emotional connections with others and afraid to risk showing any sign of weakness. In other words, many leaders act from their own fear, which creates fear in others. A leader's fear can manifest itself in arrogance, selfishness, deception, unfairness, and disrespect for others.[64]

Leaders can develop their capacity for the positive emotions of love and caring. When Walt Bettinger, CEO of Charles Schwab, was in college, he learned a lesson he tries to apply every day. The professor handed each student a blank sheet of paper and gave them one final exam question: *What's the name of the lady who cleans this building?* The students had spent four hours a night twice a week in the building for 10 weeks, encountering the cleaning lady several times a night as they went to get a soft drink or use the restroom. Bettinger says: "I didn't know Dottie's name—her name was Dottie—but I've tried to know every Dottie since."[65]

Most of us have experienced the power of love at some time in our lives. There are many different kinds of love—for example, the love of a mother for her child, romantic love, brotherly love, or the love of country, as well as the love some people feel for certain sports, hobbies, or recreational pursuits. Despite its power, the "L" word is often looked upon with suspicion in the business world.[66] However, there are a number of aspects of love that are directly relevant to work relationships and organizational performance.

Love as motivation is the force within that enables people to feel alive, connected, energized, and "in love" with life and work. Western cultures place great emphasis on the mind and the rational approach. However, it is the heart rather than the mind that powers people forward. Recall a time when you wanted to do something with all your heart, and how your energy and motivation flowed freely. Also recall a time when your head said you had to do a task, but your heart was not in it. Motivation is reduced, perhaps to the point of procrastination. There's a growing interest in helping people feel a genuine passion for their work.[67] People who are engaged rather than alienated from their work are typically more satisfied, productive, and successful.

Love as feelings involves attraction, fascination, and caring for people, work, or other things. This is what people most often think of as love, particularly in relation to romantic love between two people. However, love as feelings is also relevant in work situations. Feelings of compassion and caring for others are a manifestation of love, as are forgiveness, sincerity, respect, and loyalty, all of which are important for healthy working relationships. One personal feeling is a sense of *bliss,* best articulated for the general public by Joseph Campbell in his PBS television series and companion book with Bill Moyers, *The Power of Myth.*[68] Finding your bliss means doing things that make you light up inside, things you do for the joy of doing rather than for material rewards. Most of us experience moments of this bliss when we become so absorbed in enjoyable work activities that we lose track of time. This type of feeling and caring about work is a major source of charisma. Everyone becomes more charismatic to others when they pursue an activity they truly care about.

Love as action means more than feelings; it is translated into behavior. Stephen Covey points out that in all the great literature, love is a verb rather than a noun.[69] Love is something you do, the sacrifices you make and the giving of yourself to others. The following poignant example from the Iraq war illustrates this aspect of love.

IN THE LEAD

Cpl. Jason Dunham, United States Marine Corps; Petty Officer Michael Monsoor, United States Navy; Sgt. Rafael Peralta, United States Marine Corps; Sgt. James Witkowski, Army Reserve; Spc. Ross McGinnis, United States Army

When asked why his friend Ross McGinnis threw himself on an enemy grenade that was thrown into their Humvee, U.S. Army Staff Sgt. Ian Newland simply said, "He loved us." McGinnis was killed; the other soldiers, though wounded, survived.

During the Iraq war, at least four other U.S. soldiers—Jason Dunham and Rafael Peralta of the U.S. Marines; Michael Monsoor, a Navy EOD Technician; and Army Reserve Sgt. James Witkowski—died because they used their own bodies to shield their comrades from grenades. "What a decision that is," said Frank Farley, a professor who studies bravery. "I can't think of anything more profound in human nature."

Soldiers who survive when a comrade makes the ultimate sacrifice to save them typically struggle with feelings of guilt, depression, and anxiety and need strong counseling to cope with what has happened. However, another result is that most of them feel they need to live their lives in a way that will honor their fallen comrade. "I try not to live my life in vain for what he's done," said Newland about McGinnis's death. A Navy lieutenant with the SEALs said something similar about Peralta when he indicated that "everything pretty much revolves around what he did."[70]

These soldiers were heroic, but Ross McGinnis's father Tom McGinnis said he didn't want his son depicted as larger-than-life. "He wasn't exceptional. He was just like you and me. He made a split-second decision. He did what he thought was right."[71] Tom McGinnis's statement is a reminder that we all have the opportunity to act out of love and compassion rather than fear and indifference.

Most of us are never called upon to sacrifice our lives for others, but in all groups and organizations feelings of compassion, respect, and loyalty are translated into action, such as acts of friendliness, teamwork, cooperation, listening, understanding, and serving others above oneself. Sentiments emerge as action.

Why Followers Respond to Love

Most people yearn for more than a paycheck from their jobs. Leaders who lead with love have extraordinary influence because they meet five unspoken employee needs:

> Hear and understand me.
> Even if you disagree with me, please don't make me wrong.
> Acknowledge the greatness within me.
> Remember to look for my loving intentions.
> Tell me the truth with compassion.[72]

When leaders address these subtle emotional needs directly, people typically respond by loving their work and becoming emotionally engaged in solving problems and serving customers. Enthusiasm for work and the organization increases. People want to believe that their leaders genuinely care. From the followers' point of view, love versus fear has different motivational potential.

- **Fear-based motivation:** I need a job to pay for my basic needs (fulfilling lower needs of the body). You give me a job, and I will give you just enough to keep my job.

Fear-based motivation
motivation based on fear of losing a job

● **Love-based motivation:** If the job and the leader make me feel valued as a person and provide a sense of meaning and contribution to the community at large (fulfilling higher needs of heart, mind, and body), then I will give you all I have to offer.[73]

Many examples throughout this book illustrate what happens when positive emotion is used. One management consultant went so far as to advise that finding creative ways to love could solve every imaginable leadership problem.[74] Rational thinking and technical skills are important, but leading with love builds trust, stimulates creativity, inspires commitment, and unleashes boundless energy.

Love-based motivation
motivation based on feeling valued in the job

Leadership Essentials

■ Leaders use emotional as well as intellectual capabilities and understandings to guide organizations through a turbulent environment and help people feel energized, motivated, and cared for in the face of rapid change, uncertainty, and job insecurity. Leaders can expand the capacities of their minds and hearts through conscious development and practice.

■ Leaders should be aware of how their mental models affect their thinking and may cause "blind spots" that limit understanding. Becoming aware of assumptions is a first step toward shifting one's mental model and being able to see the world in new and different ways. Four key issues important to expanding and developing a leader's mind are independent thinking, open-mindedness, systems thinking, and personal mastery.

■ Leaders should also understand the importance of emotional intelligence. Four basic components of emotional intelligence are self-awareness, self-management, social awareness, and relationship management. Emotionally intelligent leaders can have a positive impact on organizations by helping employees grow, learn, and develop; creating a sense of purpose and meaning; instilling unity and team spirit; and basing relationships on trust and respect, which allows employees to take risks and fully contribute to the organization. Most work in organizations is done in teams, and emotional intelligence applies to teams as well as to individuals. Leaders develop a team's emotional intelligence by creating norms that foster a strong group identity, building trust among members, and instilling a belief among members that they can be effective and succeed as a team.

■ Traditional organizations have relied on fear as a motivator. Although fear does motivate people, it prevents people from feeling good about their work and often causes avoidance behavior. Fear can reduce trust and communication so that important problems and issues are hidden or suppressed. Leaders can choose to lead with love instead of fear. Love can be thought of as a motivational force that enables people to feel alive, connected, and energized; as feelings of liking, caring, and bliss; and as actions of helping, listening, and cooperating. Each of these aspects of love has relevance for organizational relationships. People respond to love because it meets unspoken needs for respect and affirmation. Rational thinking is important to leadership, but it takes love to build trust, creativity, and enthusiasm.

Discussion Questions

1. How do you feel about developing the emotional qualities of yourself and other people in the organization as a way to be an effective leader? Discuss.

2. Do you agree that people have a capacity for developing their minds and hearts beyond their current level of competency? Can you give an example? Discuss.

3. Why is it so hard for people to change their assumptions? What are some specific reasons why leaders need to be aware of their mental models?

4. Discuss the similarities and differences between mental models and open-mindedness.

5. What is the concept of personal mastery? How important is it to a leader?

6. Which of the four elements of emotional intelligence do you consider most essential to an effective leader? Why?

7. Consider fear and love as potential motivators. Which is the best source of motivation for college students? For members of a new product development team? For top executives at a media conglomerate? Why?

8. Have you ever experienced love and/or fear from leaders at work? How did you respond? Is it possible that leaders might carry love too far and create negative rather than positive results? Discuss.

9. Do you think it is appropriate for a leader to spend time developing a team's emotional intelligence? Why or why not?

10. Think about the class for which you are reading this text as a system. How might making changes without whole-systems thinking cause problems for students?

Leadership at Work

MENTORS

Think of a time when someone reached out to you as a mentor or coach. This might have been a time when you were having some difficulty, and the person who reached out would have done so out of concern for you rather than for their own self interest.

Below, briefly describe the situation, who the mentor was, and what the mentor did for you.

_____

_____

_____

Mentoring comes from the heart, is a generous act, and is usually deeply appreciated by the recipient. How does it feel to recall the situation in which a mentor assisted you?

_____

_____

_____

Share your experience with one or more students. What are the common characteristics that mentors possess based on your combined experiences?

_____

_____

_____

In Class: A discussion of experiences with mentors is excellent for small groups. The instructor can ask each group to identify the common characteristics that their mentors displayed, and each group's conclusions can be written on the board. From these lists of mentor characteristics, common themes associated with mentors can be defined. The instructor can ask the class the following key questions: What are the key characteristics of mentors? Based on the key mentor characteristics, is effective mentoring based more on a person's heart or mind? Will you (the student) reach out as a mentor to others in life, and how will you do it? What factors might prevent you from doing so?

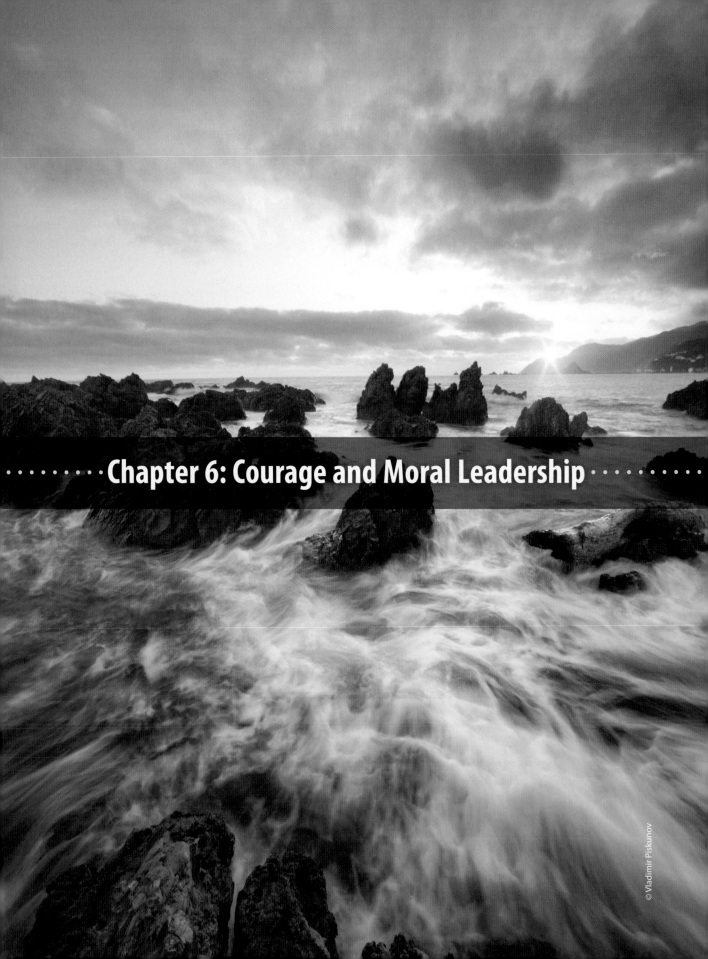

Chapter 6: Courage and Moral Leadership

© Vladimir Piskunov

Your Leadership Challenge

After reading this chapter, you should be able to:

- Combine a rational approach to leadership with a concern for people and ethics.

- Recognize your own stage of moral development and ways to accelerate your moral maturation.

- Know and use mechanisms that enhance an ethical organizational culture.

- Apply the principles of stewardship and servant leadership.

- Recognize courage in others and unlock your own potential to live and act courageously.

Chapter Outline

Xerox was in a free fall when Anne Mulcahy took over as CEO in 2000. Rather than sugarcoating the dire situation, Mulcahy candidly told shareholders that the company's business model was unsustainable and dramatic actions were needed to save the organization. Investors dumped Xerox shares, driving the already-decimated stock price even lower. Advisers urged Mulcahy to declare bankruptcy, but she chose instead to focus on a vision of restoring Xerox to greatness. Rather than becoming immobilized by a need to soothe analysts, angry shareholders, and investment bankers, Mulcahy headed out to talk to customers and employees. She implemented severe cost-cutting measures, but she refused to cut back on research and development, despite shareholder petitions to shut down all R&D.

By the time she retired in mid-2009, Mulcahy was being praised for engineering one of the most remarkable turnarounds in recent business history. Her actions led to paying off the company's debt, reinvigorating the product line and technology base, and growing sales to more than $17 billion. Mulcahy became the first woman selected by her peers to receive *Chief Executive* magazine's "CEO of the Year" award, which she promptly declared to "represent the impressive accomplishments of Xerox people around the world." Yet, of all Mulcahy's accomplishments, perhaps the most stunning was that she "had the courage to say 'no' to Wall Street."[1] Her advice for leaders navigating the current trying times? It might go something like this: Face reality; stay true to your values; focus on employees and clients; get your team aligned with a vision for renewal.

TURBULENT TIMES

As a new CEO in 2000, Anne Mulcahy certainly wasn't happy to have Xerox's stock price fall and its credit rating plummet, but she "thought it was far more credible to acknowledge that the company was broken" than to try to mask the truth.[2] Contrast her approach to that of Alan Schwartz, CEO of Bear Stearns, who told CNBC that the company's "liquidity and balance sheet are strong" just 36 hours before Bear Stearns sought emergency funding from the Federal Reserve to avoid bankruptcy and was sold to JPMorgan.[3] Mulcahy was practically ridiculed in the press in the early 2000s, but she had the courage and commitment to do what she believed was right, which included holding fast to the ethical values that had been part of what originally made Xerox a great company.

Being a real leader means learning who you are and what you stand for, and then having the courage to act. Leaders demonstrate confidence and commitment in what they believe and what they do. A deep devotion to a cause or a purpose larger than one's self sparks the courage to act, as it did for Anne Mulcahy. In addition, leadership has less to do with using other people than with serving other people. For example, Mulcahy suppressed her own fears and insecurities to give hope and strength to people who had become demoralized and hopeless. "She was leading by example," said one of Xerox's creditors. "Everybody at Xerox knew she was working hard, and that she was working hard for them."[4] Placing others ahead of oneself is a key to successful leadership, whether in politics, war, education, sports, social services, or business.

This chapter explores ideas related to courage and moral leadership. In the previous chapter, we discussed mind and heart, two of the three elements that come together for successful leadership. This chapter focuses on the third element, spirit—on the ability to look within, to contemplate the human condition, to think about what is right and wrong, to see what really matters in the world, and to have the courage to stand up for what is worthy and right. We begin by examining the situation in which most organizations currently operate, the dilemma leaders face in the modern world, and the kinds of behaviors that often contribute to an unethical organizational climate. Next we explore how leaders can act in a moral way, examine a model of personal moral development, and look at the importance of stewardship and servant leadership. The final sections of the chapter explore what courage means and how leaders develop the courage for moral leadership to flourish.

Moral Leadership Today

Every decade sees its share of political, social, and corporate villains, but the pervasiveness of ethical lapses in recent years has been astounding. In the political arena, Illinois Governor Rob Blagojevich resigned amid accusations of a wide-ranging corruption that included trying to sell the Senate seat vacated by President Barack Obama. Russia's telecom minister is on the hot seat over charges that he owns huge chunks of the industry he oversees, having surreptitiously converted telecom businesses from state ownership. In Britain, Parliament is embroiled in an explosive scandal related to politicians' expenses, with members of all parties allegedly finding myriad ways to bilk the system. U.S. military and intelligence organizations are dealing with the fallout from the Abu Ghraib prisoner abuse scandal and alleged torture of detainees at Guantanamo Bay.[5] And the names of once-revered corporations have become synonymous with greed, deceit, arrogance, or lack of moral conscience: AIG, Lehman Brothers, Enron, Bear Stearns, Countrywide, WorldCom. No wonder a recent poll found that 76 percent of Americans surveyed say corporate America's moral compass is "pointing in the wrong direction." Sixty-nine percent say executives rarely consider the public good in making decisions, and a whopping 94 percent say executives make decisions based primarily on a desire to advance their own careers.[6]

The Ethical Climate in U.S. Business

Unethical behavior can occur at all levels of organizations, but top leaders in particular are facing closer scrutiny because what goes on at the top sets the standard for the rest of the organization. In a study of *Fortune* 100 companies, fully 40 percent were found to have recently been engaged in activities that could be considered unethical.[7] Moreover, researchers concluded that the misdeeds in many cases could be traced to the failure of top executives to enforce and live up to ethical standards.

Unethical and illegal behavior can lead to serious consequences for organizations. For one thing, when employees lose trust in leaders, morale, commitment, and performance suffer. Customers who lose trust in the organization will bolt, as evidenced by the mass desertion of Arthur Andersen after the firm was found guilty of obstruction of justice for destroying tons of documents related to the Enron investigation. Investors may also withdraw their support from the company—or even file suit if they believe they've been lied to and cheated. For example, investors have filed a civil suit against Countrywide Financial's leaders, accusing them of dumping $848 million in stock in the 18 months prior to the company's sale to Bank of America. CEO Angelo Mozilo sold $474 million in stock during the same time period he was telling investors the market turmoil was a good opportunity for Countrywide.[8]

Leaders at all levels carry a tremendous responsibility for setting the ethical climate and can act as role models for others.[9] However, leaders face many pressures that challenge their ability to do the right thing. The most dangerous obstacles for leaders are personal weakness and self-interest rather than full-scale corruption.[10] Pressures to cut costs, increase profits, meet the demands of vendors or business partners, and look successful can all contribute to ethical lapses. During the boom years in the housing market, for example, many lenders, appraisers, builders, realtors, and investment firms simply got caught up in the belief that housing prices would continue to rise, and they pushed aside any concerns in the pursuit of profits. Or consider the dot-com bubble, when the practice of rewarding managers with stock options, originally intended to align the interests of managers with those of shareholders, caused basic human greed to get out of hand as managers tried to push their company's stock prices higher.[11] Leaders want their organizations to appear successful, and they can sometimes do the wrong thing just so they will look good to others. This is what happened to Bernard Ebbers, former CEO of WorldCom. Ebbers kept buying shares of WorldCom stock even as the company began to topple, and he ordered the issuing of false statements about the company's financial situation because he really thought he could turn things around and save his and the company's name.[12] The question for leaders is whether they can summon the fortitude to do the right thing despite outside pressures. "Life is lived on a slippery slope," says Harvard Business School's Richard Tedlow. "It takes a person of character to know what lines you don't cross."[13]

Action Memo

As a leader, you can put ethical values into action and set the example you want followers to live by. You can resist pressures to act unethically just to avoid criticism or achieve short-term gains.

What Leaders Do to Make Things Go Wrong

Leaders signal what matters through their behavior, and when leaders operate from principles of selfishness and greed, many employees come to see that type of behavior as okay. At the now-defunct Bear Stearns, for example, senior executives were openly arrogant and ambitious for personal successes, and they built a "sharp-elbowed, opportunistic culture" in which rules and basic standards of fairness and honor could be bent for the sake of achieving personal gain. One former Bear Stearns CEO said he "looked for managers with *PSD degrees*—poor, smart, with a deep desire to get rich."[14] Contrast his approach to hiring with that of Jamie Dimon, the CEO of JPMorgan Chase profiled in Chapter 1. Dimon says he has never, "not once," hired someone who wanted the job just for the money. "I wanted them to join because they wanted to build a great company over a long period of time," Dimon says.[15]

Action Memo

Go to Leader's Self-Insight 6.1 and complete the questions to learn your Mach score and how you might fit into a "me first" type environment.

Exhibit 6.1 compares unethical and ethical leadership by looking at 10 things leaders do that make things go wrong for the organization. The behaviors listed in column 1 contribute to an organizational climate ripe for ethical and legal abuses. Column 2 lists the opposite behaviors, which contribute to a climate of trust, fairness, and doing the right thing.[16]

Some executives are preoccupied with their own importance and take every opportunity to feed their greed or nourish their egos. They focus on having a huge salary, a big office, and other symbols of status rather than on what is good for the organization. These leaders typically pay more attention to gaining benefits for themselves rather than for the company or the larger society. Top leaders at AIG spent $400,000 on a corporate retreat at a lavish California beach resort just weeks after receiving an $85 billion rescue loan from the U.S. government. At Washington Mutual, the process of setting executive bonuses was revised so that steep losses related to the housing crisis wouldn't affect top leaders' pay. In the United Kingdom, fund manager Invesco Perpetual was sharply criticized for taking brokers clay pigeon shooting during the time the firms' clients were losing billions.[17] Executives who expect big salaries, bonuses, and perks at the same time the company is struggling, clients and customers are hurting, and employees are losing their jobs are not likely to create an environment of trust and integrity.

Also shown in Exhibit 6.1, unethical leaders may be dishonest with employees, partners, customers, vendors, and shareholders, and they regularly fail to honor their agreements or commitments to others. In a *USA Today* survey some years ago, 82 percent of CEOs said they lied about their golf scores. Sure, it's a small thing, but little by little, dishonesty can become a way of life and business.[18] Unethical leaders frequently treat people unfairly, perhaps by giving special favors

Exhibit 6.1 Comparing Unethical versus Ethical Leadership

The Unethical Leader	The Ethical Leader
Is arrogant and self-serving	Possesses humility
Excessively promotes self-interest	Maintains concern for the greater good
Practices deception	Is honest and straightforward
Breaches agreements	Fulfills commitments
Deals unfairly	Strives for fairness
Shifts blame to others	Takes responsibility
Diminishes others' dignity	Shows respect for each individual
Neglects follower development	Encourages and develops others
Withholds help and support	Serves others
Lacks courage to confront unjust acts	Shows courage to stand up for what is right

Source: Based on Donald G. Zauderer, "Integrity: An Essential Executive Quality," *Business Forum* (Fall 1992), pp. 12–16.

Leader's Self-Insight 6.1

What's Your Mach?

Leaders differ in how they view human nature and the tactics they use to get things done through others. Answer the following questions based on how you view others. Think carefully about each question and be honest about what you feel inside. Please answer whether each item below is Mostly False or Mostly True for you.

	Mostly False	Mostly True
1. Overall, it is better to be humble and honest than to be successful and dishonest.	_____	_____
2. If you trust someone completely, you are asking for trouble.	_____	_____
3. A leader should take action only when it is morally right.		
4. A good way to handle people is to tell them what they like to hear.	_____	_____
5. There is no excuse for telling a white lie to someone.	_____	_____
6. It makes sense to flatter important people.	_____	_____
7. Most people who get ahead as leaders have led very moral lives.	_____	_____
8. It is better to not tell people the real reason you did something unless it benefits you to do so.	_____	_____

	Mostly False	Mostly True
9. The vast majority of people are brave, good, and kind.	_____	_____
10. It is hard to get to the top without sometimes cutting corners.	_____	_____

Scoring and Interpretation

To compute your Mach score, give yourself one point for each Mostly False answer to items 1, 3, 5, 7, and 9, and one point for each Mostly True answer to items 2, 4, 6, 8, and 10. These items were drawn from the works of Niccolo Machiavelli, an Italian political philosopher who wrote *The Prince* in 1513 to describe how a prince can retain control of his kingdom. From 8–10 points suggests a high Machiavellian score. From 4–7 points indicates a moderate score, and 0–3 points would indicate a low "Mach" score. Successful political intrigue at the time of Machiavelli was believed to require behaviors that today would be considered ego centered and manipulative, which is almost the opposite of ethical leadership. A high Mach score today does not mean a sinister or vicious person, but probably means the person has a cool detachment, sees life as a game, and is not personally engaged with people. Discuss your results with other students, and talk about whether politicians in local or federal government, or top executives in a company like Bear Stearns, would likely have a high or a low Mach score.

Source: Adapted from R. Christie and F. L. Geis, *Studies in Machiavellianism* (New York: Academic Press, 1970).

marble: © Kirill Matkov   sunset: © Marco Regalia

or privileges to followers who flatter their egos or by promoting people based on favoritism rather than concrete business results.

Unethical leaders tend to take all the credit for successes, but they blame others when things go wrong. By taking credit for followers' accomplishments, failing to allow others to have meaningful participation in decision making, and generally treating people with discourtesy and disrespect, they diminish the dignity of others. They see followers as a means to an end, and they show little concern for treating people as individuals or helping followers develop their potential. Unethical leaders focus on their own needs and goals, whereas ethical leaders serve others.

Finally, one of the primary ways leaders contribute to an unethical and potentially corrupt organization is by failing to speak up against acts they believe are wrong. A leader who holds his tongue in order to "fit in with the guys" when colleagues are telling sexually offensive jokes is essentially giving his support for that type of behavior. If a leader knows someone is being treated unfairly by a colleague and does nothing, the leader is setting a precedent for others to behave unfairly as well. Peers and subordinates with lax ethical standards feel free to act as they choose. It is often hard to stand up for what is right, but this is a primary way in which leaders create an environment of integrity.

Acting Like a Moral Leader

When leaders forget that business is about *values* and not just economic performance, organizations and the broader society suffer. Top leaders in companies that get into trouble typically make quarterly earnings and the share price their primary purpose of business and the most important measure of individual and organizational success.[19] Moral leadership doesn't mean ignoring profit and loss, share price, production costs, and other hard measurable facts, but it does require recognizing and adhering to ethical values and acknowledging the importance of human meaning, quality, and higher purpose.[20] Henry Ford's century-old comment seems tailor-made for today's poor ethical climate: "For a long time people believed that the only purpose of industry was to make a profit. They are wrong. Its purpose is to serve the general welfare."[21]

Despite the corporate realities of greed, competition, and the drive to achieve goals and profits, leaders can act based on ethical standards and encourage others to develop and use ethical values in the workplace. *The single most important factor in ethical decision making in organizations is whether leaders show a commitment to ethics in their talk and especially their behavior.*[22] Employees learn about the values that are important in the organization by watching leaders.

Exhibit 6.2 lists some specific ways leaders act to build an environment that allows and encourages people to behave ethically. Leaders create organizational systems and policies that support ethical behavior, such as creating open-door policies that encourage employees to talk about anything without fear, establishing clear ethics codes, rewarding ethical conduct, and showing zero tolerance for violations.

Action Memo

As a leader, you can drive fear out of the organization so that followers feel comfortable reporting problems or ethical abuses. You can establish clear ethics policies, reward ethical conduct, and show zero tolerance for violations.

Exhibit 6.2 How to Act Like a Moral Leader

1. Articulate and uphold high moral principles.
2. Focus on what is right for the organization as well as all the people involved.
3. Set the example you want others to live by.
4. Be honest with yourself and others.
5. Drive out fear and eliminate undiscussables.
6. Establish and communicate ethics policies.
7. Develop a backbone—show zero tolerance for ethical violations.
8. Reward ethical conduct.
9. Treat everyone with fairness, dignity, and respect, from the lowest to the highest level of the organization.
10. Do the right thing in both your private and professional life—even if no one is looking.

Sources: Based on Linda Klebe Treviño, Laura Pincus Hartman, and Michael Brown, "Moral Person and Moral Manager: How Executives Develop a Reputation for Ethical Leadership," *California Management Review* 42, no. 4 (Summer 2000), pp. 128–142; Christopher Hoenig, "Brave Hearts," *CIO* (November 1, 2000), pp. 72–74; and Patricia Wallington, "Honestly?!" *CIO* (March 15, 2003), pp. 41–42.

Exhibit 6.3 Trans World Entertainment Corporation Code of Ethics

General Statement of Policy

- Honesty and candor in our activities, including observance of the spirit, as well as the letter of the law;
- Avoidance of conflicts between personal interests and the interests of the Company, or even the appearance of such conflicts;
- Avoidance of Company payments to candidates running for government posts, or government officials;
- Compliance with generally accepted accounting principles and controls;
- Maintenance of our reputation and avoidance of activities which might reflect adversely on the Company; and
- Integrity in dealing with the Company's assets.

Source: Trans World Entertainment Corporation Code of Ethics. n.d. Retrieved February 7, 2007, from http://www.twec.com/corpsite/corporate/code.cfm.

After a series of scandals rocked aerospace giant Boeing, for instance, CEO Jim McNerney is trying to ingrain ethical behavior into the fabric of the organization. McNerney instituted new ethics training for employees worldwide and tied managers' compensation to ethical leadership.[23] Many companies have hired high-level chief compliance officers to police managers and employees.[24] Most companies have established codes of ethics to guide employee behavior, such as the clear, concise statement used by Trans World Entertainment, shown in Exhibit 6.3. Each of the key points in Trans World's general statement of policy is described in detail in the company's complete code of ethics. However, an ethics code alone is not enough. Most importantly, leaders articulate and uphold high ethical standards, and they behave morally even if they think no one is looking. If leaders cut corners or bend the rules when they think they won't get caught, they and their organizations will ultimately suffer the consequences.

Moreover, leaders realize that what they do in their personal lives carries over to the professional arena. Leaders are a model for the organization 24 hours a day, 7 days a week. Consider Mike Price, who was fired as the University of Alabama's football coach before he ever coached a game. While in Florida participating in a golf tournament, Price spent hundreds of dollars on drinks and tips for exotic dancers, spent the night with a woman other than his wife, and ran up a $1,000 room-service bill. The university administration fired Price as a clear signal that the "boys-will-be-boys" mindset in the athletic department would no longer be tolerated.[25] A visible leadership position entails the responsibility for conducting both one's personal and professional life in an ethical manner. Leaders build ethical organizations by demonstrating the importance of serving people and society, as well as winning football games, increasing business profits, or making more money for themselves. Consider the example of Warren Buffett, the legendary chairman of Berkshire Hathaway.

IN THE LEAD

Warren Buffett, Berkshire Hathaway

Berkshire Hathaway and Warren Buffett haven't escaped the fallout from the recent economic crisis. Buffett had his worst year in business in four decades, with his holding company reporting a 62 percent drop in net income. In his early 2009 letter to shareholders, Buffett accepted the blame for some of the decline but also pointed a finger at unnamed, unethical CEOs who have left the credit market and stock market in shambles. Despite the heavy losses, Berkshire still had about $25 billion of cash on hand and was shopping for bargains while share prices of many companies were sliding.

But what makes Buffett one of corporate America's best leaders is not his investing ability, but his moral leadership. The two are, in a sense, tied together. Buffett always looks at a company's "intrinsic business value" rather than just at the stock price. He is known for his commitment to sound ethics and transparency in disclosing mistakes or failures. At annual meetings, he and his partner answer shareholder questions for more than four hours. Although Wall Street pressures boards to fire CEOs who don't produce short-term results, Buffett has a long record of retaining the CEOs of his companies. As for bending the rules, his advice to employees of Salomon Brothers when it was embroiled in a scandal with the U.S. Treasury Department seems apt for today's climate: "You don't need to play outside the lines," Buffett said. "You can make a lot of money hitting the ball down the middle."

Buffett has indeed made a lot of money. And, in 2006, he stunned the world by giving most of his $40 billion fortune to charity, with the majority committed to the Bill and Melinda Gates Foundation, which funds programs in global health, education, and financial services for the poor. As for himself, Buffett lives a modest lifestyle. He lives in the same house he bought for $31,500 in 1956, drives an old car, and eats simple meals at inexpensive restaurants. "I do not want to live like a king," Buffett says. "I just love to invest."[26]

Individuals like Warren Buffett illustrate that leaders can run successful organizations based on ethical principles. He says his fondest hope is that Berkshire Hathaway will adhere to those principles long after he is gone.

There is some evidence that doing right by employees, customers, and the community, as well as by shareholders, is good business. For example, a study of the financial performance of large U.S. corporations considered "best corporate citizens" found that they enjoy both superior reputations and superior financial performance.[27] Similarly Governance Metrics International, an independent corporate governance ratings agency in New York, reports that the stocks of companies run on more selfless principles perform better than those run in a self-serving manner.[28]

Becoming a Moral Leader

Leadership is not merely a set of practices with no association with right or wrong. All leadership practices can be used for good or evil and thus have a moral dimension. Leaders choose whether to act from selfishness and greed to diminish others or to behave in ways that serve others and motivate people to expand their potential as employees and as human beings.[29] **Moral leadership** is about distinguishing right from wrong and doing right, seeking the just, the honest, the good, and the right conduct in achieving goals and fulfilling purpose. Leaders have great influence over others, and moral leadership gives life to others and enhances the lives of others. Immoral leadership takes away from others in order to enhance oneself.[30] Moral leadership uplifts people, enabling them to be better than they were without the leader.

Specific characteristics such as ego strength, self-confidence, and a sense of independence may enable leaders to behave morally in the face of opposition. Moreover, leaders can develop these characteristics through their own hard work. People have choices about whether to behave morally. Consider the following remembrance of Viktor Frankl, who was in one of the death camps in Nazi Germany.

Moral leadership
distinguishing right from wrong and doing right; seeking the just, honest, and good in the practice of leadership

We who lived in concentration camps can remember the men who walked through the huts comforting the others, giving away their last piece of bread. They may have been few in number, but they offer sufficient proof that everything can be taken from a man but one thing: the last of the human freedoms—to choose one's attitude in any given set of circumstances. To choose one's own way.

And there were always choices to make. Every day, every hour, offered the opportunity to make a decision, a decision which determined whether you would or would not submit to those powers which threatened to rob you of your very self, your inner freedom. . . .[31]

A leader's capacity to make moral choices is related to the individual's level of moral development.[32] Exhibit 6.4 shows a simplified illustration of one model of personal moral development. At the **preconventional level,** individuals are egocentric and concerned with receiving external rewards and avoiding punishments. They obey authority and follow rules to avoid detrimental personal consequences or satisfy immediate self-interests. The basic orientation toward the world is one of taking what one can get. Someone with this orientation in a leadership position would tend to be autocratic toward others and use the position for personal advancement.

At level two, the **conventional level,** people learn to conform to the expectations of good behavior as defined by colleagues, family, friends, and society. People at this level follow the rules, norms, and values in the corporate culture. If the rules are to not steal, cheat, make false promises, or violate regulatory laws, a person at this level will attempt to obey. People at the conventional level adhere to the norms of the larger social system. If the social system says it is okay to inflate bills to the government or make achieving the bottom line more important than honesty and integrity, they will usually go along with that norm also. Often, when organizations do something illegal, many managers and employees are simply going along with the system.[33]

At the **postconventional level,** sometimes called the *principled level,* leaders are guided by an internalized set of principles universally recognized as just and right. People at this level may even disobey rules or laws that violate these principles. These internalized values become more important than the expectations of other people in the organization or community. A leader at this level is visionary, empowering, and committed to serving others and a higher cause.

Preconventional level
the level of personal moral development in which individuals are egocentric and concerned with receiving external rewards and avoiding punishments

Conventional level
the level of personal moral development in which people learn to conform to the expectations of good behavior as defined by colleagues, family, friends, and society

Postconventional level
the level of personal moral development in which leaders are guided by an internalized set of principles universally recognized as right or wrong

Exhibit 6.4 Three Levels of Personal Moral Development

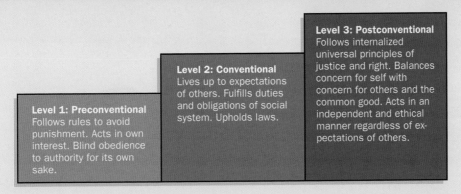

Level 1: Preconventional
Follows rules to avoid punishment. Acts in own interest. Blind obedience to authority for its own sake.

Level 2: Conventional
Lives up to expectations of others. Fulfills duties and obligations of social system. Upholds laws.

Level 3: Postconventional
Follows internalized universal principles of justice and right. Balances concern for self with concern for others and the common good. Acts in an independent and ethical manner regardless of expectations of others.

Sources: Based on Lawrence Kohlberg, "Moral Stages and Moralization: The Cognitive-Developmental Approach," in *Moral Development and Behavior: Theory, Research, and Social Issues,* ed. Thomas Likona (Austin, TX: Holt, Rinehart and Winston, 1976), pp. 31–53; and Jill W. Graham, "Leadership, Moral Development, and Citizenship Behavior," *Business Ethics Quarterly* 5, no. 1 (January 1995), pp. 43–54.

Most adults operate at level two of moral development, and some have not advanced beyond level one. Only about 20 percent of American adults reach the third, postconventional level of moral development, although most of us have the capacity to do so.[34] People at level three are able to act in an independent, ethical manner regardless of expectations from others inside or outside the organization, and despite the risk to their own reputation or safety. Impartially applying universal standards to resolve moral conflicts balances self-interest with a concern for others and for the common good. Research has consistently found a direct relationship between higher levels of moral development and more ethical behavior on the job, including less cheating, a tendency toward helpfulness to others, and the reporting of unethical or illegal acts, known as whistleblowing.[35]

Leaders can use an understanding of these stages to enhance their own and followers' moral development and to initiate training programs to move people to higher levels of moral reasoning. When leaders operate at level three of moral development, they focus on higher principles and encourage others to think for themselves and expand their understanding of moral issues.

Servant Leadership

What is a leader's moral responsibility toward followers? Is it to limit and control them to meet the needs of the organization? Is it to pay them a fair wage? Or is it to enable them to grow and create and expand themselves as human beings?

Much of the thinking about leadership today implies that moral leadership involves turning followers into leaders, thereby developing their potential rather than using a leadership position to control or limit people. The ultimate expression of this leadership approach is called *servant leadership,* which can best be understood by comparing it to other approaches. Exhibit 6.5 illustrates a continuum of leadership thinking and practice. Traditional

Exhibit 6.5 Changing Leader Focus from Self to Others

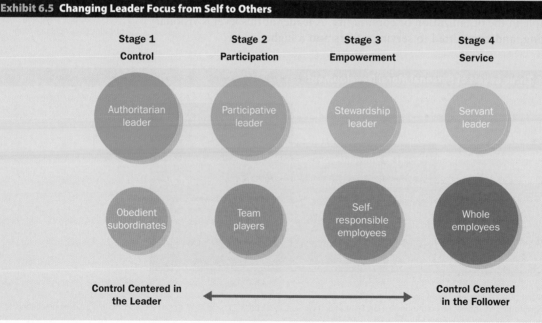

| Stage 1 Control | Stage 2 Participation | Stage 3 Empowerment | Stage 4 Service |

Authoritarian leader — Participative leader — Stewardship leader — Servant leader

Obedient subordinates — Team players — Self-responsible employees — Whole employees

Control Centered in the Leader ⟷ Control Centered in the Follower

organizations were based on the idea that the leader is in charge of subordinates and the success of the organization depends on leader control over followers. In the first stage, subordinates are passive—not expected to think for themselves but simply to do as they are told. Stage two in the continuum involves subordinates more actively in their own work. Stage three is stewardship, which represents a significant shift in mindset by moving responsibility and authority from leaders to followers.

Servant leadership represents a stage beyond stewardship, where leaders give up control and make a choice to serve employees. Along the continuum, the focus of leadership shifts from leader to followers. In the following sections, we discuss each stage of this leadership continuum in more detail.

Authoritarian Management

The traditional understanding of leadership is that leaders are good managers who direct and control their people. Followers are obedient subordinates who follow orders. In Chapter 2, we discussed the autocratic leader, who makes the decisions and announces them to subordinates. Power, purpose, and privilege reside with those at the top of the organization. At this stage, leaders set the strategy and goals, as well as the methods and rewards for attaining them. Organizational stability and efficiency are paramount, and followers are routinized and controlled along with machines and raw materials. Subordinates are given no voice in creating meaning and purpose for their work and no discretion as to how they perform their jobs. This leadership mindset emphasizes tight top–down control, employee standardization and specialization, and management by impersonal measurement and analysis.

Participative Management

Since the 1980s, many organizations have made efforts to actively involve employees. Leaders have increased employee participation through employee suggestion programs, participation groups, and quality circles. Teamwork has become an important part of how work is done in most organizations. Studies indicate that around 70 percent of the largest U.S. corporations have adopted some kind of employee participation program or shifted to a team design. However, many of these programs do not redistribute power and authority to lower-level workers.[36] The mindset is still paternalistic in that leaders determine purpose and goals, make final decisions, and decide rewards. Employees are expected to make suggestions for quality improvements, act as team players, and take greater responsibility for their own jobs, but they are not allowed to be true partners in the enterprise. Leaders are responsible for outcomes, and they may act as mentors and coaches. They have given up some of their control, but they are still responsible for the morale, emotional well-being, and performance of subordinates, which can lead to treating followers as if they are not able to think for themselves.[37]

Stewardship

Stewardship is a pivotal shift in leadership thinking. Followers are empowered to make decisions, and they have control over how they do their own jobs. Leaders give followers the power to influence goals, systems, and structures and become leaders themselves. **Stewardship** supports the belief that leaders are deeply accountable to others as well as to the organization, without trying to control others, define meaning and purpose for others, or take care of others.[38] In fact, stewardship has been called an alternative to leadership because the spotlight is

Stewardship
a belief that leaders are deeply accountable to others as well as to the organization, without trying to control others, define meaning and purpose for others, or take care of others

on the people actually doing the work, making the product, providing the service, or working directly with the customer. Four principles provide the framework for stewardship.

1. *Reorient toward a partnership assumption.* Partnership can happen only when power and control shift away from formal leaders to core employees. Partners have a right to say "no" to one another. They are totally honest with one another, neither hiding information nor protecting the other from bad news. In addition, partners (leaders and followers) are jointly responsible for defining vision and purpose and jointly accountable for outcomes.

2. *Localize decisions and power to those closest to the work and the customer.* Decision-making power and the authority to act should reside right at the point where the work gets done. This means reintegrating the "managing" and the "doing" of work, so that everyone is doing some of the core work of the organization part of the time. Nobody gets paid simply to plan and manage the work of others.

3. *Recognize and reward the value of labor.* The reward systems tie everyone's fortunes to the success of the enterprise. Stewardship involves redistributing wealth by designing compensation so that core workers can make significant gains when they make exceptional contributions. Everyone earns his or her pay by delivering real value, and the organization pays everyone as much as possible.

4. *Expect core work teams to build the organization.* Teams of workers who make up the core of the organization or division define goals, maintain controls, create a nurturing environment, and organize and reorganize themselves to respond to a changing environment and the marketplace they serve.

Action Memo

As a leader, you can apply the principles of stewardship and treat followers as true partners by sharing power and authority for setting goals, making decisions, and maintaining control over their own work and performance.

Stewardship leaders guide the organization without dominating it and facilitate followers without controlling them. Stewardship allows for a relationship between leaders and followers in which each makes significant, self-responsible contributions to organizational success. In addition, it gives followers a chance to use their minds, bodies, and spirits on the job, thereby allowing them to be whole human beings.

The Servant Leader

Servant leadership takes stewardship assumptions about leaders and followers one step further. Robert Wood Johnson, who built Johnson & Johnson from a small private company into one of the world's greatest corporations, summarized his ideas about management in the expression "to serve." In a statement called "Our Management Philosophy," Johnson went on to say, "It is the duty of the leader to be a servant to those responsible to him."[39] Johnson died decades ago, but his beliefs about the moral responsibility of a leader are as fresh and compelling (and perhaps as controversial) today as they were when he wrote them.

Servant leadership is leadership upside-down. Servant leaders transcend self-interest to serve the needs of others, help others grow and develop, and provide opportunity for others to gain materially and emotionally. In organizations, these leaders' top priority is service to employees, customers, shareholders, and

Servant leadership
leadership in which the leader transcends self-interest to serve the needs of others, help others grow, and provide opportunities for others to gain materially and emotionally

the general public. In their minds, the purpose of their existence is to serve; leadership flows out of the act of service because it enables other people to grow and become all they are capable of being.[40] Ari Weinzweig and Paul Saginaw, cofounders of Zingerman's Community of Businesses, built their $30 million food, restaurant, and training company based on servant leadership principles.

IN THE LEAD

Ari Weinzweig and Paul Saginaw, Zingerman's Community of Businesses

Ari Weinzweig and Paul Saginaw started a small delicatessen in Ann Arbor, Michigan, because they wanted to serve the best sandwiches in the world. The deli was a rousing success and was written about enthusiastically in *The New York Times*, *Esquire*, *Bon Appetit*, and many other publications. But after a decade or so, the partners noticed a problem. Business was still strong, but the deli no longer offered challenges and opportunities for growth to employees. When one manager with an MBA decided to start her own bakery to supply breads and pastries for the deli, Weinzweig and Saginaw had an idea—why not let employees start a whole community of small businesses, each with the Zingerman's name but each having its own identity, with the founding employee as an owner of the business. Thus was born Zingerman's Community of Businesses, which by 2007 consisted of 545 employees working in eight separate businesses, including a bakery, restaurant, coffee-roasting company, and catering business.

A desire to give people opportunities to grow is only one aspect of Weinzweig and Saginaw's servant leadership orientation. The two believe that the higher you rise in an organization, the harder you have to work for other people. They treat employees like customers and, within reason, do their bidding. When they visit the businesses, the partners are constantly asking employees, *What can I do for you?* "Sometimes I'm the note-taker. . . . Sometimes I'm on my hands and knees wiping up what people spilled," says Weinzweig.

The third aspect of being a servant leader for the partners is always putting the good of the organization and its people above personal goals and desires. Mutual trust, integrity, and respect are the values on which Zingerman's operates. Profit is not a motivator for the partners. "We've had dozens and dozens of opportunities to franchise, sell the name, take the check, and walk away," said Saginaw. Instead, as Weinzweig puts it, their goal is "to leave our world better than it was when we came here."[41]

Ari Weinzweig and Paul Saginaw illustrate that good leadership is more about serving others than taking care of oneself. Leaders in other organizations appreciate this as well. When Robert Townsend took over as head of the investment department at American Express, for example, he made it his mission to stay out of his employees' way and invest his time and energy in getting them the pay, titles, and recognition they deserved from the organization.[42] At the age of 74, Gerald Grinstein, former CEO of Delta Airlines, joined front-line employees in deep cleaning planes, scrubbing seats and carpets on his hands and knees. And IBM has incorporated service into its new leadership development program for high-potential employees. Through the Corporate Service Corps, specially selected teams of IBM employees will work with small businesses and nonprofit organizations in places like Ghana, Tanzania, Romania, and Turkey.[43] There has been an explosion of interest in the concept of leader as servant in recent years because of the emphasis in organizations on empowerment, participation, shared authority, and building a community of trust.[44]

Action Memo

As a leader, you can put the needs, interests, and goals of others above your own and use your personal gifts to help others achieve their potential. Complete the questionnaire in Leader's Self-Insight 6.2 to evaluate your leadership approach along the dimensions of authoritarian leadership, participative leadership, stewardship, and servant leadership.

Servant leadership was first described by Robert Greenleaf in his book, *Servant Leadership*. Greenleaf began developing his ideas after reading Hermann Hesse's novel, *Journey to the East*. The central character of the story is Leo, who appears as a servant to a group of men on a journey. Leo performs the lowliest, most menial tasks to serve the group, and he also cheers them with his good spirits and his singing. All goes well until Leo disappears, and then the journey falls into disarray. Years later, when the narrator is taken to the headquarters of the Order that had sponsored the original journey, he encounters Leo again. There, he discovers that Leo is in fact the titular head of the Order, a great leader.[45] Hesse's fictional character is the epitome of the servant leader, and some doubt whether real human beings functioning in the real world of organizations can ever achieve Leo's level of selflessness in service to others. However, as illustrated by the earlier examples, organizational leaders have shown that it is possible to operate from the principles of servant leadership, even in the business world.

There are four basic precepts in Greenleaf's servant leadership model:[46]

1. *Put service before self-interest.* Servant leaders make a conscious choice to use their gifts in the cause of change and growth for other individuals and for the organization. The desire to help others takes precedence over the desire to achieve a formal leadership position or to attain power and control over others. The servant leader calls for doing what is good and right for others, even if it does not "pay off" financially. In this view, the organization exists as much to provide meaningful work to the person as the person exists to perform work for the organization.

2. *Listen first to affirm others.* One of the servant leader's greatest gifts to others is listening, fully understanding the problems others face, and affirming his or her confidence in others. Servant leaders try to figure out the will of the group and then further it however they can. They don't impose their will on others. By understanding others, the servant leader can contribute to the best course of action.

3. *Inspire trust by being trustworthy.* Servant leaders build trust by doing what they say they will do, being honest with others, giving up control, and focusing on the well-being of others. They share all information, good and bad, and they make decisions to further the good of the group rather than their own interests. In addition, trust grows from trusting others to make their own decisions. Servant leaders gain trust because they give everything away—power, control, rewards, information, and recognition.

4. *Nourish others and help them become whole.* Servant leaders care about followers' spirits as well as their minds and bodies, and they believe in the unique potential of each person to have a positive impact on the world. A servant leader works to help others find the power of the human spirit and accept their responsibilities. This requires an openness and willingness to share in the pain and difficulties of others. Being close to people also means leaders make themselves vulnerable to others and are willing to show their own pain and humanity.

Think about situations in which you were in a formal or informal leadership role in a group or organization. Imagine using your personal approach as a leader. To what extent does each of the following statements characterize your leadership? Please answer whether each item below is Mostly False or Mostly True for you.

	Mostly False	Mostly True
1. My actions meet the needs of others before my own.	____	____
2. I explicitly enable others to feel ownership for their work.	____	____
3. I like to consult with people when making a decision.	____	____
4. I'm a perfectionist.	____	____
5. I like to be of service to others.	____	____
6. I try to learn the needs and perspectives of others.	____	____
7. I consciously utilize the skills and talents of others.	____	____
8. I am assertive about the right way to do things.	____	____
9. I give away credit and recognition to others.	____	____
10. I believe that others have good intentions.	____	____
11. I quickly inform others of developments that affect their work.	____	____
12. I tend to automatically take charge.	____	____
13. I encourage the growth of others, expecting nothing in return.	____	____
14. I value cooperation over competition as a way to energize people.	____	____
15. I involve others in planning and goal setting.	____	____
16. I put people under pressure when needed.	____	____

Scoring and Interpretation

There are four subscale scores that represent four dimensions of leadership. For the dimension of authoritarian leadership, give yourself one point for each Mostly True response to questions 4, 8, 12, and 16. For the dimension of participative leadership, give yourself one point for each Mostly True response to questions 2, 6, 10, and 14. For the dimension of stewardship, give yourself one point for each Mostly True response to questions 3, 7, 11, and 15. For the dimension of servant leadership, give yourself one point for each Mostly True response to questions 1, 5, 9, and 13.

My leadership scores are:

Authoritarian: _____
Participative: _____
Stewardship: _____
Servant: _____

These scores represent the four aspects of leadership called authoritarian, participative, stewardship, and servant as described in the text and illustrated in Exhibit 6.5. A score of 3–4 on any of these dimensions would be considered above average, and a score of 0–1 is below average.

Compare your four scores to each other to understand your approach to stewardship and servant leadership. On which of the four dimensions would you like to have the highest score? The lowest? Study the specific questions on which you scored Mostly True or Mostly False to analyze your pattern of strengths and weaknesses. It is not possible to display all four dimensions of leadership simultaneously, so you should think about the dimension you want to emphasize to reflect your leader ideal.

marble: © Kirill Matkov   sunset: © Marco Regalia

Servant leadership can mean something as simple as encouraging others in their personal development and helping them understand the larger purpose in their work. ServiceMaster, which cleans and maintains hospitals, schools, and other buildings, provides a good example. Leaders care how employees feel about themselves, about their work, and about the people they interact with.

They instill a sense of dignity, responsibility, and meaningfulness in menial tasks like scrubbing floors and cleaning toilets. One employee who works in a hospital, for example, says she sees herself as part of a team that helps sick people get well.[47]

Leadership Courage

Serving others and doing the right thing is not always easy. Leaders sometimes have to reach deep within themselves to find the strength and courage to resist temptations or to stand up for moral principles when others may ridicule them or when they may suffer financially or emotionally for their actions.

Some would say that without courage, leadership cannot exist. However, for many leaders, particularly those working in large organizations, the importance of courage is easily obscured—the main thing is to get along, fit in, and do whatever brings promotions and pay raises. In a world of stability and abundance, leaders can often forget even the *meaning* of courage, so how can they know where to find it when they need it? In the following sections, we examine the nature of leadership courage and discuss some ways courage is expressed in organizations. The final section of the chapter explores the sources of leadership courage.

What Is Courage?

Many people know intuitively that courage can carry you through deprivation, ridicule, and rejection and enable you to achieve something about which you care deeply. Courage is both a moral and a practical matter for leaders. A lack of courage is what allows greed and self-interest to overcome concern for the

Consider **This!**
Is It Worth the Risk?

To *laugh* . . . is to risk appearing the fool.

To *weep* . . . is to risk appearing sentimental.

To *reach out* . . . is to risk involvement.

To *expose feelings* . . . is to risk exposing your true self.

To *place your ideas and dreams before a crowd* . . . is to risk rejection.

To *love* . . . is to risk not being loved in return.

To *live* . . . is to risk dying.

To *hope* . . . is to risk despair.

To *try* . . . is to risk failure.

But risks must be taken, because the greatest hazard in life is to risk nothing. Those who risk nothing do nothing and have nothing.

They may avoid suffering and sorrow, but they cannot learn, feel, change, grow, or love.

Chained by their certitude, they are slaves; they have forfeited their freedom.

Only one who risks is free.

© Janet Rand

common good.[48] The courage to take risks has always been important for living a full, rewarding life, as discussed in the *Consider This* box. Yet the courage to resist jumping on the bandwagon and taking unnecessary or unethical risks is equally important. For today's organizations, things are constantly changing, and leaders thrive by solving problems through trial and error. They create the future by moving forward in the face of uncertainty, by taking chances, by acting with courage.[49] The defining characteristic of **courage** is the ability to step forward through fear. Courage doesn't mean the absence of doubt or fear, but the ability to act in spite of them. As U.S. Senator John McCain puts it, "Fear is the opportunity for courage, not proof of cowardice."[50]

In fact, if there were no fear or doubt, courage would not be needed. People experience all kinds of fears, including fear of death, mistakes, failure, embarrassment, change, loss of control, loneliness, pain, uncertainty, abuse, rejection, success, and public speaking. It is natural and right for people to feel fear when real risk is involved, whether the risk be losing your life, losing your job, losing the acceptance of peers, or losing your reputation. Consider that Charles Darwin put off publishing his *Origin of Species* for two decades because he feared public scorn and ridicule from his peers.[51] But many fears are learned and prevent people from doing what they want. True leaders step through these learned fears to accept responsibility, take risks, make changes, speak their minds, and fight for what they believe.

Courage Means Accepting Responsibility Leaders make a real difference in the world when they are willing to step up and take personal responsibility. Some people just let life happen to them; leaders make things happen. Courageous leaders create opportunities to make a difference in their organizations and communities. One societal example is Barbara Johns, an ordinary 16-year-old who made an extraordinary difference during the Civil Rights movement in the South. Johns led students of her segregated high school on a 2-week strike after a bus full of white students refused to pick her up. The NAACP stepped in and helped the young people sue for an integrated school. The Johns family home was burned the same year. Other young people took a stand too, with some children as young as grade school being jailed for protesting the segregation of lunch counters, community centers, or sports leagues.[52]

Leaders also demonstrate courage by openly taking responsibility for their failures and mistakes, rather than avoiding blame or shifting it to others. The acceptance of responsibility in many of today's large organizations seems nonexistent. At Lehman Brothers, for instance, CEO Richard Fuld refused to admit mistakes as Lehman teetered on the brink of collapse. After the firm went bankrupt following a shocking $4 billion quarterly loss and the breakdown of buyout negotiations with Bank of America, Fuld blamed Lehman's failure on inaction on the part of government and a general loss of confidence in the financial markets. Testifying before a congressional committee, Fuld calmly stated that he took all "prudent and appropriate" measures to fulfill his fiduciary duties.[53]

Courage Often Means Nonconformity Leadership courage means going against the grain, breaking traditions, reducing boundaries, and initiating change. Leaders are willing to take risks for a larger, ethical purpose, and they encourage others to do so. Consider the following example from the U.S. military.

Courage
the ability to step forward through fear

IN THE LEAD

Colonel Sean McFarland and Captain Travis Patriquin, United States Army

The U.S. military's role in helping Iraq move from a country plagued by increasing violence to one with glimmers of hope is made up of the stories of mostly anonymous soldiers and officers working quietly, courageously, and unconventionally day by day. One of those stories is that of Capt. Travis Patriquin and his boss, Col. Sean McFarland. When McFarland's brigade was sent to Ramadi, he was given broad guidance for calming the intense violence there.

Realizing that U.S. rules and conventional approaches don't work in Iraq, McFarland and Patriquin, who spoke Arabic, began negotiations with local Sunni sheiks, some of whom had mixed loyalties in the war. The strategy involved moving troops off of big remote bases directly into Ramadi's most dangerous neighborhoods, as well as finding ways to give the sheiks what they wanted. Superiors were wary and some openly opposed the tactic, but McFarland and Patriquin forged ahead, courting local sheiks "over cigarettes and endless cups of tea." The end result of long, complex negotiations was an alliance between more than 50 tribal sheiks and U.S. forces to fight al Qaeda in Iraq. Since McFarland's brigade left Ramadi, an additional 150 or so sheiks have joined in the alliance.

McFarland said he was willing to try just about anything to win over the population to help reduce the violence. "The prize in the counterinsurgency fight is not terrain," says McFarland. "It's the people. When you've secured the people, you have won the war. The sheiks lead the people."[54]

Despite the skepticism of senior officers, McFarland and Patriquin (as well as the tribal sheiks) had the courage to take unconventional steps to lessen the violence in Iraq. Patriquin was later killed by a roadside bomb. Sheik Sattar Al-Risha named a police station in Ramadi for him. Less than a year later, Sheik Sattar was also killed. However, the peace the two men had courageously helped bring to Ramadi held.[55]

Going against the status quo can be difficult. It's often easier to stay with what is familiar, even if it will lead to certain failure, than to initiate bold change. A naval aviator once said that many pilots die because they choose to stay with disabled aircraft, preferring the familiarity of the cockpit to the unfamiliarity of the parachute.[56] Similarly, many leaders hurt their organizations and their own careers by sticking with the status quo rather than facing the difficulty of change. Most leaders initiating change find some cooperation and support, but they also encounter resistance, rejection, loneliness, and even ridicule. Taking chances means making mistakes, enduring mockery or scorn, being outvoted by others, and sometimes failing miserably.

> ### Action Memo
>
> As a leader, you can develop the backbone to accept personal responsibility for achieving desired outcomes, going against the status quo, and standing up for what you believe. You can learn to push beyond your comfort zone and break through the fear that limits you.

Courage Means Pushing Beyond the Comfort Zone To take a chance and improve things means leaders have to push beyond their comfort zone. When people go beyond the comfort zone, they encounter an internal "wall of fear." A social experiment from 30 years ago illustrates the wall of fear that rises when people push beyond their comfort zone. To explore the web of unwritten rules that govern people's behavior on New York City subways, Dr. Stanley Milgram asked his first-year graduate students to board a crowded train and ask someone for a seat. Milgram's focus of interest soon shifted to the students themselves, as the

Leader's Self-Insight 6.3

Assess Your Moral Courage

Think about situations in which you either assumed or were given a leadership role in a group or organization. Imagine using your own courage as a leader. To what extent does each of the following statements characterize your leadership? Please answer whether each item below is Mostly False or Mostly True for you.

	Mostly False	Mostly True
1. I risk substantial personal loss to achieve the vision.	_____	_____
2. I take personal risks to defend my beliefs.	_____	_____
3. I say no even if I have a lot to lose.	_____	_____
4. I consciously link my actions to higher values.	_____	_____
5. I don't hesitate to act against the opinions and approval of others.	_____	_____
6. I quickly tell people the truth, even when it is negative.	_____	_____
7. I feel relaxed most of the time.	_____	_____
8. I speak out against organizational injustice.	_____	_____
9. I stand up to people if they make offensive remarks.	_____	_____
10. I act according to my conscience even if it means I lose status and approval.	_____	_____

Scoring and Interpretation

Each question above pertains to some aspect of displaying courage in a leadership situation. Add up your points for Mostly True answers: _____. If you received a score of 7 or higher, you have real potential to act as a courageous leader. A score below 3 indicates that you avoid difficult issues or have not been in situations that challenge your moral leadership. Is your score consistent with your understanding of your own courage? Look at the individual questions for which you scored Mostly False or Mostly True and think about your specific strengths and weaknesses. Compare your score to that of other students. How might you increase your courage as a leader? Do you want to?

seemingly simple assignment proved to be extremely difficult, even traumatic. Most students found it decidedly uncomfortable to bluntly ask someone for a seat. One now says of the experiment: "I was afraid I was going to throw up."[57] People may encounter the internal wall of fear when about to ask someone for a date, confront the boss, break off a relationship, launch an expensive project, or change careers. Facing the internal wall of fear is when courage is needed most.

> **Action Memo**
>
> *Assess your level of leadership courage by completing the exercise in Leader's Self-Insight 6.3.*

Courage Means Asking for What You Want and Saying What You Think Leaders have to speak out to influence others. However, the desire to please others—especially the boss—can sometimes block the truth. Everyone wants approval, so it is difficult to say things when you think others will disagree or disapprove. Author and scholar Jerry Harvey tells a story of how members of his extended family in Texas decided to drive 40 miles to Abilene for dinner on a hot day when the car air conditioning did not work. They were all miserable. Talking about it afterward, each person admitted they had not wanted to go but went along to please the others. The **Abilene Paradox** is the name Harvey uses to describe the tendency of people to not voice their true thoughts because they want to please others.[58] Courage means speaking your mind even when you know others may disagree with you and may even deride you. Courage also

Abilene Paradox
the tendency of people to resist voicing their true thoughts or feelings in order to please others and avoid conflict

means asking for what you want and setting boundaries. It is the ability to say no to unreasonable demands from others, as well as the ability to ask for what you want to help achieve the vision.

Courage Means Fighting for What You Believe Courage means fighting for valued outcomes that benefit the whole. Leaders take risks, but they do so for a higher purpose. For example, Peter Rost, a physician formerly with Pfizer Inc., took a stand calling for legislation to allow the import of lower-priced medicines from Canada and elsewhere, a practice Pfizer and other U.S. drug companies strongly oppose. Rost took the career risk because he believed the legislation would benefit the large number of sick people in the United States who have trouble affording the medicines they need.[59] Taking risks that do not offer the possibility of valuable and ethical outcomes is at best foolish and at worst evil. Leaders at companies such as Lehman Brothers and Bear Stearns, for example, pushed risk to the limits, but they did so primarily for selfish reasons. Courage doesn't mean doing battle to destroy the weak, feed one's ego, or harm others. It means doing what you believe is right, even when this goes against the status quo and possibly opens you to failure and personal sacrifice.

How Does Courage Apply to Moral Leadership?

There are many people working in organizations who have the courage to be unconventional, to step up and take responsibility, to do what they believe is right, and to treat employees and customers as whole human beings who deserve respect. Balancing profit with people, self-interest with service, and control with stewardship requires individual moral courage.

Acting Like a Moral Leader Requires Personal Courage To practice moral leadership, leaders have to know themselves, understand their strengths and weaknesses, know what they stand for, and often be nonconformists. Honest self-analysis can be painful, and acknowledging one's limitations in order to recognize the superior abilities of others takes personal strength of character. In addition, moral leadership means building relationships, which requires listening, having significant personal experiences with others, and making yourself vulnerable—qualities that frighten many people. Yet, by getting close and doing what is best for others— sharing the good and the bad, the pain and anger as well as the success and the joy—leaders bring out the best qualities in others.[60]

An example of this in practice is when William Peace had to initiate a layoff as general manager of the Synthetic Fuels Division of Westinghouse. Peace had the courage to deliver the news about layoffs personally. He took some painful blows in the face-to-face meetings he held with the workers to be laid off, but he believed allowing people to vent their grief and anger at him and the situation was the moral thing to do. His action sent a message that leaders valued employees as human beings with feelings. Thus employees rededicated themselves to helping save the division.[61] For Peace, the courage to practice moral leadership by personally facing employees gained respect, renewed commitment, and higher performance, even though he suffered personally in the short run.

Opposing Unethical Conduct Requires Courage **Whistleblowing** means employee disclosure of illegal, immoral, or unethical practices in the organization.[62] One recent example comes from Japan, where Kiroku Akahane, a sales executive at Meat Hope, revealed that the company routinely mixed pork, mutton, and chicken in products it labeled as pure ground beef.[63] Akahane took the step even

Whistleblowing
employee disclosure of illegal, immoral, or unethical practices in the organization

though it meant he lost his job, became treated like an outcast in his community, and was even shunned by some relatives.

Whistleblowing has become widespread in recent years, but it is still highly risky for employees, who may lose their jobs, be ostracized by coworkers, or be transferred to undesirable positions. David Windhauser, the former controller of Trane, a heating and cooling company owned by American Standard, was fired after reporting that managers were fraudulently reporting expenses on financial statements.[64] Most whistleblowers realize they may suffer financially and emotionally, but they act courageously to do what they think is right.

Finding Personal Courage

How does a leader find the courage to step through fear and confusion, to act despite the risks involved? All of us have the potential to live and act courageously, if we can push through our own fears. Most of us have learned fears that limit our comfort zones and stand in the way of being our best and accomplishing our goals. We have been conditioned to follow the rules, to not rock the boat, to go along with things we feel are wrong so others will like and accept us. There are a number of ways leaders can unlock the courage within themselves, including committing to causes they believe in, connecting with others, harnessing anger, and developing their skills.

Action Memo

As a leader, you can find your personal courage by committing to something you deeply believe in. You can welcome potential failure as a means of growth and development and build bonds of caring and mutual support with family, friends, and colleagues to reduce fear.

Believe in a Higher Purpose   Courage comes easily when we fight for something we really believe in. Leaders who have a strong emotional commitment to a larger vision or purpose find the courage to step through fear. Kailash Satyarthi, head of the South Asian Coalition on Child Servitude, receives regular threats and two of his coworkers have been killed, but Satyarthi continues striving to free India's millions of children forced to work in bonded labor.[65] He doesn't risk his life just for the thrill of it. He does so for a cause he deeply believes in—the dignity of all human beings. In business organizations, too, courage depends on belief in a higher vision. Lawrence Fish, who retired as chairman, president, and CEO of Citizens Financial Group in 2009, built Citizens into a banking powerhouse, but he said, "If we just make money, we'll fail." Fish is known for his volunteer efforts and commitment to the community, and his unconventional approach to operating a bank efficiently but with heart. Throughout his career, Fish has experienced both tremendous success and downright failure, but he has maintained the courage to pursue a vision that business is as much about doing good in the world as it is about making money.[66]

Draw Strength from Others   Caring about others and having support from others is a potent source of courage in a topsy-turvy world. Leaders who genuinely care about the people they work with will take risks to help those people grow and succeed. Having the support of others is also a source of courage, and the best leaders aren't afraid to lean on others when they need to. People who feel alone in the world take fewer risks because they have more to lose.[67] Being part of an organizational team that is supportive and caring, or having a loving and supportive family at home, can reduce the fear of failure and help people take risks they otherwise wouldn't take. Consider the example of Daniel Lynch, CEO of ImClone. When he took over the top job, things were about as bad as they could get. Founder Sam Waksal had been hauled off in handcuffs for alleged insider trading, the financial state of the company was in a shambles, and the company's application for Food

Leader's Bookshelf

Courage Goes to Work: How to Build Backbones, Boost Performance, and Get Results

By Bill Treasurer

TURBULENT TIMES

Bill Treasurer, the author of *Courage Goes to Work*, grew up in a household where lessons about courage were treated as importantly as lessons about history or arithmetic. That gave him an early understanding of courage as a skill that is developed with practice and strengthened when it is used. The founder and chief encouragement officer at Giant Leap Consulting, Treasurer draws upon his experiences helping people and organizations be more courageous to give us all some tips in this book.

Three Types of Courage

"Courage is, most often, a behavioral response to a challenge," writes Treasurer. "As a manager, you have a responsibility, indeed an obligation, to activate the courage of those around you." To tap into and strengthen one's own courage and the courage of followers, leaders can understand three types of courage that are important in the workplace.

- **Try Courage.** This is the courage to take initiative, to "step up to the plate" rather than playing it safe. To help followers practice try courage skills, leaders help people build on their strengths, provide challenging assignments that require people to stretch themselves, encourage novel approaches and experimentation, accept mistakes, and reward persistence in the face of obstacles.

- **Trust Courage.** The second type of courage is the courage to trust and rely on others. Leaders trust others to gain trust in return. They give people the benefit of the doubt, and they give employees lots of latitude in how to accomplish their tasks. Leaders build trust courage by respecting followers, being honest but kind and courteous, and getting to know people on an emotional level. They can help followers practice trust courage by encouraging them to open up about their feelings, desires, dreams, and fears.

- **Tell Courage.** "I have come to believe that the TELL Courage bucket is the one most in need of filling," says Treasurer. When people are afraid to speak up about mistakes, voice contrary opinions, question their leaders, and point out wrongdoing, companies suffer, as many leaders have learned in recent years. Leaders build tell courage by encouraging people to speak up, genuinely listening to others, not taking things personally, avoiding blame and defensiveness, and, when appropriate, acting on what they are told.

Modeling Courage

"When your behaviors are directed by courageous impulses, you are operating out of your best and bravest self," writes Treasurer. "When other people witness your newfound behaviors . . . they gradually step into their own courage, too." To help others find and develop their courage means leaders must first find and develop their own.

Courage Goes to Work, by Bill Treasurer, is published by Berrett-Koehler.

marble: © Ioannis Drimilis   library: www.istockphoto.com/nikada

and Drug Administration (FDA) approval of a key cancer drug had just been rejected. Over a two-year period, Lynch led a remarkable turnaround by focusing on getting the financial house in order, restoring trust among employees, and getting approval for the new cancer drug. Lynch didn't hesitate to tell people he needed their help, and managers and employees rose to the challenge. According to chief financial officer Michael Howerton, the camaraderie that emerged as people struggled through the difficulties together gave them the courage to keep putting one foot in front of the other, no matter how bad things looked.[68]

Harness Frustration and Anger If you have ever been really angry about something, you know that it can cause you to forget about fear of failure, fear of embarrassment, or fear that others won't like you. In organizations, we can also see the power of frustration and anger. After he was paralyzed in a motorcycle accident, Glenn McIntyre got angry every time he stayed at a hotel. His anger and frustration over how poorly hotels served disabled guests gave him the courage to stop feeling sorry for himself and start a new business, Access Designs. The firm helps hotels such as Quality Suites and Renaissance Ramada redesign their space to be more usable for disabled travelers.[69]

Leaders can harness their anger to deal with difficult situations. When someone has to be fired for just cause, a supervisor may put if off until some incident makes her angry enough to step through the fear and act. Sometimes, outrage over a perceived injustice can give a mild-mannered person the courage to confront the boss head on.[70] In addition, getting mad at yourself may be the motivation to change. Anger, in moderate amounts, is a healthy emotion that provides energy to move forward. The challenge is to harness anger and use it appropriately.

Develop Your Skills Although harnessing frustration and anger can be useful for finding courage, "flying off the handle" is typically not beneficial for achieving positive outcomes. In most cases within organizations, finding courage is a deliberate act rather than an instantaneous response.[71] You can develop courage-type skill step-by-step, starting with courage in small situations to strengthen yourself for bigger challenges. Courageous leaders are not reckless and foolhardy; they typically are people who have developed the skills and resources they need to take a difficult stand or pursue a tough course of action. In addition, courageous leaders can develop courageous followers by modeling courage in their own behavior and by helping people practice courage, as described in this chapter's Leader's Bookshelf.

To behave courageously, leaders clarify their personal and organizational goals and know what steps need to be taken to achieve them. They weigh the importance of the issue at hand and the risks and benefits of taking action. For example, Lieutenant General Claudia J. Kennedy, the first female three-star general in the U.S. Army, went through a rigorous risk–benefit analysis before reporting a fellow officer who had plagiarized a research paper at an army school. She didn't want to be seen as a "snitch," and she didn't want to hurt a colleague, but she felt a strong allegiance to the Army's high standards. In the end, Kennedy decided that her personal integrity and her loyalty to the Army's standards were most important, and she discreetly reported the misdeed.[72] Courage can be thought of as a decision-making skill that is developed through conscious thought and practice.

Leadership Essentials

- This chapter explored a number of ideas concerning moral leadership and leadership courage. People want honest and trustworthy leaders. However, the ethical climate in many organizations is at a low point. Leaders face pressures that challenge their ability to do the right thing—pressures to cut costs, increase profits, meet the demands of various stakeholders, and look successful. Creating an ethical organization requires that leaders act based on moral principles.

- Leaders cause things to go wrong in the organization when they excessively promote self-interest, practice deception and breach agreements, and lack the courage to confront unjust acts. Ethical leaders are humble, honest, and straightforward. They maintain a concern for the greater good, strive for fairness, and demonstrate the courage to stand up for what is right. Acting as a moral leader means demonstrating the importance of serving people and society as well as increasing profits or personal gain.

■ One personal consideration for leaders is the level of moral development. Leaders use an understanding of the stages of moral development to enhance their own as well as followers' moral growth. Leaders who operate at higher stages of moral development focus on the needs of followers and universal moral principles.

■ Ideas about control versus service between leaders and followers are changing and expanding, reflected in a continuum of leader–follower relationships. The continuum varies from authoritarian managers to participative managers to stewardship to servant leadership. Leaders who operate from the principles of stewardship and servant leadership can help build ethical organizations.

■ The final sections of the chapter discussed leadership courage and how leaders can find their own courage. Courage means the ability to step forward through fear, to accept responsibility, to take risks and make changes, to speak your mind, and to fight for what you believe. Two expressions of courage in organizations are moral leadership and ethical whistleblowing. Sources of courage include belief in a higher purpose, connection with others, harnessing anger, and developing courage as a skill.

Discussion Questions

1. What are some pressures you face as a student that challenge your ability to do the right thing? Do you expect to face more or fewer pressures as a leader? Discuss what some of these pressures might be.

2. If most adults are at a conventional level of moral development, what does this mean for their potential for moral leadership?

3. Do you feel that the difference between authoritarian leadership and stewardship should be interpreted as a moral difference? Discuss.

4. If you were in a position similar to Kiroku Akahane at Meat Hope, what do you think you would do? Why?

5. Should serving others be placed at a higher moral level than serving oneself? Discuss.

6. If you find yourself avoiding a situation or activity, what can you do to find the courage to move forward? Explain.

7. If it is immoral to prevent those around you from growing to their fullest potential, are you being moral?

8. Leaders at AIG argued that they were obligated to pay bonuses to executives even after the company was bailed out by the U.S. government because of the company's contracts with these executives. Do you think this is a legitimate argument from an ethical standpoint? Discuss.

9. Do you agree that it is important for leaders to do the right thing even if no one will ever know about it? Why or why not?

10. A consultant recently argued that the emphasis on corporate governance and social responsibility has distracted leaders from key business issues such as serving customers and beating competitors. Do you agree? Should leaders put business issues first or ethical issues first?

Leadership at Work

SCARY PERSON

Think of a person in your life right now who is something of a scary person for you. Scary people are those you don't really know but who are scary to you because you anticipate that you won't like them, perhaps because you don't like the way they act or look from a distance, and hence you avoid building relationships with them. A scary person might be a student at school, someone at work, a neighbor, or someone you are aware of in your social circle.

Scary people trigger a small amount of fear in us—that is why we avoid them and don't really get to know them. A test of courage is whether you can step through your fear. You will experience fear many times as a leader.

For this exercise, your assignment is to reach out to one or more scary persons in your life. Invite the person for lunch or just walk up and introduce yourself and start a conversation. Perhaps you can volunteer to work with the person on an assignment. The key thing is to step through your fear and get to know this person well enough to know what he or she is really like.

After you have completed your assignment, share what happened with another person. Were you able to reach out to the scary person? What did you discover about the scary person? What did you discover about yourself by doing this activity? If you found the exercise silly and refused to do it, you may have let fear get the better of you by rationalizing that the assignment has little value.

In Class: The instructor can give this assignment to be done prior to a specific class. During class it is a good exercise for students to discuss their scary person experiences among themselves in small groups. The instructor can ask students to report to their groups about the scary person, revealing as many details as they are comfortable with, explaining how they summoned the courage to reach out, and the result. After the groups have finished their exchange, the instructor can ask a couple of student volunteers to report their experiences to the entire class. Then students can be asked questions such as: Looking back on this experience, what is courage? How was it expressed (or not) in this exercise? How will fear and courage be part of organizational leadership?

Chapter 7: Followership

© Vladimir Piskunov

Your Leadership Challenge

After reading this chapter, you should be able to:

- Recognize your followership style and take steps to become a more effective follower.

- Understand the leader's role in developing effective followers.

- Apply the principles of effective followership, including responsibility, service, challenging authority, participating in change, and knowing when to leave.

- Implement the strategies for effective followership at school or work.

- Know what followers want from leaders and what leaders expect from followers.

- Use feedback and leadership coaching to help followers grow and achieve their potential.

Chapter Outline

Irvin D. Yalom, a professor of psychiatry and author of the novels *Lying on the Couch* and *When Nietzsche Wept*, has some interesting stories from his counseling experience with clients in individual and group therapy. One woman ranted at length in a group therapy session about her boss, who never listened and refused to pay her any respect. There's nothing funny about a bad boss, but the interesting thing about this client was that as her work with Yalom continued, her complaints about her terrible boss persisted through three different jobs with three different supervisors.[1] It is likely that not only she but also her supervisors, colleagues, and the companies where she worked suffered due to her unproductive relationships with leaders.

Contrast this woman's attitude and approach to that of Marcia Reynolds, who once worked for a micromanaging boss who was always criticizing and correcting her work. Reynolds decided to stop resenting his micromanaging and instead "act as though he were the world's best boss with the world's best employee." Instead of complaining and pushing back when her boss micromanaged, Reynolds was cheerful and helpful. She says an interesting thing happened: "When I stopped resisting, he started trusting me. When there was no longer any resistance, he quit fighting. Doing that really empowered me." As her boss increasingly trusted Reynolds, his micromanaging continued to abate, their relationship continued to improve, and both were happier and more productive.[2]

Leadership and followership are closely intertwined. Effective followers can shape productive leader behavior just as effective leaders develop people into good followers. In this chapter, we examine the important role of followership, including the nature of the follower's role, the different styles of followership that individuals express, and how effective followers behave. The chapter explores how followers develop their personal potential to be more effective, looks at what leaders want from followers, and discusses strategies for managing up. Finally, we look at what followers want from leaders and examine the leader's role in developing effective followers through feedback and coaching.

The Role of Followers

Followership is important in the discussion of leadership for several reasons. Without followers there are no leaders. Organizing into hierarchies is a natural phenomenon in both the human and animal kingdoms. Researchers studying wolves, chimpanzees, and even chickens have long known that social pecking order promotes the welfare of the group because some individuals act as leaders and others as followers.[3] The same thing applies to humans. For any group or organization to succeed, there must be people who willingly and effectively follow just as there must be those who willingly and effectively lead. Leadership and followership are fundamental roles that individuals shift into and out of under various conditions. Everyone—leaders included—is a follower at one time or another. Indeed, most individuals, even those in positions of authority, have some kind of boss or supervisor. Individuals are more often followers than leaders.[4]

Second, recall that the definition of a leader from Chapter 1 referred to an influence relationship among leaders and followers. This means that in a position of leadership, an individual is influenced by the actions and the attitudes of followers. In fact, the contingency theories introduced in Chapter 3 are based on how leaders adjust their behavior to fit situations, especially their followers. Thus, the nature of leader–follower relationships involves reciprocity, the mutual exchange of influence.[5] The followers' influence upon a leader can enhance the leader or accentuate the leader's shortcomings, as illustrated in the opening examples.[6]

Third, many of the qualities that are desirable in a leader are the same qualities possessed by an effective follower. In addition to demonstrating initiative, independence, commitment to common goals, and courage, a follower can provide enthusiastic support of a leader, but not to the extent that the follower fails to challenge a leader who is unethical or threatens the values or objectives of the organization.[7] One corporate governance consultant, for example, points out that ineffective followers are as much to blame for ethical and legal lapses within organizations as are crooked leaders.[8] Followers have a responsibility to speak up when leaders do things wrong.

Both leader and follower roles are proactive; together they can achieve a shared vision. The military often provides insight into the interaction of leadership and followership. A performance study of U.S. Navy personnel found that the outstanding ships were those staffed by followers who supported their leaders but also took initiative and did not avoid raising issues or concerns with their superiors. Consider how West Point trains future military leaders by emphasizing the role of followership.

IN THE LEAD

U.S. Military Academy, West Point

At West Point, everyone leads and everyone follows. It's a 24-hour leadership laboratory where people learn that leadership and followership are two sides of the same whole.

An important lesson is that leaders are nothing without followers. "You learn from the beginning that you're not in a position of leadership because you're smarter or better," says cadet Joe Bagaglio. "As soon as you think you know it all, you get burned."

Each spring, West Point graduates nearly 1,000 men and women who leave with a bachelor's degree and a commission as second lieutenant in the United States Army. After a 6-week leave, these new graduates take their first jobs as military officers in places like Kosovo, Guam, Afghanistan, or Iraq. Most of us think of West Point as a place of rules, rigidity, structure, and conformity, and to a great extent, it is. Cadets learn to subordinate their self-interest for the good of the whole, because that's what they'll be called upon to do when they graduate. Cadets also learn to rely on the competencies of followers and their own judgment. They learn that everyone is part of the team and no one individual—no matter his or her rank—is more important than the mission of the whole. The entire community relies on this interdependence.

At West Point, every action is an opportunity to learn, to gain new experience, and to grow in understanding. Formal leaders are always pushing followers—and themselves—to get out of their comfort zone so that they expand their capacity for leadership. "Everyone's a teacher," says cadet Chris Kane, a platoon leader in Company C-2 at West Point. "That's what I love about this place. We're all teachers."[9]

In any organization, leaders can help develop effective followers, just as effective followers develop better leaders. The performance of followers, leaders, and the organization are variables that depend on one another.

Styles of Followership

Despite the importance of followership and the crucial role that followers play in the success of any endeavor, research on the topic is limited. One theory of followership was proposed by Robert E. Kelley, who conducted extensive interviews with leaders and followers and came up with five styles of followership.[10] These followership styles are categorized according to two dimensions, as illustrated in Exhibit 7.1. The first dimension is the quality of independent, **critical thinking** versus dependent, **uncritical thinking**. Critical thinking means approaching subjects, situations, and problems with thoughtful questions and in an unbiased way, gathering and assessing ideas and information objectively, and mentally penetrating into underlying implications of various alternatives. This recalls our discussion of mindfulness in Chapter 5; independent critical thinkers are mindful of the effects of their and other people's behavior on achieving organizational goals. They are aware of the significance of their own actions and the actions of others. They can weigh the impact of decisions on the vision set forth by a leader and offer constructive criticism, creativity, and innovation. Conversely, a dependent, uncritical thinker does not consider possibilities beyond what he or she is told, does not contribute to the cultivation of the organization, and accepts the leader's ideas without assessing or evaluating them.

According to Kelley, the second dimension of followership style is *active versus passive behavior*. An active individual participates fully in the organization, engages in behavior that is beyond the limits of the job, demonstrates a sense of ownership, and initiates problem solving and decision making. A passive individual is characterized by a need for constant supervision and prodding by superiors. Passivity is often regarded as laziness; a passive person does nothing that is not required and avoids added responsibility.

The extent to which one is active or passive and is a critical, independent thinker or a dependent, uncritical thinker determines whether he or she is an

Critical thinking
thinking independently and being mindful of the effects of one's own and other people's behavior on achieving the organization's vision

Uncritical thinking
failing to consider possibilities beyond what one is told; accepting the leader's ideas without thinking

Exhibit 7.1 Followership Styles

Independent, critical thinking

Alienated	Effective
Pragmatic Survivor	
Passive	Conformist

Passive ← → **Active**

Dependent, uncritical thinking

Source: Adapted from *The Power of Followership* by Robert E. Kelley, p. 97. Copyright © 1992 by Consultants to Executives and Organizations, Ltd. Used by permission of Doubleday, a division of Random House, Inc.

alienated follower, a passive follower, a conformist, a pragmatic survivor, or an effective follower, as shown in Exhibit 7.1.

The **alienated follower** is a passive, yet independent, critical thinker. Alienated followers are often effective followers who have experienced setbacks and obstacles, perhaps promises broken by superiors. Thus, they are capable, but they focus exclusively on the shortcomings of the organization and other people. Often cynical, alienated followers are able to think independently, but they do not participate in developing solutions to the problems or deficiencies they see. For example, Barry Paris spent more than 10 years writing on and off for the *Pittsburgh Post-Gazette,* where he was known for his bad attitude and lack of enthusiasm and teamwork. Eventually Paris realized that he wasted that time ruminating over what he perceived as the hypocrisy of journalistic objectivity. "I could never resign myself to it," says Paris. Thus, rather than doing his best and trying to help others maintain standards of integrity and objectivity, he allowed hostility and cynicism to permeate his work.[11]

The **conformist** participates actively in the organization but does not utilize critical thinking skills in his or her task behavior. In other words, a conformist typically carries out any and all orders regardless of the nature of those tasks. The conformist participates willingly, but without considering the consequences of what he or she is being asked to do—even at the risk of contributing to a harmful endeavor. For example, the thousands of people who can't pay their mortgages and are losing their homes can blame not only top managers in firms like Countrywide, Fannie Mae, and IndyMac Bank who embraced the rampant sale of subprime mortgages (sometimes called *liars' loans*), but also many conformist managers and employees who blindly went along with the strategy. A conformist is concerned only with avoiding conflict. This style often results from rigid rules and authoritarian environments in which leaders perceive subordinate recommendations as a challenge or threat.[12]

The **pragmatic survivor** has qualities of all four extremes—depending on which style fits with the prevalent situation. This type of follower uses whatever style best benefits his or her own position and minimizes risk. Within any given company, some 25 to 35 percent of followers tend to be pragmatic survivors,

Action Memo

Complete the questionnaire in Leader's Self-Insight 7.1 to evaluate how well you carry out a followership role.

Alienated follower
a person in the organization who is a passive, yet independent, critical thinker

Conformist
a follower who participates actively in the organization but does not utilize critical thinking skills in his or her task behavior

Pragmatic survivor
a follower who has qualities of all four extremes (alienated, effective, passive, conformist), depending on which style fits with the prevalent situation

Leader's Self-Insight 7.1

The Power of Followership

For each of the following statements, please answer whether each item is Mostly False or Mostly True for you. Think of a specific but typical followership situation and how you acted.

	Mostly False	Mostly True
1. Does your work help you fulfill some higher societal or personal goal that is important to you?	___	___
2. Are you highly committed to and energized by your work and organization, giving them your best ideas and performance?	___	___
3. Does your enthusiasm also spread to and energize your coworkers?	___	___
4. Instead of waiting for or merely accepting what the leader tells you, do you personally figure out the most critical activities for achieving the organization's priority goals?	___	___
5. Do you actively develop a distinctive competence in those critical activities so that you become more valuable to the leader and the organization?	___	___
6. When starting a new job or assignment, do you quickly build a record of successes in tasks that are important to the leader?	___	___
7. Do you take the initiative to seek out and successfully complete assignments that go above and beyond your job?	___	___
8. When you are not the leader of a group project, do you still contribute at a high level, often doing more than your share?	___	___
9. Do you independently think up and champion new ideas that will contribute significantly to the leader's or the organization's goals?	___	___
10. Do you try to solve the tough problems (technical or organizational), rather than look to the leader to do it?	___	___
11. Do you help out your coworkers, making them look good even when you do not get any credit?	___	___
12. Do you help the leader or group see both the upside potential and downside risks of ideas or plans, playing the devil's advocate if need be?	___	___

	Mostly False	Mostly True
13. Do you understand the leader's needs, goals, and constraints, and work hard to meet them?	___	___
14. Do you actively and honestly own up to your strengths and weaknesses rather than put off evaluation?	___	___
15. Do you act on your own ethical standards rather than the leader's or the group's standards?	___	___
16. Do you assert your views on important issues, even though it might mean conflict with your group or reprisals from the leader?	___	___

Scoring and Interpretation

Questions 1, 4, 9, 10, 12, 14, 15, and 16 measure "independent thinking." Sum the number of Mostly True answers checked and write your score below.

Questions 2, 3, 5, 6, 7, 8, 11, and 13 measure "active engagement." Sum the number of Mostly True answers checked and write your score below.

Independent Thinking Total Score = _____

Active Engagement Total Score = _____

These two scores indicate how you carry out your followership role. A score of 2 or below is considered low. A score of 6 or higher is considered high. A score of 3–5 is in the middle. Based on whether your score is high, middle, or low, assess your followership style below.

Followership Style	Independent Thinking Score	Active Engagement Score
Effective	High	High
Alienated	High	Low
Conformist	Low	High
Pragmatist	Middling	Middling
Passive	Low	Low

How do you feel about your followership style? Compare your style to others. What might you do to be more effective as a follower?

Source: From Robert E. Kelley, *The Power of Followership: How to Create Leaders People Want to Follow and Followers Who Lead Themselves,* pp. 89–97. Copyright © 1992 by Consultants to Executives and Organizations, Ltd. Used by permission of Doubleday, a division of Random House, Inc.

marble: © Kirill Markov   sunset: © Marco Regalia

avoiding risks and fostering the status quo, often for political reasons. Government appointees often demonstrate this followership style because they have their own agendas and a short period of time in which to implement them. They may appeal to the necessary individuals, who themselves have a limited time to accomplish goals and are therefore willing to do whatever is necessary to survive in the short run. Pragmatic survivors also may emerge when an organization is going through desperate times, and followers find themselves doing whatever is needed to get themselves through the difficulty.[13]

The **passive follower** exhibits neither critical, independent thinking nor active participation. Being passive and uncritical, these followers display neither initiative nor a sense of responsibility. Their activity is limited to what they are told to do, and they accomplish things only with a great deal of supervision. The assistant manager at one large hotel found herself having to supervise her boss's daughter, who failed to follow procedures, had to be told over and over when and how to perform tasks, and showed little interest in the job, reflecting the characteristics of a passive follower.[14] Passive followers leave the thinking to their leaders. Sometimes, however, this style is the result of a leader who expects and encourages passive behavior. Followers learn that to show initiative, accept responsibility, or think creatively is not rewarded, and may even be punished by the leader, so they grow increasingly passive. Passive followers are often the result of leaders who are overcontrolling of others and who punish mistakes.[15]

The **effective follower** is both a critical, independent thinker and active in the organization. Effective followers behave the same toward everyone, regardless of their positions in the organization. They do not try to avoid risk or conflict. Rather, effective followers have the courage to initiate change and put themselves at risk or in conflict with others, even their leaders, to serve the best interest of the organization.

Characterized by both mindfulness and a willingness to act, effective followers are essential for an organization to be effective. They are capable of self-management, they discern strengths and weaknesses in themselves and in the organization, they are committed to something bigger than themselves, and they work toward competency, solutions, and a positive impact. Dawn Marshall, a cashier at Pathmark, illustrates the characteristics of the effective follower.

IN THE LEAD

Dawn Marshall, Pathmark

Five hours into her shift, four harried customers line up at Dawn Marshall's cash register at the Pathmark supermarket in Upper Derby, Pennsylvania. Eight minutes and 27 bags later, they're all out the door with smiles on their faces. Few people would think Marshall has a glamorous or influential job—but she treats it like the most significant job in the world.

Marshall specializes in giving people a little bit of luxury in the mundane chore of grocery shopping. She's a good cashier, but her forte is bagging. Marshall knows how to pack the flimsy plastic bags so that eggs don't get broken, bread doesn't get squashed, and ground beef doesn't leak all over the cereal boxes. She even won a National Grocers Association contest as the best bagger in America, based on speed, bag-building technique, style, and attitude. "I believe it's an art that should be taken seriously," Marshall says of her work. Many Pathmark customers agree. They're tired of cashiers and baggers who simply throw the stuff in bags without giving a care for the customer's convenience or needs. One customer admits that she shops at Pathmark rather than a store closer to her home because of Marshall. "I like her attitude," says the customer. "Clone her."

Passive follower
a person in an organization who exhibits neither critical, independent thinking nor active participation

Effective follower
a critical, independent thinker who actively participates in the organization

> Even though Marshall works on her feet all day and often has to put up with rude or insensitive customers, she handles whatever comes her way with a positive attitude. For Marshall, her job is not bagging groceries, but making people's lives easier. Thus, she approaches her work with energy and enthusiasm, striving to do her best in every encounter. She doesn't need close supervision or someone pushing her to work harder. The busier it is, the better she likes it.[16]

Dawn Marshall has taken what some would consider a boring, low-paying job and imbued it with meaning and value. She accepts responsibility for her own personal fulfillment and finds ways to expand her potential and use her capacities to serve the needs of others and the organization. Effective followers like Dawn Marshall also act as leaders by setting an example and using a positive attitude to inspire and uplift other people.

Effective followers are far from powerless—and they know it. Therefore, they do not despair in their positions, nor do they resent or manipulate others. This chapter's *Consider This* provides highlights from a speech given by Nelson Mandela that explains his meaning of effective followership.

Action Memo

As a leader, you can also be an effective follower. You can think independently and critically instead of blindly accepting what your superiors tell you. Rather than dwelling on the shortcomings of others, you can look for solutions.

Demands on the Effective Follower

Effective followership is not always easy. The discussion of courage and integrity in Chapter 6 applies to followers as well as leaders. Indeed, followers sometimes experience an even greater need for these qualities because of their subordinate position. To be effective, followers have to know what they stand for and be willing to express their own ideas and opinions to their leaders, even though this might mean risking their jobs, being demeaned, or feeling inadequate.[17] Effective followers have the courage to accept responsibility, challenge authority, participate in change, serve the needs of the organization, and leave the organization when necessary.[18]

Consider **This!**
Our Deepest Fear

Our deepest fear is not that we are inadequate, Our deepest fear is that we are powerful beyond measure.

It is our light, not our darkness, that most frightens us.

We ask ourselves, who am I to be brilliant, gorgeous, talented and fabulous?

Actually, who are you NOT to be? You are a child of God.

Your playing small doesn't serve the world.

There's nothing enlightened about shrinking so that other people won't feel insecure around you.

We were born to make manifest the glory . . . that is within us.

It's not just in some of us; it's in everyone.

And as we let our own light shine, we unconsciously give other people permission to do the same.

As we are liberated from our own fear, our presence automatically liberates others.

Source: From the 1994 Inaugural Speech of Nelson Mandela.

© majaiva

The Courage to Assume Responsibility The effective follower feels a sense of personal responsibility and ownership in the organization and its mission. Thus, the follower assumes responsibility for his or her own behavior and its impact on the organization. Effective followers do not presume that a leader or an organization will provide them with security, permission to act, or personal growth. Instead, they initiate the opportunities through which they can achieve personal fulfillment, exercise their potential, and provide the organization with the fullest extent of their capabilities. Emiliana "Millie" Barela has been cleaning rooms for 32 years at Antlers at Vail, a Colorado ski lodge. She takes pride in her work and sees her job as an important part of creating a good experience for guests. Barela takes it upon herself to get to know guests and put their interests and needs first.[19]

Action Memo

As a follower, you can assume responsibility for your own personal development, behavior, and work performance. You can look for opportunities to make a difference, seek to meet organizational needs, serve others, and work toward the common good.

The Courage to Challenge Effective followers don't sacrifice their personal integrity or the good of the organization in order to maintain harmony. If a leader's actions and decisions contradict the best interests of the organization, effective followers take a stand. Obedience is considered a high virtue in military organizations, for example, but the U.S. Army teaches soldiers that they have a duty to disobey illegal or immoral orders.[20] Good leaders want followers who are willing to challenge them for the good of the organization. Rob Hummel, head of international postproduction at Dreamworks SKG, once promoted a manager who was known for being "difficult." Why? Because he knew this manager's willingness to speak truthfully to higher-ups was a strength to the organization.[21] Leaders are human and make mistakes. Effective leaders depend on followers who have the courage to challenge them.

Action Memo

As a follower, you can support your leaders through difficult times, but have the courage to challenge your superiors when their behavior or decisions contradict the best interests of the organization.

The Courage to Participate in Transformation Effective followers view the struggle of corporate change and transformation as a mutual experience shared by all members of the organization. When an organization undergoes a difficult transformation, effective followers support the leader and the organization. They are not afraid to confront the changes and work toward reshaping the organization. David Chislett, of Imperial Oil's Dartmouth, Nova Scotia refinery, was faced with this test of courage. The refinery was the least efficient in the industry and the board of directors gave management nine months to turn things around. Chislett's bosses asked him to give up his management position and return to the duties of a wage earner as part of an overall transformation strategy. He agreed to the request, thereby contributing to the success of the refinery's transformation.[22]

The Courage to Serve An effective follower discerns the needs of the organization and actively seeks to serve those needs. Just as leaders can serve others, as discussed in the previous chapter, so can followers. A follower can provide strength to the leader by supporting the leader and by contributing to the organization in areas that complement the leader's position. By displaying the will to serve others over themselves, followers act for the common mission of the organization with a passion that equals that of a leader. Timothy D. Cook, who is second in command at Apple, is known as an exceptional follower.

IN THE LEAD

Timothy D. Cook, Apple Inc.

As CEO of Apple, Steve Jobs provides the pizzazz for employees and the public alike. But it is Timothy Cook who makes sure things run smoothly behind the scenes. "He's the story behind the story," says one former Apple executive.

Cook was originally hired in 1998 as a senior vice president of operations and has made a steady climb up the ranks to now serve as chief operating officer and second-in-command. Cook counters the CEO's quick, unpredictable temper with his quiet, thoughtful manner. Jobs can concentrate on the big picture and ideas for snazzy new products because he knows Cook is taking care of the nuts and bolts of the business. Far from being a "yes-man," Cook has his own ideas about how things should be done, and industry insiders see his stamp on the company. Yet he is content to play "Spock" to Steve Jobs' "Captain Kirk," using his analytical and detail-oriented mind to offset Jobs' more intuitive, emotional approach. Like Spock supporting Captain Kirk, Cook doesn't hesitate to push Jobs' boundaries to help him, and the organization, become better. And just as Kirk never hesitated to beam down to a planet and leave Spock in charge, Jobs has confidently placed the company in the hands of Cook during his bouts of poor health in recent years.

For now, Cook is content to keep a low profile but have a high impact at Apple. Yet his contributions have caught the attention of other technology companies, and he is routinely solicited for CEO jobs. If Cook takes the step to top leader, he can hope to have a second-in-command who is as courageous in serving as he has been at Apple.[23]

The Courage to Leave Sometimes organizational or personal changes create a situation in which a follower must withdraw from a particular leader–follower relationship. People might know they need new challenges, for example, even though it is hard to leave a job where they have many friends and valued colleagues. If followers are faced with a leader or an organization unwilling to make necessary changes, it is time to take their support elsewhere. In addition, a follower and leader may have such strong differences of opinion that the follower can no longer support the leader's decisions and feels a moral obligation to leave. U.S. General John Batiste turned down a promotion and resigned because he felt he could no longer support civilian leaders' decisions regarding Iraq. The role of military officers is to advise civilian leaders and then carry out orders even when they disagree. Gen. Batiste spent weeks torn between his sense of duty and respect for the chain of command and a feeling that he owed it to his soldiers to speak out against leaders' decisions. Ultimately, believing he could no longer serve his leaders as he should, the general had the courage to leave the job, even though it meant the end of a lifelong career he highly valued.[24]

Developing Personal Potential

How do followers expand their potential to be critical, independent thinkers who make active contributions to their organizations? Later in this chapter, we will discuss the crucial role of leaders in developing effective followers. However, followers can expand their own capabilities by developing and applying personal leadership qualities in both their private and work lives. One well-known and widely acclaimed approach to helping people deal courageously with life's changes and challenges is Stephen Covey's *The Seven Habits of Highly Effective People*.[25] Covey defines a habit as the intersection of knowledge, skill, and desire.

His approach to personal and interpersonal effectiveness includes seven habits arranged along a maturity continuum, from dependence to independence to interdependence, as illustrated in Exhibit 7.2. Each habit builds on the previous one so that individuals grow further along the maturity continuum as they develop these personal effectiveness habits.

In organizations, many people fall into a mindset of dependency, expecting someone else to take care of everything and make all the decisions. The *dependent* person is comparable to the passive follower we described earlier, displaying neither initiative nor a sense of personal responsibility. Dependent people expect someone else to take care of them and blame others when things go wrong. An *independent* person, on the other hand, has developed a sense of self-worth and an attitude of self-reliance. Independent people accept personal responsibility and get what they want through their own actions. To be a truly effective follower—or a leader—requires a further step to *interdependence,* the realization that the best things happen by working cooperatively with others, that life and work are better when one experiences the richness of close interpersonal relationships.

Action Memo

As a leader or follower, you can expand your potential by consciously developing and applying leadership qualities in your personal and work life. You can move from dependence and passivity toward greater self-reliance and interdependence based on positive, productive relationships with others.

From Dependence to Independence

Covey's first three habits deal with self-reliance and self-mastery. Covey calls these *private victories* because they involve only the individual follower growing from dependence to independence, not the follower in relationship with others.[26]

Habit 1: Be Proactive® Being proactive means more than merely taking initiative; it means being responsible for your own life. Proactive people recognize that

---

Exhibit 7.2 The Maturity Continuum®

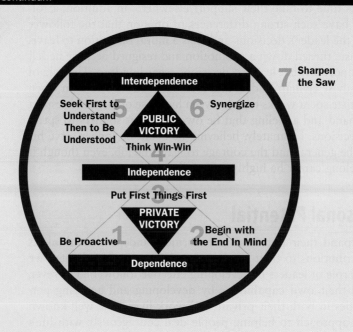

Source: © 1989 Franklin Covey Co. The Maturity Continuum is a registered trademark of Franklin Covey Co. All rights reserved. Reprinted with permission. *The 7 Habits of Highly Effective People* are registered trademarks of Franklin Covey Co. Used with permission.

they have the ability to choose and to act with integrity. They don't blame others or life's circumstances for their outcomes. Eleanor Roosevelt was talking about being proactive when she observed that, "No one can make you feel inferior without your consent."[27] Proactive people know that it is not what happens to them but how they respond to it that ultimately matters.

Habit 2: Begin with the End in Mind® This means to start with a clear mental image of your destination. For each individual, beginning with the end in mind means knowing what you want, what is deeply important to you, so that you can live each day in a way that contributes to your personal vision. In addition to clarifying goals and plans, this habit entails establishing guiding principles and values for achieving them.

Habit 3: Put First Things First® This habit encourages people to gain control of time and events by relating them to their goals and by managing themselves. It means that, rather than getting tangled up dealing with things, time, and activities, we should focus on preserving and enhancing *relationships* and on accomplishing *results*.

Effective Interdependence

The first three habits build a foundation of independence, from which one can move to interdependence—caring, productive relationships with others—which Covey calls *public victories*. Moving to effective interdependence involves open communication, effective teamwork, and building positive relationships based on trust, caring, and respect, topics that are discussed throughout this book. No matter what position you hold in the organization, when you move to interdependence, you step into a leadership role.

Habit 4: Think Win–Win® To think win–win means understanding that without cooperation, the organization cannot succeed. When followers understand this, they cooperate in ways that ensure their mutual success and allow everyone to come out a winner. Win–win is a frame of mind and heart that seeks agreements or solutions that are mutually beneficial and satisfying.

Habit 5: Seek First to Understand, Then to Be Understood® This principle is the key to effective communication. Many people don't listen with the intent to understand; they are too busy thinking about what they want to say. Seeking first to understand requires being nonjudgmental and able to empathize with the other person's situation. *Empathetic listening* gets inside another person's frame of reference so that you can better understand how that person feels. Chapter 9 discusses communication in detail.

Habit 6: Synergize® Synergy is the combined action that occurs when people work together to create new alternatives and solutions. In addition, the greatest opportunity for synergy occurs when people have different viewpoints, because the differences present new opportunities. The essence of synergy is to value and respect differences and take advantage of them to build on strengths and compensate for weaknesses.

Habit 7: Sharpen the Saw® This habit encompasses the previous six—it is the habit that makes all the others possible. "Sharpening the saw" is a process of using and continuously renewing the physical, mental, spiritual, and social aspects of your life. To be an effective follower or an effective leader requires living a balanced life. For example, John Barr founded Barr Devlin, an investment bank that specializes in utility mergers, but he is also a writer who has published four volumes of poetry.[28]

What Leaders Want from Followers

If followers don't do their jobs well, leaders and the organization suffer. One aspect of being a good follower is to understand what leaders want and need. Leaders and organizational situations vary, but here are a few things every good leader wants from his or her followers:[29]

1. *A Make-It-Happen Attitude.* Leaders don't want excuses. They want results. A leader's job becomes smoother when he or she has followers who are positive and self-motivated, who can get things done, who accept responsibility, and who excel at required tasks. Leaders value those people who take responsibility when they see something that needs to be done or a problem that needs to be solved. In addition, people who are innovative and creative, who propose ideas and alternatives, are highly important to the leader's success. Have you ever sat in a meeting where everyone, including the boss, seems confused and uncertain—and then one person introduces a significant new idea or insight? Right then, the tempo changes and things move forward. Leaders depend on the ideas and actions of followers.

2. *A Willingness to Collaborate.* Leaders are responsible for much more in the organization than any individual follower's concerns, feelings, and performance. Each follower is a part of the leader's larger system and should realize that his or her actions affect the whole. Larry Bossidy, former chairman and CEO of AlliedSignal and of Honeywell, tells about a conflict between the heads of manufacturing and marketing at one organization. Because the two managers didn't communicate with one another, inventories were always out of whack. The CEO finally had to fire them both because their refusal to cooperate was hurting the organization. They got their jobs back when they jointly called and said they got the point and would change their behavior.[30]

3. *The Motivation to Stay Up-to-Date.* Bosses want followers to know what is happening in the organization's industry or field of endeavor. In addition, they want people to understand their customers, their competition, and how changes in technology or world events might affect the organization. Most people try to learn all they can in order to get a job, but they sometimes grow complacent and fail to stay current with what's going on outside the narrow confines of their day-to-day work.

4. *The Passion to Drive Your Own Growth.* Similarly, leaders want followers who seek to enhance their own growth and development rather than depending solely on the leader to do it. This chapter's Leader's Bookshelf describes an approach followers can take to drive their own development and suggests that the best performers are not necessarily people with innate talent but those who take responsibility for continuously improving themselves. Improvement efforts might include taking classes or seminars, but there are many other ways people can drive their professional growth. Anything that exposes an individual to new people and ideas can enhance personal and professional development. One example is when followers

marble: © Ioannis Drimilis library: www.istockphoto.com/nikada

Leader's Bookshelf

Talent Is Overrated: What *Really* Separates World-Class Performers from Everybody Else
by Geoff Colvin

In *Talent Is Overrated*, Geoff Colvin, *Fortune* magazine's senior editor-at-large, presents recent research showing that achieving success in any endeavor, whether it be selling products, investing, playing golf, or leading a team, requires *deliberate practice*, which means practice that explicitly aims to improve performance, reaches just beyond one's current level of competence, provides feedback on results, and involves a high level of repetition.

Applying the Principles Every Day

Colvin shows how each of us can take charge of our own growth and improvement by applying the principles of deliberate practice in our everyday work:

- *Before the Work*. The starting point is to set a clear, specific goal for how you want to improve in some aspect of your work. This should be an immediate goal for what you will be working on that day, not a big, long-range goal. In addition, it should focus more on process than on outcome. For example, rather than a goal to win a big account, the goal might be to discern the customer's unspoken needs. Then, develop specific plans and techniques for how you will achieve the goal.

- *During the Work*. The most critical aspect of this stage is close self-observation. For example, elite long-distance runners focus intently on their stride, their breathing, and so forth. Even if your work is purely mental, you can practice "stepping outside yourself" to monitor what is happening in your own mind, assess your thinking, and question how things are going. For example, if the customer raises an unexpected problem during the negotiation, you can take a mental pause to observe your own mental processes: Do I fully understand why the customer has this objection? What am I feeling? What different strategy should I try?

- *After the Work*. This is the feedback segment, in which you evaluate your own practice activities. The key is to be specific and compare your performance to some measure that stretches just beyond your current capability. When you're stretching yourself, though, you're going to make mistakes. The final step is deciding how to respond. Let's say you didn't win the customer account and, moreover, you left the meeting feeling like a whipped puppy. If you want to improve your performance, don't blame the customer's unreasonable demands; consider ways you can better discern what the customer really wants and needs for next time.

Sounds Like Hard Work! Is It Worth It?

"It isn't just companies that have to keep kicking up their performance more than they ever did before," writes Colvin. He asserts that people are "under unprecedented pressure to develop their own abilities more highly than was ever necessary before. . . ." In today's tough global environment, taking responsibility for one's own development could make the difference between winners and losers.

Talent Is Overrated, by Geoff Colvin, is published by Portfolio/Penguin Group.

---

actively network with others inside and outside the organization. Another is when followers take on difficult assignments, which demonstrates a willingness to face challenges, stretch their limits, and learn.

Strategies for Managing Up

There is growing recognition that how followers manage their leaders is just as important as how their leaders manage them.[31] Most followers at some point complain about the leader's deficiencies, such as a failure to listen, to encourage, or to recognize followers' efforts.[32] Sometimes, though, we need to look in the mirror before blaming our leaders for an unsatisfying or unproductive relationship. Effective followers transform the leader–follower relationship by striving to improve their leaders rather than just criticizing them. To be effective, followers develop a meaningful, task-related relationship with their bosses that enables

Leader's Self-Insight 7.2
Are You an Annoying Follower?

1. If you think there might be a mistake in something you've done, what do you do?
   A. Fess up. It's better to share your concerns up front so your boss can see if there is a problem and get it corrected before it makes him look bad.
   B. Try to hide it. Maybe there isn't really a problem, so there's no use in making yourself look incompetent.

2. How do you handle a criticism from your boss?
   A. Poke your head in her door or corner her in the cafeteria multiple times to make sure everything is okay between the two of you.
   B. Take the constructive criticism, make sure you understand what the boss wants from you, and get on with your job.

3. You're in a crowded elevator with your boss after an important meeting where you've just landed a million-dollar deal. You:
   A. Celebrate the victory by talking to your boss about the accomplishment and the details of the meeting.
   B. Keep your mouth shut or talk about non–business-related matters.

4. Your boss has an open-door policy and wants people to feel free to drop by her office any time to talk about anything. You pop in just after lunch and find her on the phone. What do you do?
   A. Leave and come back later.
   B. Wait. You know most of her phone calls are quick, so she'll be free in a few minutes.

5. You've been called to the boss's office and have no idea what he wants to talk about.
   A. You show up on time, empty-handed, and ask the boss what you need to bring with you.
   B. You show up on time with a pen, paper, and your calendar or mobile device.

6. You've been trying to get some face time with your boss for weeks and luckily catch him or her in the bathroom. You:
   A. Take care of personal business and get out of there.
   B. Grab your chance to schmooze with the boss. You might not get another any time soon.

Here are the appropriate follower behaviors:

1. **A.** Honest self-assessment and fessing up to the boss builds mutual confidence and respect. Nothing destroys trust faster than incompetence exposed after the fact.

2. **B.** David Snow, former president and COO of Empire Blue Cross and Blue Shield, refers to insecure, thin-skinned people who have to check in frequently after a criticism as *door swingers*. Door swingers are annoying in both our personal and work lives. Just get on with things.

3. **B.** You have no idea who else is in the elevator. Keep your mouth shut. You can crow about the new deal later in private.

4. **A.** There's nothing worse than having someone hovering while you're trying to carry on a phone conversation. Leave a note with your boss's assistant or come back later.

5. **B.** You can usually be safe in assuming your boss hasn't called you in for idle chitchat. Never show up without a pen and paper to make notes.

6. **A.** At best, to use the bathroom as a place to try to impress the boss makes you look desperate. It also shows a lack of tact and judgment.

Most of these seem obvious, but based on interviews with leaders, subordinates commit these sins over and over in the workplace. Keep these missteps in mind so you don't become an annoying follower.

Source: Based on William Speed Weed, Alex Lash, and Constance Loizos, "30 Ways to Annoy Your Boss," *MBA Jungle* (March–April 2003), pp. 51–55.

marble: © Kirill Matkov   sunset: © Marco Regalia

them to add value to the organization even when their ideas disagree with those of the leader.[33] You might have experienced this with a special teacher or coach. For example, students who are especially interested in a class sometimes challenge the professor on a topic as a way to expand the professor's thinking and enhance the learning experience for everyone.

Followers should also be aware of behaviors that can annoy leaders and interfere with building a quality relationship.

Action Memo

Leader's Self-Insight 7.2 gives you a chance to see if you're guilty of being an annoying follower.

One business magazine interviewed powerful people about their pet peeves and identified more than two dozen misdemeanors that followers often commit without being aware of it.

Most relationships between leaders and followers are characterized by some emotion and behavior based on authority and submission. Leaders are authority figures and may play a disproportionately large role in the mind of a follower. The relationships between leaders and followers are not unlike those between parents and children, and individuals may engage old family patterns when entering into leader–follower relationships.[34] Effective followers, conversely, typically perceive themselves as the equals of their leaders, not inherently subordinate.[35] Exhibit 7.3 illustrates the strategies that enable followers to overcome the authority-based relationship and develop an effective, respectful relationship with their leaders.

Be a Resource for the Leader

Effective followers align themselves with the purpose and the vision of the organization. They ask the leader about vision and goals and work to achieve them. In this way, followers are a resource of strength and support for the leader. This alignment involves understanding the leader's goals, needs, strengths and weaknesses, and organizational constraints. An effective follower can complement the leader's weaknesses with the follower's own strengths.[36] Similarly, effective followers indicate their personal goals and the resources they bring to the organization. Effective followers inform their leaders about their own ideas, beliefs, needs, and constraints. The more leaders and followers can know the day-to-day activities and problems of one another, the better resources they can be for each other. At one organization, a group of disabled employees took advantage of a board meeting to issue rented wheelchairs to the members, who then tried to move around the factory in them. Realizing what the workers faced, the board got the factory's ramps improved, and the employees became a better resource for the organization.[37]

Exhibit 7.3 Ways to Influence Your Leader

Be a Resource for the Leader	**Help the Leader Be a Good Leader**
Determine the leader's needs.	Ask for advice.
Zig where leader zags.	Tell leader what you think.
Tell leader about you.	Find things to thank leader for.
Align self to team purpose/vision.	
Build a Relationship	View the Leader Realistically
Ask about leader at your level/position.	Give up idealized expectations.
Welcome feedback and criticism, such as "What experience led you to that opinion?"	Don't hide anything.
	Don't criticize leader to others.
Ask leader to tell you company stories.	Disagree occasionally.

Help the Leader Be a Good Leader

Good followers seek the leader's counsel and look for ways the leader can help improve their skills, abilities, and value to the organization. They help their leaders be good leaders by simply saying what they need in order to be good followers. If a leader believes a follower values his or her advice, the leader is more likely to give constructive guidance rather than unsympathetic criticism.

Action Memo

As a leader, you can use strategies for managing up to create an equitable and respectful relationship with your superiors. You can help your supervisor be the best he or she can be by getting beyond submissive feelings and behaviors, recognizing that leaders are fallible, and being a resource for the leader.

A leader can also become a better leader when followers compliment the leader and thank him or her for behavior that followers appreciate, such as listening, rewarding followers' contributions, and sharing credit for accomplishments.[38] If a leader knows what followers appreciate, the leader is more likely to repeat that behavior. Sometimes, effective followers have to find diplomatic ways to let leaders know when their behavior is counterproductive.

Asking for advice, thanking the leader for helpful behaviors, modeling the behavior you want, and being honest about areas that need improvement are important ways followers can influence the conduct of leaders and help them be better leaders.

Build a Relationship with the Leader

Effective followers work toward a genuine relationship with their leaders, which includes developing trust and speaking honestly on the basis of that trust.[39] By building a relationship with a leader, a follower makes every interaction more meaningful to the organization. Furthermore, the relationship is imbued with mutual respect rather than authority and submission. Wes Walsh used mindful initiatives to create a relationship with his boss that maximized his own upward influence.

IN THE LEAD

Wes Walsh

When Wes Walsh came under an autocratic manager, his position predecessor warned him to either stay away from the infamously autocratic boss or else be prepared to give up any influence over the unit operations. Walsh decided to ignore this advice. Instead, he started dropping by his boss's office on a regular basis to discuss production progress. Walsh also sought approval on very small matters because they were virtually impossible for his boss to oppose. Walsh continued these frequent, informal interactions over a lengthy period of time before moving on to more consequential matters.

Eventually, major projects had to be addressed. For example, an increase in the volume of materials processed had rendered Walsh's unit too slow and too limited to adequately serve the increased production. In response, Walsh first requested his boss to devote a couple of hours to him at some designated point in the near future. When the appointed time arrived, Walsh took his boss on a lengthy tour of the plant, pointing out the volume of material scattered about waiting to be processed. He supplemented this visual evidence with facts and figures.

The boss was compelled to acknowledge the problem. Thus, he asked for Walsh's proposal, which Walsh had carefully prepared beforehand. Although the boss had rejected identical proposals from Walsh's predecessor, this time the boss almost immediately approved the sum of $150,000 for updating the unit equipment.[40]

Wes Walsh's conscious effort to interact and get his boss comfortable saying yes on small matters set a precedent for a pattern of respect that was not lost even on his autocratic superior.

Followers can generate respect by asking questions about the leader's experiences in the follower's position, actively seeking feedback, and clarifying the basis for specific feedback and criticism from the leader. Followers can also ply the leader for company stories.[41] By doing so, followers are getting beyond submissive behavior by asking leaders to be accountable for their criticism, to have empathy for the followers' position, and to share history about something both parties have in common—the organization.

View the Leader Realistically

Unrealistic follower expectations is one of the biggest barriers to effective leader–follower relationships. To view leaders realistically means to give up idealized images of them. Understanding that leaders are fallible and will make many mistakes leads to acceptance and the potential for an equitable relationship. The way in which a follower perceives his or her leader is the foundation of their relationship. It helps to view leaders as they really are, not as followers think they should be.[42]

Similarly, effective followers present realistic images of themselves. Followers do not try to hide their weaknesses or cover their mistakes, nor do they criticize their leaders to others.[43] Hiding things is symptomatic of conforming and passive followers. Criticizing leaders to others merely intensifies estrangement and reinforces the mindset of an alienated follower. These kinds of alienated and passive behaviors can have negative—and sometimes disastrous—consequences for leaders, followers, and the organization. Only positive things about a leader should be shared with others. It is an alienated follower who complains without engaging in constructive action. Instead of criticizing a leader to others, it is far more constructive to directly disagree with a leader on matters relevant to the department's or organization's work.

What Followers Want from Leaders

Throughout much of this chapter, we've talked about demands on followers and how followers can become more effective and powerful in the organization. However, the full responsibility doesn't fall on the follower. Good followers are created partly by leaders who understand their requirements and obligations for developing people.[44] Leaders have a duty to create a leader–follower relationship that engages whole people rather than treats followers as passive sheep who should blindly follow orders and support the boss.

Research indicates that followers have expectations about what constitutes a desirable leader.[45] Exhibit 7.4 shows the top four choices in rank order based on surveys of followers about what they desire in leaders and colleagues.

Exhibit 7.4 Rank Order of Desirable Characteristics

Desirable Leaders Are	Desirable Colleagues (Followers) Are
Honest	Honest
Forward-thinking	Cooperative
Inspiring	Dependable
Competent	Competent

Source: Adapted from James M. Kouzes and Barry Z. Posner, Credibility: *How Leaders Gain and Lose It, Why People Demand It* (San Francisco: Jossey-Bass, 1993), p. 255.

Followers want their leaders to be honest, forward-thinking, inspiring, and competent. A leader must be worthy of trust, envision the future of the organization, inspire others to contribute, and be capable and effective in matters that will affect the organization. In terms of competence, leadership roles may shift from the formal leader to the person with particular expertise in a given area.

Followers want their fellow followers to be honest and competent, but also dependable and cooperative. Thus, desired qualities of colleagues share two qualities with leaders—honesty and competence. However, followers themselves want other followers to be dependable and cooperative, rather than forward-thinking and inspiring. The hallmark that distinguishes the role of leadership from the role of followership, then, is not authority, knowledge, power, or other conventional notions of what a follower is not. Rather, the distinction lies in the clearly defined leadership activities of fostering a vision and inspiring others to achieve that vision. Chapter 13 discusses vision in detail, and Chapter 14 describes how leaders shape cultural values that support achievement of the vision. The results in Exhibit 7.4 also underscore the idea that behaviors of effective leaders and followers often overlap. Followers do not want to be subjected to leader behavior that denies them the opportunity to make valued contributions. Leaders have a responsibility to enable followers to fully contribute their ideas and abilities. Three specific ways leaders enhance the abilities and contributions of followers are by offering clarity of direction, giving honest, constructive feedback, and providing coaching.

Action Memo

As a leader, you can learn to give and receive feedback that contributes to growth and improvement rather than fear and hard feelings.

Clarity of Direction

It is the leader's job to clearly communicate where the group or organization is going and why.[46] Creating an inspiring vision is only one aspect of setting direction. Followers also need specific, unambiguous goals and objectives, on both an individual and team level. Numerous studies have shown that clear, specific, challenging goals enhance people's motivation and performance.[47] Having clear goals lets people know where to focus their attention and energy and enables them to feel a sense of pride and accomplishment when goals are achieved. Providing clarity of direction enables followers to manage their own behaviors and track their own progress. In addition, it provides a basis for understanding leader decisions regarding bonuses, salary increases, or promotions.

Another aspect of clarifying direction is helping followers see how their own individual jobs fit in the larger context of the team, department, and total enterprise. This is one reason many leaders use open-book management. When people can see the bigger financial picture, they have a perspective on where the organization stands and how they can contribute.

Frequent, Specific, and Immediate Feedback

When managers were asked in a McKinsey & Company survey what factors contributed to their growth and development, respondents ranked "candid, insightful feedback" as one of the most important elements. Unfortunately, most also indicated that their supervisors did not do a good job of providing such feedback.[48] Effective leaders see feedback as a route to improvement and development, not as something to dread or fear. When a leader provides feedback, it signals that the leader cares about the follower's growth and career development and wants to help the person achieve his or her potential.[49]

Action Memo

Before reading on, answer the questions in Leader's Self-Insight 7.3 to learn how you may manage performance feedback from your boss.

Leader's Self-Insight 7.3

Receiving Feedback

The following items describe ways you might act toward receiving feedback from a supervisor. Think about a job you had, or just imagine how you would behave if you had a job, and answer the questions below. Indicate whether each item below is Mostly False or Mostly True for you.

	Mostly False	Mostly True
1. After performing a task well, I would cheerfully greet my supervisor, hoping that this would lead to a conversation about my work.	_____	_____
2. After performing poorly, I might try to schedule outside appointments or take a sick day to avoid my supervisor.	_____	_____
3. I would confess about my poor performance to my supervisor immediately, but have several solutions prepared to show that I would not make the same mistake twice.	_____	_____
4. After performing well, I might display my excellent work to my coworkers and hope they might relay some positive remarks to my supervisor.	_____	_____
5. After performing poorly, I might go the other way when I saw my supervisor coming or otherwise avoid contact for awhile.	_____	_____
6. I would inform my boss that I wasn't able to complete my assignment on time but that I would stay late that night to finish it.	_____	_____
7. After performing well, I would ask my supervisor about my performance to draw his/her attention to my success.	_____	_____
8. After performing poorly, I would try to avoid eye contact with my supervisor so that he/she didn't start a conversation with me about my performance.	_____	_____
9. After performing poorly, I would immediately show my supervisor that I was taking responsibility for my performance by taking corrective measures.	_____	_____

Scoring and Interpretation

Most followers want to perform well and receive appropriate recognition, and most followers sometimes experience poor performance. These questions provide some indication of how you manage feedback from your supervisor. Questions 1, 4, and 7 indicate your "feedback seeking" behavior and indicate the extent to which you want your boss to know about your good work and provide you with positive feedback. Questions 2, 5, and 8 indicate your "feedback avoiding" behavior when your performance is poor. Questions 3, 6, and 9 indicate your "feedback mitigating" behavior to correct the outcome when your performance is poor. Record the number of Mostly True responses below for each set of questions. A score of 3 would be considered high, and a score of 0 or 1 would be low for each type of behavior.

Feedback seeking (1, 4, 7): _____. "Feedback seeking" is a personal preference because good performance serves your supervisor well, and whether you want feedback from your boss is up to you. A high score indicates you want feedback, but any score indicates appropriate followership.

Feedback avoiding (2, 5, 8): _____. In terms of followership, "feedback avoiding" behavior is perhaps least effective for serving your boss. Avoiding poor performance feedback means you may have trouble confronting reality and fear negative evaluation. A low score here is characteristic of a good follower.

Feedback mitigating (3, 6, 9): _____. "Feedback mitigating" behavior is very effective follower behavior because you take personal responsibility to correct poor outcomes and keep your boss informed. A high score indicates good followership.

Source: Adapted from Sherry E. Moss, Enzo R. Valenzi, and William Taggart, "Are You Hiding from Your Boss? The Development of a Taxonomy and Instrument to Assess the Feedback Management Behaviors of Good and Bad Performers," *Journal of Management* 29, no. 4 (2003), pp. 487–510. Used with permission.

Feedback occurs when a leader uses evaluation and communication to help individuals learn about themselves and improve.[50] Many people face significant challenges in giving and receiving feedback, particularly negative feedback.[51] One problem is that feedback is often "saved up" for annual evaluation time. Effective leaders, though, provide both positive and negative constructive feedback on an ongoing basis. If someone handles a difficult task, for instance, the leader offers feedback on the spot rather than letting the person wonder how effective he or she was, perhaps imagining the worst. If you've ever given a class presentation and received no feedback from either the professor or other students, for example, your imagination likely began to conjure up a highly negative rather than a positive evaluation of your performance. As former advertising account executive Ryan Broderick said, "hearing something is better than hearing nothing."[52]

Followers appreciate positive feedback, but they also want to know when they aren't doing what is expected of them, and they want the feedback to be specific enough to enable them to do better. Leaders who avoid giving any critical feedback "achieve kindness in the short term but heartlessness in the long run, dooming the problem employee to non-improvement."[53] Here are some ways leaders can provide feedback that benefits followers and takes less of an emotional toll on both leader and follower:[54]

1. *Make it timely.* People shouldn't have to wait for an annual review to know how they're doing or how they can improve. Leaders should give feedback as soon as possible after they observe a behavior or action they want to correct or reinforce. Often, this means immediately, such as when a leader says, "Great job on the presentation, Sal, and you used graphics very effectively. The only place I see it could have been better would be including some specifics like past sales figures. Do you know where to find that information or would you like me to set up a meeting with our sales manager?" If leaders wait to offer feedback, it should be only long enough to gather necessary information or to marshal their thoughts and ideas.

2. *Focus on the performance, not the person.* Feedback should not be used simply to criticize a person or to point out faults. A person who feels like he or she is being attacked personally will not learn anything from the feedback. The focus should always be on how the follower can improve. Leaders have to point out work that is poorly done, but it is equally important to reinforce work that is done well. This helps people learn from what they do right, and softens the impact of negative feedback.

3. *Make it specific.* Effective feedback describes the precise behavior and its consequences, and explains why the leader either approves of the behavior or thinks there is a need for improvement. The leader might provide illustrations and examples to clarify what behavior is considered effective, and he or she always checks for understanding rather than assuming the follower knows what actions the leader wants.

4. *Focus on the desired future, not the past.* Good leaders don't drag up the failures and mistakes of the past. In addition, if it is clear that a follower's mistake was a one-time occurrence and not likely to be repeated, the leader will let it go rather than offering negative feedback. Effective feedback looks toward the future, minimizes fault-finding, and describes the desired behaviors and outcomes.

Feedback
using evaluation and communication to help individuals and the organization learn and improve

Coaching to Develop Potential

Coaching takes feedback a step further to help followers upgrade their skills and enhance their career development. **Leadership coaching** is a method of directing or facilitating a follower with the aim of improving specific skills or achieving a specific development goal, such as developing time management skills, enhancing personal productivity, or preparing for new responsibilities. At Xerox, for example, former CEO Anne Mulcahy acted as a leadership coach for her successor, Ursula Burns. Burns is a master problem-solver, but she admits she needs to listen better instead of "letting my big mouth drive the discussion," and she lacks Mulcahy's patience, diplomacy,

Action Memo

As a leader, you can make feedback a regular habit and remember to include positive comments and praise as well as critical feedback. As a follower, you can view feedback as a chance to improve yourself. Reframe negative feedback in a way that helps you take positive action toward what you want out of your work and life.

and mastery at getting people lined up to support decisions and actions. These are areas in which Mulcahy's coaching helped Burns expand her capabilities for being a CEO.[55] Coaching doesn't mean trying to change people and make them something other than what they are. Instead, it means helping followers realize their potential.[56]

To understand what it means to be a coach, consider the difference in mindset and behavior required for managing versus coaching:

Managing	Coaching[57]
Telling	Empowering
Judging	Facilitating
Controlling	Developing
Directing	Supporting; removing obstacles

Rather than telling followers what to do, directing and controlling their behavior, and judging their performance, which is a traditional management role, coaching involves empowering followers to explore, helping them understand and learn, providing support, and removing obstacles that stand in the way of their ability to grow and excel.

Coaching generally follows a four-step process, as illustrated in Exhibit 7.5.[58] *Observations* are visible occurrences in which the leader identifies a performance gap or an opportunity to help a follower improve in a specific area. For example, Raj, the assistant director of a social services agency, notices that Janine, program manager for job services, routinely stays late to re-do or complete the work of people in her department. Following this observation, the next step is for Raj to talk with Janine about her behavior and strive for agreement that there is a problem or a chance to improve her leadership by learning to delegate more effectively. Step 2, *discussion and agreement*, is an essential part of coaching. A leader who tries to coach a follower who sees no need for coaching is wasting his or her time. The follower has to be interested in improving and have a shared understanding of the areas that need work. The third step involves *creating and following a coaching plan* with specific goals, action steps, measures of success, and a timeline for Janine to delegate more effectively. The plan might include specific training sessions, times when Raj and Janine will meet to work toward the goals. Leaders also take advantage of opportunities to coach on the spot.[59] For example, if Raj notices Janine handling a routine departmental task, he can encourage her development by asking her if one of her subordinates could handle the task instead. Throughout the active coaching process, the leader is providing ongoing feedback, as well as listening to

Leadership coaching
a method of directing or facilitating a follower with the aim of improving specific skills or achieving a specific development goal

Exhibit 7.5 The Leadership Coaching Process

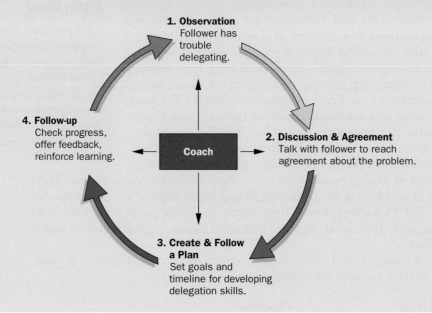

Source: Based on "Closing Gaps and Improving Performance: The Basics of Coaching," excerpt, originally published as Chapter 4 of *Performance Management: Measure and Improve the Effectiveness of Your Employees* (Boston, MA: Harvard Business School Press, 2006).

feedback from the follower regarding the coaching process. *Follow-up*, the final step in coaching, means setting a date to check the follower's progress, reinforcing learning, discussing any problems and ways the leader can help, and looking for opportunities for additional coaching and feedback.

Leaders can take either a directive coaching or a supportive coaching approach. **Directive coaching**, which involves showing or telling a person what needs to be done and how to do it, is closest to a traditional managing role. This approach is most helpful when the leader is coaching a follower who is inexperienced in a particular job or whose performance needs immediate improvement. The leader might instruct a new employee who needs to develop skills in the leader's area of expertise, show the person the most expedient way to handle tasks, and provide answers to the employee's questions. **Supportive coaching**, such as the coaching provided by Anne Mulcahy to Ursula Burns, described earlier, involves helping others create their own solutions. Supportive coaching is built on a more collaborative relationship with the follower. Rather than providing direct answers or telling the follower what to do, the leader facilitates follower learning, such as by asking questions to guide the individual's thinking, allowing the individual to learn through trial and error, and serving as a resource and supporter for the follower's journey of discovery and development. The leader helps the follower think critically about his or her own performance and judge progress toward achieving goals.

One of the primary benefits followers describe from leadership coaching is the opportunity to receive clear, direct feedback about their performance, which underscores the fact, discussed in the previous section, that many leaders fail to effectively provide feedback. Exhibit 7.6 shows other factors that followers find useful from coaching, including gaining a new perspective, getting advice on handling specific organizational situations, dealing with organizational politics, and receiving encouragement and support.[60]

Directive coaching
helping a follower develop by showing or telling the follower what needs to be done and how to do it

Supportive coaching
facilitating follower learning by asking questions, allowing the individual to learn through trial and error, and serving as a resource for the follower's journey of discovery and development

Exhibit 7.6 Follower Benefits from Coaching

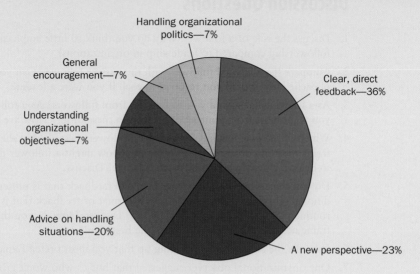

Source: "The Business Leader as Development Coach," *PDI Portfolio* (Winter 1996), p. 6; and Personnel Decisions International, http://www.personneldecisions.com.

Leadership Essentials

- The important role of followership in organizations is increasingly recognized. People are followers more often than leaders, and effective leaders and followers share similar characteristics. An effective follower is both independent and active in the organization. Being an effective follower depends on not becoming alienated, conforming, passive, or a pragmatic survivor.

- Effective followership is not always easy. Effective followers display the courage to assume responsibility, to challenge their leaders, to participate in transformation, to serve others, and to leave the organization when necessary. Strategies for being an effective follower include being a resource, helping the leader be a good leader, building a relationship with the leader, and viewing the leader realistically.

- Leaders want followers who are positive and self-motivated, who take action to get things done, who accept responsibility, and who excel at required tasks. Followers want both their leaders and their colleagues to be honest and competent. However, they want their leaders also to be forward-thinking and inspirational. The two latter traits distinguish the role of leader from follower. Followers want to be led, not controlled. They also want leaders to create an environment that enables people to contribute their best. Three specific ways leaders enhance the abilities and contributions of followers are by offering clarity of direction, giving honest, constructive feedback, and providing coaching.

- Followers want feedback that is timely and specific, focuses on performance rather than the person, and focuses on the future rather than dragging up mistakes of the past. Leaders can use directive or supportive coaching to help followers improve specific skills or achieve a specific development goal.

Discussion Questions

1. Discuss the role of a follower. Why do you think so little emphasis is given to followership compared to leadership in organizations?

2. Compare the alienated follower with the passive follower. Can you give an example of each? How would you respond to each if you were a leader?

3. As a leader, what would you want most from followers? As a follower, what would you want most from your leader? How do these differ? How are they the same?

4. Which of the five demands on effective followers described in the chapter do you feel is most important? Least important? How might a follower derive the courage to behave in new ways to be more effective? Discuss.

5. Do you think you would respond better to feedback that is presented using a traditional scheduled performance review format or feedback that is presented as a routine part of everyday work activities? Discuss. How do you think leaders should frame negative feedback to achieve the best results?

6. Describe the strategy for managing up that you most prefer. Explain.

7. One organizational observer suggested that bosses who won't give negative feedback to followers who need it cause even more damage in the long run than those who fly off the handle when a follower makes a mistake. Do you agree? Discuss.

8. Is the will to leave a job the ultimate courage of a follower, compared to the will to participate in transformation? Which would be hardest for you?

9. What does leadership coaching mean to you? How should leaders decide which followers they will provide with coaching?

Leadership at Work

FOLLOWER ROLE PLAY

You are a production supervisor at Hyperlink Systems. Your plant produces circuit boards that are used in Nokia cell phones and IBM computers. Hyperlink is caught in a competitive pricing squeeze, so senior management hired a consultant to study the production department. The plant manager, Sue Harris, asked that the consultant's recommendations be implemented immediately. She thought that total production would increase right away. Weekly production goals were set higher than ever. You don't think she took into account the time required to learn new procedures, and plant workers are under great pressure. A handful of workers have resisted the new work methods because they can produce more circuit boards using the old methods. Most workers have changed to the new methods, but their productivity has not increased. Even after a month, many workers think the old ways are more efficient, faster, and more productive.

You have a couple of other concerns with Harris. She asked you to attend an operations conference, and at the last minute sent another supervisor instead, without any explanation. She has made other promises of supplies and equipment to your section, and then has not followed through. You think she acts too quickly without adequate implementation and follow-up.

You report directly to Harris and are thinking about your responsibility as a follower. Write below specifically how you would handle this situation. Will you confront her with the knowledge you have? When and where will you meet with her? What will you say? How will you get her to hear you?

_____

_____

_____

What style—effective, conformist, passive, alienated—best describes your response to this situation? Referring to Exhibit 7.3, which strategy would you like to use to assist Harris?

_____

_____

_____

In Class: The instructor can ask students to volunteer to play the role of the plant manager and the production supervisor. A few students can take turns role-playing the production supervisor in front of the class to show different approaches to being a follower. Other students can be asked to provide feedback on each production supervisor's effectiveness and on which approach seems more effective for this situation.

Source: Based on K. J. Keleman, J. E. Garcia, and K. J. Lovelace, *Management Incidents: Role Plays for Management Development* (Dubuque, Iowa: Kendall Hunt Publishing Company, 1990), pp. 73–75, 83.

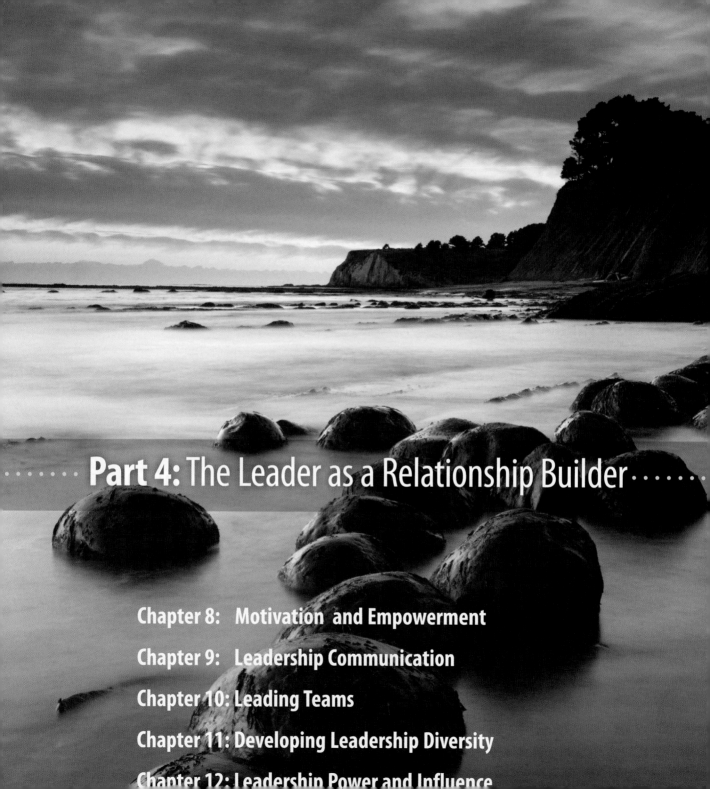

Part 4: The Leader as a Relationship Builder

Chapter 8: Motivation and Empowerment

Your Leadership Challenge

After reading this chapter, you should be able to:

- Recognize and apply the difference between intrinsic and extrinsic rewards.

- Motivate others by meeting their higher-level needs.

- Apply needs-based theories of motivation.

- Implement individual and systemwide rewards.

- Avoid the disadvantages of "carrot-and-stick" motivation.

- Implement employee engagement programs and empowerment to meet higher-level needs.

Chapter Outline

When Joie de Vivre Hospitality took over the Hotel Carlton in San Francisco, annual turnover was around 50 percent. In the hotel industry, where about 90 percent of employees are low-skilled and low-paid, that's about average, but the new leadership team knew it didn't have to be that way. Hervé Blondel, the new Hotel Carlton general manager, decided to treat employees like partners. He started by finding out what they needed in order to do their jobs better. For Theophilus McKinney, who oversaw the front desk, it was working evenings instead of days and rearranging the phones so they were easier to answer—and, oh yes, being allowed to wear the funky shoes he prefers. For Anita Lum and her colleagues in housekeeping, it was pretty simple, too— new vacuum cleaners that did what they were supposed to do. The previous management had refused to replace the aging vacuums, but Blondel bought a new one for each member of the housekeeping staff, and the company now replaces them every year. The new leaders also give people more leeway in serving guests and encourage them to participate in decisions that directly affect their jobs.

Within a few years under fresh leadership, annual turnover at Hotel Carlton was down to less than 10 percent. Customer satisfaction had improved too, with the Hotel Carlton rising from near the lowest among Joie de Vivre properties to near the highest. "It seems that this company cares about us . . . ," says Lum. Front-desk worker Emelie Dela Cruz adds that "we're all just happier." Caring about employees and helping them see their jobs as valuable and fun are top priorities for Joie de Vivre leaders. CEO Chip Conley says it is important to "focus on the impact they're making rather than just the task of cleaning the toilet."[1]

Many other leaders have found that creating an environment where people feel valued is a key to high motivation. This chapter explores motivation in organizations and examines how leaders can bring out the best in followers. We examine the difference between intrinsic and extrinsic rewards and discuss how these rewards meet the needs of followers. Individuals have both lower and higher needs, and there are different methods of motivation to meet those needs. The chapter presents several theories of motivation, with particular attention to the differences between leadership and conventional management methods for creating a motivated workforce. The final sections of the chapter explore empowerment, employee engagement programs, and other recent motivational tools that do not rely on traditional reward and punishment methods.

Leadership and Motivation

Most of us get up in the morning, go to school or work, and behave in ways that are predictably our own. We usually respond to our environment and the people in it with little thought as to why we work hard, invest extra time and energy in certain classes, or spend our leisure time pursuing specific recreational or volunteer activities. Yet all these behaviors are motivated by something. **Motivation** refers to the forces either internal or external to a person that arouse enthusiasm and persistence to pursue a certain course of action. Employee motivation affects productivity, so part of a leader's job is to channel followers' motivation toward the accomplishment of the organization's vision and goals.[2] The study of motivation helps leaders understand what prompts people to initiate action, what influences their choice of action, and why they persist in that action over time.

Exhibit 8.1 illustrates a simple model of human motivation. People have basic needs, such as for friendship, recognition, or monetary gain, which translate into an internal tension that motivates specific behaviors with which to fulfill the need. To the extent that the behavior is successful, the person is rewarded when the need is satisfied. The reward also informs the person that the behavior was appropriate and can be used again in the future.

The importance of motivation, as illustrated in Exhibit 8.1, is that it can lead to behaviors that reflect high performance within organizations. Studies have found that high employee motivation and high organizational performance and profits go hand in hand.[3] An extensive survey by the Gallup organization, for example, found that when all of an organization's employees are highly motivated and performing at their peak, customers are 70 percent more loyal, turnover

Motivation
the forces either internal or external to a person that arouse enthusiasm and persistence to pursue a certain course of action

Exhibit 8.1 A Simple Model of Motivation

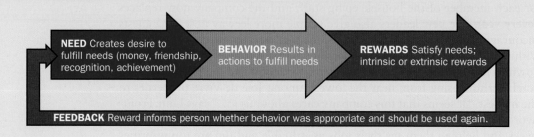

NEED Creates desire to fulfill needs (money, friendship, recognition, achievement) → BEHAVIOR Results in actions to fulfill needs → REWARDS Satisfy needs; intrinsic or extrinsic rewards

FEEDBACK Reward informs person whether behavior was appropriate and should be used again.

drops by 70 percent, and profits jump 40 percent.[4] Leaders can use motivation theory to help satisfy followers' needs and simultaneously encourage high work performance. When workers are not motivated to achieve organizational goals, the fault is often with the leader.

Intrinsic and Extrinsic Rewards

Rewards can be either intrinsic or extrinsic, systemwide or individual. Exhibit 8.2 illustrates the categories of rewards, combining intrinsic and extrinsic rewards with those that are applied systemwide or individually.[5] **Intrinsic rewards** are the internal satisfactions a person receives in the process of performing a particular action. Solving a problem to benefit others may fulfill a personal mission, or the completion of a complex task may bestow a pleasant feeling of accomplishment. An intrinsic reward is internal and under the control of the individual, such as to engage in task behavior to satisfy a need for competency and self-determination.

Conversely, **extrinsic rewards** are given by another person, typically a supervisor, and include promotions and pay increases. Because they originate externally as a result of pleasing others, extrinsic rewards compel individuals to engage in a task behavior for an outside source that provides what they need, such as money to survive in modern society. Think about the difference in motivation for polishing a car if it belongs to you versus if you work at a car wash. Your good feelings from making your own car shine would be intrinsic. However, buffing a car that is but one of many in a day's work requires the extrinsic reward of a paycheck.[6]

Rewards can be given systemwide or on an individual basis. **Systemwide rewards** apply the same to all people within an organization or within a specific category or department. **Individual rewards** may differ among people within the same organization or department. An extrinsic, systemwide reward could be insurance benefits or vacation time available to an entire organization or category of people, such as those who have been with the organization for six months or more. Cynthia Bertucci Kaye, the founder and CEO of Logical Choice Technologies, instituted a profit-sharing program as an extrinsic systemwide reward. She set a gross profit goal and told employees if they achieved it by the end of the year, 10 percent of the profit would be split equally among employees who had been with the company for at least a year.[7] An intrinsic, systemwide reward might be the sense of pride that comes from within by virtue of working for a "winning" organization. As an example, employees at online mortgage lender Quicken Loans, which ranked Number 2 on *Fortune* magazine's 2008 list

Intrinsic rewards
internal satisfactions a person receives in the process of performing a particular action

Extrinsic rewards
rewards given by another person, typically a supervisor, such as pay increases and promotions

Systemwide rewards
rewards that apply the same to all people within an organization or within a specific category or department

Individual rewards
rewards that differ among individuals within the same organization or department

---

Exhibit 8.2 Examples of Intrinsic and Extrinsic Rewards

	Extrinsic	Intrinsic
Individual	Large merit increase	Feeling of self-fulfillment
Systemwide	Insurance benefits	Pride in being part of a "winning" organization

Source: Adapted from Richard M. Steers, Lyman W. Porter, and Gregory A. Bigley, *Motivation and Leadership at Work,* 6th ed. (New York: McGraw-Hill, 1996), p. 498. Reprinted with permission of the McGraw-Hill Companies.

TURBULENT TIMES

of "100 Best Companies to Work For," experience an intrinsic systemwide reward from working at a company recognized for its smart, ethical approach to doing business. While other firms were pushing subprime mortgages, Quicken stuck to a more conservative and ethical business model.[8]

An extrinsic, individual reward is a promotion, pay raise, or bonus check. At pipeline operator and refinery NuStar Energy, a spinoff of Valero, employees can get bonuses of up to $10,000 based on performance.[9] An intrinsic, individual reward would be a sense of self-fulfillment that an individual derives from his or her work. Oprah Winfrey provides an example. Winfrey is an Emmy award-winning television talk show host and is personally worth an estimated $1.5 billion. Yet Winfrey says she has never been motivated by money or a desire for power and prestige. Instead, she feels rewarded by serving others—uplifting, enlightening, encouraging, and transforming how people see themselves.[10]

Action Memo

As a leader, you can provide extrinsic rewards, such as promotions, pay raises, and praise, but also help followers achieve intrinsic rewards and meet their higher-level needs for accomplishment, growth, and fulfillment.

Although extrinsic rewards are important, leaders work especially hard to help followers achieve intrinsic rewards—both individually and systemwide. They strive to create an environment where people feel valued and feel that they are contributing to something worthwhile.

Higher versus Lower Needs

Intrinsic rewards appeal to the "higher" needs of individuals, such as for accomplishment, competence, fulfillment, and self-determination. Extrinsic rewards appeal to the "lower" needs of individuals, such as for material comfort and basic safety and security. Exhibit 8.3 outlines the distinction between conventional

Exhibit 8.3 Needs of People and Motivation Methods

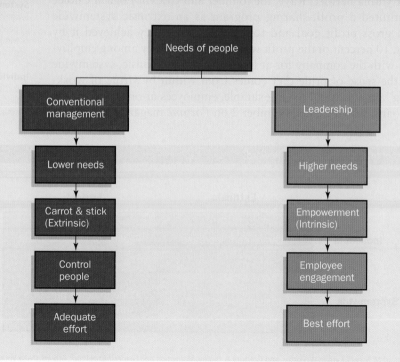

Source: Adapted from William D. Hitt, *The Leader–Manager: Guidelines for Action* (Columbus, OH: Battelle Press, 1988), p. 153.

management and leadership approaches to motivation based on people's needs. Conventional management approaches often appeal to an individual's lower, basic needs and rely on extrinsic rewards and punishments to motivate subordinates to behave in desired ways. These approaches are effective, but they are based on controlling the behavior of people by manipulating their decisions about how to act. The higher needs of people may be unmet in favor of utilizing their labor in exchange for external rewards. Under conventional management, people perform adequately to receive rewards or avoid punishments, because they will not necessarily derive intrinsic satisfaction from their work.

The leadership approach strives to motivate people by providing them with the opportunity to satisfy higher needs and become intrinsically rewarded. Employees in companies that are infused with a social mission, and that find ways to enrich the lives of others, are typically more highly motivated because of the intrinsic rewards they get from helping other people.[11] Leaders at any company can enable people to find meaning in their work. At FedEx, for example, many employees take pride in getting people the items they need on time, whether it be a work report that is due, a passport for a holiday trip to Jamaica, or an emergency order of medical supplies.[12] Remember, however, that the source of an intrinsic reward is internal to the follower. Thus, what is intrinsically rewarding to one individual may not be so to another. One way in which leaders try to enable all followers to achieve intrinsic rewards is by giving them more control over their own work and the power to affect outcomes. When leaders empower others, allowing them the freedom to determine their own actions, subordinates reward themselves intrinsically for good performance. They may become creative, innovative, and develop a greater commitment to their objectives. Thus motivated, they often achieve their best possible performance.

Ideally, work behaviors should satisfy both lower and higher needs, as well as serve the mission of the organization. Unfortunately, this is often not the case. The leader's motivational role, then, is to create a situation that integrates the needs of people—especially higher needs—and the fundamental objectives of the organization.

Needs-Based Theories of Motivation

Needs-based theories emphasize the needs that motivate people. As illustrated earlier in Exhibit 8.1, needs are the source of an internal drive that motivates behavior to fulfill the needs. An individual's needs are like a hidden catalog of the things he or she wants and will work to get. To the extent that leaders understand follower needs, they can design the reward system to direct energies and priorities toward attainment of shared goals.

Hierarchy of Needs Theory

Probably the most famous needs-based theory is the one developed by Abraham Maslow.[13] Maslow's **hierarchy of needs theory** proposes that humans are motivated by multiple needs and those needs exist in a hierarchical order, as illustrated in Exhibit 8.4, wherein the higher needs cannot be satisfied until the lower needs are met. Maslow identified five general levels of motivating needs.

- *Physiological* The most basic human physiological needs include food, water, and oxygen. In the organizational setting, these are reflected in the needs for adequate heat, air, and base salary to ensure survival.
- *Safety* Next is the need for a safe and secure physical and emotional environment and freedom from threats—that is, for freedom from violence and for

Hierarchy of needs theory
Maslow's theory proposes that humans are motivated by multiple needs and those needs exist in a hierarchical order

Exhibit 8.4 Maslow's Hierarchy of Needs

Need Hierarchy	Fulfillment on the Job
Self-actualization Needs	Opportunities for advancement, autonomy, growth, creativity
Esteem Needs	Recognition, approval, high status, increased responsibilities
Belongingness Needs	Work groups, clients, coworkers, supervisors
Safety Needs	Safe work, fringe benefits, job security
Physiological Needs	Heat, air, base salary

an orderly society. In an organizational setting, safety needs reflect the needs for safe jobs, fringe benefits, and job security.

- *Belongingness* People have a desire to be accepted by their peers, have friendships, be part of a group, and be loved. In the organization, these needs influence the desire for good relationships with coworkers, participation in a work team, and a positive relationship with supervisors.
- *Esteem* The need for esteem relates to the desires for a positive self-image and for attention, recognition, and appreciation from others. Within organizations, esteem needs reflect a motivation for recognition, an increase in responsibility, high status, and credit for contributions to the organization.
- *Self-actualization* The highest need category, self-actualization, represents the need for self-fulfillment: developing one's full potential, increasing one's competence, and becoming a better person. Self-actualization needs can be met in the organization by providing people with opportunities to grow, be empowered and creative, and acquire training for challenging assignments and advancement.

According to Maslow's theory, physiology, safety, and belonging are deficiency needs. These low-order needs take priority—they must be satisfied before higher-order, or growth, needs are activated. The needs are satisfied in sequence: Physiological needs are satisfied before safety needs, safety needs are satisfied before social needs, and so on. A person desiring physical safety will devote his or her efforts to securing a safer environment and will not be concerned with esteem or self-actualization. Once a need is satisfied, it declines in importance and the next higher need is activated. When a union wins good pay and working conditions for its members, for example, basic needs will be met and union members may then want to have social and esteem needs met in the workplace.

Two-Factor Theory

Frederick Herzberg developed another popular needs-based theory of motivation called the *two-factor theory*.[14] Herzberg interviewed hundreds of workers about times when they were highly motivated to work and other times when they were dissatisfied and unmotivated to work. His findings suggested that the work characteristics associated with dissatisfaction were quite different from those pertaining to satisfaction, which prompted the notion that two factors influence work motivation.

Exhibit 8.5 illustrates the two-factor theory. The center of the scale is neutral, meaning that workers are neither satisfied nor dissatisfied. Herzberg believed that

Exhibit 8.5 Herzberg's Two-Factor Theory

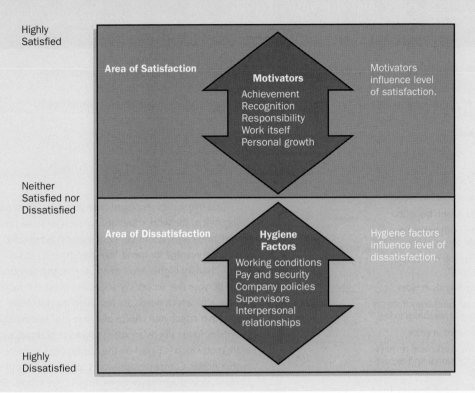

two entirely separate dimensions contribute to an employee's behavior at work. The first dimension, called **hygiene factors**, involves the presence or absence of job dissatisfiers, such as working conditions, pay, company policies, and interpersonal relationships. When hygiene factors are poor, work is dissatisfying. This is similar to the concept of deficiency needs described by Maslow. Good hygiene factors remove the dissatisfaction, but they do not in themselves cause people to become highly satisfied and motivated in their work.

The second set of factors does influence job satisfaction. **Motivators** fulfill high-level needs such as needs for achievement, recognition, responsibility, and opportunity for growth. Herzberg believed that when motivators are present, workers are highly motivated and satisfied. Thus, hygiene factors and motivators represent two distinct factors that influence motivation. Hygiene factors work in the area of lower-level needs, and their absence causes dissatisfaction. Inadequate pay, unsafe working conditions, or a noisy work environment will cause people to be dissatisfied, but their correction will not cause a high level of work enthusiasm and satisfaction. Higher-level motivators such as challenge, responsibility, and recognition must be in place before employees will be highly motivated. Leaders at Pizza Express successfully apply the two-factor theory to provide both hygiene factors and motivators, thus meeting employees' higher as well as lower needs. It's a formula that has created happy, motivated employees and a successful organization.

Action Memo

You can evaluate your current or a previous job according to Maslow's needs theory and Herzberg's two-factor theory by answering the questions in Leader's Self-Insight 8.1.

Hygiene factors
the first dimension of Herzberg's two-factor theory; involves working conditions, pay, company policies, and interpersonal relationships

Motivators
the second dimension of Herzberg's two-factor theory; involves job satisfaction and meeting higher-level needs such as achievement, recognition, and opportunity for growth

Leader's Self-Insight 8.1

Are Your Needs Met?

Think of a specific job (current or previous) you have held. If you are a full-time student, think of your classes and study activities as your job. Please answer the following questions about those work activities. Indicate whether each item is Mostly False or Mostly True for you.

	Mostly False	Mostly True
1. I feel physically safe at work.	_____	_____
2. I have good health benefits.	_____	_____
3. I am satisfied with what I'm getting paid for my work.	_____	_____
4. I feel that my job is secure as long as I want it.	_____	_____
5. I have good friends at work.	_____	_____
6. I have enough time away from my work to enjoy other things in life.	_____	_____
7. I feel appreciated at work.	_____	_____
8. People at my workplace respect me as a professional and expert in my field.	_____	_____
9. I feel that my job allows me to realize my full potential.	_____	_____
10. I feel that I am realizing my potential as an expert in my line of work.	_____	_____
11. I feel I'm always learning new things that help me to do my work better.	_____	_____
12. There is a lot of creativity involved in my work.	_____	_____

Scoring and Interpretation

Compute the number of Mostly True responses for the questions that represent each level of Maslow's hierarchy, as indicated below, and write your score where indicated:

Questions 1–2: Physiological and health needs.
Score = _____.

Questions 3–4: Economic and safety needs.
Score = _____.
Questions 5–6: Belonging and social needs.
Score = _____.
Questions 7–8: Esteem needs.
Score = _____.
Questions 9–12: Self-actualization needs.
Score = _____.

These five scores represent how you see your needs being met in the work situation. An average score for overall need satisfaction (all 12 questions) is typically 6, and the average for lower-level needs tends to be higher than for higher-level needs. Is that true for you? What do your five scores say about the need satisfaction in your job? Which needs are less filled for you? How would that affect your choice of a new job? In developed countries, lower needs are often taken for granted, and work motivation is based on the opportunity to meet higher needs. Compare your scores to those of another student. How does that person's array of five scores differ from yours? Ask questions about the student's job to help explain the difference in scores.

Re-read the 12 questions. Which questions would you say are about the *motivators* in Herzberg's Two-Factor Theory? Which questions are about *hygiene factors*? Calculate the average points for the motivator questions and the average points for the hygiene factor questions. What do you interpret from your scores on these two factors compared to the five levels of needs in Maslow's hierarchy?

Source: These questions are taken from *Social Indicators Research* 55 (2001), pp. 241–302, "A New Measure of Quality of Work Life (QWL) based on Need Satisfaction and Spillover Theories," M. Joseph Sirgy, David Efraty, Phillip Siegel and Dong-Jin Lee. Copyright © and reprinted with kind permission of Kluwer Academic Publishers.

marble: © Kirill Matkov   sunset: © Marco Regalia

IN THE LEAD

Julie MacDonald, Pizza Express

Julie MacDonald, director of human resources for Pizza Express, a chain of 350 restaurants across the United Kingdom, knew the company did a good job of motivating people who wanted to move up the organizational hierarchy, but she realized it was neglecting local restaurant managers who wanted to stay right where they were. Consequently, excellent people gradually became demotivated and headed for management jobs at the competition.

MacDonald worked with other leaders to change that. Pizza Express already provided hygiene factors such as good salaries and benefits, including bonuses of up to 30 percent of annual salary, generous maternity and paternity leave, childcare vouchers, and free meals. What was lacking was a program to meet higher-level needs for responsibility, achievement, and professional and personal growth. The answer was a program called "Exploration." One aspect is the A-Club, which all managers of top-ranked Pizza Express restaurants are eligible to join (the company does an annual review that grades restaurants from A+ to D). Members of the A-Club meet two or three times a year, sometimes for a social event such as visiting a cookery school or a fantastic restaurant, other times to participate in making important company-level decisions. Managers can also pitch personal development ideas to top bosses. One, for example, wanted to develop expertise in Italian wine. Applicants make a presentation outlining their idea, its benefits, how it will work, and what it will cost. A panel of top leaders makes a decision on the spot whether to fund the project. Managers at lower-ranked restaurants aren't overlooked, either. They participate in a personal and professional development program aimed at enabling managers to more easily communicate with one another, develop their skills, and improve their restaurants.

With the addition of these high-level motivators, Pizza Express is making sure restaurant managers stay engaged with their jobs rather than looking for greater satisfaction elsewhere. Consequently, the company has one of the lowest turnover rates in the industry.[15]

The implication of the two-factor theory for leaders is clear. People have multiple needs, and the leader's role is to go beyond the removal of dissatisfiers to the use of motivators to meet higher-level needs and propel employees toward greater enthusiasm and satisfaction.

Acquired Needs Theory

Another needs-based theory was developed by David McClelland. The **acquired needs theory** proposes that certain types of needs are acquired during an individual's lifetime. In other words, people are not born with these needs, but may learn them through their life experiences.[16] For example, the parents of Bill Strickland, who founded and runs Manchester Bidwell, a highly successful nonprofit organization that provides after-school and summer programs for at-risk young people, always encouraged him to follow his dreams. When he wanted to go south to work with the Freedom Riders in the 1960s, they supported him. His plans for tearing up the family basement and making a photography studio were met with equal enthusiasm. Strickland thus developed a *need for achievement* that enabled him to accomplish amazing results later in life.[17] Three needs most frequently studied are the need for achievement, need for affiliation, and need for power.

> **Action Memo**
>
> *As a leader, you can use good working conditions, satisfactory pay, and comfortable relationships to reduce job dissatisfaction. To spur greater follower satisfaction and enthusiasm, you can employ motivators—challenge, responsibility, and recognition.*

- *Need for achievement*—the desire to accomplish something difficult, attain a high standard of success, master complex tasks, and surpass others.
- *Need for affiliation*—the desire to form close personal relationships, avoid conflict, and establish warm friendships.
- *Need for power*—the desire to influence or control others, be responsible for others, and have authority over others.

For more than 20 years, McClelland studied human needs and their implications for management. People with a high need for achievement tend to enjoy

Acquired needs theory
McClelland's theory that proposes that certain types of needs (achievement, affiliation, power) are acquired during an individual's lifetime

work that is entrepreneurial and innovative. People who have a high need for affiliation are successful "integrators," whose job is to coordinate the work of people and departments.[18] Integrators include brand managers and project managers, positions that require excellent people skills. A high need for power is often associated with successful attainment of top levels in the organizational hierarchy. For example, McClelland studied managers at AT&T for 16 years and found that those with a high need for power were more likely to pursue a path of continued promotion over time.

In summary, needs-based theories focus on underlying needs that motivate how people behave. The hierarchy of needs theory, the two-factor theory, and the acquired needs theory all identify the specific needs that motivate people. Leaders can work to meet followers' needs and hence elicit appropriate and successful work behaviors.

Other Motivation Theories

Three additional motivation theories—the reinforcement perspective, expectancy theory, and equity theory—focus primarily on extrinsic rewards and punishments Relying on extrinsic rewards and punishments is sometimes referred to as the *carrot-and-stick approach*.[19] Behavior that produces a desired outcome is rewarded with a "carrot," such as a pay raise or promotion. Conversely, undesirable or unproductive behavior brings the "stick," such as a demotion or withholding a pay raise. Carrot-and-stick approaches tend to focus on lower needs, although higher needs can sometimes also be met.

Reinforcement Perspective on Motivation

The reinforcement approach to employee motivation sidesteps the deeper issue of employee needs described in the needs-based theories. **Reinforcement theory** simply looks at the relationship between behavior and its consequences by changing or modifying followers' on-the-job behavior through the appropriate use of immediate rewards or punishments.

Behavior modification is the name given to the set of techniques by which reinforcement theory is used to modify behavior.[20] The basic assumption underlying behavior modification is the **law of effect**, which states that positively reinforced behavior tends to be repeated, and behavior that is not reinforced tends not to be repeated. **Reinforcement** is defined as anything that causes a certain behavior to be repeated or inhibited. Four ways in which leaders use reinforcement to modify or shape employee behavior are positive reinforcement, negative reinforcement, punishment, and extinction.

Positive reinforcement is the administration of a pleasant and rewarding consequence immediately following a desired behavior. A good example of positive reinforcement is immediate praise for an employee who does a little extra in his or her work. The pleasant consequence will increase the likelihood of the excellent work behavior occurring again. Studies have shown that positive reinforcement does help to improve performance. In addition, nonfinancial reinforcements such as positive feedback, social recognition, and attention are just as effective as financial rewards.[21] Indeed, many people consider factors other than money to be more important. One study of employees at fast-food drive-throughs, for example, found that performance feedback and supervisor recognition had a significant effect on motivating employees to "up-sell," or ask customers to increase their order.[22] Nelson Motivation Inc. conducted a survey of 750 employees across a number of industries to assess the value they placed on various rewards. Cash and

Reinforcement theory
a motivational theory that looks at the relationship between behavior and its consequences by changing or modifying followers' on-the-job behavior through the appropriate use of immediate rewards or punishments

Behavior modification
the set of techniques by which reinforcement theory is used to modify behavior

Law of effect
states that positively reinforced behavior tends to be repeated and behavior that is not reinforced tends not to be repeated

Reinforcement
anything that causes a certain behavior to be repeated or inhibited

Positive reinforcement
the administration of a pleasant and rewarding consequence following a behavior

other monetary rewards came in dead last. The most valued rewards involved praise and manager support and involvement.[23]

Negative reinforcement, sometimes referred to as *avoidance learning*, is the process of withdrawing an unpleasant consequence once a behavior is improved, thereby encouraging and strengthening the desired behavior. The idea is that people will change a specific behavior to avoid the undesired result that behavior provokes. As a simple example, a supervisor who constantly reminds or nags an employee who is goofing off on the factory floor and stops the nagging when the employee stops goofing off is using negative reinforcement.

Punishment is the imposition of unpleasant outcomes on an employee in order to discourage and weaken an undesirable behavior. For example, the previously mentioned supervisor might assign the employee who is goofing off on the factory floor a particularly dirty and difficult task for the rest of the afternoon. The supervisor expects that the negative outcome will serve as a punishment and reduce the likelihood of the employee goofing off during work. The use of punishment in organizations is controversial and often criticized because it fails to indicate the correct behavior.

Extinction is the withholding of something positive, such as leader attention, praise, or pay raises. With extinction, undesirable behavior is essentially ignored. The idea is that behavior that is not reinforced with positive attention and rewards will gradually disappear. A *New York Times* reporter wrote a humorous article about how she learned to stop nagging and instead use reinforcement theory to shape her husband's behavior after studying how professionals train animals.[24] When her husband did something she liked, such as throw a dirty shirt in the hamper, she would use *positive reinforcement*, thanking him or giving him a hug and a kiss. Undesirable behaviors, such as throwing dirty clothes on the floor, on the other hand, were simply ignored, applying the principle of *extinction*.

> ### Action Memo
>
> As a leader, you can change follower behavior through the appropriate use of rewards and punishments. To establish new behaviors quickly, you can reinforce the desired behavior after each and every occurrence. To sustain the behaviors over a long time period, try reinforcing the behaviors intermittently.

Leaders can apply reinforcement theory to influence the behavior of followers. They can reinforce behavior after each and every occurrence, which is referred to as *continuous reinforcement*, or they can choose to reinforce behavior intermittently, which is referred to as *partial reinforcement*. Some of today's companies are using a continuous reinforcement schedule by offering people cash, game tokens, or points that can be redeemed for prizes each time they perform the desired behavior. Leaders at LDF Sales & Distributing, for example, tried a program called "The Snowfly Slots," developed by management professor Brooks Mitchell, to cut inventory losses. Workers received tokens each time they double-checked the quantity of a shipment. Since LDF started using Snowfly, inventory losses have fallen by 50 percent, saving the company $31,000 a year.[25]

With partial reinforcement, the desired behavior is reinforced often enough to make the employee believe the behavior is worth repeating, even though it is not rewarded every time it is demonstrated. Continuous reinforcement can be very effective for establishing new behaviors, but research has found that partial reinforcement is more effective for maintaining behavior over extended time periods.[26]

Expectancy Theory

Expectancy theory suggests that motivation depends on individuals' mental expectations about their ability to perform tasks and receive desired rewards. Expectancy theory is associated with the work of Victor Vroom, although a number

Negative reinforcement
the withdrawal of an unpleasant consequence once a behavior is improved

Punishment
the imposition of unpleasant outcomes on an employee following undesirable behavior

Extinction
the withdrawal of a positive reward, meaning that behavior is no longer reinforced and hence is less likely to occur in the future

Expectancy theory
a theory that suggests that motivation depends on individuals' mental expectations about their ability to perform tasks and receive desired rewards

of scholars have made contributions in this area.[27] Expectancy theory is concerned not with understanding types of needs, but with the thinking process that individuals use to achieve rewards.

Expectancy theory is based on the relationship among the individual's effort, the possibility of high performance, and the desirability of outcomes following high performance. Exhibit 8.6 illustrates these elements and the relationships among them. The $E > P$ expectancy is the probability that putting effort into a task will lead to high performance. For this expectancy to be high, the individual must have the ability, previous experience, and necessary tools, information, and opportunity to perform. The $P > O$ expectancy involves whether successful performance will lead to the desired outcome. If this expectancy is high, the individual will be more highly motivated. *Valence* refers to the value of outcomes to the individual. If the outcomes that are available from high effort and good performance are not valued by an employee, motivation will be low. Likewise, if outcomes have a high value, motivation will be higher. A simple example to illustrate the relationships in Exhibit 8.6 is Alfredo Torres, a salesperson at Diamond Gift Shop. If Alfredo believes that increased selling effort will lead to higher personal sales, his $E > P$ expectancy would be considered high. Moreover, if he also believes that higher personal sales will lead to a promotion or pay raise, the $P > O$ expectancy is also high. Finally, if Alfredo places a high value on the promotion or pay raise, valence is high and he will be highly motivated. For an employee to be highly motivated, all three factors in the expectancy model must be high.[28]

Like the path–goal theory of leadership described in Chapter 3, expectancy theory is personalized to subordinates' needs and goals. A leader's responsibility is to help followers meet their needs while attaining organizational goals. Fairmont Hotels & Resorts implemented an employee recognition program that lets award winners work with leaders to design the reward they want. Letting employees

Exhibit 8.6 Key Elements of Expectancy Theory

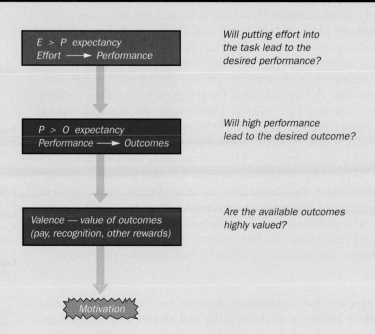

E > P expectancy
Effort ⟶ Performance

Will putting effort into the task lead to the desired performance?

P > O expectancy
Performance ⟶ Outcomes

Will high performance lead to the desired outcome?

Valence — value of outcomes (pay, recognition, other rewards)

Are the available outcomes highly valued?

Motivation

design their own rewards ensures that the reward will have high value and people will be more motivated to work for it.

According to expectancy theory, leaders enhance motivation by increasing followers' expectancy—clarifying individual needs, providing the desired outcomes, and ensuring that individuals have the ability and support needed to perform well and attain their desired outcomes. Wesley Willows, a retirement community in Rockford, Illinois, applied expectancy theory in a companywide wellness program for employees, which paid off with healthier employees and lower health-care costs.

IN THE LEAD

Bill Pratt, Wesley Willows Corporation

Leaders in companies all over the country have been inspired by *The Biggest Loser*. Given that the program has been such a hit on television, maybe a contest-style incentive program can work to help employees trim their waistlines, stop smoking, or attain other wellness goals.

At Wesley Willows, chief executive Bill Pratt invests $20,000 to $30,000 a year in an incentive-based weight loss program, which includes fees to Tangerine Wellness Inc. and rewards for workers who reach their goals. Employees who want to participate meet with a Tangerine representative who takes weight and height information and helps them formulate goals and plans for achieving them. People can participate individually or as part of a team. A customized Web site lets people track their team's progress. Incentives are also available for people who need to gain weight or who simply need to maintain their current healthy weight.

The program has been a success. About half of the company's 290 staff members participate, and they lost a cumulative 750 pounds in little over a year. Health insurance claims over a period that included the first six months of the program dropped 19 percent. An added benefit was a 30 percent drop in turnover, which Pratt attributes to the fun, collegial environment the program has brought about. "I see anywhere from 15 to 20 people out walking in groups on company grounds on a regular basis," he says.[29]

Participants in the Wesley Willows wellness program work with Tangerine Wellness representatives to set reasonable goals for weight loss and to determine action steps, so they feel confident they can achieve the goals if they put forth effort. They know that achieving goals will lead to rewards, and the rewards that are available—including cash, recognition for being on a winning team, and the reward of feeling and looking better—are highly valued. Thus, all three elements of the expectancy theory model illustrated in Exhibit 8.6 are high, which leads to high motivation.

Action Memo

Expectancy theory and reinforcement theory are widely used in all types of organizations and leadership situations. The questionnaire in Leader's Self-Insight 8.2 gives you the opportunity to see how effectively you apply these motivational ideas in your own leadership.

Equity Theory

Sometimes employees' motivation is affected not only by their expectancies and the rewards they receive, but also by their perceptions of how fairly they are treated in relation to others. **Equity theory** proposes that people are motivated to seek social equity in the rewards they receive for performance.[30] According to the theory, if people perceive their rewards as equal to what others receive for similar contributions, they will believe they are treated fairly and will be more highly motivated. When they believe they are not being treated fairly and equitably, motivation will decline.

Equity theory
a theory that proposes that people are motivated to seek social equity in the rewards they receive for performance

Leader's Self-Insight 8.2
Your Approach to Motivating Others

Think about situations in which you were in a formal or informal leadership role in a group or organization. Imagine using your personal approach as a leader, and answer the following questions. Indicate whether each item is Mostly False or Mostly True for you.

	Mostly False	Mostly True
1. I ask the other person what rewards they value for high performance.	_____	_____
2. I find out if the person has the ability to do what needs to be done.	_____	_____
3. I explain exactly what needs to be done for the person I'm trying to motivate.	_____	_____
4. Before giving somebody a reward, I find out what would appeal to that person.	_____	_____
5. I negotiate what people will receive if they accomplish the goal.	_____	_____
6. I make sure people have the ability to achieve performance targets.	_____	_____
7. I give special recognition when others' work is very good.	_____	_____
8. I only reward people if their performance is up to standard.	_____	_____
9. I use a variety of rewards to reinforce exceptional performance.	_____	_____
10. I generously praise people who perform well.	_____	_____
11. I promptly commend others when they do a better-than-average job.	_____	_____
12. I publicly compliment others when they do outstanding work.	_____	_____

Scoring and Interpretation

These questions represent two related aspects of motivation theory. For the aspect of expectancy theory, sum the points for Mostly True to questions 1–6. For the aspect of reinforcement theory, sum the points for Mostly True for questions 7–12.

The scores for my approach to motivation are:

My use of expectancy theory: _____

My use of reinforcement theory: _____

These two scores represent how you see yourself applying the motivational concepts of expectancy and reinforcement in your own leadership style. Four or more points on *expectancy theory* means you motivate people by managing expectations. You understand how a person's effort leads to performance and make sure that high performance leads to valued rewards. Four or more points for *reinforcement theory* means that you attempt to modify people's behavior in a positive direction with frequent and prompt positive reinforcement. New managers often learn to use reinforcements first, and as they gain more experience are able to apply expectancy theory.

Exchange information about your scores with other students to understand how your application of these two motivation theories compares to other students. Remember, leaders are expected to master the use of these two motivation theories. If you didn't receive an average score or higher, you can consciously do more with expectations and reinforcement when you are in a leadership position.

Sources: These questions are based on D. Whetten and K. Cameron, *Developing Management Skills*, 5th ed. (Upper Saddle River, NJ: Prentice Hall, 2002), pp. 302–303; and P. M. Podsakoff, S. B. Mackenzie, R. H. Moorman, and R. Fetter, "Transformational Leader Behaviors and Their Effects on Followers' Trust in Leader, Satisfaction, and Organizational Citizenship Behaviors," *Leadership Quarterly* 1, no. 2 (1990), pp. 107–142.

marble: © Kirill Matkov   sunset: © Marco Regalia

People evaluate equity by a ratio of inputs to outcomes. That is, employees make comparisons of what they put into a job and the rewards they receive relative to those of other people in the organization. Inputs include such things as education, experience, effort, and ability. Outcomes include pay, recognition, promotions, and other rewards. A state of equity exists whenever the ratio of one person's outcomes to inputs equals the ratio of others' in the work group. Inequity occurs when the input/outcome ratios are out of balance, such as when an employee with a high level of experience and ability receives the same salary as a new, less-educated employee. One mail-order company ran into trouble when leaders had to hire new employees quickly in a tight labor market and needed to offer the newcomers higher salaries than current employees were making in order to match what the new hires were making elsewhere. The motivation and commitment of long-time employees declined significantly, as did their performance, because they felt treated unfairly.[31] In today's environment, the opposite is occurring, with new employees in some companies, such as U.S. auto manufacturers and parts suppliers, being hired at wages much lower than those of their coworkers who were hired before the firms negotiated new labor agreements to help the companies cut costs and survive. "If I was doing the same job, working just as hard, and earning what they make," said one employee who was hired before the cut, "I'd be resentful."[32]

This discussion provides only a brief overview of equity theory. The theory's practical use has been criticized because a number of key issues are unclear. However, the important point of equity theory is that, for many people, motivation is influenced significantly by relative as well as absolute rewards. The concept reminds leaders that they should be cognizant of the possible effects of perceived inequity on follower motivation and performance.

Action Memo

As a leader, you can clarify the rewards a follower desires and ensure that he or she has the knowledge, skills, resources, and support to perform and obtain the desired rewards. You can keep in mind that perceived equity or inequity in rewards also influences motivation.

The Carrot-and-Stick Controversy

Reward and punishment motivational practices dominate organizations. According to the Society for Human Resource Management, 84 percent of all companies in the United States offer some type of monetary or nonmonetary reward system, and 69 percent offer incentive pay, such as bonuses, based on an employee's performance.[33] However, in other studies, more than 80 percent of employers with incentive programs have reported that their programs are only somewhat successful or not working at all.[34]

When used appropriately, financial incentives can be quite effective. For one thing, giving employees pay raises or bonuses can signal that leaders value their contributions to the organization. Some researchers argue that using money as a motivator almost always leads to higher performance.[35] However, despite the testimonies of numerous organizations that enjoy successful incentive programs, the arguments against the efficacy of carrot-and-stick methods are growing. Critics argue that extrinsic rewards are neither adequate nor productive motivators and may even work against the best interests of organizations. Reasons for this criticism include the following:

1. *Extrinsic rewards diminish intrinsic rewards.* Here's a story: A shopkeeper got tired of the noise of a group of children who played outside his store every afternoon. One day, he asked them to leave and promised he'd give each of them $1 to come back and play there the next day. Of course, they showed up. The shopkeeper said he would give each one 50 cents to come back the following day, and the next day 25 cents. At that point, the children said they wouldn't be back the following day because it wasn't worth it for a quarter. The shopkeeper got what he wanted by shifting the children's motivation for playing there toward earning an extrinsic reward rather than for the intrinsic pleasure they once got. The moral of the story is that the motivation to seek an extrinsic reward, whether it's a bonus or professional approval, leads people to focus on the reward rather than

on the intrinsic satisfaction they get from their jobs.[36] When people lack intrinsic rewards in their work, they lose interest and their performance levels out; it stays just adequate to reach the reward. In the worst case, people perform hazardously, such as covering up an on-the-job accident to get a bonus based on a safety target.

2. *Extrinsic rewards are temporary.* Bestowing extrinsic rewards might ensure short-term success, but not long-term quality.[37] The success of reaching immediate goals is quickly followed by the development of unintended consequences. Because people are focusing on the reward, the work they do holds no interest for them, and without interest in their work, the potential for exploration, innovation, and creativity disappears.[38] The current deadline may be met, but better ways of working will not be discovered.

3. *Extrinsic rewards assume people are driven by lower needs.* Giving people perfunctory rewards of praise and pay increases presumes that the primary reason people initiate and persist in actions is to satisfy lower needs. However, behavior is also based on yearning for self-expression, self-esteem, and positive feelings. In surveys about employee satisfaction, for example, the rewards that rank high typically don't relate to money but to aspects of work that give people a feeling of responsibility and achievement.[39] Extrinsic rewards focus on the specific goals and deadlines delineated by incentive plans rather than enabling people to facilitate their vision for a desired future, that is, to realize their possible higher needs for growth and fulfillment.[40]

4. *Organizations are too complex for carrot-and-stick approaches.* The relationships and the accompanying actions that are part of today's organizations are overwhelmingly complex.[41] By contrast, carrot-and-stick plans are quite simple, and the application of an overly simplified incentive plan to a highly complex operation usually creates a misdirected system.[42] It is difficult for leaders to interpret and reward all the behaviors that employees need to demonstrate to keep complex organizations successful over the long term. Thus, extrinsic motivators often wind up rewarding behaviors that are the opposite of what the organization wants and needs. Although managers may espouse long-term growth, for example, they reward quarterly earnings; thus, workers are motivated to act for quick returns for themselves.

Recent years have shown the damaging consequences of misdirected incentive plans. Alan Blinder, Princeton professor of economics and public affairs, points out that a fundamental cause of the recent financial crisis was the "perverse go-for-broke incentives" that rewarded people for taking excessive risks with other people's money.[43] Public outrage over skewed incentives that contributed to company failures and a global economic crisis prompted the U.S. Congress to require that boards of directors vote on the compensation plans of companies that received federal bailout funds. Other companies took the lead by voluntarily adopting these so-called "say on pay" practices early in the crisis.

IN THE LEAD

Amgen Inc., Verizon Communications, Aflac

"It is not clear that existing compensation mechanisms effectively ensure that traders take into account the long-term interests of the bank for which they work—i.e., its survival," wrote Pierre Cailleteau, chief international economist for Moody's Investors Service. He was referring to reward practices that give traders a vested interest in closing a deal, regardless of how effectively that deal delivers or fails to deliver in the long term.

During the financial meltdown of 2008–2009, it became clear that people at every level of the financial system were getting rewarded for short-term performance—if things went wrong down the line, it was someone else's problem. When it all came crashing down, there were heated demands for companies in all industries to make sure their incentive plans aligned with the interests of shareholders and the public. Amgen, a biotechnology firm, took what at the time was an unusual step. At its 2008 meeting, the firm asked shareholders to answer questions such as whether the proposed 2009 compensation plan was performance-based, whether performance goals were clearly defined and understandable, and whether the incentive plan was clearly linked to long-term strategy.

Other firms adopted similar approaches. Directors at Home Depot met with shareholders individually or in small groups to hear their concerns and get their input regarding incentives. Both Verizon Communications and Aflac, the insurer based in Columbus, Georgia, gave shareholders a vote on top executives' pay packages. Corporate governance monitors believe such practices will increase as companies look for ways to appease angry shareholders and create incentive plans that promote more ethical and socially responsible behavior.[44]

Companies such as Amgen, Verizon, and Aflac are trying to make sure their incentive plans do not inadvertently motivate the wrong types of behavior. In the financial industry, incentives originally designed to encourage innovation and beneficial risk-taking unintentionally encouraged people to push rules to the limit. Unfortunately, incentives that reward short-term performance remain the rule for many Wall Street firms, and compensation reform remains a hot topic.[45] This chapter's *Consider This* further examines how incentives can end up motivating the wrong behaviors.

5. *Carrot-and-stick approaches destroy people's motivation to work as a group.* Extrinsic rewards and punishments create a culture of competition versus a culture of cooperation.[46] In a competitive environment, one person's success is a threat to another's goals. Furthermore, sharing problems and solutions is out of the question when coworkers may use your weakness to undermine you, or when a supervisor might view the need for assistance as a disqualifier for rewards. In contrast, replacing the carrot-and-stick with methods based on meeting higher *as well as* lower needs enables a culture of collaboration marked by compatible goals; all the members of the organization are trying to achieve a shared vision. Without the effort to control behavior individually through rigid rewards, people can see coworkers as part of their success. Each person's success is mutually enjoyed because every success benefits the organization.

Incentive programs can be successful, especially when people are actually motivated by money and lower needs. However, individual incentives are rarely enough to motivate behaviors that benefit the organization as a whole. One way for leaders to address the carrot-and-stick controversy is to understand a program's strengths and weaknesses and acknowledge the positive but limited effects of extrinsic motivators. A leader also appeals to people's higher needs, and no subordinate should have work that does not offer some self-satisfaction

Consider **This!**
On the Folly of Rewarding A While Hoping for B

Managers who complain about the lack of motivation in workers might do well to examine whether the reward system encourages behavior different from what they are seeking. People usually determine which activities are rewarded and then seek to do those things, to the virtual exclusion of activities not rewarded. Nevertheless, there are numerous examples of fouled-up systems that reward unwanted behaviors, whereas the desired actions are not being rewarded at all.

In sports, for example, most coaches stress teamwork, proper attitude, and one-for-all spirit. However, rewards are usually distributed according to individual performance. The college basketball player who passes the ball to teammates instead of shooting will not compile impressive scoring statistics and will be less likely to be drafted by the pros. The big-league baseball player who hits to advance the runner rather than to score a home run is less likely to win the titles that guarantee big salaries. In universities, a primary goal is the transfer of knowledge from professors to students, yet professors are rewarded primarily for research and publication, not for their commitment to good teaching. Students are rewarded for making good grades, not necessarily for acquiring knowledge, and may resort to cheating rather than risk a low grade on their college transcript.

In business, there are often similar discrepancies between the desired behaviors and those rewarded. For example, see the table below.

Managers Hope For	But They Reward
Teamwork and collaboration	The best individual performers
Innovative thinking and risk taking	Proven methods and not making mistakes
Development of people skills	Technical achievements and accomplishment
Employee involvement and empowerment	Tight control over operations and resources
High achievement	Another year's routine effort
Commitment to quality	Shipping on time, even with defects
Long-term growth	Quarterly earnings

What do a majority of managers see as the major obstacles to dealing with fouled-up reward systems?

1. The inability to break out of old ways of thinking about reward and recognition. This includes entitlement mentality in workers and resistance by management to revamp performance review and reward systems.
2. Lack of an overall systems view of performance and results. This is particularly true of systems that promote subunit results at the expense of the total organization.
3. Continuing focus on short-term results by management and shareholders.

Motivation theories must be sound because people do what they are rewarded for. But when will organizations learn to reward what they say they want?

Sources: Steven Kerr, "An Academy Classic: On the Folly of Rewarding A, While Hoping for B," and "More on the Folly," *Academy of Management Executive* 9, no. 1 (1995), pp. 7–16.

© majaiva

as well as a yearly pay raise. Furthermore, rewards can be directly linked to behavior promoting the higher needs of both individuals and the organization, such as rewarding quality, long-term growth, or a collaborative culture.[47]

Action Memo

As a leader, you can avoid total reliance on carrot-and-stick motivational techniques. You can acknowledge the limited effects of extrinsic rewards and appeal to people's higher needs for intrinsic satisfaction.

Empowering People to Meet Higher Needs

Many leaders are shifting from efforts to control behavior through carrot-and-stick approaches to providing people with the power, information, and authority that enables them to find greater intrinsic satisfaction with their work. **Empowerment** refers to power sharing, the delegation of power or authority to subordinates in the organization.[48]

Empowerment provides strong motivation because it meets the higher needs of individuals. Research indicates that individuals have a need for *self-efficacy,* which is the capacity to produce results or outcomes, to feel they are effective.[49] Most people come into an organization with the desire to do a good job, and empowerment enables leaders to release the motivation already there. Increased responsibility motivates most people to strive to do their best.

In addition, leaders greatly benefit from the expanded capabilities that employee participation brings to the organization. This enables them to devote more attention to vision and the big picture. It also takes the pressure off of leaders when subordinates are able to respond better and more quickly to the markets they serve.[50] Frontline employees often have a better understanding than do leaders of how to improve a work process, satisfy a customer, or solve a production problem. To empower followers, leaders provide them with an understanding of how their jobs are important to the organization's mission and performance, thereby giving them a direction within which to act freely.[51] For example, after Hurricane Katrina wiped out electrical service for 195,000 customers, Mississippi Power restored service in just 12 days thanks to an empowered workforce that was able to act innovatively within certain guidelines. Crews were able to engineer their own solutions in the field rather than waiting for top–down direction.[52] The autonomy of empowered employees can create flexibility, motivation, and superior performance capabilities for an organization.[53]

Elements of Empowerment

Five elements must be in place before employees can be truly empowered to perform their jobs effectively: information, knowledge, discretion, meaning, and rewards.[54]

1. *Employees receive information about company performance.* In companies where employees are fully empowered, no information is secret. At KI, an office furniture maker, everyone is taught to think like a business owner. Each month, managers share business results for each region, customer segment, and factory with the entire workforce so that everyone knows what product lines are behind or ahead, which operations are struggling, and what they can do to help the company meet its goals.[55]

Action Memo

As a leader, you can give employees greater power and authority to help meet higher motivational needs. You can implement empowerment by providing the five elements of information, knowledge, discretion, significance, and rewards.

Empowerment
power sharing; the delegation of power or authority to subordinates in the organization

2. *Employees receive knowledge and skills to contribute to company goals.* Companies train people to have the knowledge and skills they need to personally contribute to company performance. Knowledge and skills lead to feelings of competency—the belief that one is capable of accomplishing one's job successfully.[56] For example, when DMC, which makes pet supplies, gave employee teams the authority and responsibility for assembly line shutdowns, it provided extensive training on how to diagnose and interpret line malfunctions, as well as the costs related to shut-down and start-up. Employees worked through case studies to practice line shutdowns so they would feel they had the skills to make good decisions in real-life situations.[57]

3. *Employees have the power to make substantive decisions.* Many of today's most competitive companies give employees the power to influence work procedures and organizational direction through quality circles and self-directed work teams. At BHP Copper Metals in San Manuel, Arizona, teams of tank house workers identify and solve production problems and determine how best to organize themselves to get the job done. In addition, they can even determine the specific hours they need to handle their own workloads. For example, an employee could opt to work for four hours, leave, and come back to do the next four.[58]

4. *Employees understand the meaning and impact of their jobs.* Empowered employees consider their jobs important and meaningful, see themselves as capable and influential, and recognize the impact their work has on customers, other stakeholders, and the organization's success.[59] Understanding the connection between one's day-to-day activities and the overall vision for the organization gives people a sense of direction, allowing them to fit their actions to the vision and influence the outcome of their work.[60]

5. *Employees are rewarded based on company performance.* Studies have revealed the important role of fair reward and recognition systems in supporting empowerment. By affirming that employees are progressing toward goals, rewards help to keep motivation high.[61] Leaders are careful to examine and redesign reward systems to support empowerment and teamwork. Two ways in which organizations can financially reward employees based on company performance are through profit-sharing and employee stock ownership plans (ESOPs). Through an ESOP at Van Meter Industrial, an electrical parts distributor based in Cedar Rapids, Iowa, for example, 100 percent of the equity of the company is in the hands of employees, including managers, professional staff members, technical specialists, and frontline workers. Insurer Aflac has a profit-sharing program for all employees, from call center personnel to top leaders.[62] Unlike traditional carrot-and-stick approaches, these rewards focus on the performance of the group rather than individuals. Furthermore, rewards are just one component of empowerment rather than the sole basis of motivation.

Empowerment Applications

Many of today's organizations are implementing empowerment programs, but they are empowering workers to varying degrees. At some companies, empowerment means encouraging employee ideas, whereas managers retain final authority for decisions; at others, it means giving frontline employees almost complete power to make decisions and exercise initiative and imagination.[63]

Current methods of empowering employees fall along a continuum as shown in Exhibit 8.7. The continuum runs from a situation where frontline employees have no discretion (such as on a traditional assembly line) to full empowerment where workers even participate in formulating organizational strategy. An example of full empowerment is when self-directed teams are given the power to hire, discipline, and dismiss team members and to set compensation rates. Few organizations have moved to this level of empowerment. One that has is Semco, a Brazil-based company involved in manufacturing, services, and e-business. Ricardo Semler, whose father started the company in the 1950s, believes that people will act in their own, and by extension, the organization's best interests if they are given complete freedom. Semco lets people control their work hours, location, and even pay plans. Employees also participate in all organizational decisions, including what businesses Semco should pursue. Employees can veto any new product idea or business venture. They choose their own leaders and manage themselves to accomplish goals. Information is

Action Memo

Have you felt empowered in a job you have held? Take the quiz in Leader's Self-Insight 8.3 to evaluate your empowerment experience and compare it to the experience of other students.

Exhibit 8.7 The Empowerment Continuum

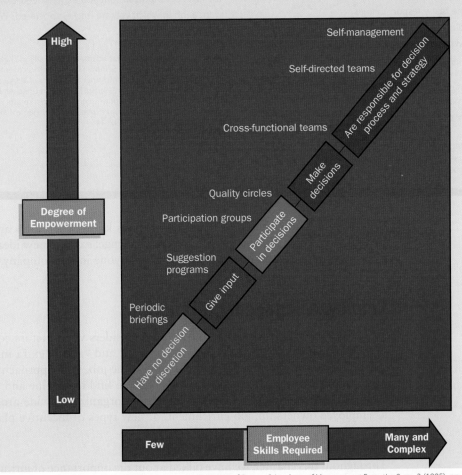

Sources: Based on Robert C. Ford and Myron D. Fottler, "Empowerment: A Matter of Degree," *Academy of Management Executive* 9, no. 3 (1995), pp. 21–31; Lawrence Holpp, "Applied Empowerment," *Training* (February 1994), pp. 39–44; and David P. McCaffrey, Sue R. Faerman, and David W. Hart, "The Appeal and Difficulties of Participative Systems," *Organization Science* 6, no. 6 (November–December 1995), pp. 603–627.

Leader's Self-Insight 8.3

Are You Empowered?

Think of a job—either a current or previous job—that was important to you, and then answer the following questions with respect to the managers above you in that job. Indicate whether each item is Mostly False or Mostly True for you.

In general, my supervisor/manager:

	Mostly False	Mostly True
1. Gave me the support I needed to do my job well.	_____	_____
2. Gave me the performance information I needed to do my job well.	_____	_____
3. Explained top management's strategy and vision for the organization.	_____	_____
4. Gave me many responsibilities.	_____	_____
5. Trusted me.	_____	_____
6. Allowed me to set my own goals.	_____	_____
7. Encouraged me to take control of my own work.	_____	_____
8. Used my ideas and suggestions when making decisions.	_____	_____
9. Made me responsible for what I did.	_____	_____
10. Encouraged me to figure out the causes and solutions to problems.	_____	_____

Scoring and Interpretation

Add one point for each Mostly True answer to the 10 questions to obtain your total score. The questions represent aspects of empowerment that an employee may experience in a job. If your score was 6 or above, you probably felt empowered in the job for which you answered the questions. If your score was 3 or below, you probably did not feel empowered. Did you feel highly motivated in that job, and was your motivation related to your empowerment? What factors explained the level of empowerment you felt? Was empowerment mostly based on your supervisor's leadership style? The culture of the organization? Compare your score with another student. Each of you take a turn describing the job and the level of empowerment you experienced. Do you want a job in which you are fully empowered? Why or why not?

Sources: These questions were adapted from Bradley L. Kirkman and Benson Rosen, "Beyond Self-Management: Antecedents and Consequences of Team Empowerment," *Academy of Management Journal* 42, no. 1 (February 1999), pp. 58–74; and Gretchen M. Spreitzer, "Psychological Empowerment in the Workplace: Dimensions, Measurements, and Validation," *Academy of Management Journal* 38, no. 5 (October 1995), pp. 1442–1465.

openly and broadly shared so that all employees know where they and the company stand. People are encouraged to seek challenge, explore new ideas and business opportunities, and question the ideas of anyone in the company.[64]

Employee Engagement Programs

The most recent thinking about motivation considers what factors contribute to people's willingness to be fully engaged at work and "go the extra mile" to contribute their creativity, energy, and passion on the job. One approach is to foster an organizational environment that helps people find true value and meaning in their work. A second approach is to implement organizationwide programs such as employee ownership, job enrichment, or new types of incentive plans.

Giving Meaning to Work Through Engagement

Throughout this chapter, we have talked about the importance of intrinsic rewards to high motivation. One way people get intrinsic rewards at work is when they feel a deep sense of importance and meaningfulness, such as people who work for a social cause or mission. However, people can find a sense of meaning and importance no matter what type of organization they work in if leaders build an environment in which people can flourish. When people feel that they're a part of something special, they are more highly motivated and committed to the success of the organization and all its members.

One path to meaning is through *employee engagement,* which researchers have found contributes to stronger organizational performance and higher profitability.[65] Internet shoe retailer Zappos takes engagement so seriously that it pays people to quit if they don't feel passionate about their work. In 2008, the "early-resignation bonus" was $1,500; the amount changes as leaders experiment to make sure the right people are being weeded out.[66] Employee **engagement** means that people enjoy their jobs and are satisfied with their work conditions, contribute enthusiastically to meeting team and organizational goals, and feel a sense of belonging and commitment to the organization. A fully engaged employee is one who is emotionally connected to the organization and actively seeks to serve the mission.[67]

It is the behavior of leaders that makes the biggest difference in whether people feel engaged at work.[68] A leader's role is not to control others, but to organize the workplace in such a way that each person can learn, contribute, and grow. Researchers at the Gallup Organization developed a metric called the Q12, a list of 12 questions that provides a way to evaluate how leaders are doing in creating an environment that provides intrinsic rewards by meeting higher-level needs. For example, one question on the Q12 concerns whether people have an opportunity at work to do what they do best. Recall from Chapter 2 the discussion of strengths and how each person has a unique set of talents and abilities. When people have an opportunity to do work that matches these natural capabilities, their satisfaction and engagement levels soar. One recent Gallup study found that organizations where leaders focused on maximizing their employees' natural talents increased employee engagement levels by an average of 33 percent a year.[69] The Q12 also evaluates characteristics such as whether employees know what is expected of them, whether they have the resources they need to perform well, whether they feel appreciated and recognized for doing good work, and whether they feel that their opinions are important. The full list of questions on the Q12 survey can be found in the book, *First Break All the Rules,* by researchers Marcus Buckingham and Curt Coffman.[70] When a majority of employees can answer the Q12 questions positively, the organization enjoys a highly motivated, engaged, and productive workforce. Buckingham has since written a new book, discussed in the Leader's Bookshelf, which takes a more in-depth look at what constitutes superior leadership.

Organizations where employees give high marks on the Q12 enjoy reduced turnover, are more productive and profitable, and enjoy greater employee and customer loyalty.[71] Yet, regrettably, Gallup's most recent semiannual Q12 survey found that 18 percent of U.S. employees are actively *disengaged.*[72] Active disengagement means that people are actively undermining their organization's success.

Leaders can identify the level of engagement in their organizations and implement strategies to facilitate full engagement and improve performance. Consider how the Medical Center of Plano (Texas) used the Q12 to spark a turnaround, as described in the following example.

Engagement
when people enjoy their jobs and are satisfied with their work conditions, contribute enthusiastically to meeting team and organizational goals, and feel a sense of belonging and commitment to the organization

Leader's Bookshelf

The One Thing You Need to Know . . . About Great Managing, Great Leading, and Sustained Individual Success

by Marcus Buckingham

Marcus Buckingham has spent two decades, including 17 years with the Gallup Organization, studying managers and leaders and how they build effective workplaces. His most recent book, *The One Thing You Need to Know . . . About Great Managing, Great Leading, and Sustained Individual Success,* brings together his thoughts in a well-written and engaging format. Buckingham points out that: "A leader's job is to rally people toward a better future." The problem, though, is that motivation can flag because most people fear the future. So how do leaders "find a way to make people excited and confident about what comes next"?

DO ONE THING: BE CLEAR

Clarity, Buckingham contends, is the most effective way to turn fear into confidence and motivation. Leaders define the future in such clear and vivid terms—through their actions, their stories, their heroes, their images, their measurements, and their rewards—that everyone can see where the organization is, where it wants to go, and how to take it there. He offers four points of clarity that leaders address:

- *Whom do we serve?* Leaders let followers know precisely whom they are trying to please. General Manager Denny Clements, for example, makes clear that the only people Toyota's Lexus Group is trying to serve are customers for whom time is their most precious commodity. Leaders don't always have to be right, Buckingham says, because there are often no right answers. They just have to be focused.
- *What is our core strength?* People know competition is tough. If leaders expect followers to feel confident about the future, they need to tell them why they're going to win. For Best Buy CEO Brad Anderson, this core strength is the quality of frontline store employees, so people get the training they need to better serve customers.
- *What is our core measurement?* Rather than looking at 15 different metrics, leaders identify the one score that will track people's progress toward the future. At Best Buy, the core measurement is employee engagement, based on the Gallup Q12 survey (discussed in this textbook).

- *What actions can we take right now?* Leaders highlight a few carefully selected actions they can take to show followers the way to the future. Some actions are symbolic and demonstrate the leader's vision of the future. Others are systemic and compel people to do things differently.

THREE DISCIPLINES OF LEADERS

"Effective leaders don't have to be passionate or charming or brilliant," says Buckingham. "What they must be is clear." To find that clarity, leaders develop three disciplines. First, they take the time to reflect so they can distill complexity into a vivid path to the future. Next, they practice the key words, images, and stories they will use to describe where they want followers to go. The third discipline involves selecting and celebrating heroes in the organization who visibly embody the future. By mastering these three disciplines, leaders can provide clarity for followers and engender confidence, motivation, and creativity to move toward the desired future.

The One Thing You Need to Know, by Marcus Buckingham, is published by The Free Press.

marble: © Ioannis Drimilis   library: www.istockphoto.com/nikada

IN THE LEAD

Harvey Fishero, Medical Center of Plano

The Medical Center of Plano is a world-class medical facility with 427 beds, more than 1,300 employees, and 900 physicians representing 70 specialties and subspecialties. But the organization competes with 29 other world-class hospitals in the Dallas–Fort Worth, Texas, area, all with great location, state-of-the-art technology, and sophisticated public relations.

Leaders knew that staying ahead of the pack required getting the very best from every employee. Unfortunately, the Medical Center had high turnover and low morale, and leaders couldn't put their finger on the reasons why. They decided to use the Gallup Q12 as a way to measure employee expectations and how well the organization was meeting them. The results were shocking: Only 18 percent of employees were *engaged*, 55 percent were *not engaged*, and 27 percent were *actively disengaged*.

CEO Harvey Fishero and other leaders guided their transformation of the Medical Center by intentionally addressing the issues covered by each of the Q12 questions, such as making sure people knew what was expected of them, had the materials and equipment needed to perform well, felt appreciated for doing good work, and so forth.

Within five years, the percentage of *actively disengaged* employees dropped to 9 percent, whereas the percentage of *engaged* employees jumped to 61 percent. Turnover declined, customer satisfaction improved, costs went down, and profits went up as employee engagement levels increased. The Medical Center of Plano was named by the *Dallas Business Journal* as a Best Place to Work in Dallas–Fort Worth, based on surveys of employees.[73]

By conscientiously implementing changes designed to meet the needs of employees based on the Q12, leaders dramatically boosted engagement and helped turn the Medical Center into the leader of Plano's medical institution pack. However, they know long-term success depends on continually looking for ways to maintain high employee engagement. In addition, leaders are expanding their efforts to measure and increase patient satisfaction and engagement as well.

Other Approaches

There are a number of other approaches to improving organizationwide motivation. Some of the most common are job enrichment programs, employee ownership, gainsharing, paying for knowledge, and paying for performance. Variable compensation and various forms of "at risk" pay are key motivational tools today and are becoming more common than fixed salaries at many companies.

Employee ownership occurs on two levels. First, empowerment can result in a psychological commitment to the mission of an organization, whereby members act as "owners" rather than employees. Second, by owning stock in the companies for which they work, individuals are motivated to give their best performances.

Hot Dog on a Stick is wholly owned by its 1,300 employees, 85 percent of whom are women and 92 percent of whom are under the age of 25. "They schedule their locations, order the food, look at the profit-and-loss statements," says CEO Fredrica Thode. "It's like being CEO of their own store."[74] Giving all employees ownership is a powerful way to motivate people to work for the good of the entire company. Employee ownership also signals that leaders acknowledge each person's role in reaching corporate goals. Employee ownership programs are usually supported by *open-book management*, which enables all employees to see and understand how the company is doing financially and how their actions contribute to the bottom line.

Gainsharing is another approach that motivates people to work together rather than focus on individual achievements and rewards. Gainsharing refers to an employee involvement program that ties additional pay to improvements in total employee performance.[75] Employees are asked to actively search for ways to make process improvements, with any resulting financial gains divided among

Action Memo

As a leader, you can build an environment that unleashes employee potential and allows people to find meaning in their work. You can also apply ideas, such as employee ownership, job enrichment, and new incentives, to motivate people toward greater cooperation and teamwork.

Employee ownership
giving employees real and psychological ownership in the organization; as owners, people are motivated to give their best performance

Gainsharing
motivational approach that encourages people to work together rather than focus on individual achievements and rewards; ties additional pay to improvements in overall employee performance

employees. One example is a gainsharing program at Meritor. Since it rewards employees for improvements in their own unit as well as companywide, the program has proven to be a powerful incentive for teamwork.[76]

Pay for knowledge programs base an employee's salary on the number of task skills he or she possesses. If employees increase their skills, they get paid more. A workforce in which individuals skillfully perform numerous tasks is more flexible and efficient. At BHP Copper Metals, for example, leaders devised a pay-for-skills program that supported the move to teamwork. Employees can rotate through various jobs to build their skills and earn a higher pay rate. Rates range from entry-level workers to lead operators. Lead operators are those who have demonstrated a mastery of skills, the ability to teach and lead others, and effective self-directed behavior.[77]

Pay for performance, which links at least a portion of employees' monetary rewards to results or accomplishments, is a significant trend in today's organizations.[78] Gainsharing is one type of pay for performance. Other examples include profit sharing, bonuses, and merit pay. In addition to the potential for greater income, pay for performance can give employees a greater sense of control over the outcome of their efforts. At Semco, described earlier, employees choose how they are paid based on 11 compensation options, which can be combined in various ways. Exhibit 8.8 lists Semco's 11 ways to pay. Semco leaders indicate that the flexible pay plan encourages innovation and risk-taking and motivates people to perform in the best interest of the company as well as themselves.

However, some pay-for-performance plans, particularly those centered on bonuses, have come under attack in recent years because they motivated people to focus on short-term achievements that reap individual rewards, with little concern for the long-term health of the organization. At companies such as AIG, Merrill Lynch, and Bear Stearns, for instance, people were focused on doing whatever it took to get a big bonus. Acknowledging that compensation was part of the problem that led to the Wall Street crisis, leaders in many companies are

Pay for knowledge
programs that base an employee's pay on the number of skills he or she possesses

Pay for performance
a program that links at least a portion of employees' monetary rewards to results or accomplishments

---

Exhibit 8.8 Semco's 11 Ways to Pay

Semco, a South American company involved in manufacturing, services, and e-business, lets employees choose how they are paid based on 11 compensation options:

1. Fixed salary
2. Bonuses
3. Profit sharing
4. Commission
5. Royalties on sales
6. Royalties on profits
7. Commission on gross margin
8. Stock or stock options
9. IPO/sale warrants that an executive cashes in when a business unit goes public or is sold
10. Self-determined annual review compensation in which an executive is paid for meeting self-set goals
11. Commission on difference between actual and three-year value of the company

Source: Ricardo Semler, "How We Went Digital Without a Strategy," *Harvard Business Review* (September–October 2000), pp. 51–58.

searching for ways to revise pay-for-performance plans so people are rewarded for boosting long-term organizational performance rather than short-term results. Morgan Stanley, for example, has increased base salaries for valued employees in order to reduce the emphasis on annual bonuses and "restore a balance between fixed and variable compensation."[79] At Analytical Graphics, top managers receive 100 percent of their bonuses only if the company achieves 110 percent of its growth targets.[80]

A final motivational technique, **job enrichment**, incorporates high-level motivators into the work, including job responsibility, recognition, and opportunities for growth, learning, and achievement. In an enriched job, the employee controls resources needed to perform well and makes decisions on how to do the work.

One way to enrich an oversimplified job is to enlarge it, that is, to extend the responsibility to cover several tasks instead of only one. Leaders at Ralcorp's cereal manufacturing plant in Sparks, Nevada, enriched jobs by combining several packing positions into a single job and cross-training employees to operate all of the packing line's equipment. Employees were given both the ability and the responsibility to perform all the various functions in their department, not just a single task. In addition, line employees became responsible for all screening and interviewing of new hires as well as training and advising one another. They also manage the production flow to and from their upstream and downstream partners—they understand the entire production process so they can see how their work affects the quality and productivity of employees in other departments. Ralcorp invests heavily in training to be sure employees have the needed operational skills as well as the ability to make decisions, solve problems, manage quality, and contribute to continuous improvement. Enriched jobs have improved employee motivation and satisfaction, and the company has benefited from higher long-term productivity, reduced costs, and happier employees.[81]

Job enrichment
a motivational approach that incorporates high-level motivators into the work, including job responsibility, recognition, and opportunities for growth, learning, and achievement

Leadership Essentials

■ This chapter introduced a number of important ideas about motivating people in organizations. Individuals are motivated to act to satisfy a range of needs. The leadership approach to motivation tends to focus on the higher needs of employees. The role of the leader is to create a situation in which followers' higher needs and the needs of the organization can be met simultaneously.

■ Needs-based theories focus on the underlying needs that motivate how people behave. Maslow's hierarchy of needs proposes that individuals satisfy lower needs before they move on to higher needs. Herzberg's two-factor theory holds that dissatisfiers must be removed and motivators then added to cause high motivation. McClelland asserted that people are motivated differently depending on which needs they have acquired.

■ Other motivation theories, including the reinforcement perspective, expectancy theory, and equity theory, focus primarily on extrinsic rewards and punishments, sometimes called *carrot-and-stick* methods of motivation. The reinforcement perspective proposes that behavior can be modified by the use of rewards and punishments. Expectancy theory is based on the idea that a person's motivation is contingent upon his or her expectations that a given behavior will result in desired rewards. Equity theory proposes that individuals' motivation is affected not only by the rewards they receive, but also by their perceptions of how fairly they are treated in relation to others. People are motivated to seek equity in the rewards they receive for performance.

- Although carrot-and-stick methods of motivation are pervasive in North American organizations, many critics argue that extrinsic rewards undermine intrinsic rewards, bring about unintended consequences, are too simple to capture organizational realities, and replace workplace cooperation with unhealthy competition.

- An alternative approach to carrot-and-stick motivation is that of empowerment, by which subordinates know the direction of the organization and have the autonomy to act as they see fit to go in that direction. Leaders provide employees with the knowledge to contribute to the organization, the power to make consequential decisions, and the necessary resources to do their jobs. Empowerment typically meets the higher needs of individuals.

- Empowerment is tied to the trend toward helping employees find value and meaning in their jobs and creating an environment where people can flourish. When people are fully engaged with their work, satisfaction, performance, and profits increase. Leaders create the environment that determines employee engagement. One way to measure how engaged people are with their work is the Q12, a list of 12 questions about the day-to-day realities of a person's job. Other current organizationwide motivational programs include employee ownership, gainsharing, pay for knowledge, pay for performance, and job enrichment.

Discussion Questions

1. Describe the kinds of needs that people bring to an organization. How might a person's values and attitudes, as described in Chapter 4, influence the needs he or she brings to work?

2. With the economy in a slump, some companies are secretively freezing pay raises or even cutting pay for some employees so they can offer substantial raises to people considered star performers. As a motivational technique, does this practice seem like a good one to you? What might be some disadvantages of this technique?

3. What do you see as the leader's role in motivating others in an organization? Consider, for example, whether employees have some responsibility to motivate themselves.

4. Do you agree that hygiene factors, as defined in Herzberg's two-factor theory, cannot provide increased satisfaction and motivation? Discuss.

5. If you were the owner of a small firm, would you prefer to implement an employee stock ownership program, a profit-sharing program, or a bonus program as a means of motivating employees? Discuss your reasons. What other motivational techniques would you employ?

6. What are the features of the reinforcement and expectancy theories that make them seem like carrot-and-stick methods for motivation? Why do they often work in organizations?

7. Why is it important for leaders to have a basic understanding of equity theory? Can you see ways in which some of today's popular compensation trends, such as gainsharing or pay for performance, might contribute to perceived inequity among employees? Discuss.

8. Do you agree that it is the behavior of leaders that largely determines employee engagement, as defined in the text? What might be some other factors that influence engagement?

9. Discuss whether you believe it is a leader's responsibility to help people find meaning in their work. How might leaders do this for employees at a fast-food restaurant? How about for employees who empty waste containers and clean restrooms at airports?

10. In some school districts, young students are rewarded for good grades and attendance with Happy Meals from McDonald's, and older students get cash rewards. What motivation theory described in the chapter does this best illustrate? Do you think this would provide positive motivation for improving grades and attendance? What might be some potential problems with this approach?

Leadership at Work

SHOULD, NEED, LIKE, LOVE

Think of a school or work task that you feel an obligation or commitment to complete, but you don't really want to do it. Write the task here:

_____

_____

_____

Think of a school or work task you do because you need to, perhaps to get the benefit, such as money or credit. Write the task here:

_____

_____

_____

Think of a school or work task you like to do because it is enjoyable or fun. Write the task here:

_____

_____

_____

Think of a task you love to do—one in which you become completely absorbed and from which you feel a deep satisfaction when finished. Write the task here:

_____

_____

_____

Now reflect on those four tasks and what they mean to you. How motivated (high, medium, low) are you to accomplish each of these four tasks? How much mental effort (high, medium, low) is required from you to complete each task?

Now estimate the percentage of your weekly tasks that you would rate as *should, need, like, love*. The combined estimates should total 100%.

Should: _____%
Need: _____%
Like: _____%
Love: _____%

If your *should* and *need* percentages are substantially higher than your *like* and *love* categories, what does that mean for you? Does it mean that you are forcing yourself to do tasks you find unpleasant? Why? Why not include more *like* and *love* tasks in your life? Might you grow weary of the *should* and *need* tasks at some point and select a new focus or job in your life? Think about this and discuss your percentages with another student in the class.

Tasks you *love* connect you with the creative spirit of life. People who do something they love have a certain charisma, and others want to follow their lead. Tasks you *like* typically are those that fit your gifts and talents and are tasks for which you can make a contribution. Tasks you do because of *need* are typically practical in the sense that they produce an outcome you want, and these tasks often do not provide as much satisfaction as the *like* and *love* tasks. Tasks you do strictly because you *should*, and which contain no *love, like,* or *need,* may be difficult and distasteful and require great effort to complete. You are unlikely to become a leader for completing *should* tasks.

What does the amount of each type of task in your life mean to you? How do these tasks relate to your passion and life satisfaction? Why don't you have more *like* and *love* tasks? As a leader, how would you increase the *like* and *love* tasks for people who report to you? Be specific.

_____

_____

_____

In Class: The instructor can have students talk in small groups about their percentages and what the percentages mean to them. Students can be asked how the categories of *should, need, like,* and *love* relate to the theories of motivation in the chapter. Do leaders have an obligation to guide employees toward tasks they like and love, or is it sufficient at work for people to perform need and should tasks?

The instructor can write student percentages on the board so students can see where they stand compared to the class. Students can be asked to interpret the results in terms of the amount of satisfaction they receive from various tasks. Also, are the percentages related to the students' stage of life?

Chapter 9: Leadership Communication

© Eric Foltz

After reading this chapter, you should be able to:

- Act as a communication champion rather than just as an information processor.
- Use key elements of effective listening and understand why listening is important to leader communication.

- Recognize and apply the difference between dialogue and discussion.
- Select an appropriate communication channel for your leadership message and effectively use nonverbal communication.

- Communicate in a way that persuades and influences others.
- Effectively communicate during times of stress or crisis.

Johnson & Johnson CEO Bill Weldon has plenty to do as top leader of an organization made up of 250 or so operating companies in 57 countries. But for Weldon, one of his most important jobs is traveling around the world talking directly with employees, especially those moving into leadership positions. Today, more than ever, those conversations focus on ethical issues and how the famed Johnson & Johnson Credo (the company's formal statement of purpose and values) applies to real-life situations. Weldon says, "It's an open dialogue about 'How could this have happened? Could it have happened in your area? What do you do to ensure it doesn't?'" Weldon knows leaders need strong communication and feedback from all around the organization to keep in touch with what is happening and make sure the company stays on track.[1]

Weldon's emphasis on open and honest communication trickles down through the organization. For example, Debra Sandler, worldwide president of McNeil Nutritionals, a J&J company, makes sure employees are trained in handling difficult conversations so they can tell her things she might not *want* to hear but *needs* to hear. That helps create an environment where people can "literally share the good news, the bad news, or any news, and there are no repercussions for that," says Calvin Schmidt, McNeil Nutritional's worldwide vice president of marketing and sales.[2]

Leadership communication has been one key to helping Johnson & Johnson maintain a successful track record and a good corporate reputation. The overall reputation of corporate America has never been worse, according to Harris Interactive's 2009 survey asking people to rate the reputations of 60 large

TURBULENT TIMES

corporations. Johnson & Johnson claimed the top spot, as it has eight times in the survey's 10-year history. In the 2009 survey, the financial services industry received the lowest industry ranking, along with the tobacco industry, but the reputation of firms in all industries declined in the 2009 survey.[3]

Leaders need good communication skills particularly during these times of weakened trust, uncertainty, and economic crisis. Motivation, which we discussed in the previous chapter, depends greatly on a leader's ability to communicate. Recall that leadership means influencing people to bring about change toward a vision, or desirable future for the organization. Leaders communicate to share the vision with others, inspire and motivate them to strive toward the vision, and build the values and trust that enable effective working relationships and goal accomplishment.

Successful leader communication also includes deceptively simple components, such as asking questions, paying attention to nonverbal communication, and actively listening to others. At Campbell Soup Company, CEO Douglas Conant has lunch every six weeks with a dozen employees from across the company to get their feedback. Intel holds "skip level" meetings, where managers meet regularly with employees two levels down to hear their ideas and opinions.[4] Unfortunately, however, research shows that many executives are not investing the time and energy to be effective communicators. Many top managers, for example, resist employee feedback because they don't want to hear negative information. Without feedback, leaders can miss important signals that something is going wrong, and the organization and all its people suffer. In addition, they often make decisions and plans that are out of alignment with employee needs or perceptions, making smooth implementation less likely.[5]

This chapter describes tools and skills that can be used to overcome the communication deficit pervading today's organizations. We examine how leaders use communication skills to make a difference in their organizations and the lives of followers.

How Leaders Communicate

Have you ever had a supervisor or instructor whose communication skills were so poor that you didn't have any idea what was expected of you or how to accomplish the job you were asked to do? On the other hand, have you experienced the communication flair of a teacher, boss, or coach who "painted a picture in words" that both inspired you and clarified how to achieve an objective?

Leadership means communicating with others in such a way that they are influenced and motivated to perform actions that further common goals and lead toward desired outcomes. **Communication** is a process by which information and understanding are transferred between a sender and a receiver, such as between a leader and an employee, an instructor and a student, or a coach and a football player. Exhibit 9.1 shows the key elements of the communication process. The sender (such as a leader) initiates a communication by *encoding* a thought or idea, that is, by selecting symbols (such as words) with which to compose and transmit a message. The message is the tangible formulation of the thought or idea sent to the receiver, and the *channel* is the medium by which the message is sent. The channel could be a formal report, a blog, a telephone call, an e-mail or text message, or a face-to-face conversation. The receiver *decodes* the symbols to interpret the meaning of the message. Encoding and decoding can sometimes cause communication errors because individual differences, knowledge, values, attitudes, and background act as filters and may create "noise" when translating

Communication
a process by which information and understanding are transferred between a sender and a receiver

from symbols to meaning. Employees and supervisors, husbands and wives, parents and children, friends and strangers all have communication breakdowns because people can easily misinterpret messages. *Feedback* is the element of the communication process that enables someone to determine whether the receiver correctly interpreted the message. Feedback occurs when a receiver responds to a leader's communication with a return message. Without feedback, the communication cycle is incomplete. Effective communication involves both the transference and the mutual understanding of information.[6] As illustrated in Exhibit 9.1, the nature of effective communication is cyclical, in that a sender and receiver may exchange messages several times to achieve a mutual understanding. The ongoing process of sending, receiving, and feedback to test understanding underlies both management and leadership communication.

Management Communication

The traditional role of a manager is that of "information processor." Managers spend some 80 percent of each working day in communication with others.[7]

Exhibit 9.1 A Circular Model of Interpersonal Communication

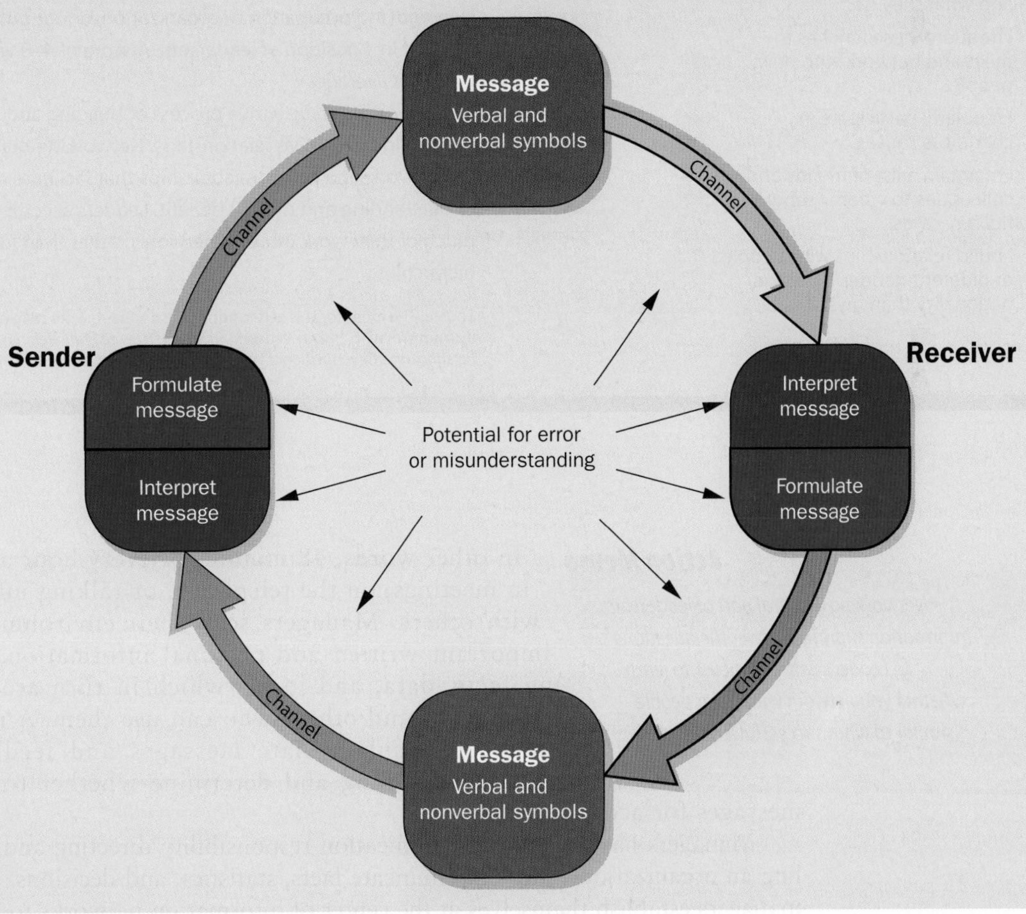

Sources: Based on Gabriela Moise, "Communication Models Used in the Online Learning Environment," *The 3rd International Conference on Virtual Learning 2008*, ICVL (http://www.icvl.eu/2008), pp. 247–254; and Wilbur Schramm, *The Process and Effects of Mass Communication*, 6th ed. (Urbana, IL: University of Illinois Press, 1965).

Leader's Self-Insight 9.1
Am I Networked?

Think about your current life as an employee or as a student. Indicate whether each of the following items is Mostly False or Mostly True for you.

	Mostly False	Mostly True
1. I learn early on about changes going on in the organization that might affect me or my job.		
2. I have a clear belief about the positive value of active networking.		
3. I am good at staying in touch with others.		
4. I network as much to help other people solve problems as to help myself.		
5. I am fascinated by other people and what they do.		
6. I frequently use lunches to meet and network with new people.		
7. I regularly participate in charitable causes.		
8. I maintain a list of friends and colleagues to whom I send holiday cards.		
9. I build relationships with people of different gender, race, and nationality than myself.		
10. I maintain contact with people from previous organizations and school groups.		
11. I actively give information to subordinates, peers, and my boss.		
12. I know and talk with peers in other organizations.		

Scoring and Interpretation

Add the number of Mostly True answers for your score: _____. A score of 9 or above indicates that you are excellent at networking and can be a networking leader. A score of 3 or below would suggest that you need to focus more on building networks, perhaps work in a slow-moving occupation or organization, or not put yourself in a position of leadership. A score of 4–8 would be about average.

Networking is the active process of building and managing productive relationships. Networking builds social, work, and career relationships that facilitate mutual understanding and mutual benefit. Leaders accomplish much of their work through networks rather than formal hierarchies.

Source: The ideas for this self-insight questionnaire were drawn primarily from Wayne E. Baker, *Networking Smart: How to Build Relationships for Personal and Organizational Success* (New York: McGraw-Hill, 1994).

marble: © Kirill Matkov   sunset: © Marco Regalia

Action Memo

Networking is a vital part of leadership information sharing. Answer the questions in Leader's Self-Insight 9.1 to learn whether you network with other people similar to what successful leaders do.

In other words, 48 minutes of every hour are spent in meetings, on the telephone, or talking informally with others. Managers scan their environments for important written and personal information, gathering facts, data, and ideas, which in turn are sent to subordinates and others who can use them. A manager then receives subordinate messages and feedback to check understanding and determine whether to modify messages for accuracy.

Managers have a huge communication responsibility directing and controlling an organization. They communicate facts, statistics, and decisions. Effective managers establish themselves at the center of information networks to facilitate the completion of tasks. Leadership communication, however, serves a different purpose.

The Leader as Communication Champion

Although leadership communication also includes the components of sending, receiving, and feedback, it is different from management communication. Leaders often communicate the big picture—the vision, as defined in Chapter 1—rather than facts and pieces of information. A leader can be seen as a communication champion.[8]

A **communication champion** is philosophically grounded in the belief that communication is essential to building trust and gaining commitment to the vision. Leaders use communication to inspire and unite people around a common sense of purpose and identity. A communication champion enables followers to "live" the vision in their day-to-day activities.[9] This chapter's *Consider This* box highlights the importance of this aspect of leader communication. People need a vision to motivate them toward the future. Learning, problem solving, decision making, and strategizing are all oriented around and stem from the vision. Furthermore, communication champions visibly and symbolically engage in communication-based activities. Whether they walk around asking questions or thoughtfully listen to a subordinate's problem, the actions of champions convey a commitment to communication. Communication isn't just about occasional meetings, formal speeches, or presentations. Leaders actively communicate through both words and actions every day. Regular communication is essential for building personal relationships with followers and keeping everyone lined up in the same direction, toward achieving the company's vision and purpose.

Exhibit 9.2 shows the leader-as-communication-champion model. By establishing an open communication climate, asking questions, actively listening to others, learning

Consider **This!**
Opening a Window to a Brighter World

A blind man was brought to the hospital. He was both depressed and seriously ill.
He shared a room with another man, and one day asked, "What is going on outside?"
The man in the other bed explained in some detail about the sunshine, the gusty winds, and the people walking along the sidewalk. The next day, the blind man again asked, "Please tell me what is going on outside today." The roommate responded with a story about the activities in a park across the way, the ducks on the pond, and the people feeding them. The third day and each day thereafter for two weeks, the blind man asked about the world outside and the other man answered, describing a different scene. The blind man enjoyed these talks, and he grew happier learning about the world seen through the window.

Then the blind man's roommate was discharged from the hospital. A new roommate was wheeled in—a tough-minded businessman who felt terrible, but wanted to get work done. The next morning, the blind man said, "Will you please tell me what is going on outside?" The businessman didn't feel well, and he didn't want to be bothered to tell stories to a blind man. So he responded assertively, "What do you mean? I can't see outside. There is no window here. It's only a wall."

The blind man again became depressed, and a few days later he took a turn for the worse and was moved to intensive care.

Source: Based on a story the author heard at a spiritual service in Santa Fe, New Mexico.

Communication champion
a person who is philosophically grounded in the belief that communication is essential to building trust and gaining commitment to a vision

© majaiva

Exhibit 9.2   The Leader as Communication Champion

Action Memo

As a leader, you can be a communication champion. You can use verbal, nonverbal, and symbolic communication to unite people around a common vision, facilitate strategic conversations, and build trust.

to discern underlying messages, and applying the practices of dialogue and the Johari Window, leaders facilitate and support *strategic conversations* that help move the organization forward. Leader communication is *purpose-directed* in that it directs everyone's attention toward the vision, values, and desired outcomes of the group or organization and persuades people to act in a way to help achieve the vision.

Leaders use many communication methods, including selecting rich channels of communication and using nonverbal communication. Leaders often use symbolic language and behavior to get their messages across and to influence others. For example, President Ronald Reagan was known as a great communicator. In communicating his message about the federal budget, Reagan spoke of a trillion dollars in terms of stacking it next to the Empire State Building. Framed this way, the message redefined the meaning of a trillion dollars, and took on a new reality for the public.

Leading Strategic Conversations

Strategic conversation refers to people talking across boundaries and hierarchical levels about the group or organization's vision, critical strategic themes, and the values that can help achieve desired outcomes. Leaders facilitate strategic conversations by (1) asking questions and actively listening to others to understand their attitudes and values, needs, personal goals, and desires; (2) setting the agenda for conversation by underscoring the key strategic themes that are linked to organizational success; and (3) selecting the right communication channels and facilitating dialogue.[10] An example of strategic conversation comes from Royal Philips Electronics, Europe's largest electronics outfit. President Gerard Kleisterlee outlined four key technology themes that he believes should define Philips' future in the industry: display, storage, connectivity, and digital video processing. These themes intentionally cross technology boundaries and require people to communicate and collaborate across departments and divisions. A strategic conversation for each theme begins with a one-day summit that brings together everyone who has relevant information to contribute—regardless of rank or job position—so that people can together gain a clear sense of goals and establish cooperative working relationships.[11]

Six key components for facilitating strategic conversations are an open communication climate, asking questions, active listening, discernment, dialogue, and a communication model known as the Johari Window.

Strategic conversation
communication that takes place across boundaries and hierarchical levels about the group or organization's vision, critical strategic themes, and values that can help achieve desired outcomes

Exhibit 9.3 Why Open the Communication Climate?

An open climate is essential for cascading vision, and cascading is essential because:

Natural Law 1: You Get What You Talk About
A vision must have ample "air time" in an organization. A vision must be shared and practiced by leaders at every opportunity.

Natural Law 2: The Climate of an Organization Is a Reflection of the Leader
A leader who doesn't embody the vision and values doesn't have an organization that does.

Natural Law 3: You Can't Walk Faster Than One Step at a Time
A vision is neither understood nor accepted overnight. Communicating the vision must be built into continuous, daily interaction so that over time followers will internalize it.

Source: Based on Bob Wall, Robert S. Slocum, and Mark R. Sobol, *Visionary Leader* (Rocklin, CA: Prima Publishing, 1992), pp. 87–89.

Creating an Open Communication Climate

Open communication means sharing all types of information throughout the organization, especially across functional and hierarchical boundaries. Open communication runs counter to the traditional flow of selective information downward from supervisors to subordinates. Good leaders want communication to flow in all directions. Communication across traditional boundaries enables leaders to hear what followers have to say, which means the organization gains the benefit of all employees' minds. The same perspectives batted back and forth between top executives don't lead to effective change, the creation of a powerful shared vision, or the network of personal relationships that keeps organizations thriving. New voices and continuous conversation involving a broad spectrum of people revitalize and enhance communication.[12]

To build an open communication climate, leaders break down conventional hierarchical and departmental boundaries that may be barriers to communication, enabling them to convey a stronger awareness of and commitment to organizational vision, goals, and values. In an open climate, a leader's communication of the vision "cascades" through an organization, as explained in Exhibit 9.3. People throughout the organization thus have a clear direction and an understanding of how they can contribute.[13] Open communication is one way Alan Mulally is helping Ford Motor Company survive these trying times in the auto industry.

IN THE LEAD

Alan Mulally, Ford Motor Company

"Communicate, communicate, communicate," says Alan Mulally, CEO of Ford Motor Company. "Everyone has to know the plan, its status, and areas that need special attention." Mulally's emphasis on open and honest communication could be one reason Ford now stands alone as an independent U.S. auto company.

One example of Mulally's attitude toward communication is the Business Plan Review, a meeting held every Thursday morning. When he arrived at Ford, there were only six or seven people reporting directly to the top leader, but Mulally quickly changed that to include every functional discipline on the executive team, because "everybody in this place had to be involved and had to know everything." He instituted color coding for reports: green for good, yellow for caution, and red for problems. In the beginning, managers were all coding their operations reports green. Mulally bluntly said,

Open communication
leaders sharing all types of information throughout the company and across all levels

"You . . . know, we lost a few billion dollars last year. Is there anything that's not going well?" Manager Mark Fields took the plunge and admitted production problems with a new car model. The whole place was deathly silent . . . then Mulally started clapping and told Fields how much he appreciated his honesty and clarity so the company can fix what's wrong. After that, people began telling the bad as well as the good. No BlackBerrys, no side conversations, and no "pontificating" are allowed at the meetings. Mulally has been known to dismiss vice presidents who "couldn't stop talking because they thought they were so damn important."

Mulally also insists that this kind of open communication cascade down through the organization. There are no secrets at Ford anymore, he points out, and managers are focused on pulling everyone together to move in the same direction. Mulally had a new vision statement, based on the theme "One Team, One Plan, One Goal," printed on plastic cards and distributed to all employees. "This is a huge enterprise, and the magic is, everybody knows the plan," he says.[14]

Action Memo

As a leader, you can create an open communication climate by sharing both good and bad information, and you can facilitate communication across groups, departments, and hierarchical levels.

Leaders at Ford, as at other organizations, want an open communication climate, because it can help to alleviate tension and conflict between departments, build trust, reaffirm employee commitment to a shared vision, and make the company more competitive.

Asking Questions

Managers typically think they should be the people with the right answers. Leadership, though, is more about being the person with the right *questions*.[15] Questions encourage people to think and empower them to find answers. Many leaders—indeed, most people in general—are unaware of the amazing power of questions. In our society, we're conditioned to come up with answers. Very young children are typically full of questions, but from an early age they're discouraged from asking them. Children may be told that questioning adults is rude or disrespectful. Students are expected to hold up their hands in class to give the right answer, and they're often chastised for an incorrect response. Leaders often assume that if someone comes to them with a problem, their job is to solve it with the correct answer. They mistakenly fear that not having an answer means followers will lose respect for them.

Asking the right kinds of questions benefits both leaders and followers in many ways.[16] What are the important questions for leaders to ask? There are two basic approaches to leader questioning. One purpose of questioning is *leader-centered*, in that it seeks to inform the leader about specific issues, investigate problems or opportunities, and gather information, ideas, or insights. This type of questioning is important because it helps leaders tap into the expertise and ideas of followers. With advances in technology and communications, no one person can master all the data and information needed to meet the challenges most organizations face. In addition, asking questions shows that leaders value the knowledge of others, care about how others feel, and are open to new ideas, which helps to build trusting, respectful relationships.[17]

Leaders also use questions for another purpose. This approach is *follower-centered*, in that it seeks to develop new insights, encourage critical thinking, expand people's awareness, and stimulate learning. One study found that 99 percent of top managers surveyed believe that critical thinking skills at all levels are crucial to the success of their organizations.[18] As the best teachers have long known, using the Socratic method—asking questions rather than giving answers—provokes critical thought and leads to deeper, more lasting learning. This type of questioning empowers followers and helps to build positive attitudes and follower self-confidence, as well.

Listening

Just as important as asking questions is listening to the responses. One of the most important tools in a leader's communication tool kit is listening, both to followers and customers.[19] It is only by listening that leaders can identify strategic themes and understand how to influence others to achieve desired outcomes. Listening helps create an open communication climate, because people are willing to share their ideas, suggestions, and problems when they think someone is listening and genuinely values what they have to say. When leaders fail to listen to employees, it sends the signal, "you don't matter," which decreases commitment and motivation.

Listening involves the skill of grasping and interpreting a message's genuine meaning. Remember that message reception is a vital link in the communication process. However, many people do not listen effectively. They concentrate on formulating what they're going to say next rather than on what is being said to them. Our listening efficiency, as measured by the amount of material understood and remembered by subjects 48 hours after listening to a 10-minute message, is, on average, no better than 25 percent.[20]

What constitutes good listening? Exhibit 9.4 gives 10 keys to effective listening and illustrates a number of ways to distinguish a bad listener from a good one.

Listening
the skill of grasping and interpreting a message's genuine meaning

Exhibit 9.4 Ten Keys to Effective Listening

Key	Poor Listener	Good Listener
1. Listen actively	Is passive, laid back	Asks questions; paraphrases what is said
2. Find areas of interest	Tunes out dry subjects	Looks for opportunities, new learning
3. Resist distractions	Is easily distracted	Fights distractions; tolerates bad habits; knows how to concentrate
4. Capitalize on the fact that thought is faster than speech	Tends to daydream with slow speakers	Challenges, anticipates, summarizes; listens between lines to tone of voice
5. Be responsive	Is minimally involved	Nods; shows interest, positive feedback
6. Judge content, not delivery	Tunes out if delivery is poor	Judges content; skips over delivery errors
7. Hold one's fire	Has preconceptions; argues	Does not judge until comprehension is complete
8. Listen for ideas	Listens for facts	Listens to central themes
9. Work at listening	No energy output; faked attention	Works hard; exhibits active body state, eye contact
10. Exercise one's mind	Resists difficult material in favor of light, recreational material	Uses heavier material as exercise for the mind

Sources: Adapted from Sherman K. Okum, "How to Be a Better Listener," *Nation's Business* (August 1975), p. 62; and Philip Morgan and Kent Baker, "Building a Professional Image: Improving Listening Behavior," *Supervisory Management* (November 1985), pp. 34–38.

Leader's Self-Insight 9.2
Listening Self-Inventory

Go through the following questions, answering No or Yes next to each question. Mark each as truthfully as you can in light of your behavior in the last few meetings or social gatherings you attended.

	No	Yes
1. I frequently attempt to listen to several conversations at the same time.		
2. I like people to give me the facts and then let me make my own interpretation.		
3. I sometimes pretend to pay attention to people.		
4. I pay attention to nonverbal communications.		
5. I usually know what another person is going to say before he or she says it.		
6. I usually respond immediately when someone has finished talking.		
7. I evaluate what is being said while it is being said.		
8. I usually formulate a response while the other person is still talking.		
9. I notice the speaker's "delivery" style, which may distract me from the content.		

	No	Yes
10. I often ask people to clarify what they have said rather than guess at the meaning.		
11. I make a concerted effort to understand other people's points of view.		
12. People feel that I have understood their point of view even when we disagree.		

Scoring and Interpretation

The correct answers according to communication theory are as follows: No for questions 1, 2, 3, 5, 6, 7, 8, and 9. Yes for questions 4, 10, 11, and 12.

If you missed only two or three questions, you strongly approve of your own listening habits and you are on the right track to becoming an effective listener in your role as a leader. If you missed four or five questions, you have uncovered some doubts about your listening effectiveness, and your knowledge of how to listen has some gaps. If you missed six or more questions, you probably are not satisfied with the way you listen, and your followers and coworkers might feel that you are not paying attention when they speak. Work on improving your active listening skills.

marble: © Kirill Matkov   sunset: © Marco Regalia

A key to effective listening is focus. A good listener's total attention is focused on the message; he isn't thinking about an unrelated problem in the purchasing department, how much work is piled up on his desk, or what to have for lunch. A good listener also listens actively, finds areas of interest, is flexible, works hard at listening, and uses thought speed to mentally summarize, weigh, and anticipate what the speaker says.

Effective listening is engaged listening. Good leaders ask lots of questions, force themselves to get out of their office and mingle with others, set up listening forums where people can say whatever is on their minds, and provide feedback to let people know they have been heard.[21] Active listening is a daily, ongoing, and vital part of every leader's job.

Action Memo

Evaluate your listening skills by answering the questions in Leader's Self-Insight 9.2.

Discerning Hot Topics

One of the most rewarding and beneficial kinds of listening involves **discernment**. By this kind of listening, a leader detects the unarticulated messages hidden below

Discernment
listening in which a leader detects unarticulated messages hidden below the surface of spoken interaction

the surface of spoken interaction, complaints, behavior, and actions. In particular, leaders try to discern "hot topics" that require leader intervention.

Hot topics are issues that are characterized by strong emotions and extreme uncertainty and that can't be resolved by resorting to facts and logic. The stakes for those involved in hot topic issues are high.[22] For example, when leaders are trying to implement major changes there are often employee fears and resentments hidden below the surface as people wonder what the changes will mean for them. Are their jobs at stake? Will they be required to do more work for the same pay? Can they adapt to the new procedures? Leaders use discernment to detect potential problems or hidden emotions. One leader dealing with a problem employee in the kitchen at an upscale restaurant got nowhere by asking outright why her sous chef had gone from consistently good performance to frequently being tardy or absent. After several days working almost full-time in the kitchen and keeping her eyes and ears open, the restaurant manager discerned that the quiet, introverted employee felt insecure and inadequate since a new head chef with a flamboyant personality had been hired. With this understanding, she got the two employees together and was able to solve the problem.

Action Memo

As a leader, you can learn to be a better listener. You can focus your total attention on what the other person is saying and work hard to listen—use eye contact; ask questions and paraphrase the message; and offer positive feedback.

In recent years, as employees face increased stress related to the economic downturn, many companies have begun teaching leaders how to discern problems that might require leader intervention. The number of employees who are irritable, insulting, or discourteous is growing as people cope with the stress of job uncertainty, overwhelming debt and tighter access to credit, and increased workloads due to downsizing. In one study, nearly half of U.S. workers report experiencing yelling and verbal abuse on the job. Another study found that 2 to 3 percent of people admit to pushing, slapping, or hitting someone at work. In some cases, it gets much worse—like the San Diego transit employee who shot and killed a foreman and a fellow mechanic just after his shift had ended. Leaders at some companies, such as Pitney Bowes, are being proactive in identifying and assisting workers who are distressed, before the problems boil over.[23]

IN THE LEAD

Pitney Bowes Corporation

Pitney Bowes provides a help line for employees to call if they notice colleagues exhibiting erratic or angry behavior. But violence simmering under the surface can be even more risky, the company learned. A guard at one Pitney Bowes facility, for example, quit his job one day, then returned a few days later and killed his replacement. Now, the company trains managers on how to discern signs of employee distress that might not be obvious—and might not even be work-related. "People bring all sorts of demons to work . . . that they shouldn't think they can solve on their on," says Michele Coleman Mayes, senior vice president and general counsel at Pitney Bowes.

Pitney Bowes has a company physician, as well as a program offering referrals to counselors. The first step, though, is often up to a discerning, caring leader to make. The company trains supervisors and managers to be acute observers as well as empathetic listeners. When leaders notice that someone seems to be having difficulty, they talk to them, push them to get help, and don't let them remain isolated. Discerning potential problems and intervening to prevent disruptive and even violent behavior has become an important aspect of every leader's job.

Other companies are also developing programs to help leaders recognize potential danger signs. Not all hot topics lead to workplace violence, but leaders stay alert to conflicts that can disrupt smooth interaction and high performance. Discerning hot topics requires that a leader genuinely care about people and pay attention to their words and behavior. If a previously highly productive employee begins to have trouble focusing on her job, something is wrong. The discerning leader steps in rather than letting the problem grow.

Dialogue

Sometimes, hot topics involve whole groups of employees, and in these cases a type of communication referred to as dialogue can help. The "roots of dialogue" are *dia* and *logos,* which can be thought of as *stream of meaning*. In **dialogue**, people together create a stream of shared meaning that enables them to understand each other and share a view of the world.[24] People may start out as polar opposites, but by actively listening and talking authentically to one another, they discover their common ground, common issues, and common dreams on which they can build a better future.

Most of us have a tendency to infuse everything we hear with our own opinions rather than being genuinely open to what others are saying. In addition, traditional business values in the United States and most other Western countries reward people for forcefully asserting their own ideas and opinions and trying to discredit or contradict others.[25] But people can engage in dialogue only when they come to a conversation free of prejudgments, personal agendas, and "right" answers. Participants in a dialogue do not presume to know the outcome, nor do they sell their convictions.

One way to understand the distinctive quality of dialogue is to contrast it with discussion.[26] Exhibit 9.5 illustrates the differences between a dialogue and a discussion. Typically, the intent of a discussion is to present one's own point of view and persuade others in the group to adopt it. A discussion is often resolved by logic or by "beating down" opposing viewpoints. Dialogue, on the other hand, requires that participants suspend their attachments to a particular point of view so that a deeper level of listening, synthesis, and meaning can emerge from the group. A dialogue's focus is to reveal feelings and build common ground, with the emphasis on inquiry rather than advocacy. Dialogue is particularly useful for conversations about difficult and emotionally charged issues—hot topics—as further discussed in this chapter's Leader's Bookshelf.

One example of using dialogue for hot topics occurred at NECX, an online marketplace that was acquired by Converge. Henry Bertolon, cofounder and CEO, introduced dialogue to improve communication after a period of rapid growth led to internal tensions. "We'd have meetings that just melted down," he says. "Everyone would scream at each other and then leave." Bertolon hired Wil Calmas, a psychologist with an MBA, to lead a series of programs to get people talking—and listening—to one another on a deeper, authentic level. People were encouraged to express fear, hostility, frustration, secret wishes—whatever feelings were affecting their lives and work. The dialogue sessions created a safe environment for people to reveal their feelings, explore ideas, and build common ground. Bertolon also believed it helped employees be loose, flexible,

Action Memo

As a leader, you can use dialogue to help people create a shared sense of meaning and purpose. You can enable people to express their hopes and fears, suspend their convictions and explore assumptions, and become motivated to search for common ground.

Dialogue
active sharing and listening in which people explore common ground and grow to understand each other and share a world view

Exhibit 9.5 Dialogue and Discussion: The Differences

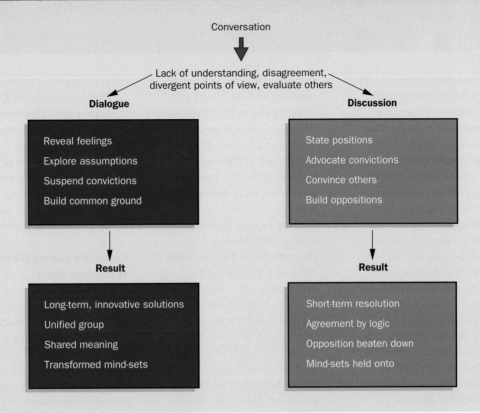

Source: Adapted from Edgar Schein, "On Dialogue, Culture, and Organizational Learning," *Organizational Dynamics* (Autumn 1993), p. 46.

and open to new ideas—ready to respond to the rapid changes taking place all around them.[27]

Both forms of communication, dialogue and discussion, can result in organizational change. However, the result of a discussion is limited to a specific topic being deliberated, whereas the result of dialogue is characterized by group unity, shared meaning, and transformed mindsets. This kind of result is far-reaching. A new, common mindset is not the same thing as agreement, because it creates a reference point from which subsequent communication can start. As new and deeper solutions are developed, a trusting relationship is built among communicators, which is important to all communication episodes that follow. Dialogue thus transforms communication and, by extension, the organization.

The Johari Window

Another framework for understanding how to improve interpersonal communication is the Johari Window. Named after the first names of its inventors, Joseph Luft and Harry Ingham, the Johari Window can be used to recognize the impact of leader communication tools such as dialogue, listening, discerning hot topics, and asking questions to improve relationships.[28]

The **Johari Window** represents information—facts, feelings, experiences, opinions, attitudes, intentions, motivations, and so forth—within or about a person in relation to others in a group, in terms of whether the information is known or

Johari Window
a framework for enhancing communication effectiveness based on interpersonal understanding by oneself and others

Leader's Bookshelf

Crucial Conversations: Tools for Talking When Stakes Are High
by Kerry Patterson, Joseph Grenny, Ron McMillan, and Al Switzler

Almost everyone has experienced the discomfort of a *crucial conversation,* which refers to a discussion where emotions run strong, opinions vary, and the stakes are high. Crucial conversations are conversations about tough issues that may cause conflict. Some examples that occur in the workplace include confronting a coworker who makes suggestive comments or behaves offensively, approaching a boss who is breaking his own safety rules, or talking to a team member who isn't keeping commitments. For most of us, the more crucial the conversation, the less likely we are to handle it well. The authors of *Crucial Conversations: Tools for Talking When Stakes Are High* take a step-by-step approach to explore tools leaders can use to help create the conditions, within themselves and others, for effectively dealing with difficult issues.

The Leader's Role in Crucial Conversations

Leaders use the technique of dialogue to keep themselves and others calm and focused when discussions turn into crucial conversations. Here are a few guidelines:

- *Encourage a free flow of information.* When it comes to controversial, risky, and emotional conversations, effective leaders find a way to get all relevant information from themselves and others into the open. At the core of every successful crucial conversation is the free flow of information and ideas, with people feeling safe enough to openly and honestly express their opinions, feelings, and theories.

- *Start with heart.* A key principle of dialogue is that the leader starts with getting his or her own heart right. In a high-risk conversation, the leader has to start with the right motives and stay calm and focused no matter what happens. To stay focused, leaders have to know what they want for themselves, for others, and for the relationship.

- *When people are at cross purposes, think CRIB.* **C**ommit to seek a mutual purpose; **R**ecognize the purpose behind the strategy; **I**nvent a mutual purpose; **B**rainstorm new strategies. When people are poles apart on what they want, leaders can use this tool to bring people back to dialogue. They first get people to commit to finding some agreement; strive to discern the true purpose behind one another's words; find broader goals that can serve as a basis for mutual purpose; and, with a mutual purpose as a grounding, brainstorm ideas for meeting each person's individual needs.

Communicating When it Matters Most

When we're angry, upset, frustrated, anxious, or otherwise influenced by strong emotions, conversation often deteriorates into *violence* or *silence,* verbally attacking the other person or verbally withdrawing. These are the times when dialogue is most important. *Crucial Conversations* offers ideas for thinking about and preparing for difficult conversations, along with specific tips and tools that can help leaders say and do the right thing.

Source: *Crucial Conversations: Tools for Talking When Stakes Are High,* by Kerry Patterson, Joseph Grenny, Ron McMillan, and Al Switzler, is published by McGraw-Hill.

marble: © Ioannis Drimilis   library: www.istockphoto.com/nikada

unknown by the individual and whether it is known or unknown by the group. The four quadrants of the Johari Window are shown in Exhibit 9.6, and each "window" is described in the following paragraphs. The lines dividing the four panes are like window shades that move as interaction progresses.

1. The "open" quadrant represents information that is known to the individual and is also known to the group. For example, I know my name, and so do you if you look at the author's name on this textbook. The information represented by the open window can include not just facts, but also feelings, motives, behaviors, wants, needs, and desires. When a new team comes together, the open area is typically small because people have little information about one another. As the process of getting to know one another continues, the window shades move down or to the right, placing more and more information into the open window. The goal is to expand

Exhibit 9.6 The Johari Window

	Known to individual	Not known to individual
Known to others in group	1. Open	2. Blind
Not known to others in group	3. Hidden	4. Unknown

Source: Based on the Johari Window model by Joseph Luft and Harry Ingham, as depicted in Alan Chapman, "Johari Window," http://www.businessballs.com/johariwindowmodel.htm (accessed May 18, 2009); and Duen Hsi Yen, "Johari Window," http://www.noogenesis.com/game_theory/johari/johari_window.html (accessed May 18, 2009).

the open quadrant for each individual involved. When people have deep self-awareness and are open to others, they are more effective. The open quadrant is where good communication and cooperation happen.

2. The "blind" quadrant includes things that are known about an individual by others but are unknown to the individual herself. As a very simple example, let's say we're having lunch in the university cafeteria and I have unknowingly gotten some food on my face. If you now tell me that I have something on my face, then the window shade moves to the right, enlarging the open quadrant's area. People typically have blind spots about many other more complex issues. For instance, team members may notice that the leader never makes eye contact, which causes some to question her sincerity. The leader is unaware of this tendency to avoid eye contact. By seeking feedback and giving empathetic feedback to others, leaders can gradually reduce the blind area so that everyone becomes more self-aware.

3. The "hidden" quadrant represents things that an individual knows about himself but keeps hidden from others. We all keep certain feelings, fears, or desires hidden from others, and it is natural to want to keep some things private. However, information that affects one's work, performance, or relationships needs to be moved out of the hidden area and into the open. One team member with a hidden fear of flying, for instance, gets cranky and uncooperative in the days before any scheduled business trip that requires flying. As soon as this person tells his teammates that he has a deep fear of flying, he has moved this bit of information out of the hidden quadrant, enlarging the open quadrant's area. Thus, people have a better understanding of why their normally agreeable and cooperative teammate has turned grumpy and disagreeable. Reducing the hidden area reduces the potential for misunderstandings and conflicts.

4. The "unknown" quadrant represents things that are unknown both to the individual and to others in the group. Unknown issues could include things like an unknown illness, repressed or subconscious feelings, undetected abilities or talents, or conditioned behaviors or attitudes. Through a process of self-discovery, people can narrow the unknown quadrant, moving more information into the "hidden" or "open" areas. An individual might discover something about himself or herself that is extremely personal and

will always remain hidden. On the other hand, someone might discover that she has a great talent for organizing events or a great love of public speaking, and this would be moved into the open area.

This discussion provides only a brief overview of the Johari Window model. The key point is that leaders can create an environment where people are learning about themselves and are more open with others. Good leaders encourage self-discovery, constructive feedback, and honest disclosure, so that communications are free of distractions, mistrust, and misunderstandings.

Communicating to Persuade and Influence

To act as a communication champion, as described earlier in this chapter, leaders don't communicate just to convey information, but to persuade and influence others. They use communication skills to sell others on the vision and influence them to behave in ways that achieve goals and help accomplish the vision.

The ability to persuade others is more critical today than ever before. The command-and-control mindset of managers telling people what to do and how to do it is gone. Employees don't just want to know *what* they should do but *why* they should do it. In addition, with new collaborative ways of working, many leaders are involved in situations where lines of authority are blurred. Companies such as Union Bank of California, Gerdau Ameristeel, and IBM are adding training programs that help people learn how to lead by influence rather than command.[29] Leaders can follow four steps to practice the art of persuasion:[30]

1. *Establish credibility.* A leader's credibility is based on the leader's knowledge and expertise as well as his or her relationships with others. When leaders have demonstrated that they make well-informed, sound decisions, followers have confidence in their expertise. Leaders also build credibility by establishing good relationships and showing that they have others' best interests at heart.

2. *Build goals on common ground.* To be persuasive, leaders describe how what they're requesting will benefit others as well as the leader. For example, when David Zugheri wanted to switch to a primarily paperless system at First Houston Mortgage, he emphasized to employees that storing customer records electronically meant they could now work from home when they needed to care for a sick child, or take a vacation and still keep track of critical accounts. "I could literally see their attitudes change through their body language," Zugheri says.[31] When people see how they will personally benefit from doing something, they're usually eager to do it. When leaders can't find common advantages, it's a good signal that they need to adjust their goals and plans.

3. *Make your position compelling to others.* Leaders appeal to others on an emotional level by using symbols, metaphors, and stories to express their messages, rather than relying on facts and figures alone. By tapping into the imaginations of their followers, leaders can inspire people to accomplish amazing results. At National Grange Mutual, a property-casualty insurance company, leaders in the claims unit picked up on a statement made by one of the company's independent agents to appeal to people's emotions and imaginations. When discussing how the claims unit should relate to customers, the agent said, "I want my customers to feel your arm go around them when they have a claim." Leaders used this evocative

image to focus employees on reengineering the claims process to provide better, faster, more caring service.[32]

4. *Connect emotionally.* Recall the discussion of emotional intelligence from Chapter 5. Good leaders sense others' emotions and adjust their approach to match the audience's ability to receive their message. Leaders use their emotional understanding to influence others in positive ways. In addition, by looking at how people have interpreted and responded to past events in the organization, leaders can get a better grasp on how followers may react to their ideas and proposals.

Persuasion is a valuable communication process that individuals can use to lead others to a shared solution or commitment. Karen Tse, founder and director of International Bridges to Justice, provides an excellent example of a persuasive leader. She was just 37 years old when she founded an organization that would change the lives of thousands of prisoners in places like China, Cambodia, and Vietnam by training public defenders and raising awareness of human rights abuses. Tse persuades by connecting emotionally to people, whether it is a businessman she's asking for a donation or a prison guard she's encouraging to allow prisoners daily exercise. Rather than fighting against the "bad," Tse says she tries to find the good in each person and work with that part of them to make changes. One Cambodian prison director who initially told Tse he would beat prisoners down "like rats" eventually worked with her to improve the prison's dark, dank cells, build a garden, and implement exercise classes for prisoners and guards.[33]

> **Action Memo**
>
> As a leader, you can increase your credibility by becoming knowledgeable and building positive relationships with others. You can show how your plans will benefit followers and tap into their imagination and emotions to inspire support.

To be persuasive and act a communication champion, leaders must communicate frequently and easily with others in the organization. Yet for some individuals, communication experiences are unrewarding, so they may consciously or unconsciously avoid situations where communication is required.[34] The term *communication apprehension* describes this avoidance behavior, and is defined as "an individual's level of fear or anxiety associated with either real or anticipated communication with another person or persons."[35]

Selecting Rich Communication Channels

One key to effective communication is selecting the right channel for relaying the message. A **channel** is a medium by which a communication message is carried from sender to receiver. A leader may discuss a problem face-to-face, use the telephone, write a memo or letter, use e-mail, send a text message, post a message on a blog or Web page, or put an item in a newsletter, depending on the nature of the message.

The Continuum of Channel Richness

Research has attempted to explain how leaders select communication channels to enhance communication effectiveness.[36] Studies have found that channels differ in their capacity to convey information. **Channel richness** is the amount of information that can be transmitted during a communication episode. The channels available to leaders can be classified into a hierarchy based on information richness, as illustrated in Exhibit 9.7.

The richness of an information channel is influenced by three characteristics: (1) the ability to handle multiple cues simultaneously; (2) the ability to facilitate rapid, two-way feedback; and (3) the ability to establish a personal focus for the communication. Face-to-face discussion is the richest medium, because it permits

Channel
a medium by which a communication message is carried from sender to receiver

Channel richness
the amount of information that can be transmitted during a communication episode

Exhibit 9.7 A Continuum of Channel Richness

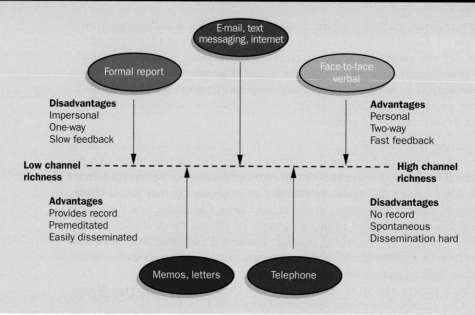

direct experience, multiple information cues, immediate feedback, and personal focus. Face-to-face discussions facilitate the assimilation of broad cues and deep, emotional understanding of the situation. Tony Burns, former CEO of Ryder Systems, always preferred handling things face-to-face. "You can look someone in the eyes," he explains. "You can tell by the look in his eyes or the inflection of his voice what the real problem or question or answer is."[37] Telephone conversations are next in the richness hierarchy. Eye contact, gaze, posture, and other body language cues are missing, but the human voice still carries a tremendous amount of emotional information.

> **Action Memo**
>
> *Complete the questions in Leader's Self-Insight 9.3 to learn your level of communication apprehension.*

Electronic messaging, such as through e-mail, text messages, social networking sites, or group services such as Twitter, is increasingly being used for communications that were once handled over the telephone. Although these channels lack both visual and verbal cues, they allow for rapid feedback and can be personalized. Blogs provide a way to get information to a wide audience and also permit rapid feedback.[38]

Print media such as notes and letters can be personalized, but they convey only the cues written on paper and are slow to provide feedback. Impersonal written media, including fliers, bulletins, and standard computer reports, are the lowest in richness. The channels are not focused on a single receiver, use limited information cues, and do not permit feedback.

It is important for leaders to understand that each communication channel has advantages and disadvantages, and that each can be an effective means of communication in the appropriate circumstances.[39] Channel selection depends on whether the message is routine or nonroutine. Routine communications are simple and straightforward, such as a product price change. Routine messages convey data or statistics or simply put into words what people already understand and agree on. Routine messages can be efficiently communicated through a channel lower in richness. Written or electronic communications also are effective when the audience is widely dispersed or when the communication is

Leader's Self-Insight 9.3
Communication Apprehension

The following questions are about your feelings toward communication with other people. Indicate whether each item is Mostly False or Mostly True for you. There are no right or wrong answers. Many of the statements are similar to other statements. Do not be concerned about this. Work quickly and just record your first impressions.

	Mostly False	Mostly True
1. I look forward to expressing myself at meetings.	_____	_____
2. I hesitate to express myself in a group.	_____	_____
3. I look forward to an opportunity to speak in public.	_____	_____
4. Although I talk fluently with friends, I am at a loss for words on the platform.	_____	_____
5. I always avoid speaking in public if possible.	_____	_____
6. I feel that I am more fluent when talking to people than most other people are.	_____	_____
7. I like to get involved in group discussions.	_____	_____
8. I dislike using my body and voice expressively.	_____	_____
9. I'm afraid to speak up in a conversation.	_____	_____
10. I would enjoy presenting a speech on a local television show.	_____	_____

Scoring and Interpretation

Give yourself 1 point for each Mostly False answer to questions 2, 4, 5, 8, and 9. Give yourself 1 point for each Mostly True answer to questions 1, 3, 6, 7, and 10.

Your total points: _____

This personal assessment provides an indication of how much apprehension (fear or anxiety) you feel in a variety of communication settings. Total scores may range from 0 to 10. A score of 3 or less indicates that you are more apprehensive about communication than the average person. A score of 8 or above indicates a low level of communication apprehension. Scores between 4 and 7 indicate average apprehension.

Individual questions is this exercise pertain to four common situations—public speaking, meetings, group discussions, and interpersonal conversations. Study the individual questions to see which situations create more apprehension for you. To be an effective communication champion, you should work to overcome communication anxiety. Interpersonal conversations create the least apprehension for most people, followed by group discussions, larger meetings, and then public speaking. Compare your scores with another student. What aspect of communication creates the most apprehension for you? How do you plan to reduce your communication apprehension?

Source: Adapted from J. C. McCroskey, "Validity of the PRCA as an Index of Oral Communication Apprehension," *Communication Monographs* 45 (1978), pp. 192–203. Used with permission.

"official" and a permanent record is required.[40] On the other hand, nonroutine messages typically concern issues of change, conflict, or complexity that have great potential for misunderstanding. Nonroutine messages often are characterized by time pressure and surprise. Leaders can communicate nonroutine messages effectively only by selecting a rich channel.

Leaders should select a channel to fit the message. Following layoffs, for example, people are fearful and worried about their own jobs. Many leaders, not knowing what to say, send out a written notice and hide in their offices. Good leaders, on the other hand, know face-to-face communication is the way to keep morale and productivity high. At one construction company that had to lay off employees, the CEO called employees together and told them how the mortgage crisis and downturn in the housing market was affecting their company. He acknowledged that he couldn't promise there wouldn't be more layoffs, but as he explained what was going on,

Action Memo

As a leader, you can choose rich forms of communication, such as face to face or the telephone, when an issue is complex, emotionally charged, or especially important. For a routine, straightforward message, you can use a written or electronic form of communication.

the emotions in the room became calmer because people knew what to prepare for.[41] Most leader communication by its very nature is comprised of nonroutine messages. Although leaders make good use of all channels, they don't let anything substitute for the rich face-to-face channel when important issues are at stake.

Effectively Using Electronic Communication Channels

Electronic communication has become a fact of life in today's organizations. New technologies provide highly efficient ways of communicating and can be particularly useful for routine messages. Text messaging, which allows people to share shorthand messages instantly, has rapidly grown in use and is becoming more common than e-mail in some organizations.[42] Many of today's leaders, as in the following example, are also using blogs to keep in closer touch and rebuild trust among employees, customers, shareholders, and the public.

IN THE LEAD

James F. Albaugh, Boeing Integrated Defense Systems, and Randy Baseler, Boeing Commercial Airplanes

"I've always been a big believer in open and honest dialogue that gets the issues on the table," says James Albaugh, the chief executive of Boeing Integrated Defense Systems. Albaugh's view hasn't always been shared by other Boeing executives. Indeed, defense contractors and aerospace companies in general aren't known for their openness. Yet after a series of ethical scandals rocked the giant company, Boeing leaders are embracing a new approach to communication.

One aspect of the once-secretive company's attempt to build an open communication climate is the use of both external and internal blogs. Randy Baseler, vice president for marketing at Boeing Commercial Airplanes, for example, started a public blog to share the company's view on products and marketing strategies—and comments are welcome. The blog has exposed Boeing to some stinging criticism, but leaders believe the openness will lead to more constructive dialogue with customers and the public. Employees, too, are seeing a more open approach to communication. Internal blogs, such as one used by Albaugh at Boeing Integrated Defense Systems, get conversations going and enable people to raise issues or point out problems anonymously.

It's too soon to say whether Boeing executives' use of blogs and other communication strategies will result in a more productive, open, and ethical climate. Operating in an industry built on security clearances and classified government projects, secrecy is woven into the fiber of the organization. Some issues may always require secrecy, yet leaders are making a sincere effort to break down walls where possible, be more open with employees and the public, prevent the kind of ethical lapses that have occurred in recent years, and restore trust.[43]

Action Memo

As a leader, you can avoid letting electronic communications become a complete substitute for human interactions. You can resist the urge to criticize or complain in an electronic message, and never send an e-mail when you are angry or upset.

Electronic communication has many advantages, but there are disadvantages as well. The proliferation of electronic media has contributed to *poorer* communication in many organizations. Employees who work in offices down the hall from one another will often send an e-mail or text message rather than communicating face to face. One employee reported that he was fired via e-mail—by a manager who sat five feet away in the same office.[44] Even for less traumatic messages, electronic methods can increase the potential for communication errors. Leaders can come across as sounding cold, arrogant, or insensitive when they attempt to discuss delicate or complex issues via e-mail. Things that might be handled smoothly in a face-to-face conversation or over the phone turn into massive problems by fostering resentment, bitterness, and hard feelings.[45]

Another equally disturbing concern, one psychiatrist argues, is that the growing use of technology for communicating has created hidden problems for both individuals and organizations by depriving people of the "human moments" that are needed to energize people, inspire creativity, and support emotional well-being.[46] People need to interact with others in physical space to build the connections that create great organizations. Electronic communication is here to stay, and the key for leaders is to benefit from the efficiencies of new technologies while preventing their unintended problems. Here are some tips for effectively using electronic communication:

- *Combine high-tech and high-touch.* Never allow electronic communication to take the place of human connections. People who work together should meet face to face on a regular basis, and leaders should get to know their followers in real as well as virtual space. Many companies that use virtual workers require that they come into the office at least once a month for unstructured face time.[47] A real-estate developer in Boston has a free-pizza day once a week when widely scattered workers can come by, sit around the table in his office, and just talk.[48]
- *Consider the circumstances.* People who know one another well and have worked together a long time can typically communicate about more complex issues via electronic means than can people who have a new working relationship.[49] When people have a long-term working relationship, there is less potential for misunderstandings and hard feelings. In addition, when all parties involved have a good grasp of the issues being discussed, electronic channels can be used effectively. A leader of a longstanding, well-functioning team could thus use e-mail more extensively than the leader of a team that has just been formed.
- *Think twice and read twice before you hid the "Send" button.* Many people feel pressured to respond to electronic messages quickly, which can create unintended problems.[50] Before you hit *send*, slow down and think about whether the message is something you want out there in cyberspace where anyone might read it. Don't send an electronic message when you are angry or upset. This is a situation that definitely calls for richer communication channels. Never send an electronic message without reading it at least twice. Give the same attention to your electronic messages as you would to a memo or letter, and be as courteous to the receiver as if you were delivering the message in person.

Exhibit 9.8 lists some further dos and don'ts concerning subjects appropriate for electronic mail.

Nonverbal Communication

Leaders don't just communicate in words. Leaders are watched, and their appearance, behavior, actions, and attitudes are symbolic messages to others. Indeed, **nonverbal communication**, that is, messages transmitted through actions, behavior, facial expressions, and tone of voice, accounts for over one-half of the entire message received in a personal encounter.[51] Even the selection of a communication channel can convey a symbolic message. In other words, people attach meaning to the channel itself.

Nonverbal communication
messages transmitted through action and behavior

Exhibit 9.8 Dos and Don'ts of Electronic Mail

Do

- Use e-mail to set up meetings, to recap spoken conversations, or to follow up on information already discussed face to face.
- Keep e-mail messages short and to the point. Many people read e-mail on handheld devices, which have small screens.
- Use e-mail to prepare a group of people for a meeting. For example, it is convenient to send the same documents to a number of people and ask them to review the materials before the meeting.
- Use e-mail to transmit standard reports.
- Act like a newspaper reporter. Use the subject line to grab the reader's attention and reflect what the message is about. Put the most important information in the first paragraph. Answer any questions—who, what, when, where, why, and how—that are pertinent.

Don't

- Use e-mail to discuss something with a colleague who sits across the aisle or down the hall from you. Take the old-fashioned approach of speaking to each other.
- Say anything negative about a boss, friend, or colleague via e-mail. And don't forward the negative comments of others.
- Use e-mail to start or perpetuate a feud. If you get an e-mail that tempts you to respond in a scathing manner, stop yourself. You may be misinterpreting the message. Even if you're not, take the high road.
- Write anything in an e-mail you wouldn't want published in a newspaper. E-mail with sensitive or potentially embarrassing information has an uncanny way of leaking out.

Sources: Based on "15 Dos and Don'ts" box in Andrea C. Poe, "Don't Touch That 'Send' Button," *HR Magazine* (July 2001), pp. 74–80; Michael Goldberg, "The Essential Elements of E-Mail," *CIO* (June 1, 2003), p. 24; and Mary Lynn Pulley and Jane Hilberry, *Get Smart! How E-Mail Can Make or Break Your Career and Your Organization* (Colorado Springs, CO: Get Smart! Publishing, 2007).

Reports and memos typically convey formality and legitimize a message. Personal visits from a leader are interpreted as a sign of teamwork and caring.[52]

Many people don't realize that they are communicating all the time, without saying a word, by their facial expressions, body language, and actions.[53] For example, Marcia Finberg had always had a friendly relationship with her boss at a Phoenix hospital, so she knew something was wrong when he suddenly started avoiding her. The boss didn't want to tell Finberg that her position was being terminated and she was out of a job, but his actions clearly screamed a negative message to Finberg.[54] On a more positive note, consider how a new general manager at a manufacturing facility used nonverbal communication to convey the importance of cost-cutting. In his first months on the job, the new plant manager noticed that when members of the management team had to travel, they flew first class. Rather than issuing a directive that first-class travel was not allowed, the plant manager always flew coach. Soon, everyone throughout the company was flying coach.[55]

> **Action Memo**
>
> *As a leader, you can symbolize important messages through your appearance, body language, facial expressions, and daily actions. You can be more effective by using management by wandering around. You can get out and mingle with followers and customers to learn about their ideas, problems, and needs through informal observation and conversation.*

Leaders strive to be aware of what they signal to others in addition to verbal messages. Research suggests that if there is a discrepancy between a person's verbal and nonverbal communication, the nonverbal is granted more weight by the interpreter.[56] In interpreting a leader's nonverbal cues, followers determine the extent to which a leader's actions correspond with his or her verbal messages. If a leader talks about customer service, but spends no time with customers, followers would likely place little value on service. If a leader talks about valuing employee feedback but stays in her office with the door closed most of the time, followers will doubt the sincerity of her words. One way leaders nonverbally communicate the value of feedback is by practicing *management by wandering around* (MBWA).[57] MBWA means that leaders leave their offices and speak directly to employees as they work. These impromptu encounters send symbolic positive messages to followers that leaders care about their ideas, opinions, and feelings.

Communicating in a Crisis

A leader's skill at communicating becomes even more crucial during times of rapid change, uncertainty, or crisis. Over the past few years, the sheer number and scope of crises—everything from terrorist attacks, workplace shootings, and a potential flu pandemic, to corporate failures, leader ethical lapses, and widespread economic turmoil—have made communication a more demanding job for leaders. Organizations face small crises every day, such as the loss of computer data, charges of racial discrimination, a factory fire, or the need for downsizing. When leaders at Internet shoe retailer Zappos realized the economic downturn was hurting their business, CEO Tony Hsieh met with other executives to clarify how they should handle the situation. They decided the company needed to lay off 124 of their 1,500 employees and agreed on generous severance packages. Wanting to get the word out quickly to alleviate stress and uncertainty, Hsieh announced the decisions in an e-mail, on his blog, and with Twitter. Employees being let go were notified personally. It was a difficult time, but the response to how leaders handled the situation from both departing staffers and those remaining was generally positive.[58]

Communicating in a crisis has always been part of a leader's job, but the world has become so fast, interconnected, and complex that unexpected events happen more frequently and often with greater and more painful consequences. For example, the rapid global spread of the H1N1 flu virus in 2009 affected leaders and organizations in countries around the world. Leaders at the U.S. National Pork Producers Council, for instance, were in perpetual crisis mode as the media's references to the virus as "swine flu" led to a swift decline in sales of pork, restrictions on imports of U.S. pork products, and a devastating drop in hog prices for farmers.[59] To be prepared for communicating in a crisis, leaders can develop four skills:[60]

1. *Stay calm; listen harder.* A leader's emotions are contagious, so leaders have to stay calm and focused. Perhaps the most important part of a leader's job in a crisis situation is to absorb people's fears and uncertainties, which means listening is more important than ever. Leaders also tailor their messages to reflect hope and optimism at the same time they acknowledge the danger and difficulties, thus giving comfort, inspiration, and hope to others. "You do not pass uncertainty down to your team members," said Eugene Kranz, the NASA flight director charged with returning the crippled *Apollo 13* spacecraft safely to earth in 1970. "No matter what is going on around you, you have to be cooler than cool."[61]

2. *Be visible.* When people's worlds have become ambiguous and uncertain, they need to feel that someone is in control. Many leaders underestimate just how important their presence is during a crisis.[62] They have a tendency to want to hide, gather information, think things through, deal with their own emotions, and develop a strategy for tackling the problem. However, being a leader means stepping out immediately, both to reassure followers and respond to public concerns. For example, after cases of listeriosis that led to the deaths of 20 people in Canada were linked to tainted meat from Maple

Leaf Foods, CEO Michael McCain immediately appeared in a television ad to express his sorrow, issue a heartfelt apology, and acknowledge the company's safety failings. McCain felt it was important to put speed of communication above strict accuracy.[63] In contrast to that openness, leaders in U.S. financial institutions have been sharply criticized for their failure to quickly step forward during the recent financial crisis.[64]

3. *Tell the truth.* Leaders gather as much information from as many diverse sources as they can, do their best to determine the facts, and then "get the awful truth out" to employees and the public as soon as possible.[65] Rumor control is critical. Duke University provides both a negative and a positive example of the importance of getting the truth out.

IN THE LEAD

Duke University and Duke University Hospital

Several years ago, doctors at Duke University Hospital made one of the worst mistakes in modern medical history—transplanting the wrong heart and lungs into 17-year-old Jesica Santillan, who later died. Although the story was already out, it took nine days for Duke leaders to fully admit the hospital's mistake. By that time, the organization's image was severely damaged, and rumors of unauthorized medical experiments and doctors pulling the plug against the family's wishes were rampant. To counteract the damage, Duke's health chief and the surgeons involved in the transplant went on CBS's *60 Minutes* to tell the whole story and offer a mournful public apology.

In contrast to that debacle, Duke University handled a situation several years later much more effectively. The university was thrust into crisis when three members of its lacrosse team were charged with beating, strangling, and raping an African-American exotic dancer the team had hired for a party where team members were drinking heavily. Duke President Richard Brodhead immediately accepted responsibility for the incident, offered an apology, and began steps for taking corrective action. He indicated that the facts of the rape case were not established, and that the players were presumed innocent until proven guilty (charges against all three players were eventually dropped when the victim's story changed). However, Brodhead acknowledged that several members of the lacrosse team had clearly acted inappropriately. From the time the incident happened until the end of the case, Brodhead communicated regularly through various media with students and parents, alumni, employees, and the public. As he explained on *60 Minutes*, Brodhead realized he "had to take personal leadership of this issue from day one."[66]

4. *Communicate a vision for the future.* In a crisis situation, leaders have to deal with the physical and emotional needs of people, but they also need to get back to work as soon as possible. The group, organization, or community has to keep going, and most people want to be a part of the rebuilding process, to feel that they have something to look forward to. Moments of crisis present excellent opportunities for leaders to communicate a vision for the future that taps into people's emotions and desires for something better. When Xerox was facing bankruptcy some years ago, CEO Anne Mulcahy wrote and shared with employees a fictitious *Wall Street Journal* article describing Xerox five years in the future, outlining the things Xerox wanted to accomplish as if they had already been achieved and presenting the company as a thriving, forward-thinking organization.[67] By giving people vision and hope, Mulcahy set the stage for a remarkable turnaround.

Action Memo

As a leader, you can learn to be an effective crisis communicator. By remaining calm and focused, you can acknowledge people's concerns and fears, provide accurate and up-to-date information, and help people see a better tomorrow.

Leadership Essentials

■ Effective communication is an essential element of leadership. Leaders are communication champions who inspire and unite people around a common sense of purpose and identity. They lead strategic conversations that get people talking across boundaries about the vision, key strategic themes, and the values that can help the group or organization achieve desired outcomes.

■ Six elements that facilitate strategic conversations are an open communication climate, asking questions, active listening, discernment, dialogue, and the Johari Window. Open communication is essential for building trust, and it paves the way for more opportunities to communicate with followers, thus enabling the organization to gain the benefits of all employees' minds. However, leaders must be active listeners and must learn to discern hidden undercurrents and hot topics that may create problems for the group or organization. It is through listening and discernment that leaders identify strategic issues and build productive relationships that help the organization succeed. When active listening spreads throughout a group, a type of communication referred to as dialogue occurs. Through dialogue, people discover common ground and together create a shared meaning that enables them to understand each other and share a view of the world. The Johari Window framework can be used by leaders to help create an environment where people are more open and honest, which facilitates better communication.

■ Leader communication is purpose-directed, and an important element is persuading others to act in ways that achieve goals and accomplish the vision. Four steps for practicing the art of persuasion are to establish credibility, build goals on common ground, make your position compelling, and connect with others on an emotional level. Leaders use rich communication channels and nonverbal as well as verbal communication.

■ Electronic communication channels present new challenges for leader communication. Electronic channels can be very advantageous if used appropriately, but their use increases the potential for communication errors, and these channels are not effective for complex or sensitive messages.

■ The final point emphasized in this chapter is that effective communication becomes even more crucial during times of rapid change and crisis. Four critical skills for communicating in a crisis are to remain calm, be visible, "get the awful truth out," and communicate a vision for the future.

Discussion Questions

1. How do you think leadership communication differs from conventional management communication?

2. Board members at some companies are opening the lines of communication so shareholders can voice their concerns about executive compensation and corporate governance. Do you think this is a good idea? What might be some risks associated with this type of open communication?

3. A manager in a communication class remarked, "Listening seems like minimal intrusion of oneself into the conversation, yet it also seems like more work." Do you agree or disagree? Discuss.

4. How does dialogue differ from discussion? Give an example of each from your experience.

5. Some senior executives believe they should rely on written information and computer reports because these yield more accurate data than face-to-face communications do. Do you agree? Discuss.

6. What communication channel would you choose to communicate an impending companywide layoff? News about the company picnic? New corporate quality goals that will require significant changes in how your subordinates perform their tasks? Explain your choices.

7. If you wanted to communicate nonverbally with your team to create a sense of trust and teamwork, what would you do?

8. How do leaders use communication to influence and persuade others? Think of someone you have known who is skilled in the art of persuasion. What makes this person an effective communicator?

9. Does the Johari Window seem like a good framework for leaders who want to create better communications among team members? Can you think of potential problems a leader might encounter when applying the Johari Window?

10. Think about a recent crisis, such as the decline and fall of large financial institutions, the H1N1 (swine flu) scare, or the 2009 shooting rampage at Fort Hood Army base, and discuss how you think leaders handled crisis communication.

Leadership at Work

LISTEN LIKE A PROFESSIONAL

The fastest way to become a great listener is to act like a professional listener, such as a clinical psychologist who uses listening to heal another person. Therapists drop their own point of view to concentrate on the patient's point of view. The therapist listens totally, drawing out more information rather than thinking about a response.

The next time you are in a conversation in which the other person talks about some problem or concern, practice professional listening by doing the following:

1. Hold a steady gaze on the person's left eye (not the nose or face, but the left eye)— use a soft gaze, not a hard stare.

2. Remove your thoughts and opinions from the conversation—quell your mind chatter and your desire to say something in response.

3. Suspend judgment—rather than critically analyzing what is being said, feel empathy as if you are walking in the other person's shoes.

4. Draw out the other person's thoughts with brief questions and paraphrasing. Repeat the professional listening approach at least three times with different people to get comfortable with it.

List your thoughts on how the other people responded to your listening, and what it felt like to you.

Other person responded:

1. _____

   _____

   _____

2. _____

   _____

   _____

3. _____
_____
_____

What I felt:

1. _____
_____
_____

2. _____
_____
_____

3. _____
_____
_____

In Class: The instructor can divide students into pairs—listener and speaker—in class to practice this exercise. The "speaking" students can be asked to talk about some small problem or annoyance they encountered in the previous day or two. The "listening" students can be given instructions to not speak during the first trial, and instead just maintain a soft gaze into the speaker's left eye and respond only with body language (facial expressions and nods). The speaking students should continue until they have nothing more to say or until they feel an emotional shift and the problem seems to have disappeared. After students switch roles and play both speaker and listener, the instructor can ask the class for perceptions of what happened and what they were feeling during the conversation.

It works well to have the students choose a second pairing, and redo the exercise with a new problem. The only difference the second time is that the "listener" role is given fewer restrictions, so the listener can make brief comments such as to paraphrase or ask a short question. The listeners, however, should keep spoken comments to a minimum and definitely should not offer their own ideas or point of view. After the students finish, the instructor can gather opinions about what the experience was like for both the speaker and the listener. Key questions include the following: What did it feel like to listen rather than respond verbally to what another person said? What is the value of this professional listening approach? In what situations is professional listening likely to be more or less effective? If the instructor desires, the exercise can be done a third time to help students get more comfortable with a true listening role.

Source: Adapted from Michael Ray and Rochelle Myers, *Creativity in Business* (New York: Broadway Books, 2000), pp. 82–83.

Chapter 10: Leading Teams

© Eric Foltz

Your Leadership Challenge

After reading this chapter, you should be able to:

- Turn a group of individuals into a collaborative team that achieves high performance through shared mission and collective responsibility.

- Identify challenges associated with teamwork and explain why people

sometimes have negative feelings about working in a team.

- Understand and handle the stages of team development, and design an effective team in terms of size, diversity, and levels of interdependence.

- Develop and apply the personal qualities of effective team leadership for traditional, virtual, and global teams.

- Handle conflicts that inevitably arise among members of a team.

Chapter Outline

"Working together for the common good is not normally a function for us out on the PGA Tour," said Olin Browne, a PGA (Professional Golf Association) Tour player. "We play as individuals." But to win against the heavily favored Europeans at the Ryder Cup competition meant a group of 12 individual U.S. players had to function as a team. The captain of the U.S. team, Paul Azinger, decided to divide the 12-man group into three sub-teams, called pods, assigning each pod an assistant captain. Azinger relied on the help of a team-building specialist to put together members who could work well with one another. The pods did all their practices together and were paired only with other pod members in the competition. When all was said and done, the U.S. team pulled off a surprising victory over the European squad. The win was largely due to the teamwork. The pods "allowed the players, without any formal training, to feed off each other and help each other . . . ," said Browne. "In the larger 12-man group, some guys with quieter personalities might have been lost in the shuffle."[1]

The sports world is full of stories of underdog teams that have won championships against a group of players who were better individually but did not make up a better team.[2] For leaders in business and nonprofit organizations, as well, creating effective teams is a key to better performance. Teams are becoming the basic building block of organizations.

Teams can provide benefits for both organizations and employees through higher productivity, quality improvements, greater flexibility and speed, a flatter management structure, increased employee involvement and satisfaction, and lower turnover.[3] However, teams present greater leadership challenges than does the traditional hierarchical organization. This chapter explores team leadership. We define various types of teams, look at how teams develop, and examine characteristics that influence team effectiveness. The chapter then explores topics such as cohesiveness and performance, task and socioemotional roles of team members, and the leader's personal role in building effective teams. The new challenge of leading virtual and global teams is also discussed. The final part of the chapter looks at how leaders manage team conflict, including using negotiation.

Teams in Organizations

Teams are not right for every situation, but much work in organizations is *interdependent*, which means that individuals and departments rely on other individuals and departments for information or resources in order to accomplish their work. When tasks are highly interdependent, a team can be the best approach for ensuring the level of coordination, information sharing, and exchange of materials necessary for successful task accomplishment.

What Is a Team?

A **team** is a unit of two or more people who interact and coordinate their work to accomplish a shared goal or purpose.[4] This definition has three components. First, teams are made up of two or more people. Teams can be large, but most have fewer than 15 people. Second, people in a team work together regularly. People who do not interact regularly, such as those waiting in line at the company cafeteria or riding together in the elevator, do not compose a team. Third, people in a team share a goal, whether it is building a car, placing mentally challenged clients in job training, or writing a textbook. Today's students are frequently assigned to complete assignments in teams. In this case, the shared goal is to complete the task and receive an acceptable grade. However, in many cases, student teams are given a great deal of structure in terms of team roles and responsibilities, time frame, activities, and so forth. In a work setting, these elements are typically much more ambiguous and have to be worked out within the team.

A team is a group of people, but the two are not one and the same. A professor, coach, or employer can put together a *group* of people and never build a *team*. For example, the 2004 U.S. Olympic basketball team was made up entirely of superstar players, yet the members never coalesced as a team, instead functioning as a group of individual players. The team came in third and lost to Lithuania. In contrast, the 1980 U.S. hockey team that beat the Soviets to win gold at the Lake Placid Olympics consisted of a bunch of no-name players. Coach Herb Brooks picked players based on their personal chemistry—how they worked together as a team—rather than on their individual abilities and egos.[5] Only when people sublimate their individual needs and desires and synthesize their knowledge, skills, and efforts toward accomplishment of a communal goal do they become a team. This chapter's *Consider This* illustrates the spirit and power of teamwork.

Team
a unit of two or more people who interact and coordinate their work to accomplish a shared goal or purpose

Consider **This!**
Lessons from Geese

Fact 1: As each goose flaps its wings, it creates an "uplift" for the birds that follow. By flying in a "V" formation, the whole flock adds 71 percent greater flying range than if each bird flew alone.

Lesson: People who share a common direction and sense of community can get where they are going quicker and easier because they are traveling on the thrust of one another.

Fact 2: When a goose falls out of formation, it suddenly feels the drag and resistance of flying alone. It quickly moves back into formation to take advantage of the lifting power of the bird immediately in front of it.

Lesson: If we have as much sense as a goose, we stay in formation with those headed where we want to go. We are willing to accept their help and give our help to others.

Fact 3: When the lead goose tires, it rotates back into the formation and another goose flies to the point position.

Lesson: It pays to take turns doing the hard tasks and sharing leadership. Like geese, people are interdependent on each other's skills, capabilities, and unique arrangement of gifts, talents, or resources.

Fact 4: The geese flying in formation honk to encourage those up front to keep up their speed.

Lesson: We need to make sure our honking is encouraging. In groups where there is encouragement, the production is much greater. The power of encouragement (to stand by one's heart or core values and encourage the heart and core of others) is the quality of honking we seek.

Fact 5: When a goose gets sick, wounded, or shot down, two geese drop out of the formation and follow it down to help and protect it. They stay until it dies or is able to fly again. Then, they launch out with another formation or catch up with the flock.

Lesson: If we have as much sense as a goose, we will stand by each other in difficult times as well as when we are strong.

Source: 1991 Organizational Development Network. Original author unknown.

© majaiva

Exhibit 10.1 lists the primary differences between a group and a team. A team achieves high levels of performance through shared leadership, a sense of purpose, and collective responsibility by all members working toward a common goal. Teams are characterized by equality; in the best teams, there are no individual "stars" and everyone sublimates individual ego to the good of the whole. The Leader's Bookshelf further discusses characteristics of teams that lead to high performance.

All organizations are made up of groups of people who work together to accomplish specific goals. Although not all organizations use teams as they are defined in Exhibit 10.1, many of the leadership ideas presented in this chapter can also be applied in leading other types of groups.

Exhibit 10.1 Differences Between Groups and Teams

Group	Team
Has a designated, strong leader	Shares or rotates leadership roles
Individual accountability	Mutual and individual accountability (accountable to each other)
Identical purpose for group and organization	Specific team vision or purpose
Performance goals set by others	Performance goals set by team
Works within organizational boundaries	Not inhibited by organizational boundaries
Individual work products	Collective work products
Organized meetings, delegation	Mutual feedback, open-ended discussion, active problem solving

Source: Based on Jon R. Katzenbach and Douglas K. Smith, "The Discipline of Teams," *Harvard Business Review* (March–April 1995), pp. 111–120; and Milan Moravec, Odd Jan Johannessen, and Thor A. Hjelmas, "Thumbs Up for Self-Managed Teams," *Management Review* (July–August 1997), pp. 42–47 (chart on p. 46).

The Dilemma of Teams

If you've been in a class where the instructor announced that part of the grade would be based on a team project, you probably heard a few groans. The same thing happens in organizations. Leaders should understand that some people love the idea of teamwork, others hate it, and many people have both positive and negative emotions about working as part of a team. There are three primary reasons teams present a dilemma for people:

- *We Have to Give Up Our Independence.* When people become part of a team, their success depends on the team's success; therefore, they are dependent on how well other people perform, not just on their own individual initiative and actions. In addition, whereas most people are comfortable with the idea of making sacrifices in order to achieve their own individual success, teamwork demands that they make sacrifices for *group* success.[6] The idea is that each person should put the team first, even if at times it hurts the individual.
- *We Have to Put Up with Free Riders.* Teams are sometimes made up of people who have different work ethics. The term **free rider** refers to a team member who attains benefits from team membership but does not actively participate in and contribute to the team's work. You might have experienced this frustration in a student project team, where one member put little effort into the project but benefited from the hard work of others when grades were handed out. Free riding is sometimes called *social loafing* because some members do not exert equal effort.[7] The potential for free riding might be one reason a survey found that 40 to 60 percent of people (depending on gender and age) like working in teams to learn from others, but no more than 36 percent report they like working in teams to complete tasks.[8]
- *Teams Are Sometimes Dysfunctional.* Some companies have had great success with teams, but there are also numerous examples of how teams in organizations fail spectacularly.[9] A great deal of research and team experience over the past few decades has produced significant insights into what causes teams to succeed or fail. The evidence shows that how teams are managed plays the most critical role.[10] Exhibit 10.2 lists five dysfunctions that are common in teams and describes the contrasting desirable characteristics that effective leaders develop in their teams.[11]

Free rider
a team member who attains benefits from team membership but does not actively participate in and contribute to the team's work

Leader's Bookshelf

Great Business Teams: Cracking the Code for Standout Performance

by Howard M. Guttman

Management consultant and author Howard Guttman believes high-performance organizations begin with great teams. In his book, *Great Business Teams*, Guttman draws on research into the inner workings of several dozen high-performance teams at companies such as Johnson & Johnson, L'Oreal, Novartis, and Mars Drinks.

Characteristics of Great Teams

Whether it is a top leadership team, a cross-functional project team, or a self-directed product development team, Guttman says great teams share five key characteristics:

1. **They are led by high-performance leaders.** Leaders of great teams put power and authority in the hands of the team. They see their job as making sure all members are clear about and committed to the business strategy and operational goals, understand their roles and responsibilities, and adhere to specific ground rules for decision making and interpersonal behavior.

2. **They have members who act as leaders.** Members of great teams act as leaders by embracing responsibility, exerting influence to accomplish tasks, and holding one another accountable for results. Everyone's performance—even the leader's—is subject to scrutiny and feedback.

3. **They abide by protocols.** Ambiguity kills effective teamwork, says Guttman. To achieve high performance, everyone on the team needs to be clear about what the team as a whole is going to accomplish, what each individual will contribute, how the team will carry out its tasks, and how members are expected to interact with one another.

4. **They are never satisfied.** On a high-performance team, self-monitoring, self-evaluation, and continually raising the performance bar are the norm.

5. **They have a supportive performance management system.** To get great teamwork, the organization's performance management and reward systems have to support the expected team behaviors.

Why Teams?

Guttman believes today's organizations and the challenges they face are too complex for formal leaders to make all the decisions. He argues that companies can best succeed with distributed leadership, in which key decisions are made by layers of self-directed teams that are jointly accountable for performance.

Great Business Teams, by Howard Guttman, is published by John Wiley & Sons.

Exhibit 10.2 Five Common Dysfunctions of Teams

Dysfunction	Effective Team Characteristics
Lack of trust—People don't feel safe to reveal mistakes, share concerns, or express ideas.	**Trust**—Members trust one another on a deep emotional level; feel comfortable being vulnerable with one another.
Fear of conflict—People go along with others for the sake of harmony; don't express conflicting opinions.	**Healthy conflict**—Members feel comfortable disagreeing and challenging one another in the interest of finding the best solution.
Lack of commitment—If people are afraid to express their true opinions, it's difficult to gain their true commitment to decisions.	**Commitment**—Because all ideas are put on the table, people can eventually achieve genuine buy-in around important goals and decisions.
Avoidance of accountability—People don't accept responsibility for outcomes; engage in finger-pointing when things go wrong.	**Accountability**—Members hold one another accountable rather than relying on managers as the source of accountability.
Inattention to results—Members put personal ambition or the needs of their individual departments ahead of collective results.	**Results orientation**—Individual members set aside personal agendas to focus on what's best for the team. Collective results define success.

Source: Based on Patrick Lencioni, *The Five Dysfunctions of a Team* (New York: John Wiley & Sons, 2002).

marble: © Ioannis Drimillis   library: www.istockphoto.com/nikada

How Teams Develop

Smoothly functioning teams don't just happen. They are built by leaders who take specific actions to help people come together as a team. One important point for leaders to understand is that teams develop over time.[12]

Research suggests that teams develop over several stages. Exhibit 10.3 shows one model of the stages of team development.[13] These stages typically occur in sequence, although there can be overlap. Team leaders should recognize the stages of development and help teams move through them successfully.

Forming The **forming** stage of development is a period of orientation and getting acquainted. Team members find out what behavior is acceptable to others, explore friendship possibilities, and determine task orientation. Uncertainty is high, because no one knows what the ground rules are or what is expected of them. Members will usually accept whatever power or authority is offered by either formal or informal leaders. The leader's challenge at this stage of development is to facilitate communication and interaction among team members to help them get acquainted and establish guidelines for how the team will work together. It is important at this stage that the leader try to make everyone feel comfortable and like a part of the team. Leaders can draw out shy or quiet team members to help them establish relationships with others.

Forming
stage of team development that includes orientation and getting acquainted

---

Exhibit 10.3 Stages of Team Development

Source: Based on the stages of small group development in Bruce W. Tuckman, "Developmental Sequence in Small Groups," *Psychological Bulletin* 63 (1965), pp. 384–399; and B. W. Tuckman and M. A. Jensen, "Stages of Small Group Development Revisited," *Group and Organizational Studies* 2 (1977), pp. 419–427.

Storming During the **storming** stage, individual personalities emerge more clearly. People become more assertive in clarifying their roles. This stage is marked by conflict and disagreement. Team members may disagree over their perceptions of the team's mission or goals. They may jockey for position or form subgroups based on common interests. The team is characterized by a general lack of unity and cohesiveness. It is essential that teams move beyond this stage or they will never achieve high performance. The leader's role is to encourage participation by each team member and help people find their common vision and values. Members need to debate ideas, surface conflicts, disagree with one another, and work through the uncertainties and conflicting perceptions about team tasks and goals.

Action Memo

As a leader, you can guide your team through its stages of development. Early on you can help members know one another, and then encourage participation and common purpose, followed by clarifying goals and expectations. Finally, you can concentrate on helping the team achieve high performance.

Norming At the **norming** stage, conflict has been resolved and team unity and harmony emerge. Consensus develops as to who the natural team leaders are, and members' roles are clear. Team members come to understand and accept one another. Differences are resolved and members develop a sense of cohesiveness. This stage typically is of short duration and moves quickly into the next stage. The team leader should emphasize openness within the team and continue to facilitate communication and clarify team roles, values, and expectations.

Performing During the **performing** stage, the major emphasis is on accomplishing the team's goals. Members are committed to the team's mission. They interact frequently, coordinate their actions, and handle disagreements in a mature, productive manner. Team members confront and resolve problems in the interest of task accomplishment. At this stage, the team leader should concentrate on facilitating high task performance and helping the team self-manage to reach its goals.

Leaders at Lucasfilm Ltd., the creator of *Star Wars*, *Pirates of the Caribbean*, and *Transformers*, understand that personal contact and face-to-face communication are important for rapidly building individuals into a team. They brought the company's disparate units—such as special effects shop Industrial Light and Magic (ILM), the LucasArts video game company, Lucasfilm Animation, and others—together in one huge $350 million complex so teams can quickly reach the performing stage of development.[14] At Lucasfilm, multidisciplinary teams rapidly form around specific projects, complete the job, and then disband, which is the final stage in the team development model, adjourning.

Adjourning The **adjourning** stage occurs in committees and teams that have a limited task to perform and are disbanded afterward. During this stage, the emphasis is on wrapping up and gearing down. Task performance is no longer a top priority and leaders frequently focus on team members' social and emotional needs. People may feel heightened emotionality, strong cohesiveness, and depression or regret over the team's disbandment. At this point, the leader may wish to signify the team's disbanding with a ritual or ceremony, perhaps giving out certificates or awards to signify closure and completeness.

Team Types and Characteristics

In the following sections, we look at various types of teams that have traditionally been used in organizations and examine some characteristics that are important

Storming
stage of team development in which individual personalities and conflicts emerge

Norming
stage of team development in which conflicts have been resolved and team unity emerges

Performing
stage of team development in which the major emphasis is on accomplishing the team's goals

Adjourning
stage of team development that occurs in committees and teams that have a limited task to perform; the emphasis is on wrapping up, gearing down, and signifying closure

Exhibit 10.4   Evolution of Teams and Team Leadership

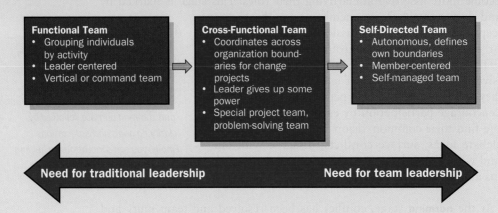

to team dynamics and performance. Later in the chapter, we will discuss the new challenge of leading virtual and global teams.

Traditional Types of Teams

Exhibit 10.4 illustrates three fundamental types of teams used in today's organizations: functional teams, cross-functional teams, and self-directed teams.

Functional Teams A **functional team** is part of the traditional vertical hierarchy. This type of team is made up of a supervisor and his or her subordinates in the formal chain of command. Sometimes called a *vertical team* or a *command team*, the functional team can include three or four levels of hierarchy within a department. Typically, a functional team makes up a single department in the organization. For example, the quality control department at Blue Bell Creameries in Brenham, Texas, is a functional team that tests all incoming ingredients to make sure only the best products go into the company's ice cream. A financial analysis department, a human resources department, and a sales department are all functional or vertical teams. Each is created by the organization within the vertical hierarchy to attain specific goals through members' joint activities.

Cross-Functional Teams As the name implies, **cross-functional teams** are made up of members from different functional departments within the organization. Employees are generally from about the same hierarchical level in the organization, although cross-functional teams sometimes cross vertical as well as horizontal boundaries. Cross-functional teams typically have a specific team leader and coordinate across boundaries to lead projects of special importance, such as creating a new product in a manufacturing organization or developing an interdisciplinary curriculum in a middle school. Georgetown Preparatory School in North Bethesda, Maryland, used a cross-functional team to develop a flu preparedness plan.

Functional team
team made up of a supervisor and subordinates in the formal chain of command

Cross-functional team
team made up of members from different functional departments within an organization

IN THE LEAD

Georgetown Preparatory School

When the H1N1 (swine flu) outbreak hit, Georgetown Preparatory School, the oldest all-boys Catholic school in the United States, was ready. Georgetown began thinking about a flu preparedness plan during the avian flu scare several years ago. Leaders wanted to develop a plan that would both address the ongoing threat of seasonal flu and prepare for a flu pandemic, should it happen. "Our discussions on preparedness became no less important than those regarding curriculum, teaching methods, and character education," says Margaret Frazier, academic dean at Georgetown.

To share knowledge and responsibility all across the school community, leaders put together a cross-functional team made up of teachers, coaches, administrators, support staff, and outside consultants. The result was FluPrep, a plan that makes everyone aware of what they can do individually and collectively to combat seasonal influenza, as well as to learn about and prepare for other, more deadly health threats. The team addressed a number of difficult questions, such as how to encourage "responsible absence," whether to track foreign travel of students and staff, at what point the school would close should an outbreak occur, and how to use distance learning.

Few schools have addressed preparedness needs on this level, and Georgetown was much better equipped than many educational institutions for dealing with the H1N1 threat in 2009. "In this age of global connectedness and virulent infectious disease . . . preparedness may be the subject of greatest importance," Frazier says. FluPrep is an evolving plan, and Georgetown Prep continues to use a cross-functional approach to involve everyone across the school community.[15]

As with the FluPrep team at Georgetown Preparatory School, cross-functional teams are generally involved in projects that affect several departments and therefore require that many views be considered. Cross-functional teams facilitate information sharing across functional boundaries, generate suggestions for coordinating the departments represented, develop new ideas and solutions for existing organizational problems, and assist in developing new practices or policies.

The members of one type of cross-functional team, the *problem-solving* or *process-improvement* team, meet voluntarily to discuss ways to improve quality, efficiency, and the work environment. Their recommendations are proposed to top executives for approval. Another frequent application of cross-functional teams is for change projects, especially new product innovation, because effectively developing new products and services requires coordination across many departments. These are sometimes called *special project* teams. One example comes from Healthwise, a nonprofit organization that works with numerous health-care organizations and online health sites like WebMD. The company used a special project team made up of doctors, other health specialists, writers, and technical people to create a new product line called HealthMastery Campaigns. HealthMastery is a series of programs that e-mails information, surveys, and reminders to consumers on topics such as asthma, back problems, or smoking cessation, fitting with the company's goal of providing information to help consumers make informed health-care decisions.[16]

Action Memo

As a leader, you can create a cross-functional team to handle a change project, such as product innovation, that requires coordination across departmental boundaries. Use a problem-solving or process-improvement team to initiate ideas for improving quality and efficiency.

Evolution to Self-Directed Teams Cross-functional teams may gradually evolve into self-directed teams, which represent a fundamental change in how work is organized. Exhibit 10.4 illustrates the evolution of teams and team leadership. The functional team groups individuals by common skill and activity within the traditional structure. Leadership is based on the vertical hierarchy. In cross-functional teams, members have more freedom from the hierarchy, but the team typically is still leader-centered and leader-directed. The leader is most often assigned by the organization and is usually a supervisor or manager from one of the departments represented on the team. Leaders do, however, give up some of their control and power at this stage in order for the team to function effectively.

In the next stage of evolution, team members work together without the ongoing direction of managers, supervisors, or assigned team leaders.[17] Self-directed teams are member-centered rather than leader-centered and -directed. Hundreds of companies, including ICU Medical, Consolidated Diesel, Whole Foods, the Mayo Clinic, IBM, and Edy's Grand Ice Cream, are using self-directed teams. Empirical studies have shown that self-directed teams are associated with higher job satisfaction.[18] Job satisfaction increases partly because working in self-directed teams enables people to feel challenged, find their work meaningful, feel more control over their work lives, and develop a stronger sense of identity with the organization.[19]

Self-directed teams typically consist of 5 to 20 members who rotate jobs to produce an entire product or service or at least one complete aspect or portion of a product or service (for example, engine assembly or insurance claims processing).[20] Self-directed teams often are long-term or permanent in nature, although many of today's fast-moving companies, such as Lucasfilm, described earlier, also use temporary self-directed teams that come together to work on a specific project and then disband when their work is done. Self-directed teams typically include three elements:

1. The team includes workers with varied skills and functions, and the combined skills are sufficient to perform a major organizational task, thereby eliminating barriers among departments and enabling excellent coordination.

2. The team is given access to resources such as information, financial resources, equipment, machinery, and supplies needed to perform the complete task.

3. The team is empowered with decision-making authority, which means that members have the freedom to select new members, solve problems, spend money, monitor results, and plan for the future.

In self-directed teams, members take over duties such as scheduling work or vacations, ordering materials, and evaluating performance. Self-directed teams are typically not completely autonomous, in that organizational leaders set overall direction and monitor the team's work on a regular basis. However, these teams are effectively trained to work with minimum supervision, and members are jointly responsible for making decisions and solving problems. At Whole Foods, each store has approximately eight self-directed teams, each responsible for a department such as seafood, produce, or checkout. The teams have a tremendous amount of discretion related to staffing, pricing, product selection, and so forth.[21] Self-directed teams at ICU Medical, a maker of medical devices, have even instituted changes over the objections of top leaders. Founder and CEO George Lopez says he has never vetoed a team decision. He believes teams work only if people have the authority to make important decisions.[22] Leaders in companies such as ICU Medical and Whole Foods believe critical decisions should be made by those who will be most directly affected by the consequences.

Self-directed teams typically elect one of their own to serve as team leader, and the leader may change each year. Some teams function without a designated leader, so anyone may play a leadership role depending on the situation. For example, the emergency trauma team at Massachusetts General

Self-directed teams
teams made up of members who work with minimum supervision and rotate jobs to produce a complete product or service

Action Memo

As a leader, you can use a self-directed team when members are capable of working without active supervision. Give the team access to the money, equipment, supplies, and information needed to perform its project or task, and empower the team with decision-making authority.

Hospital performs so smoothly that the team switches leaders seamlessly, depending on the crisis at hand. With each new emergency, direction may come from a doctor, intern, nurse, or technician—whoever is particularly experienced with the problem at hand.[23]

Understanding Team Characteristics

One of a leader's most important jobs is to get the team designed right by considering such characteristics as size, diversity, and interdependence. The quality of team design has a significant impact on the success of a team.[24]

Size More than 30 years ago, psychologist Ivan Steiner examined what happened each time the size of a team increased, and he proposed that team performance and productivity peaked at about five—a quite small number. He found that adding additional members beyond five caused a decrease in motivation, an increase in coordination problems, and a general decline in performance.[25] Since then, numerous studies have found that smaller teams perform better, though most researchers say it's impossible to specify an optimal team size. One recent investigation of team size based on data from 58 software development teams found that the best-performing teams ranged in size from three to six members.[26] Results of a Gallup poll in the United States show that 82 percent of employees agree that small teams are more productive.[27] In another survey of white-collar workers, 54 percent of respondents said they prefer working in groups of three.[28]

Teams should be large enough to take advantage of diverse skills, yet small enough to permit members to feel an intimate part of a community. A summary of research on size suggests that small teams show more agreement, ask more questions, and exchange more opinions. Members want to get along with one another. Small teams report more satisfaction and enter into more personal discussions, and members feel a greater sense of cohesiveness and belonging. Large teams (generally defined as 12 or more members) tend to have more disagreements and differences of opinion. Subgroups often form and conflicts among them may occur. Demands on leaders are greater in large teams, because there is less member participation. Large teams also tend to be less friendly and members do not feel that they are part of a cohesive community.[29] As a general rule, it is more difficult to satisfy members' needs in large teams, forcing leaders to work harder to keep members focused and committed to team goals.

Diversity Because teams require a variety of skills, knowledge, and experience, it seems likely that heterogeneous teams would be more effective because members bring diverse abilities, information, and ways of thinking to bear on a project or problem. In general, research supports this idea, showing that heterogeneous teams produce more innovative solutions to problems than do homogeneous teams.[30] Diversity within a team can be a source of creativity. One international business consultant uses the 1960s rock sensation The Beatles to illustrate the importance of diversity to creative teamwork, pointing out how personality differences, distinct abilities, and collegial competition among the four band members contributed to their phenomenal success.[31] Within organizations, too, diversity can contribute to a healthy level of conflict that leads to better decision making. Among top management teams, for example, low levels of conflict are associated with poor decision making. Furthermore, many of these low-conflict teams reflect little diversity among members.[32] Consider the example of Mark IV Transportation & Logistics.

IN THE LEAD

Jerry Giampaglia, Mark IV Transportation & Logistics

Members of the top management team at Mark IV Transportation & Logistics don't have much interest in socializing together on weekends. They are so different in their lifestyles and interests that they can't seem to find much to talk about outside of work. But that's just fine with CEO Jerry Giampaglia, who has seen this diverse team accomplish amazing results, driving revenue from $3 million to $20 million in five years. "We're nothing alike when we're outside this company," Giampaglia says, "but when we walk through those doors, we're clicking."

For a decade, Mark IV was run by a tightly knit group of friends and family, mostly men, who thought alike, acted alike, and often met for drinks or sporting events after work. It was an agreeable and satisfying work environment. The trouble was, Mark IV was in a rut, providing the same three basic services as every other courier service in town and unable to push past the $3 million mark in revenues. Giampaglia had an insight that things were likely to stay the same as long as the company was run by the same homogeneous top management team. So he started filling open positions with a more diverse mix of people that he likely would have shunned in the past.

Now, meetings are often raucous and consensus isn't easy to achieve. People argue opinions back and forth and challenge one another's assumptions. The disagreements have sparked new ideas and new ways of thinking. Mark IV now customizes its services to meet the needs of clients. "In the old company, the challenges found us and we sweated them out," Giampaglia says. "Now, we create challenges and love finding solutions."[33]

Jerry Giampaglia discovered what many leaders now know: Team diversity can provide a healthy level of disagreement that sparks innovation and leads to better decision making. However, despite the value of some conflict, conflict that is too strong or is not handled appropriately can limit team members' satisfaction and performance. For example, a new product team at a company that manufactures and sells upscale children's furniture found their differing perspectives and working styles to be a significant source of conflict during crunch times. Members who needed peace and quiet were irked at those who wanted music playing in the background. Compulsively neat members found it almost impossible to work with those who liked working among stacks of clutter. Fortunately, this team was able to overcome these divisive issues for the sake of the project.[34] Teams made up of highly diverse members tend to have more difficulty learning to work well together, but, with effective leadership and conflict resolution, the problems seem to dissolve over time. Managing team conflict will be discussed in more detail later in the chapter.

Interdependence **Interdependence** means the extent to which team members depend on each other for information, resources, or ideas to accomplish their tasks. Tasks such as performing surgery or directing military operations, for example, require a high degree of interaction and exchange, whereas tasks such as assembly-line manufacturing require very little.[35]

Three types of interdependence can affect teams: pooled, sequential, and reciprocal.[36] In **pooled interdependence,** the lowest form of interdependence, members are fairly independent of one another in completing their work, participating on a team, but not *as* a team.[37] They may share a machine or a common secretary, but most of their work is done independently. An example might be a sales team, with each salesperson responsible for his or her own sales area and

Interdependence
the extent to which team members depend on each other for information, resources, or ideas to accomplish their tasks

Pooled interdependence
the lowest form of team interdependence; members are relatively independent of one another in completing their work

customers, but sharing the same appointment secretary. Salespersons need not interact to accomplish their work and little day-to-day coordination is needed.[38]

Sequential interdependence is a serial form wherein the output of one team member becomes the input to another team member. One member must perform well in order for the next member to perform well, and so on. Because team members have to exchange information and resources and rely upon one another, this is a higher level of interdependence. An example might be an engine assembly team in an automobile plant. Each team member performs a separate task, but his work depends on the satisfactory completion of work by other team members. Regular communication and coordination are required to keep work running smoothly.

The highest level of interdependence, **reciprocal interdependence,** exists when team members influence and affect one another in reciprocal fashion. The output of team member A is the input to team member B, and the output of team member B is the input back again to team member A. Reciprocal interdependence characterizes most teams performing knowledge-based work. For example, the Federal Bureau of Investigation (FBI) uses Cyber Action Teams, or CATs, made up of agents, computer forensics experts, and specialists in computer code to fight computer crimes such as new viruses, worms, and other rogue programs. This kind of work doesn't move forward in a logical, step-by-step fashion. Instead, reciprocal tasks require "an open-ended series of to-and-fro collaborations, iterations, and reiterations" among team members.[39] With reciprocal teams, each individual member makes a contribution, but only the team as a whole "performs."

Leaders are responsible for facilitating the degree of coordination and communication needed among team members, depending on the level of team interdependence. Top executives at Ford Motor Company, for example, created the conditions to support a high level of interdependence for the team developing the Escape Hybrid SUV, enabling members to complete an extraordinarily complex project on a tight time schedule. All team members were located on the same floor at headquarters to enable close interaction. Problems were often solved in hallway chats or over lunch in the nearby cafeteria. Top managers gave the team nearly complete autonomy so that decisions could be made quickly. Getting the Escape Hybrid SUV right required hundreds of back-and-forth discussions and thousands of adjustments to the hardware, software, and wiring of the vehicle.[40] The vehicle was a resounding success when it was introduced, and applying the hybrid technologies developed during the project is key to Ford's future.[41]

When team interdependence is high, true team leadership, which involves empowering the team to make decisions and take action, is especially important to high performance. However, for teams with low interdependence, traditional leadership, individual rewards, and granting authority and power to individuals rather than the team may be appropriate.[42]

Team Effectiveness

Team effectiveness can be defined as achieving four performance outcomes—innovation/adaptation, efficiency, quality, and employee satisfaction.[43] *Innovation/ adaptation* means the degree to which teams affect the organization's ability to

---

Action Memo

As a leader, you can improve team effectiveness by paying attention to the size, diversity, and interdependence of your team. When interdependence among members is high, empower team members to make decisions and initiate action together.

Sequential interdependence
serial form of interdependence in which the output of one team member becomes the input to another team member

Reciprocal interdependence
highest form of team interdependence; members influence and affect one another in reciprocal fashion

Team effectiveness
the extent to which a team achieves four performance outcomes: innovation/ adaptation, efficiency, quality, and employee satisfaction

learn and to rapidly respond to environmental needs and changes. *Efficiency* pertains to whether the team helps the organization attain goals using fewer resources. *Quality* refers to achieving fewer defects and exceeding customer expectations. *Satisfaction* pertains to the team's ability to maintain employee commitment and enthusiasm by meeting the personal needs of its members. In the following sections, we discuss issues that influence team effectiveness, including team cohesiveness and performance; team task and socioemotional roles; and the personal impact of the team leader.

Team Cohesiveness and Effectiveness

Team cohesiveness is defined as the extent to which members stick together and remain united in the pursuit of a common goal.[44] Members of highly cohesive teams are committed to team goals and activities, feel that they are involved in something significant, and are happy when the team succeeds. Members of less cohesive teams are less concerned about the team's welfare.

Determinants of Cohesiveness Leaders can use several factors to influence team cohesiveness. One is team *interaction*. The greater the amount of contact between team members and the more time they spend together, the more cohesive the team. Through frequent interaction, members get to know one another and become more devoted to the team. Another factor is *shared mission and goals*. When team members agree on purpose and direction, they will be more cohesive.

The most cohesive teams are those that feel they are involved in something immensely relevant and important—that they are embarking on a journey together that will make the world better in some way. An aerospace executive, recalling his participation in an advanced design team, put it this way: "We even walked differently than anybody else. We felt we were way out there, ahead of the whole world."[45] A third factor is *personal attraction* to the team, meaning members find their common ground and enjoy being together. Members like and respect one another.

The organizational context can also affect team cohesiveness. When a team is in moderate *competition* with other teams, its cohesiveness increases as it strives to win. Finally, *team success* and the favorable evaluation of the team's work by outsiders add to cohesiveness. When a team succeeds and others in the organization recognize this success, members feel good and their commitment to the team will be higher.

Consequences of Team Cohesiveness The consequences of team cohesiveness can be examined according to two categories: morale and performance. As a general rule, employee *morale* is much higher in cohesive teams because of increased communication, a friendly atmosphere, loyalty, and member participation in decisions and activities. High team cohesiveness has almost uniformly positive effects on the satisfaction and morale of team members.[46]

With respect to team *performance*, it seems that cohesiveness and performance are generally positively related, although research results are mixed. Cohesive teams can sometimes unleash enormous amounts of employee energy and creativity. One explanation for this is the research finding that working in a team increases individual motivation and performance. Simply interacting with others has an energizing effect.[47] In relation to this, one study found that cohesiveness

---

Action Memo

As a leader, you can facilitate team cohesiveness by providing members with opportunities to interact and know one another. You can use friendly competition with other teams to increase cohesion, and work with top leaders to develop high performance norms for the team.

Team cohesiveness
the extent to which members stick together and remain united in the pursuit of a common goal

---

Action Memo

Cohesiveness is generally considered an attractive feature of teams. Leader's Self-Insight 10.1 gives you a chance to measure the cohesiveness of a team you have been involved in at school or work.

marble: © Kirill Matkov   sunset: © Marco Regalia

Leader's Self-Insight 10.1

Is Your Team Cohesive?

Think of a specific team of which you are or were recently a part, either at work or school, and answer the following questions about your perception of the team. Indicate whether each item is Mostly False or Mostly True for you.

	Mostly False	Mostly True
1. Members are proud to tell others they are part of the team.	_____	_____
2. Members are willing to put a great deal of effort into their work for the team to be successful.	_____	_____
3. Members sometimes try to make other team members look bad.	_____	_____
4. Members are willing to "talk up" the team's work with other employees as being good for the organization.	_____	_____
5. Members seem to take personal advantage of each other's mistakes.	_____	_____
6. Members really care about the success of the team.	_____	_____

	Mostly False	Mostly True
7. Members feel there is not much to be gained by sticking with this team's project.	_____	_____
8. Members of this team really like spending time together.	_____	_____

Scoring and Interpretation

Give yourself 1 point for each Mostly False answer to questions 3, 5, and 7 and 1 point for each Mostly True answer to questions 1, 2, 4, 6, and 8. Sum your points for the 8 questions: _____. These questions pertain to team cohesion—the extent to which team members like, trust, and respect one another and are united toward a common goal. These questions were originally designed to assess the commitment of hospital upper-management teams to joint strategic decisions. If your score is 6 or higher, your team would be considered high in cohesion—members are committed to one another and the team's goal. A score of 0–2 indicates below-average team cohesion.

Source: Adapted from Robert S. Dooley and Gerald E. Fryxell, "Attaining Decision Quality and Commitment from Dissent: The Moderating Effects of Loyalty and Competence in Strategic Decision-Making Teams," *Academy of Management Journal* 42, no. 4 (1999), pp. 389–402.

is more closely related to high performance when team interdependence is high, requiring frequent interaction, coordination, and communication, as discussed earlier in this chapter.[48] However, cohesiveness can also *decrease* performance in some cases. One matter of particular concern is **groupthink,** which refers to the tendency of people in cohesive groups to suppress contrary opinions. People slip into groupthink when the desire for harmony outweighs concerns over decision quality. When members of highly cohesive teams put team unity first, they sometimes censor personal opinions and are reluctant to question or challenge the opinions of others.

Another factor influencing performance is the relationship between teams and top leadership. One study surveyed more than 200 work teams and correlated job performance with cohesiveness.[49] Highly cohesive teams were more productive when team members felt supported by organizational leaders and less productive when they sensed hostility and negativism from leaders.

Meeting Task and Socioemotional Needs

Another important factor in team effectiveness is ensuring that the needs for both task accomplishment and team members' socioemotional well-being are met. Recall from Chapter 3 the discussion of situational leadership and the metacategories of task-oriented and relationship-oriented behaviors described in that chapter (Exhibit 3.2). Task-oriented behavior places primary concern on tasks

Groupthink
the tendency of people in cohesive groups to suppress contrary opinions

Task-specialist role
team leadership role associated with initiating new ideas, evaluating the team's effectiveness, seeking to clarify tasks and responsibilities, summarizing facts and ideas for others, and stimulating others to action

Socioemotional role
team leadership role associated with facilitating others' participation, smoothing conflicts, showing concern for team members' needs and feelings, serving as a role model, and reminding others of standards for team interaction

and production and is generally associated with higher productivity, whereas relationship-oriented behavior emphasizes concern for followers and relationships and is associated with higher employee satisfaction.

For a team to be successful over the long term, both task-oriented behavior and relationship-oriented behavior are required within the team. That is, the team must both maintain its members' satisfaction and accomplish its task. These requirements are met through two types of team leadership roles, as illustrated in Exhibit 10.5. A *role* might be thought of as a set of behaviors expected of a person occupying a certain position, such as that of team leader. The **task-specialist role** is associated with behaviors that help the team accomplish its goal, such as initiating new ideas, evaluating facts, and proposing solutions. The **socioemotional role** includes behaviors that maintain people's emotional well-being, such as facilitating the participation of others, smoothing over conflicts, showing concern for others, and maintaining harmony.[50]

Ideally, a team leader is able to play both task-specialist and socioemotional roles to some extent. At Marriott, strengthening both task-oriented and relationship-oriented skills is a primary goal for team leader training, because teams headed by leaders with both types of skills are typically more productive and innovative.[51] In any case, it is the leader's responsibility to make sure both task and socioemotional needs are met, whether through the leader's own behaviors or through the actions and behaviors of other team members.

Action Memo

As a leader, you can make sure that both the task and socioemotional needs of team members are met so that people experience both friendly support and goal accomplishment.

The Team Leader's Personal Role

Successful teams begin with confident and effective team leaders. Harvard Business School professors studying surgery teams have found that the attitude and actions of the team leader, and the quality of the leader's interactions with

Exhibit 10.5 Two Types of Team Leadership Roles

Task-Specialist Role	Socioemotional Role
Initiate ideas. Propose solutions and stimulate new ways of looking at problems.	*Encourage others.* Be warm and receptive; draw others out and encourage their contributions.
Give opinions. Offer opinions on task solutions; give candid feedback on others' suggestions.	*Reconcile differences.* Smooth over conflicts; reduce tension and help others resolve differences.
Seek information. Ask for facts to clarify tasks, responsibilities, and suggestions.	*Provide friendship and support.* Act friendly and supportive; show concern for members' feelings.
Pull ideas together. Relate various ideas to the problem at hand; summarize suggestions.	*Go along with the team.* Be willing to compromise and go along with others' ideas; follow and remind others of agreed-upon norms for behavior.
Stimulate action. Energize others and spur the team to action when interest wanes.	*Maintain harmony.* Seek to identify and correct dysfunctional behavior or problems with team interactions.

Source: Based on Robert A. Baron, *Behavior in Organizations*, 2nd ed. (Boston: Allyn & Bacon, 1986); Don Hellriegel, John W. Slocum, Jr., and Richard W. Woodman, *Organizational Behavior*, 8th ed. (Cincinnati, OH: South-Western, 1998), p. 244; and Gary A. Yukl, *Leadership in Organizations*, 4th ed. (Upper Saddle River, NJ: Prentice Hall, 1998), pp. 384–387.

team members, are crucial to team effectiveness and the success of the surgery.[52] However, leading a team requires a shift in mindset and behavior for those who are accustomed to working in traditional organizations where managers make the decisions.

Most people can learn the new skills and qualities needed for team leadership, but it is not always easy. To be effective team leaders, people have to be willing to change themselves, to step outside their comfort zone and let go of many of the assumptions that have guided their behavior in the past. Here we will discuss four specific changes leaders can make to develop a foundation for effective team leadership.[53]

Recognize the Importance of Shared Purpose and Values

Team leaders articulate a clear and compelling vision so that everyone is moving in the same direction. Having a compelling purpose is one of the key elements of effective teams.[54] A team can't succeed if everyone is floundering around wondering why the team exists and where it is supposed to be going, or if people are going in different directions rather than pulling together for a common purpose.

Leaders also shape team norms and values that are important for accomplishing the vision. A **team norm** is a belief about appropriate conduct that is shared by members and guides their behavior. Norms are important because they define the boundaries of acceptable behavior and provide a frame of reference for team members' actions.[55] The team leader's expectations can significantly influence what norms and values the team adopts and how strongly they persist.[56] For example, NFL Commissioner Roger Goodell made it his mission to establish norms that promote positive conduct and censure player misbehavior. In today's environment, the boys-will-be-boys mentality is no longer acceptable to many fans and the general public. Eventually the norms were formalized in a zero-tolerance personal conduct policy, formulated in concert with the Players Association. These norms have helped protect football's image despite the misbehavior of some individual players.[57]

Build Consensus

Although a team's fundamental purpose may be defined by top executives in an organization, effective team leaders don't simply "hand down" a team vision and authoritatively declare the goals and methods for achieving it. Good team leaders work to understand the interests, goals, values, and opinions of team members in order to define and articulate what the team stands for and how it should function.[58] Rather than putting themselves above the team, they respectfully listen to members and strive to build a shared team identity that shapes action toward achieving the larger goal. Effective teamwork depends on the cooperation and support of all members, and teams function at their best when individual members see the team's interest as their own interest. Thus, leaders work to build consensus rather than issuing orders. Good leaders share power, information, and responsibility, and they allow team members who do the work to have a say in how to do it. They have faith that the team as a collective identity is capable of making good decisions, even if the decisions might not be the ones the leader as an individual would make.

Admit Your Mistakes

The best team leaders are willing to make themselves vulnerable by admitting they don't know everything. Being an effective team leader means enabling all members to contribute their unique skills, talents, and ideas. Leaders can serve as a *fallibility model* by admitting their ignorance and mistakes and asking for help, which lets people know that problems, errors, and concerns can be discussed openly without fear of appearing incompetent.[59] When Bruce Moravec was asked to lead a team to

Team norm
a belief about appropriate conduct that is shared by team members and guides their behavior

Leader's Self-Insight 10.2

Assess Your Team Leadership Skills

Answer the following questions based on what you have done as a team leader, or think you would do, related to the team situations and attitudes described. Check either Mostly False or Mostly True for each question.

	Mostly False	Mostly True
1. An important part of leading a team is to keep members informed almost daily of information that could affect their work.	___	___
2. I love communicating online to work on tasks with team members.	___	___
3. Generally, I feel somewhat tense while interacting with team members from different cultures.	___	___
4. I nearly always prefer face-to-face communications with team members over e-mail.	___	___
5. I enjoy doing things in my own way and in my own time.	___	___
6. If a new member were hired, I would expect the entire team to interview the person.	___	___
7. I become impatient when working with a team member from another culture.	___	___
8. I suggest a specific way each team member can make a contribution to the project.	___	___
9. If I were out of the office for a week, most of the important work of the team would get accomplished anyway.	___	___
10. Delegation is hard for me when an important task has to be done right.	___	___
11. I enjoy working with people with different accents.	___	___
12. I am confident about leading team members from different cultures.	___	___

Scoring and Interpretation

The answers for effective team leadership are as follows: Give yourself 1 point for each Mostly True answer to questions 1, 2, 6, 8, 9, 11, and 12. Give yourself 1 point for each Mostly False answer to questions 3, 4, 5, 7, and 10. If your score is 9 or higher, you certainly understand the ingredients to be a highly effective team leader. If your score is 3 or lower, you might have an authoritarian approach to leadership, or are not comfortable with culturally diverse team membership or virtual team communications, such as e-mail.

Questions 1, 5, 6, 8, 9, and 10 pertain to authoritarian versus participative team leadership. Questions 3, 7, 11, and 12 pertain to cultural differences. Questions 2 and 4 pertain to virtual team communications. Which aspects of team leadership reflect your leader strengths? Which reflect your weaknesses? Team leadership requires that the leader learn to share power, information, and responsibility, be inclusive of diverse members, and be comfortable with electronic communications.

Source: Adapted from "What Style of Leader Are You or Would You Be?" in Andrew J. DuBrin, *Leadership: Research Findings, Practice, and Skills*, 3rd ed. (Boston: Houghton Mifflin Company, 2001), pp. 126–127; and James W. Neuliep and James C. McCroskey, "The Development of Intercultural and Interethnic Communication Apprehension Scales," *Communication Research Reports*, 14, no. 2 (1997), pp. 145–156.

marble: © Kirill Markov sunset: © Marco Regalia

Action Memo

Complete the exercise in Leader's Self-Insight 10.2 to evaluate your capacity for team leadership.

design a new fuselage for the Boeing 757, he had to gain the respect and confidence of people who worked in areas he knew little about. "You don't want to pretend you're more knowledgeable about subjects other people know more about," Moravec advises. "That dooms you to failure. . . . They're the experts."[60]

Provide Support and Coaching to Team Members

Good team leaders make sure people get the training, development opportunities, and resources they need and that they are adequately rewarded for their contributions to the organization. Rather than always thinking about oneself and how to get the next promotion or salary increase, effective team leaders spend their time taking care of team members. Most team members share the critically important needs for recognition and support. Dan Schulman, now CEO of Virgin Mobile USA, learned early in his career the value of recognizing the contributions of others. After his sister died unexpectedly at the age of 20, Schulman says he stopped caring about his work, but team members rallied around him and made sure the project was successful. When Schulman gave his report, he openly told his boss that he had little to do with the project's success, that it was due to the team. When leading future teams, Schulman says he found that giving credit to team members made the teams more cohesive and more effective.[61]

> **Action Memo**
>
> As a leader, you can articulate a clear and compelling vision for the team to help members see their work as meaningful and important. You can make room for everyone to contribute and provide people with the training, support, and coaching they need to excel.

Although team leaders have to keep people focused on accomplishing tasks, as we discussed earlier, research shows that the soft leadership skills concerned with building positive relationships are especially important for creating a high-performance team.[62] Team effectiveness, productivity, and learning are strengthened when team leaders provide support to team members, reinforce team identity and meaning, work to maintain interpersonal relationships and group cohesiveness, and offer training and coaching to enhance members' self-leadership skills.

The Leader's New Challenge: Virtual and Global Teams

Being a team leader is even more challenging when people are scattered in different geographical locations and may be separated by language and cultural differences as well. Virtual and global teams are a reality for many of today's leaders. Exhibit 10.6 illustrates the primary differences between conventional types of teams and today's virtual and global teams. Conventional types of teams discussed earlier in this chapter meet and conduct their interactions face to face in the same physical space. Team members typically share similar cultural backgrounds and characteristics. The key characteristics of virtual and global teams, on the other hand, are (1) spatial distance limits face-to-face interaction, and (2) the use of technological communication is the primary means of connecting team members.[63] Members of virtual and global teams are scattered in different locations, whether it be different offices and business locations around the country or around the world. Most communication is handled via telephone, fax, e-mail, instant messaging, virtual document sharing, videoconferencing, and other media. In some virtual teams, members share the same dominant culture,

Exhibit 10.6 Differences Between Conventional, Virtual, and Global Teams

Type of Team	Spatial Distance	Communications	Member Cultures	Leader Challenge
Conventional	Colocated	Face to face	Same	High
Virtual	Scattered	Mediated	Same	Higher
Global	Widely scattered	Mediated	Different	Very high

but global teams are often made up of members whose cultural values vary widely. The leadership challenge is thus highest for global teams because of the increased potential for misunderstandings and conflicts.

Virtual Teams

A **virtual team** is made up of geographically or organizationally dispersed members who share a common purpose and are linked primarily through advanced information and telecommunications technologies.[64] Team members use e-mail, voice mail, videoconferencing, Internet and intranet technologies, and various forms of collaboration software to perform their work rather than meeting face to face.

Action Memo

As a leader, you can help a virtual team perform even with limited control and supervision. You can select members who thrive in a virtual environment, arrange opportunities for periodic face-to-face meetings, and ensure that members understand the goals and performance standards.

Uses of Virtual Teams   Virtual teams, sometimes called *distributed teams*, may be temporary cross-functional teams that work on specific projects, or they may be long-term, self-directed teams. Virtual teams sometimes include customers, suppliers, and even competitors to pull together the best minds to complete a project. Using virtual teams allows organizations to tap the best people for a particular job, no matter where they are located, thus enabling a fast response to competitive pressures. When IBM needs to staff a project, it gives a list of skills needed to the human resources department, which provides a pool of people who are qualified. The team leader then puts together the best combination of people for the project, which often means pulling people from many different locations. IBM estimates that about a third of its employees participate in virtual teams.[65]

Leading the Virtual Team   Despite their potential benefits, there is growing evidence that virtual teams are typically less effective than teams whose members meet face to face.[66] The team leader can make a tremendous difference in how well a virtual team performs, but virtual teams bring significant leadership challenges.[67] Leaders of conventional teams can monitor how team members are doing and if everything is on track, but virtual team leaders can't see when or how well people are working. Virtual team leaders have to trust people to do their jobs without constant supervision, and they learn to focus more on results than on the process of accomplishing them. Too much control can kill a virtual team, so leaders have to give up most of their control and yet at the same time provide guidance, encouragement, support, and development. The ideas presented earlier regarding the team leader's personal role are applicable to virtual teams as well. In addition, to be successful, virtual team leaders can master the following skills:[68]

- *Select the right team members.* Effective virtual team leaders put a lot of thought into getting the right mix of people on the team. Team members need the right mix of technical, interpersonal, and communication skills to work effectively in a virtual environment. In addition, leaders make clear to the team why each member was chosen to participate, thus giving people a basis for trust in others' abilities and commitment. Choosing people who have open, honest, and trusting personalities is also a plus. As with other types of teams, small virtual teams tend to be more cohesive and work together more effectively. However, diversity of views and experiences is also important to the success of a virtual team. Diversity is usually built into virtual teams because when leaders can pick the right people for the job, no matter where they are located, members usually reflect diverse backgrounds and viewpoints.[69]

Virtual team
a team made up of geographically or organizationally dispersed members who share a common purpose and are linked primarily through advanced information technologies

- *Use technology to build relationships.* Leaders make sure people have opportunities to know one another and establish trusting relationships. At Mobil Corp., leaders bring virtual team members together in one location at the beginning of a project so they can begin to build personal relationships and gain an understanding of their goals and responsibilities.[70] These intense meetings allow the team to rapidly go through the *forming* and *storming* stages of development, as discussed earlier in this chapter. Studies of virtual teams suggest these processes are best accomplished at the same time and in the same place.[71] However, leaders also apply technology to build relationships, and they encourage non–task-related communication, such as the use of online social networking where people can share photos, thoughts, and personal biographies. In a study of which technologies make virtual teams successful, researchers found that round-the-clock virtual work spaces, where team members can access the latest versions of files, keep track of deadlines and timelines, monitor one another's progress, and carry on discussions between formal meetings, got top marks.[72]

- *Agree on ground rules.* Leaders make everyone's roles, responsibilities, and authority clear from the beginning. All team members need to explicitly understand both team and individual goals, deadlines, and expectations for participation and performance. When roles and expectations are clear, trust can develop more easily. It is also important that leaders define a clear context so that people can make decisions, monitor their own performance, and regulate their behavior to accomplish goals. Another important point is shaping norms of full disclosure and respectful interaction. Team members need to agree on communications etiquette, such as whether good-natured flaming is okay or off limits, rules for "verbalizing" online when members are shifting mental gears or need more feedback, whether there are time limits on responding to voice mail or e-mail, and so forth.

As the use of virtual teams grows, there is growing understanding of what makes them successful. Some experts suggest that leaders solicit volunteers as much as possible for virtual teams, and interviews with virtual team members and leaders support the idea that members who truly want to work as a virtual team are more effective.[73] At Nokia, most virtual teams are made up of people who volunteered for the task.

IN THE LEAD

Nokia

In a study of 52 virtual teams in 15 leading multinational companies, London Business School researchers found that Nokia's teams were among the most effective, even though they were made up of people working in several different countries, across time zones and cultures.

What makes Nokia's teams so successful? Nokia leaders are careful to select people who have a collaborative mindset, and they form many teams with volunteers who are highly committed to the task or project. The company also tries to make sure some members of a team have worked together before, providing a base for trusting relationships. Making the best use of technology is critical. In addition to a virtual work space that team members can access 24 hours a day, Nokia provides an online resource where virtual workers are encouraged to post photos and share personal information. With the inability of members to get to know each other being one the biggest barriers to effective virtual teamwork, encouraging and supporting social networking has paid off for Nokia.[74]

Global Teams

As the example of Nokia shows, virtual teams are frequently also global teams, which means people are working together not only across spatial distances but across time barriers and cultural and language differences as well. **Global teams** are work teams made up of culturally diverse members who live and work in different countries and coordinate some part of their activities on a global basis.[75] Rob Nicholson, a programmer for IBM in England, shares tasks with team members in India and Canada. Intel uses teams of chip designers in Israel, India, and the United States.[76] The research unit of BT Labs has researchers spread across several countries who work in global teams to investigate virtual reality, artificial intelligence, and other advanced technologies.[77] A survey of 103 firms found that nearly half now use global teams for new product development. Moreover, one out of every five teams in these companies is likely to be global.[78] Global teams bring many advantages, but they also present significant leadership challenges. When the executive council of *CIO* magazine asked global chief information officers to rank their company's greatest challenges, managing virtual global teams ranked as the most pressing issue.[79]

Why Global Teams Often Fail   All of the difficulties of virtual teamwork are magnified in the case of global teams because of the added problem of language and cultural barriers.[80] Building trust is even more difficult when people bring different norms, values, attitudes, and patterns of behavior to the team. An "us against them" mentality can easily develop, which is just the opposite of what organizations want from global teams.[81] Consider what happened in one team made up of members from India, Israel, Canada, the United States, Singapore, Spain, Brussels, Great Britain, and Australia:

> *"Early on…team members were reluctant to seek advice from team-mates who were still strangers, fearing that a request for help might be interpreted as a sign of incompetence. Moreover, when teammates did ask for help, assistance was not always forthcoming. One team member confessed to carefully calculating how much information she was willing to share. Going the extra mile on behalf of a virtual teammate, in her view, came at a high price of time and energy, with no guarantee of reciprocation."*[82]

A survey found that top executives in organizations that use global teams consider building trust and overcoming communication barriers the two most important—but also the two most difficult—leader tasks related to the success of global teams.[83] Thus, the greatest barriers to effective global teamwork relate to lack of people skills for dealing with teammates from other cultures, rather than to lack of technical knowledge or commitment. Communication barriers can be formidable in global teams. Not only do global teams have to cope with different time zones and conflicting schedules, but members also often speak different languages. And even when members can communicate in the same language, they still might have a hard time understanding one another because of cultural differences. Members from different cultures often have different beliefs about such things as authority, decision making, and time orientation. For example, some cultures, such as the United States, are highly focused on "clock time," and tend to follow rigid schedules, whereas many other cultures have a more relaxed, cyclical concept of time. These different

Action Memo

As a leader, you can provide language and cross-cultural training for a global team and guide members to set aside their preconceived ideas and assumptions for behavior.

Global teams
teams made up of culturally diverse members who live and work in different countries and coordinate some part of their activities on a global basis

cultural attitudes toward time can affect work pacing, team communications, and the perception of deadlines.[84]

Leading the Global Team Increasingly, the expertise, knowledge, and skills needed to complete a project are scattered around the world. In addition, as discussed earlier, diversity can be a powerful stimulus for creativity and the development of better alternatives for problem solving. All of the guidelines for leading traditional and virtual teams apply to global teams as well. For example, a strong sense of shared purpose can help bridge language and culture gaps. In addition, global team leaders can improve success by incorporating the following ideas:[85]

- *Manage language and culture.* Organizations using global teams can't skimp on training. Language and cross-cultural education can help overcome linguistic and cultural hurdles. Language training encourages more direct and spontaneous communication by limiting the need for translators. Understanding one another's cultures can also enrich communications and interpersonal relationships. For the team to succeed, all team members have to gain an appreciation of cultural values and attitudes that are different from their own. Xplane, a consulting and design firm in Portland, Oregon, that acquired a small firm in Madrid, uses a year-round employee exchange program, renting apartments in Portland and Madrid and sending team members back and forth for cultural learning visits.[86]
- *Stretch minds and behavior.* As team members learn to expand their thinking and embrace cultural differences, they also learn to develop a shared team culture. In global teams, all members have to be willing to deviate somewhat from their own values and norms and establish new norms for the team.[87] Leaders can work with team members to set norms and guidelines for acceptable behavior. These guidelines can serve as a powerful self-regulating mechanism, enhance communications, enrich team interactions, and help the team function as an integrated whole.

Handling Team Conflict

As one would expect, there is an increased potential for conflict among members of global and virtual teams because of the greater chances for miscommunication and misunderstandings. Studies of virtual teams indicate that how they handle internal conflicts is critical to their success, yet conflict within virtual teams tends to occur more frequently and take longer to resolve. Moreover, people in virtual teams tend to engage in more inconsiderate behaviors such as name-calling or insults than do people who work face to face.[88] Some people aren't cut out for virtual teamwork and show a greater propensity for shirking their duties or giving less than their full effort when working in a virtual environment, which can lead to team conflicts.[89] Cultural value differences, little face-to-face interaction, and lack of on-site monitoring make it harder to build team identity and commitment.

Whenever people work together in teams, some conflict is inevitable. Whether leading a virtual team or a team whose members work side-by-side, bringing conflicts out into the open and effectively resolving them is one of the team leader's most important jobs.

Conflict refers to hostile or antagonistic interaction in which one party attempts to thwart the intentions or goals of another. Conflict is natural and occurs in all teams and organizations. It can arise between members of a team

Conflict
antagonistic interaction in which one party attempts to thwart the intentions or goals of another

or between teams. Too much conflict can be destructive, tear relationships apart, and interfere with the healthy exchange of ideas and information needed for team development and cohesiveness.[90] High-performing teams typically have lower levels of conflict, and the conflict is more often associated with tasks than with interpersonal relationships. In addition, teams that reflect healthy patterns of conflict are usually characterized by high levels of trust and mutual respect.[91]

Causes of Conflict

Leaders can be aware of several factors that cause conflict among individuals or teams. Whenever teams compete for scarce resources, such as money, information, or supplies, conflict is almost inevitable. Conflicts also emerge when task responsibilities are unclear. People might disagree about who has responsibility for specific tasks or who has a claim on resources, and leaders help members reach agreement. Another reason for conflict is simply because individuals or teams are pursuing conflicting goals. Consider the following example.

IN THE LEAD

The *Los Angeles Times*

The *Los Angeles Times* has long been one of the most respected names in journalism. The winner of several Pulitzer Prizes, the *Times* is one of only a handful of newspapers with a claim to national standing. But in recent years, the newspaper has had a heck of a time trying to keep good editors. In less than four years, three seasoned editors came and went from the top editorial position. Moreover, the paper has seen the departure of several other high-level editors after short tenures, many of which came as a result of conflict between the business need to cut costs versus the editorial need to maintain high quality.

All newspapers are facing seriously tough circumstances, but the *Los Angeles Times* has been hit particularly hard, battered by years of flagging circulation even before the housing slump and declining economy cut deeply into ad revenues. Thus, the never-ending battle between the business side of the organization (goals of reducing costs and luring advertisers) and the news side (goals of providing quality news) became an all-out war at the *Times*. Though the conflict is complex, most former editors say they left because an excessive emphasis on goals of cost-cutting has cut the heart out of the storied newspaper.[92]

The *Times'* parent company, Tribune Company, which owns the *Chicago Tribune* and acquired the Los Angeles paper in 2000, filed for bankruptcy protection in late 2008. Although the tensions that have plagued the *Times* can't be blamed directly for the Tribune Company's woes, the inability of leaders to effectively manage goal conflicts made it even more difficult for the organization to weather the "perfect storm" of forces roiling the media industry and the broader economy.[93]

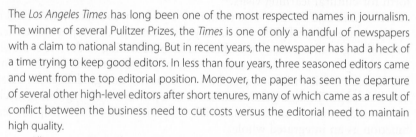

Action Memo

As a leader, you can adopt the best approach for handling a team conflict. Choose among the competing, avoiding, compromising, accommodating, or collaborating styles based on the degree of assertiveness and cooperativeness needed to manage the situation.

A final cause of conflict relates to interpersonal clashes caused by basic differences in personality, values, and attitudes, as described in Chapter 4. It sometimes happens that two people simply do not get along with one another and will never see eye to eye on any issue. Often, the only solution is to separate the parties and reassign them to other teams where they can be more productive.

Styles to Handle Conflict

Teams as well as individuals develop specific styles for dealing with conflict, based on the desire to satisfy their own concerns versus the other party's concerns. Exhibit 10.7 describes five styles of handling conflict. How an individual approaches conflict is measured along two dimensions: *assertiveness* and *cooperation*. Effective leaders and team members vary their style to fit a specific situation, as each style is appropriate in certain circumstances.[94]

1. The *competing style,* which reflects assertiveness to get one's own way, should be used when quick, decisive action is vital on important issues or unpopular actions, such as during emergencies or urgent cost-cutting.

2. The *avoiding style,* which reflects neither assertiveness nor cooperativeness, is appropriate when an issue is trivial, when there is no chance of winning, when a delay to gather more information is needed, or when a disruption would be costly.

3. The *compromising style* reflects a moderate amount of both assertiveness and cooperativeness. It is appropriate when the goals on both sides are equally important, when opponents have equal power and both sides want to split the difference, or when people need to arrive at temporary or expedient solutions under time pressure.

4. The *accommodating style* reflects a high degree of cooperativeness, which works best when people realize that they are wrong, when an issue is more important to others than to oneself, when building social credits for use in later discussions, or when maintaining cohesiveness is especially important.

5. The *collaborating style* reflects a high degree of both assertiveness and cooperativeness. This style enables both parties to win, although it may require substantial dialogue and negotiation. The collaborating style is

Exhibit 10.7 A Model of Styles to Handle Conflict

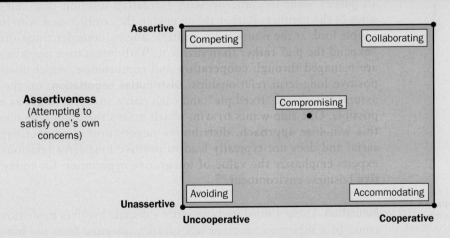

Source: Adapted from Kenneth Thomas, "Conflict and Conflict Management," in M. D. Dunnette, ed., *Handbook of Industrial and Organizational Behavior* (New York: John Wiley & Sons, 1976), p. 900. Used by permission of Marvin D. Dunnette.

important when both sets of concerns are too important to be compromised, when insights from different people need to be merged into an overall solution, or when the commitment of both sides is needed for a consensus.

Each approach can be successful, depending on the people involved and the situation. In a study of conflict in virtual teams, researchers found that the competing and collaborating styles had a positive effect on team performance.[95] The effectiveness of the competing style might be related to the use of electronic communication, in that team members don't interpret the individual's approach as being aggressive and are more willing to accept a quick resolution.

Action Memo

Which conflict-handling style do you tend to use most frequently? Answer the questions in Leader's Self-Insight 10.3 to find out. Try to think of conflict situations you've been involved in where each of the styles might be appropriate.

Other Approaches

The various styles of handling conflict illustrated in Exhibit 10.7 are especially effective for an individual to use when he or she disagrees with another. But what can a team leader do when conflict erupts among others? Research suggests several techniques that help resolve conflicts among people or teams.

Vision A compelling vision can pull people together. A vision is for the whole team and cannot be attained by one person. Its achievement requires the cooperation of conflicting parties. To the extent that leaders can focus on a larger team or organizational vision, conflict will decrease because the people involved see the big picture and realize they must work together to achieve it.

Bargaining/Negotiating Bargaining and negotiating mean that the parties in conflict engage in give-and-take discussions and consider various alternatives to reach a joint decision that is acceptable to both sides. Conflicting parties may embark upon negotiation from different perspectives and with different intentions, reflecting either an *integrative* approach or a *distributive* approach. **Integrative negotiation** is based on a win–win assumption, in that all parties want to come up with a creative solution that can benefit both sides of the conflict. Rather than viewing the conflict as a win–lose situation, people look at the issues from multiple angles, consider trade-offs, and try to "expand the pie" rather than divide it. With integrative negotiation, conflicts are managed through cooperation and compromise, which fosters trust and positive long-term relationships. **Distributive negotiation,** on the other hand, assumes there is a "fixed pie" and each party attempts to get as much of it as possible. One side wants to win, which means the other side must lose. With this win–lose approach, distributive negotiation is competitive and adversarial and does not typically lead to positive long-term relationships.[96] Most experts emphasize the value of integrative negotiation for today's collaborative business environment.[97]

Integrative negotiation
a cooperative approach to negotiation in which conflicting parties attempt to reach a win–win solution

Distributive negotiation
adversarial negotiation in which conflicting parties compete to win the most resources and give up as little as possible

Mediation Using a third party to settle a dispute involves mediation. A mediator could be a supervisor, another team leader, someone from the human resources department, or an outside ombudsman. The mediator can discuss the conflict with each party and work toward a solution. For example, Alan Siggia and Richard Passarelli, cofounders of Sigmet, which designs data processors that turn weather radar signals into graphic displays used by meteorologists, were feeling overwhelmed dealing with the interpersonal conflicts within their small company. The leaders contracted with Work Well Together, a Boston consulting firm, to

Leader's Self-Insight 10.3
How Do You Handle Team Conflict?

Think of some disagreements you have had with a team member, a student group, manager, friend, or coworker. Then answer the following questions based on how frequently you engage in each behavior. There are no right or wrong answers. Indicate whether each item is Mostly False or Mostly True for you.

	Mostly False	Mostly True
1. I shy away from topics that might cause a dispute.		
2. I strongly assert my opinion in a disagreement.		
3. I suggest solutions that combine others' points of view.		
4. I give in a little when other people do the same.		
5. I avoid a person who wants to discuss a topic of disagreement.		
6. I combine arguments into a new solution from the ideas raised in a dispute.		
7. I will split the difference to reach a settlement.		
8. I am quick to agree when someone I am arguing with makes a good point.		
9. I keep my views to myself rather than argue.		
10. I try to include other people's ideas to create a solution they will accept.		
11. I offer trade-offs to reach solutions in a disagreement.		
12. I try to smooth over disagreements by making them seem less serious.		
13. I hold my tongue rather than argue with another person.		

	Mostly False	Mostly True
14. I raise my voice to get other people to accept my position.		
15. I stand firm in expressing my viewpoints during a disagreement.		

Scoring and Interpretation

Five categories of conflict-handling strategies are measured in this instrument: competing, avoiding, compromising, accommodating, and collaborating. By comparing your scores on the following five scales, you can see your preferred conflict-handling strategy.

To calculate your five scores, give yourself 1 point for each Mostly True answer for the three items indicated.

Competing: Items 2, 14, 15: _____
Avoiding: Items 1, 5, 9: _____
Compromising: Items 4, 7, 11: _____
Accommodating: Items 8, 12, 13: _____
Collaborating: Items 3, 6, 10: _____

Briefly review the text material (page 317) about these five strategies for handling conflict. Which of the five strategies do you use the most? Which strategy do you find the most difficult to use? How would your strategy differ if the other person was a family member rather than a team member? Are there some situations where a strategy in which you are weak might be more effective? Explain your scores to another student and listen to the explanation for his or her scores. How are your conflict-handling strategies similar or different?

Source: Adapted from "How Do You Handle Conflict?" in Robert E. Quinn et al., *Becoming a Master Manager* (New York: John Wiley & Sons, 1990), pp. 221–223.

send in a mediator who listens to employee problems and helps leaders devise solutions to conflicts.[98] If a solution satisfactory to all parties cannot be reached, the parties may be willing to turn the conflict over to the mediator and abide by his or her solution.

Facilitating Communication One of the most effective ways to reduce conflict is to help conflicting parties communicate openly and honestly. As conflicting parties exchange information and learn more about one another, suspicions diminish and teamwork becomes possible. A particularly promising avenue for reducing conflict

Action Memo

As a leader, you can use techniques, such as bargaining and negotiation, third-party mediation, facilitating communication, and focusing people on a common vision, to aid in resolving a conflict.

is through dialogue, as discussed in Chapter 9. Dialogue asks that participants suspend their attachments to their own viewpoint so that a deeper level of listening, synthesis, and meaning can evolve from the interaction. Individual differences are acknowledged and respected, but rather than trying to figure out who is right or wrong, the parties search for a joint perspective.

Each of these approaches can be helpful in resolving conflicts between individuals or teams. Effective leaders use a combination of these on a regular basis—such as articulating a larger vision and continuously facilitating communication—to keep conflict at a minimum while the team moves forward.

Leadership Essentials

■ Many leaders today are called upon to facilitate teams rather than manage direct-report subordinates. Teams can be effective in providing the coordination and information sharing needed to accomplish interdependent tasks. However, teams present a dilemma for many people. Individuals have to give up their independence and sometimes make sacrifices for the good of the team. Other potential problems are free riders and dysfunctional teams.

■ Functional teams typically are part of the traditional organization structure. Cross-functional teams, including problem-solving teams, process-improvement teams, and special project teams, often represent an organization's first move toward greater team participation. Cross-functional teams may evolve into self-directed teams, which are member-centered rather than leader-centered and -directed. Two recent types of teams—virtual teams and global teams—have resulted from advances in technology, changing employee expectations, and the globalization of business.

■ Teams go through stages of development and change over time. Guiding a team through these stages is an important part of team leadership. In addition, leaders have to get the team designed right by considering such factors as size, diversity, and interdependence and ensuring that task and socioemotional roles are filled. These considerations help to determine team effectiveness. The leader's personal role is also crucial. People typically have to change themselves to become good team leaders. Four principles that provide a foundation for team leadership are to recognize the importance of shared purpose and values, build consensus, admit your mistakes, and provide support and coaching to team members.

■ These principles apply to virtual and global teams as well. However, being a team leader is even more challenging when people are scattered in different geographic locations and may be separated by language and cultural differences. To create effective, smoothly functioning virtual teams, leaders select team members who have the skills and temperaments to work virtually, use technology to build trusting relationships, and agree on ground rules for the team. For global teams, leaders also have to manage language and cultural differences and guide people to stretch their minds and behavior to establish a shared culture for the team.

■ Virtual and global teams increase the potential for misunderstanding, disagreements, and conflicts. However, all teams experience some conflict because of scarce resources, faulty communication, goal conflicts, power and status differences, or personality clashes. Leaders use varied styles to handle conflict. In addition, they employ the following techniques to help resolve conflicts: unite people around a shared vision, use bargaining and negotiation, bring in a mediator, and help conflicting parties communicate openly and honestly, particularly through dialogue.

Discussion Questions

1. What is the difference between a "team" and a "group"? Describe your personal experience with each.

2. Discuss the differences between a cross-functional team and a self-directed team. Do you believe self-directed teams could be effectively used in certain types of organizations? Explain.

3. What do you consider the primary advantages of an organization using virtual and global teams? What are some of the disadvantages?

4. Why might a person need to go through significant personal changes to be an effective team leader? What are some of the changes required?

5. Describe the three levels of interdependence and explain how they affect team leadership.

6. The chapter suggests that very small teams (say, three to six members) perform better, and most people prefer to work in small teams. However, many companies use teams of 100 or more people to perform complex tasks, such as creating and developing a new product. Do you think a unit of that size can truly function as a team? Discuss.

7. What are the stages of team development? As the leader of a virtual team, how would you facilitate the team's development through each stage?

8. Discuss the relationship between team cohesiveness and performance.

9. What style of handling conflict do you typically use? Can you think of instances where a different style might have been more productive?

10. If you were the leader of a team developing a new computer game, and conflicts arose related to power and status differences among team members, what would you do? How might you use the various conflict resolution techniques described in the chapter?

Leadership at Work

TEAM FEEDBACK

Think back to your most recent experience working in a team, either at work or school. Write down your answers to the following questions about your role in the team.

What did the team members appreciate about you?

_____

_____

_____

What did the team members learn from you?

_____

_____

_____

What could the team members count on you for?

_____

_____

_____

How could you have improved your contribution to the team?

_____

_____

_____

Evaluate your answers. What is the overall meaning of your answers? What are the implications for your role as a team member? As a team leader?

_____

_____

_____

In Class: "Team Feedback" is an excellent exercise to use for student feedback to one another after a specific team class project or other activities done together during the class. If there were no assigned team activities, but students have gotten to know each other in class, they can be divided into groups and provide the information with respect to their participation in the class instead of in the student team.

The instructor can ask the student groups to sit in a circle facing one another. Then one person will volunteer to be the focal person, and each of the other team members will tell that team member the following:

- What I appreciate about you
- What I learned from you
- What I could count on you for
- My one suggestion for improvement as a team leader/member

When the team members have given feedback to the focal person, another team member volunteers to hear feedback, and the process continues until each person has heard the four elements of feedback from every other team member.

The key questions for student learning are: "Are you developing the skills and behaviors to be a team leader?" If not, what does that mean for you? If you are now providing team leadership, how can you continue to grow and improve as a team leader?

Source: Thanks to William Miller for suggesting the questions for this exercise.

Chapter 11: Developing Leadership Diversity

© Eric Foltz

After reading this chapter, you should be able to:

- Understand and reduce the difficulties faced by minorities in organizations.

- Apply an awareness of the dimensions of diversity and multicultural issues in your everyday life.

- Encourage and support diversity to meet organizational needs.

- Consider the role of cultural values and attitudes in determining how to deal with employees from different cultures or ethnic backgrounds.

- Break down your personal barriers that may stand in the way of becoming an inclusive leader.

When Mike Pitcher first joined LeasePlan USA as head of sales and marketing, he met with representatives of the company's top customers to learn about their needs. He was surprised to find that most of the representatives were women. Pitcher noticed, as well, that the majority of the vehicle-leasing company's 450 employees were female. However, LeasePlan's leadership structure was firmly rooted in the good-old-boy network of the traditionally male-dominated industry. These observations were part of what spurred LeasePlan's leaders to embark on an effort to diversify the company's leadership and change its culture. Today, Pitcher is CEO of LeasePlan, and six of the company's top 14 executives are women. Each year, 30 female employees are selected to participate in a program that includes skills assessment, career coaching, and networking events. LeasePlan also has programs aimed at helping minority employees move into leadership positions. Pitcher sees the company's diversity initiative as a strategic investment. "Our sustainable competitive advantage is our people," he says.[1]

LeasePlan is among the many companies recognizing that valuing and supporting diverse employees pays off. Today's best leaders realize that diversity sparks innovation, leads to better decision making, and spurs growth. Employment agency Randstad pairs young "20-something" employees with older, experienced workers so that both can learn from each other.[2] Merrill Lynch uses global teams to smoothly negotiate cross-cultural deals. At PepsiCo, which is now led by CEO Indra K. Nooyi, an Indian-born woman, leaders attributed one percentage point of its 7.4 percent revenue growth to new products directly inspired by diversity efforts.[3] The benefits of diversity are one reason the face of America's organizations is beginning to change, with women and minorities slowly moving into upper-level leadership positions. However, there are still many challenges for creating diverse organizations with inclusive cultures. One of the most important roles for leaders in the coming years will be developing a solid base of diverse leadership talent. "In any organization in America, you will see diversity at the bottom of the house," says Roberta (Bobbi) Gutman, vice president and director of global diversity at Motorola. "But to get it higher up takes the clout and the wingspan of company leadership."[4]

This chapter explores the topic of diversity and multiculturalism. First, we look at the difficulties leaders encounter in leading people who are different from themselves. Then we define diversity, explore the value of diversity for organizations, and look at the challenges minorities face in organizations. Next, we examine a style of leadership that can support a more inclusive work environment, take a closer look at global diversity, and explore how leaders can increase their cultural intelligence. Finally, we discuss the personal stages of leader diversity awareness and the personal qualities for leading diverse workplaces.

Leading People Who Aren't Like You

You've recently gotten the promotion you've longed for, worked for, and know you deserve. The job of managing the Northern New England district office of Allyn & Freeson Investments required relocating, but your family enthusiastically made the move. Your children seem to be adjusting well to their new school and your wife likes her job at the local bank. If only things were as smooth at Allyn & Freeson. The all-white staff seems to be throwing up roadblocks in every direction. Nobody seems to even talk to you unless they're asked a direct question or forced to make a response to your greeting of "Good morning." Traveling to the branch offices isn't much better, and many of the local managers have inexplicably stopped sending in their weekly reports. You knew being the first African-American district manager in the area was going to be a bit of a challenge, but the sense of isolation you feel is more powerful than you anticipated. Even in the branch offices, you've met only two other African-Americans, and they're in low-level clerical positions.[5]

Action Memo

Complete the exercise in Leader's Self-Insight 11.1 to learn about the values you will bring to leading people who are diverse and not like you.

Welcome to the real world of diverse leadership. As more women and minorities move up the management hierarchy, they're often finding it a lonely road to travel. Even for someone who has experienced a degree of racism or sexism at lower organizational levels, stepping into a position of higher authority can be a real eye-opener. Racism and sexism in the workplace often show up in subtle ways—the disregard by a subordinate for an assigned chore; a lack of urgency in completing an important assignment; the ignoring of comments or suggestions made at a team meeting. Many minority leaders struggle daily with the problem of delegating authority and responsibility to employees who show them little respect.

How does an African-American, Asian, or Hispanic manager lead an all-white workforce, or a female manager lead a workforce of mostly males? What happens when a 29-year-old is promoted to a position of authority over a group of mostly 50- to 60-year-old middle managers? These questions are being asked more and more often in today's diverse organizations. Consider Clarence Otis, CEO of Darden Restaurants (Olive Garden, Red Lobster), one of only a handful

Leader's Self-Insight 11.1
Values Balancing

For each of the following pairs of values, select the one that is most descriptive of you. Even if both qualities describe you, you must choose one.

1. Analytical _____ Compassionate _____
2. Collaborative _____ Decisive _____
3. Competitive _____ Sociable _____
4. Loyal _____ Ambitious _____
5. Resourceful _____ Adaptable _____
6. Sensitive to others _____ Independent _____
7. Self-reliant _____ Uniting _____
8. Helpful _____ Persistent _____
9. Risk-taker _____ Contented _____
10. Interested _____ Knowledgeable _____
11. Responsible _____ Encouraging _____
12. Tactful _____ Driven _____
13. Forceful _____ Gentle _____
14. Participating _____ Achievement-oriented _____
15. Action-oriented _____ Accepting _____

Scoring and Interpretation

The words above represent two leadership values: "capacity for collaboration" and "personal initiative." "Personal initiative" is represented by the first word in the odd-numbered rows and the second word in the even-numbered rows. "Capacity for collaboration" is represented by the first word in the even-numbered rows and by the second word in the odd-numbered rows. Add the number of words circled that represent each value and record the number:

Personal Initiative: _____
Capacity for Collaboration: _____

Capacity for collaboration represents feminine values in our culture, and if you circled more of these items, you may be undervaluing your personal initiative. Personal initiative represents masculine values, and more circled words here may mean you are undervaluing your capacity for collaboration. How balanced are your values? How will you lead someone with values very different from yours?

Gender is a trait of diversity. How prevalent in organizations are feminine and masculine values? Read the rest of this chapter to learn which values are associated with successful leadership.

Source: Based on Donald J. Minnick and R. Duane Ireland, "Inside the New Organization: A Blueprint for Surviving Restructuring, Downsizing, Acquisitions and Outsourcing." *Journal of Business Strategy* 26 (2005), pp. 18–25; and A. B. Heilbrun, "Measurement of Masculine and Feminine Sex Role Identities as Independent Dimensions." *Journal of Consulting and Clinical Psychology* 44 (1976), pp. 183–190.

marble: © Kirill Matkov   sunset: © Marco Regalia

of African-American CEOs running *Fortune 500* companies; Rachelle Hood, the African-American woman hired to transform Denny's Restaurants from an icon of racism after a series of discrimination lawsuits; or Cathy Lanier, the white female chief of the Washington, D.C., Metropolitan Police, who leads a mostly black and male workforce. These and other minority leaders face enormous challenges.

Although today's college students have been called the "post-racial generation," in many organizations people who fall outside the traditional U.S. model of the middle-aged white male manager still have a hard time being successful. The cultural values and organizational systems in many companies do not genuinely support and value diversity. By the end of this chapter, we hope you will better understand some of the challenges, as well as some leadership strategies that can help make organizations more inclusive and provide a better working environment for all people.

Diversity Today

The goal for today's leaders is to recognize that each person can bring value and strengths to the workplace based on his or her own combination of diverse characteristics. Organizations establish workforce diversity programs to promote the hiring, inclusion, and career advancement of diverse employees and to ensure that differences are accepted and respected in the workplace.

Definition of Diversity

Workforce diversity means a workforce made up of people with different human qualities or who belong to various cultural groups. From the perspective of individuals, **diversity** refers to all the ways in which people differ, including dimensions such as age, race, marital status, physical ability, income level, and lifestyle.[6] Decades ago, most companies defined diversity in terms of a very limited set of dimensions, but today's organizations are embracing a much more inclusive definition that recognizes a spectrum of differences that influence how people approach work, interact with each other, derive satisfaction from their work, and define who they are as people in the workplace.[7]

Exhibit 11.1 illustrates the difference between the traditional model and a more inclusive model of diversity. The dimensions of diversity shown in the traditional model reflect primarily inborn differences that are immediately observable, such as race, gender, age, and physical ability. However, the inclusive model of diversity includes *all* of the ways in which people differ, including dimensions of diversity that can be acquired or changed throughout one's lifetime. These dimensions may have less impact than those in the traditional model but nevertheless affect a person's self-definition and world view and impact the way the person is viewed by others.

For example, veterans of the war in Iraq may have been profoundly affected by their military experience and may be perceived differently from other people. An employee living in a public housing project will be perceived differently from one who lives in an affluent part of town. Women with children are perceived differently in the work environment than those without children. Secondary dimensions such as work style and skill level are particularly relevant in the organizational setting.[8]

Workforce diversity
a workforce made up of people with different human qualities or who belong to various cultural groups

Diversity
differences among people in terms of age, ethnicity, gender, race, or other dimensions

---

Exhibit 11.1 Traditional vs. Inclusive Models of Diversity

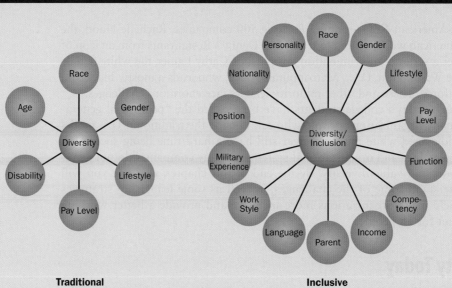

Traditional

Inclusive

Source: Reproduced by permission. Anthony Oshiotse and Richard O'Leary, "Corning Creates an Inclusive Culture to Drive Technology Innovation and Performance," *Wiley InterScience, Global Business and Organizational Excellence* 26, no. 3 (March–April 2007), p. 12.

Changing Attitudes Toward Diversity

Attitudes toward diversity are changing partly because they have to as leaders respond to significant changes in our society, including demographic changes and globalization.[9] In the United States, the minority population is now roughly 100.7 million, making about one in three U.S. residents a minority. Around 32 million people speak Spanish at home, and nearly half of these people say they don't speak English very well.[10] White, American-born males now make up less than half the U.S. workforce, with many more women, people of color, and immigrants seeking employment opportunities.[11]

The other factor contributing to increased acceptance of diversity is globalization. Leaders are emphasizing cross-cultural understanding so that people can work smoothly across borders. "The speed of global business is accelerating diversity," says Pauline Ning Brody, a Shanghai-born diversity consultant and former director of global sales for Colgate-Palmolive.[12] An unprecedented number of foreign-born CEOs now run major companies in the United States, Britain, and several other countries.[13] Employees with global experience and cultural sensitivity are in high demand because at least some aspect of almost every business today cuts across national boundaries. As the following example shows, corporations aren't the only organizations seeking a diverse workforce to cope with the challenges of globalization.

IN THE LEAD

Secret Intelligence Service (M16)

James Bond need not apply. Britain's secret spy agency, M16, has embarked on an intense campaign to recruit women and minorities, not the white males who have long been the face of M16. The agency's recruiting Web site encourages women, including mothers, to apply and assures them they won't be used as "seductresses." Applications from disabled candidates are also welcomed. But the biggest push is for ethnic minorities who speak languages such as Arabic, Persian, Mandarin, Urdu, and the Afghan languages of Dari and Pashto.

For intelligence agencies, diversity is considered *mission critical*. With terrorism being the key challenge, security agencies in the United States as well as Britain are seeking a multicultural workforce to act as receptionists, linguists, operational agents, technology officers, security guards, and so forth.

For Britain's M16, the push for more minority applicants is starting to pay off. In 2007, 40 percent of recruits from open recruiting were women and 11 percent were ethnic minorities. As Britain moves toward passage of a new "Equality Bill" that will strengthen discrimination laws and allow organizations to give preference to minorities, M16 is getting a head start. Pola Uddin, the first Muslim woman in the House of Lords, said it's about time James Bond got a taste of affirmative action.[14]

Intelligence and security agencies recognize the importance of having people who understand and can fit in with the diverse and ever-changing global landscape. As the head of human resources for M16 put it ". . . [all] agencies have to show that they're making positive efforts [to diversify], but for us it means much more."[15]

The Value of Organizational Diversity

There is no question that organizations have to change to reflect the new global reality. However, there are a number of other reasons leaders want to incorporate diversity.

Recent research supports the idea that diversity adds value to organizations and can contribute to a firm's competitive advantage.[16] For one thing, leaders can use internal diversity to meet the needs of diverse customers. Culture plays an important role in determining the goods, entertainment, social services, and household products that people use, so organizations are recruiting minority employees who can understand how diverse people live and what they want and need. In addition, having a diverse workforce can build stronger connections with diverse customers. "Our country's consumer base is so varied," says Shelley Willingham-Hinton, president of the National Organization for Diversity in Sales and Marketing. "I can't think of how a company can succeed without having that kind of diversity with their employees."[17]

When customers see and interact with people like themselves, they feel better about doing business with the company. Allstate Insurance intentionally tries to hire people who look like, sound like, and think like the company's clients. At the Sunnyside neighborhood office in Queens, New York, one of the most ethnically diverse communities in the country, customers often relate to sales reps like members of their family, consulting them on problems that might have no relation to insurance. Mike Kalkin, the agent who heads up the office (and who is himself from an immigrant family), often recruits employees from within the community because they understand the local population's unique needs. A different situation exists at a northwestern Arkansas office, where a growing retired population means placing more emphasis on serving the needs of older customers.[18]

Action Memo

As a leader, you can hire and promote people from diverse cultures and with diverse human characteristics. You can use organizational diversity to improve creativity and decision making, better serve customers, and enhance organizational flexibility.

When organizations support diversity, people feel valued for what they can bring to the organization, which leads to higher morale. A story from furniture manufacturer Herman Miller, told in the *Consider This* box, illustrates that each of us has unique talents and gifts. In addition, people can build better relationships at work when they develop the skills to understand and accept cultural differences.

Finally, diversity contributes to greater organizational learning and flexibility and leads to stronger performance, as discussed in the previous chapter on teams. Recruiting and valuing diverse individuals enables organizations to attract and retain the best human talent. A survey commissioned by *The New York Times* found that 91 percent of job seekers think diversity programs make a company a better place to work, and nearly all minority job seekers said they would prefer to work in a diverse workplace.[19] Another survey of MBA candidates shows that companies that make a strong commitment to diversity appeal to both white and minority MBAs looking for jobs.[20]

A diverse workforce contributes to *diversity of thought*, which is a critical element for high performance.[21] People who differ in various ways, whether it be race, cultural background, physical ability, educational level, lifestyle, age, marital status, or other dimensions, are more likely to have diverse opinions and perspectives. This diversity of thought means there is a broader and deeper base of ideas, opinions, and experiences for problem solving, creativity, and innovation. If everyone thinks alike, the organization suffers. As Bell Atlantic CEO Ivan Seidenberg put it, "If everybody in the room is the same, you'll get a lot fewer arguments and a lot worse answers."[22] Referring to our discussion of team diversity in the previous chapter, diverse groups tend to be more creative than homogeneous groups in part because of the different opinions and perspectives people can bring to the problem or issue. According to the results of one study,

Consider **This!**
Honoring Our Diversity of Gifts

One day the millwright died.

My father, being a young manager at the time, did not particularly know what he should do when a key person died, but thought he ought to go visit the family. He went to the house and was invited to join the family in the living room. There was some awkward conversation—the kind with which many of us are familiar.

The widow asked my father if it would be all right if she read aloud some poetry. Naturally, he agreed. She went into another room, came back with a bound book, and for many minutes, read selected pieces of beautiful poetry. When she finished, my father commented on how beautiful the poetry was and asked who wrote it. She replied that her husband, the millwright, was the poet.

It is now nearly sixty years since the millwright died, and my father and many of us at Herman Miller continue to wonder: Was he a poet who did millwright's work, or was he a millwright who wrote poetry?

***

Understanding diversity enables us to see that each of us is needed. . . .

The simple act of recognizing diversity in corporate life helps us to connect the great variety of gifts that people bring to the work and service of the organization. Diversity allows each of us to contribute in a special way, to make our special gift a part of the corporate effort.

Source: From *Leadership Is an Art*, by Max DePree, copyright © 1987 by Max DePree. Used with permission of Doubleday, a division of Random House, Inc.

© majaiva

companies that rate high on creativity and innovation have a higher percentage of women and nonwhite male employees than less innovative companies.[23]

Challenges Minorities Face

Creating an inclusive organizational environment where all individuals feel respected, valued, and able to develop their unique talents is difficult. Most people, including leaders, have a natural tendency toward **ethnocentrism,** which refers to the belief that one's own culture and subculture are inherently superior to other cultures.[24] Moreover, studies by social psychologists suggest that there is a natural tendency among humans to identify themselves with a particular group and to feel antagonistic and discriminatory toward other groups.[25] In high school, the jocks are aligned against the geeks, for instance. In hospital cafeterias, the surgeons sit in one area and the medical residents in another. In newspaper offices, the editorial folks are antagonistic toward the advertising people. The combination of this natural force toward separation, ethnocentric viewpoints, and a standard set of cultural assumptions and practices creates a number of challenges for minority employees and leaders.

Ethnocentrism
the belief that one's own culture and subculture are inherently superior to other cultures

Action Memo

Take the quiz in Leader's Self-Insight 11.2 to evaluate your personal degree of passive bias and think about ways you can become more diversity-aware.

Leader's Self-Insight 11.2
A Passive Bias Quiz

Check either No or Yes for each of the following questions.

	No	Yes
1. What you notice first about people around you are the characteristics that make them different from you.	____	____
2. You make it a general rule never to discuss the subjects of race, ethnicity, politics, age, religion, gender, and sexuality when you are at work.	____	____
3. When others make bigoted remarks or jokes, you either laugh or say nothing because you don't want to seem sensitive or self-righteous.	____	____
4. When you see publications that are targeted at an ethnic, gender, or religious group that you do not represent, you usually ignore them.	____	____
5. When you look for a mentor or protégé, you pick someone like yourself.	____	____
6. If someone tells you about a cultural difference that you have never heard of, you don't ask questions about it.	____	____
7. You are affiliated with organizations that practice subtle discrimination, but you say nothing because you didn't create the rules.	____	____
8. Before you hire someone for a position, you have a vague picture in mind of what the ideal candidate would look like.	____	____

	No	Yes
9. Your conversations make use of phrases like "you people" or "our kind."	____	____
10. You avoid talking about cultural differences when dealing with people different from you because you're afraid of saying the wrong thing.	____	____
11. When complimenting someone from a different background, you might say, "You are nothing like the others" or "I really don't think of you as a _____.	____	____
12. There are people in your organization whom you like and respect but would feel uncomfortable introducing to your family or close friends.	____	____

Scoring and Interpretation

Give yourself five points for each "yes" answer. The appropriate score for today's world is "0." However, if you scored less than 20, you're probably making a good attempt to eliminate personal passive bias. A score of 20 to 40 means you need to watch it—you reveal passive bias that is inappropriate in organizations and society. If you scored more than 40, your level of bias could get you into trouble. You should definitely consider ways to become more diversity-aware and culturally sensitive.

Source: Adapted from Lawrence Otis Graham, *Proversity: Getting Past Face Values and Finding the Soul of People* (New York: John Wiley & Sons, 1997). Used with permission of Lawrence Otis Graham.

marble: © Kirill Matkov   sunset: © Marco Regalia

Prejudice, Stereotypes, and Discrimination

Prejudice
an adverse feeling or opinion formed without regard for the facts

Stereotype
a rigid, exaggerated, irrational, and typically negative belief or image associated with a particular group of people

Discrimination
treating people differently based on prejudicial attitudes and stereotypes

One significant problem in many organizations is **prejudice**, which is an adverse feeling or opinion formed without regard for the facts. Prejudiced people tend to view those who are different as deficient. An aspect of prejudice is stereotyping. A **stereotype** is a rigid, exaggerated, irrational, and typically negative belief or image associated with a particular group of people. When a leader and company act out prejudicial attitudes toward people who are the targets of their prejudice, **discrimination** has occurred.[26] Paying a woman less than a man for the same work is gender discrimination. Refusing to hire someone because he or she has a different ethnicity is ethnic discrimination. For example, some years ago, the manager of the mergers and acquisitions department of a major bank encountered resistance from senior leaders because she wanted to hire an Indian applicant who wore a turban.[27]

Such discrimination is not only unethical but also illegal in the United States. Leaders should be aware that there are a number of federal and state laws that prohibit various types of discrimination. Wal-Mart is facing a huge class-action lawsuit alleging that the retailer discourages the promotion of women to management positions and pays them less than men across all job positions.[28] Numerous other companies, including Mitsubishi, EMC Corporation, FedEx Express, Allied Aviation Services, eBay, and Abercrombie & Fitch, have been hit by suits alleging the companies broke laws that prohibit discrimination on the basis of race, gender, age, physical disability, or other diverse characteristics.

Blatant discrimination is not as widespread as in the past, but passive—and sometimes unconscious—bias is still a big problem in the workplace. Consider a report from the National Bureau of Economic Research (titled "Are Greg and Emily More Employable Than Lakisha and Jamal?"), which shows that employers sometimes unconsciously discriminate against job applicants based solely on the Afrocentric or African-American–sounding names on their resume. In interviews prior to the research, most human resource managers surveyed said they expected only a small gap and some expected to find a pattern of reverse discrimination. The results showed instead that white-sounding names got 50 percent more callbacks than African-American–sounding names, even when skills and experience were equal.[29] Prejudicial attitudes are deeply rooted in our society as well as in our organizations. Sociologist William Bielby proposes that people have innate biases and, left to their own devices, they will automatically discriminate. *Unconscious bias theory* suggests that white males, for example, will inevitably slight women and minorities because people's decisions are influenced by unconscious prejudice.[30]

It takes intentional leadership actions to change the status quo. Leaders can establish conditions that limit the degree of unconscious bias that goes into hiring and promotion decisions. Corporations such as BP and Becton Dickinson, for example, use tools to measure unconscious as well as conscious bias in their diversity training programs.[31]

Action Memo

As a leader, you can appreciate differences among people but shed stereotypes and prejudicial attitudes. You can avoid discrimination and view differences among people as positive or neutral.

Unequal Expectations

A survey by Korn Ferry International found that 59 percent of minority managers surveyed had observed a racially motivated double standard in the delegation of assignments.[32] Their perceptions are supported by a study that showed minority managers spend more time in the "bullpen" waiting for their chance and then have to prove themselves over and over again with each new assignment. Another study found that white managers gave more negative performance ratings to African-American leaders and white subordinates and more positive ratings to white leaders and African-American subordinates, affirming the widespread acceptance of these employees in their stereotypical roles.[33] The perception by many minorities is that no matter how many college degrees they earn, how many hours they work, how they dress, or how much effort and enthusiasm they invest, they are never considered to "have the right stuff."[34]

Women trying to advance in their careers often find themselves in a double bind. They have learned that they need to act and think like men to succeed, but they are criticized when they do so. The band of acceptable behavior is much more narrow for women leaders than for men. Many career women identified with the harsh scrutiny given to Katie Couric when she took over the *CBS Evening News* and to Hillary Clinton during the 2008 presidential campaign—criticized on the one hand for being too feminine or on the other hand for being too strong and aggressive. When women managers are assertive and competitive like their male colleagues, they are often judged in performance reviews as being too tough, abrasive, or not supportive of their employees. Conversely, if they behave in stereotypically feminine ways of showing care and concern for others, they're typically judged as being less competent. One study found that women managers are rarely perceived by their peers and supervisors as both competent and likable.[35]

The Glass Ceiling

Another issue is the **glass ceiling**, an invisible barrier that separates women and minorities from top leadership positions. They can look up through the ceiling, but prevailing attitudes are invisible obstacles to their own advancement. Research has also suggested the existence of "glass walls" that serve as invisible barriers to important lateral movement within the organization. Glass walls bar experience in areas such as line supervision or general management that would enable women and minorities to advance to senior-level positions.[36]

Although a few women and minorities have moved into highly visible top leadership positions, such as Ursula Burns at Xerox, Kenneth Chenault at American Express, Ellen Kullman at DuPont, and Indra Nooyi at PepsiCo, most women and minorities are still clustered at the bottom of the organizational hierarchy. Women have made significant strides in recent years, but they still represent only a small percentage of top executives and board members in America's 500 largest companies.[37] In 2009, a record 15 women were CEOs of *Fortune* 500 companies. Only eight African-Americans have ever made it to the top of *Fortune* 500 companies, and in 2009, that number had slipped to five. In July 2009, Ursula Burns made history as the first African-American woman to rise to the top of a *Fortune* 500 company.[38] However, both male and female African-Americans and Hispanics continue to hold only a small percentage of all management positions in the United States.[39]

Leaders in other countries are struggling with similar diversity issues. A report on executive talent in the United Kingdom, for example, indicates that although employees on the front lines "reflect the rich diversity of 21st century Britain," the executive suite is overwhelmingly "white, male, able-bodied, and of a certain age—[with] a photo of their wife and kids . . . on the desk."[40] Criticism of gender inequality in Germany is growing, as most European Union countries have narrowed the wage gap between men and women, but pay disparity in Germany remains wide.[41] Japanese companies, too, face mounting criticism about the scarcity of women in management positions. In Japan, women make up 41 percent of the workforce but occupy less than 3 percent of high-level management positions.[42]

Some women get off the fast track before they ever encounter the glass ceiling, which has been referred to as the *opt-out trend*. In a survey of nearly 2,500 women and 653 men, 37 percent of highly qualified women report that they have voluntarily left the workforce at some point in their careers, compared to only 24 percent of similarly qualified men.[43] Women leaders sometimes feel that the cost of climbing the corporate ladder is too high. Indeed, successful career women do frequently give up personal time, outside friendships, or hobbies because they still do most of the child care and housework in addition to their business responsibilities. Exhibit 11.2 shows the discrepancy between high-achieving men and women in terms of the time they devote to domestic duties, based on one survey. Today, an increasing number of successful women are negotiating with companies to achieve greater flexibility and work–life balance, a trend that is appreciated by both men and women, as described in the Leader's Bookshelf.

Glass ceiling
an invisible barrier that separates women and minorities from top leadership positions

Womenomics is in part a celebration of the fact that women are becoming more powerful in corporate America, in part a how-to guide for women to "stop juggling and struggling and finally start living and working the way you want," and in part a description of how organizations are changing in response to greater diversity in the workplace.

Building a Saner Workplace

The authors of *Womenomics*—Claire Shipman, a correspondent for *Good Morning America*, and *BBC World News America* anchor Katty Kay—suggest that women who have proved their value to the organization can successfully negotiate to achieve greater work–life balance. However, in their book, they also profile some companies where corporate leaders are taking the first step.

- **Capital One Financial.** Leaders at Capital One surveyed female employees to find out what they most

wanted in their work lives. The top answer was flexibility. A follow-up survey that went to everyone discovered that most male employees wanted the same thing. The company implemented its *Flexible Work Arrangements* program to let people design their own schedules with their managers.

- **KPMG.** Workaholics are no longer welcome at this accounting firm. KPMG uses wellness scorecards to find out whether someone is working too many hours or skipping vacations. If so, a manager does an intervention. The firm also offers its staff compressed workweeks, flexible hours, telecommuting, job sharing, and even reduced workloads.

- **Kaye/Bassman International.** This recruiting firm in Plano, Texas, takes a simple approach: It asks each employee what he or she wants. Whether it is to work from home

or to have afternoons off to spend with the kids, in almost every case the request is granted. CEO Jeff Kaye says the flexible approach has led to greater productivity.

No More One-Size-Fits-All

Shipman and Kay point out that the change in mindset has come about not only because of women's concerns but also because sought-after technologically savvy young employees—male and female—are demanding more flexibility in their work lives. "The one-size-fits-all workplace doesn't work," Kathleen Chistensen of the Alfred P. Sloan Foundation is quoted as saying. "Employees increasingly feel more entitled to say: 'I need and I want to work in a certain way.'"

Womenomics, by Claire Shipman and Katty Kay, is published by Harper Business.

marble: © Ioannis Drimilis   library: www.istockphoto.com/nikada

---

Exhibit 11.2 Primary Domestic Responsibilities of High-Achieving Men and Women

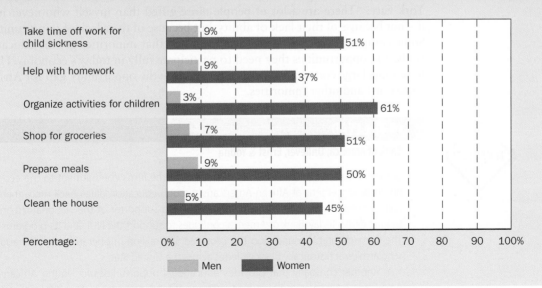

Source: National Parenting Association, as reported in Sylvia Ann Hewlett, "Executive Women and the Myth of Having It All," *Harvard Business Review* (April 2002), pp. 66–73.

Action Memo

As a leader, you can fight ethnocentric attitudes. You can create an environment in which people value diverse ways of thinking, dressing, or behaving, and you can help break down the barriers of unequal expectations, stereotypes, unequal pay, and the glass ceiling. You can close the opportunity gap so minorities have an equal chance to succeed.

Although some women voluntarily leave the fast track, there are many who genuinely want to move up the corporate ladder but find their paths blocked. Fifty-five percent of executive women surveyed by Catalyst said they aspire to senior leadership levels.[44] In addition, a survey of 103 women voluntarily leaving executive jobs in *Fortune* 1000 companies found that corporate culture was cited as the number-one reason for leaving.[45] The greatest disadvantages for women leaders stem largely from prejudicial attitudes and a heavily male-oriented corporate culture.[46] Some years ago, when Procter & Gamble asked the female executives it considered "regretted losses" (that is, high performers the company wanted to retain) why they left their jobs, the most common answer was that they didn't feel valued by the company.[47]

The Opportunity Gap

A final challenge is the lack of opportunities for many minorities. In some cases, people fail to advance to higher levels in organizations because they haven't been able to acquire the necessary education and skills. For example, although educational opportunities for African-Americans have improved in recent years, black Americans still have only 79 percent of the status of white Americans in this area, according to a report by the National Urban League. Overall educational spending on black students is approximately 82 percent of the amount spent on white students, which contributes to greater struggles for black students and a higher dropout rate, especially among young men.[48] Only about 60 percent of Hispanics complete high school, and both African-Americans and Hispanics lag behind whites in college attendance. Among Native Americans who complete high school, only 10 percent go to college, and of those only about half graduate. A 2008 report by the American Council on Education indicates that Hispanic and Native American young adults have even less education than their parents' generation.[49]

Eric Adolphe, president and CEO of Optimus Corporation, who managed to stay in college because of a scholarship from the National Association Council for Minorities in Engineering, recalls many of the kids he grew up with in New York City: "There are a lot of people more gifted than myself who never made it—not because of their lack of ability, but because of their lack of opportunity."[50] Some companies are taking the lead to ensure that minorities get the education, skills, and opportunities they need to participate fully in today's economy. Here's how some large corporations are trying to close the opportunity gap for African-Americans and other minorities.

IN THE LEAD

Bank of America, Unilever, Ernst & Young

Leaders at Bank of America are proud to say that the firm's commitment to the economic advancement of African-Americans through education dates back more than half a century, when the company first became a supporter of the National Urban League (NUL). Today, Bank of America continues to support the NUL and its programs. The firm's charitable foundation has provided $16 million in operating support and scholarships at historically black colleges across the United States.

Another company that provides educational opportunities for young African-Americans is Unilever, a global manufacturer of food, personal-care, and home-care products. As founding and continuing corporate sponsor of the Jackie Robinson

Foundation, the company offers two scholarships: the Ralph E. Ward Achievement Award (for academic excellence) and the Unilever Legacy of Leadership Award (for community excellence). Unilever is also a big supporter of INROADS, an organization that helps minority young people launch business careers.

Ernst & Young (E & Y) has provided millions of dollars in scholarships for undergraduate and graduate minority students majoring in accounting, information technology, engineering, finance, and other disciplines. An innovative program called Your Master Plan gives recent college graduates a chance to work at E & Y while they pursue a master's degree in accounting, paid for by the firm. In an industry that is one of the least racially diverse in the nation, Ernst & Young is taking solid steps to build a pipeline of minority candidates to be the leaders of tomorrow.[51]

Companies such as Bank of America, Unilever, and Ernst & Young recognize that supporting educational opportunities for minority students is one important way to ensure that minority candidates have a more equitable chance of advancing in the workplace.

Ways Women Lead

One aspect of diversity that is of particular interest in organizations today is the way in which women's style of leadership may differ from men's. As women move into higher positions in organizations, it has been observed that they often use a style of leadership that is highly effective in today's turbulent, culturally diverse environment.[52]

There is some evidence that men may become less influential in the U.S. workforce, with women becoming dominant players, because the women's approach is more attuned to the needs and values of a multicultural environment. For example, there's a stunning gender reversal in U.S. education, with girls taking over almost every leadership role from kindergarten to graduate school. Women of all races and ethnic groups are outpacing men in earning bachelor's and master's degrees. In one recent year, women made up 58 percent of undergraduate college students.[53] Among 25- to 29-year-olds, 32 percent of women have college degrees, compared to 27 percent of men. Women are rapidly closing the M.D. and Ph.D. gap, and they make up about half of all U.S. law students, half of all undergraduate business majors, and about 30 percent of MBA candidates. The number of female graduates in traditionally male-dominated disciplines such as engineering and computer science is also rapidly climbing. In addition, studies show that women students are more achievement-oriented, less likely to skip classes, spend more time studying, and typically earn higher grades.[54] Overall, women's participation in both the labor force and civic affairs has steadily increased since the mid-1950s, whereas men's participation has slowly but steadily declined.[55]

Women as Leaders

According to James Gabarino, an author and professor of human development at Cornell University, women are "better able to deliver in terms of what modern society requires of people—paying attention, abiding by rules, being verbally competent, and dealing with interpersonal relationships in offices."[56] His observation is supported by the fact that female managers are typically rated higher by subordinates on interpersonal skills as well as on factors such as task behavior, communication, ability to motivate others, and goal accomplishment.[57] As illustrated in Exhibit 11.3, one survey of followers rated women leaders significantly higher than men on several characteristics that are crucial for developing fast, flexible, adaptive organizations. Female leaders were rated as having more idealized influence, providing more inspirational motivation, being more individually considerate, and offering more intellectual stimulation.[58] *Idealized influence* means that followers identify with and want to emulate the leader; the leader is trusted and respected, maintains high standards, and is considered to have power because of who she is rather than what position she holds. *Inspirational motivation* is derived from the leader who appeals emotionally and symbolically to employees' desire to do a good job and help achieve organizational goals. *Individual consideration* means each follower is treated as an individual but all are treated equitably; individual needs are recognized, and assignments are delegated to followers to provide learning opportunities. One of the strengths of Cynthia Carroll, the first female leader of global mining company Anglo American, for example, is "getting the most out of each individual." Carroll is also bringing a new mindset to Anglo American that is helping the company become more global in its approach, reflecting intellectual stimulation.[59] *Intellectual stimulation* means questioning current methods and challenging employees to think in new ways. In addition to these qualities, women leaders were judged by subordinates in the survey as more effective and satisfying to work for and were considered able to generate extra levels of effort from employees.

There is increasing evidence that companies where women make up a significant percentage of board members and senior management perform better than those with only a few women in high-level positions. One study by Catalyst found that *Fortune 500* companies with three or more women on the board achieve, on average, an 83 percent higher return on equity than those with minimal female representation.[60]

Is Leader Style Gender-Driven?

Several researchers have examined the question of whether women lead differently than men. Leadership traits traditionally associated with white, American-born males include aggressiveness or assertiveness, rational analysis, and a "take charge" attitude. Male leaders tend to be competitive and individualistic and prefer working in vertical hierarchies. They rely on formal authority and position in their dealings with subordinates.

Exhibit 11.3 Comparison of Male and Female Leaders by Their Subordinates

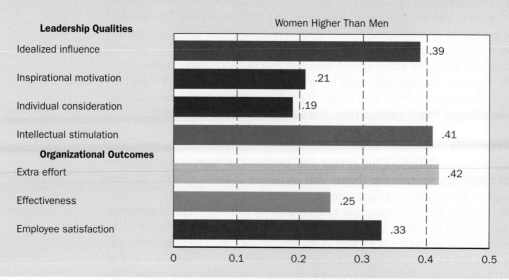

Note: *Ratings of leaders were on a scale of 1–5. Women leaders were rated higher, on average, by the amount indicated for each item.*
Source: Based on Bernard M. Bass and Bruce J. Avolio, "Shatter the Glass Ceiling: Women May Make Better Managers," *Human Resource Management* 33, no. 4 (Winter 1994), pp. 549–560.

Some women also reflect these characteristics, of course, but research has found that, in general, women prefer less competitive environments than men, tend to be more collaborative, and are more concerned with relationship building, inclusiveness, participation, and caring.[61] Female leaders such as Deborah Kent, the first woman to head a vehicle assembly plant for Ford Motor, or Terry Kelly, CEO of W. L. Gore & Associates, are often more willing to share power and information, to encourage employee development, and to strive to enhance others' feelings of self-worth. "It does no good have a diverse workforce if you don't listen to their opinions and thoughts," says Kent. "I treat people the way I want to be treated."[62]

Professor and author Judy B. Rosener has called women's approach to leadership **interactive leadership**.[63] The leader favors a consensual and collaborative process, and influence derives from relationships rather than position power and authority. Some psychologists have suggested that women may be more relationship-oriented than men because of different psychological needs stemming from early experiences. This difference between the relationship orientations of men and women has sometimes been used to suggest that women cannot lead effectively because they fail to exercise power. However, whereas male leaders may associate effective leadership with a top-down command-and-control process, women's interactive leadership seems appropriate for the future of diversity, globalization, and learning organizations. Cindy Szadokierski applies interactive leadership to handle the complex and demanding job of managing operations for United Airlines in Chicago.

Action Memo

As a leader, you can choose to employ an interactive, collaborative leadership style. You can develop personal relationships with your followers and make everyone feel like an important part of things.

IN THE LEAD

Cindy Szadokierski, United Airlines

Twenty-five years ago, Cindy Szadokierski quit her job teaching high school French and went to work as a reservations agent for United Airlines. Today, she is vice president in charge of operations for United's largest hub at O'Hare International Airport.

From the beginning of her career with United, Szadokierski wanted to be in operations because she liked the idea of bridging the gap between what goes on in the field and what happens at headquarters. As she oversees 4,000 employees and 600 flights a day, her favorite times are the weekly afternoon walkabouts on the O'Hare ramp and the weekly morning strolls through the terminal. Why? Because they give her a chance to connect with employees and customers. Pete McDonald, chief operating officer of United's parent, UAL Corporation, says there were serious operations problems at O'Hare, so they put "the most communicative person" in the job. Szadokierski applies many of the same skills she used as a teacher: planning, setting expectations, motivating, and teaching people everything from technical aspects to the softer side of building relationships.

Her approach to leadership is more collaborative than command-and-control. In addition to learning from employees and customers during her weekly ramp and terminal outings, Szadokierski meets regularly with her leadership team to talk about what's going right, what's going wrong, and how to fix any problems. "We plan very, very carefully and collaboratively," Szadokierski says. "[But] when things don't go right, I sit down with my team, dig to find out what failed, and put processes in place so that it doesn't reoccur.... We have to expose our failures and issues so we can find answers and be better."[64]

Although the values associated with interactive leadership, such as inclusion, relationship building, and caring, are generally considered "feminine"

Interactive leadership
a leadership style in which people develop personal relationships with followers, share power and information, empower employees, and strive to enhance others' feelings of self-worth

values, interactive leadership is not gender-specific. These values are becoming increasingly valuable for both male and female leaders. Today's flatter, team-based organizations are no longer looking for top-down authority figures but for more collaborative and inclusive approaches to leadership.[65]

Again, the interactive leadership style is not exclusive to women. Any leader can learn to adopt a more inclusive style by paying attention to nonverbal behavior and developing skills such as listening, empathy, cooperation, and collaboration.[66]

Global Diversity

One of the most rapidly increasing sources of diversity is globalization, which means that leaders are confronting diversity issues across a broader stage than ever before. For leaders interacting with people from other cultures, even something as seemingly simple as a handshake can be confusing, as illustrated in Exhibit 11.4. If the proper way to shake hands can vary so widely, no wonder managers have trouble knowing how to act when doing business with people from or in other countries.

Leaders can get a handle on the challenges of global diversity by understanding the sociocultural environment and by developing cultural intelligence to know how to behave appropriately.

Action Memo

Social value differences can significantly affect leadership, working relationships, and organizational functioning. Answer the questions in Leader's Self-Insight 11.3 to better understand the social values of your classmates or coworkers.

The Sociocultural Environment

Social and cultural differences may provide more potential for difficulties and conflicts than any other source. For instance, after hundreds of mostly Somali Muslim employees walked out to protest not being allowed extra break times to pray during Ramadan, leaders at a JBS Swift & Company meatpacking plant in Omaha, Nebraska, altered their policies so the workers could pray at the appropriate times. That, however, led to protests by non-Muslim workers, who alleged "preferential treatment," causing leaders to reconsider allowing extra breaks for prayer. The tensions and conflicts led to a near-riot, and Swift's leaders are still trying to resolve the issues that have arisen between the different groups.[67]

Exhibit 11.4 How Do You Shake Hands?

Culture	Preferred Style of Handshake
Asian	Gentle (shaking hands is unfamiliar and uncomfortable for some Asians; the exception is the Korean, who usually prefers a firm handshake)
British	Soft
French	Light and quick; repeated on arrival and departure; not offered to superiors
German	Brusque and firm; repeated on arrival and departure
Latin American	Moderate grasp; repeated frequently.
Middle Eastern	Gentle; repeated frequently
North American	Firm

Source: From *Bridging Cultural Barriers for Corporate Success* by Sondra Thiederman. Copyright © 1991. Lexington Books. Reprinted by permission of the author.

Leader's Self-Insight 11.3

Social Values

Instructions: Different social groups (work colleagues, family, professional groups, and national, religious, and cultural groups) are all around us. Focus on the group of individuals whom you consider to be your colleagues (e.g., team members, coworkers, classmates). Respond to each of the following statements and indicate its level of importance to your colleague group on the scale of (1) Not at all important to (5) Very important.

How Important Is It:	Not at All Important			Very Important	
1. To compromise one's wishes to act together with your colleagues?	1	2	3	4	5
2. To be loyal to your colleagues?	1	2	3	4	5
3. To follow norms established by your colleagues?	1	2	3	4	5
4. To maintain a stable environment rather than "rock the boat"?	1	2	3	4	5
5. To not break the rules?	1	2	3	4	5
6. To be a specialist or professional rather than a manager?	1	2	3	4	5
7. To have an opportunity for high earnings?	1	2	3	4	5
8. To have an opportunity for advancement to higher-level jobs?	1	2	3	4	5
9. To work with people who cooperate well with one another?	1	2	3	4	5
10. To have a good working relationship with your manager?	1	2	3	4	5
11. To have a manager that gives detailed instructions?	1	2	3	4	5
12. To avoid disagreement with a manager?	1	2	3	4	5

Scoring and Interpretation

There are four subscale scores that measure the four social values described by Hofstede. For the dimension of individualism–collectivism, compute your average score based on responses to questions 1, 2, and 3. For the dimension of uncertainty avoidance, compute your

average score based on responses to questions 4, 5, and 6. For the dimension of masculinity–femininity, reverse score your responses to questions 9 and 10 (5 = 1, 4 = 2, 2 = 4, and 1 = 5) and then compute your average score for questions 7, 8, 9, and 10. For the dimension of power distance, compute the average score for questions 11 and 12.

My average social value scores are:
Individualism–collectivism (I–C) _____.
Uncertainty avoidance (UA) _____.
Masculinity–femininity (M–F) _____.
Power distance (PD) _____.

An average score of 4 or above on the I–C scale means that *collectivism* is a social value in your colleague group, and a score of 2 or below means that the value of *individualism* dominates. A score of 4 or above on the UA scale means that your group values the absence of ambiguity and uncertainty (*high uncertainty avoidance*), and a score of 2 or below means that uncertainty and unpredictability are preferred. A score of 4 or above on the M–F scale means that *masculinity* is a social value in your colleague group, and a score of 2 or below means that the value of *femininity* dominates. A score of 4 or above on the PD scale means that *high power distance*, or hierarchical differences, is a social value in your colleague group, and a score of 2 or below means that the value of *low power distance*, or equality, dominates.

Compare your four scores to one another to understand your perception of the different values. On which of the four values would you like to score higher? Lower? Analyze the specific questions on which you scored higher or lower to analyze the pattern of your group's social values. Show your scores to a student from another country and explain what they mean. How do your social values differ from the social values of the international student? How do these social values differ across the nationalities represented in your class?

Source: Adapted from Geert Hofstede, *Culture's Consequences* (London: Sage Publications, 1984); and D. Matsumoto, M. D. Weissman, K. Preston, B. R. Brown, and C. Kupperbausch, "Context-Specific Measurement of Individualism–Collectivism on the Individual Level: The Individualism–Collectivism Interpersonal Assessment Inventory," *Journal of Cross-Cultural Psychology* 28, no. 6 (1997), pp. 743–767.

Cultural factors have also created problems for managers in some U.S. corporations trying to transfer their diversity policies and practices to European divisions. Policies designed to address diversity issues in the United States don't take into consideration the complex social and cultural systems in Europe. In Britain, for example, class distinctions are as big an aspect of diversity as race, gender, or disability.[68] Even the meaning of the term *diversity* can present problems. In many European languages, the closest word implies separation rather than the inclusion sought by U.S. diversity programs.[69] Foreign firms doing business in the United States face similar challenges understanding and dealing with diversity issues. C. R. "Dick" Shoemate, chairman and CEO of Bestfoods, says, "It takes a special kind of leadership to deal with the differences in a multicountry, multicultural organization. . . ." Bestfoods uses cross-border assignments and extensive individual coaching to train people to lead a multicultural workforce.[70]

Social Value Systems

Research done by Geert Hofstede on IBM employees in 40 countries discovered that mindset and cultural values on issues such as individualism versus collectivism strongly influence organizational and employee relationships and vary widely among cultures.[71] Exhibit 11.5 shows examples of how countries rate on four significant dimensions.

Power distance
how much people accept equality in power; high power distance reflects an acceptance of power inequality among institutions, organizations, and individuals; low power distance means people expect equality in power

Uncertainty avoidance
the degree to which members of a society feel uncomfortable with uncertainty and ambiguity and thus support beliefs and behaviors that promise certainty and conformity

- *Power distance.* High **power distance** means people accept inequality in power among institutions, organizations, and individuals. Low power distance means people expect equality in power. Countries that value high power distance are Malaysia, the Philippines, and Panama. Countries that value low power distance include Denmark, Austria, and Israel.

- *Uncertainty avoidance.* High **uncertainty avoidance** means that members of a society feel uncomfortable with uncertainty and ambiguity and thus support beliefs and behaviors that promise certainty and conformity. Low uncertainty avoidance means that people have a high tolerance for the unstructured, the unclear, and the unpredictable. High uncertainty avoidance cultures include

Exhibit 11.5 Rank Orderings of 10 Countries Along Four Dimensions of National Value System

Country	Power[a]	Uncertainty[b]	Individualism[c]	Masculinity[d]
Australia	7	7	2	5
Costa Rica	8	2 (tie)	10	9
France	3	2 (tie)	4	7
India	2	9	6	6
Japan	5	1	7	1
Mexico	1	4	8	2
Sweden	10	10	3	10
Thailand	4	6	9	8
United States	6	8	1	4

[a]1 = highest power distance; 10 = lowest power distance
[b]1 = highest uncertainty avoidance; 10 = lowest uncertainty avoidance
[c]1 = highest individualism; 10 = highest collectivism
[d]1 = highest masculinity; 10 = highest femininity

Source: From Dorothy Marcic, *Organizational Behavior and Cases,* 4th ed. (St. Paul, MN: West, 1995). Based on Geert Hofstede, *Culture's Consequences* (London: Sage Publications, 1984); and *Cultures and Organizations: Software of the Mind* (New York: McGraw-Hill, 1991).

Greece, Portugal, and Uruguay. Singapore and Jamaica are two countries with low uncertainty avoidance values.

- *Individualism and collectivism.* **Individualism** reflects a value for a loosely knit social framework in which individuals are expected to take care of themselves. **Collectivism** is a preference for a tightly knit social framework in which people look out for one another and organizations protect their members' interests. Countries with individualist values include the United States, Great Britain, and Canada. Countries with collectivist values are Guatemala, Ecuador, and Panama.
- *Masculinity and femininity.* **Masculinity** reflects a preference for achievement, heroism, assertiveness, work centrality, and material success. **Femininity** reflects the values of relationships, cooperation, group decision making, and quality of life. Japan, Austria, and Mexico are countries with strong masculine values. Countries with strong feminine values include Sweden, Norway, Denmark, and the former Yugoslavia. Both men and women subscribe to the dominant value in masculine or feminine cultures.

Terry Neill, a managing partner at a London-based change management practice, uses Hofstede's findings in his work with companies. Based on his experiences with global companies such as Unilever PLC, Shell Oil, and BP, Neill points out that the Dutch, Irish, Americans, and British are generally quite comfortable with open argument. However, Japanese and other Asian employees often feel uneasy or even threatened by such directness.[72] In many Asian countries, leaders perceive the organization as a large family and emphasize cooperation through networks of personal relationships. In contrast, leaders in Germany and other central European countries typically strive to run their organizations as impersonal well-oiled machines.[73] How leaders handle these and other cultural differences can have tremendous impact on the satisfaction and effectiveness of diverse employees.

Developing Cultural Intelligence

Although understanding the sociocultural environment and social value differences is crucial, a person cannot expect to know everything necessary to be prepared for every conceivable situation. Thus, in a multicultural environment, leaders will be most successful if they are culturally flexible and able to easily adapt to new situations and ways of doing things. In other words, they need cultural intelligence. **Cultural intelligence (CQ)** refers to a person's ability to use reasoning and observation skills to interpret unfamiliar gestures and situations and devise appropriate behavioral responses.[74] Developing a high level of CQ enables a person to interpret unfamiliar situations and adapt quickly. Rather than a list of global "dos and don'ts," CQ is a practical learning approach that enables a person to ferret out clues to a culture's shared understandings and respond to new situations in culturally appropriate ways.

Cultural intelligence includes three components that work together: cognitive, emotional, and physical.[75] The cognitive component involves a person's observational and learning skills and the ability to pick up on clues to understanding. The emotional aspect concerns one's self-confidence and self-motivation. A leader has to believe in his or her ability to understand and assimilate into a different culture. Difficulties and setbacks are triggers to work harder, not a cause to give up. The third component of CQ, the physical, refers to a person's ability to shift his or her speech patterns, expressions, and body language to be in tune with people from a different culture. Most people aren't equally strong

Individualism
a value for a loosely knit social framework in which individuals are expected to take care of themselves

Collectivism
a preference for a tightly knit social framework in which people look out for one another and organizations protect their members' interests

Masculinity
a preference for achievement, heroism, assertiveness, work centrality, and material success

Femininity
a preference for relationships, cooperation, group decision making, and quality of life

Cultural intelligence
the ability to use reasoning and observation to interpret unfamiliar situations and devise appropriate behavioral responses

in all three areas, but maximizing cultural intelligence requires that they draw upon all three facets.

Developing high CQ requires that a leader be open and receptive to new ideas and approaches. Ken Powell, CEO of General Mills, says taking an international assignment early in his career was "unsettling," but one of the best things he did.[76] Working in a different country is one of the best ways people can stretch beyond their comfort zone and develop a broader, more global perspective. One study found that people who adapt to global management most easily are those who have grown up learning how to understand, empathize, and work with others who are different from themselves. For example, Singaporeans consistently hear English and Chinese spoken side by side. The Dutch have to learn English, German, and French, as well as Dutch, to interact and trade with their economically dominant neighbors. English Canadians must not only be well-versed in American culture and politics, but they also have to consider the views and ideas of French Canadians, who, in turn, must learn to think like North Americans, members of a global French community, Canadians, and Quebecois.[77] People who have grown up without this kind of language and cultural diversity, which includes most leaders in the United States, typically have more difficulties with foreign assignments, but willing managers from any country can learn to open their minds and appreciate other viewpoints.

Leadership Implications

A study of executives in five countries found that although the globalization of business seems to be leading to a convergence of managerial values and attitudes, executives in different countries differ significantly in some areas, which can create problems for leadership.[78] To lead effectively in a diverse global environment, leaders should be aware of cultural and subcultural differences. Chapter 3 examined contingency theories of leadership that explain the relationship between leader style and a given situation. It is important for leaders to recognize that culture affects both style and the leadership situation. For example, in cultures with high uncertainty avoidance, a leadership situation with high task structure as described in Chapter 3 is favorable, but those in low uncertainty avoidance cultures prefer less-structured work situations. Research into how the contingency models apply to cross-cultural situations is sparse. However, all leaders need to be aware of the impact that culture may have and consider cultural values in their dealings with employees and colleagues.

How behavior is perceived differs from culture to culture. An American manager nearly blew a deal with a Korean company because he complained directly to higher-level managers when he had difficulty getting the information he needed from his Korean counterparts. In the United States, such an approach would be acceptable, but in Korea, it was seen as a sign of disrespect. The lower-level Korean managers were horrified and embarrassed; the upper-level managers were offended; and the crisis was resolved only when top-level managers from the United States made a trip to Korea to apologize and show respect.[79] As another example, to criticize a subordinate in private directly is considered appropriate behavior in individualistic societies such as the United States. However, in Japan, which values collectivism over individualism, the same leader behavior would be seen as inconsiderate. Japanese employees lose face if they are

Action Memo

As a leader, you can develop cultural intelligence. You can study other languages and cultures and form relationships with people from different countries. You can learn to be sensitive to differences in social value systems, and find creative ways to address delicate diversity issues.

criticized directly by a supervisor. The expectation is that people will receive criticism information from peers rather than directly from the leader.[80]

Becoming an Inclusive Leader

One goal for today's global organizations is to ensure that *all* people—women, ethnic minorities, younger people, gays and lesbians, the disabled, older people, racial minorities, as well as white males—are given equal opportunities and treated with fairness and respect.[81] Strong, culturally sensitive leadership can move organizations toward a more inclusive culture, where all individuals are valued and respected for the unique abilities they bring to the workplace.

Stages of Personal Diversity Awareness

Leaders vary in their sensitivity and openness to other cultures, attitudes, values, and ways of doing things. Exhibit 11.6 shows a model of five stages of individual diversity awareness and actions.[82] The continuum ranges from a defensive,

Exhibit 11.6 Stages of Personal Diversity Awareness

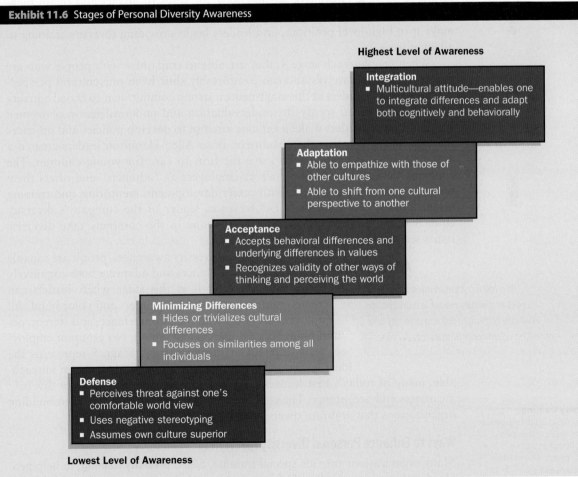

Highest Level of Awareness

Integration
- Multicultural attitude—enables one to integrate differences and adapt both cognitively and behaviorally

Adaptation
- Able to empathize with those of other cultures
- Able to shift from one cultural perspective to another

Acceptance
- Accepts behavioral differences and underlying differences in values
- Recognizes validity of other ways of thinking and perceiving the world

Minimizing Differences
- Hides or trivializes cultural differences
- Focuses on similarities among all individuals

Defense
- Perceives threat against one's comfortable world view
- Uses negative stereotyping
- Assumes own culture superior

Lowest Level of Awareness

Source: Based on M. Bennett, "A Developmental Approach to Training for Intercultural Sensitivity," *International Journal of Intercultural Relations* 10 (1986), pp. 179–196.

ethnocentric attitude, in which leaders meet the minimum legal requirements regarding affirmative action and sexual harassment, to a complete understanding and acceptance of people's differences, in which leaders value diversity as an inherent part of the organizational culture.

People at stage 1 see differences as a threat against their own comfortable world view and frequently use negative stereotyping or express prejudicial attitudes. Leaders at this stage of diversity awareness consider themselves successful if their legal record is good. They may view women and minorities as a "problem" that must be dealt with. Typically, these leaders promote a few minorities to executive-level jobs to meet legal requirements. At stage 2, people attempt to minimize differences and focus on the similarities among all people. This is the stage where unconscious and subtle bias is most evident, because people have moved beyond openly prejudicial attitudes. Leaders don't adequately recognize or respond to the challenges minorities and women face in the organization. When an individual moves to stage 3 of diversity awareness, he or she accepts cultural differences and recognizes the validity of other ways of thinking and doing things. Here, leaders become proactive and acknowledge that addressing issues of gender, race, disability, and so forth is important not just for the minority employees but also for the health of the organization. They recognize that women and minorities can bring needed insight into developing and marketing products for new customers, so they look for ways to attract and retain high-quality minority employees. In stage 3 organizations, more women and minorities make it to high-level positions, and leaders begin providing diversity training to all employees.

When people reach stage 4, they are able to empathize with people who are different from themselves and can comfortably shift from one cultural perspective to another. Leaders at this stage make a strong commitment to broad equality and community and rectify the undervaluation and underutilization of women and minorities. Leaders make a genuine attempt to develop policies and practices that are inclusive rather than exclusive. Booz Allen Hamilton leaders created a new program for women who leave the firm to care for young children. The company designates valued female ex-employees as "adjuncts" and offers them work on short projects, along with career development, mentoring, and training opportunities.[83] At UPS, the CEO serves as leader of the company's diversity council because he believes it makes everyone in the company take diversity issues seriously.

Action Memo

As a leader, you can advance to higher stages of diversity awareness and action. You can commit to valuing diversity and providing equal opportunities for everyone.

At stage 5 of diversity awareness, people are capable of integrating differences and adapting both cognitively and behaviorally. It is at this stage where leaders can create organizations that are gender- and color-blind. All employees are judged on their competence, and stereotypes and prejudices are completely erased. No group of employees feels different or disadvantaged. Stage 5 represents the ideal leader and organization. Although it may seem unreachable, many of today's best leaders are striving to achieve this stage of diversity awareness and acceptance. The commitment of top leaders is critical to building organizations that embrace diversity in all aspects of the business.

Ways to Enhance Personal Diversity Awareness

Diversity training
training designed to help people become aware of their own biases, become sensitive to and open to people different from themselves, and learn skills for communicating and working effectively in a diverse workplace

Many organizations provide special training, called **diversity training**, to help people identify their own cultural boundaries, prejudices, and stereotypes and develop the skills for managing and working in a diverse workplace. Leaders can also seek training on their own to improve their diversity awareness and skills. Working or living within a multicultural context requires a person to use interaction skills that transcend the skills that are typically effective when dealing with others from one's own in-group.[84]

The first step in training is for leaders to become aware of the assumptions they make and to increase their sensitivity and openness to those who are different from themselves. A basic aim of personal development in this area is to recognize that hidden and overt biases direct our thinking about specific individuals and groups. If leaders can recognize that they prejudge people and that this tendency needs to be consciously addressed in communications with and treatment of others, they have taken an important first step toward more inclusive leadership.

The next step is developing diversity skills, that is, learning how to communicate and work effectively in a diverse environment. Rather than just attempting to increase understanding and sensitivity, leaders develop concrete skills they can use in everyday situations, such as how to handle conflict in a constructive manner or how to modify nonverbal communication such as body language and facial expression.[85] Verizon Communications uses an online training tool where leaders can tap into various diversity scenarios that might occur in the workplace and see how to manage them in an appropriate way.[86] In addition to training provided by the organization, leaders can seek diversity training through a variety of online sources, videotapes or DVDs, and outside consulting firms.

Personal Qualities for Leading Diverse People

Four characteristics have been identified as important for inclusive leadership.[87]

- *A personal, long-range vision that recognizes and supports a diverse organizational community.* Leaders should have long-term plans to include employees of various ethnic and cultural groups, races, ages, and so on at all levels of the organization. In addition, they express the vision through symbols and rituals that reinforce the value of a diverse workforce.
- *A broad knowledge of the dimensions of diversity and awareness of multicultural issues.* Leaders need a basic knowledge of the various dimensions of diversity as discussed earlier in this chapter. They put this knowledge into action through the use of inclusive language and showing respect for differences.
- *An openness to change themselves.* Leaders in diverse organizations encourage feedback from their employees, can accept criticism, and are willing to change their behavior. It is leaders' behavior that has the most impact on whether diversity is truly valued within the organization. At Baxter Healthcare Corp., for example, chairman and CEO Harry Jansen Kraemer, Jr., writes a newsletter called *CEO Update* for the company intranet. Rather than just talking about business issues, he includes a section updating people on his family life. For women who are juggling career and family, it is a clear signal that the company values family and considers work–life balance important.[88]
- *Mentoring and empowerment of diverse employees.* Leaders take an active role in creating opportunities for all employees to use their unique abilities. They also offer honest feedback and coaching as needed, and they reward those in the organization who show respect to all individuals.

Action Memo

As a leader, you can create a personal vision for a diverse community. You can use words, symbols, and leadership actions to create an organizational culture that includes the participation of all people regardless of race, age, gender, cultural or ethnic group, or physical ability.

Once leaders examine and change themselves, they can lead change in the organization. Diversity presents many challenges, yet it also provides leaders with an exciting opportunity to build organizations as integrated communities in which all people feel encouraged, respected, and committed to common purposes and goals. Consider how leaders at Denny's Restaurants have improved diversity awareness to transform the company from an icon of racism to a paragon of diversity.

IN THE LEAD

Denny's Restaurants

It was a spring morning in 1993 when six African-American Secret Service agents sat waiting for their food at Denny's for more than an hour while their white colleagues ate. Their meals arrived just before they had to leave. The highly publicized incident led to other revelations of discrimination against African-American customers and employees—and to a series of racial discrimination lawsuits. Thirteen years later, a Denny's executive received the "We Share the Dream Award" at the 18th annual Dr. Martin Luther King Jr. Awards Dinner. How did Denny's go from worst to first? It comes down to top leader commitment and some serious training to improve diversity awareness and behavior.

After settling the discrimination lawsuits in 1994, Denny's hired Rachelle Hood as its first chief diversity officer. Hood got the company to hire more than 100 diversity trainers and implemented training at every level. Every single person at Denny's—not just managers, dishwashers, and servers, but also media planners and leased security guards—attends diversity training with specific guidelines on how to apply diversity understanding and sensitivity to working in the restaurant business. In the "We Can" training program, for example, employees learn a three-step model: (1) *prevention,* such as how to behave in order to reduce the possibility of a guest or fellow employee feeling that he or she has been discriminated against; (2) *intervention,* which teaches people to "acknowledge, apologize, and act" when something goes wrong; and (3) *managing escalation,* in which employees learn how to genuinely listen, show empathy, and reduce the anger and frustration level. Denny's spends several million dollars a year on building awareness, and its diversity training system is one of the most comprehensive in the industry.

Hood cemented diversity awareness by working with managers to increase supplier diversity, developing marketing campaigns targeting minority customers, and tying managers' bonus pay to meeting diversity goals. In 1993, only one of the chain's franchises was minority-owned, the company had no minority suppliers, and the board was made up primarily of white males. Today, however, things are very different:

- More than 40 percent of Denny's franchises are owned by minorities.
- During a recent 10-year period, Denny's contracted nearly $1 billion for goods and services with minority suppliers, with African-Americans accounting for 48 percent of the business. That represents around 18 percent of the company's contracts, as compared to a national average of 3 to 4 percent.
- Forty-four percent of the board of directors is composed of women and people of color.
- Minority employees represent 41 percent of Denny's overall management and 59 percent of the workforce.[89]

Thanks to these advancements, *Black Enterprise* magazine named Denny's one of the best corporations for African-Americans, and *Fortune* ranked Denny's in its list of "America's 50 Best Corporations for Minorities" two years in a row. Denny's turnaround is one of the best examples of how far and how fast a company can progress with strong leadership and an aggressive approach to culture change.

Leadership Essentials

■ One main point of this chapter is that diversity is a fact of life in today's world, and leaders can create change in organizations to keep pace with the changing environment. The U.S. population, the workforce, and the customer base are changing. In addition, organizations are operating in an increasingly global world, which means dealing with diversity on a broader stage than ever before.

■ Diversity is defined as all the ways in which people differ. This definition has been broadened in recent years to be more inclusive and recognize a broad spectrum of characteristics. The inclusive definition of diversity embraces not only dimensions such as gender and race, but also characteristics such as work style, nationality, and income level.

■ There are several reasons why organizations are recognizing the need to value and support diversity. Diversity helps organizations build better relationships with diverse customers and helps develop employee potential. A diverse workforce provides diversity of thought and a broader and deeper base of experience for creativity and problem solving. One aspect of diversity of recent interest is women's style of leadership, referred to as interactive leadership. The values associated with interactive leadership, such as inclusion and relationship building, are emerging as valuable qualities for both male and female leaders in the twenty-first century.

■ Today's leaders face significant challenges leading people who are different from themselves. The first step for leading diverse people is understanding the hardships that people who do not fit the mainstream white, U.S.-born, male culture often endure. These include prejudice, stereotypes, and discrimination; unequal expectations; the glass ceiling; and the opportunity gap.

■ Another important issue is global diversity. Leaders can be aware of the impact culture may have, understand social and cultural value differences, and develop cultural intelligence.

■ People differ in their level of diversity awareness and their sensitivity to other cultures, values, and ways of doing things. Leaders evolve through stages of personal diversity awareness and action, ranging from minimum efforts to meet affirmative action guidelines to valuing diversity as an integral part of organizational culture. Strong, culturally sensitive leadership is the only way organizations can become inclusive. Leaders first change themselves by developing personal characteristics that support diversity. They use these personal characteristics to change the organization. The ultimate goal for leaders in the twenty-first century is to build organizations as integrated communities in which all people feel encouraged, respected, and committed to common purposes and goals.

Discussion Questions

1. How might a leader's role and responsibility change as a company becomes more diverse? Explain.

2. Why is diversity of thought important for today's organizations? Do you think an organization can have diversity of thought if all employees are of the same race and approximately the same age and background?

3. What is interactive leadership, and why might this approach be increasingly important in the twenty-first century?

4. Discuss ways in which low power distance as a social value among followers could affect their interaction with a leader who displays high power distance.

5. Why do you think many women *opt out* from seeking higher levels of corporate leadership? Discuss why you think this either is or is not a trend that might hurt organizations over the next decade.

6. How would you lead a group of people who are different from you?

7. Why is it important for today's leaders to develop cultural intelligence? Do you think a leader who has never had experience with people different from himself or herself can develop the ability to smoothly adapt to culturally different ways of thinking and behaving? Discuss.

8. Recall a leader you worked for. At what stage of personal diversity awareness (refer to Exhibit 11.6) was this leader? Explain. At what stage of diversity awareness are you?

9. Do you think people and organizations can ever become gender- and color-blind? Discuss.

10. The chapter described a conflict at a meatpacking plant over providing break times for Muslims to pray. How might leaders accommodate the needs of diverse groups without offending other groups or appearing to show favoritism?

Leadership at Work

PERSONAL DIVERSITY

Each of us feels different in many ways from the average behavior or expectations that other people seem to value. This reflects our own feelings of diversity. The differences you feel compared to others could be about your physical characteristics (height, age, skin color), but also could reflect a difference in your thinking style, feelings, personality, or behavior, especially when you feel different from what other people expect or what you perceive are the social norms. Write in the following list six ways you feel different from others:

1. _____ 4. _____
2. _____ 5. _____
3. _____ 6. _____

Now answer the following questions with respect to your perceived diversity. What are your feelings about being different?

_____
_____
_____

Which elements of diversity are you proud of? Why?

_____
_____
_____

What element would you like to change to be less diverse? Why?

_____
_____
_____

How do your differences contribute to a student team or work organization?

_____

_____

_____

In Class: This exercise can be adapted for group discussion in class about underlying diversity. The instructor can ask students to sit in teams of three to five members in a circle facing each other. A student (focal person) then volunteers to describe the way he or she feels different from others based on the previous list. Other students take turns providing feedback to the focal person on what the perceived differences mean to them with respect to team or class contributions. Each student takes a turn as the focal person, describing their feelings of being different and hearing feedback from others on the perception and impact of those differences.

Here are the key questions for this exercise: What did you learn about perceived diversity and interpersonal relations? What does it mean when our differences appear larger to ourselves than they appear to others? How does personal diversity affect team or organizational performance? (A list can be written on the board.)

Chapter 12: Leadership Power and Influence

© Eric Foltz

Your Leadership Challenge

After reading this chapter, you should be able to:

- Use power and politics to help accomplish important organizational goals.

- Practice aspects of charismatic leadership by pursuing a vision or idea that you care deeply about and want to share with others.

- Apply the concepts that distinguish transformational from transactional leadership.

- Use coalitional leadership to build alliances that can help you achieve important goals for the organization.

- Identify types and sources of power in organizations and know how to increase power through political activity.

- Describe structural, human resource, political, and symbolic frames of

reference and identify your dominant leadership frame.

- Use the influence tactics of rational persuasion, friendliness, reciprocity, developing allies, direct appeal, and scarcity.

Chapter Outline

How did a poor African-American girl growing up with a single mom in inner-city Chicago turn into one of the most recognized names in financial services? Intelligence, hard work, integrity, and a strong work ethic are part of the answer. But what has really helped Mellody Hobson not only survive but thrive in the white male–dominated world of investing is her political skill. Hobson, who is today president of mutual fund company Ariel Investments, started at Ariel as a student intern and joined full time after college graduation. She immediately started networking, making friends and supporters that she's kept to this day. Hobson hangs out with celebrities like George Lucas and Ciara, enjoys talking with teachers and school children on Chicago's South Side, counts Warren Buffett, Dick Parsons, and Jamie Dimon among her friends, sits on the boards of Estée Lauder, Starbucks, and the Chicago Public Library, has hosted fundraisers for Barack Obama since his first Senate campaign, worked with Richard Daley to improve Chicago public schools, and loves mingling with Formula One race fans, where she cheers on Lewis Hamilton, the first black racer. "She finds a way to find a connection with virtually anyone," says David Geffen, cofounder of Dreamworks, where Hobson also sits on the board.

Hobson's networking skill has helped her achieve what she wants for herself and for Ariel Investments. Even when she was a 25-year-old new employee,

Hobson was able to influence Ariel founder John Rogers and board members regarding a critical strategic decision—to strengthen Ariel as a brand focused on value investing by separating it from the Calvert Group, which focused on social investing (the two firms were involved in a joint venture). Rogers says he was initially shocked by Hobson's boldness, but Hobson used information, networking, and personal persuasion to convince him it was the right decision. "She went out and did a lot of heavy lifting and convinced our board and myself it was the right thing to do."[1]

Mellody Hobson had little formal power as a young Ariel employee, but she already understood how to use politics and influence to get things done. Successful leaders like Hobson take the time to build relationships both inside and outside the organization and to talk informally about important projects and priorities. All leaders use power and influence to have an impact on their organizations.

This chapter explores the topic of leadership power and influence in detail. The chapter opens with a consideration of three types of influential leadership. We next examine what we mean by the terms *power* and *influence,* consider different leader frames of reference that affect how leaders think about and use power, look at some sources and types of power, and outline ways leaders exercise power and influence through political activity. Finally, we briefly consider some ethical aspects of using power and influence.

Three Kinds of Influential Leadership

New leaders often think of leadership power as something granted by an organization through the leader's position. However, leaders also have power that doesn't depend on job authority, and they influence people through a variety of means. Three types of influential leadership that rely on a leader's personal characteristics and relationships rather than on a formal position of authority are transformational, charismatic, and coalitional leadership.

Transformational Leadership

Transformational leadership is characterized by the ability to bring about significant change in both followers and the organization. Transformational leaders have the ability to lead changes in an organization's vision, strategy, and culture as well as promote innovation in products and technologies.

One way to understand transformational leadership is to compare it to transactional leadership.[2] The basis of **transactional leadership** is a transaction or exchange process between leaders and followers. The transactional leader recognizes followers' needs and desires and then clarifies how those needs and desires will be satisfied in exchange for meeting specified objectives or performing certain duties. Thus, followers receive rewards for job performance, whereas leaders benefit from the completion of tasks. Transactional leaders focus on the present and excel at keeping the organization running smoothly and efficiently. They are good at traditional management functions such as planning and budgeting and generally focus on the impersonal aspects of job performance. Transactional leadership can be quite effective. However, because it involves a commitment to "follow the rules," transactional leadership maintains stability within the organization rather than promoting change.

Transactional skills are important for all leaders. However, in a world in which success often depends on continuous change, organizations also

Transformational leadership
leadership characterized by the ability to bring about significant change in followers and the organization

Transactional leadership
a transaction or exchange process between leaders and followers

need transformational leadership.[3] Rather than analyzing and controlling specific transactions with followers using rules, directions, and incentives, transformational leadership focuses on intangible qualities such as vision, shared values, and ideas in order to build relationships, give larger meaning to separate activities, and provide common ground to enlist followers in the change process. Transformational leadership is based on the personal values, beliefs, and qualities of the leader rather than on an exchange process between leaders and followers.

Studies support the idea that transformational leadership has a positive impact on follower development, performance, and even organizational profitability.[4] Moreover, transformational leadership skills can be learned and are not ingrained personality characteristics. Transformational leadership differs from transactional leadership in four significant areas.[5]

> ### Action Memo
>
> *As a leader, you can act like a transformational leader by rallying people around an inspiring vision, expressing optimism about the future, helping followers develop their potential, and empowering people to make change happen.*

1. *Transformational leadership develops followers into leaders.* Instead of strictly controlling people, transformational leaders give followers greater freedom to control their own behavior. Transformational leadership rallies people around a mission and vision and defines the boundaries within which followers can operate to accomplish goals. The transformational leader arouses in followers an awareness of problems and issues and helps people look at things in new ways so that productive change can happen.

2. *Transformational leadership elevates the concerns of followers from lower-level physical needs (such as for safety and security) to higher-level psychological needs (such as for self-esteem and self-actualization).* Lower-level needs are met through adequate wages, safe working conditions, and other considerations, but the transformational leader also pays attention to each individual's need for growth and development. Therefore, the leader sets examples and assigns tasks not only to meet immediate needs but also to elevate followers' needs and abilities to a higher level and link them to the organization's mission. Transformational leaders change followers so that they are empowered to change the organization.

3. *Transformational leadership inspires followers to go beyond their own self-interests for the good of the group.* Transformational leaders motivate people to do more than originally expected. They make followers aware of the importance of change goals and outcomes and, in turn, enable them to transcend their own immediate interests for the sake of the whole organization.

4. *Transformational leadership paints a vision of a desired future state and communicates it in a way that makes the pain of change worth the effort.*[6] The most significant role of the transformational leader may be to find a vision for the organization that is significantly better than the old one and to enlist others in sharing the dream. It is the vision that launches people into action and provides the basis for the other aspects of transformational leadership we have just discussed. Change can happen only when people have a sense of purpose as well as a desirable picture of where the organization is going. Without vision, there can be no transformation.

Effective leaders exhibit both transactional and transformational leadership patterns. They accentuate not only their abilities to build a vision and empower and energize others, but also the transactional skills of designing structures, control systems, and reward systems that can help people achieve the vision.[7]

Charismatic Leadership

Charisma has been called "a fire that ignites followers' energy and commitment, producing results above and beyond the call of duty."[8] **Charismatic leaders** have an emotional impact on people and inspire them to do more than they would normally do, despite obstacles and personal sacrifice. They may speak emotionally about putting themselves on the line for the sake of a cause and they are perceived as people who persist in spite of great odds against them. Charismatic leaders often emerge in troubled times, whether in society or in organizations, because a strong, inspiring personality can help to reduce stress and anxiety among followers. For example, Amr Khaled emerged as a young, charismatic Muslim religious leader in Egypt during the Mideast crisis of the early twenty-first century. Khaled's sermons, delivered in an emotional, impassioned manner, touched people who were searching for a moderate approach to living as a good Muslim.[9]

Charismatic leadership and transformational leadership are not the same. Whereas transformational leadership seeks to increase follower engagement and empowerment, charismatic leadership typically instills both awe and submission in followers.[10] Followers admire both charismatic and transformational leaders, want to identify with them, and have a high degree of trust in them. However, transformational leadership motivates people not just to follow the leader personally, but also to believe in the need for change and be willing to make sacrifices for the sake of the vision rather than just out of admiration for the leader.

Charisma can be used for good or ill, but applied wisely and ethically, it can lift the entire organization's level of energy and performance. Charismatic leaders can raise people's consciousness about new possibilities and motivate them to transcend their own interests for the sake of the team, department, or organization. Although charisma itself cannot be learned, there are aspects of charismatic leadership that anyone can use. For one thing, charisma comes from pursuing activities that you have a true passion for.[11] Charismatic leaders are engaging their emotions in everyday work life, which makes them energetic, enthusiastic, and attractive to others. Their passion for a mission inspires people to follow them and galvanizes people to action. Consider Martin Luther King, Jr., and his passion for the cause of equality. One organizational leader with this type of passion is Major Tony Burgess, the U.S. Army tactical officer attached on a full-time basis to Company C-2 at West Point. Burgess says he "fell in love with leading," and his passion for commanding an Army company shows in his leadership.[12]

A number of studies have identified the unique qualities of charismatic leaders, documented the impact they have on followers, and described the behaviors that help them achieve remarkable results.[13] Exhibit 12.1 compares distinguishing characteristics of charismatic and noncharismatic leaders.[14]

Charismatic leaders create an atmosphere of change and articulate an idealized vision of a better future. They have an ability to communicate complex ideas and goals in clear, compelling ways, so that people understand and identify with their message. Charismatic leaders also act in unconventional ways and use unconventional means to transcend the status quo and create change.

Action Memo

As a leader, you can use aspects of charismatic leadership by articulating a vision, making personal sacrifices to help achieve it, and appealing to people's emotions more than to their minds. Expand your charismatic potential by pursuing activities that you genuinely love.

Charismatic leaders
leaders who have the ability to inspire and motivate people to do more than they would normally do, despite obstacles and personal sacrifice

Exhibit 12.1 Distinguishing Characteristics of Charismatic and Noncharismatic Leaders

	Noncharismatic Leaders	Charismatic Leaders
Likableness:	Shared perspective makes leader likable	Shared perspective and idealized vision make leader likable and an honorable hero worthy of identification and imitation
Relation to status quo:	Tries to maintain status quo	Creates atmosphere of change
Future goals:	Limited goals not too discrepant from status quo	Idealized vision that is highly discrepant from status quo
Articulation:	Weak articulation of goals and motivation to lead	Strong and inspirational articulation of vision and motivation to lead
Behavior:	Uses available means to achieve goals within framework of the existing order	Uses unconventional means to transcend the existing order
Influence:	Primarily authority of position and rewards	Transcends position; personal power based on expertise and respect and admiration for the leader

Source: Jay A. Conger and Rabindra N. Kanungo and Associates, *Charismatic Leadership: The Elusive Factor in Organizational Effectiveness* (San Francisco: Jossey-Bass, 1988), p. 91.

The final quality shared by charismatic leaders is that their source of influence comes from personal characteristics rather than a formal position of authority. People admire, respect, and identify with the leader and want to be like him or her. Although charismatic leaders may be in formal positions of authority, charismatic leadership transcends formal organizational position because the leader's influence is based on personal qualities rather than the power and authority granted by the organization.

Action Memo

Complete the questions in Leader's Self-Insight 12.1 to learn how a supervisor of yours rates on transformational leadership. Then, answer the questions for how you would behave in a leadership situation.

Coalitional Leadership

Transformational and charismatic leadership both suggest it is the individual leader who acts as a catalyst for bringing about valuable change toward achieving a goal or vision. Yet in most cases, successful change results from a *coalition* of people rather than the efforts of a single leader. **Coalitional leadership** involves building a coalition of people who support the leader's goals and can help influence others to implement the leader's decisions and achieve the goals.[15] Coalitional leaders observe and understand patterns of interaction and influence in the organization. They are skilled at developing relationships with a broad network of people and can adapt their behavior and approach to diverse people and situations. Coalitional leaders develop positive relationships both within and outside the organization, and they spend time learning others' views and building mutually beneficial alliances.

There are four steps for effective coalitional leadership:[16]

1. *Coalitional leaders do lots of interviews.* Leaders conduct informal interviews with people from all across the organization to gather

Coalitional leadership
leadership that involves developing allies and building a coalition of people who support the leader's goals and can help influence others to implement the leader's decisions and achieve the goals

Leader's Self-Insight 12.1
Transformational Leadership

Think of a situation where someone (boss, coach, teacher, group leader) was in a leadership position over you. Indicate whether each of the following items is Mostly False or Mostly True for you.

In general, the leader over me:

	Mostly False	Mostly True
1. Listened carefully to my concerns	___	___
2. Showed conviction in his/her values	___	___
3. Helped me focus on developing my strengths	___	___
4. Was enthusiastic about our mission	___	___
5. Provided coaching advice for my development	___	___
6. Talked optimistically about the future	___	___
7. Encouraged my self-development	___	___
8. Fostered a clear understanding of important values and beliefs	___	___
9. Provided feedback on how I was doing	___	___
10. Inspired us with his/her plans for the future	___	___
11. Taught me how to develop my abilities	___	___
12. Gained others' commitment to his/her dream	___	___

Scoring and Interpretation

These questions represent two dimensions of transformational leadership. For the dimension of *develops followers into leaders*, sum your Mostly True responses to questions 1, 3, 5, 7, 9, and 11. For the dimension of *inspires followers to go beyond their own self-interest*, sum your Mostly True responses for questions 2, 4, 6, 8, 10, and 12.

The scores for my leader are:

Develops followers into leaders: _____

Inspires followers to go beyond their own self-interest: _____

These two scores represent how you saw your leader on two important aspects of transformational leadership. A score of 5 or above on either dimension is considered high because many leaders do not practice transformational skills in their leadership or group work. A score of 2 or below would be below average. Compare your scores with other students to understand your leader's practice of transformational leadership. How do you explain your leader's score?

Remember, the important learning from this exercise is about yourself, not your leader. Analyzing your leader is simply a way to understand the transformational leadership concepts. How would you rate on the dimensions of *developing followers into leaders* or *inspiring followers to go beyond their own self-interest?* These are difficult skills to master. Answer the 12 questions for yourself as a leader. Analyze your pattern of transformational leadership as revealed in your 12 answers.

Source: Adapted from Sherry E. Moss, Enzo R. Valenzi, and William Taggart, "Are You Hiding from Your Boss? The Development of a Taxonomy and Instrument to Assess the Feedback Management Behaviors of Good and Bad Performers," *Journal of Management* 29, no. 4 (2003), pp. 487–510. Used with permission.

marble: © Kirill Matkov   sunset: © Marco Regalia

Action Memo

Take the short quiz in Leader's Self-Insight 12.2 to help you determine whether you have the potential to be a charismatic leader.

information and get a clear sense of the challenges and opportunities they face. Asking open-ended questions and listening to others enables the leader to learn about the needs and goals of others, find out who believes in and supports the change, who might be opposed and why, and who has ideas, opinions, and expertise that can contribute to accomplishing the desired goals. In addition to interviews, leaders talk informally with people whenever they get a chance. Consider the following example from ServiceMaster.

Leader's Self-Insight 12.2

Have You Got Charisma?

This short quiz will help you determine whether you have characteristics that are associated with charismatic leaders. Circle the answer that best describes you.

1. I am most comfortable thinking in
   a. Generalities
   b. Specifics
2. I worry most about
   a. Current competitive issues
   b. Future competitive issues
3. I tend to focus on
   a. The opportunities I've missed
   b. The opportunities I've seized
4. I prefer to
   a. Promote traditions and procedures that have led to success in the past
   b. Suggest new and unique ways of doing things
5. I tend to ask
   a. How can we do this better?
   b. Why are we doing this?
6. I believe
   a. There's always a way to minimize risk
   b. Some risks are too high
7. I tend to persuade people by using
   a. Emotion
   b. Logic

8. I prefer to
   a. Honor traditional values and ways of thinking
   b. Promote unconventional beliefs and values
9. I would prefer to communicate via
   a. A written report
   b. A one-page chart
10. I think this quiz is
    a. Ridiculous
    b. Fascinating

Scoring and Interpretation

The following answers are associated with charismatic leadership:

1. a; 2. b; 3. a; 4. b; 5. b; 6. a; 7. a; 8. b; 9. b; 10. b

If you responded in this way to seven or more questions, you have a high charisma quotient and may have the potential to be a charismatic leader. If you answered this way to four or fewer questions, your charisma level is considered low. Do you believe a person can develop charisma?

Source: Based on "Have You Got It?" a quiz that appeared in Patricia Sellers, "What Exactly Is Charisma?" *Fortune* (January 15, 1996), pp. 68–75. The original quiz was devised with the assistance of leadership expert Jay Conger.

IN THE LEAD

Jim Goetz, ServiceMaster

After 10 hours of meetings focused on the company's new Six Sigma initiative, all Jim Goetz wanted to do was head to his hotel room. As CIO of ServiceMaster, Goetz wanted to develop an Internet-based system for collecting, reporting, and sharing information and delivering Six Sigma improvements.

He suspected that some managers in the branches and divisions, who had been accustomed to initiating and implementing their own projects, wouldn't be happy about a centralized system. So, as tired as he was, Goetz headed toward the lobby and the hotel lounge. He approached people from all divisions and talked with them over a beer or a coffee, probing for their feelings about the Six Sigma initiative, their goals and interests, and their expectations for how IT could help them meet their own department's or division's objectives.

Several hours later, as Goetz finally settled in his room, he understood the major challenges he faced: selling frontline branch employees on the ease of the new system and convincing division managers of the value of centralized implementation. More importantly, Goetz now had a pretty good idea of who his allies were and who was strongly opposed. He was already formulating ideas for how he could bring other people into a coalition by aligning the project with their own interests.[17]

2. *Coalitional leaders visit customers and other stakeholders.* Coalitional leaders also solicit the views and input of customers as well as other potentially influential stakeholders, such as board members, government agencies, creditors, or others. Jan Frank found that this was a big part of her job bringing change to California's State Compensation Insurance Fund, which receives no taxpayer money but is treated as an arm of state government. When Frank took over in 2007, the agency was reeling from financial scandal, ethical violations, and a criminal investigation. In addition to talking with managers, employees, and board members about her plans and goals for repairing the agency's credibility, Frank also met regularly with lawmakers and regulators to solicit their input regarding operations. She knew their support was crucial to implementing her plans and achieving what she wanted for the agency.[18]

3. *Coalitional leaders develop a map of stakeholder buy-in.* Leaders typically find that there are some people who strongly support their goals and plans, some who adamantly oppose them, and a large percentage who could swing either way. As illustrated in Exhibit 12.2, in mapping the level of buy-in for any significant change, about 10 percent of people can typically be classified as *advocates*, those stakeholders inside and outside the organization who are strong supporters and will help lead the change effort. Another

Exhibit 12.2 Mapping Stakeholder Buy-In

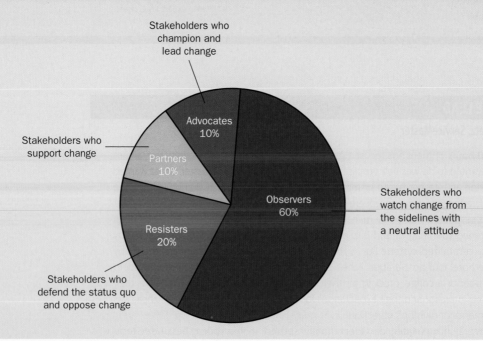

Source: Data are adapted from materials supplied by ExperiencePoint, Inc., in conjunction with the GlobalTech simulation, 2007.

10 percent might be *partners,* who support and encourage the change but will not actively lead it. Twenty percent are typically strongly opposed to the change. These *resisters* might even disrupt or sabotage change efforts. The remaining 60 percent are classified as *observers* because they have a neutral attitude toward the proposed ideas and changes.[19]

4. *Coalitional leaders break down barriers and promote cross-silo cooperation.* The final critical step in coalitional leadership is continually breaking down barriers and promoting cooperation and collaboration across departments, divisions, and levels. For example, when Colin Powell was U.S. Chairman of the Joint Chiefs of Staff, he regularly brought together the heads of the Army, Air Force, Navy, and Marines so they could understand one another's viewpoints.[20] Cross-enterprise understanding and cooperation is essential to achieving a larger vision.

Power, Influence, and Leadership

All leadership relies on the use of power to influence others and get things done.[21] Power is often defined as the potential ability of one person to influence others to carry out orders[22] or to do something they otherwise would not have done.[23] Other definitions stress that power is the ability to achieve goals or outcomes that power holders desire.[24] The achievement of desired outcomes is the basis of the definition used here. **Power** is the potential ability of one person in an organization to influence other people to bring about desired outcomes. It is the potential to influence others within the organization with the goal of attaining desired outcomes for power holders. Potential power is realized through the processes of politics and influence.[25] **Influence** refers to the effect a person's actions have on the attitudes, values, beliefs, or actions of others. Whereas power is the capacity to cause a change in a person, influence may be thought of as the degree of actual change. For example, as a child you may have had the experience of playing a game you didn't really want to play because one person in the group influenced others to do what he or she wanted. Or you may have changed your college major because of the influence of someone important in your life, or shifted your beliefs about some social issue based on the influence of political or religious leaders.

Hard Versus Soft Power

Most discussions of power include five types that are available to leaders.[26] Exhibit 12.3 illustrates the five types of leader power, categorized as either *hard power* or *soft power.* Hard power is power that stems largely from a person's position of authority. This is the kind of power that enables a supervisor to influence subordinates with the use of rewards and punishments, allows a manager to issue orders and expect them to be obeyed, or lets a domineering CEO force through his or her own decisions without regard for what anyone else thinks. Hard power includes legitimate, reward, and coercive power, which are defined largely by the organization's policies and procedures. However, it is important to remember that position power and leadership are not the same thing. As we discussed in Chapter 1, a person might hold a formal position of authority and yet not be a leader.

Effective leaders don't rely solely on the hard power of their formal position to influence others. Soft power includes expert power and referent power, which are based on personal characteristics and interpersonal relationships more than on a position of authority. In today's world, soft power is, more than ever, the tool of the leader. Consider that Jeffrey Immelt, CEO of General

Power
the potential ability of one person to influence other people to bring about desired outcomes

Influence
the effect a person's actions have on the attitudes, values, beliefs, or actions of others

Exhibit 12.3 Five Types of Leader Power

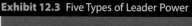

Hard Power	Soft Power
Legitimate: Based on leader holding a formal position or title. People accept leader's right to issue orders or direct activities.	**Expert:** Based on leader's special knowledge or skills. People trust and respect decisions because of leader's expertise.
Reward: Based on leader having the ability to provide or withhold rewards. People comply in order to obtain desired rewards.	**Referent:** Based on leader's personal characteristics. People admire and respect leader, like to be around him or her, and adopt the leader's viewpoint.
Coercive: Based on leader's ability punish or recommend punishment. follow orders to avoid punishments.	to People

- Legitimate
- Reward
- Coercive

- Expert
- Referent

Hard (Position) Power   Soft (Personal) Power

Electric, considers himself a failure if he exercises his formal authority more than seven or eight times a year. The rest of the time, Immelt is using softer means to persuade and influence others and to resolve conflicting ideas and opinions.[27] Even the United States military is talking about the importance of building relationships rather than using brute force. Defense Secretary Robert Gates, for instance, says that in the battle for hearts and minds abroad, the United States has to be "good at listening to others" rather than just good at kicking down doors, and the Army's new stability operations field manual openly talks about the value of soft power.[28] Wesley Clark, former supreme commander of NATO who led the mission against Serb President Slobodan Milosevic, suggests that, for leaders in businesses as well as nations, building a community of shared interests should be the first choice, rather than using threats, intimidation, and raw power.[29]

Each of the five types of leader power illustrated in Exhibit 12.3 is discussed in detail in the following paragraphs.

Legitimate Power **Legitimate power** is the authority granted from a formal position in an organization. For example, once a person has been selected as a supervisor, most employees accept that they are obligated to follow his or her direction with respect to work activities. Certain rights, responsibilities, and prerogatives accrue to anyone holding a formal leadership position. Followers accept the legitimate rights of formal leaders to set goals, make decisions, and direct activities.

Legitimate power
authority granted from a formal position

Reward Power Power that stems from the authority to bestow rewards on other people is called **reward power**. For example, appointed leaders may have access to formal rewards, such as pay increases or promotions. Moreover, organizations allocate huge amounts of resources downward from top leaders. Leaders control resources and their distribution. Lower-level followers depend on leaders for the financial and physical resources to perform their tasks. Leaders with reward power can use rewards to influence subordinates' behavior.

Coercive Power The opposite of reward power is **coercive power**. It refers to the power to punish or recommend punishment. Supervisors have coercive power when they have the right to fire or demote subordinates, criticize, or withdraw pay increases. For example, if a salesman does not perform as well as expected, the sales manager has the coercive power to criticize him, reprimand him, put a negative letter in his file, and hurt his chance for a raise. Coercive power is the negative side of legitimate and reward power.

Expert Power Power resulting from a leader's special knowledge or skill regarding tasks performed by followers is referred to as **expert power**. When a leader is a true expert, subordinates go along with recommendations because of his or her superior knowledge. Leaders at supervisory levels often have experience in the production process that gains them promotion. At top management levels, however, leaders may lack expert power because subordinates know more about technical details than they do. People throughout the organization with expertise and knowledge can use it to influence or place limits on decisions made by people above them in the organization.[30]

Referent Power This kind of power comes from leader personality characteristics that command followers' identification, respect, and admiration so they want to emulate the leader. When workers admire a supervisor because of the way he or she deals with them, the influence is based on referent power. **Referent power** depends on the leader's personal characteristics rather than on a formal title or position and is especially visible in the area of charismatic leadership. For example, Steve Jobs clearly has strong position power as CEO of Apple, but it is referent power and expert power that make him one of the most famous and most powerful leaders in the world.

Action Memo

As a leader, you can expand your personal power by developing good relationships and acquiring advanced knowledge and experience. You can use power to gain the commitment of others to achieve the vision. Use position power when appropriate, but don't overdo it.

IN THE LEAD

Steve Jobs, Apple

He has been called a "narcissistic perfectionist with a volcanic temper." He has also been referred to as a "master communicator," "the model of a charismatic leader," "a tantalizingly elusive figure," and "one of the greatest business leaders of all time."

If any business leader commands a rock star–like following, it is Steve Jobs. In 1982, Jobs (scruffily bearded and riding his bike to work) appeared in a *National Geographic* photo-essay about the microchip revolution. His personality was portrayed as symbolic of a culture that would change the world. Decades later, Apple employees, customers, and the press still can't get enough of Jobs. The tale of how he dropped out of college, cofounded Apple, got fired from his own company, returned years later to save it, and then transformed it by creating a whole new business with the iPod and iPhone is the stuff of legend. He is famously secretive about his personal life, but thousands of news articles pry into it, such as when he took a leave of absence for undisclosed health reasons in 2009 (the world later learned that Jobs had a liver transplant).

Reward power
authority to bestow rewards on other people

Coercive power
authority to punish or recommend punishment

Expert power
authority resulting from a leader's special knowledge or skill

Referent power
authority based on personality characteristics that command followers' attention, respect, and admiration so that they want to emulate the leader

Despite his unpredictable temper, many people inside and outside of Apple admire and respect—some would say *worship*—Steve Jobs. They tell their "Steve-Jobs-yelled-in-my-face" stories with pride. His energizing personality and his refusal to "sell out" make people want to be around him and want to be *like* him. Indeed, one magazine article commented that the amazing staff loyalty he inspires has turned Apple into "Steve Jobs with a thousand lives." In addition, Jobs has proved that he is both a technological wizard and a master of innovation and insight into customer needs, giving him expert as well as referent power.[31]

Charismatic leadership, such as that of Steve Jobs, is intensely based on the relationship between leader and followers and relies heavily on either referent or expert power. However, all good leaders make use of these types of power rather than using position power alone. The *Consider This* box talks about the far-reaching impact of referent power.

Follower Responses to the Use of Power

Leaders use the various types of power to influence others to do what is necessary to accomplish organizational goals. The success of any attempt to influence is a matter of degree, but there are three distinct outcomes that may result from the use of power: compliance, resistance, and commitment, as illustrated in Exhibit 12.4.[32]

When people successfully use hard, position power (legitimate, reward, coercive), the response is compliance. **Compliance** means that people follow the directions of the person with power, whether or not they agree with those directions. They will obey orders and carry out instructions even though they may not like it. The problem is that in many cases, followers do just enough work as is necessary to satisfy the leader and may not contribute their full potential. Recall our earlier definition of *observers* in the discussion of coalitional leadership. These people don't actively resist or sabotage the leader's efforts, but

Consider **This!**
The Ripple Effect

Do you want to be a positive influence in the world? First, get your own life in order. Ground yourself in this single principle so that your behavior is wholesome and effective. If you do that, you will earn respect and be a powerful influence.

Your behavior influences others through a ripple effect. A ripple effect works because everyone influences everyone else. Powerful people are powerful influences.

If your life works, you influence your family.

If your family works, your family influences the community.

If your community works, your community influences the nation.

If your nation works, your nation influences the world.

If your world works, the ripple effect spreads throughout the cosmos.

Source: John Heider, *The Tao of Leadership: Leadership Strategies for a New Age* (New York: Bantam Books, 1985), p. 107. Copyright 1985 Humanic Ltd., Atlanta, GA. Used with permission.

Compliance
following the directions of the person with power, regardless of how much agreement there is with that person's directions

Exhibit 12.4 Responses to the Use of Power

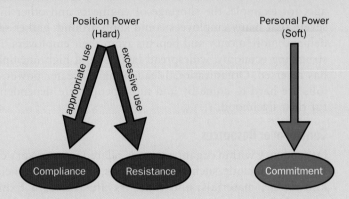

they don't fully participate in achieving the vision. However, if the use of hard power, especially the use of coercion, exceeds a level people consider legitimate, some followers will actively resist the attempt to influence. **Resistance** means that employees will deliberately try to avoid carrying out instructions or they will attempt to disobey orders. Thus, the effectiveness of leaders who rely solely on position power is limited.

The follower response most often generated by soft, personal, and interpersonal power (expert, referent) is commitment. People become *partners* or *advocates,* rather than resisters or observers, as defined earlier. **Commitment** means that followers adopt the leader's viewpoint and enthusiastically carry out instructions. Needless to say, commitment is preferred to compliance or resistance. Although compliance alone may be enough for routine matters, commitment is particularly important when the leader is promoting change. Change carries risk or uncertainty, and follower commitment helps to overcome fear and resistance associated with change efforts. Successful leaders exercise both personal and position power to influence others.

Sources of Leader Power

The five types of power provide a basis for much of a leader's influence. In organizations, however, additional sources of power and influence have been identified.[33]

Dependency

You probably know from personal experience that when a person has control over something that others want and need, that person is quite powerful. People in organizations, as elsewhere, gain power when others depend on them—for information, resources, cooperation, and so forth. The more people depend on someone, the greater that person's power.[34] For instance, an executive assistant who has control over access to the CEO may have more power than a vice president because people depend on her to get their views heard by the top leader.

Organizational leaders have power over employees to some extent because people depend on them for their jobs. However, the nature of dependency relationships between leaders and subordinates in organizations fluctuates depending on economic circumstances. When unemployment is low and jobs

Resistance
the act of disobeying orders or deliberately avoiding carrying out instructions

Commitment
adopting the leader's viewpoint and enthusiastically carrying out instructions

are plentiful, people feel less dependent on their supervisors, and managers are more dependent on employees because they are hard to replace. Only a few years ago, for example, the shortage of engineers and other high-tech talent was so severe that many employees could shop around, gather several offers, and then demand more money and benefits from their employers.[35] Not so today. With a struggling economy, widespread layoffs, and high unemployment, the situation has reversed. Organizational leaders have greater power over workers because jobs are hard to come by and most people are dependent on the organization for their livelihood.

Control over Resources

Dependency within organizations is related to a person's control over resources. Resources include such things as jobs, rewards, financial support, expertise, knowledge, materials, and time. As illustrated in Exhibit 12.5, people are more dependent—therefore leaders and organizations have more control and power—when resources are high on three characteristics—importance, scarcity, and nonsubstitutability.[36] People in the organization must perceive the resource to be *important*—that is, if nobody wants what you've got, it is not going to create dependency. Resources can be important for a variety of reasons. For example, they may be essential elements of a key product, they may directly generate sales, or they may be critical to reducing or avoiding uncertainty for the organization's top decision makers. Chief information officers have gained a tremendous amount of power in many organizations because of the critical role of IT for both business and nonprofit organizations. Similarly, ethics and compliance officers are highly powerful today because they help reduce uncertainty for top leaders concerning ethical lapses and financial malfeasance.

Scarcity refers to whether the resource is easy or difficult to obtain. A resource that is difficult or expensive to acquire is more valuable and creates more dependency than one that is widely available. Leaders and employees with specialized knowledge illustrate this aspect of dependency. In traditional companies moving

Exhibit 12.5 Characteristics That Affect Dependency and Power in Organizations

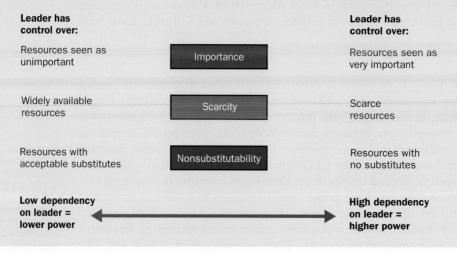

Leader has control over:		Leader has control over:
Resources seen as unimportant	Importance	Resources seen as very important
Widely available resources	Scarcity	Scarce resources
Resources with acceptable substitutes	Nonsubstitutability	Resources with no substitutes
Low dependency on leader = lower power	⟵————————⟶	**High dependency on leader = higher power**

toward e-business, some young Internet-savvy managers have gained power over senior leaders who have little computer expertise.

The third characteristic, *nonsubstitutability*, means that leaders or employees with control over resources with no viable substitute will have more power. A somewhat amusing example comes from Evan Steingart's consumer products company. A low-level inventory-transfer clerk had to sign off on the shipment of all goods. Arrogant salespeople who felt they were "above" the clerk and treated him badly would find themselves at a disadvantage, as the clerk would have a long list of things to do before he could get to their shipping order, and the salespeople had no recourse but to wait.[37]

Control over Information

One critical resource in organizations is information. Despite the trend toward empowerment and broader information sharing, the fact remains that some people will almost always have access to more information than others. Furthermore, they can withhold or divulge this information in ways designed to achieve their desired outcomes.[38] As a negative illustration of this, financial aid leaders at some colleges and universities received "consultant fees," tuition reimbursement, and other perks from several student-loan companies in exchange for providing information that recommended those companies over others to students. The financial aid directors had control of information about various lending agencies, and they could choose to disclose information and shape student decisions that best served their own personal interests. On a more positive note, Attorney General Andrew Cuomo selectively released information to the public as he began investigating the allegations, thereby influencing big banks and colleges to come clean by admitting the sweetheart deals and spurring legislation to protect students from conflicts of interest.[39]

Control over information—which involves both access to information and control over how and to whom it is distributed—is an important source of power for leaders. To some extent, access to information is determined by a person's position in the organization. Top leaders typically have access to more information than do lower-level supervisors or other employees. They can release information selectively to influence others and shape actions and decisions. However, control over information can also be a source of power for lower-level leaders and employees. Employees who have exclusive access to information needed by leaders to make decisions gain power as a result. For example, top executives may be dependent on the production manager for analyzing and interpreting complex operations data.

Action Memo

As a leader, you can gain power by gaining control over resources and increasing your knowledge. You can use information to shape decisions and actions, and stay alert to ways you can help the organization cope with critical uncertainties.

Increasing Power Through Political Activity

Acquiring and using power is largely a political process. **Politics** involves activities to acquire, develop, and use power and other resources to obtain desired future outcomes when there is uncertainty or disagreement about choices.[40] Politically skillful leaders strive to understand others' viewpoints, needs, desires, and goals, and use their understanding to influence people to act in ways that help the leader accomplish his or her goals for the team or organization.[41]

For example, leaders at most organizations engage in some degree of political activity aimed at influencing government policies, because government choices

Politics
activities to acquire, develop, and use power and other resources to obtain desired future outcomes when there is uncertainty or disagreement about choices

represent a critical source of uncertainty for businesses as well as nonprofit organizations.[42] Consider proposed federal legislation that will allow government oversight of many kinds of exotic financial instruments, such as credit default swaps, that were a major cause of the recent financial crisis. Although most people agree some level of regulation is needed, leaders at finance companies will likely be lobbying to insure that the reforms "preserve the widespread availability of swaps and other important risk management tools," as the CEO of one trade group put it.[43]

Individuals also engage in political activity within organizations. Although some people have a negative view of politics, the appropriate use of political behavior serves organizational goals. Politics is a natural process for resolving differences among organizational interest groups.[44] Political behavior can be either a positive or negative force. Uncertainty and conflict are natural in organizations, and politics is the mechanism for accomplishing things that can't be handled purely through formal policies or position power.

Leader Frames of Reference

The appropriate use of power and politics to get things done is an important aspect of leadership. Before exploring political tactics, let's consider leadership frames of reference and how a political approach combines with other leadership philosophies.

A **frame** is a perspective from which a leader views the world, and it influences how the leader interacts with followers, makes decisions, and exercises power. Four leader frames of reference illustrated in Exhibit 12.6 are structural, human resource, political, and symbolic.[45] Leaders often begin with a limited structural perspective and develop the other frames as they mature and climb higher in their leadership development, thus achieving a more balanced mindset and approach.

Frame
a perspective from which a leader views the world; influences how the leader interacts with followers, makes decisions, and exercises power

The Structural Frame The organization as a machine is the dominant image in the structural frame of reference. Leaders strive for machine-like efficiency and value

Exhibit 12.6 Four Leader Frames of Reference

1. Structural
Mindset: Sees organization as machine, economics, plans
Emphasis: Goals, systems, efficiency, formal authority

2. Human Resource
Mindset: Sees organization as family, belonging, clan
Emphasis: People, relationships, engagement

3. Political
Mindset: Sees organization as jungle, power, schemes
Emphasis: Resource allocation, negotiation, coalition building

4. Symbolic
Mindset: Sees organization as theater, spiritual meaning, dreams
Emphasis: Vision, culture & values, inspiration

Source: Based on Lee G. Bolman and Terrence E. Deal, *Reframing Organizations* (San Francisco: Jossey-Bass, 1991); and L. G. Bolman and T. E. Deal, "Leadership and Management Effectiveness: A Multi-Frame, Multi-Sector Analysis," *Human Resource Management* 30, no. 4 (Winter 1991), pp. 509–534. Thanks to Roy Williams for suggesting the stair sequence.

hard data and analysis for decision making. The **structural frame** places emphasis on plans, goal setting, and clarifying expectations as a way to provide order, efficiency, and stability. Leaders rely heavily on the power and authority granted through their organizational position to influence others (position power), and they emphasize clear job descriptions, rules and procedures, and administrative systems. This frame views the organization as a rational system and strives for clarity of direction and control of results.

The Human Resource Frame According to the **human resource frame**, people are the organization's most valuable resource. This frame defines problems and issues in interpersonal terms and looks for ways to adjust the organization to meet human needs. Leaders do not rely solely on their position power to exert influence. Instead, they focus on relationships and often lead through empowerment and engagement. Leaders use the human resource perspective to involve followers and give them opportunities for personal and professional development. The images in this view are a sense of family, belonging, and the organization as a clan.

The Political Frame The **political frame** views organizations as arenas of ongoing conflict or tension over the allocation of scarce resources. Leaders spend their time networking and building coalitions to influence decisions and actions. As with the coalitional leadership style we discussed earlier in this chapter, leaders with this frame of reference strive to build a power base and they use both position and personal power to achieve desired results. The mindset in the political frame is to be aware of the organization as a jungle. Power and politics are considered a natural and healthy part of organizational life.

Action Memo

Use each of the structural, human resource, political, and symbolic frames of reference to maximize your leadership effectiveness. Complete the questionnaire in Leader's Self-Insight 12.3 to understand your dominant frame.

The Symbolic Frame To use full leadership potential requires that leaders also develop a fourth frame of reference—the **symbolic frame**—in which leaders perceive the organization as a system of shared meaning and values. Rather than relying only on the use of formal power or the use of political tactics, leaders focus on shared vision, culture, and values to influence others. The dominant image is to see the organization as theater. Leaders are concerned with spirit and meaning, and they focus on harnessing followers' dreams and emotions for the benefit of the organization and all of its people.

Each of the four frames of reference provides significant possibilities for enhancing leadership effectiveness, but each is incomplete. Many new leaders have not yet developed a political frame. Leaders can first understand their own natural frame, recognize its limitations, and then learn to integrate multiple frames to achieve their full leadership potential.

Political Tactics for Asserting Leader Influence

A leader's power is useless unless it is applied to influence others to implement decisions, facilitate change, and accomplish goals, which requires both skill and willingness. The Leader's Bookshelf describes a few strategies leaders can apply when they need to influence people to change their behavior. Not all attempts to use power result in actual influence. Some power moves are rejected by followers, particularly if they are seen to be self-serving. Leaders have to determine the best approach for using their power—that is, the approach that is most likely to influence others—by considering the individuals, groups, and situations

Structural frame
a leader frame of reference that places emphasis on planning, setting goals, and clarifying expectations as a way to provide order, efficiency, and stability

Human resource frame
a leader frame of reference that defines problems and issues in interpersonal terms and looks for ways to adjust the organization to meet human needs

Political frame
a leader frame of reference that views the organization as an arena of conflict or tension over the allocation of scarce resources

Symbolic frame
a leader frame of reference that perceives the organization as a system of shared meaning and focuses on shared vision, culture, and values to influence others

Leader's Self-Insight 12.3
Your Leadership Orientation

This questionnaire asks you to describe yourself as a leader. For each of the following items, give the number "4" to the phrase that best describes you, "3" to the item that is next best, and on down to "1" for the item that is least like you.

1. My strongest skills are:
   _____ a. Analytical skills
   _____ b. Interpersonal skills
   _____ c. Political skills
   _____ d. Flair for drama
2. The best way to describe me is:
   _____ a. Technical expert
   _____ b. Good listener
   _____ c. Skilled negotiator
   _____ d. Inspirational leader
3. What has helped me the most to be successful is my ability to:
   _____ a. Make good decisions
   _____ b. Coach and develop people
   _____ c. Build strong alliances and a power base
   _____ d Inspire and excite others
4. What people are most likely to notice about me is my:
   _____ a. Attention to detail
   _____ b. Concern for people
   _____ c. Ability to succeed in the face of conflict and opposition
   _____ d. Charisma
5. My most important leadership trait is:
   _____ a. Clear, logical thinking
   _____ b. Caring and support for others
   _____ c. Toughness and aggressiveness
   _____ d. Imagination and creativity
6. I am best described as:
   _____ a. An analyst
   _____ b. A humanist
   _____ c. A politician
   _____ d. A visionary

Scoring and Interpretation

Compute your scores as follows:

Structural = 1a + 2a + 3a + 4a + 5a + 6a =

_____

Human Resource = 1b + 2b + 3b + 4b + 5b + 6b =

_____

Political = 1c + 2c + 3c + 4c + 5c + 6c =

_____

Symbolic = 1d + 2d + 3d + 4d + 5d + 6d =

_____

Your answers reveal your preference for four distinct leader orientations or frames of reference. The higher your score, the greater your preference. A low score may mean a blind spot. "Structural" means to view the organization as a machine that operates with efficiency to be successful. "Human Resource" means to view the organization primarily as people and to treat the family well to succeed. "Political" means to view the organizations as a competition for resources and the need to build alliances to succeed. "Symbolic" means to view the organization as a system of shared meaning and values and to succeed by shaping the culture.

Do you view politics in a positive or negative light? Most new leaders succeed first by using either or both of the structural or people orientations. New leaders often have a blind spot about politics. As managers move up the hierarchy, they learn to be more political or they miss out on key decisions. The symbolic view usually comes last in a leader's development. Compare your scores to other students and see which orientations are more widely held.

Source: © 1988, Leadership Frameworks, 440 Boylston Street, Brookline, Massachusetts 02146. All rights reserved. Used with permission.

involved.[46] In addition, they understand the basic principles that can cause people to change their behavior or attitudes.

Leaders frequently use a combination of influence strategies, and people who use a wider variety of tactics are typically perceived as having greater power and influence. One survey of a few hundred leaders identified more than 4,000 different techniques by which these people were able to influence others to do what the

marble: © Ioannis Drimilis   library: www.istockphoto.com/nikada

Leader's Bookshelf

Influencer: The Power to Change Anything
by Kerry Patterson, Joseph Grenny, David Maxfield, Ron McMillan, and Al Switzler

Leaders face a challenge every day in trying to get people to do what needs to be done, because it often means changing people's attitudes, habits, loyalties, and ways of thinking. The authors of *Influencer: The Power to Change Anything* assert that people change only when they (1) believe it will be worth it, and (2) believe they can do what is asked of them.

How to Be a Successful Influencer

Influencer describes and illustrates six strategies leaders can use to accomplish the two requirements. "Not everyone will become influencers with a capital 'I,'" they admit, "but everyone can learn and apply the methods and strategies the world's best influencers use every day." Here are four of the strategies, two related to motivation and two related to ability:

- *Make the undesirable desirable.* Leaders need to connect with people on a personal basis to understand what they want and help them discover links between their personal goals and organizational goals. When Ralph Heath, now president of Lockheed Martin Aeronautics, had to move a new fighter jet from drawing board to production in only 18 months, he spent weeks interviewing people at all levels to understand their needs, frustrations, and aspirations. Later, people were willing to listen to him because they knew he had taken their needs and goals into account.

- *Harness peer pressure.* "When seeking influence tools that have an impact on profound and persistent problems, no resource is more powerful . . . than the persuasion of people who make up our social network," the authors write. Leaders seek out those who can influence others and make sure people feel praised, emotionally supported, and encouraged by those around them when they exhibit the desired behaviors.

- *Develop people's skills.* Good leaders make sure people have the technical, interpersonal, and emotional skills and abilities they need to enact the new behaviors. To build confidence, leaders break large challenges into discrete parts, with clear achievable goals for each part. They provide rapid feedback to alleviate fear and uncertainty.

- *Change the environment.* "Given that things are far easier to change than people, and that these things can then have a permanent impact on how people behave," the authors suggest that leaders change the physical environment to enhance people's ability to change. Emery Air Freight pioneered the idea of using sturdy, reusable, uniform-sized containers, but leaders couldn't get employees to fill them properly. A simple change—drawing a "Fill to Here" line on the inside of every container—solved the problem.

Practical Application and Support

Compelling case studies from business, health care, social science, and other disciplines are woven throughout to illustrate how each of the strategies can be applied to real problems. In addition, the authors provide a list of additional tools and resources for those who want to strengthen their influence skills.

Influencer: The Power to Change Anything, by Kerry Patterson, Joseph Grenny, David Maxfield, Ron McMillan, and Al Switzler, is published by McGraw-Hill.

leader wanted.[47] However, the myriad successful influence tactics used by leaders fall into basic categories of influence actions. Exhibit 12.7 lists seven principles for asserting leader influence. Notice that most of these involve the use of soft, personal power, rather than relying solely on hard, position power or the use of rewards and punishments.

1. *Use rational persuasion.* Perhaps the most frequently used influence tactic is rational persuasion, which means using facts, data, and logical arguments to persuade others that a proposed idea or request is the best way to complete a task or accomplish a desired goal. It can be effective whether

Exhibit 12.7 Seven Principles for Asserting Leader Influence

1. Use rational persuasion.
2. Make people like you.
3. Rely on the rule of reciprocity.
4. Develop allies.
5. Ask for what you want.
6. Remember the principle of scarcity.
7. Extend formal authority with expertise and credibility.

the influence attempt is directed upward toward superiors, downward toward subordinates, or horizontally, because most people have faith in facts and analysis.[48] Rational persuasion is most effective when a leader has technical knowledge and expertise related to the issue (expert power), although referent power is also used. Frequently, some parts of a rational argument cannot be backed up with facts and figures, so people have to believe in the leader's credibility to accept his or her argument.

2. *Make people like you.* We all know it's easier to say yes to someone we like than to someone we don't like.[49] One author of a book on influence tells a story about an American working in Saudi Arabia, who learned that getting information or action from government offices was easy when he'd drop by, drink tea, and chat for awhile.[50] Cultural values in Saudi Arabia put great emphasis on personal relationships, but people in all cultures respond to friendliness and consideration. When a leader shows concern for others, demonstrates trust and respect, and treats people fairly, people are more likely to want to help and support the leader by doing what he or she asks. In addition, most people will like a leader who makes them feel good about themselves. Leaders never underestimate the importance of praise.

3. *Rely on the rule of reciprocity.* A primary way to turn power into influence is to share what you have—whether it be time, resources, services, or emotional support. There is much research indicating that most people feel a sense of obligation to give something back in return for favors others do for them.[51] This is one reason that organizations like Northrup Grumman, Kraft Foods, and Pfizer make donations to the favorite charities of House and Senate members. Leaders attempt to curry favor with lawmakers whose decisions can significantly affect their business.[52] The "unwritten law of reciprocity" means that leaders who do favors for others can expect others to do favors for them in return. Leaders also elicit the cooperative and sharing behavior they want from others by first demonstrating it with their own actions.[53] Some researchers argue that the concept of exchange—trading something of value for what you want—is the basis of all other influence tactics. For example, rational persuasion works because the other person sees a benefit from going along with the plan, and making people like you is successful because the other person receives liking and attention in return.[54]

4. *Develop allies.* Reciprocity also plays an important role in developing networks of allies, people who can help the leader accomplish his or

Action Memo

As a leader, you can use political activity to achieve important organizational goals when there is uncertainty or disagreement about choices. You can develop connections with powerful people by volunteering for difficult projects and serving on committees.

her goals. Leaders can influence others by taking the time to talk with followers and other leaders outside of formal meetings to understand their needs and concerns, as well as to explain problems and describe the leader's point of view.[55] Leaders consult with one another and reach a meeting of minds about a proposed decision, change, or strategy.[56] A leader can expand his or her network of allies by reaching out to establish contact with additional people. Some leaders expand their networks through the hiring, transfer, and promotion process. Identifying and placing in key positions people who are sympathetic to the desired outcomes of the leader can help achieve the leader's goals.

One study found that political skill, particularly network-building, has a positive impact on both followers' perceptions of a leader's abilities and performance as well as on the actual, objective performance of the work unit.[57] Sheila Bair, chair of the Federal Deposit Insurance Corporation, has enhanced her reputation and power base by courting allies to support her views on how to fix the troubled U.S. financial system.

IN THE LEAD

Sheila Bair, Federal Deposit Insurance Corporation

As chair of the Federal Deposit Insurance Corporation (FDIC), Sheila Bair has emerged as one of the most powerful, as well as the most courageous, people in Washington. She was one of the first to propose helping distressed homeowners and stop foreclosures with loan modifications and has stood her ground against intense criticism. Her strong lobbying efforts have given the FDIC and Bair increasing power. "She very likely will be the only agency head to come out of this crisis with an enhanced reputation," said Carmen Fine, president and chief executive of the Independent Community Bankers of America. When her term as chair expires in 2011, Bair will likely be well positioned for another high-level job. *Forbes* magazine ranked her the second-most powerful woman in the world, behind only German Chancellor Angela Merkel.

Bair is a skilled politician who first learned the value of developing allies when she worked for former U.S. Senate Majority Leader Robert Dole. People who have negotiated with her say she is always willing to listen. "We don't always agree," said Carmen Fine, "but her door has always been open and she consults with everyone."

Although Washington regulators try to present a united front, sources have said that behind the scenes Bair and U.S. Treasury Secretary Timothy Geithner disagree strongly over how to fix the financial mess. Bair has developed steadfast allies within the Obama administration, and even some people who once called for ousting her as FDIC chair have allegedly swung their support her way. "Eventually, Sheila will be the way we go," said Christopher Whalen, head of consulting firm Institutional Risk Analytics. "She could eventually be the next Secretary of the Treasury."[58]

---

5. *Ask for what you want.* Sheila Bair also employs another technique for influencing people, which is to be clear about what you want and openly ask for it. Even opponents praise her knack for being forceful at the right times in order to achieve her goals. Bair has obtained greater power for the FDIC partly because she clearly asked for it. If leaders do not ask, they seldom receive. Political activity is effective only when the leader's vision, goals, and desired changes are made explicit so the organization can respond. Leaders can use their courage to be assertive, saying what

they believe to persuade others. An explicit proposal may be accepted simply because other people have no better alternatives. Also, an explicit proposal for change or for a specific decision alternative will often receive favorable treatment when other options are less well defined. Effective political behavior requires sufficient forcefulness and risk-taking to at least try to achieve desired outcomes.[59]

6. *Remember the principle of scarcity.* This principle means that people usually want more of what they can't have. When things are less available, they become more desirable. An interesting dissertation study on the purchase decisions of wholesale beef buyers found that buyers more than doubled their orders when they were told that because of weather conditions there was likely to be a scarcity of foreign beef in the near future. Interestingly, though, their orders increased 600 percent when they were informed that no one else had that information yet.[60] Retailers often use this principle by sending advance notice of sales to credit card holders, making them feel they're getting information that the general shopping public doesn't have. Leaders can learn to frame their requests or offers in such a way as to highlight the unique benefits and exclusive information being provided. One approach is to selectively release information that is not broadly available and that supports the leaders' ideas or proposals. Letting people know they're getting a sneak peak at information captures their interest and makes them more likely to support the leader's position.

Action Memo

As a leader, you can influence others by using rational persuasion, developing allies, and expanding your expertise and credibility. Remember that people respond to friendliness and consideration, and they typically feel obligated to return favors.

7. *Extend formal authority with expertise and credibility.* The final principle for asserting influence is the leader's legitimate authority in the organization. Legitimate authorities are in a position to be particularly influential. However, research has found that the key to successful use of formal authority is to be knowledgeable, credible, and trustworthy. Leaders who become known for their expertise, who are honest and straightforward with others, and who develop relationships and inspire trust can exert greater influence than those who simply try to issue orders.[61] In addition, effective leaders keep the six previous influence principles in mind, realizing that influence depends primarily on personal rather than position power.

Leaders can use an understanding of these tactics to assert influence and get things done. When leaders ignore political tactics, they may find themselves failing without understanding why. For example, at the World Bank, Paul Wolfowitz tried to wield power without building the necessary relationships he needed to assert influence.

IN THE LEAD

Paul Wolfowitz, World Bank

After former Deputy Secretary of Defense Paul Wolfowitz lost his bids to become defense secretary or national security advisor in the Bush administration, he jumped at the chance to be the new president of World Bank. But Wolfowitz doomed his career at World Bank from the start by failing to develop relationships and build alliances.

Most World Bank leaders had been in their positions for many years when Wolfowitz arrived, and they were accustomed to "promoting each other's interests and scratching each other's backs," as one board member put it. Wolfowitz came in and tried to assert his own ideas, goals, and formal authority without considering the interests, ideas, and goals of others. He quickly alienated much of the World Bank leadership team and board by adopting a single-minded position on key issues and refusing to consider alternative views. Rather than attempting to persuade others to his way of thinking, Wolfowitz issued directives to senior bank officers, either personally or through his handpicked managers. Several high-level officers resigned following disputes with the new president.

Eventually, the board asked for Wolfowitz's resignation. "What Paul didn't understand is that the World Bank presidency is not inherently a powerful job," said one former colleague. "A bank president is successful only if he can form alliances with the bank's many fiefdoms. Wolfowitz didn't ally with those fiefdoms. He alienated them."[62]

Wolfowitz realized too late that he needed to use a political approach rather than trying to force his own agenda. Even when a leader has a great deal of power, political tactics are more effective than force for turning power into influence.

Ethical Considerations in Using Power and Politics

Harry Truman once said that leadership is the ability to get people to do what they don't want to do and like it.[63] His statement raises an important issue: Leadership is an opportunity to use power and influence to accomplish important organizational goals, but power can also be abused.

One consideration is the difference between *personalized* leaders and *socialized* leaders.[64] This distinction refers primarily to the leader's approach to the use of power.[65] Personalized leaders are typically selfish, impulsive, and exercise power for their own self-centered needs and interests rather than for the good of the organization. Socialized leaders exercise power in the service of higher goals that will benefit others and the organization as a whole. Personalized leaders are characterized as self-aggrandizing, nonegalitarian, and exploitative, whereas socialized leaders are empowering, egalitarian, and supportive. Personalized behavior is based on caring about self; socialized behavior is based on valuing others.

> **Action Memo**
>
> As a leader, you can be ethical in your use of power and politics. You can build long-term productive relationships to achieve important goals and benefit the entire team or organization.

A specific area in which the unethical use of power is of increasing concern for organizations is sexual harassment. People in organizations depend on one another—and especially on leaders—for many resources, including information, cooperation, and even their jobs. When access to resources seems to depend on granting sexual favors or putting up with sexually intimidating or threatening comments, the person in a dependent position is being personally violated, whether or not the leader actually withholds the resources. Partly in response to pressures from the courts, many organizations are developing policies and procedures that protect individuals from sexual harassment on the job and offer mechanisms for reporting complaints. Sexual harassment is not just unethical; it is illegal, and it is a clear abuse of power.

However, there are many other situations in organizations that are not so clear-cut, and leaders may sometimes have difficulty differentiating ethical from unethical uses of power and politics. Exhibit 12.8 summarizes some criteria that can guide ethical actions. First and foremost is the question of whether the action is motivated by self-interest or whether it is consistent with the organization's goals. One Internet company has a rule that any employee

Exhibit 12.8 Guidelines for Ethical Action

| Is the action consistent with the organization's goals, rather than being motivated purely by self-interest? | Does the action respect the rights of individuals and groups affected by it? | Does the action meet the standards of fairness and equity? | Would you wish others to behave in the same way if the action affected you? | Ethical Choice |

Sources: Based on G. F. Cavanaugh, D. J. Mobert, and M. Valasques, "The Ethics of Organizational Politics," *Academy of Management Journal,* (June 1981), pp. 363–374; and Stephen P. Robbins, *Organizational Behavior,* 8th ed. (Upper Saddle River, NJ: Prentice Hall, 1998), p. 422.

can be terminated for a political act that is in the individual's own self-interest rather than in the interest of the company, or that harms another person in the organization.[66] Once a leader answers this primary question, there are several other questions that can help determine whether a potential influence action is ethical, including whether it respects the rights of individuals and groups affected by it, whether it meets the standards of fairness, and whether the leader would want others to behave in the same way. If a leader answers these questions honestly, they can serve as a guide to whether an intended act is ethical.

In the complex world of organizations, there will always be situations that are difficult to interpret. The most important point is for leaders to be aware of the ethical responsibilities of having power and take care to use their power to help rather than harm others. Leaders should think not in terms of getting their own way, but rather in terms of building long-term productive relationships that can achieve goals and benefit the entire organization.

Leadership Essentials

■ This chapter looked at how leaders use power and political processes to influence others and get things done. Three types of influential leadership that rely strongly on a leader's personal characteristics and relationships are transformational, charismatic, and coalitional leadership. Charismatic leaders have an emotional impact on people. They create an atmosphere of change, articulate an idealized vision of the future, inspire faith and hope, and frequently incur personal risks to influence followers. Transformational leaders also create an atmosphere of change, and they inspire followers not just to follow them personally but also to believe in the vision. Transformational leaders inspire followers to go beyond their own self-interest for the good of the whole. Coalitional leadership involves developing a coalition of people who can help influence others to implement the leader's decisions and achieve the leader's desired goals. To have broad influence, leaders develop relationships with others, listen to others' needs and goals, and promote cooperation.

■ All leaders use power and politics to influence people and accomplish goals. Power is the ability to influence others to reach desired outcomes. The best-known types of power are legitimate, reward, expert, referent, and coercive, which are associated with a leader's position and personal qualities. Three distinct outcomes may result from the use of power: compliance, resistance, and commitment. The effective use of position power generally leads to follower compliance, whereas the excessive use of position power—particularly coercive power—may result in resistance. The follower response most often generated by personal power is commitment.

- A key aspect of power is that it is a function of dependency, which is related to a person's control over resources and control over information. Dependency is greatest for resources that are highly important, scarce, and have no readily available substitutes.

- Power is acquired, developed, and exercised through political activities. Having a political perspective on the organization is important, because leaders need to use politics to accomplish important goals. A political perspective can be combined with other leader frames of reference. Frames of reference influence how the leader interacts with followers, makes decisions, and exercises power. Four leader frames of reference are structural, human resource, political, and symbolic. Leaders typically begin with a structural frame and develop other frames of reference as they mature in their leadership responsibilities and understanding.

- Leaders use a wide variety of influence tactics, but they fall within some broad categories based on general principles for asserting influence. Seven principles for asserting leader influence are rational persuasion, liking and friendliness, reciprocity, developing allies, direct appeal, scarcity, and formal authority. One important consideration for leaders is how to use power and politics ethically and responsibly. Ethical leaders use power to serve the organization's goals, respect the rights of individuals and groups, and strive to be fair in their dealings with others.

Discussion Questions

1. Lord Acton, a British historian of the late 19th century, said that "power tends to corrupt; absolute power corrupts absolutely," suggesting that a person's sense of morality lessens as his or her power increases. Do you agree? Considering this idea, is it ethical for leaders to try to increase their power? Discuss.

2. What do you consider the most important difference between transformational leadership and transactional leadership? Between transformational and charismatic leadership? How is transformational leadership similar to charismatic leadership?

3. Assume you are on a search committee to replace the CEO of a large financial services firm like Citigroup. Which do you think would be more valuable for a new top leader trying to solve the problems within that organization—charismatic, transformational, or coalitional leadership? What about for a new top leader of a small private university? Discuss.

4. Which of the four organizational frames of reference do you most admire? How do you think this frame of reference could be beneficial or detrimental to your leadership capability?

5. A recent magazine article suggested that young college graduates just entering the workforce are refusing to "play the political game." Why might this be the case? If politics is important for getting things done, can these people succeed as leaders? Discuss.

6. Which types of power would you rely on to implement an important decision quickly? Which types would you consider most valuable for sustaining power over the long term?

7. How does control over information give power to a person? Have you ever used control over information to influence a decision with friends or coworkers? Explain.

8. Describe ways in which you might increase your personal power.

9. Which of the seven influence tactics would you be most comfortable with as leader of a study group? Of a work team? Discuss.

10. A leadership observer said in an interview that most women leaders view power differently than men do and prefer a collaborative, relationship-oriented use of power. If this is the case, what does it suggest about women leaders' abilities to accomplish goals? What does it suggest about women's ability to rise to higher organizational levels? Discuss.

Leadership at Work

CIRCLE OF INFLUENCE

How do you personally try to influence others? Think carefully about how you get others to agree with you or do something you want. Watch the way you influence others in a team, at home, or during your work. Make a list of your influence tactics:

1. _____   4. _____
2. _____   5. _____
3. _____   6. _____

Of the influence and political tactics discussed in the chapter, which ones do you typically not use?

_____

_____

_____

During the next two days, your assignment is to (1) monitor the influence tactics you typically use, and (2) try one new tactic that you don't normally use. The new influence tactic you will try is:

_____

_____

Another important concept is called the *circle of influence*. Think carefully about the people who have influence *over you*. These people are your circle of influence. You may have one circle of influence at work, another at home, and others for your social life or career. Write down the people who would have some influence over you at work or school:

_____

_____

_____

This is your circle of influence.

A person's circle of influence can be important when you really want to influence that person. If someone doesn't respond to your normal influence attempts, think about identifying the individual's circle of influence—the people who have influence over him or her. You can then influence people in the "circle" as an indirect way to influence the person you want to change.

Pick an individual at work or school, or even your instructor, and plot out that person's circle of influence. List the key people you believe are in the person's circle of influence:

_____

_____

_____

How would you get more information on the person's true circle of influence?

_____

_____

_____

How can you use your knowledge of the person's circle to have influence over him/her? What are possible disadvantages of using this approach to influence someone?

In Class: The instructor can ask students to sit in small groups of three to five people and share the circles of influence they identified for themselves. After listing the circle of influence at work or school, students can also talk about the circles of people who might influence them in their professional, social, or family activities. Key questions for this discussion are: What are the common themes in the students' circles of influence? When and how could the circle idea be applied to influence someone? How might it be misapplied and backfire on your effort to influence another?

istockphoto.com/AVTG

Part 5: The Leader as Social Architect

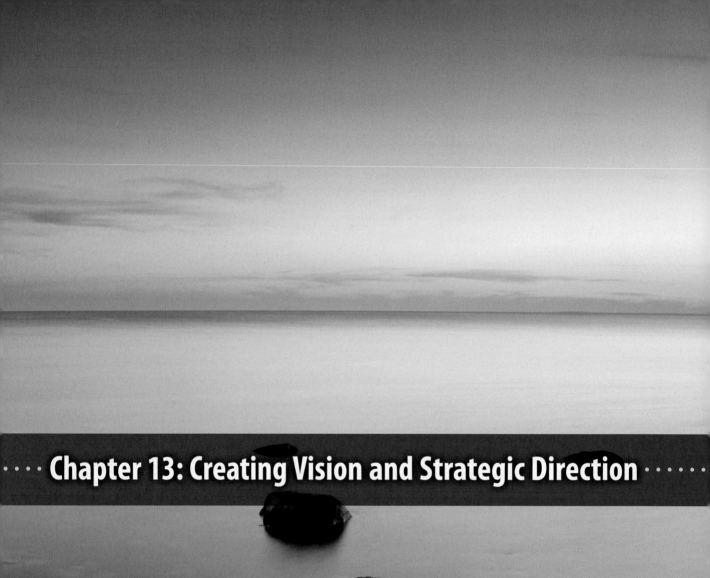

Chapter 13: Creating Vision and Strategic Direction

istockphoto.com/AVTG

Your Leadership Challenge

After reading this chapter, you should be able to:

- Explain the relationship among vision, mission, strategy, and mechanisms for execution.

- Create your personal leadership vision.

- Use the common themes of powerful visions in your life and work.

- Describe four basic approaches for framing a noble purpose that followers can believe in.

- Understand how leaders formulate and implement strategy.

- Apply the elements of effective strategy.

Chapter Outline

R ay Anderson runs a carpet company. If you were looking for an industry to blame for the destruction of our natural environment, the carpet business would rank right up there—massive consumption of fossil fuels, heavy use of water, and tons of debris going into landfills. But several years ago, Ray Anderson had a different vision: What if his company, Interface Inc., could be a model of environmental sustainability? People thought he was crazy—a carpet company a paragon of corporate environmental virtue?

Anderson bucked the conventional thinking and declared that Interface would eliminate its environmental footprint by 2020, and make money in the process. After the initial shock, customers and employees became inspired by the ambitious vision. Investors took a little longer to "see the green light," but growing sales proved Anderson was onto something. The emotional appeal of Anderson's vision stirred an almost cult-like following. Today, Interface is a leader in the industry, as well as a leader in environmental sustainability. Between 1994 and 2008, the company cut its use of fossil fuels by 45 percent and its water and landfill use by 80 percent. Sales in the last quarter before the economic slump hit were almost $300 million. The recent downturn has hurt Interface, and leaders have been forced to make some tough business decisions, including laying off 500 people and closing manufacturing operations in Belleville, Ontario.

However, Anderson points out that staying focused on the vision helped Interface weather the last downturn. When the industry lost 37 percent in sales between 2001 and 2004, Interface lost only about half that percentage, thanks in part to its focus on sustainability. Anderson is working overtime to explain the

TURBULENT TIMES

current cost-cutting decisions, listen to employees, respond to their concerns, and keep people directed toward the future.[1]

One of the most important functions of a leader is to articulate and communicate a compelling vision that will motivate and energize people toward the future. Ray Anderson's idealistic vision of sustainability inspired and energized people because employees want to work toward something greater than just making money for shareholders. Good leaders are always looking forward, setting a course for the future and getting everyone moving in the same direction. Lorraine Monroe, former principal of the renowned Frederick Douglass Academy in Harlem and founder of the Lorraine Monroe Leadership Institute, refers to a leader as "the drum major, the person who keeps a vision in front of people and reminds them of what they're about." People naturally "gravitate toward leaders who have a vision," Monroe says. "When people see that you love your work, they want to catch your energy."[2]

In this chapter, we first provide an overview of the leader's role in creating the organization's future. Then, we examine what vision is, the underlying themes that are common to effective visions, and how vision works on multiple levels. The distinction between vision and the organization's mission is also explained. We then discuss how leaders formulate vision and strategy and the leader's contribution to achieving the vision and mission.

Strategic Leadership

Superior organizational performance is not a matter of luck. It is determined largely by the choices leaders make. Top leaders are responsible for knowing the organization's environment, considering what it might be like in 5 or 10 years, and setting a direction for the future that everyone can believe in. Strategic leadership is one of the most critical issues facing organizations.[3] **Strategic leadership** means the ability to anticipate and envision the future, maintain flexibility, think strategically, and work with others to initiate changes that will create a competitive advantage for the organization in the future.[4] In a fast-changing world, leaders are faced with a bewildering array of complex and ambiguous information, and no two leaders will see things the same way or make the same choices.

The complexity of the environment and the uncertainty of the future can overwhelm a leader. Thus, many are inclined to focus on internal organizational issues rather than strategic activities. It is easier and more comforting for leaders to deal with routine, operational issues where they can see instant results and feel a sense of control. In addition, many leaders are inundated with information and overwhelmed by minutiae. They may have difficulty finding the quiet time needed for "big-picture thinking." One study looked at the time executives in various departments spend on long-term, strategic activities and found discouraging results. In the companies studied, 84 percent of finance executives' time, 70 percent of information technology executives' time, and 76 percent of operational managers' time is focused on routine, day-to-day activities.[5] Another study found that, on average, senior executives spend less than 3 percent of their energy on building a corporate perspective for the future, and in some companies, the average is less than 1 percent.[6] Yet no organization can thrive for the long term without a clear viewpoint and framework for the future.

Exhibit 13.1 illustrates the levels that make up the domain of strategic leadership. Strategic leadership is responsible for the relationship of the external environment to choices about vision, mission, strategy, and their execution.[7]

Strategic leadership
the ability to anticipate and envision the future, maintain flexibility, think strategically, and initiate changes that will create a competitive advantage for the organization in the future

Exhibit 13.1 The Domain of Strategic Leadership

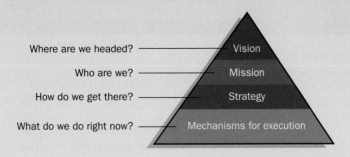

At the top of Exhibit 13.1 is a clear, compelling vision of where the organization wants to be in 5 to 10 years. A vision is an aspiration for the future and answers the question "Where are we headed?"[8] The vision works in concert with the company's mission—its core values, purpose, and reason for existence. Mission answers the question "Who are we as an organization?" The next level in Exhibit 13.1, strategy, responds to the question "How do we achieve the vision?" Strategy provides direction for translating the vision into action and is the basis for the development of specific mechanisms to help the organization achieve goals. Execution specifies "What do we do right now?" Strategies are intentions, whereas execution is through the basic organizational architecture (structure, incentives) that makes things happen. Each level of the hierarchy in Exhibit 13.1 supports the level above it. Each part of this framework will be discussed in the remainder of this chapter.

Action Memo

As a leader, you can learn to think strategically. You can anticipate and envision the future, and initiate changes that can help the group or organization thrive over the long term.

Leadership Vision

A **vision** is an attractive, ideal future that is credible yet not readily attainable. It is an ambitious view of the future that everyone involved can believe in, one that can realistically be achieved, yet one that offers a future that is better in important ways than what now exists. In the early 1950s, Sony Corporation wanted to "[b]ecome the company most known for changing the worldwide poor-quality image of Japanese products."[9] Since that time, Japanese companies have become known for quality, but in the 1950s this was a highly ambitious goal that fired people's imaginations and sense of national pride. Sometimes, visions are brief, compelling, and slogan-like, easily communicated to and understood by everyone in the organization. For example, Coca-Cola's "A Coke within arm's reach of everyone on the planet," Canon's "Beat Xerox," and Komatsu's "Encircle Caterpillar" serve to motivate all employees.

Exhibit 13.2 lists a few more brief vision statements that let people know where the organization wants to go in the future. Not all successful organizations have such short, easily communicated slogans, but their visions are powerful because leaders paint a compelling picture of where the organization wants to go. The vision expressed by civil rights leader Martin Luther King, Jr., in his "I Have a Dream" speech is a good example of how leaders paint a vision in words. King articulated a vision of racial harmony, where discrimination was nonexistent,

Vision
an attractive, ideal future that is credible yet not readily attainable

Action Memo

Go to Leader's Self-Insight 13.1 and answer the questions to learn where you stand with respect to a personal vision.

Leader's Self-Insight 13.1
My Personal Vision

How much do you think about the positive outcomes you want in your future? Do you have a personal vision for your life? Indicate whether each of the following items is Mostly False or Mostly True for you.

	Mostly False	Mostly True
1. I can describe a compelling image of my future.		
2. Life to me seems more exciting than routine.		
3. I have created very clear life goals and aims.		
4. I feel that my personal existence is very meaningful.		
5. In my life, I see a reason for being here.		
6. I have discovered a satisfying "calling" in life.		
7. I feel that I have a unique life purpose to fulfill.		
8. I will know when I have achieved my purpose.		
9. I talk to people about my personal vision.		
10. I know how to harness my creativity and use my talents.		

Scoring and Interpretation

Add the number of Mostly True answers for your score: _____. A score of 7 or above indicates that you are in great shape with respect to a personal vision. A score of 3 or below would suggest that you have not given much thought to a vision for your life. A score of 4–6 would be about average.

Creating a personal vision is difficult work for most people. It doesn't happen easily or naturally. A personal vision is just like an organizational vision in that it requires focused thought and effort. Spend some time thinking about a vision for yourself and write it down.

Source: The ideas for this questionnaire were drawn primarily from Chris Rogers, "Are You Deciding on Purpose?" *Fast Company* (February/March 1998), pp. 114–117; and J. Crumbaugh, "Cross-Validation of a Purpose-in-Life Test Based on Frankl's Concepts," *Journal of Individual Psychology* 24 (1968), pp. 74–81.

marble: © Kirill Matkov   sunset: © Marco Regalia

and he conveyed the confidence and conviction that his vision would someday be achieved.

Strong, inspiring visions have been associated with higher organizational performance and greater employee motivation and satisfaction.[10] Employees want to know where the organization is going so they know where to focus their energies. When people are encouraged by a picture of what the organization can be in the future, they can help take it there. Consider what happened at one biotechnology firm. The CEO spoke with a consultant about his inability

Exhibit 13.2   Examples of Brief Vision Statements

Apple: To make a contribution to the world by making tools for the mind that advance humankind.

Unilever: To be the foremost company meeting daily needs across the world in foods, cleaning, and personal care.

Ritz-Carlton (Amelia Island) engineering department: To boldly go where no hotel has gone before—free of all defects.

New York City Transit: No graffiti.

BP: Beyond Petroleum.

Egon Zehnder: Be the worldwide leader in executive search.

Sources: Examples from Pieter Klaas Jagersma, "Aspiration and Leadership," *Journal of Business Strategy* 28, no. 1 (2007), pp. 45–52; Jon R. Katzenbach and the RCL Team, *Real Change Leaders: How You Can Create Growth and High Performance in Your Company* (New York: Times Business, 1995), pp. 68–70; Andrew Campbell and Sally Yeung, "Creating a Sense of Mission," *Long Range Planning* (August, 1991), pp. 10–20; Alan Farnham, "State Your Values, Hold the Hot Air," *Fortune* (April 19, 1993), pp. 117–124; and Christopher K. Bart, "Sex, Lies, and Mission Statements," *Business Horizons* (November–December 1997), pp. 23–28.

to get agreement among his leadership team regarding problems and priorities. After the consultant asked about the vision for the company, the CEO realized he hadn't clearly articulated one. He took the team on an offsite meeting specifically to create a vision of where they wanted the company to go. With this vision as a guide, it was easy to resolve specific issues because everyone knew the direction.[11]

Leaders in nonprofit organizations also create visions so people know where the organization wants to go. For example, leaders at the Greater Chicago Food Depository have a vision of transforming the nonprofit agency from an organization that just feeds the hungry to one that helps end hunger. The agency sponsors an intense 12-week program aimed at teaching low-income, low-skilled workers the basics of cooking, along with life skills such as punctuality, teamwork, commitment, and personal responsibility, with the goal of landing each person a good job. Poverty is a big problem, and its causes are many and complex, but leaders know people can't begin to move up unless they have jobs. The vision of helping people change their lives has energized employees in a way that simply providing food to low-income clients never did.[12] Vision is just as important for nonprofit agencies like the Greater Chicago Food Depository, the United Way, and the Salvation Army as it is for businesses such as Coca-Cola, Google, or General Electric. Indeed, nonprofits sometimes need vision even more than do businesses, since they operate without the regular feedback provided by profit and loss.[13]

In Exhibit 13.3, vision is shown as a guiding star, drawing everyone along the same path toward the future. Vision is based in the current reality but is concerned with a future that is substantially different from the status quo.[14] Taking the group or organization along this path requires leadership. Compare this to rational management (as described in Chapter 1), which leads to the status quo.

Exhibit 13.3 The Nature of the Vision

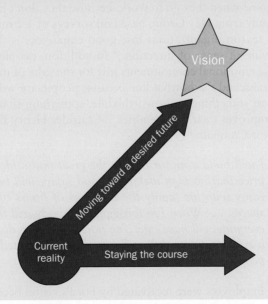

Source: Based on William D. Hitt, *The Leader–Manager: Guidelines for Action* (Columbus, OH: Battelle Press, 1988).

What Vision Does

Vision works in a number of important ways. An effective vision provides a link between today and tomorrow, serves to energize and motivate employees toward the future, provides meaning for people's work, and sets a standard of excellence and integrity in the organization.[15]

Vision Links the Present to the Future Vision connects what is going on right now with what the organization aspires to. A vision is always about the future, but it begins with the here and now. At Google, employees are guided by a vision of unifying data and information around the world, one day totally obliterating language barriers via the Internet.[16] They create services that meet current needs, but they also strive to envision and create products and services that encourage other, broader applications.

In organizations, the pressures to meet deadlines, make the big sale, solve immediate problems, and complete specific projects are very real. Some have suggested that leaders need "bifocal vision," the ability to take care of the needs of today and meet current obligations while also aiming toward dreams for the future.[17] The ability to operate on both levels can be seen in a number of successful companies, such as DuPont. Top executives routinely review short-term operational goals with managers throughout the company, reflecting a focus on the present. However, DuPont has succeeded over the long haul because of its leaders' ability to keep an eye on the future and shift gears quickly to take advantage of new opportunities. Since its beginning, DuPont's business portfolio has shifted from gunpowder to specialty chemicals, and today, the company is moving into biotechnology and life sciences.[18]

Action Memo

As a leader, you can articulate an optimistic vision for the future that will inspire and challenge people to give their best. Evaluate your potential for visionary leadership by completing the questionnaire in Leader's Self-Insight 13.2.

Vision Energizes People and Garners Commitment People want to feel enthusiastic about their work. Many people commit their time and energy voluntarily to projects they believe in—a political campaign, community events, or environmental causes, for example. These same people often leave their energy and enthusiasm at home when they go to work, because they don't have anything to inspire them. A study from Hay Group based on surveys of 1.2 million employees suggests that one reason organizations lose good employees is the lack of a clear vision that provides a sense of direction.[19] In addition, people are not generally willing to make emotional commitments just for the sake of increasing profits. Vision needs to transcend the bottom line because people are willing, and even eager, to commit to something truly worthwhile, something that makes life better for others or improves their communities.[20] Consider Henry Ford's original vision for Ford Motor Company:

> *I will build a motor car for the great multitude. . . . It will be so low in price that no man making a good salary will be unable to own one and enjoy with his family the blessings of hours of pleasure in God's open spaces. . . . When I'm through, everybody will be able to afford one, and everyone will have one. The horse will have disappeared from our highways, the automobile will be taken for granted [and we will give many people] employment at good wages.[21]*

Employees were motivated by Ford's vision because they saw an opportunity to make life better for themselves and others.

Leader's Self-Insight 13.2
Visionary Leadership

Think about a situation in which you either assumed or were given a leadership role in a group. Imagine your own behavior as a leader. To what extent do the following statements characterize your leadership? Indicate whether each of the following items is Mostly False or Mostly True for you.

	Mostly False	Mostly True
1. I have a clear understanding of where we are going.	_____	_____
2. I work to get others committed to our desired future.	_____	_____
3. I initiate discussion with others about the kind of future I would like us to create together.	_____	_____
4. I show others how their interests can be realized by working toward a common vision.	_____	_____
5. I look ahead and forecast what I expect in the future.	_____	_____
6. I make certain that the activities I manage are broken down into manageable chunks.		_____
7. I seek future challenges for the group.	_____	_____
8. I spend time and effort making certain that people adhere to the values and outcomes that have been agreed on.	_____	_____

	Mostly False	Mostly True
9. I inspire others with my ideas for the future.	_____	_____
10. I give special recognition when others' work is consistent with the vision.	_____	_____

Scoring and Interpretation

The odd-numbered questions pertain to creating a vision for the group. The even-numbered questions pertain to implementing the vision. Calculate your score for each set of questions. Which score is higher? Compare your scores with other students.

This questionnaire pertains to two dimensions of visionary leadership. Creating the vision has to do with whether you think about the future, whether you are excited about the future, and whether you engage others in the future. Implementing the vision is about the extent to which you communicate, allocate the work, and provide rewards for activities that achieve the vision. Which of the two dimensions is easier for you? Are your scores consistent with your understanding of your own strengths and weaknesses? What might you do to improve your scores?

Vision Gives Meaning to Work People also need to find dignity and meaning in their work. Even employees performing routine tasks can find pride in their work when they have a larger purpose for what they do. For example, an insurance clerk who thinks of her job as helping victims of fire or burglary put their lives back in order will feel very differently than one who thinks of his job as "processing insurance claims."[22] "People want to accomplish great things," advises former UPS CEO Michael L. Eskew. "They want to make a difference. Leaders need to say 'This is where we are going,' and then, 'this is why we need you.'"[23] People are drawn to companies that offer them a chance to do something meaningful. Today, prospective employees often ask about a company's vision when interviewing for a job because they want to know what the organization aims for and how, or whether, they will fit in.

Vision Establishes a Standard of Excellence and Integrity A powerful vision frees people from the mundane by providing them with a challenge that requires them to give their best. In addition, vision provides a measure by which employees can gauge their contributions to the organization. Most workers welcome the

marble: © Kirill Matkov sunset: © Marco Regalia

chance to see how their work fits into the whole. Think of how frustrating it is to watch a movie when the projector is out of focus. Today's complex, fast-changing business environment often seems just like that—out of focus.[24] A vision is the focus button. It clarifies an image of the future and lets people see how they can contribute. A vision presents a challenge—asking people to go where they haven't gone before. A powerful vision that defies conventional thinking is one of the key traits shared by many companies that rank on *Business Week*'s BW50 list of high-performing organizations. Gilead Sciences landed high on the list for four consecutive years thanks to leadership vision.

IN THE LEAD

John Martin, Gilead Sciences

Many pharmaceutical companies see providing HIV treatments as a necessary public service. Since the majority of HIV victims live in developing countries and can't afford high-cost drugs, leaders think it doesn't pay to incur significant development costs to improve the standard treatments, which require patients to take dozens of pills a day.

John Martin and other leaders at Gilead Sciences, though, saw things differently. Gilead, they decided, would create HIV treatments that are cheaper and more convenient than standard drugs. Martin challenged his scientists with a vision of creating a single-dose treatment that could be provided at a lower cost. The first four efforts failed, but eventually Gilead came out with Atripla, a single pill taken at bedtime that combines myriad compounds that are released into the bloodstream at different times.

Atripla costs just $1,300 a month—expensive, of course, but less than standard HIV drugs. Gilead and other companies continue searching for an HIV vaccine, but in the meantime, the new treatment has both improved the lives of patients and helped Gilead's bottom line. The company's profits tripled in four years.[25]

Action Memo

As a leader, you can frame a vision that sets a standard of excellence and integrity, connects to core values, and helps people find meaning in their work.

Visions such as the one at Gilead Sciences clarify and connect to the core values and ideals of the organization and thus set a standard of integrity for employees. A good vision brings out the best in people by illuminating important values, speaking to people's hearts, and letting them be part of something bigger than themselves. Because good visions present a challenge, they encourage people to be creative, take risks, think in unconventional ways, and find new approaches. This chapter's *Consider This* box discusses three qualities a powerful vision can inspire.

Common Themes of Vision

Five themes are common to powerful, effective visions: they have broad, widely shared appeal; they help organizations deal with change; they encourage faith and hope for the future; they reflect high ideals; and they define both the organization's destination and the basic rules to get there.

Vision Has Broad Appeal   Although it may seem obvious that a vision can be achieved only through people, many visions fail to adequately involve employees. Isolated top leaders may come up with a grand idea that other employees find ridiculous, or they might forget that achieving the vision requires understanding and commitment throughout the organization. For example, in 1994, most people thought Ray Anderson's idea of turning a carpet company into an environmental leader was insane. If he had not been able to involve managers, engineers, employees,

Consider **This!**
Vision's Offspring

A compelling vision inspires and nurtures three qualities, here personified as individuals. Do you think followers would benefit from contact with the following "people" in an organization?

Clarity

My visits to Clarity are soothing now. He never tells me what to think or feel or do but shows me how to find out what I need to know. . . . He presented me with a sketchbook and told me to draw the same thing every day until the drawing started to speak to me.

Commitment

Commitment has kind eyes. He wears sturdy shoes. . . . You can taste in [his] vegetables that the soil has been cared for. . . . He is a simple man, and yet he is mysterious. He is more generous than most people. His heart is open. He is not afraid of life.

Imagination

Some people accuse Imagination of being a liar. They don't understand that she has her own ways of uncovering the truth. . . . Imagination has been working as a fortune-teller in the circus. She has a way of telling your fortune so clearly that you believe her, and then your wishes start to come true. . . . Her vision is more complex, and very simple. Even with the old stories, she wants us to see what has never been seen before.

Source: J. Ruth Gendler, *The Book of Qualities* (New York: Harper & Row, 1988), pp. 15, 43, and 55. Used with permission.

© majaiva

customers, and investors in the vision, it could never become a reality. The vision cannot be the property of the leader alone.[26] The ideal vision is identified with the organization as a whole, not with a single leader or even a top leadership team. It "grabs people in the gut" and motivates them to work toward a common end.[27] It allows each individual to act independently but in the same direction.

Vision Deals with Change Effective visions help the organization achieve bold change. The National Institute for Learning Disabilities existed for 25 years, providing services to a narrow segment of the educational market. Then, leaders formulated a bold vision for broadening the scope of the organization and serving a million students by 2020. The so-called "2020 Vision" presented a tremendous challenge that required leaders and employees to stretch their thinking and change how they provide services.[28] Change can be frightening, but a clear sense of direction helps people face the difficulties and uncertainties involved in the change process. When employees have a guiding vision, everyday decisions and actions throughout the organization respond to current problems and challenges in ways that move the organization toward the future rather than maintain the status quo.

Vision Encourages Faith and Hope Vision exists only in the imagination—it is a picture of a world that cannot be observed or verified in advance. The future is shaped by people who believe in it, and a powerful vision helps people believe that they can be effective, that there is a better future they can move to through their own commitment and actions. Vision is an emotional appeal to our fundamental human needs and desires—to feel important and useful, to believe we can make a real difference in the world.[29] For example, John F. Kennedy's vision for NASA to send a man to the moon by the end of the 1960s was so powerful that hundreds of thousands of people throughout the world believed in a future they couldn't see.[30]

Vision Reflects High Ideals Good visions are idealistic. Visions that portray an uplifting future have the power to inspire and energize people. When Kennedy announced the "man on the moon" vision, NASA had only a small amount of the knowledge it would need to accomplish the feat. Yet in July 1969, the vision became a reality. William F. Powers, who worked at NASA during the 1960s, later helped Ford Motor Company develop an idealistic vision for the world's first high-volume, aerodynamically styled car that featured fuel economy (the 1980s Taurus). It was a big risk for Ford at a time when the company was down and out. But leaders portrayed this as a chance not only to save the company but also to establish a whole new path in automotive engineering, which tapped into employees' imaginations and idealism.[31]

Vision Defines the Destination and the Journey A good vision for the future includes specific outcomes that the organization wants to achieve. It also incorporates the underlying values that will help the organization get there. For example, a private business school might specify certain outcomes such as a top-20 ranking, placing 90 percent of students in summer internships, and getting 80 percent of students into jobs by June of their graduating year. Yet in the process of reaching those specific outcomes, the school wants to increase students' knowledge of business, ethical values, and teamwork, as well as prepare them for lifelong learning. Additionally, the vision may espouse underlying values such as no separation between fields of study or between professors and students, a genuine concern for students' welfare, and adding to the body of business knowledge. A good vision includes both the desired future outcomes and the underlying values that set the rules for achieving them.

A Vision Works at Multiple Levels

Most of the visions we have talked about so far are for the company as a whole. However, divisions, departments, and individuals also have visions, which are just as important and powerful. Successful individuals usually have a clear mental picture of their vision and how to achieve it. People who do not have this clear vision of the future have less chance of success. Three young Pepperdine University graduates started an organization to help other young people find and pursue their personal vision.

IN THE LEAD

Roadtrip Productions

Several years ago, Mike Marriner, Nathan Gebhard, and Brian McAllister set out in a neon-green Fleetwood RV on an epic pilgrimage to find out what they wanted to do with their lives. One thing they knew: They weren't ready and willing to play it safe and follow the expected paths of medicine, consulting, and the family landfill business.

Armed with a video camera, the three interviewed successful leaders in a wide variety of professions, asking questions such as: "When you were our age, what were you thinking?" and "How did you get to where you are?" The answers all boiled down to this simple message, says McAllister: "Block out the noise and really pave your own road guided by what lights you up." Following their three-month, 17,342-mile journey across the country, the three founded Roadtrip Productions to help other young people experience their own journeys and find their own visions. Roadtrip has evolved into a PBS television series, three books, and an online community. It has formed partnerships with career centers at numerous colleges in the United States and Britain.

The Roadtrip founders believe many young people are desperately searching for meaning in their work but don't know how to find it or lack the confidence to pursue it. Marriner suggests that most people know deep down what they're passionate about, but they lack the confidence or courage to pursue that vision. They have been conditioned to look for the safe paths and to pick jobs, careers, or other pursuits where they feel confident they can be successful. Yet, as Howard Schultz, chairman and former CEO of Starbucks, told the team during his interview, success shouldn't be the target. Instead, success comes from pursuing your vision.[32]

Roadtrip also reminds people that making an initial career choice is just one aspect of a personal vision that will grow and change over time. Some successful organizations ask employees to write a personal vision statement because leaders know that people who have a vision of where they want their lives to go are more effective. In addition, this enables leaders to see how an employee's personal vision and the team or organizational vision can contribute to one another.

Organizational visions grow and change as well. Within organizations, top leaders develop a vision for the organization as a whole, and at the same time a project team leader five levels beneath the CEO can develop a vision with team members for a new product they are working on. Leaders of functional departments, divisions, and teams can use vision with the same positive results as do top leaders. The vision becomes the common thread connecting people, involving them personally and emotionally in the organization.[33] In innovative companies, every group or department creates its own vision, as long as the vision is in line with the overall company's direction.

When every person understands and embraces a vision, the organization becomes self-adapting. Although each individual acts independently, everyone is working in the same direction. In the new sciences, this is called the principle of self-reference. **Self-reference** means that each element in a system will serve the goals of the whole system when the elements are imprinted with an understanding of the whole. Thus, the vision serves to direct and control people for the good of themselves and the organization.

To develop a shared vision, leaders share their personal visions with others and encourage others to express their dreams for the future. This requires openness, good listening skills, and the courage to connect with people on an emotional level. A leader's ultimate responsibility is to be in touch with the hopes and dreams that drive employees and find the common ground that binds personal dreams into a shared vision for the organization. As one successful top leader put it, "My job, fundamentally, is listening to what the organization is trying to say, and then making sure it is forcefully articulated."[34] Another successful leader refers to leadership as "discovering the company's destiny and having the courage to follow it."[35]

Action Memo

As a leader, you can create a shared vision so that every individual, team, and department is moving in the same direction. You can help people see the values, activities, and objectives that will attain the vision.

Self-reference
a principle stating that each element in a system will serve the goals of the whole system when the elements are imprinted with an understanding of the whole

Mission
the organization's core broad purpose and reason for existence

Mission

Mission is not the same thing as a company's vision, although the two work together. The **mission** is the organization's core broad purpose and reason for existence. It defines the company's core values and reason for being, and it provides a basis for creating the vision. Whereas vision is an ambitious desire for the future, mission is what the organization "stands for" in a larger sense.

What Mission Does

Whereas visions grow and change, the mission persists in the face of changing technologies, economic conditions, or other environmental shifts. It serves as the glue that holds the organization together in times of change and guides strategic choices and decisions about the future. The mission defines the enduring character—the spiritual DNA—of the organization and can be used as a leadership tool to help employees find purpose in their work.[36] Companies with strong missions that give people purpose, such as Medtronic's "To restore people to full life and health" or Liberty Mutual Company's "Helping people live safer, more secure lives" typically attract better employees, have better relationships with external parties, and perform better in the marketplace over the long term.[37] Particularly in today's environment, people are drawn to companies that have a clear purpose that goes beyond enhancing shareholder wealth. The Leader's Bookshelf describes some values and operating principles of companies that believe their purpose is not to enrich shareholders but to serve the greater good.

Recall the discussion of intrinsic rewards from Chapter 8. When people connect their jobs to a higher cause or purpose, the work itself becomes a great motivator. The Gallup organization's Q12 study, also discussed in Chapter 8, has found that when employees believe the company's mission makes their job important, they are typically more engaged with their work, feel a greater sense of pride and loyalty, and are more productive. Exhibit 13.4 compares the Gallup results for those who agree that the mission makes their job important to those who do not feel that the mission of the company makes their job important. The differences are quite striking. For example, 60 percent of respondents who agreed that the mission makes their job important reported feeling engaged with their work, whereas none of the respondents who disagreed felt engaged with their work. Sixty-six percent would

Exhibit 13.4 The Power of a Strong Mission

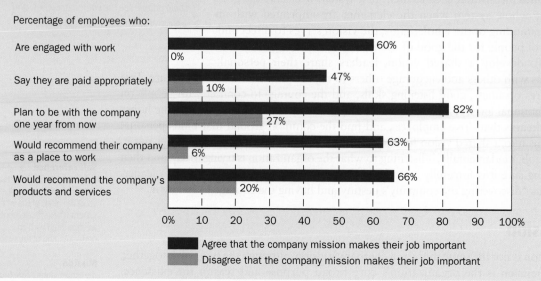

Source: Susan Ellingwood, "On a Mission," *Gallup Management Journal* (Winter 2001), pp. 6–7.

In *Firms of Endearment*, Rajendra Sisodia, David Wolfe, and Jagdish Sheth posit that the world has entered an "age of transcendence," in which people are searching for meaning in their lives that goes beyond "the world that is materialistically defined by . . . most traditional business enterprises." They profile leaders and companies that champion "a new humanistic vision" that embraces the common welfare rather than striving just to create shareholder wealth.

Share of Heart, Not Share of Wallet

"Firms of endearment" are defined as companies in which leaders strive to align and serve the interests of all stakeholder groups—customers, employees, partners, and communities, as well as shareholders. Here are some values and operating principles that firms of endearment live by.

- *Their executive salaries are relatively modest*. In 2005 (the most recent year for which figures were available when the book was written), the average CEO of an S&P 500 company received nearly $11.75 million in total compensation. In contrast, Costco paid its CEO Jim Sinegal $350,000 plus a $200,000 bonus. In that year, Costco had sales of $57 billion, and its stock value increased 40 percent over the two-year period ending July 2006.

- *They show a genuine passion for customers and connect emotionally with them*. New Balance offers more shoe widths than other major athletic footwear companies because the company was founded on the values of comfort and healing. Fit and performance are more important than style. The slogan, "Connect with Yourself; Achieve New Balance," resonates with customers seeking to find balance and meaning in their lives.

- *Development of employees is a high priority*. At The Container Store, people receive 235 hours of training during the first year alone, and at least 160 hours a year after that. UPS has an "Earn and Learn" program, which invests millions in tuition and books for part-time employees to attend college and become more eligible for promotion to full-time positions.

- *They honor the spirit, not just the letter, of the law and apply uniformly high operating standards around the world*. Honda's Green Factory program has required that every Honda facility reduce emissions and energy use, reuse more raw materials, and recycle manufacturing materials. Honda plants worldwide comply with the toughest environmental management standards.

Making the World a Better Place

The mission of Timberland, says CEO Jeffrey Swartz, is "to make the world a better place." To some extent, all the companies profiled in *Firms of Endearment* are striving toward that goal. The authors point out that the book is about good leadership, which can enable companies to achieve superior performance and high returns to investors while at the same time serving a higher purpose.

Firms of Endearment: How World-Class Companies Profit from Passion and Purpose, by Rajendra S. Sisodia, David B. Wolfe, and Jagdish N. Sheth, is published by Wharton School Publishing.

marble: © Ioannis Drimilis library: www.istockphoto.com/nikada

recommend their company's products or services, compared to only 20 percent of those who did not believe the mission made their job important.[38]

Typically, the mission is made up of two critical parts: the core values and the core purpose. The *core values* guide the organization "no matter what." As Ralph Larsen, former CEO of Johnson & Johnson, explained it, "The core values embodied in our Credo might be a competitive advantage, but that is not *why* we have them. We have them because they define for us what we stand for, and we would hold them even if they became a competitive *dis*advantage in certain situations."[39] Johnson & Johnson's core values led the company, for example, to voluntarily remove Tylenol from the market after product tampering led to the cyanide poisoning of some Tylenol capsule users, even though this act cost the company more than $100 million.

Exhibit 13.5 Mission, Vision, and Values of DuPont Canada

Our Mission

Sustainable Growth: Increasing shareholder and societal value while reducing our environmental footprint.

Our Vision

Our vision is to be the world's most dynamic science company, creating sustainable solutions essential to a better, safer, healthier life for people everywhere.

We will be a pacesetter in improving every aspect of our operations with a total commitment to meeting the needs of our customers in Canada and abroad with continuously improving, high-value offerings.

Our Core Values

Safety, concern and care for people, protection of the environment, and personal and corporate integrity are this company's highest values, and we will not compromise them.

Life. Improved by DuPont Science

Source: "DuPont Mission, Vision, and Values," DuPont Canada Web site, "Our Company; Company at a Glance: Our Mission, Vision, Values," http://www2.dupont.com/Our_Company/en_CA/glance/vision (accessed April 10, 2007).

The mission also includes the company's *core purpose*. The core values and core purpose are frequently expressed in a *mission statement*. Exhibit 13.5 shows the vision, mission, and core values of DuPont Canada. Consider how DuPont's specific vision grows out of the company's mission and works with it.

A Framework for Noble Purpose

An effective mission statement doesn't just describe products or services; it captures people's idealistic motivations for why the organization exists. Most successful companies have missions that proclaim a noble purpose of some type, such as Mary Kay's "to enrich the lives of women," or Wal-Mart Stores' mission "to give ordinary folk the chance to buy the same things as rich people."[40]

Leaders are responsible for framing a noble purpose that inspires and leads followers to high performance and helps the organization maintain a competitive advantage. People like to have a sense that what they are doing matters and makes a positive difference in the world.

Exhibit 13.6 describes four basic approaches leaders take in framing an organizational purpose that can tap into people's desire to contribute and feel that their work is worthwhile.[41] Each of these approaches is described in more detail in the following paragraphs.

Action Memo

As a leader, you can keep in mind what the organization stands for in a broader sense—its core purpose and values—and create the vision around that central mission.

Discovery Many people are inspired by the opportunity to find or create something new. Discovery for its own sake can serve as a noble purpose, as it does for employees at Google, where people are energized by the psychic rewards they get from working on intellectually stimulating and challenging technical problems.[42] As another example, leaders at Samsung Electronics reenergized the company by focusing employees on discovery rather than imitation, transforming Samsung into a world-class innovator rather than a manufacturer known for cheap, low-quality knockoffs. This shift in purpose led to amazing results at Samsung.[43] This type of purpose inspires people to see the adventure in their work and experience the joy of a pioneering or entrepreneurial spirit.

Exhibit 13.6 A Leader's Framework for Noble Purpose

Purpose	Description	Basis for Action	Examples
Discovery	Finding the new	Pioneer, entrepreneur	Google, 3M, Virgin
Excellence	Being the best	Fulfillment	Berkshire Hathaway, Apple, BMW
Altruism	Providing service	Happiness	ServiceMaster, Dollar General
Heroism	Being effective	Achievement	Microsoft, Dell, ExxonMobil

Source: Nikos Mourkogiannis, *Purpose: The Starting Point of Great Companies* (New York: Palgrave Macmillan, 2006); and Nikos Mourkogiannis, "The Realist's Guide to Moral Purpose," *strategy+business* Issue 41 (Winter 2005), pp. 42–53.

Excellence With this approach, rather than emphasizing discovery, leaders focus people on being the best, both on an individual and an organizational level. Apple, for instance, didn't invent the MP3 player or the smartphone, but instead focused on making the best possible version of these products.[44] In addition, excellence is defined by the work itself rather than by customers. Indeed, organizations that pursue excellence would rather turn customers away than compromise their quality. Consider that Apple has always built high-quality, cleverly designed computers, yet it holds less than 10 percent of the personal computer market. Leaders would like to increase their share of the market, but they aren't willing to sacrifice their commitment to high quality and what they consider superior technology.[45] In companies with excellence as a guiding purpose, managers and employees are treated as valuable resources and provided with support to perform at their peak. People are motivated by the opportunity to experience intrinsic rewards and personal fulfillment.

Altruism Many nonprofit organizations are based on a noble purpose of altruism because they emphasize serving others, but businesses can use this approach as well. For example, leaders at Dollar General stress the purpose of giving low-income people a good deal, not just making sales and profits. Even a car manufacturer can have a noble purpose, as leaders at Honda have shown.

IN THE LEAD

Tetsuo Iwamura and Ben Knight, Honda Motor Corporation

In the 1970s, Honda leaders adopted the motto "Blue skies for our children" as a guideline for future vehicle development, says Ben Knight, head of Honda engineering in North America. Two decades later, when competitors were raking in profits building big, gas-guzzling pickups and sport utility vehicles, Honda never strayed from its mission of building fuel-efficient, environmentally friendly cars like the Accord, Civic, and new Fit subcompact. Honda has posted the highest average fuel efficiency of any automaker for its overall vehicle lineup over the past 15 years.

Today, Honda is reaping the rewards of its commitment to fuel efficiency. When gas prices skyrocketed, Honda's sales kept going up while others, even Toyota's, were going down. The company could barely keep up with the demand for its vehicles, while other companies were struggling to reduce their bloated inventories of pickups and

SUVs. "Honda is a philosophy-driven company," says Tetsuo Iwamura, president of Honda North America. "Even when the large SUVs and trucks were big sellers, they did not fit with our philosophy."

During the mid-1990s glory days of larger vehicles, some dealers pressured Honda to offer a full-size pickup and a car with a V-8 engine, but leaders believed doing so would hurt the company in the long run. Honoring the purpose was more important than reaping quick profits. "We have a saying that we want to make Honda the company that society wants to exist," said Iwamura.[46]

Honda's mission clearly places it in the category of altruism as a guiding purpose. Any company that puts a high premium on customer service can be considered to fall in this category as well. Marriott, for instance, encapsulates its purpose in the slogan, "The Spirit to Serve."[47] The basis of action for this type of purpose is to increase personal happiness. Most people feel good when they are doing something to help others or make their communities or the world a better place.

Heroism The final category, heroism, means the company's purpose is based on being strong, aggressive, and effective. Companies with this basis of noble purpose often reflect almost an obsession with winning. Bill Gates imbued Microsoft with a goal of putting the Windows operating system into every personal computer, for example.[48] At General Electric, former CEO Jack Welch wanted the company to strive to be number one or number two in each industry in which it did business. As another example, Southwest Airlines was founded with a heroic goal of winning against much larger competitors such as American and Delta. With this approach, the basis of action is people's desire to achieve and to experience *self-efficacy*, as described in Chapter 8. People want to feel capable of being effective and producing results.

Companies that remain successful over the long term have top executives who lead with a noble purpose. A well-chosen noble purpose taps into the emotions and instincts of employees and customers and can contribute to better morale, greater innovativeness, and higher employee and organizational performance.

Strategy in Action

Strong missions that reflect a noble purpose and guiding visions are both important, but they are not enough alone to make strong, powerful organizations. For organizations to succeed, they need ways to translate vision, values, and purpose into action, which is the role of strategy. **Strategic management** refers to the set of decisions and actions used to formulate and implement specific strategies that will achieve a competitively superior fit between the organization and its environment so as to achieve organizational goals.[49]

It is the leader's job to find this fit and translate it into action. When leaders link vision and strategic action, they can make a real difference for their organization's future. Research has shown that strategic thinking and planning for the future can positively affect a company's performance and financial success.[50] One study found that as much as 44 percent of the variance in profitability of major firms can be attributed to strategic leadership.[51]

Deciding How to Achieve the Vision

Strategy can be defined as the general plan of action that describes resource allocation and other activities for dealing with the environment and helping the

Strategic management
the set of decisions and actions used to formulate and implement specific strategies that will achieve a competitively superior fit between the organization and its environment so as to achieve organizational goals

Strategy
the general plan of action that describes resource allocation and other activities for dealing with the environment and helping the organization attain its goals

organization attain its goals and achieve the vision. In formulating strategy, leaders ask questions such as "Where is the organization now? Where does the organization want to be? What changes and trends are occurring in the competitive environment? What courses of action can help us achieve our vision?"

Developing effective strategy requires actively listening to people both inside and outside the organization, as well as examining trends and discontinuities in the environment that can be used to gain an edge. Rather than reacting to environmental changes, strategic leaders study the events that have already taken place and act based on their anticipation of what the future might be like.[52] An example is Progressive Insurance, which was the first to offer rate quotes online. Other companies had the same information about the growth of personal computers and the Internet, but they didn't interpret it in the same way or formulate the same strategy for taking advantage of the new technology. Good leaders anticipate, look ahead, and prepare for the future based on trends they see in the environment today, which often requires radical thinking.

Innovative thinking carries a lot of risk. Sometimes leaders have to shift their strategy several times before they get it right.[53] In addition, strategy necessarily changes over time to fit shifting environmental conditions. To improve the chances for success, leaders develop strategies that focus on three qualities: core competence, developing synergy, and creating value for customers.

An organization's **core competence** is something the organization does extremely well in comparison to competitors. Leaders try to identify the organization's unique strengths—what makes their organization different from others in the industry. L.L. Bean succeeds with a core competence of excellent customer service and a quality guarantee. A customer can return a purchase at any time and get a refund or exchange, no questions asked. One story told about the company is that a manager approached a young boy with his mother and commented that his L.L. Bean jacket was frayed at the sleeves and collar. The mother commented that it was no wonder, considering how much he had worn it, but the manager said, "That shouldn't happen; we need to replace that for you."[54]

Synergy occurs when organizational parts interact to produce a joint effect that is greater than the sum of the parts acting alone. As a result the organization may attain a special advantage with respect to cost, market power, technology, or employee skills. One way companies gain synergy is through alliances and partnerships. North General Hospital, a small community hospital in Harlem that caters mostly to the poor and elderly, had lost money every year since it was founded in 1979—until 2005, when leaders focused on a new strategy that included an alliance with Mount Sinai Medical Center, one of New York City's most prominent teaching hospitals. In return for an annual fee, North General uses Mount Sinai physicians and surgeons who perform highly specialized procedures and treat specific diseases that affect African-Americans in high rates. The deal boosts revenue for Mount Sinai, as well, and brings in more patients because North General acts as a referral service for patients with complex medical issues.[55]

Focusing on core competencies and attaining synergy help companies create value for their customers. **Value** can be defined as the combination of benefits received and costs paid by the customer.[56] For example, Panera Bread doesn't have the lowest costs for sandwiches and other food and drink products, but it works hard to create an environment where people want to spend time. "If you give people food they want, in an environment that they want, they will spend a

Action Memo

As a leader, you can prepare for the future based on trends in the environment today. Don't be afraid to think radically. You can shift your strategies to fit changing conditions.

Core competence
something the organization does extremely well in comparison to competitors

Synergy
the interaction of organizational parts to produce a joint effect that is greater than the sum of the parts

Value
the combination of benefits received and costs paid by the customer

dollar or two more, they will go out of their way for it," says CEO Ron Shaich.[57] Delivering value to the customer is at the heart of strategy.

Strategy formulation integrates knowledge of the environment, vision, and mission with the company's core competence in such a way as to attain synergy and create value for customers. When these elements are brought together, the company has an excellent chance to succeed in a competitive environment. But to do so, leaders have to ensure that strategies are executed—that actual behavior within the organization reflects the desired direction.

Deciding How to Execute

Strategy execution means using specific mechanisms, techniques, or tools for directing organizational resources to accomplish strategic goals. This is the basic architecture for how things get done in the organization. Strategy execution, sometimes called *implementation*, is the most important as well as the most difficult part of strategic management, and leaders must carefully and consistently manage the execution process to achieve results.[58] One survey found that only 57 percent of responding firms reported that managers successfully implemented the new strategies they had devised over the past three years.[59] Other research has estimated that as much as 70 percent of all business strategies never get implemented, reflecting the complexity of strategy execution.[60]

Strategy execution involves using several tools or parts of the organization that can be adjusted to put strategy into action. Strong leadership is one of the most important tools for strategy execution. Followers need *line of sight* to the organization's strategic objectives, which means they understand the goals and how their actions will contribute to achieving them.[61] Leaders create the environment that determines whether people understand and feel committed to achieving the company's strategic objectives. When leaders clearly communicate a vision, spell out specific strategic goals, openly share information, and involve employees in making decisions that affect their jobs and the organization, people can see how their individual actions contribute to achieving the larger goals.[62] In addition, open communication and employee involvement increase trust, and people who trust their leaders are typically more supportive of strategy and put forth more effort to implement strategic decisions.[63]

Strategy is also executed through organizational elements such as structural design, pay or reward systems, budget allocations, and organizational rules, policies, or procedures. Leaders make decisions about changes in structure, systems, policies, and so forth, to support the company's strategic direction. They should take care, however, that these decisions promote ethical and socially responsible behavior on the part of employees rather than encouraging them to meet the strategic goals at any price. For instance, Wells Fargo leaders have been praised for a growth strategy that included goals of expanding financial services to minority customers and neighborhoods. However, recent allegations shed a much more negative light on the bank's leaders. Former employees have said the company offered rewards to loan officers to aggressively push subprime mortgages in minority communities. One claimed the bank gave bonuses to loan officers who steered minority borrowers who should have qualified for prime loans toward higher-interest subprime loans instead.[64]

A more positive example comes from The Home Depot. CEO Frank Blake has loosened rules, revised procedures, and shifted reward systems to emphasize quality customer service in support of a strategy that takes Home Depot back to its roots as a source of not only products but also help and information. Former CEO Bob Nardelli's strategy of dominating the wholesale housing-supply

Strategy formulation
integrating knowledge of the environment, vision, and mission with the core competence in such a way as to attain synergy and create customer value

Strategy execution
putting strategy into action by adjusting various parts of the organization and directing resources to accomplish strategic goals

business created fast growth but also led to low morale and poor customer service. Blake has sold off the supply unit to invest in an "army of orange aprons" at the retail stores.[65]

Leaders make decisions every day—some large and some small—that support company strategy. Exhibit 13.7 provides a simplified model for how leaders make strategic decisions. The two dimensions considered are whether a particular choice will have a high or low strategic impact on the business and whether execution of the decision will be easy or difficult. A change that both produces a high strategic impact and is easy to execute would be a leader's first choice for putting strategy into action. For example, leaders at Payless Shoe Source shifted the company's strategy to try to appeal to young, fashion-conscious women with trendier shoes at reasonable prices, or as CEO Matt Rubel put it, to "democratize fashion." One of the first steps leaders took was to give the stores a new look. The tall, crowded wire racks were replaced with low countertops and displays arranged by fashion rather than by size. The walls are curved to give a feeling of movement and energy. Even the lighting is strategic. Modern white ceiling lamps brighten the whole store and accent lamps highlight the higher-fashion items. "It makes a $12 shoe look like a $20 shoe," says Rubel. The redesign of stores was easy to execute and is already having a big strategic impact. As one fashion-conscious shopper said, "Everything looks so much nicer. Is this Payless?"[66]

Some strategic decisions, however, are much more difficult to execute. For example, pursuing growth through mergers and acquisitions can present difficulties of blending production processes, accounting procedures, corporate cultures, and other aspects of the organizations into an effectively functioning whole. Structural reorganization, such as a shift to horizontal teams or breaking a corporation into separate divisions, is another example of a high-risk decision. Leaders frequently initiate major changes despite the risks and difficulties because the potential strategic payoff is very high.

Leaders also sometimes pursue activities that have a low strategic impact but which are relatively easy to execute. Incremental improvements in products, work processes, or techniques are examples. Over time, incremental improvements can have an important effect on the organization. In addition,

Exhibit 13.7 Making Strategic Decisions

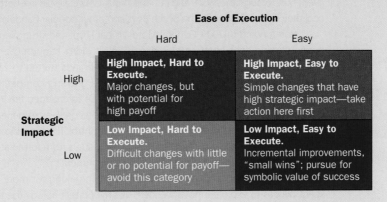

Source: Adapted from Amir Hartman and John Sifonis, with John Kador, *Net Ready: Strategies for the New E-conomy* (New York: McGraw-Hill, 2000), p. 95.

small changes can symbolize improvement and success to people within the organization. It may be important for leaders to produce quick, highly visible improvements to boost morale, keep people committed to larger changes, or keep followers focused on the vision. For example, the manager of a purchasing department wanted to re-engineer the purchasing process to increase efficiency and improve relationships with suppliers. He wanted requisitions and invoices to be processed within days rather than the several weeks it had been taking. Employees were skeptical that the department could ever meet the new standards and pointed out that some invoices currently awaiting processing were almost two months old. The manager decided to make some simple revisions in the flow of paperwork and employee duties, which enabled the department to process all the old invoices so that no remaining invoice was more than a week old. This "small win" energized employees and helped keep them focused on the larger goal.[67] The positive attitude made execution of the larger change much smoother.

The final category shown in Exhibit 13.7 relates to changes that are both difficult to execute and have low strategic impact. An illustration of a decision in this category was the attempt by new management at a highly successful mailorder clothing company to implement teams. In this case, the decision was not made to support a new strategic direction but simply to try out a new management trend—and it was a miserable failure that cost the organization much time, money, and employee goodwill before the teams were finally disbanded.[68] Effective leaders try to avoid making decisions that fall within this category.

The Leader's Contribution

Although good leadership calls for actively involving everyone, leaders are still ultimately responsible for establishing direction through vision and strategy. When leadership fails to provide direction, organizations flounder. General Motors provides both a positive and a negative example.

IN THE LEAD

General Motors

In the 1920s, Alfred P. Sloan formulated a vision and strategy of innovation that set GM on course to become the world's largest automaker. By offering "a car for every purse and purpose," GM surpassed Ford in 1932 and owned 50 percent of the U.S. auto market by the late 1950s. Through the 1950s and into the 1960s, GM's cars sold like hotcakes and were so cool they inspired songs by the Beach Boys and other popular bands of the time.

Flash-forward to 2009. General Motors is bankrupt and struggling to survive, practically begging consumers to buy its vehicles. It didn't happen over night. The high cost of GM's strategy of offering a multiplicity of brands started to cause problems in the 1970s, largely due to spikes in oil prices and growing competition from foreign automakers. Instead of crafting a focused response to changed environmental conditions, leaders began a juggling act. Internal tensions grew as some leaders pushed for innovation and others pushed for stronger cost control. This "fighting over the steering wheel that controlled GM's direction" distracted leaders from formulating a clear vision and strategy that responded to shifts in the environment.

Without a clear focus, GM has been bumbling along for more than 30 years. It spent billions to explore innovative ideas like hybrid technology (begun in the 1970s), the Saturn small-car company in the 1980s, and the EV1 electric vehicle in the 1990s, then failed to provide the projects with adequate funding because they cost too much or weren't providing enough immediate profit.[69]

GM lost its way because leaders couldn't agree on a clear direction for the organization. Innovation, once part of the company's DNA, got pushed to the back burner in favor of efficiency, but without a strategic focus the company's resources were spread way too thin. For instance, Saturn was originally a success, but the company failed to introduce any new models for five years, effectively starving the promising division. GM filed for Chapter 11 bankruptcy in early June 2009, and new leadership is focusing resources on just four core brands to try to save the once-renowned automaker.[70]

To keep organizations competitive, leaders consciously adopt a focused vision and strategy and make sure everyone's activities move the organization in the right direction.

Stimulating Vision and Action

In the waiting lounge of a fine lakeside restaurant, a sign reads, "Where there is no hope in the future, there is no power in the present." The owner explains its presence there by telling the story of how his small, picturesque village with its homes and businesses was sacrificed to make way for a flood-control project. After losing their fight to reverse the decision, most business leaders simply let their businesses decline and die. Soon, the only people who came to the village did so to eat at the cheery little diner, whose owner became the butt of jokes because he continued to work so hard. Everyone laughed when he chose to open a larger and fancier restaurant on the hill behind the village. Yet, when the flood-control project was finally completed, he had the only attractive restaurant on the edge of a beautiful, newly constructed lake that drew many tourists. Anyone could have found out, as he did, where the edge of the lake would be, yet most of the business owners had no vision for the future. The restaurant owner had a vision and he took action on it.

Hopes and dreams for the future are what keep people moving forward. However, for leaders to make a real difference, they have to link those dreams with strategic actions. Vision has to be translated into specific goals, objectives, and plans so that employees know how to move toward the desired future. An old English churchyard saying applies to organizations as it does to life:

Life without vision is drudgery.

Vision without action is but an empty dream.

Action guided by vision is joy and the hope of the earth.[71]

Exhibit 13.8 illustrates four possibilities of leadership in providing direction. Four types of leaders are described based on their attention to vision and attention to action. The person who is low both on providing vision and stimulating action is *uninvolved,* not really a leader at all. The leader who is all action and little vision is a *doer.* He or she may be a hard worker and dedicated to the job and the organization, but the doer is working blind. Without a sense of purpose and direction, activities have no real meaning and do not truly serve the organization, the employees, or the community. The *dreamer,* on the other hand, is good at providing a big idea with meaning for self and others. This leader may effectively inspire others with a vision, yet he or she is weak on executing strategic action. The vision in this case is only a dream, a fantasy, because it has little chance of ever becoming reality. To be an *effective leader,* one both dreams big *and* transforms those dreams into significant strategic action, either through one's own activities or by hiring other leaders who can effectively execute the vision and strategy.

Action Memo

Strategic management is one of the most critical jobs of a leader, but leaders may exhibit different strategy styles that can be effective. Leader's Self-Insight 13.3 lets you determine your strengths based on two important ways leaders can bring creativity to strategic management.

Leader's Self-Insight 13.3
Your Strategy Style

Think about *how you handle challenges and issues* in your current or a recent job. Then circle "A" or "B" for each of the following items depending on which is generally more descriptive of your behavior. There are no right or wrong answers. Respond to each item as it best describes how you respond to work situations.

1. When keeping records, I tend to
   A. be very careful about documentation.
   B. be more haphazard about documentation.

2. If I run a group or a project, I
   A. have the general idea and let others figure out how to do the tasks.
   B. try to figure out specific goals, time lines, and expected outcomes.

3. My thinking style could be more accurately described as
   A. linear thinker, going from A to B to C.
   B. thinking like a grasshopper, hopping from one idea to another.

4. In my office or home, things are
   A. here and there in various piles.
   B. laid out neatly or at least in reasonable order.

5. I take pride in developing
   A. ways to overcome a barrier to a solution.
   B. new hypotheses about the underlying cause of a problem.

6. I can best help strategy by making sure there is
   A. openness to a wide range of assumptions and ideas.
   B. thoroughness when implementing new ideas.

7. One of my strengths is
   A. commitment to making things work.
   B. commitment to a dream for the future.

8. For me to work at my best, it is more important to have
   A. autonomy.
   B. certainty.

9. I work best when
   A. I plan my work ahead of time.
   B. I am free to respond to unplanned situations.

10. I am most effective when I emphasize
    A. inventing original solutions.
    B. making practical improvements.

Scoring and Interpretation

For Strategic Innovator style, score one point for each "A" answer circled for questions 2, 4, 6, 8, and 10 and for each "B" answer circled for questions 1, 3, 5, 7, and 9. For Strategic Adaptor style, score one point for each "B" answer circled for questions 2, 4, 6, 8, and 10, and for each "A" answer circled for questions 1, 3, 5, 7, and 9. Which of your two scores is higher and by how much? The higher score indicates your Strategy Style.

Strategic Innovator and Strategic Adaptor are two important ways leaders bring creativity to strategic management. Leaders with an adaptor style tend to work within the situation as it is given and improve it by making it more efficient and reliable. They succeed by building on what they know is true and proven. Leaders with the innovator style push toward a new paradigm and want to find a new way to do something. Innovators like to explore uncharted territory, seek dramatic breakthroughs, and may have difficulty accepting an ongoing strategy. Both innovator and adaptor styles are essential to strategic management, but with different approaches. The Strategic Adaptor asks, "How can I make this better?" The Strategic Innovator asks, "How can I make this different?" Strategic Innovators often use their skills in the formulation of whole new strategies, and Strategic Adaptors are often associated with strategic improvements and strategy execution.

If the difference between the two scores is 2 or less, you have a mid-adaptor/innovator style, and work well in both arenas. If the difference is 4–6, you have a moderately strong style and probably work best in the area of your strength. And if the difference is 8–10, you have a strong style and almost certainly would want to work in the area of your strength rather than in the opposite domain.

Sources: Adapted from Dorothy Marcic and Joe Seltzer, *Organizational Behavior: Experiences and Cases* (Cincinnati: South-Western, 1998), pp. 284–287; and William Miller, *Innovation Styles* (Dallas, TX: Global Creativity Corporation, 1997). The adaptor-innovator concepts are from Michael J. Kirton, "Adaptors and Innovators: A Description and Measure," *Journal of Applied Psychology* 61, no. 5 (1976), p. 623.

Exhibit 13.8 Linking Strategic Vision and Strategic Action

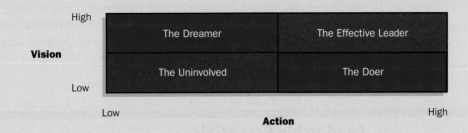

Source: Based on William D. Hitt, *The Leader–Manager: Guidelines for Action* (Columbus, OH: Battelle Press, 1988), p. 7.

How Leaders Decide

To determine strategic direction for the future, leaders look inward, outward, and forward. Leaders scan both the internal and external organizational environment to identify trends, threats, and opportunities for the organization.

Organizations need both a broad and inspiring vision and an underlying plan for how to achieve it. To decide and map a strategic direction, leaders strive to develop industry foresight based on trends in technology, demographics, government regulation, values, and lifestyles that will help them identify new competitive advantages. One approach leaders take in setting a course for the future is through hard analysis. Situation analysis, for example, includes a search for SWOT—strengths, weaknesses, opportunities, and threats that affect organizational performance. Leaders using situation analysis obtain external information from a variety of sources, such as customers, government reports, suppliers, consultants, or association meetings. They gather information about internal strengths and weaknesses from sources such as budgets, financial ratios, profit and loss statements, and employee surveys. Another formula often used by leaders is a five-force analysis developed by Michael Porter, who studied a number of businesses and proposed that strategy is often the result of five competitive forces: potential new entrants into an industry; the bargaining power of buyers; the bargaining power of suppliers; the threat of substitute products; and rivalry among competitors. By carefully examining these five forces, leaders can develop effective strategies to remain competitive.

Vision and strategy have to be based on a solid factual foundation, but too much rationality can get in the way of creating a compelling vision. Leaders do conduct rational analysis, but successful visions also reflect their personal experiences and understandings.[72] When leaders rely solely on formal strategic planning, competitor analysis, or market research, they miss new opportunities. Consider that when Ted Turner first talked about launching a 24-hour news and information channel in the 1970s, many dismissed him as delusional. Every source of conventional wisdom, from market research to broadcast professionals, said the vision was crazy and bound to fail. Yet Turner looked at emerging social and demographic trends, listened to his intuition, and launched a global network that generates 35 percent gross margins.[73]

Action Memo

As a leader, you can combine vision with action. You can make a difference for your team or organization by both having big dreams and transforming them into significant strategic action.

To formulate a vision, leaders also look inward to their hopes and dreams, and they listen to the hopes and dreams of followers. Foresight and the ability to see future possibilities emerge not just from traditional strategic planning tools and formulas, but from curiosity, instinct and intuition, emotions, deep thinking, personal experience, and hope. To connect with people's deeper yearning for something great, vision can transcend the rational. Although it is based on reality, it comes from the heart rather than the head.

Leadership Essentials

▪ Leaders establish organizational direction through vision and strategy. They are responsible for studying the organization's environment, considering how it may be different in the future, and setting a direction everyone can believe in. The shared vision is an attractive, ideal future for the organization that is credible yet not readily attainable. A clear, powerful vision links the present and the future by showing how present actions and decisions can move the organization toward its long-range goals. Vision energizes employees and gives them an inspiring picture of the future to which they are eager to commit themselves. The vision can also give meaning to work and establish a standard of excellence by presenting a challenge that asks all workers to give their best.

▪ The mission includes the company's core values and its core purpose or reason for existence. Visions for the future change, whereas the mission should persist, as a reflection of the enduring character of the organization. Effective leaders frame a noble purpose that inspires followers and helps the organization maintain a competitive advantage. To frame an organizational purpose that helps people find their work meaningful, leaders can choose among four basic concepts as the basis of purpose: discovery, excellence, altruism, and heroism.

▪ Strategic management is the serious work of figuring out how to translate vision and mission into action. Strategy is a general plan of action that describes resource allocation and other activities for dealing with the environment and helping the organization reach its goals. Like vision, strategy changes, but successful companies develop strategies that focus on core competence, develop synergy, and create value for customers. Strategy is executed through the systems and structures that are the basic architecture for how things get done in the organization.

▪ Leaders decide on direction through rational analysis as well as intuition, personal experience, and hopes and dreams. Leaders make a real difference for their organization only when they link vision to strategic action, so that vision is more than just a dream. Superior organizational performance is not a matter of luck. It is determined by the decisions leaders make.

Discussion Questions

1. A management consultant said that strategic leaders are concerned with vision and mission, while strategic managers are concerned with strategy. Do you agree? Discuss.

2. A vision can apply to an individual, a family, a college course, a career, or decorating an apartment. Think of something you care about for which you want the future to be different from the present and write a vision statement for it.

3. If you worked for a company like Apple or Google that has a strong vision for the future, how would that affect you compared to working for a company that did not have a vision?

4. Do you agree with the principle of self-reference? In other words, do you believe if people know where the organization is trying to go, they will make decisions that support the desired organizational outcome?

5. What does it mean to say that the vision can include a description of both the journey and the destination?

6. Many visions are written and hung on a wall. Do you think this type of vision has value? What would be required to imprint the vision within each person?

7. What is the difference between mission and vision? Can you give an example of each?

8. Do you think every organization needs a noble purpose in order to be successful over the long term? Discuss. Name one company that seems to reflect each category of noble purpose as defined in the chapter.

9. Strategic vision and strategic action are both needed for a leader to be effective. Which do you think you are better at doing? Why?

10. If vision is so important, why do analysts and commentators sometimes criticize a new CEO's emphasis on formulating a vision for a company that is struggling to survive? Discuss.

Leadership at Work

FUTURE THINKING

Think of some problem you have in your life right now. It could be any problem you are having at school, home, or work that you would like to solve. Write a few words that summarize the problem:

_____

_____

_____

Now write brief answers to the following questions for that specific problem. (Do not look ahead to the next set of four questions. This exercise is more effective if the questions are seen in sequence.)

1. Why do I have this problem?

_____

_____

_____

2. Who/what caused this problem?

_____

_____

_____

3. What stands in the way of a solution?

_____

_____

_____

4. How likely is it that I'll solve this problem?

_____

_____

_____

After you have answered these four questions, write down what are you feeling about the problem.

_____

_____

_____

Now, for the same problem, write brief answers to the following four questions.

1. What do I really want instead of this problem? (Your answer equals your desired future outcome.)

_____

_____

_____

2. How will I know I've achieved this future outcome? (What will I see, hear, and feel?)

_____

_____

_____

3. What resources do I need to pursue this future outcome?

_____

_____

_____

4. What is the first step I can take to achieve this outcome?

_____

_____

_____

After you have answered these four questions, what are you feeling about the problem?

_____

_____

_____

The human mind is effective at focusing on problems to diagnose what is wrong and who is to blame. The first four questions reflect that approach, which is called *problem-focused thinking*.

The second set of four questions reflects a different approach, called *outcome-directed thinking*. It focuses the mind on future outcomes and possibilities rather than on the causes of the problem. Most people feel more positive emotion, more creative ideas, and more optimism about solving the problem after answering the second four questions compared to the first four questions. Shifting the mind to the future harnesses the same power that a vision has to awaken creativity and inspire people to move forward. Future thinking is using the idea of future vision on a small, day-to-day scale.

In Class: This exercise is very effective when each student selects a problem, and then students interview each other about their problems. Students should work in pairs—one acting the role of leader and the other acting as a subordinate. The subordinate describes his or her problem (one minute), and then the leader simply asks the first four questions (*changing each "I" to "you"*) and listens to the answers (four minutes). Then the two students can switch leader/ subordinate roles and repeat the process for the same four questions. The instructor can then gather students' observations about what they felt when answering the four questions.

Then, students can be instructed to find a new partner, and the pairs can again adopt the role of leader and subordinate. The subordinate will relate the same problem as before to the leader, but this time the leader will ask the second four questions (outcome-directed thinking, *again changing each "I" to "you"*). After the subordinate answers the four questions, the pair switches leader/subordinate roles and repeats the process. Then the instructor can ask for student observations about how they felt answering these four questions compared to the first four questions. Generally the reaction is quite positive. The key questions for students to consider are: How did the questions about future outcomes affect your creative thoughts for solving the problem compared to the first four questions that were problem-oriented? As a leader, can you use future-oriented questions in your daily life to shape your thinking and the thinking of others toward more creative problem solving? Future-oriented thinking is a powerful leadership tool.

Sources: This approach to problem solving was developed by Robert P. Bostrom and Victoria K. Clawson of Bostrom and Associates, Columbia, Missouri, and this exercise is based on a write-up appearing in *Inside USAA*, the company newsletter of USAA (September 11, 1996), pp. 8–10; and Victoria K. Clawson and Robert P. Bostrom, "Research-Driven Facilitation Training for Computer-Supported Environments," *Group Decision and Negotiation* 5 (1996), pp. 7–29.

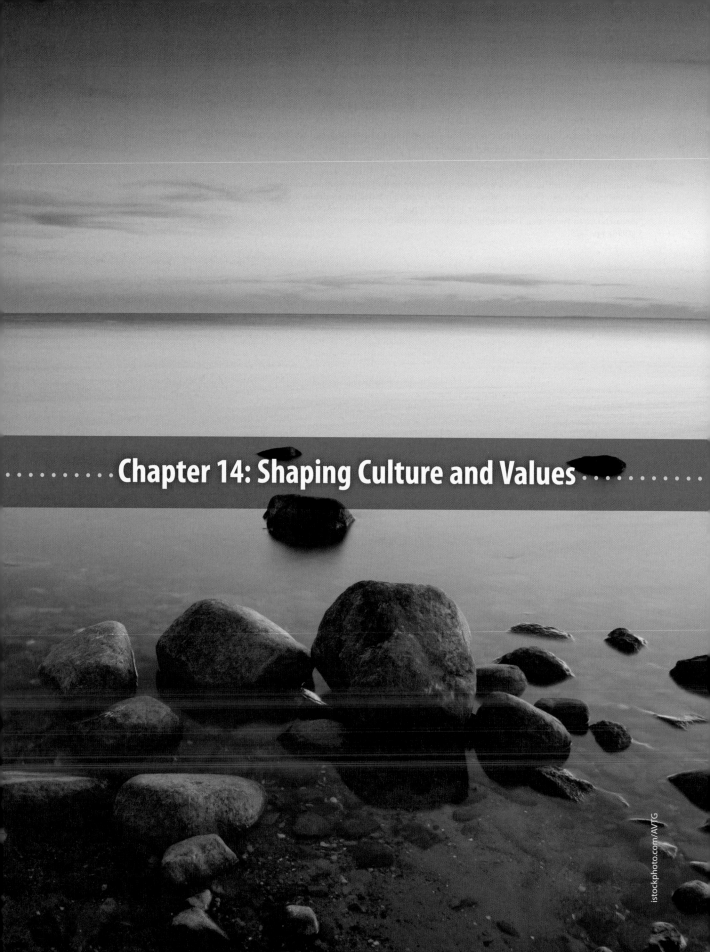

Chapter 14: Shaping Culture and Values

istockphoto.com/AVTG

Your Leadership Challenge

After reading this chapter, you should be able to:

- Understand why shaping culture is a critical function of leadership.

- Recognize the characteristics of an adaptive, as opposed to an unadaptive, culture.

- Understand and apply how leaders shape culture and values through ceremonies, stories, symbols,

language, selection and socialization, and daily actions.

- Identify the cultural values associated with adaptability, achievement, clan, and bureaucratic cultures and the environmental conditions associated with each.

- Act as an ethical leader and instill ethical values in the organizational culture.

- Apply the principles of spiritual leadership to help people find deeper life meaning and a sense of membership through work.

Chapter Outline

As CEO of Zappos.com, Tony Hsieh's top goal is not selling the most shoes over the Internet. His real priority is making employees and customers happy. Most Zappos employees are hourly call center workers. They get paid less than the industry average (even Hsieh makes only $36,000 a year) and don't get fancy perks, but they talk about the company with an almost religious zeal. Zappos employees might not have an onsite fitness center, but they do have a nap room and a full-time life coach they can talk to if they need guidance or if they're just having a bad day. People are encouraged to let their unique personalities come out at work, and they are given the autonomy to do whatever it takes to "wow" customers. Employees are guided by a set of 10 core values, including "Create fun and a little weirdness," "Be humble," and "Pursue growth and learning." Managers are required to spend 10 to 20 percent of their time goofing off with the people they manage, and after-hours get-togethers for parades, happy hours, and pajama parties are common. When interviewing applicants, leaders look for creativity, individuality, and a positive attitude, and they create conditions that allow those qualities to flourish. The unique culture at Zappos has helped the company grow rapidly in sales and profits, as well as landed it at Number 23 as the highest-ranking newcomer on *Fortune*'s list of the Best Companies to Work For. "If we get the culture right," Hsieh says, "most of the other stuff, like the brand and the customer service, will just happen."[1]

In the previous chapter, we talked about creating an inspiring vision and defining the strategies to help achieve it. Successful leaders recognize that culture is a core element in helping the organization meet strategic goals and attain the vision. Leaders align people with the vision by influencing organizational culture and shaping the environment that determines morale and performance. Corporate culture is powerful because it affects a company's performance for better or worse. Thriving companies such as Google, Southwest Airlines, and Apple have often attributed their success to the cultures their leaders helped create. On the other hand, dysfunctional cultures or the wrong cultural values have been blamed for many of the problems at companies like Enron, Bear Stearns, and General Motors.

This chapter explores ideas about organizational culture and values, and the role of leaders in shaping them. Most leaders recognize that culture is an important mechanism for attracting, motivating, and retaining talented employees, a capability that may be the single best predictor of overall organizational excellence.[2] One long-term study discovered that organizations with strong cultures outperform organizations with weak cultures two-to-one on several primary measures of financial performance.[3] The first section of this chapter describes the nature of corporate culture and its importance to organizations. Then we turn to a consideration of how shared values can help the organization stay competitive and how leaders influence cultural values for high performance. Leaders emphasize specific cultural values depending on the organization's situation. The final section of the chapter briefly discusses ethical and spiritual values and how values-based leadership shapes an organization's cultural atmosphere.

Action Memo

Some leaders incorporate spiritual values as part of the corporate culture. Complete Leader's Self-Insight 14.1, "How Spiritual Are You," before reading the rest of this chapter.

Organizational Culture

As the world has grown more turbulent, the concept of culture has become increasingly important to organizational leaders because the new environment often calls for new values and fresh approaches to doing business. Most leaders now understand that when a company's culture fits the needs of its external environment and company strategy, employees can create an organization that is tough to beat.[4]

What Is Culture?

Some people think of culture as the character or personality of an organization. How an organization looks and "feels" when you enter it is a manifestation of the organizational culture. For example, if you visit headquarters at ExxonMobil, you would likely get a sense of formality the minute you walk in the door. Most employees are in conventional business attire, desks are neat and orderly, and the atmosphere is tinged with competitiveness and a rigorous, analytical approach to taking care of business. "They're not in the fun business," said one oil industry analyst. "They're in the profit business."[5] At a company such as Zappos, though, where fun is a core value, employees may be wearing jeans and sneakers, sport pierced lips or noses, and have empty pizza boxes, coffee cups, and drink bottles on their desks. Both of these companies are highly successful, but the underlying cultures are very different.

Culture can be defined as the set of key values, assumptions, understandings, and norms that is shared by members of an organization and taught to new members as correct.[6] *Norms* are shared standards that define what behaviors are

Culture
the set of key values, assumptions, understandings, and norms that is shared by members of an organization and taught to new members as correct

acceptable and desirable within a group of people. At its most basic, culture is a pattern of shared assumptions and beliefs about how things are done in an organization. As organizational members cope with internal and external problems, they develop shared assumptions and norms of behavior that are taught to new members as the correct way to think, feel, and act in relation to those problems.[7]

Culture can be thought of as consisting of three levels, as illustrated in Exhibit 14.1, with each level becoming less obvious.[8] At the surface level are visible artifacts, such as manner of dress, patterns of behavior, physical symbols, organizational ceremonies, and office layout—all the things one can see, hear, and observe by watching members of the organization. Consider some observable aspects of culture at John Lewis, a successful retailer in Great Britain. People working in John Lewis stores are typically older than staff members at other retailers and are called partners, not employees. Everyone shares in company profits and has a say in how the business is run. The entrance to leaders' offices is small and functional rather than ostentatious, and stores exude an air of simplicity, calmness, and order.[9] At a deeper level of culture are the expressed values and beliefs, which are not observable but can be discerned from how people explain and justify what they do. These are values that members of the organization hold at a conscious level. For example, John Lewis partners consciously know that dependability, service, and quality are highly valued and rewarded in the company culture.

Some values become so deeply embedded in a culture that organizational members may not be consciously aware of them. These basic, underlying assumptions are the essence of the culture. At John Lewis, these assumptions might include (1) that the company cares about its employees as much as it expects them to care about customers, (2) that individual employees should think for themselves and do what they believe is right to provide exceptional customer service, and (3) that trust and honesty are an essential part of successful business relationships. Assumptions generally start out as expressed values, but over time they become more deeply embedded and less open to question—organization

Exhibit 14.1 Levels of Corporate Culture

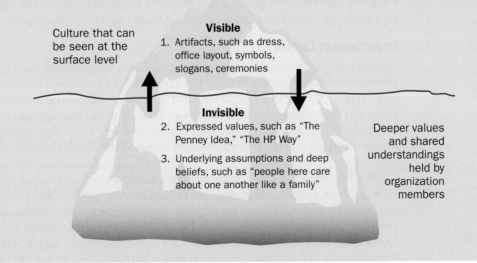

Culture that can be seen at the surface level

Visible
1. Artifacts, such as dress, office layout, symbols, slogans, ceremonies

Invisible
2. Expressed values, such as "The Penney Idea," "The HP Way"
3. Underlying assumptions and deep beliefs, such as "people here care about one another like a family"

Deeper values and shared understandings held by organization members

Think about your current life. Indicate whether each of the following items is Mostly False or Mostly True for you.

	Mostly False	Mostly True
1. I often reflect on the meaning of life.	_____	_____
2. I want to find a community where I can grow spiritually.	_____	_____
3. I have made real personal sacrifices in order to make the world a better place.	_____	_____
4. Sometimes when I look at an ordinary thing I feel that I am seeing it fresh for the first time.	_____	_____
5. I sometimes have unexpected flashes of insight or understanding while relaxing.	_____	_____
6. It is important to me to find meaning and mission in the world.	_____	_____
7. I often feel a strong sense of unity or connection with all the people around me.	_____	_____
8. I have had experiences that made my role in life clear to me.	_____	_____
9. After reflecting on something for a long time, I have learned to trust my feelings rather than logical reasons.	_____	_____
10. I am often transfixed by loveliness in nature.	_____	_____

Scoring and Interpretation

Spiritual leadership engages people in higher values and mission, and tries to create a corporate culture based on love and community rather than fear and separation. Spiritual leadership is not for everyone, but when spiritual ideals guide a leader's behavior, an excellent culture can be created. Values-based and spiritual leadership are discussed later in the chapter.

Add the number of Mostly True answers for your score: _____. A score of 7 or above indicates that you are highly spiritual and will likely become a values-based or spiritual leader. A score of 4–6 would suggest that you are spiritually average. A score of 0–3 means that you may be skeptical about developing spiritual awareness.

Source: Based on Kirsi Tirri, Petri Nokelainen, and Martin Ubani, "Conceptual Definition and Empirical Validation of the Spiritual Sensitivity Scale," *Journal of Empirical Theology* 19, no. 1 (2006), pp. 37–62; and Jeffrey Kluger, "Is God in Our Genes?" *Time* (October 25, 2004), pp. 62–72.

members take them for granted and often are not even aware of the assumptions that guide their behavior, language, and patterns of social interaction.

Importance of Culture

When people are successful at what they undertake, the ideas and values that led to that success become institutionalized as part of the organization's culture.[10] Culture gives employees a sense of organizational identity and generates a commitment to particular values and ways of doing things. Culture serves two important functions in organizations: (1) it integrates members so that they know how to relate to one another, and (2) it helps the organization adapt to the external environment.

Internal Integration Culture helps members develop a collective identity and know how to work together effectively. It is culture that guides day-to-day working relationships and determines how people communicate in the organization, what behavior is acceptable or not acceptable, and how power and status are allocated. Culture can imprint a set of unwritten rules inside employees' minds, which can be very powerful in determining behavior, thus affecting organizational performance.[11]

Many organizations are putting increased emphasis on developing strong cultures that encourage teamwork, collaboration, and mutual trust.[12] In an environment of trust, people are more likely to share ideas, be creative, and be generous with their knowledge and talents.

Action Memo

As a leader, you can pay attention to organizational culture and develop an awareness of how cultural values, norms, and beliefs influence people's behavior in the organization.

External Adaptation Culture also determines how the organization meets goals and deals with outsiders. The right cultural values can help the organization respond rapidly to customer needs or the moves of a competitor. Culture can encourage employee commitment to the core purpose of the organization, its specific goals, and the basic means used to accomplish goals.

The culture should embody the values and assumptions needed by the organization to succeed in its environment. If the competitive environment requires speed and flexibility, for example, the culture should embody values that support adaptability, collaboration across departments, and a fast response to customer needs or environmental changes. Consider how the cultural values at Cisco encourage internal behaviors that meet the needs of its competitive environment.

IN THE LEAD

John Chambers, Cisco Systems

Cisco Systems has been called the plumber of the technology world. It makes the routers, switches, and advanced network technologies that keep data moving round-the-clock and around the world. When the dot-com bubble burst at the beginning of the century, Cisco went from being the most highly valued company in the world to fighting for its life. After the initial shock, CEO John Chambers and other leaders started positioning Cisco for the future, which included changing the independent "cowboy culture" that encouraged people to compete with each other for power, resources, and success, creating barriers to cooperation.

The new environment called for stronger collaboration and a faster response to shifting technology needs. Trust and openness became the new key values. Today, it is unacceptable for people at Cisco not to share their ideas, knowledge, and resources. Executives are rewarded based on how well the entire business performs, rather than just their individual units, so they share responsibility for one another's success. Rather than having proposals and suggestions sent to top executives for approval, a network of councils and boards that cross functional, departmental, and hierarchical lines are empowered to launch new businesses. That keeps people working together and speeds innovation. One board made up of volunteer self-identified "sports freaks" built a product called StadiumVision, which allows venue owners to push video and digital content such as advertising to fans in the stadium. Now a multibillion-dollar business, StadiumVision came together in less than 4 months, without the CEO ever being involved in decision making. Command and control is a thing of the past, Chambers asserts, with the future belonging to those companies that build leadership throughout the organization.

The change didn't come easily, and around 20 percent of Cisco's executives left the company because they couldn't adjust to the new cultural values. Those who stayed, though, argue that today's increasingly interconnected world requires breaking down barriers internally as well as with customers, partners, and suppliers. Rather than just being a technical advisor, Cisco also offers guidance on how other companies can transition to a more collaborative way of working. "We've added culture to our core competencies," says Chambers.[13]

At Cisco, a strong culture helps bind people together, making the organization a community rather than just a collection of individuals. However, the culture also encourages adaptation to the environment in order to keep the organization healthy and profitable. This chapter's *Consider This* highlights the importance of individual learning and adaptability. Just like people, organizational cultures have to grow and change to meet new challenges.

Consider **This!**
Here Is Your Assignment

1. You will receive a body.
   You may like it or not, but it will be yours for the entire period this time around.

2. You will learn lessons.
   You are enrolled in a full-time, informal school called life. Each day in this school you will have the opportunity to learn lessons. You may like the lessons or think them irrelevant and stupid.

3. There are no mistakes, only lessons.
   Growth is a process of trial and error, experimentation. The "failed" experiments are as much a part of the process as the experiment that ultimately "works."

4. A lesson is repeated until it is learned.
   A lesson will be presented to you in various forms until you have learned it; then you can go on to the next lesson.

5. Learning lessons does not end.
   There is no part of life that does not contain its lessons. If you are alive, there are lessons to be learned.

6. "There" is no better than "here."
   When your "there" has become a "here," you will simply obtain another "there" that will, again, look better than "here."

7. Others are merely mirrors of you.
   You cannot love or hate something about another person unless it reflects to you something you love or hate about yourself.

8. What you make of your life is up to you.
   You have all the tools and resources you need; what you do with them is up to you. The choice is yours.

9. The answers lie inside you.
   The answers to life's questions lie inside you. All you need to do is look, listen, and trust.

10. Whether you think you can or can't, in either case you'll be right. Think about it.

© majaiva

Culture Strength, Adaptation, and Performance

Culture strength
the degree of agreement among employees about the importance of specific values and ways of doing things

Culture strength refers to the degree of agreement among employees about the importance of specific values and ways of doing things. If widespread consensus exists, the culture is strong and cohesive; if little agreement exists, the culture is weak.[14] The effect of a strong culture is not always a positive one. Sometimes a strong culture can encourage the wrong values and cause harm to the organization and its members. Think of Bear Stearns, which had a strong, highly competitive corporate culture that supported pushing everything to the limits in the pursuit of wealth. As long as an employee was making money for the firm, leaders took a hands-off approach, which allowed increasingly risky and sometimes unethical behavior. Accustomed to this swashbuckling culture, former Bear Stearns traders who now work for JPMorgan (which acquired parts of the firm) are having a hard time adjusting to JPM's culture of accountability.[15]

A strong culture increases employee cohesion and commitment to the values, goals, and strategies of the organization, but companies can sometimes have unethical values or values that are unhealthy for the organization because they don't fit the needs of the environment. Research at Harvard into some 200 corporate cultures found that a strong culture does not ensure success unless it also encourages a healthy adaptation to the external environment.[16] A strong culture that does not encourage adaptation can be more damaging to an organization than a weak culture. For example, fixing the insular, overly bureaucratic culture at General Motors is a top priority for the U.S. government, which is now majority owner of the automaker. For decades, any outside leader who came in and advocated for change at GM got pushed out of the company or left in frustration. Products were held up, decisions delayed, and problems never solved because of a culture that discouraged dissent, inhibited collaborative teamwork, and promoted extensive study and documentation for even minor matters like changing the design of a headlight. "Addressing cultural issues is just as fundamental to our assignment as addressing the balance sheet or financing," said the lead adviser to the White House on the auto industry.[17]

Adaptive Cultures

As illustrated in Exhibit 14.2, adaptive corporate cultures have different values and behavior from unadaptive cultures. In adaptive cultures, leaders are concerned with customers and those internal people, processes, and procedures that bring about useful change. In unadaptive cultures, leaders are concerned with themselves or their own special projects, and their values tend to discourage risk taking and change. Thus, a strong culture is not enough, because an unhealthy culture may encourage the organization to march resolutely in the wrong direction. Healthy cultures help companies adapt to the external environment.

An organization's culture may not always be in alignment with the needs of the external environment. The values and ways of doing things may reflect what worked in the past. The difference between desired and actual values and behaviors is called the **culture gap**.[18] Many organizations have some degree of culture gap, though leaders often fail to realize it. An important step toward shifting the culture toward more adaptive values is to recognize when people are adhering to the wrong values or when important values are not held strongly enough.[19]

Culture gaps can be immense, particularly in the case of mergers. The integration of FedEx and Kinko's, for example, has been rocky because of their very different corporate cultures. Kinko's always had a somewhat freewheeling culture, reflected in a statement made by one former worker: "I had cornrows and green hair and no one seemed to mind." FedEx, on the other hand, has a culture based on structure, uniformity, and discipline. Five years after FedEx bought the copy-center company, managers are still struggling to implement the culture change they feel is needed.[20]

Culture gap
the difference between desired and actual values and behaviors

Exhibit 14.2 Adaptive Versus Unadaptive Cultures

	Adaptive Organizational Culture	Unadaptive Organizational Culture
Visible behavior	Leaders pay close attention to all their constituencies, especially customers, and initiate change when needed to serve their legitimate interests, even if it entails taking some risks.	Managers tend to behave somewhat insularly, politically, and bureaucratically. As a result, they do not change their strategies quickly to adjust to or take advantage of changes in their business environments.
Expressed values	Leaders care deeply about customers, stockholders, and employees. They also strongly value people and processes that can create useful change (e.g., leadership initiatives up and down the management hierarchy).	Managers care mainly about themselves, their immediate work group, or some product (or technology) associated with that work group. They value the orderly and risk-reducing management process much more highly than leadership initiatives.
Underlying assumption	Serve whole organization, trust others.	Meet own needs, distrust others.

Source: Reprinted with the permission of The Free Press, a Division of Simon & Schuster Adult Publishing Group, from *Corporate Culture and Performance* by John P. Kotter and James L. Heskett. Copyright © 1992 by Kotter Associates, Inc., and James L. Heskett. All rights reserved.

Despite the popularity of mergers and acquisitions as a corporate strategy, many fail. Studies by consulting firms such as McKinsey & Company, the Hay Group, and others suggest that performance declines in almost 20 percent of acquired companies after acquisition. Some experts claim that 90 percent of mergers never live up to expectations.[21] One reason for this is the difficulty of integrating cultures. Organizational leaders should remember that the human systems—in particular, the norms and values of corporate culture—are what make or break any change initiative. The problem of integrating cultures increases in scope and complexity with global companies and cross-cultural mergers or acquisitions.

Action Memo

To improve your understanding of adaptive versus unadaptive cultures, go to Leader's Self-Insight 14.2 and assess the cultural values of a place you have worked.

The High-Performance Culture

Culture plays an important role in creating an organizational climate that enables learning and innovative response to challenges, competitive threats, or new opportunities. A strong culture that encourages adaptation and change enhances organizational performance by energizing and motivating employees, unifying people around shared goals and a higher mission, and shaping and guiding employee behavior so that everyone's actions are aligned with strategic priorities. Thus, creating and influencing an adaptive culture is one of the most important jobs for organizational leaders. The right culture can drive high performance.[22]

A number of studies have found a positive relationship between culture and performance.[23] In *Corporate Culture and Performance*, Kotter and Heskett provided evidence that companies that intentionally managed cultural values outperformed similar companies that did not.[24] Some companies have developed systematic ways to measure and manage the impact of culture on organizational performance. At Caterpillar Inc., leaders used a tool called the Cultural Assessment Process (CAP) to give top executives hard data documenting millions of dollars in savings they could attribute directly to cultural factors.[25] Even the U.S. government

Leader's Self-Insight 14.2
Working in an Adaptive Culture

Think of a specific full-time job you have held. Indicate whether each of the following items is Mostly False or Mostly True according to your perception of the managers above you when you held that job.

	Mostly False	Mostly True
1. Good ideas got serious consideration from management above me	_____	_____
2. Management above me was interested in ideas and suggestions from people at my level in the organization.	_____	_____
3. When suggestions were made to management above me, they received fair evaluation.	_____	_____
4. Management did not expect me to challenge or change the status quo.	_____	_____
5. Management specifically encouraged me to bring about improvements in my workplace.	_____	_____
6. Management above me took action on recommendations made from people at my level.	_____	_____
7. Management rewarded me for correcting problems.	_____	_____
8. Management clearly expected me to improve work unit procedures and practices.	_____	_____
9. I felt free to make recommendations to management above me to change existing practices.	_____	_____
10. Good ideas did not get communicated upward because management above me was not very approachable.	_____	_____

Scoring and Interpretation

To compute your score: Give yourself one point for each Mostly True answer to questions 1, 2, 3, 5, 6, 7, 8, and 9 and for each Mostly False answer to questions 4 and 10. Total points: _____.

An adaptive culture is shaped by the values and actions of top and middle managers. When managers actively encourage and welcome change initiatives from below, the organization will be infused with values for change. These 10 questions measure your management's openness to change. A typical average score for management openness to change is about 4. If your average score was 5 or higher, you worked in an organization that expressed cultural values of adaptation. If your average score was 3 or below, the culture was probably unadaptive.

Thinking back to your job, was the level of management openness to change correct for that organization? Why? Compare your score to that of another student, and take turns describing what it was like working for the *managers above you*. Do you sense that there is a relationship between job satisfaction and management's openness to change? What specific manager characteristics and corporate values accounted for the openness (or lack of) in the two jobs?

Sources: Based on S. J. Ashford, N. P. Rothbard, S. K. Piderit, and J. E. Dutton, "Out on a Limb: The Role of Context and Impression Management in Issue Selling," *Administrative Science Quarterly* 43 (1998), pp. 23–57; and E. W. Morrison and C. C. Phelps, "Taking Charge at Work: Extrarole Efforts to Initiate Workplace Change," *Academy of Management Journal* 42, (1999), pp. 403–419.

is recognizing the link between culture and effectiveness. The U.S. Office of Personnel Management created its Organizational Assessment Survey as a way for federal agencies to measure aspects of culture and shift values toward high performance.[26]

Strong adaptive cultures that facilitate high performance often incorporate the following values:

1. *The whole is more important than the parts and boundaries between parts are minimized.* People are aware of the whole system, how everything fits together, and the relationships among various organizational parts. All members consider how their actions affect other parts and the total organization. This emphasis on the whole reduces boundaries both within

the organization and with other companies. Although subcultures may form, everyone's primary attitudes and behaviors reflect the organization's dominant culture. The free flow of people, ideas, and information allows coordinated action and continuous learning.

2. *Equality and trust are primary values.* The culture creates a sense of community and caring for one another. The organization is a place for creating a web of relationships that allows people to take risks and develop to their full potential. The emphasis on treating everyone with care and respect creates a climate of safety and trust that allows experimentation, mistakes, and learning. Managers emphasize honest and open communications as a way to build trust.

3. *The culture encourages risk taking, change, and improvement.* A basic value is to question the status quo and to take risks that are in the interest of the company and its stakeholders. Constant questioning of assumptions opens the gates to creativity and improvement. The culture rewards and celebrates the creators of new ideas, products, and work processes. To symbolize the importance of taking risks, an adaptive culture may also reward those who fail in order to learn and grow.

In addition, high-performance cultures emphasize both values and solid business performance as the drivers of organizational success. Leaders align values with the company's day-to-day operations—hiring practices, performance management, budgeting, criteria for promotions and rewards, and so forth. A study of corporate values by Booz Allen Hamilton and the Aspen Institute found that leaders in companies that report superior financial results typically put a high emphasis on values and link them directly to the way they run the organization.[27] For example, at Cisco Systems, described earlier, the performance review and reward systems were revised to reflect the emphasis on values of collaboration, openness, and trust.[28]

Cultural Leadership

An organization exists only because of the people who are a part of it, and those people both shape and interpret the character and culture of the organization. That is, an organization is not a slice of objective reality; different people may perceive the organization in different ways and relate to it in different ways. Leaders in particular formulate a viewpoint about the organization and the values that can help people achieve the organization's mission, vision, and strategic goals. Therefore, leaders enact a viewpoint and a set of values that they think are best for helping the organization succeed. A primary way in which leaders influence norms and values to build a high-performance culture is through *cultural leadership.*

A **cultural leader** defines and uses signals and symbols to influence corporate culture. Cultural leaders influence culture in two key areas:

1. *The cultural leader articulates a vision for the organizational culture that employees can believe in.* This means the leader defines and communicates central values that employees believe in and will rally around. Values are tied to a clear and compelling mission, or core purpose.

2. *The cultural leader heeds the day-to-day activities that reinforce the cultural vision.* The leader makes sure that work procedures and reward systems match and reinforce the values. Actions speak louder than words, so cultural leaders "walk their talk."[29]

Cultural leader
a leader who actively uses signals and symbols to influence corporate culture

For values to guide the organization, leaders model them every day. Canada's WestJet Airlines, which ranked in a survey for three years in a row as having Canada's most admired corporate culture, provides an illustration. Employees (called simply "people" at WestJet) regularly see CEO Clive Beddoe and other top leaders putting the values of equality, teamwork, participation, and customer service into action. At the end of a flight, for example, everyone on hand pitches in to pick up garbage–even the CEO. Leaders spend much of their time chatting informally with employees and customers, and they regularly send notes of thanks to people who have gone above and beyond the call of duty. Top executives have been known to visit the call center on Christmas Day to help out or to thank people for working the holiday. Leaders don't receive perks over and above anyone else. There are no assigned parking spaces and no club memberships. Every person at WestJet is treated like first-class, exactly the way leaders want employees to treat every passenger on a WestJet flight.[30]

Creating and maintaining a high-performance culture is not easy in today's turbulent environment and changing workplace, but through their words—and particularly their actions—cultural leaders let everyone in the organization know what really counts. Some of the mechanisms leaders use to enact cultural values are organizational rites and ceremonies, stories, symbols, and specialized language. In addition, they emphasize careful selection and socialization of new employees to keep cultures strong. Perhaps most importantly, leaders signal the cultural values they want to instill in the organization through their day-to-day behavior.

Action Memo

As a leader, you can build a high-performance culture that is strong and adaptive by showing concern for customers and other stakeholders in the external environment and by supporting people and projects that bring about useful change. You can be alert to culture gaps and influence values to close them.

Ceremonies

A **ceremony** is a planned activity that makes up a special event and is generally conducted for the benefit of an audience. Leaders can schedule ceremonies to provide dramatic examples of what the company values. Ceremonies reinforce specific values, create a bond among employees by allowing them to share an important event, and anoint and celebrate employees who symbolize important achievements.[31]

A ceremony often includes the presentation of an award. At Mary Kay Cosmetics, one of the most effective companies in the world at using ceremonies, leaders hold elaborate award ceremonies at an annual event called "Seminar," presenting jewelry, furs, and luxury cars to high-achieving sales consultants. The most successful consultants are introduced by film clips like the ones used to present award nominees in the entertainment industry.[32] These ceremonies recognize and celebrate high-performing employees and help bind sales consultants together. Even when they know they will not personally be receiving awards, consultants look forward to Seminar all year because of the emotional bond it creates with others.

Stories

A **story** is a narrative based on true events that is repeated frequently and shared among employees. Leaders can use stories to illustrate the company's primary values. For example, leaders at Ritz-Carlton hotels tell a story about a beach attendant who was stacking chairs for the evening when a guest asked if he would leave out two chairs. The guest wanted to return to the beach in the evening and propose to his girlfriend. Although the attendant was going off duty,

Ceremony
a planned activity that makes up a special event and is generally conducted for the benefit of an audience

Story
a narrative based on true events that is repeated frequently and shared among employees

he not only left out the chairs, but he also stayed late, put on a tuxedo, and escorted the couple to their chairs, presenting them with flowers and champagne and lighting candles at their table. The story is firmly entrenched in Ritz-Carlton's folklore and symbolizes the value of going above and beyond the call of duty to satisfy customers.[33]

In some cases, stories may not be supported by facts, but they are consistent with the values and beliefs of the organization. At Nordstrom, for example, leaders do not deny the story about a customer who got his money back on a defective tire, even though Nordstrom does not sell tires. The story reinforces the company's no-questions-asked return policy.[34]

Symbols

Another tool for conveying cultural values is the **symbol.** A symbol is an object, act, or event that conveys meaning to others. In a sense, stories and ceremonies are symbols, but leaders can also use physical artifacts to symbolize important values. For example, at the headquarters of Mother, a London-based advertising agency known for its strong culture and offbeat ads, there are no private offices. In fact, except for the restrooms, there are no doors in the whole place. This headquarters design symbolizes and reinforces the cultural values of open communication, collaboration, creativity, and egalitarianism.[35]

Specialized Language

Language can shape and influence organizational values and beliefs. Leaders sometimes use slogans or sayings to express key corporate values. Slogans can easily be picked up and repeated by employees. For example, at Averitt Express, the slogan "Our driving force is people" applies to customers and employees alike. The culture emphasizes that drivers and customers, not top executives, are the power that fuels the company's success.

Leaders also express and reinforce cultural values through written public statements, such as corporate mission statements or other formal statements that express the core values of the organization. When Sidney Taurel, who became chairman and CEO of Eli Lilly and Company in 1999, wanted to create a more adaptive culture able to respond to the demands of the global marketplace, he worked with other leaders to develop a formal statement of how to put Lilly's core values (respect for all people, honesty and integrity, and striving for excellence) into action. The statement includes descriptions and mottos such as "Model the values: Show us what you're made of," "Implement with integrity, energy, and speed: Provide the powder and supply the spark," and "Get results through people: Set people up to succeed."[36]

Selection and Socialization

To maintain cultural values over time, leaders emphasize careful selection and socialization of new employees. Companies with strong, healthy cultures, such as Genentech, Nordstrom, and Zappos, described in the chapter opening example, often have rigorous hiring practices. At biotechnology firm Genentech, job candidates often go through as many as 20 interviews because leaders want to be sure they hire people with the right values. "We're extremely nonhierarchical," says CEO Art Levinson. "We're not wearing ties. People don't call us doctor." Candidates who ask too many questions about salary, title, and personal advancement are quickly weeded out. Genentech wants people who care about

Symbol
an object, act, or event that conveys meaning to others

the science and about the company's mission, not about fancy offices and titles.[37]

Once the right people are hired, the next step is socializing them into the culture. **Socialization** is the process by which a person learns the values, norms, perspectives, and expected behaviors that enable him or her to successfully participate in the group or organization.[38] When people are effectively socialized, they "fit in," because they understand and adopt the norms and values of the group. Socialization is a key leadership tool for transmitting the culture and enabling it to survive over time. Leaders act as role models for the values they want new employees to adopt, as well as implement formal training programs, which may include pairing the newcomer with a key employee who embodies the desired values.

Action Memo

As a leader, you can shape cultural values through rites and ceremonies, stories, symbols, and language. You can keep the culture strong by carefully selecting and socializing people, and by making sure your actions match the espoused values.

Newcomers learn about values by watching other employees, as well as paying attention to what gets noticed and rewarded by leaders. But good leaders don't leave socialization to chance. Zappos provides new hires with four weeks of training, which includes learning about the company's values. At The Walt Disney Company, all new employees attend training sessions to learn about Disney's unique culture, where employees are referred to as "cast members," work either "on stage" or "backstage," and wear "costumes" rather than uniforms. After their initial training, each new hire is paired with a role model to continue the socialization process.[39]

Formal socialization programs can be highly effective. One study of recruits into the British Army surveyed newcomers on their first day and then again eight weeks later. Researchers compared the findings to a sample of experienced "insider" soldiers and found that after eight weeks of training, the new recruits' norms and values had generally shifted toward those of the insiders.[40] Another field study of around 300 people from a variety of organizations found that formal socialization was associated with less stress for newcomers, less ambiguity about expected roles and behaviors, and greater job satisfaction, commitment, and identification with the organization.[41]

Daily Actions

One of the most important ways leaders build and maintain the cultures they want is by signaling and supporting important cultural values through their daily actions. Employees learn what is valued most in a company by watching what attitudes and behaviors leaders pay attention to and reward, how leaders react to organizational crises, and whether the leader's own behavior matches the espoused values.[42] Amerisource CEO Dave Yost supports values of frugality and egalitarianism by answering his own phone, flying coach, and doing without fancy perks and stylish office furniture.[43] Good leaders understand how carefully they are watched by employees.

Leaders can also change unadaptive cultures by their actions. For example, at Marriott, as at many hotels, the pursuit of superior round-the-clock performance led to a deeply ingrained culture of *face time*—the more hours a manager put in, the better. Eventually, this philosophy made it tough for Marriott to find and keep talented people. When leaders wanted to instill values that encouraged work–life balance and an emphasis on results rather than hours worked, one of their most important steps was to make a point of leaving work early whenever possible. Encouraging lower-level managers to take more time off did no good until top leaders demonstrated the new value with their own behavior.[44]

Socialization
the process by which a person learns the cultural values, norms, and behaviors that enable him to "fit in" with a group or organization

Through ceremonies, stories, symbols, language, selection and socialization practices, and their own behavior, leaders shape culture. When culture change is needed to adapt to the environment or bring about smoother internal integration, leaders are responsible for instilling new values.

The Competing Values Approach to Shaping Culture

Organizational values are the enduring beliefs that have worth, merit, and importance for the organization. The economic crisis, the breakdown of corporate ethics and responsibility that contributed to it, and the crash of once-thriving companies have brought values to the forefront. Unhealthy cultural values played a crucial role in many of the mistakes these companies made.[45] Ethical values will be discussed later in the chapter. Changes in the nature of work, globalization, increasing diversity in the workforce, and other shifts in the larger society have also made the topic of values one of considerable concern to leaders. They are faced with such questions as, "How can I determine what cultural values are important? Are some values 'better' than others? How can the organization's culture help us be more competitive?"

In considering what values are important for the organization, leaders consider the external environment and the company's vision and strategy. Cultures can vary widely across organizations; however, organizations within the same industry often share similar values because they are operating in similar environments.[46] Key values should embody what the organization needs to be effective. Rather than looking at values as either "good" or "bad," leaders look for the right combination. The correct relationship among cultural values, organizational strategy, and the external environment can enhance organizational performance.

Organizational cultures can be assessed along many dimensions, such as the extent of collaboration versus isolation among people and departments, the importance of control and where control is concentrated, or whether the organization's time orientation is short-range or long-range.[47] Here, we will focus on two specific dimensions: (1) the extent to which the competitive environment requires flexibility or stability; and (2) the extent to which the organization's strategic focus and strength is internal or external. Four categories of culture associated with these differences, as illustrated in Exhibit 14.3, are adaptability, achievement, clan, and bureaucratic.[48] These four categories relate to the fit among cultural values, strategy, structure, and the environment, with each emphasizing specific values, as shown in the exhibit.

An organization may have cultural values that fall into more than one category, or even into all categories. However, successful organizations with strong cultures will lean more toward one particular culture category.

Action Memo

Determine your own cultural preferences by completing the exercise in Leader's Self-Insight 14.3.

Adaptability Culture

The **adaptability culture** is characterized by strategic leaders encouraging values that support the organization's ability to interpret and translate signals from the environment into new behavior responses. Employees have autonomy to make decisions and act freely to meet new needs, and responsiveness to customers is highly valued. Leaders also actively create change by encouraging and rewarding creativity, experimentation, and risk taking. A good example of an adaptability culture is Google, a company whose values promote individual initiative, experimentation, risk taking, and entrepreneurship.

Organizational values
the enduring beliefs that have worth, merit, and importance for the organization

Adaptability culture
culture characterized by values that support the organization's ability to interpret and translate signals from the environment into new behavior responses

Exhibit 14.3 Four Corporate Cultures

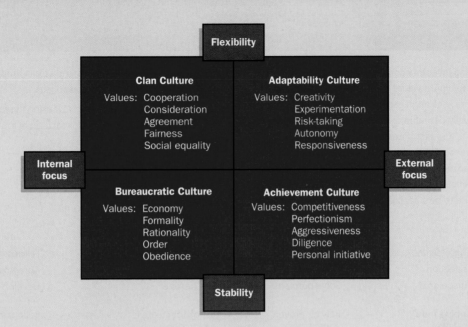

Sources: Based on Paul McDonald and Jeffrey Gandz, "Getting Value from Shared Values," *Organizational Dynamics* 21, no. 3 (Winter 1992), pp. 64–76; Deanne N. Den Hartog, Jaap J. VanMuijen, and Paul L. Koopman, "Linking Transformational Leadership and Organizational Culture," *The Journal of Leadership Studies* 3, no. 4 (1996), pp. 68–83; Daniel R. Denison and Aneil K. Mishra, "Toward a Theory of Organizational Culture and Effectiveness," *Organizational Studies* 6, no. 2 (March–April 1995), pp. 204–223; Robert Hooijberg and Frank Petrock, "On Cultural Change: Using the Competing Values Framework to Help Leaders Execute a Transformational Strategy," *Human Resource Management* 32, no. 1 (1993), pp. 29–50; and R. E. Quinn, *Beyond Rational Management: Mastering the Paradoxes and Competing Demands of High Performance* (San Francisco: Jossey-Bass, 1998).

IN THE LEAD

Sergey Brin and Larry Page, Google

As Google founders Sergey Brin and Larry Page once famously wrote, "Google is not a conventional company." Google tries to keep people thinking in unconventional ways to help the company keep innovating. Consider the flier posted on the door of every bathroom stall at corporate headquarters. Titled "Testing on the Toilet," the flier offers a quiz designed to challenge the brains of software engineers (the quiz changes every few weeks).

Fortune magazine called it "chaos by design." *The Washington Post* referred to it as a "culture of fearlessness." Whatever you call it, Google's culture works. The atmosphere inside Google feels like a university, where brainy graduate students have fun, work long and hard, and engage in academic debates about ideas that are treated like matters of global importance. They can bring their dogs to work, do their laundry on site, work out in the gym, study Mandarin, Japanese, Spanish, or French, and eat at any of 11 free gourmet cafeterias. Engineers, the "big men" (and women) on campus, spend 20 percent of their time working on their own ideas. Everyone is encouraged to propose outrageously ambitious ideas often, and teams are assigned to explore whether they will work. A lot of them don't, but some take off spectacularly.

The hiring process is designed to find out if the candidate is *Googley*. "It's an ill-defined term," says chief culture officer Stacy Sullivan, but it basically means "not someone too traditional or stuck in ways done traditionally by other companies."[49]

Leader's Self-Insight 14.3
Culture Preference Inventory

The following inventory consists of 14 sets of four responses that relate to typical values or situations facing leaders in organizations. Although each response to a question may appear equally desirable or undesirable, your assignment is to rank the four responses in each row according to your preference. Think of yourself as being in charge of a major department or division in an organization. Rank the responses in each row according to how much you would like each one to be a part of your department. There are no correct or incorrect answers; the scores simply reflect your preferences for different responses.

Rank each of the four in each row using the following scale. You must use all four numbers for each set of four responses.
1. Would not prefer at all
2. Would prefer on occasion
4. Would prefer often
8. Would prefer most of all

	I	II	III	IV
1.	Aggressiveness	Cost efficiency	Experimentation	Fairness
2.	Perfection	Obedience	Risk taking	Agreement
3.	Pursue goals	Solve problems	Be flexible	Develop people's careers
4.	Apply careful analysis	Rely on proven approaches	Look for creative approaches	Build consensus
5.	Initiative	Rationality	Responsiveness	Collaboration
6.	Highly capable	Productive and accurate	Receptive to brainstorming	Committed to the team
7.	Be the best in our field	Have secure jobs	Recognition for innovations	Equal status
8.	Decide and act quickly	Follow plans and priorities	Refuse to be pressured	Provide guidance and support
9.	Realistic	Systematic	Broad and flexible	Sensitive to the needs of others
10	Energetic and ambitious	Polite and formal	Open-minded	Agreeable and self-confident
11.	Use key facts	Use accurate and complete data	Use broad coverage of many options	Use limited data and personal opinion
12.	Competitive	Disciplined	Imaginative	Supportive
13.	Challenging assignments	Influence over others	Achieving creativity	Acceptance by the group
14.	Best solution	Good working environment	New approaches or ideas	Personal fulfillment

Scoring and Interpretation

Add the points in each of the four columns—I, II, III, IV. The sum of the point columns should be 210 points. If your sum does not equal 210 points, check your answers and your addition.

The scores represent your preference for I, achievement culture; II, bureaucratic culture; III, adaptability culture; and IV, clan culture. Your personal values are consistent with the culture for which you achieved the highest score, although all four sets of values exist within you just as they exist within an organization. The specific values you exert as a leader may depend on the group situation, particularly the needs of the external environment. Compare your scores with other students and discuss their meaning. Are you pleased with your preferences? Do you think your scores accurately describe your values?

Source: Adapted from Alan J. Rowe and Richard O. Mason, *Managing with Style: A Guide to Understanding, Assessing, and Improving Decision Making* (San Francisco: Jossey-Bass, 1987).

With rapid growth, Google's culture is showing signs of strain. The company zoomed from a few hundred people at headquarters to more than 20,000 in locations scattered around the world, and the processes needed to manage a large corporation hinder some of its creativity and flexibility. In addition, the global economic downturn has led to stronger top-down management and more control of risks and costs. Leaders are shifting the anything-goes culture as they look for ways to ensure the company continues to thrive during hard times. Nevertheless, they are also consciously trying to keep the heart of the culture intact. As one said, "Our unique culture is part of what makes Google Google."[50] Many technology and Internet-based companies, like Google, use the adaptability type of culture, as do many companies in the marketing, electronics, and cosmetics industries, because they must move quickly to satisfy customers.

Achievement Culture

The **achievement culture** is characterized by a clear vision of the organization's goals, and leaders focus on the achievement of specific targets such as sales growth, profitability, or market share. An organization concerned with serving specific customers in the external environment but without the need for flexibility and rapid change is suited to the achievement culture. This is a results-oriented culture that values competitiveness, aggressiveness, personal initiative, and the willingness to work long and hard to achieve results. An emphasis on winning is the glue that holds the organization together.[51]

Netflix provides an example of an achievement culture. Founder and CEO Reed Hastings hires the best people he can find, gives them big salaries and luxury perks, and provides them with the autonomy they need to get results. In the company's quest to become the top purveyor of online movies, Hastings says money is no object when recruiting talent. Those who perform are handsomely rewarded with generous raises and bonuses and allowed to take as much vacation time as they want. If people don't live up to the high standards, they are given a decent severance and shown the door. It's what marketing manager Heather McIlhany refers to as a tough, fulfilling, "fully-formed adult" culture.[52]

Action Memo

As a leader, you can align the organization's culture to its strategy and the needs of the external environment. You can choose to implement the appropriate culture (adaptability, achievement, clan, or bureaucratic) depending on environmental requirements and the organization's strategic focus.

Clan Culture

The **clan culture** has an internal focus on the involvement and participation of employees to meet changing expectations from the external environment. More than any other, this culture places value on meeting the needs of organization members. Companies with clan cultures are generally friendly places to work, and employees may seem almost like a family. Leaders emphasize cooperation, consideration of both employees and customers, and avoiding status differences. Leaders put a premium on fairness and reaching agreement with others.

One company that achieves success with a clan culture is In-N-Out Burger, a fast-food chain with 232 stores in the Western United States. Founders Harry and Esther Snyder created a corporate culture based on the idea that running a successful fast-food business depends on one thing: treating the people on the front lines right. One of the most important values at In-N-Out is taking care of employees and making sure they have whatever they need to be satisfied and productive.[53] This chapter's Leader's Bookshelf further describes In-N-Out Burger's unique corporate culture.

Achievement culture
culture characterized by a clear vision of the organization's goals and leaders' focus on the achievement of specific targets

Clan culture
culture with an internal focus on the involvement and participation of employees to meet changing expectations from the external environment

Leader's Bookshelf

In-N-Out Burger: A Behind-the-Counter Look at the Fast-Food Chain That Breaks All the Rules
by Stacy Perman

In-N-Out Burger was founded by Harry and Esther Snyder in 1948, but the values they instilled—such as quality, service, and treating people right—have remained an important part of In-N-Out's culture to this day. Stacy Perman's entertaining book provides an in-depth history of In-N-Out Burger and includes a glimpse into a corporate culture that is unique in the fast-food industry.

Treat People Right
Customers love In-N-Out Burger. The company enjoys cult-like status and causes "burger jams" every time it opens a new location. The Snyders believed that to treat customers right, you have to treat employees right. Here are a couple of the leadership principles that created a strong employee-focused culture:

- *Instill a sense of pride.* Employees, called *associates,* are made to feel like part of an important enterprise. They get extensive training and feedback and are given

opportunities to advance. Perman points out that "many part-timers came for a summer job and stayed for a career." The company believes in promoting from within, and about 80 percent of store managers started at the very bottom of the company, picking up trash. Local managers feel like owners of their stores, and some have been with the company for 20 years or more. When managers took a Christmas outing to a performance of *The Nutcracker,* the late Rich Snyder, who was president of In-N-Out at the time, asked them to wear tuxedos. "He thought they stood shoulder to shoulder with any blue-chip manager and wanted them to feel that way, too."

- *Put your money where your mouth is.* In-N-Out has always paid employees $2 to $3 above minimum wage, and some store managers make more than $100,000 a year. Some years ago, a consultant advised In-N-Out leaders that they could "save a ton of money" by slashing salaries. Rich

Snyder was furious at the suggestion. The company also has generous benefits, including 401(k) plans, paid vacations for part-time workers, and health, dental, and vision plans for full-timers. Rich Snyder established the tradition of holding company picnics and other family-like events and sending managers who met their goals on first-class trips to Europe.

This Culture Works
In-N-Out has one of the lowest turnover rates in the fast-food industry and beats both Burger King and McDonald's on per-store sales. The company is still family-owned; leaders have resisted going public or franchising because they don't want to grow too fast and lose the values that make In-N-Out unique.

In-N-Out Burger: A Behind-the-Counter Look at the Fast-Food Chain That Breaks All the Rules, by Stacy Perman, is published by HarperBusiness.

marble: © Ioannis Drimilis   library: www.istockphoto.com/nikada

Bureaucratic Culture

The **bureaucratic culture** has an internal focus and consistency orientation for a stable environment. The culture supports a methodical, rational, orderly way of doing business. Following the rules and being thrifty are valued. The organization succeeds by being highly integrated and efficient.

Safeco Insurance has functioned well with a bureaucratic culture. Employees take their coffee breaks at an assigned time, and a dress code specifies white shirts and suits for men and no beards. However, employees like this culture—reliability is highly valued and extra work isn't required. The bureaucratic culture works for the insurance company, and Safeco succeeds because it can be trusted to deliver on insurance policies as agreed.[54] In today's fast-changing world, very few organizations operate in a stable environment, and most leaders are shifting away from bureaucratic cultures because of a need for greater flexibility.

Bureaucratic culture
culture with an internal focus and consistency orientation for a stable environment

Each of the four cultures can be successful. The relative emphasis on various cultural values depends on the organization's strategic focus and the needs of the external environment. Leaders might have preferences for the values associated with one type of culture, but they learn to adjust the values they emulate and encourage, depending on the needs of the organization. It is the responsibility of leaders to ensure that organizations don't get "stuck" in cultural values that worked in the past but are no longer successful. As environmental conditions and strategy change, leaders work to instill new cultural values to help the organization meet new needs.

Ethical Values in Organizations

Of the values that make up an organization's culture, ethical values are considered highly important for leaders and have gained renewed emphasis in today's era of financial scandals and moral lapses. Ethics is difficult to define in a precise way. In general, **ethics** is the code of principles and values that governs the behavior of a person or group with respect to what is right or wrong. Ethics sets standards as to what is good or bad in conduct and decision making.[55] Many people believe that if you are not breaking the law, then you are behaving in an ethical manner, but ethics often goes far beyond the law.[56] The law arises from a set of codified principles and regulations that are generally accepted in society and are enforceable in the courts. Although current laws often reflect minimum ethical standards, not all ethical standards are codified into law. For example, prior to the Wall Street meltdown that came about because of millions of bad subprime mortgage loans, there were no laws preventing mortgage companies from providing what some have called "ninja loans" (no income, no job, no assets).[57] However, ethical leaders would hold that giving loans to people who most likely cannot afford the payments in order to increase your loan volume is unethical.

Most organizations that remain successful over the long term have leaders who include ethical values as part of the formal policies and informal cultures of their companies. Commentators on the recent crisis in the mortgage system, for instance, point out that a big part of the problem was a lack of ethical values that guided employee behavior. "Technical economics is crucial to understanding the crisis, but only goes so far," one wrote. "There was a hint that more than technical factors were involved when subprime loans were referred to as 'liar's loans.'"[58] In response to the recent crisis, some business schools and students are taking a fresh look at how future business leaders are trained.

IN THE LEAD

Harvard Business School, Columbia Business School, Yale School of Management, Wharton School of the University of Pennsylvania

Some members of the 2009 graduating class of Harvard Business School did something unusual. They signed a voluntary student-led pledge saying that the goal of a business leader is to "serve the greater good" and promising that they will act responsibly and ethically and refrain from advancing their "own narrow ambitions" at the expense of others.

At Harvard and other business schools, there has been an explosion of interest in ethics classes and activities that focus on personal and corporate responsibility. Many

Ethics
the code of moral principles and values that governs the behavior of a person or group with respect to what is right and wrong

students, as well as educators, are recognizing a need to give future leaders a deeper understanding of how to practice ethical leadership rather than just how to make money. At Columbia Business School, which requires an ethics course, students formed a popular "Leadership and Ethics Board" that sponsors lectures and other activities. Yale School of Management has developed sessions in its core curriculum related to the recent crisis and worked with the Aspen Institute to create a curriculum aimed at teaching business students how to act on their values at work. About 55 business schools are using all or part of the curriculum in pilot programs.

Professor Diana C. Robertson at the Wharton School of the University of Pennsylvania says she sees a generational shift, with today's students expressing a greater concern for how organizations affect the community, the lives of employees, and the natural environment. "There is a feeling that we want our lives to mean something more and to run organizations for the greater good," said Max Anderson, one of the organizers of Harvard's pledge. "No one wants to have their future criticized as a place filled with unethical behaviors."[59]

Changing how future leaders are trained could be one key to solving the ethics deficit pervading our organizations. As Bill George, retired CEO of Medtronic, once said: "I am appalled at the extent to which business leaders are caught up in the game of greed. We have idolized the wrong leaders, associating image with leadership and confusing stock price with corporate value."[60] The standards for ethical conduct are embodied within each employee as well as within the organization itself. In a survey about unethical conduct in the workplace, more than half of the respondents cited poor leadership as a factor.[61] Leaders can create and sustain a climate that emphasizes ethical behavior for all employees.

Values-Based Leadership

Ethical values in organizations are developed and strengthened primarily through **values-based leadership**, a relationship between leaders and followers that is based on shared, strongly internalized values that are advocated and acted upon by the leader.[62] Leaders influence ethical values through their personal ethics and by practicing spiritual leadership. These leaders give meaning to followers by connecting their deeply held values to organizational goals.

Personal Ethics

Employees learn about values from watching leaders. Values-based leaders generate a high level of trust and respect from employees, based not just on stated values, but on the courage, determination, and self-sacrifice they demonstrate in upholding those values. For example, Jim Hackett, CEO of Steelcase, wanted to build a corporate culture of "unyielding integrity," but his personal integrity was put to the test when the company faced a decision regarding fire-retardant products. Steelcase had great success selling a new line of panels that could be used either for cubicles or to cover floor-to-ceiling walls. The company soon discovered, though, that rules governing walls were stricter than those for cubicles and the new product might not be up to the higher fire standards in some locations. Hackett asked for research into the matter, and some executives (and even some customers) advised him to just ignore the issue since fire codes vary so much from one municipality to another. Hackett, though, knew this was a time to put his values into action. He quietly recalled the panels and replaced them with ones that would meet the strictest fire codes, even though the decision was

Values-based leadership
a relationship between leaders and followers that is based on shared, strongly internalized values that are advocated and acted upon by the leader

expensive and time-consuming for the company and caused Hackett and other top managers to lose their annual performance bonuses. The U.S. Department of Defense had some of the Steelcase panels, and after the September 11, 2001, terrorist attack on the Pentagon, leaders there told Hackett the fires likely "would have spread in a far more disastrous outcome" if the new fire-retardant material had not been used.[63]

Several factors contribute to an individual leader's ethical stance. Every individual brings a set of personal beliefs, values, personality characteristics, and behavior traits to the job. The family backgrounds and spiritual beliefs of leaders often provide principles by which they conduct business. Personality characteristics such as ego strength, self-confidence, and a strong sense of independence may enable leaders to make ethical decisions even if those decisions might be unpopular.

Action Memo

Answering the questions in Leader's Self-Insight 14.4 will give you an idea of how you feel about some ethical issues that students typically face.

One important personal factor is the leader's stage of moral development, as described in Chapter 6, which affects an individual's ability to translate values into behavior.[64] For example, some people make decisions and act only to obtain rewards and avoid punishment for themselves. Others learn to conform to expectations of good behavior as defined by society. This means willingly upholding the law and responding to the expectations of others. At the highest level of moral development are people guided by high internal standards. These are self-chosen ethical principles that don't change with reward or punishment. Leaders can strive to develop and adhere to higher principles so that their daily actions reflect important ethical values.

Leaders have to discover their own personal ethical values and actively communicate values to others through both words and actions.[65] When faced with difficult decisions, values-based leaders know what they stand for, and they have the courage to act on their principles, as Jim Hackett did at Steelcase. In addition, by clearly communicating and modeling the ethical standards they expect others to live by, leaders can empower people throughout the organization to make decisions within that framework.

Spiritual Values

Managers who incorporate spiritual values in addition to the traditional mental and behavioral aspects of leadership tend to be successful as leaders. Values and practices considered as spiritual ideals include integrity, humility, respect, appreciation for the contributions of others, fair treatment, and personal reflection.[66] This approach to leadership can be effective because many people are struggling with how to combine their spiritual journey and their work life. Some companies have put chaplains on the payroll to help people as they struggle with problems that might or might not relate to the business. "You're at work 8 to 10 hours a day," says Tim Embry, owner of American LubeFast, a chain of oil change companies. "Work is where people are at and where they need to be cared for."[67]

Polls have reported that American managers as well as workers would like deeper fulfillment on the job, and evidence suggests that workplace spirituality programs provide people with better mental and physical health, an enhanced sense of self-worth, and greater personal growth, while organizations benefit from increased productivity along with reduced absenteeism and turnover.[68]

However, even leaders who don't provide formal spirituality programs can lead with spiritual values. For example, the CEO of staffing firm Kforce says spiritual values helped guide his company's choice of a new software vendor. One vendor's price was higher, but it won the bid because its leaders were more ethical

Cheating is a common problem on college campuses today; 67 percent of students confess that they have cheated at least once. Many pressures cause students to engage in unethical behavior, and these are similar to pressures they will later face in the workplace. Answer the following questions to see how you think and feel about certain student behaviors that could be considered unethical. Circle a number on the scale from 1–5 based on the extent to which you approve of the behavior described, with 5 = Strongly approve and 1 = Strongly disapprove. *Please answer based on whether you approve or disapprove of the behavior, not whether you have ever acted in such a way.*

	Strongly disapprove				Strongly approve
1. Receiving a higher grade through the influence of a family or personal connection	1	2	3	4	5
2. Communicating answers to a friend during a test	1	2	3	4	5
3. Using a faked illness as an excuse for missing a test	1	2	3	4	5
4. Visiting a professor's office frequently to seek help in a course	1	2	3	4	5
5. "Hacking" into the university's computer system to change your grade	1	2	3	4	5
6. Getting extra credit because the professor likes you	1	2	3	4	5
7. Using formulas programmed into your pocket calculator during an exam	1	2	3	4	5
8. Attending commercial test preparatory courses such as those offered by Kaplan	1	2	3	4	5
9. Asking a friend to sign you in as attending when you are absent from a large class	1	2	3	4	5
10. Peeking at your neighbor's exam during a test	1	2	3	4	5
11. Brown-nosing your professor	1	2	3	4	5
12. Overhearing the answers to exam questions when your neighbor whispers to another student	1	2	3	4	5
13. Using a term paper that you purchased or borrowed from someone else	1	2	3	4	5
14. Contributing little to group work and projects but receiving the same credit and grade as other members	1	2	3	4	5

	Strongly disapprove				Strongly approve
15. Hiring someone or having a friend take a test for you in a very large class	1	2	3	4	5
16. Comparing work on assignments with classmates before turning the work in to the instructor	1	2	3	4	5
17. Receiving favoritism because you are a student athlete or member of a campus organization	1	2	3	4	5
18. Using unauthorized "crib notes" during an exam	1	2	3	4	5
19. Taking advantage of answers you inadvertently saw on another student's exam	1	2	3	4	5
20. Having access to old exams in a particular course that other students do not have access to	1	2	3	4	5
21. Receiving information about an exam from someone in an earlier section of the course who has already taken the test	1	2	3	4	5
22. Being allowed to do extra work, which is not assigned to all class members, to improve your grade	1	2	3	4	5

Scoring and Interpretation

There are five subscale scores that reflect your attitudes and beliefs about different categories of behavior.

For the category of *actively benefiting from unethical action,* sum your scores for questions 2, 5, 10, 13, 15, and 18 and divide by 6: _____.

For the category of *passively benefiting from questionable action,* sum your scores for questions 1, 6, 11, 14, 17, 20, and 22 and divide by 7: _____.

For the category of *actively benefiting from questionable action,* sum your scores for questions 3, 7, 9, and 21 and divide by 4: _____.

For the category of *acting on an opportunistic situation,* sum your scores for questions 12 and 19 and divide by 2: _____.

For the category of *no harm/no foul* (actions perceived to cause no harm to anyone are considered okay), sum your scores for questions 4, 8, and 16 and divide by 3: _____.

The higher the score, the more you find that category of behaviors acceptable. When the scale was administered to 291 students in marketing and finance classes at a medium-sized university, the mean scores were

Personal Ethical Beliefs (*continued*)

as follows: *actively benefiting from unethical behavior*: 1.50; *passively benefiting from questionable action*: 2.31; *actively benefiting from questionable action*: 2.46; *acting on an opportunistic situation*: 2.55; and *no harm/no foul*: 4.42. How do your scores compare to these averages? The students in this sample had high approval for the *no harm/no foul category*. Do you agree that these behaviors are acceptable? Why might some people consider them unethical? If you feel comfortable doing

so, compare your scores to another student's and discuss your beliefs about categories that you strongly disapprove or strongly approve of.

Source: Mohammed Y. A. Rawwas and Hans R. Isakson, "Ethics of Tomorrow's Business Managers: The Influence of Personal Beliefs and Values, Individual Characteristics, and Situational Factors," *Journal of Education for Business* (July 2000), p. 321. Reprinted with permission of the Helen Dwight Reid Educational Foundation. Published by Heldref Publications, 1319 Eighteenth St., NW, Washington, DC 20036-1802. Copyright © 2000.

than those in the less costly firm. **Spiritual leadership** is the display of values, attitudes, and behaviors necessary to intrinsically motivate oneself and others toward a sense of spiritual expression through calling and membership.[69] As illustrated in Exhibit 14.4, spiritual leaders start by creating a vision through which organization participants experience a sense of calling that gives meaning to their work. An appropriate vision would have broad appeal, reflect high ideals, and establish a standard of excellence. Second, spiritual leaders establish a corporate culture based on altruistic love. Altruistic love includes forgiveness, genuine caring, compassion, kindness, honesty, patience, courage, and appreciation, which enables people to experience a sense of membership and feel understood. Spiritual leaders also engage hope/faith to help the organization achieve desired outcomes. Faith is demonstrated through action. Faith means believing in the ability to excel, exercising self-control, and striving for excellence to achieve a personal best. A leader's hope/faith includes perseverance, endurance, stretch goals, and a clear expectation of victory through effort.[70] As illustrated in Exhibit 14.4, spiritual leadership behaviors enable employees to have a sense of calling that provides deeper life meaning through work. Spiritual

Action Memo

As a leader, you can be ethical and act on high moral principles in your daily behavior. You can practice spiritual leadership to help people find deeper fulfillment in their jobs.

Spiritual leadership
the display of values, attitudes, and behaviors necessary to intrinsically motivate oneself and others toward a sense of spiritual expression through calling and membership

Exhibit 14.4 Model of Spiritual Leadership

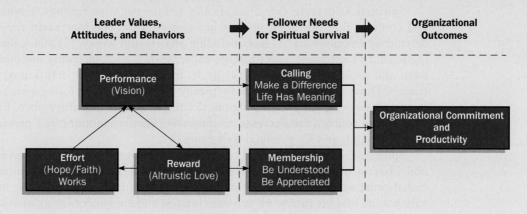

Source: L.W. Fry, "Toward a Theory of Spiritual Leadership," *The Leadership Quarterly* 14 (2003), pp. 693–727. Used with permission.

leadership also provides a sense of membership through a work community in which one feels understood and appreciated. The outcome for the organization is improved commitment and productivity.

One example of spiritual leadership comes from CitiMortgage, where a new chief executive is tackling what he calls the riskiest job he has ever done.

IN THE LEAD

Sanjiv Das, CitiMortgage

India-born Sanjiv Das, who took over as president and CEO of CitiMortgage in July 2008 in the midst of the housing crisis, has two primary goals: (1) to boost the morale of 10,000 employees who are dealing with the agony of the crisis coupled with shrinking public respect for their industry; and (2) to keep people from losing their homes. In his mind, the two goals are related. By keeping people focused on the help they can offer to alleviate the financial pressure of those caught in economic turmoil, Das is helping employees find purpose, meaning, and self-respect.

Like many companies, CitiMortgage has worked with borrowers who have missed several payments to restructure their loans. However, Citi has gone further than many banks. Das pioneered a first-of-its-kind program to temporarily lower payments and waive interest and penalties for borrowers who had lost their jobs. In addition, Citi implemented a program to preemptively reach out to approximately 500,000 homeowners who were not late on their payments but might fall behind without help. "These homeowners are often too embarrassed or worried, or simply don't know how to ask . . . for help," Das said. He believes early intervention is one of the best ways to bring down the foreclosure rate, keep people in their homes, help struggling communities, and boost the economy.

Das says his leadership approach is based in the spiritual values he learned growing up in Delhi—such as maintaining purpose and integrity during difficult times and helping others rather than trying to acquire more materials goods for oneself. "The No. 1 thing I talk about [to employees] are the customers. Each day, my business is to keep them in their homes, no matter what. That goes back to the values I was brought up with."[71]

Clearly, Sanjiv Das faces a tough leadership situation, and CitiMortgage, like many other companies in the finance and housing industries, is struggling for its very survival. However, Das's spiritual leadership is having an impact on both employee morale and business results. His approach to doing business is helping ease the anxiety and sense of failure that have sapped employee morale.

Spiritual leadership can dramatically reduce negative feelings, emotions, and conflicts that are often present in organizations. The four main types of destructive emotions are (1) fear, including anxiety and worry; (2) anger, including hostility, resentment, and jealousy; (3) sense of failure, including discouragement and depressed mood; and (4) pride, including prejudice, selfishness, and conceit. These destructive emotions typically arise from fear of losing something important or not getting something one desires. A more loving atmosphere based on care and concern can decrease or eliminate negative emotions and provide a stronger foundation for personal well-being.[72]

Spiritual leadership is related to ideas discussed in Chapter 8 on motivation and Chapter 6 on moral leadership. The spiritual leader addresses followers' higher order needs for membership and self-actualization. This is intrinsic motivation at its best because work provides interest and enjoyment for its own sake.

People are actively engaged in tasks they find meaningful, interesting, or fun. Intrinsic motivation is typically associated with better learning, higher performance, and enhanced well-being. Spiritual leadership often provides substantial autonomy and self-management, for example, through participation in empowered teams that direct activities and do work that is significant and meaningful. An employee's task involvement is under the control of the individual or team, thereby providing feedback and satisfaction through achievement, performance, and problem solving. Servant leadership, discussed in Chapter 6, holds that business organizations can create a positive impact on employees and the community. The spiritual leader, like the servant leader, engages people in work that provides both service and meaning.

Leadership Essentials

- Leaders influence organizational culture and ethical values. Culture is the set of key values, norms, and assumptions that is shared by members of an organization and taught to new members as correct. Culture serves two critically important functions—to integrate organizational members so they know how to relate to one another and to help the organization adapt to the environment.

- Strong, adaptive cultures have a positive impact on organizational outcomes. Creating and influencing an adaptive culture is important because the right culture can drive high performance. Leaders build high performance cultures by emphasizing both values and solid business operations as the drivers of organizational success.

- A culture gap exists when an organization's culture is not in alignment with the needs of the external environment or company strategy. Leaders use ceremonies, stories, symbols, specialized language, selection, and socialization to instill and strengthen the needed cultural values. In addition, leaders influence cultural values most strongly through their daily actions.

- Leaders consider the external environment and the company's vision and strategy in determining which values are important for the organization. Four types of culture may exist in organizations: adaptability, achievement, clan, and bureaucratic. Each type emphasizes different values, although organizations may have values that fall into more than one category.

- Of the values that make up an organization's culture, ethical values are among the most important. Ethics is the code of moral principles and values that governs the behavior of a person or group with respect to what is right or wrong. Leaders shape ethical values through values-based leadership. Leaders' personal beliefs and level of moral development influence their personal ethics. For organizations to be ethical, leaders have to be openly and strongly committed to ethical conduct in their daily actions. Many good leaders practice spiritual leadership, which means displaying values, attitudes, and behaviors that motivate people toward a sense of spiritual expression through calling and membership. The principles of spiritual leadership can improve both organizational performance and employee well-being.

Discussion Questions

1. Describe the culture for an organization you are familiar with. Identify the physical artifacts and discuss what underlying values and assumptions these suggest. What did you learn?

2. Name one or two companies in the news that seem to have strong corporate cultures, and describe whether the results have been positive or negative. Discuss how a strong culture could have either positive or negative consequences for an organization.

3. As a leader, how might you recognize a culture gap? What techniques might you use to influence and change cultural values when necessary?

4. Compare and contrast the achievement culture with the clan culture. What are some possible *disadvantages* of having a strong clan culture? A strong achievement culture?

5. If you were the leader of a small technology firm, how might you imprint in people's minds the values shown in Exhibit 14.2 for adaptive cultures in order to create a high performance culture? Be specific with your ideas.

6. Discuss the meaning of *calling* and *membership,* as related to spiritual leadership. Identify an organization or leader that uses these concepts. To what extent were these concepts present where you have worked?

7. If a leader directs her health-care company to reward hospital managers strictly on hospital profits, is the leader being ethically responsible? Discuss.

8. Some mortgage company leaders have said that providing subprime mortgages was based on the noble purpose of giving poor people a chance to participate in the American dream of home ownership. Discuss your opinion of this explanation.

9. Some people believe that all good leadership is spiritual in nature. Others think spiritual values have no place at work. Discuss these two opposing viewpoints.

10. In a survey of 20,000 people in 16 European countries plus Russia, Turkey, and the United States, 55 percent of respondents said cheating in business is more common than it was 10 years ago. Do you believe this is truly the case, or can you think of other explanations? Discuss.

Leadership at Work

WALK THE TALK

Often in an organization the culture is characterized both by what people say (talk) and by what people actually do (walk). When this happens, there is a gap between organizational leaders' espoused values and the values in action within the company. One example would be an espoused value of "a balanced life for employees," whereas managers and employees are actually expected to work nights and weekends to meet demanding performance goals. This is the difference between the "walk" and the "talk" in an organization.

Your assignment for this exercise is to think of one example in your own student or work experience where the walk and talk in a corporate culture did not align. Why do you think the gap occurred? Then interview four other people for examples of when an organization's espoused values did not align with the values in action. Also ask them why they think the walk and talk differed. Summarize the findings from your interviews:

My example (and why):

_____

_____

_____

_____

_____

Second person's examples (and why):

_____

_____

_____

_____

Third person's examples (and why):

_____

_____

_____

_____

Fourth person's examples (and why):

_____

_____

_____

_____

Fifth person's examples (and why):

_____

_____

_____

_____

What patterns and themes do you see in the responses? Is there a common type of walk/talk gap? What is the most common reason why these gaps occur? Which is the real culture—the leader's espoused values or the values in action?

In Class: Students can be organized into small groups in class and do this exercise all at once. Each person in the circle can give examples from student or work experiences of an organization's walk not fitting its talk and explain why he or she thinks the gaps occurred. Then students can identify the common themes from their discussion. The instructor can help students probe into this issue by writing good examples from students on the board and asking students to help identify key themes. Students can be engaged to discuss the walk versus talk phenomenon via key questions, such as: What does it mean to you when you discover a walk/talk gap in your organization? Are espoused values or values-in-action more indicative of a company's culture (or are both the culture)? Are walk/talk gaps likely to be associated with an adaptive culture? A strong culture? Do symbols, stories, ceremonies, and other signals of corporate culture mean what they imply?

Chapter 15: Leading Change

istockphoto.com/AVTG

Your Leadership Challenge

After reading this chapter, you should be able to:

- Recognize social and economic pressures for change in today's organizations.

- Implement the eight-stage model of planned change.

- Use appreciative inquiry to engage people in creating change by focusing on the positive and learning from success.

- Expand your own and others' creativity and facilitate organizational innovation.

- Use techniques of communication, training, and participation to overcome resistance to change.

- Effectively and humanely address the negative impact of change.

Chapter Outline

O ver a recent two-year period, financial services companies laid off 400,000 employees in the United States, with nearly 150,000 of those being let go in the fourth quarter of 2008 alone, when the economic crisis hit its peak.[1] Some banks, like IndyMac, were seized and restructured by the U.S. Federal Deposit Insurance Corporation (FDIC). Others, like the giant Citigroup, remained intact but received billions of dollars of bailout funds from the U.S. government—and the scrutiny and meddling that came with it. The long-term future of the firm that a decade ago rewrote the rules of finance by creating a global financial supermarket is uncertain. The one thing that is clear is that Citigroup has to change. After decades of expansion, Citi's leaders are now trying to shrink the company to a manageable size. They are returning to the use of the name Citicorp, and going back to the core business of banking. "Citigroup . . . was put together in a random fashion that wasn't market based," said one banking expert. Citi's executives, currently led by CEO Vikram Pandit (under pressure from the FDIC to step down), are struggling to cut costs, decrease the percentage of risky assets, get the right mix of leadership talent, and come up with a focused strategy to get the organization back on track.[2]

Citigroup is not alone. Most companies in the financial services industry are facing a need for dramatic change after the mortgage crisis and the Wall Street meltdown. Complicating the challenge for the big U.S. financial firms is that many expert managers and traders are turning away from these established firms to take their chances with innovative start-up companies or foreign banks that don't face the tighter government regulations being imposed on the big institutions.[3]

This chapter explores how leaders in companies such as Citigroup facilitate change, creativity, and innovation. We first look briefly at the need for change in today's organizations and examine a step-by-step framework for leading change. We explore the appreciative inquiry technique and how it can be used to lead both major changes and ongoing, everyday change. Next, the chapter examines how leaders facilitate innovation by fostering creative people and organizations. The final sections of the chapter consider why people resist change and how leaders can overcome resistance and help people cope with the potentially negative consequences of change.

Change or Perish

Recall from our definition used throughout this book that leadership is about change rather than stability. In recent years, though, the pace of change has increased dramatically, presenting significant challenges for leaders trying to keep pace with shifts in the external environment.

Change is necessary if organizations are to survive and thrive, and the sharp downturn in the economy is forcing leaders in all industries to take a fresh look at how they do business. The recent turmoil is not only pressuring leaders to rethink the economics of their business but has also brought changes in social attitudes that require new leadership responses.[4] From big, highly visible corporations such as Citigroup and General Motors, to government agencies such as the Securities and Exchange Commission (SEC) and the Central Intelligence Agency (CIA), to small companies, colleges and universities, and nonprofit organizations, the need for change is on every leader's mind. The pressing need for change management is reflected in the fact that many organizations are hiring "transformation officers" who are charged with radically rethinking and remaking either the entire organization or major parts of it.[5] Even the U.S. Army has undergone massive changes in recent years to fight a new kind of war. Rather than launching an all-out assault, the Army is struggling to learn that "the more force you use when battling insurgents, the less effective you are," as stated in the organization's new counterinsurgency doctrine.[6]

As illustrated in Exhibit 15.1, environmental forces such as rapid technological changes, a globalized economy, shifting geopolitical forces, increasing government regulation, changing markets, the growth of e-business, and the swift spread of information via the Internet are creating more threats as well as more opportunities for organizational leaders. A big problem for today's organizations is the failure to adapt to all these changes in the environment. Although there are many reasons for this problem, a primary solution is better change leadership. Leaders serve as the role models for change and provide the motivation and communication to keep change efforts moving forward. Strong, committed leadership is crucial to successful change, and research has identified some key characteristics of leaders who can accomplish successful change projects:[7]

Action Memo

Before reading the rest of the chapter, complete the questions in Leader's Self-Insight 15.1 to see how innovative you are in your personal life.

- They define themselves as change leaders rather than people who want to maintain the status quo.
- They demonstrate courage.
- They believe in employees' capacity to assume responsibility.

- They are able to assimilate and articulate values that promote adaptability.
- They recognize and learn from their own mistakes.
- They are capable of managing complexity, uncertainty, and ambiguity.
- They have vision and can describe their vision for the future in vivid terms.

Washington, D.C., Metropolitan Police Chief Cathy Lanier illustrates many of the characteristics of a change leader.

Exhibit 15.1 Forces Driving the Need for Leading Organizational Change

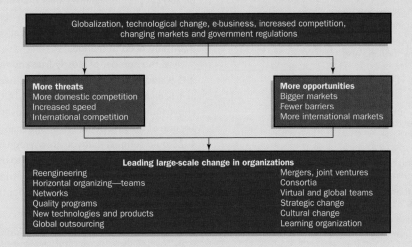

Source: Adapted with permission of The Free Press, a division of Simon & Schuster Adult Publishing Group, from *The New Rules: How to Succeed in Today's Post-Corporate World* by John P. Kotter. Copyright © 1995 by John P. Kotter. All rights reserved.

IN THE LEAD

Cathy Lanier, Washington, D.C., Metropolitan Police

"We went from beating people up, wrestling them, handcuffing them, to 'How do we prevent these things from happening?'" said Al Durham, assistant chief of the Washington, D.C., Metropolitan Police. The change in attitude has come largely because of the leadership of the new police chief, Cathy Lanier.

Lanier, a single mother and one of only three women ever picked to be the top cop in a major U.S. city, never had any interest in maintaining the status quo. She came into the job with a goal of changing the culture of crime fighting. She tries hard not to let supervisors and administrators get between her and the beat cops, and she pushes everyone in the department to get close to the people who are involved in and hurt by crime. "Even as a patrol cop, if you work hard, if you focus, you can make major changes in people's lives every single day," Lanier says.

Lanier gives out her business card (and often her private cell phone number) to everyone she meets, and she seeks the advice of people on the front lines of crime fighting. "I hate chain of command," Lanier says about her leadership style. She wants to make sure people inside and outside the department can take their concerns, gripes, or advice directly to her. Lanier has been sharply criticized for some of her decisions, but she doesn't care. What she cares about is building trust with local neighborhoods and stopping crime. Regarding her controversial decision to set up street-corner checkpoints in the Trinidad neighborhood after a night of extreme violence, Washington Mayor Adrian Fenty said that "... instead

marble: © Kirill Matkov   sunset: © Marco Regalia

Leader's Self-Insight 15.1
How Innovative Are You?

Think about your current life. Indicate whether each of the following items is Mostly False or Mostly True for you.

	Mostly False	Mostly True
1. I am always seeking out new ways to do things.	_____	_____
2. I consider myself creative and original in my thinking and behavior.	_____	_____
3. I prefer to be slow to accept a new idea.	_____	_____
4. I rarely trust new gadgets until I see whether they work for people around me.	_____	_____
5. I am usually one of the last people among my peers to adopt something new.	_____	_____
6. I like to feel that the old way of doing things is the best way.	_____	_____
7. In a group or at work I am often skeptical of new ideas.	_____	_____
8. I typically buy new foods, gear, and other innovations before other people.	_____	_____
9. My behavior influences others to try new things.	_____	_____
10. I like to spend time trying out new things.	_____	_____

Scoring and Interpretation

Innovativeness reflects an awareness of the need to innovate and a positive attitude toward change. Innovativeness is also thought of as the degree to which a person adopts innovations earlier than other people in the peer group. Innovativeness is a positive thing for leaders today because individuals and organizations are faced with a constant need to change.

Add the number of Mostly True answers to items 1, 2, 8, 9, and 10 and the Mostly False answers to items 3, 4, 5, 6, and 7 for your score: _____. A score of 8 or above indicates that you are very innovative and likely are one of the first people to adopt changes. A score of 4–7 would suggest that you are average or slightly above average in innovativeness compared to others. A score of 0–3 means that you may prefer the tried and true and hence be slow and skeptical about adopting new ideas or innovations.

Source: Based on H. Thomas Hurt, Katherine Joseph, and Chester D. Cook, "Scales for the Measurement of Innovativeness," *Human Communication Research* 4, no. 1 (1977), pp. 58–65.

of going with an antiquated policy, she sat in the room with a bunch of people and said, 'Well, let's figure out something new.' She took a lot of heat for it, but she stood firm."

Lanier has brought significant change to the Metropolitan Police by believing in and supporting cops from the lowest to the highest level of the force, articulating values that emphasize building trust and preventing crime, and having the courage to do what she thinks is right.[8]

Change does not happen easily, but good leaders throughout the organization can facilitate change and help their organizations adapt to external threats and new opportunities. One does not need to be a top leader to be a change leader. In the following section, we examine a framework for leading change, and later in the chapter we will give some tips for how leaders can overcome resistance to change.

A Framework for Leading Change

When leading a major change project, it is important for leaders to recognize that the change process goes through stages, each stage is important, and each may require a significant amount of time. Leaders are responsible for guiding employees and the organization through the change process.

Exhibit 15.2 presents an eight-stage model of planned change developed by John Kotter.[9] To successfully implement change, leaders pay careful attention to each stage. Skipping stages or making critical mistakes at any stage can cause the change process to fail.

1. At stage 1, leaders *establish a sense of urgency* that change is really needed. Crises or threats will thaw resistance to change. One good example is the shifting relationship between General Motors (GM) and the United Auto Workers (UAW). GM leaders' efforts to build a more collaborative relationship typically met with resistance from UAW leaders until bankruptcy proved the urgent need for working more closely together. Today, the UAW owns 17.5 percent of GM's stock—the union wanted cash for the money GM owed it, but gave in for the sake of the whole enterprise. In addition, the crisis convinced the UAW to pledge not to strike before 2015, ceding leverage at the bargaining table and giving GM a better chance to survive.[10] In many cases, though, there is no obvious crisis and leaders have to "find a rallying cry" that focuses people on a clear need for change.[11] Leaders carefully scan the external and internal environment— looking at competitive conditions; market position; social, technological, and demographic trends; profit and loss; operations; and other factors. After identifying potential crises or problems, they find ways to communicate the information broadly and dramatically.

2. Stage 2 involves *establishing a coalition* with enough power to guide the change process and then developing a sense of teamwork among the group. For the change process to succeed, there must be a shared commitment to the need and possibilities for organizational transformation. Middle managers will seek top leader support in the coalition. It is also essential that lower-level managers become involved. Mechanisms such as off-site retreats can get people together and help them develop a shared assessment of problems and how to approach them. At MasterBrand Industries,

Exhibit 15.2 The Eight-Stage Model of Planned Organizational Change

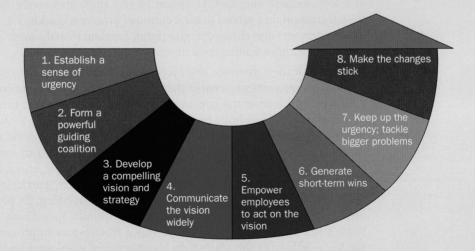

Source: John P. Kotter, *Leading Change* (Boston: Harvard Business School Press, 1996), p. 21.

for example, transformation began with an off-site meeting of some 75 key managers who examined the need for change and discussed ways to remake MasterBrand into a team-based organization.[12]

3. Stage 3 requires *developing a vision and strategy*. Leaders are responsible for formulating and articulating a compelling vision that will guide the change effort, and then developing the strategies for achieving that vision. A picture of a highly desirable future motivates people to change. David Davoudpour, owner, chairman, and CEO of Shoney's, a chain of casual restaurants that pioneered the all-you-can-eat salad bar and breakfast buffet, is inspiring managers and franchise owners with a vision of restoring Shoney's to its glory days. The chain, founded in the 1940s, once boasted 1,200 restaurants nationwide but shrank to less than 300 and neared bankruptcy because leaders failed to change with the times. Davoudpour's strategy includes revamping the décor, offering fresher, healthier food and more contemporary menu items, and providing coherent headquarters leadership to maintain consistency and quality.[13]

4. In stage 4, leaders use every means possible to widely *communicate the vision and strategy*. At this stage, the coalition of change agents should set an example by modeling the new behaviors needed from employees. They must communicate about the change at least 10 times more than they think necessary. Transformation is impossible unless a majority of people in the organization are involved and willing to help, often to the point of making personal sacrifices. At Yellow Freight System, CEO Bill Zollars regularly visited terminals across the country to communicate his vision of transforming Yellow Freight from a traditional trucking company to a one-stop-shop for a range of customers' logistics and transportation needs. "Repetition is important, especially when you're trying to change the way a company thinks about itself," Zollars advises. "You're trying to create new behaviors."[14]

5. Stage 5 involves *empowering employees throughout the organization to act on the vision*. This means getting rid of obstacles to change, which may require revising systems, structures, or procedures that hinder or undermine the change effort. People are empowered with knowledge, resources, and discretion to make things happen. Leaders at Yellow Freight, for example, invested in a sophisticated, integrated IT system to give employees on the front lines the information they needed to solve customer problems quickly. The management system was also changed to give people freedom to make many decisions themselves without waiting for a supervisor to review the problem.

6. At stage 6, leaders *generate short-term wins*. Leaders plan for visible performance improvements, enable them to happen, and celebrate employees who were involved in the improvements. Major change takes time, and a transformation effort loses momentum if there are no short-term accomplishments that employees can recognize and celebrate. A good example comes from the U.S. Mint, where Philip Diehl wanted to transform the clumsy, slow-moving government bureaucracy into a fast, energetic organization that was passionate about serving customers, particularly coin collectors. Diehl publicly set an early goal of processing 95 percent of orders within six weeks. Even though that sounds agonizingly slow in today's fast-paced business world, it was a tremendous improvement for the Mint. Achieving this short-term goal energized employees and kept the transformation efforts moving.[15] A highly visible and successful short-term

accomplishment boosts the credibility of the change process and renews the commitment and enthusiasm of employees.

7. Stage 7 *keeps up the urgency,* building on the credibility and momentum achieved by short-term wins to *tackle bigger problems.* Successful change leaders don't simply declare victory after small wins and become complacent. They use courage and perseverance to give people the energy and power to take on more difficult issues. This often involves changing systems, structures, and policies; hiring and promoting people who can implement the vision; and making sure employees have the time, resources, and authority they need to pursue the vision. Leaders at one company striving to improve collaboration, for example, found employees' energy flagging after they had achieved a short-term goal that improved on-time and complete shipments from 50 percent to 99 percent. Leaders decided to invest significant time and money in reconfiguring the plant to increase interaction of production and office personnel, thereby creating a feeling of community that reinforced and continued the change effort in a highly visible way.[16]

> ### Action Memo
>
> *As a leader, you can develop the personal characteristics to be a change leader. To improve the success of a major change, you can follow the eight-stage model for leading change, remembering to devote the necessary time, energy, and resources to each stage.*

8. Stage 8 is where leaders *make the changes stick.*[17] The transformation isn't over until the changes have well-established roots. Leaders instill new values, attitudes, and behaviors so that employees view the changes not as something new but as a normal and integral part of how the organization operates. They use many of the ideas we discussed in Chapter 14 for changing organizational culture, such as tapping into people's emotions, telling vivid stories about the new organization and why it is successful, selecting and socializing employees to fit the desired culture, and acting on the espoused values so that people know what leaders care about and reward. Leaders celebrate and promote people who act according to the new values. This stage also requires developing a means to ensure leadership development and succession so that the new values and behaviors are carried forward to the next generation of leadership.

> ### Action Memo
>
> *Answer the questions in Leader's Self-Insight 15.2 to see if you have what it takes to initiate changes and follow the eight-stage model of change.*

Stages in the change process generally overlap, but each is important for successful change to occur. When dealing with a major change effort, leaders can use the eight-stage change process to provide a strong foundation for success.

Appreciative Inquiry

One of the most exciting approaches to leading change is a process known as appreciative inquiry. **Appreciative inquiry (AI)** engages individuals, teams, or the entire organization in creating change by reinforcing positive messages and focusing on learning from success.[18] Rather than looking at a situation from the viewpoint of what is wrong and who is to blame for it, AI takes a positive, affirming approach by asking, "What is possible? What do we want to achieve?" For example, rather than looking at a problem such as decreasing sales, AI would investigate what makes sales increase. Appropriately framing a topic—to investigate what is right rather than what is wrong—is critical to the success of appreciative inquiry because it gets people away from blame, defensiveness, and denial and sets a positive framework for change. As David Cooperrider, co-creator of

Appreciative inquiry
a technique for leading change that engages individuals, teams, or the entire organization by reinforcing positive messages and focusing on learning from success

Think specifically of your current or a recent full-time job. Please answer the following 10 questions according to *your perspective and behaviors in that job*. Indicate whether each item is Mostly False or Mostly True for you.

	Mostly False	Mostly True
1. I often tried to adopt improved procedures for doing my job.	_____	_____
2. I often tried to change how my job was executed in order to be more effective.	_____	_____
3. I often tried to bring about improved procedures for the work unit or department.	_____	_____
4. I often tried to institute new work methods that were more effective for the company.	_____	_____
5. I often tried to change organizational rules or policies that were nonproductive or counterproductive.	_____	_____
6. I often made constructive suggestions for improving how things operate within the organization.	_____	_____
7. I often tried to correct a faulty procedure or practice.	_____	_____
8. I often tried to eliminate redundant or unnecessary procedures.	_____	_____

	Mostly False	Mostly True
9. I often tried to implement solutions to pressing organizational problems.	_____	_____
10. I often tried to introduce new structures, technologies, or approaches to improve efficiency.	_____	_____

Scoring and Interpretation

Please add the number of items for which you marked Mostly True, which is your score: _____. This instrument measures the extent to which people take charge of change in the workplace. Change leaders are seen as change initiators. A score of 7 or above indicates a strong take-charge attitude toward change. A score of 3 or below indicates an attitude of letting someone else worry about change.

Before change leaders can champion large planned change projects via the model in Exhibit 15.2, they often begin by taking charge of change in their workplace area of responsibility. To what extent do you take charge of change in your work or personal life? Compare your score with other students' scores. How do you compare? Do you see yourself being a change leader?

Source: *Academy of Management Journal* by E. W. Morrison and C. C. Phelps. Copyright 1999 by Academy of Management. Reproduced with permission of Academy of Management in the format Textbook via Copyright Clearance Center.

marble: © Kirill Matkov   sunset: © Marco Regalia

the AI methodology, puts it, ". . . the more you study the true, the good, the better, the possible within living human systems, the more the capacity for positive transformation."[19] AI can be applied on either a large or small scale.

Leading a Major Change

Appreciative inquiry can accelerate large-scale organizational change by positively engaging a large group of people in the change process, including leaders and employees, as well as people from outside the organization, such as customers or clients, partners, and other stakeholders.

Once a topic has been identified for exploration, the group follows a four-stage appreciative inquiry process, as illustrated in Exhibit 15.3.[20]

1. **Discovery**. In the discovery stage, people identify "the best of what exists"—the organization's key strengths and best practices. This stage is about discovering the unique qualities of the group that have contributed to success. Leaders interview people, asking them to tell stories that identify the best of their experiences with the organization. During an AI session focused on building a winning culture at American Express,

Exhibit 15.3 Four Stages of Appreciative Inquiry

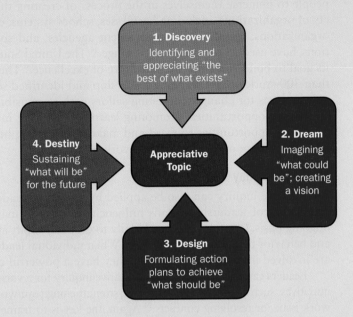

Source: Gabriella Giglio, Silvia Michalcova, and Chris Yates, "Instilling a Culture of Winning at American Express," *Organization Development Journal* 25, no. 4 (Winter 2007), pp. 33–37.

for example, leaders asked people to describe an instance when they felt the most proud working for the company. Based on these stories, people together identify common themes.

2. **Dream.** Next, people reflect on what they learned during the discovery stage and imagine what it would be like if these extraordinary experiences were the norm—what if people at American Express, for instance, experienced the kind of environment every day that made them feel proud of working for American Express? The dream stage is about imagining "what could be" and creating a shared vision of the best possible future, grounded in the reality of what already exists. By allowing people to express their dreams for the future, AI inspires hope and energy for change.

3. **Design.** The design stage formulates action plans for transforming dreams into reality. This involves people making decisions about what the organization needs to do in order to be what it wants to be. At American Express, people identified the values that would support the kind of culture they wanted, the leadership behaviors that would instill and support the values, and the structures, systems, and processes that would keep the new cultural values alive.

4. **Destiny.** The final stage of AI is creating a destiny by translating the ideas identified in the previous stages into concrete action steps. This involves both celebrating the best of what exists and pushing forward to realize the dream by creating specific programs, activities, and other tangible forces that will implement the design and ensure the continuation of change begun during the AI process. For example, specific changes in training programs, performance evaluation, and reward systems were part of the destiny stage at American Express.

Using the AI methodology for a large-scale change may involve hundreds of people over a period of several days and may be conducted off-site to enable people to immerse themselves in the process of creating the future. A wide variety of organizations, including businesses, school systems, churches and religious organizations, communities, government agencies, and social service organizations, have used AI for large-scale change.[21] The United States Navy applied AI in its goal to build "an empowered culture of excellence." The Navy collected more than 300 stories of outstanding leadership and identified seven themes that provided a basis for change: entrusting sailors with responsibility; treating mistakes as learning opportunities; promoting learning; investing in others' development; providing opportunities to excel and make a difference; bestowing appreciation and recognition; and building teamwork.[22]

Leading Everyday Change

Appreciative inquiry can also be applied by individual leaders on a smaller scale. The nature of leadership means influencing people in many small ways on an ongoing basis. Good leaders work daily to gradually shift attitudes, assumptions, and behavior toward a desired future. When individual leaders in an organization are involved in daily change efforts, they have a powerful cumulative effect.[23]

Leaders can use the tools of appreciative inquiry for a variety of everyday change initiatives, such as developing followers, strengthening teamwork, solving a particular work issue, or resolving conflicts.[24] Again, the key is to frame the issue in a positive way and keep people focused on improvement rather than looking at what went wrong. Jim Gustafson provides an example of the everyday use of appreciative inquiry.

IN THE LEAD

Jim (Gus) Gustafson, U.S. Cellular

Jim (Gus) Gustafson, currently director of strategic leadership research and development for U.S. Cellular, has a Gandhi quote painted on the wall of his office in huge letters: "Be the change you wish to see in the world."

Gustafson has long believed that leadership means serving others, and he uses appreciative inquiry on an everyday basis to coach followers and help them achieve their potential and make their best contribution. One example comes from the time Gustafson took over as leader of sales and marketing for a major electrical manufacturer. While sitting in on several employees' performance reviews with the outgoing leader, Gustafson noticed that two employees in particular were treated by the outgoing leader with disrespect and disinterest as they were given poor evaluations of their performance. Gustafson began treating the two as if they were critical to the success of the organization and giving them opportunities to contribute and excel. They lived up to the higher expectations, and both were eventually promoted to leadership positions in other parts of the organization.

One key to the change in behavior was Gustafson's use of appreciative inquiry. Gustafson asked questions such as "What have you done in the last six months that you are most proud of?" "What is your greatest source of job satisfaction?" and "What motivates you to excel?" He worked with followers to identify how they could be satisfied and productive, carrying forward the best from their past but moving toward a better future. Using appreciative inquiry created more open and honest communication, improved performance, and inspired a more trusting, collaborative environment. Gustafson continues to use appreciative inquiry as a way to stimulate learning and change and to create a community where people work for and with one another. "Collectively people can achieve much more than each could separately," he says. "When people really understand this, they will dream bigger dreams and strive for higher possibilities."[25]

Leading for Innovation

The American Management Association asked 500 CEOs the question: "What must one do to survive in the twenty-first century?" The top answer? "Practice creativity and innovation."[26] It is somewhat troubling, then, that innovation has been a top target for cost-cutting as the economy has slumped. In a 2009 survey by *BusinessWeek* and the Boston Consulting Group, more CEOs said that spending on innovation will be flat or down than since the first survey in 2005.[27]

Leaders in many companies, though, are finding creative ways to encourage and support the creation and implementation of new ideas. Effective leaders find ways to promote creativity in the departments where it is most needed. For example, some organizations, such as hospitals, government agencies, and non-profit organizations, may need frequent changes in policies and procedures, and leaders can promote creativity among administrative workers. For companies that rely on new products, leaders promote the generation and sharing of ideas across departments and, increasingly, with outsiders. In most successful companies, leaders want everyone to be searching both inside and outside the company for new ideas to solve problems and meet customer needs.

One of the best ways for leaders to facilitate continuous change is to create an environment that nourishes creativity. **Creativity** is the generation of ideas that are both novel and useful for improving efficiency or effectiveness of an organization.[28] Creative people come up with ideas that may meet perceived needs, solve problems, or respond to opportunities and are therefore adopted by the organization. However, creativity itself is a process rather than an outcome, a journey rather than a destination. One of the most important tasks of leaders today is to harness the creative energy of all employees to spur innovation and further the interests of the organization.

The Creative Organization

Leaders can build an environment that encourages creativity and helps the organization be more innovative. Five elements of innovative organizations are listed in the left column of Exhibit 15.4, and each is described in the following paragraphs.[29] These elements correspond to the characteristics of creative individuals, listed in the right column of the exhibit.

Alignment For creative acts that benefit the organization to occur consistently, the interests and actions of everyone should be aligned with the organization's purpose, vision, and goals. Leaders make clear what the company stands for, consistently promote the vision, and clarify specific goals. In addition, they make a commitment of time, energy, and resources to activities that focus people on innovation. Many organizations set up separate creative departments or venture teams. One popular approach is the **idea incubator**. An idea incubator provides a safe harbor where ideas from people throughout the organization can be developed without interference from company bureaucracy or politics.[30] Yahoo! started an off-site incubator to speed up development of ideas and be more competitive with Google. Dubbed "Brickhouse" and located in a hip section of San Francisco, the idea incubator gets about 200 ideas submitted each month and a panel sorts out the top 5 to 10. "The goal is to take the idea, develop it, and make sure it's seen by senior management quickly," says Salim Ismail, head of Brickhouse.[31]

Creative Values You may have noticed that most children have a natural desire to explore and create. Unfortunately, this desire is sometimes squelched early in life

Creativity
the generation of ideas that are both novel and useful for improving efficiency and effectiveness of the organization

Idea incubator
a safe harbor where ideas from employees throughout the organization can be developed without interference from company bureaucracy or politics

Exhibit 15.4 Characteristics of Innovative Organizations and Creative People

The Innovative Organization	The Creative Individual
Alignment	Commitment
	Focused approach
Creative values	Interdependence
	Persistence
	Energy
Unofficial activity	Self-confidence
	Nonconformity
	Curiosity
Open culture	Open-mindedness
	Conceptual fluency
	Enjoys variety
Team collaboration	Social competence
	Emotionally expressive
	Loves people

Source: Based on Alan G. Robinson and Sam Stern, *Corporate Creativity: How Innovation and Improvement Actually Happen* (San Francisco: Berrett-Koehler, 1997); Rosabeth Moss Kanter, "The Middle Manager as Innovator," *Harvard Business Review* (July–August 1982), pp. 104–105; and James Brian Quinn, "Managing Innovation: Controlled Chaos," *Harvard Business Review* (May–June 1985), pp. 73–84.

by classroom teachers who insist on strict adherence to the rules. Good leaders find ways to unleash deep-seated employee motivation for creativity and innovation. At W. L. Gore, best known for Gore-Tex fabrics, leaders basically did away with the rules so that people feel free to explore and experiment. There are no bosses at Gore; people explore ideas on their own and recruit others who believe in and want to work on the idea. That's how Gore got into businesses as diverse as Glide dental floss, Ride-On bike cables, and Elixir guitar strings.[32] Leaders can encourage an entrepreneurial spirit by instilling values of curiosity, exploration, and informed risk-taking. This **corporate entrepreneurship** can produce a higher-than-average number of innovations. One important outcome is to facilitate idea champions. **Idea champions** are people who passionately believe in an idea and fight to overcome natural resistance and convince others of its value. Change does not happen by itself. Personal energy and effort are needed to successfully promote a new idea. Champions make sure valuable ideas get accepted and carried forward for implementation.

Unofficial Activity For creativity to flourish, employees need to be able to experiment and dream outside of their regular job description. Leaders can give people free time for activities that are not officially sanctioned. One study of creativity found that in almost every case the essence of the creative act came during the "unofficial" time period.[33] Dream time is what makes it possible for companies to go where they never expected to. The classic example is 3M's Post-it Notes, one of the five most popular 3M products and one that resulted from an engineer's free-time experiments with another worker's "failure"—a not-very-sticky glue. 3M lets employees spend 15 percent of their time on any project of their own choosing, without management approval.[34] Another company that encourages unofficial activity is Google, Number 2 on *BusinessWeek*'s 2009 list of most innovative companies, where engineers spend 20 percent of their time on projects outside their regular jobs.[35] Google's founders once tracked the success of ideas management had backed versus those that had been executed by employees

Corporate entrepreneurship
internal entrepreneurial spirit that includes values of exploration, experimentation, and risk taking

Idea champions
people who passionately believe in a new idea and actively work to overcome obstacles and resistance

without direction or support from above, and they found a higher success rate among the ideas developed through unofficial activities.[36]

Open Culture Highly innovative companies maintain an open culture and look everywhere for new ideas. Leaders can encourage openness by rotating people into different jobs, allowing them time off to participate in volunteer activities, and giving them opportunities to mix with people different from themselves. One aerospace company uses the phrase *Get out of Kansas!* to stress the importance of looking for novel ideas in the world outside company walls.[37] Organizations can give people opportunities to work with customers, suppliers, and people outside the industry, which contributes to a flow of fresh ideas. Executives at Productos Cementos Mexicanos ride in cement trucks to get ideas about customer needs. Sloan Kettering Cancer Center worked with design firm IDEO, which took clinic staff to follow patients from their homes and through their treatments, leading to significant improvements in patient care.[38] Today's most successful companies are including customers, strategic partners, suppliers, and other outsiders directly in the innovation process, which is often called **open innovation**.[39] Companies such as Kraft Foods, General Mills, LEGO, Threadless, and Peugeot, for example, invite people to submit ideas over the Internet.[40] Apple allows a community of third-party software developers to create applications for the iPhone and deliver them directly to users.[41] Consumer products firm Procter & Gamble achieved an 85 percent increase in the success rate of innovation efforts thanks largely to open innovation. The Leader's Bookshelf further describes Procter & Gamble's highly successful approach to innovation.

Team Collaboration Although many individuals have creative ideas, most innovations are generated by groups of people working together. Rather than leave people stuck in their departmental silos, smart leaders find ways to get people communicating and collaborating across boundaries. Leaders at one company, for example, said they had lots of employees capable of coming up with good ideas, but they still weren't innovating. To kick-start collaboration across departments, the company held an off-site conference designed to get people from different specialties who had complementary skills and talents talking to one another. Everyone was given an electronic name tag that contained information about the person's skills and interests. When an employee approached someone with complementary skills, the badge would light up and flash a welcome such as "Hi, Susan. We should be talking about biochemistry."[42] Many companies use internal Web sites that encourage cross-organizational collaboration. For example, Arup Group, a British engineering services company, developed an online "knowledge map" that shows the company's different areas of expertise and how departments and employees are connected to one another in terms of important information flows.[43]

Leaders at companies such as Google, Arup Group, and Procter & Gamble use the characteristics of innovative organizations—alignment, creative values, unofficial activity, open culture, and team collaboration—to ignite creativity in specific departments or the entire organization.

Many organizations that want to encourage innovation also strive to hire people who display the characteristics of creative individuals, as listed in the right-hand column of Exhibit 15.4. Creative people are often known for open-mindedness, curiosity, independence, self-confidence, persistence, and a focused approach to problem solving. Clearly,

Open innovation
including customers, strategic partners, suppliers, and other outsiders directly in the innovation process

Action Memo

As a leader, you can help the organization be more innovative. You can encourage curiosity, playfulness, and exploration, give people time for unofficial activities, and promote an open culture. You can also build in mechanisms for cross-functional collaboration and information sharing.

Leader's Bookshelf

The Game Changer: How You Can Drive Revenue and Profit Growth with Innovation

by A. G. Lafley and Ram Charan

When A. G. Lafley, who had spent his entire career at Procter & Gamble, was promoted to CEO, the giant consumer products firm was flailing. Few observers expected this company lifer could bring the change needed to revive P&G, but within a few years, Lafley had turned the company into one of the brightest stars in the business world. How did he do it? By "integrating innovation into *everything* we do," says Lafley. In *The Game Changer*, written with consultant Ram Charan, Lafley describes how to be a master at innovation.

How to Be a Game Changer

Not all companies can spend $200 million a year on R&D, as Procter & Gamble does, but Lafley and Charan argue that anyone can create an organizational structure and culture that nurtures and supports innovation. Here are a few of the guidelines:

- **Make the Customer Boss.** "Regardless of the original source of innovation . . . the consumer must be at the center of the innovation process from beginning to end," Lafley says. In an immersion process called "Living It," P&G researchers live in people's homes for several days at a time to come up with ideas based directly on consumer needs. One product that resulted from living with lower-income families in Mexico was Downy Single Rinse, a fabric softener designed for a simple "wash, add softener, rinse" cycle. P&G learned that most Mexican women like to use softener, but many in rural areas have to carry water a mile or more, and most machines require that water be manually added and extracted. Cutting the usual six-step laundry cycle to three was a godsend for many families.

- **Open Up.** By revising structures and systems, Lafley radically shifted the mindset at P&G from an insular attitude resistant to ideas "not-invented-here" to one that is open to ideas from and collaboration with anyone, even competitors. He and Gil Cloyd, head of R&D, set a goal in 2000 to get 50 percent of the company's innovation from outside the organization by the end of the decade. Lafley says that in 2000 (when the figure was 10 percent), he doubted he'd see 50 percent in his lifetime, but the company reached the goal in 2007.

- **Build a Culture with Four Cs and an O.** Creating a culture of innovation is essential. That means in addition to Openness, the culture supports Connectedness, Collaboration, Curiosity, and Courage. Lafley supports courage, for example, by celebrating what he calls *Lafley's 11 Biggest Innovation Failures*. "Courage and a higher sense of purpose sustain the energy of people as they withstand the ups and downs and uncertainties inherent in the innovation process."

For Leaders Everywhere

The numerous rich examples, not only from P&G but also from innovative companies such as Nokia, Samsung, Google, and Toyota, make *The Game Changer* a fun, inspiring read. In addition, each chapter ends with an "Ask Yourself on Monday Morning" section that lists questions leaders can ask themselves to determine how they are—or are not—contributing to an environment that encourages change and innovation.

The Game Changer, by A. G. Lafley and Ram Charan, is published by Crown Business.

marble: © Ioannis Drimilis   library: www.istockphoto.com/nikada

these characteristics are stronger in some people than in others. However, research on creativity suggests that everyone has roughly equal creative potential. The problem is that many people don't use that potential. Leaders can help both individuals and organizations be more creative.

Leading Creative People

Leaders of today's organizations have compelling reasons to encourage creativity. They need employees to continually be contributing ideas in order to respond to new challenges. People can be more creative when they are open-minded, curious, and willing to take risks. Leaders can increase individual creativity by facilitating brainstorming, lateral thinking, and creative intuition.

Action Memo

Complete the exercise in Leader's Self-Insight 15.3 to see if you have a creative personality.

Brainstorming A good way leaders can encourage creativity is to set up brainstorming sessions. Assume your organization faces a problem such as how to reduce losses from shoplifting, speed up checkout, reduce food waste, or lessen noise from a machine room. **Brainstorming** uses a face-to-face interactive group to spontaneously suggest a wide range of creative ideas to solve the problem. The keys to effective brainstorming are:[44]

1. *No criticism.* Group members should not criticize or evaluate ideas in any way during the spontaneous generation of ideas. All ideas are considered valuable.

2. *Freewheeling is welcome.* People should express any idea that comes to mind, no matter how weird or fanciful. Brainstormers should not be timid about expressing creative thinking. As a full-time developer of ideas at Intuit said, "It's more important to get the stupidest idea out there and build on it than not to have it in the first place."[45]

3. *Quantity desired.* The goal is to generate as many ideas as possible. The more ideas the better. A large quantity of ideas increases the likelihood of finding excellent solutions. Combining ideas is also encouraged. All ideas belong to the group and members should modify and extend ideas whenever possible.

One improvement in the brainstorming process is to have people write down their ideas before coming to the brainstorming session, and then to go back and write down ideas immediately after the session. Taking advantage of each person's before and after thinking will increase creative output.[46] Brainstorming has been found to be highly effective for quickly generating a wide range of creative alternatives. After all the ideas are expressed and recorded, the group can have another session to discuss and evaluate which ideas or combination will best solve the problem.

Some companies are practicing an extreme type of brainstorming, based on the popularity of television reality shows, that puts people together for an extended time period to come up with ideas. Under a program called Real Whirled, for example, Whirlpool sends teams of eight people to live together for seven weeks—and to use Whirlpool appliances for cooking and cleaning, of course. Best Buy has used a similar program, with teams of people who previously didn't know one another living together for 10 weeks in a Los Angeles apartment complex. A new service, Best Buy Studio, which provides Web-design consulting for small businesses, came directly out of ideas hatched at one of the sessions.[47]

Another recent approach, called **electronic brainstorming**, or *brainwriting*, brings people together in an interactive group over a computer network.[48] People can submit ideas as well as read and extend others' ideas. Austin, Texas–based ad agency GSD&M uses electronic brainstorming sessions that include outsiders as well as employees to quickly come up with ideas for ad campaigns. Leaders say the sessions generate thousands of ideas, and keeping things anonymous "keeps the boss and the new hire on the same level."[49] Studies show that electronic brainstorming generates about 40 percent more ideas than individuals brainstorming alone, and 25 percent to 200 percent more ideas than regular brainstorming groups, depending on group size.[50] Why? Primarily because people participate anonymously, the sky's the limit in terms of what they feel free to say. Creativity also increases because people can write down their ideas immediately, avoiding

Brainstorming
a technique that uses a face-to-face group to spontaneously suggest a broad range of ideas to solve a problem

Electronic brainstorming
bringing people together in an interactive group over a computer network; sometimes called *brainwriting*

Leader's Self-Insight 15.3
Do You Have a Creative Personality?

In the following list, check each adjective that you believe accurately describes your personality. Be very honest. Check all the words that fit your personality.

1. affected _____
2. capable _____
3. cautious _____
4. clever _____
5. commonplace _____
6. confident _____
7. conservative _____
8. conventional _____
9. egotistical _____
10. dissatisfied _____
11. honest _____
12. humorous _____
13. individualistic _____
14. informal _____
15. insightful _____
16. intelligent _____
17. narrow interests _____
18. wide interests _____
19. inventive _____
20. mannerly _____
21. original _____
22. reflective _____
23. resourceful _____
24. self-confident _____
25. sexy _____
26. snobbish _____
27. sincere _____
28. submissive _____
29. suspicious _____
30. unconventional _____

Scoring and Interpretation

Add one point for checking each of the following words: 2, 4, 6, 9, 12, 13, 14, 15, 16, 18, 19, 21, 22, 23, 24, 25, 26, and 30. Subtract one point for checking each of the following words: 1, 3, 5, 7, 8, 10, 11, 17, 20, 27, 28, and 29. The highest possible score is +18 and the lowest possible score is –12.

The average score for a set of 256 assessed males on this creativity scale was 3.57, and for 126 females was 4.4. A group of 45 male research scientists and a group of 530 male psychology graduate students both had average scores of 6.0, and 124 male architects received an average score of 5.3. A group of 335 female psychology students had an average score of 3.34. If you received a score above 6.0, your personality would be considered above average in creativity.

This adjective checklist was validated by comparing the respondents' scores to scores on other creativity tests and to creativity assessments of respondents provided by expert judges of creativity. This scale does not provide perfect prediction of creativity, but it is reliable and has moderate validity. Your score probably indicates something about your creative personality compared to other people.

To what extent do you think your score reflects your true creativity? Compare your score to others in your class. What is the range of scores among other students? Which adjectives were most important for your score compared to other students? Can you think of types of creativity this test might not measure? How about situations where the creativity reflected on this test might not be very important?

Source: Harrison G. Gough, "A Creative Personality Scale for the Adjective Check List," *Journal of Personality and Social Psychology* 37, no. 8 (1979), pp. 1398–1405.

the possibility that a good idea might slip away while the person is waiting for a chance to speak in a face-to-face group.

With electronic brainstorming, social inhibitions and concerns are circumvented, which typically allows for a broader range of participation. A shy, insecure person's idea gets the same chance at being heard as that of the outgoing, confident hotshot. Another advantage is that electronic brainstorming can potentially be done with groups made up of employees from around the world, as well as outsiders, further increasing the diversity of ideas. For example, GSD&M invites outsiders from widely different backgrounds—from economists to video gamers—to brainstorm ideas for ad campaigns for the PGA Tour, Southwest Airlines, AT&T, the U.S. Air Force, and other clients.[51]

Lateral Thinking Most of a person's thinking follows a regular groove and somewhat linear pattern from one thought to the next. But linear thinking does not often provide a creative breakthrough. Linear thinking is when people take a problem or idea and then build sequentially from that point. A more creative approach is to use lateral thinking. **Lateral thinking** can be defined as a set of systematic techniques used for changing mental concepts and perceptions and generating new ones.[52] With lateral thinking, people move "sideways" to try different perceptions, different concepts, and different points of entry to gain a novel solution. Lateral thinking appears to solve a problem by an unorthodox or apparently illogical method. Lateral thinking makes an unusual mental connection that is concerned with possibilities and "what might be."

Companies as diverse as Boeing, Nokia, IBM, and Nestlé have trained people to use lateral thinking as a way to help the organization meet the demands of a rapidly changing global environment.[53] To stimulate lateral thinking, leaders provide people with opportunities to use different parts of their brain and thus to make novel, creative connections. When people take time off from working on a problem and change what they are doing, it is possible to activate different areas of the brain. If the answer isn't in the part of the brain being used, it might be in another that can be stimulated by a new experience. For example, a NASA scientist was taking a shower in a German hotel while pondering how to fix the distorted lenses in the Hubble telescope in 1990. Nobody could figure out how to fit a corrective mirror into the hard-to-reach space inside the orbiting telescope. The engineer noticed the European-style showerhead mounted on adjustable rods. This perception connected with the Hubble problem as he realized that corrective mirrors could be extended into the telescope on similar folding arms. Lateral thinking came to the rescue.[54]

Action Memo

As a leader, you can expand the creative potential of yourself and others by using the techniques of brainstorming, lateral thinking, and creative intuition.

To facilitate the creative flash from people, some managers reorganize frequently to mix people into different jobs and responsibilities, or they hire people with diverse experiences. Frequent change can be unsettling, but it keeps people's minds fresh and innovative. Having someone with a real estate background run a bank branch brings a fresh perspective to problems. People with diverse skills challenge the status quo when developing strategies or responses to customers.[55]

Personal approaches to stretch your mind when solving problems could include behaviors such as changing your sleeping hours, taking a different route to work, reading a different newspaper or listening to a different radio station, meeting new people, trying new recipes, or changing your restaurant, recreation, or reading habits, all of which might stimulate a new part of the brain and trigger a lateral response. Unilever Best Foods asks 1,500 managers to leave their offices, laboratories, or factories for three days, twice a year, to visit customers and learn more about them. Card designers at American Greetings are free to change their work location, enjoy a library of hundreds of magazines and thousands of books, and confer with counterparts in other industries, such as automotive and appliance manufacturers.[56]

Alex Osborn, the originator of brainstorming, developed many creative techniques. One effective technique that is widely used to stimulate lateral thinking is the checklist in Exhibit 15.5. The checklist seems to work best when there is a current product or service that needs to be improved. If the problem is to modify a cell phone design to increase its sales, for example, the checklist verbs in Exhibit 15.5 can stimulate an array of different perceptions about the item being analyzed.

An exercise of *considering opposites* will also stretch the mind in a lateral direction. Physical opposites include back/front, big/small, hard/soft, and slow/fast. Biological opposites include young/old, sick/healthy, male/female, and

Lateral thinking
a set of systematic techniques for changing mental concepts and generating new ones

Exhibit 15.5 Lateral Thinking Checklist

Verb	Description
Put to other uses?	New ways to use as is? Other uses if modified?
Adapt?	What else is like this? What other idea does this suggest?
Modify?	Change meaning, color, motion, sound, odor, form, shape? Other changes?
Magnify?	What to add: Greater frequency? Stronger? Larger? Plus ingredient? Exaggerate?
Minify?	What to subtract: Eliminate? Smaller? Slower? Lower? Shorter? Lighter? Split up? Less frequent?
Substitute?	Who else instead? What else instead? Other place? Other time?
Rearrange?	Other layout? Other sequence? Change pace?
Reverse?	Transpose positive and negative? How about opposites? Turn it backward? Turn it upside down? Reverse role?
Combine?	How about a blend, an alloy, an assortment, an ensemble? Combine units? Combine purposes? Combine appeals? Combine ideas?

Source: Based on Alex Osborn, *Applied Imagination* (New York: Charles Scribner's Sons, 1963).

tortoise/hare. Management opposites would be bureaucratic/entrepreneurial, or top-down/bottom-up. Business opposites are buy/sell, profit/loss, and hire/fire.[57]

Action Memo

Right now, see if you can think of three additional opposites in each of the categories of physical, biological, management, and business. Look at opposites to stretch your thinking for a problem you face.

Creative Intuition The creative flash of insight leaders want to awaken is actually the second stage of creativity. The first stage is data gathering. The mind is gathering data constantly, especially when you are studying background material on a problem to be solved. Then the creative insight bubbles up as an intuition from the deeper subconscious. It may be hard to trust that intuitive process because it seems "soft" to many business executives. The subconscious mind remembers all experiences that the conscious mind has forgotten. Intuition has a broader reach than any analytical process focused solely on the problem at hand.

Where or when do you get your best ideas? The most popular response is "in the shower." One man got good ideas so consistently in the shower that he regularly experienced a 20-minute mental core dump of ideas. He purchased a piece of clear plastic and a grease pencil to write down the creative ideas while in his "think tank." Creativity often occurs during a mental pause, a period of mixed tension and relaxation. In the shower, or while exercising, driving, walking, or meditating, the mind reverts to a neutral, somewhat unfocused state in which it is receptive to issues or themes that have not been resolved. A temporary activity that is relatively simple and mindless can provide the moment for a creative flash from deep in the subconscious. If the analytical part of the mind is too focused and active, it shuts down the spontaneous part. Thus, the semi-relaxed mental "pause" is like putting the analytical left brain on hold and giving room for the intuitive right brain to find the solution in the subconscious mind.[58] C. S. Lewis, author of *The Chronicles of Narnia*, was fond of long, contemplative walks to facilitate his creative juices. Similarly, Jerry Kathman, president and CEO of brand design agency LPK, says he gets many of his ideas during his morning jog.[59] Exercise is often considered a good way to give the mind a chance to work freely. One study suggested that a single aerobic workout is enough to kick the brains of college students into high gear for a couple of hours. Thus, physical exercise may be as effective as the shower for triggering the appropriate relaxed state that enables creative intuition to break through.[60]

To understand your own creative intuition, consider the following problems. Each set of three words has something in common.[61] Do not over-analyze. Instead just relax and see if the common element pops up from your intuition.

1. April   locker room   bride-to-be
2. curtain   fisherman   nuclear reactor
3. rat   blue   cottage
4. envy   golf   beans
5. bowling alley   tailor   wrestling match

Don't rush to find the answers. Give your intuitive subconscious time to work. After it's finished working on these problems, consider the following question you might be asked if you interview for a job at Microsoft: *How would you weigh a large jet aircraft without a scale?* This question combines logical thinking and intuition. Before reading on, how might you compute the airplane's weight doing something that is technologically feasible even if not realistic?[62]

The next challenge may appear to have no solution until your intuition shows you the obvious answer. In the following illustration, remove three matches to leave four.[63]

Here is another problem that may force your mind to respond from a different place to get the answer. The matches are an equation of Roman numerals made from ten matches. The equation is incorrect. Can you correct the equation without touching the matches, adding new matches, or taking away any matches?

Have you given adequate time to your creative intuition? The answers to these creative challenges follow:

For the word sets, the correct answers are (1) shower, (2) rods, (3) cheese, (4) green, and (5) pins.

One answer to weighing the jet aircraft would be to taxi the jet onto a ship big enough to hold it. You could put a mark on the hull at the water line and then remove the jet and reload the ship with items of known weight until it sinks to the same mark on the hull. The weight of the items will equal the weight of the jet.

The answer to the first match puzzle depends on how you interpret the word "four." Rather than counting four matches, remove the matches at the top, bottom, and right and the answer is obvious—the Roman numeral IV. For the second match puzzle, you can solve this problem by looking at it from a different perspective— turn the page upside down. Did your creative intuition come up with good answers?

Implementing Change

Leaders frequently see innovation, change, and creativity as a way to strengthen the organization, but many people view change only as painful and disruptive. A critical aspect of leading people through change is understanding that resistance to change is natural—and that there are often legitimate reasons for it. This chapter's *Consider This* box takes a lighthearted look at why employees may resist changes in some overly bureaucratic organizations.

The underlying reason why employees resist change is that it violates the **personal compact** between workers and the organization.[64] Personal compacts are the reciprocal obligations and commitments that define the relationship between

Consider **This!**
Dealing with a Dead Horse

Ancient wisdom says that when you discover you are astride a dead horse, the best strategy is to dismount. In government and other overly bureaucratic organizations, many different approaches are tried. Here are some of our favorite strategies for dealing with the "dead horse" scenario:

1. Change the rider.
2. Buy a stronger whip.
3. Beat the horse harder.
4. Shout at and threaten the horse.
5. Appoint a committee to study the horse.
6. Arrange a visit to other sites to see how they ride dead horses.
7. Increase the standards for riding dead horses.
8. Appoint a committee to revive the dead horse.
9. Create a training session to improve riding skills.
10. Explore the state of dead horses in today's environment.
11. Change the requirements so that the horse no longer meets the standards of death.
12. Hire an external consultant to show how a dead horse can be ridden.
13. Harness several dead horses together to increase speed.
14. Increase funding to improve the horse's performance.
15. Declare that no horse is too dead to ride.
16. Fund a study to determine if outsourcing will reduce the cost of riding a dead horse.
17. Buy a computer program to enhance the dead horse's performance.
18. Declare a dead horse less costly to maintain than a live one.
19. Form a work group to find uses for dead horses. And . . . if all else fails . . .
20. Promote the dead horse to a supervisory position. Or, in a large corporation, make it a Vice President.

Source: Author unknown. Another version of this story may be found at http://www.abcsmallbiz.com/funny/deadhorse.html.

© majaiva

Personal compact
the reciprocal obligations and commitments that define the relationship between employees and the organization

employees and organizations. They include such things as job tasks, performance requirements, evaluation procedures, and compensation packages. These aspects of the compact are generally clearly defined and may be in written form. Other aspects are less clear-cut. The personal compact incorporates elements such as mutual trust and dependence, as well as shared values. When employees perceive that change violates the personal compact, they are likely to resist. For example, a new general manager at the Dallas–Fort Worth Marriott wanted to change the incentive system to offer bonuses tied to the hotel's financial performance, but employees balked. "They were thinking, 'Here comes the Wicked Witch of the West taking my stuff away,'" the manager said. There are tools available to help leaders implement innovation and change.

Tools for Implementation

Leaders can improve the chances for a successful outcome by following the eight-stage model discussed earlier in this chapter and using appreciative inquiry for both large and small changes. In addition, leaders mobilize people for change by engaging their hearts as well as their minds. Effective leaders use elements such as storytelling, metaphor, humor, symbolism, and a personal touch to reach people on an emotional level and sell them on proposed changes.[65] Emotional connections are essential for persuading and influencing others; thus, leaders should not overlook the importance of emotional elements to overcome resistance to change.[66]

Action Memo

As a leader, you can understand the reasons for resistance to change and use tools such as communication, training, and follower participation to overcome resistance. Use coercion only as a last resort and when the change is urgent.

Leaders also use a number of specific implementation techniques to smooth the change process.

- *Communication and training.* Open and honest communication is perhaps the single most effective way to overcome resistance to change because it reduces uncertainty, gives people a sense of control, clarifies the benefits of the change, and builds trust. In one study of change efforts, the most commonly cited reason for failure was that employees learned of the change from outsiders.[67] Top leaders concentrated on communicating with the public and shareholders, but failed to communicate with the people who would be most intimately affected by the changes—their own employees. It is important that leaders communicate with people face-to-face rather than relying solely on newsletters, memos, or electronic communication. For example, the CEO of one information technology company embarking on a major restructuring held a meeting with all employees to explain the changes, answer questions, and reassure people that the changes were not going to result in job losses.[68]

  Employees frequently also need training to acquire skills for their role in the change process or their new responsibilities. Good change leaders make sure people get the training they need to feel comfortable with new tasks, such as when Canadian Airlines International spent a year and a half training employees in new procedures before changing its entire reservations, airport, cargo, and financial systems.[69]

- *Participation and involvement.* Participation involves followers in helping to design the change. Although this approach is time-consuming, it pays off by giving people a sense of control over the change activity. They come to understand the change better and become committed to its successful implementation. A study of the implementation and adoption of new computer technology at two companies, for example, showed a much smoother implementation process at the company that introduced the change using a participatory approach.[70]

- *Coercion.* As a last resort, leaders overcome resistance by threatening employees with the loss of jobs or promotions or by firing or transferring them. Coercion may be necessary in crisis situations when a rapid response is needed. For example, a number of top managers at Coca-Cola had to be reassigned or let go after they refused to go along with a new CEO's changes for revitalizing the sluggish corporation.[71] Coercion may also be needed for administrative changes that flow from the top down, such as downsizing the workforce. However, as a general rule, this approach to change is not advisable because it leaves people angry at leaders, and the change may be sabotaged.

Leaders at Raytheon Missile Systems faced an urgent need for change, but they wisely realized that participation and involvement, communication, and training would lead to far better results than trying to force the changes on employees.

IN THE LEAD

Raytheon Missile Systems

In the early 2000s, leaders at Raytheon Missile Systems (RMS) were reeling from the challenges brought about by the merger of four different companies into one. Employees were from different geographical areas; used different processes, methods, and tools; held different corporate cultural values and norms; and even used different words for the same products or technologies.

Top leaders put together a core change team to write a clear vision for change that would align the entire organization into one smoothly functioning manufacturing operation. The team also created a powerful change procedure that included bite-sized action steps the factories could take to achieve manufacturing improvement goals. However, leaders realized that imposing these changes from above might provoke strong resistance. So, they set up three off-site workshops that involved people from all parts of the organization and assigned subgroups to tackle the issue of describing steps needed to achieve manufacturing excellence. With facilitation from change team members, the employee groups developed descriptions that were parallel to those originally developed by the change team but which were also richer and more detailed.

Next, leaders actively involved factory managers in the changes by assigning them to assess one another's operations. In short order, factory managers were helping one another implement the best manufacturing methods of the entire organization across boundaries. Leaders set broad improvement goals for each factory, but they allowed the factory manager to determine the specific elements to improve during each year of the five-year improvement plan. Training was provided to help managers and improvement teams accomplish results faster.[72]

The change journey at Raytheon Missile Systems was not without challenges, but by communicating with employees, allowing people to participate in the change, actively involving factory managers, and providing training, leaders overcame most of the resistance and facilitated a smoother implementation. After two years, they decided to apply for the Shingo Prize for Excellence in Manufacturing as a way to gauge the organization's progress. Surprisingly, RMS won the award on its first attempt, which served both as a reminder of how far the organization had come and a way to celebrate and reward factory managers for all their hard work.

The Two Faces of Change

Effectively and humanely leading change is one of the greatest challenges for leaders. The nature and pace of change in today's environment can be exhilarating, but it can also be inconvenient, painful, and downright scary. Particularly with the recent economic slump, people are feeling a lot of fear and anxiety. Even when a change appears to be good for individual employees as well as the organization, it can lead to decreased morale, lower commitment, and diminished trust if not handled carefully. In addition, some changes that may be necessary for the good of the organization can cause real, negative consequences for individual employees, who may experience high levels of stress, be compelled to quickly learn entirely new tasks and ways of working, or possibly lose their jobs.

Some of the most difficult changes are those related to structure, such as redefining positions and responsibilities, reengineering the company, redesigning jobs, departments, or divisions, or downsizing the organization. In many cases, these types of changes mean that some people will be seriously hurt because they will lose their jobs. Numerous organizations have experienced widespread layoffs in recent years. This is one of the most difficult situations leaders face; they have to handle the layoffs in a way that eases the pain and tension for departing employees and maintains the trust, morale, and performance of employees who remain with the organization.

Leadership and Downsizing

Downsizing refers to intentionally reducing the size of a company's workforce. Massive downsizing became a common practice after the Wall Street meltdown led to a global economic crisis, as discussed in Chapter 1. On one Monday in January 2009 alone, companies announced more than 75,000 job cuts around the world, including 20,000 at Caterpillar, the largest maker of construction and mining equipment, 8,000 at wireless provider Sprint Nextel, and 7,000 at home supply retailer Home Depot.[73] That came on the heels of millions of job cuts in 2008, not only in the beleaguered financial services and auto industries, but at electronics firms, software companies, transportation companies, media organizations, telecommunications firms, and colleges and universities, as well.

Although experts have found that massive downsizing has often not achieved the intended benefits, and in some cases has significantly harmed the organization,[74] for some companies in recent years, it became a necessary means of survival. Other companies searched for creative ways to avoid layoffs, including freezing salaries or cutting pay and benefits, shortening the workweek, implementing work-sharing programs, and asking employees to take unpaid furloughs.[75] FedEx instituted pay cuts for 36,000 salaried employees, including top leaders, in an effort to avoid layoffs. CEO Fred Smith took the biggest cut, at 20 percent; other senior executives took cuts of around 8 to 10 percent; and salaried employees saw their pay cut by 5 percent.[76]

Even in good economic times, there are situations when downsizing is a necessary part of a thoughtful restructuring of assets or other important change initiatives.[77] Anytime job cuts are made, leaders should be prepared for increased conflict and stress, stronger resistance to change, and a decrease in morale, trust, and employee commitment.[78] A number of techniques can help leaders smooth the downsizing process and ease tensions for employees who leave as well as those who remain.[79] For one thing, leaders need to be open and honest about a pending layoff, even when they're not certain exactly what is going to happen. At Aruba Networks, leaders held a companywide meeting to explain that layoffs were going to be required in order to save the company.[80] Leaders should provide

Downsizing
intentionally reducing the size of a company's workforce

advance notice with as much information as possible to employees who will be let go, and they should remember that U.S. law requires companies with 100 or more employees to give 60 days' written notice of a mass layoff or plant closing. Leaders can also involve employees in shaping the criteria for which jobs will be cut or which employees will leave the company. Other options are to offer incentive packages for employees to leave voluntarily or to offer alternative work arrangements such as job-sharing and part-time work.

Action Memo

As a leader, you can be compassionate when making changes such as downsizing that will hurt some people in the organization. You can provide assistance to displaced employees, and remember to address the emotional needs of remaining employees to help them stay motivated and productive.

Providing assistance to displaced employees, such as through training programs, severance packages, extended benefits, outplacement assistance, and counseling services for both employees and their families, can ease the trauma associated with a job loss. In addition, this shows remaining employees that leaders care about people, which can help to ease employees' feelings of confusion, guilt, anger, and sadness over the loss of colleagues. Many companies also provide counseling to help remaining employees handle the emotional difficulties associated with the downsizing.

Even the best-led organizations may sometimes need to lay off employees in a turbulent environment. Leaders can attain positive results if they handle downsizing in a way that enables remaining organization members to be motivated, productive, and committed to a better future.

Leadership Essentials

■   The important point of this chapter is that tools and approaches are available to help leaders facilitate creativity and innovation and manage change. Change is inevitable, and the increased pace of change in today's global environment has led to even greater problems for leaders struggling to help their organizations adapt. A major factor in the failure of organizations to adapt to changes in the global environment is the lack of effective change leadership. Leaders who can successfully accomplish change typically define themselves as change leaders, describe a vision for the future in vivid terms, and articulate values that promote change and adaptability. Change leaders are courageous, are capable of managing complexity and uncertainty, believe in followers' capacity to assume responsibility for change, and learn from their own mistakes.

■   Major changes can be particularly difficult to implement, but leaders can help to ensure a successful change effort by following the eight-stage model of planned change—establish a sense of urgency; create a powerful coalition; develop a compelling vision and strategy; communicate the vision; empower employees to act; generate short-term wins; keep up the energy and commitment to tackle bigger problems; and institutionalize the change in the organizational culture.

■   An exciting approach to change management known as appreciative inquiry engages individuals, teams, or the entire organization in creating change by reinforcing positive messages and focusing on learning from success. Rather than looking at a situation from the viewpoint of what is wrong and who is to blame, AI takes a positive, affirming approach and follows the stages of discovery, dream, design, and destiny. Appreciative inquiry is powerful for leading both major changes and smaller, everyday changes.

◼ Leading for innovation is a significant challenge for today's leaders. One way is by creating an environment that nourishes creativity in particular departments or the entire organization. Five elements of innovative organizations are alignment, creative values, unofficial activity, open culture, and team collaboration. These correspond to characteristics of creative individuals. Creative people are less resistant to change. Although some people demonstrate more creativity than others, research suggests that everyone has roughly equal creative potential. Leaders can increase individual creativity by facilitating brainstorming, lateral thinking, and creative intuition.

◼ Implementation is a critical aspect of any change initiative. Leaders should strive to understand why people resist a change. They can use communication and training, participation and involvement, and—as a last resort—coercion to overcome resistance. Leaders should recognize that change can have negative as well as positive consequences. One of the most difficult situations leaders may face is downsizing. They can use techniques to help ease the stress and hardship for employees who leave as well as maintain the morale and trust of those who remain.

Discussion Questions

1. How are Kotter's eight-stage framework for change and the appreciative inquiry method similar? How are they different? Explain.

2. Think of a problem situation you would like to change at work, school, or home and describe how you would frame the topic and approach the change using appreciative inquiry.

3. Do you think creative individuals and creative organizations have characteristics in common? Discuss.

4. How could you increase the number of novel and useful solutions you can come up with to solve a problem?

5. What advice would you give a leader who wants to increase innovation in her department?

6. How would you suggest a leader overcome resistance to a change that is going to cause some people to lose their jobs?

7. Why are idea champions considered to be essential to innovation? Do you think these people would be more important in a large organization or a small one? Discuss.

8. Planned change is often considered ideal. Do you think unplanned change could be effective? Discuss. Can you think of an example?

9. Is the world really changing faster today, or do people just assume so?

10. Do you believe the recent Wall Street meltdown will lead to any lasting changes in U.S. financial services institutions? What kinds of lasting changes do you envision? What about companies in other industries?

Leadership at Work

ORGANIZATIONAL CHANGE ROLE PLAY

You are the new director of the Harpeth Gardens not-for-profit nursing home. Harpeth Gardens is one of 20 elder-care centers managed by Franklin Resident Care Centers. Harpeth Gardens has 56 patients and is completely responsible for their proper hygiene, nutrition, and daily recreation. Many of the patients can move about by themselves, but several require physical assistance for eating, dressing, and moving about the nursing home. During daytime hours, the head of nursing is in charge of the four certified nursing assistants (CNAs) who work on the floors. During the night shift, a registered nurse is on duty, along with three CNAs. The same number of CNAs are on duty over the weekend, and either the head of nursing or the registered nurse is on call.

Several other staff also report to you, including the heads of maintenance, bookkeeping/MIS, and the cafeteria. The on-call physician stops by Harpeth Gardens once a week to check on the residents. You have 26 full- and part-time employees who cover the different tasks and shifts.

During your interviews for the director's job, you became aware that the previous director ran a very tight ship, insisting that the best way to care for nursing home patients was by following strict rules and procedures. He personally approved almost every decision, including decisions for patient care, despite not having a medical degree. Turnover has been rather high and several beds are empty because of the time required to hire and train new staff. Other elder-care facilities in the area have a waiting list of people wanting to be admitted.

At Harpeth Gardens, the non-nursing offices have little interaction with nurses or each other. Back-office staff people seem to do their work and go home. Overall, Harpeth Gardens seems to you like a dreary place to work. People seem to have forgotten the compassion that is essential for patients and each other working in a health-care environment. You believe that a new strategy and culture are needed to give more responsibility to employees, improve morale, reduce turnover, and fill the empty beds. You have read about concepts for leading organizational change and would like to implement some new ideas to make the culture at Harpeth Gardens more creative, decentralized, and participative. You decide to start with the idea of engaging employees in decision making and encouraging more direct collaboration between departments. If those two ideas work, then you will implement other changes.

During your first week as the director, you have met all the employees, and you have confirmed your understanding of the previous director's rigid approach. You call a meeting of all employees for next Friday afternoon.

Your assignment for this exercise is to decide how you will implement the desired changes and what you will tell employees at the employee meeting. Start by deciding how you will accomplish each of the first three steps in the model in Exhibit 15.2. Write your answers to these three questions:

How will you get employees to feel a sense of urgency?

_____

_____

_____

How will you form a guiding coalition, and who will be in it?

_____

_____

_____

What is your compelling vision?

_____

_____

_____

Your next task is to prepare a *vision speech* to employees for the changes you are about to implement. In this speech, explain your dream for Harpeth Gardens and the urgency of this change. Explain exactly what you believe the changes will involve and why the employees should agree to the changes and help implement them. Sketch out the points you will include in your speech:

_____

_____

_____

In Class: The instructor can divide the class into small groups to discuss the answers to questions 1 to 3 and to brainstorm the key points to cover in the vision speech to employees. After student groups have decided what the director will say, the instructor can ask for volunteers from a few groups to actually give the speech to employees that will start the Harpeth Gardens transition toward a learning organization. The key questions are: Did the speech touch on the key points that inspire employees to help implement changes? Did the speech convey a high purpose and a sense of urgency? Did the speech connect with employees in a personal way, and did it lay out the reality facing Harpeth Gardens?

LEADERSHIP DEVELOPMENT: CASES FOR ANALYSIS

Chapter 1 Cases

SALES ENGINEERING DIVISION

When DGL International, a manufacturer of refinery equipment, brought in John Terrill to manage its Sales Engineering division, company executives informed him of the urgent situation. Sales Engineering, with 20 engineers, was the highest-paid, best-educated, and least-productive division in the company. The instructions to Terrill: Turn it around. Terrill called a meeting of the engineers. He showed great concern for their personal welfare and asked point blank: "What's the problem? Why can't we produce? Why does this division have such turnover?"

Without hesitation, employees launched a hail of complaints. "I was hired as an engineer, not a pencil pusher." "We spend over half of our time writing asinine reports in triplicate for top management, and no one reads the reports." "We have to account for every penny, which doesn't give us time to work with customers or new developments."

After a two-hour discussion, Terrill began to envision a future in which engineers were free to work with customers and join self-directed teams for product improvement. Terrill concluded he had to get top management off the engineers' backs. He promised the engineers, "My job is to stay out of your way so you can do your work, and I'll try to keep top management off your backs, too." He called for the day's reports and issued an order effective immediately that the originals be turned in daily to his office rather than mailed to headquarters. For three weeks, technical reports piled up on his desk. By month's end, the stack was nearly three feet high. During that time no one called for the reports. When other managers entered his office and saw the stack, they usually asked, "What's all this?" Terrill answered, "Technical reports." No one asked to read them.

Finally, at month's end, a secretary from finance called and asked for the monthly travel and expense report. Terrill responded, "Meet me in the president's office tomorrow morning."

The next morning the engineers cheered as Terrill walked through the department pushing a cart loaded with the enormous stack of reports. They knew the showdown had come.

Terrill entered the president's office and placed the stack of reports on his desk. The president and the other senior executives looked bewildered.

"This," Terrill announced, "is the reason for the lack of productivity in the Sales Engineering division. These are the reports your people require every month. The fact that they sat on my desk all month shows that no one reads this material. I suggest that the engineers' time could be used in a more productive manner, and that one brief monthly report from my office will satisfy the needs of the other departments."

QUESTIONS

1. Does John Terrill's leadership style fit the definition of leadership in Exhibit 1.1? Explain.
2. With respect to Exhibit 1.4, in what leadership era is Terrill? In what era is headquarters?
3. What approach would you have taken in this situation?

STUDER INTERNATIONAL

At 7:30 A.M., Dean Adams hit the snooze alarm for the third time, but he knew he could never go back to sleep. Rubbing his eyes and shaking off a headache, Adams first checked his BlackBerry and read an urgent message from his boss, explaining that Sue Chan, chief security analyst, had resigned this morning and needed to be replaced immediately. Frustrated, Adams lumbered toward the shower, hoping it would energize him to face another day. After last night's management meeting, which had ended after midnight, he was reeling from the news that his Wall Street employer, Studer International, was spiraling toward a financial meltdown.

Adams scratched his head and wondered, "How could one of the world's largest insurance companies plummet from being the gold standard in the industry to one struggling for survival?" At the end of 2007, Studer had $100 billion in annual revenues, 65 million customers, and 96,000 employees in 130 countries. One year later and staggered by losses stemming from the credit crisis, Studer teetered on the brink of failure and was in need of emergency government assistance. Studer had been a victim of the meltdown in the credit markets. The collapse of this respected financial institution sent shock waves throughout the world's economy.

Within Studer's Manhattan office, Adams and his coworkers felt growing pressure to respond to this crisis quickly and ethically. But morale was sagging and decision making was stalled. New projects were on hold, revenues weren't coming in fast enough, and job cuts were imminent. Finger-pointing and resignations of key managers had become commonplace. Strong leadership was needed to guide employees to stay the course. Adams knew his first priority was to replace Sue Chan. When leaving the meeting last night, his boss had told him, "It's critical that we keep key managers in place as we weather this storm. If we lose any, be sure you replace them with ones who can handle the stress and can make tough, maybe even unpopular, decisions."

Working up a sweat as he rushed into his office, Adams began sorting through the day's priorities. His first task would be to consider internal candidates to replace Chan. He pondered the characteristics required of a chief securities analyst and scribbled them on a notepad: experienced in security and regulatory issues; strong decision-making skills; high ethical standards; able to make job cuts; comfortable slashing budgets; and respected for calm leadership. Adams immediately thought of Julie Cobb, a senior analyst who had been vocal about her desire to move up and had recently shown steady leadership as the organization started to crumble.

Cobb had worked her way up through the organization, becoming a respected expert in her field. She had developed a strong team of loyal employees and made training and job development a priority. She was likable, sensitive to her employees, and a consensus builder. While many managers within Studer had made questionable business decisions, Julie had held herself to a high ethical standard and created a culture of integrity. Cobb was focused on the future—a go-getter who knew how to get results.

With the future of the company at stake, however, Adams wondered if Cobb could handle the tough challenges ahead. Although he valued her team-building skills, she could be soft when it came to holding employees accountable. A large part of her motivation was to have people like her. When she reported a shortfall in earnings in the last company meeting and came under fire, she'd become defensive and didn't want to point fingers at employees who were to blame. In fact, Adams recalled another instance when Cobb recoiled at the thought of firing an employee who had developed a pattern of poor attendance while caring for her sick husband. She confessed a hesitation to confront poor performers and employees struggling to balance home and work life.

Adams stirred his morning coffee and wondered aloud, "Is Julie Cobb capable of balancing kindness and toughness during a crisis? Can I count on her to be decisive and focused on top- and bottom-line results? Is she too much of a people pleaser? Will it impact her ability to lead successfully?"

QUESTIONS

1. What leadership skills are necessary in a corporate environment characterized by instability and turmoil? Has Julie Cobb demonstrated any of these skills in her current position?

2. Would you promote someone into a key leadership position who is considered a "people pleaser"? Explain.

3. Leo Durocher, baseball manager from 1939 to 1972, once said, "Nice guys finish last." Apply that idea to leadership within an organization. Is it possible for a manager who demonstrates kindness and concern for employees to achieve both top-line (total sales) and bottom-line (profits) results simultaneously?

Chapter 2 Cases

CONSOLIDATED PRODUCTS

Consolidated Products is a medium-sized manufacturer of consumer products with nonunionized production workers. Ben Samuels was a plant manager for Consolidated Products for 10 years, and he was very well liked by the employees there. They were grateful for the fitness center he built for employees, and they enjoyed the social activities sponsored by the plant several times a year, including company picnics and holiday parties. He knew most of the workers by name, and he spent part of each day walking around the plant to visit with them and ask about their families or hobbies.

Ben believed that it was important to treat employees properly so they would have a sense of loyalty to the company. He tried to avoid any layoffs when production demand was slack, figuring that the company could not afford to lose skilled workers that are so difficult to replace. The workers knew that if they had a special problem, Ben would try to help them. For example, when someone was injured but wanted to continue working, Ben found another job in the plant that the person could do despite having a disability. Ben believed that if you treat people right, they would do a good job for you without close supervision or prodding. Ben applied the same principle to his supervisors, and he mostly left them alone to run their departments as they saw fit. He did not set objectives and standards for the plant, and he never asked the supervisors to develop plans for improving productivity and product quality.

Under Ben, the plant had the lowest turnover among the company's five plants, but the second worst record for costs and production levels. When the company was acquired by another firm, Ben was asked to take early retirement, and Phil Jones was brought in to replace him.

Phil had a growing reputation as a manager who could get things done, and he quickly began making changes. Costs were cut by trimming a number of activities such as the fitness center at the plant, company picnics and parties, and the human relations training programs for supervisors. Phil believed that human relations training was a waste of time; if employees don't want to do the work, get rid of them and find somebody else who does.

Supervisors were instructed to establish high performance standards for their departments and insist that people achieve them. A computer monitoring system was introduced so that the output of each worker could be checked closely against the standards. Phil told his supervisors to give any worker who had substandard performance one warning, and then if performance did not improve within two weeks, to fire the person. Phil believed that workers don't respect a supervisor who is weak and passive. When Phil observed a worker wasting time or making a mistake, he would reprimand the person right on the spot to set an example. Phil also checked closely on the performance of his supervisors. Demanding objectives were set for each department, and weekly meetings were held with each supervisor to review department performance. Finally, Phil insisted that supervisors check with him first before taking any significant actions that deviated from established plans and policies.

As another cost-cutting move, Phil reduced the frequency of equipment maintenance, which required machines to be idled when they could be productive. Since the machines had a good record of reliable operation, Phil believed that the current maintenance schedule was excessive and was cutting into production. Finally, when business was slow for one of the product lines, Phil laid off workers rather than finding something else for them to do.

By the end of Phil's first year as plant manager, production costs were reduced by 20 percent and production output was up by 10 percent. However, three of his seven supervisors left to take other jobs, and turnover was also high among the machine operators. Some of the turnover was due to workers who were fired, but competent machine operators were also quitting, and it was becoming increasingly difficult to find any replacements for them. Finally, there was increasing talk of unionizing among the workers.[53]

QUESTIONS

1. Compare the leadership traits and behaviors of Ben Samuels and Phil Jones.
2. Which leader do you think is more effective? Why? Which leader would you prefer to work for?
3. If you were Phil Jones' boss, what would you do now?

D. L. WOODSIDE, SUNSHINE SNACKS

D. L. Woodside has recently accepted the position of research and development director for Sunshine Snacks, a large snack food company. Woodside has been assistant director of research at Skid's, a competing company, for several years, but it became clear to him that his chances of moving higher were slim. So, when Sunshine was looking for a new director, Woodside jumped at the chance.

At Skid's, Woodside had worked his way up from the mail room, going to school at night to obtain first a bachelor's degree and eventually a Ph.D. Management admired his drive and determination, as well as his ability to get along with just about anyone he came in contact with, and they gave him opportunities to work in various positions around the company over the years. That's when he discovered he had a love for developing new products. He had been almost single-handedly responsible for introducing four new successful product lines at Skid's. Woodside's technical knowledge and understanding of the needs of the research and development department were excellent. In addition, he was a tireless worker—when he started a project, he rarely rested until it was finished, and finished well.

Despite his ambition and his hard-charging approach to work, Woodside was considered an easy-going fellow. He liked to talk and joke around, and whenever anyone had a problem they'd come to Woodside rather than go to the director. Woodside was always willing to listen to a research assistant's personal problems. Besides that, he would often stay late or come in on weekends to finish an assistant's work if the employee was having problems at home or difficulty with a particular project. Woodside knew the director was a hard taskmaster, and he didn't want anyone getting into trouble over things they couldn't help. In fact, he'd been covering the mistakes of George, an employee who had a drinking problem, ever since he'd been appointed assistant director. Well, George was on his own now. Woodside had his own career to think about, and the position at Sunshine was his chance to finally lead a department rather than play second fiddle.

At Sunshine, Woodside is replacing Henry Meade, who has been the director for almost 30 years. However, it seems clear that Meade has been slowing down over the past few years, turning more and more of his work over to his assistant, Harmon Davis. When Woodside was first introduced to the people in the research department at Sunshine, he sensed not only a loyalty to Davis, who'd been passed over for the top job because of his lack of technical knowledge, but also an undercurrent of resistance to his own selection as the new director.

Woodside knows he needs to build good relationships with the team, and especially with Davis, quickly. The company has made it clear that it wants the department to initiate several new projects as soon as possible. One reason they selected Woodside for the job was his successful track record with new product development at Skid's.[54]

QUESTIONS

1. What traits does Woodside possess that might be helpful to him as he assumes his new position? What traits might be detrimental?

2. Would you consider Woodside a people-oriented or a task-oriented leader? Discuss which you think would be best for the new research director at Sunshine.

3. How might an understanding of individualized leadership theory be useful to Woodside in this situation? Discuss.

Chapter 3 Cases

ALVIS CORPORATION

Kevin McCarthy is the manager of a production department in Alvis Corporation, a firm that manufactures office equipment. After reading an article that stressed the benefits of participative management, Kevin believes that these benefits could be realized in his department if the workers are allowed to participate in making some decisions that affect them. The workers are not unionized. Kevin selected two decisions for his experiment in participative management.

The first decision involved vacation schedules. Each summer the workers are given two weeks' vacation, but no more than two workers can go on vacation at the same time. In prior years, Kevin made this decision himself. He would first ask the workers to indicate their preferred dates, and he considered how the work would be affected if different people were out at the same time. It was important to plan a vacation schedule that would ensure adequate staffing for all of the essential operations performed by the department. When more than two workers wanted the same time period, and they had similar skills, he usually gave preference to the workers with the highest productivity.

The second decision involved production standards. Sales had been increasing steadily over the past few years, and the company recently installed some new equipment to increase productivity. The new equipment would allow Kevin's department to produce more with the same number of workers. The company had a pay incentive system in which workers received a piece rate for each unit produced above a standard amount. Separate standards existed for each type of product, based on an industrial engineering study conducted a few years earlier. Top management wanted to readjust the production standards to reflect the fact that the new equipment made it possible for the workers to earn more without working any harder. The savings from higher productivity were needed to help pay for the new equipment.

Kevin called a meeting of his 15 workers an hour before the end of the workday. He explained that he wanted them to discuss the two issues and make recommendations. Kevin figured that the workers might be inhibited about participating in the discussion if he were present, so he left them alone to discuss the issues. Besides, Kevin had an appointment to meet with the quality control manager. Quality problems had increased after the new equipment was installed, and the industrial engineers were studying the problem in an attempt to determine why quality had gotten worse rather than better.

When Kevin returned to his department just at quitting time, he was surprised to learn that the workers recommended keeping the standards the same. He had assumed they knew the pay incentives were no longer fair and would set a higher standard. The spokesman for the group explained that their base pay had not kept up with inflation and the higher incentive pay restored their real income to its prior level.

On the vacation issue, the group was deadlocked. Several of the workers wanted to take their vacations during the same two-week period and could not agree on who should go. Some workers argued that they should have priority because they had more seniority, whereas others argued that priority should be based on productivity, as in the past. Since it was quitting time, the group concluded that Kevin would have to resolve the dispute himself. After all, wasn't that what he was being paid for?[33]

QUESTIONS

1. Analyze this situation using the Hersey–Blanchard model and the Vroom–Jago model. What do these models suggest as the appropriate leadership or decision style? Explain.

2. Evaluate Kevin McCarthy's leadership style before and during his experiment in participative management.

3. If you were Kevin McCarthy, what would you do now? Why?

FINANCE DEPARTMENT

Ken Osborne stared out the window, wondering what he could do to get things back on track. When he became head of the finance department of a state government agency, Osborne inherited a group of highly trained professionals who pursued their jobs with energy and enthusiasm. Everyone seemed to genuinely love coming to work every day. The tasks were sometimes mundane, but most employees liked the structured, routine nature of the work. In addition, the lively camaraderie of the group provided an element of fun and excitement that the work itself sometimes lacked.

Ken knew he'd had an easy time of things over the last couple of years—he had been able to focus his energies on maintaining relationships with other departments and agencies and completing the complex reports he had to turn in each month. The department had practically run itself. Until now. The problem was Larry Gibson, one of the department's best employees. Well-liked by everyone in the department, Gibson had been a key contributor to developing a new online accounting system, and Ken was counting on him to help with the implementation. But everything had changed after Gibson attended a professional development seminar at a prestigious university. Ken had expected him to come back even more fired up about work, but lately Larry was spending more time on his outside professional activities than he was on his job. "If only I'd paid more attention when all this began," Ken thought, as he recalled the day Larry asked him to sign his revised individual development plan. As he'd done in the past, Ken had simply chatted with Larry for a few minutes, glanced at the changes, and initialed the modification. Larry's revised plan included taking a more active role in the state accountants' society, which he argued would enhance his value to the agency as well as improve his own skills and professional contacts.

Within a month, Ken noticed that most of Gibson's energy and enthusiasm seemed to be focused on the society rather than the finance department. On "first Thursday," the society's luncheon meeting day, Larry spent most of the morning on the phone notifying people about the monthly meeting and finalizing details with the speaker. He left around 11 A.M. to make sure things were set up for the meeting and usually didn't return until close to quitting time. Ken could live with the loss of Gibson for one day a month, but the preoccupation with society business seemed to be turning his former star employee into a part-time worker. Larry shows up late for meetings, usually doesn't participate very much, and seems to have little interest in what is going on in the department. The new accounting system is floundering because Larry isn't spending the time to train people in its effective use, so Ken is starting to get complaints from other departments. Moreover, his previously harmonious group of employees is starting to whine and bicker over minor issues and decisions. Ken has also noticed that people who used to be hard at work when he arrived in the mornings seem to be coming in later and later every day.

"Everything's gone haywire since Larry attended that seminar," Ken brooded. "I thought I was one of the best department heads in the agency. Now, I realize I haven't had to provide much leadership until now. Maybe I've had things too easy."[34]

QUESTIONS

1. Why had Ken Osborne's department been so successful even though he has provided little leadership over the past two years?

2. How would you describe Osborne's current leadership style? Based on the path–goal theory, which style do you think he might most effectively use to turn things around with Larry Gibson?

3. If you were in Osborne's position, describe how you would evaluate the situation and handle the problem.

Chapter 4 Cases

INTERNATIONAL BANK

Top executives and board members of a large international bank in New York are meeting to consider three finalists for a new position. The winning candidate will be in a high-profile job, taking charge of a group of top loan officers who have recently gotten the bank into some risky financial arrangements in Latin America. The bank had taken a financial bath when the Mexican peso collapsed, and the board voted to hire someone to directly oversee this group of loan officers and make sure the necessary due diligence is done on major loans before further commitments are made. Although the bank likes for decisions to be made as close to the action level as possible, they believe the loan officers have gotten out of hand and need to be reined in. The effectiveness of the person in this new position is considered to be of utmost importance for the bank's future. After carefully reviewing resumés, the board selected six candidates for the first round of interviews, after which the list of finalists was narrowed to three. All three candidates seem to have the intellect and experience to handle the job. Before the second-round interview, the board has asked their regular consulting firm to review the candidates, conduct more extensive background checks, and administer personality tests. A summary of their reports on the three candidates follows:

A.M. This candidate has a relatively poor self-concept and exhibits a fear of the unknown. She is somewhat of an introvert and is uncomfortable using power openly and conspicuously. A.M.'s beliefs about others are that all people are inherently noble, kind, and disposed to do the right thing, and that it is possible to influence and modify the behavior of anyone through logic and reason. Once a person's shortcomings are pointed out to her, A.M. will try to help the person overcome them. She believes that all employees can be happy, content, and dedicated to the goals of the organization.

J.T. J.T. is an extravert with a strong drive for achievement and power. He likes new experiences and tends to be impulsive and adventurous. He is very self-assured and confident in his own abilities, but highly suspicious of the motives and abilities of others. J.T. believes the average person has an inherent dislike for work and will avoid responsibility when possible. He is very slow to trust others, but does have the ability over time to develop close, trusting relationships. In general, though, J.T. believes most people must be coerced, controlled, and threatened to get them to do their jobs well and to the benefit of the organization.

F.C. This candidate is also an extravert, but, although she is competitive, F.C. does not seem to have the strong desire for dominance that many extraverts exhibit. F.C. is also highly conscientious and goal-oriented, and will do whatever she believes is necessary to achieve a goal. F.C. has a generally positive attitude toward others, believing that most people want to do their best for the organization. F.C. does, though, seem to have a problem forming close, personal attachments. Her lively, outgoing personality enables her to make many superficial acquaintances, but she seems to distrust and avoid emotions in herself and others, preventing the development of close relationships.

Sources: This case is based on information in "Consultant's Report" in John M. Champion and Francis J. Bridges, *Critical Incidents in Management: Decision and Policy Issues*, 6th ed. (Homewood, IL: Irwin, 1989), pp. 55–60; and James Waldroop and Timothy Butler, "Guess What? You're Not Perfect," *Fortune* (October 16, 2000), pp. 415–420.

QUESTIONS

1. Based only on the consultant's summary, which of the three candidates would you select as a leader for the group of loan officers? Discuss and defend your decision.

2. The selection committee is more divided than before on who would be best for the job. What additional information do you think you would need to help you select the best candidate?

3. How much weight do you think should be given to the personality assessment? Do you believe personality tests can be useful in predicting the best person for a job? Discuss.

ENVIRONMENTAL DESIGNS INTERNATIONAL

When Lee Keiko returned from a quick lunch, she scanned her e-mail inbox for the message she had been dreading. She found it, labeled "high priority," among a dozen other e-mails and sank back in her chair as she mentally prepared to open it. Keiko felt a tightening in her stomach as she clicked on the message and braced herself for the assault she had grown to expect from Barry Carver, her boss at Environmental Designs International (EDI), a rapidly growing "green" company that specializes in retrofitting commercial buildings to improve their energy efficiency.

The primary clients of EDI are owners of skyscrapers who renovate their buildings to reduce energy use and cut down on greenhouse gas emissions, a contributor to global warming. Within these towering skyscrapers, the largest energy guzzlers are lighting, cooling, and heating. Owners of New York City's Empire State Building expect to reduce the skyscraper's energy use by 38 percent by the year 2013 at an annual savings of $4.4 million after this 78-year-old building is retrofitted.

Keiko had expected Carver's scathing e-mail and knew he would lambaste her and her team for missing last Friday's deadline for submitting a proposal to retrofit a 60-story Chicago skyscraper to meet new federal green standards. Keiko had warned Carver of the possible delay in completing the proposal due to changing federal regulations for energy efficiency. It was truly out of her hands. She had even consulted with the client to alert them of the delay, and they had agreed to an extended deadline.

Nevertheless, Carver was angry about the delay and fired off an e-mail that was brusque and insensitive. "I depend on you to meet deadlines and work effectively with regulatory agencies. Your ineptness may cost us this important project," he exclaimed in his e-mail to Keiko. "Why aren't you as committed to this project as I am? I can't do this alone," he stated. This was one more example of how Carver often made life miserable for his subordinates, verbally attacking them to get results. Carver had also started alienating his peers. During a recent meeting to discuss the replacement of thousands of windows in the Chicago skyscraper, Carver embarrassed a colleague by accusing him of selecting a vendor without doing a price comparison among vendors. "How can I value your recommendation, Troy, if you fail to do your homework? I need new prices by Friday!" shouted Carver.

Carver was a highly skilled architect and responsible for managing a team of designers in EDI's Chicago office. Although his abrupt personality had helped him climb the corporate ladder, his intimidating communication style was beginning to create problems and hamper his ability to get results. Carver learned in his performance review that his work relationships were suffering and the complaints about him were increasing. Even his longtime peers were avoiding him as much as possible and finding ways to work around him.

Sensitive to the growing animosity toward him, Carver began to reconsider how he interacted with his staff and peers. He felt motivated to begin using some of the tools he had recently learned in the executive education course he had just completed. During one of the skills-assessment activities, Carver learned that he could get better results by communicating more gently, building consensus, and working in a more team-oriented manner. Further, he realized he had to find ways to handle his anger and frustration when dealing with federal regulatory agencies and the inevitable delays that hampered progress on big construction projects. As he thought about the skills-assessment, Carver wondered if he could soften his image and perhaps even be considered for a senior management position he was eyeing in EDI's Los Angeles office.

Sources: Based on information in Gerry Yemen, Erika H. James, and James G. Clawson, "Nicholas Gray: The More Things Change . . . ," Darden Business Publishing, University of Virginia, Copyright 2003; and Mireya Navarro, "The Empire State Building Plans a Growth Spurt, Environmentally," *The New York Times* (April 7, 2009), p. A25.

QUESTIONS

1. "At the senior management level, you get hired for competence. You get fired for personality." In your opinion, is this statement true or false? How does it relate to Barry Carver and his current leadership style?

2. Identify the behaviors described in this case that were damaging to Barry Carver's work relationships. Why would a manager behave this way? What negative consequences did these behaviors have on his peers and subordinates?

3. How realistic is it that Carver (or anyone) can change his own leadership skills? What kind of help might he need?

Chapter 5 Cases

THE NEW BOSS

Sam Nolan clicked the mouse for one more round of solitaire on the computer in his den. He'd been at it for more than an hour, and his wife had long ago given up trying to persuade him to join her for a movie or a rare Saturday night on the town. The mind-numbing game seemed to be all that calmed Sam down enough to stop agonizing about work and how his job seemed to get worse every day.

Nolan was chief information officer at Century Medical, a large medical products company based in Connecticut. He had joined the company four years ago, and since that time Century had made great progress integrating technology into its systems and processes. Nolan had already led projects to design and build two highly successful systems for Century. One was a benefits-administration system for the company's human resources department. The other was a complex Web-based purchasing system that streamlined the process of purchasing supplies and capital goods. Although the system had been up and running for only a few months, modest projections were that it would save Century nearly $2 million annually. The new Web-based system dramatically cut the time needed for processing requests and placing orders. Purchasing managers now had more time to work collaboratively with key stakeholders to identify and select the best suppliers and negotiate better deals.

Nolan thought wearily of all the hours he had put in developing trust with people throughout the company and showing them how technology could not only save time and money but also support team-based work, encourage open information sharing, and give people more control over their own jobs. He smiled briefly as he recalled one long-term HR employee, 61-year-old Ethel Moore. She had been terrified when Nolan first began showing her the company's intranet, but she was now one of his biggest supporters. In fact, it had been Ethel who had first approached him with an idea about a Web-based job posting system. The two had pulled together a team and developed an idea for linking Century managers, internal recruiters, and job applicants using artificial intelligence software on top of an integrated Web-based system. When Nolan had presented the idea to his boss, executive vice president Sandra Ivey, she had enthusiastically endorsed it. Within a few weeks the team had authorization to proceed with the project.

But everything began to change when Ivey resigned her position 6 months later to take a plum job in New York. Ivey's successor, Tom Carr, seemed to have little interest in the project. During their first meeting, Carr had openly referred to the project as a waste of time and money. He immediately disapproved several new features suggested by the company's internal recruiters, even though the project team argued that the features could double internal hiring and save millions in training costs. "Just stick to the original plan and get it done. All this stuff needs to be handled on a personal basis anyway," Carr countered. "You can't learn more from a computer than you can talking to real people—and as for internal recruiting, it shouldn't be so hard to talk to people if they're already working right here in the company." Carr seemed to have no understanding of how and why technology was being used. He became irritated when Ethel Moore referred to the system as "Web-based." He boasted that he had never visited Century's intranet site and suggested that "this Internet obsession" would blow over in a few years anyway. Even Ethel's enthusiasm couldn't get through to him. "Technology is for those people in the IS department. My job is people, and yours should be, too," Carr shouted. Near the end of the meeting, Carr even jokingly suggested that the project team should just buy a couple of good filing cabinets and save everyone some time and money.

Nolan sighed and leaned back in his chair. The whole project had begun to feel like a joke. The vibrant and innovative human resources department his team had imagined now seemed like nothing more than a pipe dream. But despite his frustration, a new thought entered Nolan's mind: "Is Carr just stubborn and narrow-minded or does he have a point that HR is a people business that doesn't need a high-tech job posting system?"

Sources: Based on Carol Hildebrand, "New Boss Blues," *CIO Enterprise*, Section 2 (November 15, 1998), pp. 53–58; and Megan Santosus, "Advanced Micro Devices' Web-Based Purchasing System," *CIO*, Section 1 (May 15, 1998), p. 84. A version of this case originally appeared in Richard L. Daft, *Organization Theory and Design*, 7th ed. (Cincinnati, OH: South-Western, 2001), pp. 270–271.

QUESTIONS

1. Describe the two different mental models represented in this story.
2. What are some of the assumptions that shape the mindset of Sam Nolan? Of Tom Carr?
3. Do you think it is possible for Carr to shift to a new mental model? If you were Sam Nolan, what would you do?

THE USS *FLORIDA*

The atmosphere in a Trident nuclear submarine is generally calm and quiet. Even pipe joints are cushioned to prevent noise that might tip off a pursuer. The Trident ranks among the world's most dangerous weapons—swift, silent, armed with 24 long-range missiles carrying 192 nuclear warheads. Trident crews are the cream of the Navy crop, and even the sailors who fix the plumbing exhibit a white-collar decorum. The culture aboard ship is a low-key, collegial one in which sailors learn to speak softly and share close quarters with an ever-changing roster of shipmates. Being subject to strict security restrictions enhances a sense of elitism and pride. To move up and take charge of a Trident submarine is an extraordinary feat in the Navy—fewer than half the officers qualified for such commands ever get them. When Michael Alfonso took charge of the USS *Florida*, the crew welcomed his arrival. They knew he was one of them—a career Navy man who joined up as a teenager and moved up through the ranks. Past shipmates remembered him as basically a loner, who could be brusque but generally pleasant enough. Neighbors on shore found Alfonso to be an unfailingly polite man who kept mostly to himself.

The crew's delight in their new captain was short-lived. Commander Alfonso moved swiftly to assume command, admonishing his sailors that he would push them hard. He wasn't joking—soon after the *Florida* slipped into deep waters to begin a postoverhaul shakedown cruise, the new captain loudly and publicly reprimanded those whose performance he considered lacking. Chief Petty Officer Donald MacArthur, chief of the navigation division, was only one of those who suffered Alfonso's anger personally. During training exercises, MacArthur was having trouble keeping the boat at periscope depth because of rough seas. Alfonso announced loudly, "You're disqualified." He then precipitously relieved him of his diving duty until he could be recertified by extra practice. Word of the incident spread quickly. Crew members, accustomed to the Navy's adage of "praise in public, penalize in private," were shocked. It didn't take long for this type of behavior to have an impact on the crew, according to Petty Officer Aaron Carmody: "People didn't tell him when something was wrong. You're not supposed to be afraid of your captain, to tell him stuff. But nobody wanted to."

The captain's outbursts weren't always connected with job performance. He bawled out the supply officer, the executive officer, and the chief of the boat because the soda dispenser he used to pour himself a glass of Coke one day contained Mr. Pibb instead. He exploded when he arrived unexpectedly at a late-night meal and found the fork at his place setting missing. Soon, a newsletter titled *The Underground* was being circulated by the boat's plumbers, who used sophomoric humor to spread the word about the captain's outbursts over such petty matters. By the time the sub reached Hawaii for its "Tactical Readiness Evaluation," an intense week-long series of inspections by staff officers, the crew was almost completely alienated. Although the ship tested well, inspectors sent word to Rear Admiral Paul Sullivan that something seemed to be wrong on board, with severely strained relations between captain and crew. On the Trident's last evening of patrol, much of the crew celebrated with a film night—they chose *The Caine Mutiny* and *Crimson Tide*, both movies about Navy skippers who face mutinies and are relieved of command at sea. When Humphrey Bogart, playing the captain of the fictional USS *Caine*, exploded over a missing quart of strawberries, someone shouted, "Hey, sound familiar?"

When they reached home port, the sailors slumped ashore. "Physically and mentally, we were just beat into the ground," recalls one. Concerned about reports that the crew seemed "despondent," Admiral Sullivan launched an informal inquiry that eventually led him to relieve Alfonso of his command. It was the first-ever firing of a Trident submarine commander. "He had the chance of a lifetime to experience the magic of command, and he squandered it," Sullivan said. "Fear and intimidation lead to certain ruin." Alfonso himself seemed dumbfounded by Admiral Sullivan's actions, pointing out that the USS *Florida* under his command posted "the best-ever grades assigned for certifications and inspections for a postoverhaul Trident submarine."

Source: Based on Thomas E. Ricks, "A Skipper's Chance to Run a Trident Sub Hits Stormy Waters," *The Wall Street Journal* (November 20, 1997), pp. A1, A6.

QUESTIONS

1. Analyze Alfonso's impact on the crew in terms of love versus fear. What might account for the fact that he behaved so strongly as captain of the USS *Florida*?

2. Which do you think a leader should be more concerned about aboard a nuclear submarine—high certification grades or high-quality interpersonal relationships? Do you agree with Admiral Sullivan's decision to fire Alfonso? Discuss.

3. Discuss Commander Alfonso's level of emotional intelligence in terms of the four components listed in the chapter. What advice would you give him?

Chapter 6 Cases

SYCAMORE PHARMACEUTICALS

"Did you see the report on CNN last night, claiming Sycamore manipulated scientific studies on Osteoporin?" asked Cole Dominguez, as he rushed into John Blake's office, quickly shutting the door behind him. "I can't believe this has leaked out. If the FDA pulls this drug from the market, we can kiss next quarter's big bonus goodbye," he exclaimed. Blake had seen the report and had expected Sycamore, a global pharmaceutical company, to come under fire for promoting its popular rheumatoid arthritis drug, Osteoporin, for the treatment of other diseases like Crohn's disease and lupus—despite negative scientific studies that challenged its effectiveness. But the aggressive marketing campaign was well underway when the unfavorable studies came in. Sycamore's top management chose to suppress the unflattering finds and move ahead with a systematic marketing strategy that created an illusion of Osteoporin's effectiveness and offered financial incentives to doctors for prescribing the drug even in cases where there was no evidence it would work.

John Blake sat back in his chair and nervously ran his fingers through his hair. He exhaled deeply and looked at Dominguez, saying, "We knew we were taking a risk, Cole, aggressively marketing a drug without scientific studies to back up our claims that it worked. The CNN report is only the beginning, my friend. You and I should expect to be called to reveal everything we know. Ethically, Sycamore is responsible for publishing reports on its drugs, even the ones that aren't so flattering."

Dominguez knew his position on the situation. He would stand by the Sycamore management team and back them up, no matter what. He needed this job and knew he had been following orders. Dominguez recalled an e-mail from the CEO in 2008 that said, " . . . we should avoid publishing anything that damages Osteoporin's marketing success. Do not report anything that is negative. Delay these reports as long as legally possible." Dominguez wondered aloud, "Weren't we just following orders?"

Following the report on CNN, Sycamore's communications department went on high alert and moved into crisis mode. Press releases and the corporate blog were issuing the same message to build credibility and put out the rapidly growing fire. In part, the statement said, "Sycamore is committed to the safe distribution of Osteoporin and the communication of medically or scientifically significant results of all studies, regardless of outcome."

Blake shuddered as he read the blog and glanced up at his frantic colleague. "You knew this was going to happen, didn't you Cole? How long can deception like this stay under wraps? Don't we have a responsibility to the poor man or woman popping that pill every day? They think it's helping them. It probably isn't. This just feels so wrong," he said as he buried his head in his hands.

Their conversation was interrupted by a knock at the door. Blake waved in the general manager, who asked if they would both meet individually with an FDA representative that afternoon to answer questions about their knowledge of the timing and content of the scientific studies on Osteoporin for the treatment of Crohn's disease and lupus. Blake's gut feeling was that he needed to be honest with the FDA, but he knew he would likely be fired or demoted if he didn't support management. He also knew that pulling Osteoporin from the market would result in severe losses for Sycamore and the loss of a significant bonus for himself.

Source: Based on Gardiner Harris, "Document Details Plan to Promote Costly Drug," *The New York Times* (September 2, 2009), http://www.nytimes.com/2009/09/02/business/02drug.html?_r=1&emc=eta1 (accessed September 30, 2009); and Keith J. Winstein, "Suit Alleges Pfizer Spun Unfavorable Drug Studies," *The Wall Street Journal* (October 8, 2008), p. B1.

QUESTIONS

1. What would you advise John Blake to do? Why? What are reasons both for and against being honest with the FDA?

2. Do you believe it would take courage for Blake to honestly reveal the timing and content of the scientific studies? What sources of courage might he call upon to help him make his decision?

3. Discuss possible reasons why Dominguez and Blake went along with the deception in the first place. Would you have participated in suppressing the negative studies? Explain why or why not.

THE BOY, THE GIRL, THE FERRYBOAT CAPTAIN, AND THE HERMITS

There was an island, and on this island there lived a girl. A short distance away there was another island, and on this island there lived a boy. The boy and the girl were very much in love with each other.

The boy had to leave his island and go on a long journey, and he would be gone for a very long time. The girl felt that she must see the boy one more time before he went away. There was only one way to get from the island where the girl lived to the boy's island, and that was on a ferryboat that was run by a ferryboat captain. And so the girl went down to the dock and asked the ferryboat captain to take her to the island where the boy lived. The ferryboat captain agreed and asked her for the fare. The girl told the ferryboat captain that she did not have any money. The ferryboat captain told her that money was not necessary: "I will take you to the other island if you will stay with me tonight."

The girl did not know what to do, so she went up into the hills on her island until she came to a hut where a hermit lived. We will call him the first hermit. She related the whole story to the hermit and asked for his advice. The hermit listened carefully to her story, and then told her, "I cannot tell you what to do. You must weigh the alternatives and the sacrifices that are involved and come to a decision within your own heart."

And so the girl went back down to the dock and accepted the ferryboat captain's offer. The next day, when the girl arrived on the other island, the boy was waiting at the dock to greet her. They embraced, and then the boy asked her how she got over to his island, for he knew she did not have any money. The girl explained the ferryboat captain's offer and what she did. The boy pushed her away from him and said, "We're through. That's the end. Go away from me. I never want to see you again," and he left her.

The girl was desolate and confused. She went up into the hills of the boy's island to a hut where a second hermit lived. She told the whole story to the second hermit and asked him what she should do. The hermit told her that there was nothing she could do, that she was welcome to stay in his hut, to partake of his food, and to rest on his bed while he went down into the town and begged for enough money to pay the girl's fare back to her own island.

When the second hermit returned with the money for her, the girl asked him how she could repay him. The hermit answered, "You owe me nothing. We owe this to each other. I am only too happy to be of help." And so the girl went back down to the dock and returned to her own island.

QUESTIONS

1. List in order the characters in this story that you like, from most to least. What values governed your choices?

2. Rate the characters on their level of moral development. Explain.

3. Evaluate each character's level of courage. Discuss.

Chapter 7 Cases

GENERAL PRODUCTS BRITAIN

Carl Mitchell was delighted to accept a job in the British branch office of General Products, Inc., a multinational consumer products corporation. Two months later, Mitchell was miserable. The problem was George Garrow, the general manager in charge of the British branch, to whom Mitchell reported.

Garrow had worked his way into the general manager's position by "keeping his nose clean" and not making mistakes, which he accomplished by avoiding controversial and risky decisions. As Mitchell complained to his wife, "Any time I ask him to make a decision, he just wants us to dig deeper and provide 30 more pages of data, most of which are irrelevant. I can't get any improvements started."

Garrow seemed terrified of departing from the status quo, but Mitchell was planning changes to the line of frozen breakfast foods he was in charge of and needed Garrow's support. While competitors were introducing new frozen breakfast products, Garrow clung to what was familiar—a 1990s package design and breakfast foods that were laden with fat and sodium. Sales were stagnating and grocers were giving shelf space to more successful products. Running out of patience and struggling to stay motivated, Mitchell decided to make one last attempt to persuade Garrow to revamp the frozen breakfast line. After Garrow agreed to listen to his ideas, Mitchell went to work, scrambling to pull together the extensive data he knew would be required to make Garrow feel comfortable rolling out a new line of frozen breakfast foods for the health-conscious consumer.

For the next four weeks, Mitchell and two product managers worked extensive overtime, gathering data and developing a plan. They studied competitors, researched consumer breakfast habits, and hired a Chicago design firm to mock up a new package design. They even met with a dietician to analyze the fat and sugar content of the most popular breakfast foods and develop healthier options. Believing he had a solid plan, Mitchell then held focus groups to fine-tune the final details of the plan. Finally, Mitchell and the product managers prepared a PowerPoint deck and practiced their presentation. They were ready to present their ideas to Garrow.

On the morning of the presentation, Mitchell was ecstatic. Looking to one of the product managers, Mitchell said, "This plan is brilliant. Thanks for all your creative work on a tight schedule. I can hardly wait to present our data and product plan. We're all exhausted, but there's going to be a payoff."

Unfortunately, Garrow didn't share this enthusiasm. He was quiet during the presentation and looked at his watch several times. Sensing Garrow's uneasiness, Mitchell quickly wrapped up his presentation, saying, "As supported by our research presented this morning, I am convinced General Products can successfully launch the following low-fat, low-sugar frozen breakfast items: a home-style, organic wheat waffle and a breakfast sandwich made of low-fat yogurt and whole wheat cereal wafers."

After an uncomfortably long silence, Garrow cleared his voice, shifted in his chair, and said, "You know, this is a huge investment, Carl. I'd like to see you build a more solid case with some additional research on these two breakfast options. Shouldn't we be offering a low-carb option, too? And what about teenagers? You didn't mention them in your presentation. They don't even eat breakfast, do they? Can you get me some answers to these questions? And let's take this slow, Carl. Just be patient. We don't want to rush; we need to cover all our bases."

Soon after this meeting, Mitchell's two best product managers quit, burned out and frustrated with the lack of support and the demand for additional pointless data.

QUESTIONS

1. How would you evaluate Mitchell as a follower? How would you evaluate his courage and style?
2. If you were Mitchell, would you confront Garrow and share your honest feelings and frustrations?
3. If you were Garrow's boss and Mitchell came to see you, what would you say?

JAKE'S PET LAND

Adam Gerrit glanced up from the cash register as his first customers of the day walked into Jake's Pet Land, a neighborhood pet store that is part of a small, regional chain. A young boy, obviously distraught, reluctantly placed a shoebox on the counter. "We have a problem," whispered the boy's dad, "and I would like to get a refund." Cautiously, Adam lifted the lid of the shoebox and found an ebony-colored chinchilla hunched in the corner of the box, huddled in wood chips and barely breathing. Normally inquisitive and active, the chinchilla was obviously sick. The boy's father, a loyal customer for several years, handed Adam a receipt. Adam knew the refund policy by heart: "The health of exotic animals is guaranteed for seven days after purchase. No refunds are granted after seven days." The chinchilla had been purchased 10 days ago, but Adam, as a long-time employee, knew his manager would agree to bend the rules in this case and grant this customer a full refund. Putting the policy manual out of his mind, Adam handed the customer a full refund of $125, saying to the distraught boy, "I'm sorry your little buddy didn't make it. Would you like to look for another pet?" Although he had clearly stretched the return policy rules, Adam felt confident that his store manager, Phillip Jordan, would support his decision.

Jordan did support Adam's decision to bend company rules if it meant retaining a loyal customer. Although the store's thick policy manual called for strict adherence to established procedures, Jordan encouraged employees to think independently when meeting the needs of customers. Jordan also felt strongly about building camaraderie among his small staff, even if it meant straying outside the edicts in the policy manual. For example, Jordan bought the entire staff pizza and soft drinks as a reward for their cheerful attitude when asked to stay late to clean out the stockroom after the store closed. While they restocked shelves and mopped the stockroom floor, his employees told stories, traded jokes, and enjoyed helping each other complete the job quickly. Jordan was proud of the productive yet friendly culture he had created, even if his district manager would frown on some of his decisions.

Without surprise, Jordan's store steadily increased revenue, up 5.4 percent from the previous year. Employees were motivated and enthusiastic. One factor contributing to the store's success was low employee turnover. Again setting company policy aside, Jordan retained his employees by offering slightly higher wages, granting small promotions with increased responsibilities, and rewarding "VIP" employees with free passes to a local theme park. Because all of the employees were pet owners, he also allowed employees to take home overstocked pet supplies and free samples of new pet foods. This loyalty to employees resulted in a successful store. But Jordan knew his district manager would abruptly end all of these practices if he knew about them, so Jordan learned to keep guarded secrets.

Trouble began when Jordan was transferred to another store, closer to his home, and a new manager with a completely different managerial style was brought in. Wedded to rules and procedures, Jan Whitall was driven by order and discipline. On Whitall's first day on the job, she set the tone for her tenure with this announcement: "The company's new compensation policy will be strictly followed in this store, and some of you will have your pay reduced to adhere to the new pay scales. This is uncomfortable for me, but it's the result of some questionable decisions by your previous manager." The morale of top performers, including Adam, plummeted. By the end of Whitall's first month, she had fired an employee for violating the store's return policy. The employee had granted a full refund for a ball python after the seven-day return period. Another employee was publicly reprimanded for giving a customer a sample of a new organic pet food to try before purchasing it. Stunned by these actions, employees became indignant and bristled under her tight authority. The friendly, warm culture had vanished. Adam Gerrit confided to his coworker, "I've applied for a position at the pet superstore down the road. Before I resign, I'm going to talk to Jan and see if she can lighten up on the rules."

Mustering his courage, Adam tapped on Whitall's office door and asked if he could talk with her. Putting down her reading glasses and pushing away the financial reports in front of her, Whitall motioned for him to sit down. "I'm worried about morale around here," Adam began. "Some of our best workers are leaving and I'm considering it, too. Under our previous manager, I loved coming to work and enjoyed the friendship of coworkers and customers. Now, everyone is in a sour mood and we've lost some customers." Taking a deep breath, he continued. "If you are willing to be more flexible with the company policies, I would be willing to stay." Unflustered, Whitall kept her firm stance. "Adam," she explained, "I'm responsible to the district manager, who long suspected that the previous manager wasn't adhering to company policies. It's my intention to do my job the way I've been instructed, and I'm sorry to hear you will be leaving."

As Adam left her office with his head down, Whitall mused to herself that the district manager would be proud of her ability to stand firm. In fact, he had recently complimented her on her approach. Neither realized that sales would take a surprising dip in the next quarter.

QUESTIONS

1. Which store manager—Phillip Jordan or Jan Whitall—would you prefer working for? How did each leader's style affect the culture of the pet store? Explain.

2. What kind of follower was Adam Gerrit? In general, what characteristics of followers do you admire? What characteristics would you want them to display when working for you?

3. If you were the district manager, which store manager would you prefer to have working for you? Why? In your opinion, which manager did a better job of managing up? Which manager did a better job of managing down?

Chapter 8 Cases

MONTEGO BAY

Lisa Mahoney stared intently at her computer screen, scrolling quickly through the disappointing quarterly sales reports for her store. For three years, Mahoney had flourished in her role as a store manager for Montego Bay, a retailer selling distinctive women's apparel in an upscale outdoor mall in Pasadena. Mahoney was discouraged that sales were down 3.5 percent from last year and weary of the challenges that faced her. She knew 20 underperforming stores would be closed over the next 18 months, and she wanted to protect her store and her employees from layoffs. She wondered how to keep employees hopeful and working hard during the economic downturn.

Theresa Daley, operations director for Montego Bay, asked Mahoney to join her for lunch to discuss a new initiative. Seated together at an outdoor café, Daley told Mahoney, "We're under a lot of pressure to improve store performance," as she squeezed a fresh lemon into her glass of water. "I would like to try out a new, computerized scheduling system in your store for six months to see if it will improve productivity and reduce payroll costs. You have an excellent track record, Lisa. If we see improvements in your store after six months, we may implement it in other Montego Bay stores."

Mahoney learned that the new system had several goals: (1) to improve labor efficiencies by determining how many employees should be working at any given time; (2) to automatically schedule the most productive salespeople to work the hours with the most customer traffic; and (3) to increase sales by turning more browsers into buyers. Mahoney agreed to the trial period but worried that the new system would disrupt the productive and collegial work environment she had created at the Pasadena store.

Despite her concerns, Mahoney announced the new plan to her sales staff and was ready to give it a go. The new system tracked employees' daily "performance metrics": sales per hour, units sold, and dollars per transaction. Based on these data, the system generated work schedules for each employee, giving the most successful salespeople prime work hours when the store was bustling with customers. The system also recorded sales per employee. Employees with low performance metrics were scheduled for slower time slots or left off the schedule. Almost immediately, Mahoney's worst fears became reality—employee morale took a nosedive and long-term employees started grumbling about the new system.

"What do you mean, I can't work on Saturday," moaned Sylvia, stunned that the system didn't find her productive enough to work on a prime sales day. "I have always worked Saturdays. Plus, my hours have been cut from 40 hours to 12 this week!" she exclaimed. "I can't even cover my living expenses with these hours." Sylvia had lost her Saturday shift and full-time work status to a new, more aggressive salesperson who had generated more sales. Recognizing the game that had to be played to win the best hours, Sylvia started out-hustling other employees and becoming aggressive with customers. Other employees did the same, snatching customers as they came in the door or pushing products that customers didn't want. Anger and frustration brewed among the sales staff as they outmaneuvered each other to close more sales. Employees seemed motivated to work hard but not the way Mahoney wanted. After the six-month trial period drew to a close, the employees bitterly voiced their complaints.

Mahoney listened attentively, but she knew her options were limited. Before the system was installed, she would create the weekly schedules and accommodate personal preferences. But the new system automatically generated work schedules based solely on performance metrics. Her high-performing, motivated staff was feeling devalued, and the friendly work environment was shattered. Despite these disadvantages, however, sales were up 2.8 percent and labor costs were down 5 percent at the end of the six-month trial.

QUESTIONS

1. What theories of motivation underlie the switch to the new, computerized scheduling system? Why are employees working harder? Why aren't they happier?

2. If you were Lisa Mahoney, what factors would you use to evaluate the success of the six-month trial period? Would you stick with this automated scheduling system? What will you propose to Theresa Daley for the future?

3. In your opinion, how would the new system impact customers? How would employee behavior change customers' shopping experiences?

CUB SCOUT PACK 81

Things certainly have changed over the past six years for Cub Scout Pack 81. Six years ago, the pack was on the verge of disbanding. There were barely enough boys for an effective den, and they had been losing membership for as long as anyone could remember. The cub master was trying to pass his job on to any parent foolish enough to take the helm of a sinking ship, and the volunteer fire department that sponsored the pack was openly considering dropping it.

But that was six years ago. Today the pack has one of the largest memberships of any in the Lancaster/Lebanon Council. It has started its own Boy Scout troop, into which the Webelos can graduate, and it has received a presidential citation for its antidrug program. The pack consistently wins competitions with other packs in the Council, and the fire department is very happy about its sponsorship. Membership in the pack is now around 60 cubs at all levels, and they have a new cub master.

"Parents want their boys to be in a successful program," says Cub Master Mike Murphy. "Look, I can't do everything. We depend on the parents and the boys to get things done. Everybody understands that we want to have a successful program, and that means we all have to participate to achieve that success. I can't do it all, but if we can unleash the energy these boys have, there isn't anything in the Cub Scout Program we can't do!"

It was not always like that. "About five years ago we placed fourth for our booth in the Scout Expo at the mall," says Mike. "Everybody was surprised! Who was Pack 81? We were all elated! It was one of the best things to happen to this pack in years. Now, if we don't win at least something, we're disappointed. Our kids expect to win, and so do their parents."

Fourth place at the Scout Expo eventually led to several first places. Success leads to success, and the community around Pack 81 knows it.

"Last year, we made our annual presentation to the boys and their parents at the elementary school. We were with several other packs, each one trying to drum up interest in their program. When everyone was finished, the boys and their parents went over to the table of the pack that most interested them. We must have had well over half of the people at our table. I was embarrassed! They were standing six or seven deep in front of our table, and there was virtually nobody in front of the others."

Source: "Case IV: Cub Scout Pack 81," in *2001–02 Annual Editions: Management,* Fred H. Maidment, ed. (Guilford, CT: McGraw-Hill/Dushkin, 2001), p. 130.

QUESTIONS

1. What are some of Mike Murphy's basic assumptions about motivation?

2. Why do you think he has been so successful in turning the organization around?

3. How would you motivate people in a volunteer organization such as the Cub Scouts?

Chapter 9 Cases

THE SUPERINTENDENT'S DIRECTIVE

Educational administrators are bombarded by requests for innovation at all educational levels. Programs to upgrade math, science, and social science education, state accountability plans, new approaches to administration, and other ideas are initiated by teachers, administrators, interest groups, reformers, and state regulators. In a school district, the superintendent is the key leader; in an individual school, the principal is the key leader.

In the Carville City School District, Superintendent Porter has responsibility for 11 schools—eight elementary, two junior high, and one high school. After attending a management summer course, Porter sent the following e-mail to the principal of each school:

> "Please request that teachers in your school develop a set of performance objectives for each class they teach. A consultant will be providing instructions for writing the performance objectives during the August 10 in-service day. The deadline for submitting the performance objectives to my office is September 21."

Mr. Weigand, principal of Earsworth Elementary School, forwarded Porter's e-mail to his teachers with the following message:

> "Please see the forwarded e-mail from Superintendent Porter. As he explains, you will need to write performance objectives for each course you

teach. These are due one month from today. This afternoon, during the in-service meeting, you will receive training on how to write these performance objectives."

After receiving this e-mail, several teachers at the elementary school responded with a flurry of hastily written e-mail responses. One well-respected and talented teacher wrote the following e-mail, accidentally sending it to Mr. Weigand instead of her colleagues:

> "This is nonsense! I should be spending my time focused on the lesson plan for the new advanced English class the board of education approved. Porter is clueless and has no idea the demands we are facing in the classroom. We never even hear from him until he wants us to complete some empty exercise. I am going to start looking for a school district that values my time!"

Mr. Weigand was stunned by this e-mail, wondering if he was close to losing a valuable teacher who was admired by her peers and others in the school system. He knew this e-mail had been written in haste and that this teacher would be embarrassed to know that he had received it. He was concerned that other teachers may have reacted in similar ways to his e-mail. He also wondered how to respond to the angry e-mail and how to improve morale at the start of a new school year.

QUESTIONS

1. Evaluate the e-mail communications of Mr. Porter and Mr. Weigand. To what extent are they communicating effectively about the new performance objectives? Explain. If you were a teacher, how would you have felt after receiving the e-mail? Why?

2. If you were Mr. Weigand, how would you respond to the angry teacher? Be specific about how you would communicate with her and what you would say. How could he have communicated differently about the performance objectives to influence the teachers more positively?

3. Identify the mistakes that the teacher made when composing and sending her e-mail message.

THE SADDLE CREEK DELI

The Saddle Creek Deli serves fresh sandwiches and hearty salads at moderate prices to skiers in the bustling ski resort town of Vail, Colorado. The deli is known for its cozy ambiance, Western décor, and two-story stone fireplace. Catering to skiers, the Saddle Creek Deli serves fresh meals in a hurry to people taking a break from the slopes and is located 10 minutes from a popular ski lift. Large windows provide a dazzling view of the nearby mountains. The deli's major attraction, however, is a high-quality, old-fashioned soda fountain that specializes in superior ice cream sundaes and sodas. Business has grown steadily during the seven years of operation.

The deli has been so successful that Richard Purvis, owner and manager, decided to hire a manager so that he could devote more time to other business interests. After a month of quiet recruitment and interviewing, he selected Paul McCarthy, whose prior experience included the supervision of a small restaurant in a nearby resort hotel.

During the first few weeks, McCarthy seemed to perform his work efficiently. According to his agreement with Purvis, McCarthy was paid a straight salary plus a percentage of the amount he saved the business monthly, based on the previous month's operating expenses. All other employees were paid a straight hourly rate.

After a month on the job, McCarthy single-handedly decided to initiate a cost-saving program designed to increase his earnings. He changed the wholesale meat and cheese suppliers, lowering both his cost and product quality in the process. Arbitrarily, he reduced the size and portion of everything on the menu, including the fabulous sundaes and sodas. McCarthy then focused on reducing payroll costs by cutting back on the number of employees working a shift and reducing fringe benefits. During a tense staff meeting to announce these changes, McCarthy tersely stated, "You can expect to see some changes in your hours starting next week. I see too many people sitting around with not enough to do." Next, he announced that he was discontinuing the one-dollar meals for employees working more than five hours and eliminating the 20 percent employee discount. As he concluded his announcements, he asked if anyone had any questions. No one dared speak. McCarthy shrugged his shoulders and quickly left the meeting.

Frustrated, the employees streamed out of the meeting and quietly grumbled about the changes. "Why tell him what we really think," some mused. Employees believed McCarthy had made up his mind, so they braced themselves for the fallout. Soon after, employees started noticing the negative consequences of McCarthy's hasty, cost-cutting decisions. During the busy lunch hour, for example, customers would storm out after waiting 20 minutes for a sandwich. Others would grumble to servers about the smaller portions and then leave a meager tip. Many employees heard customers complain about the dirt and grime collecting in the dining area and restrooms. Employees started to burn out from listening to constant complaints and trying to do the work of two people. Tension mounted and resentment toward McCarthy grew.

Meanwhile, Purvis became aware of the overhaul McCarthy was undertaking at the deli. When questioned by the owner about the impact of his new practices, McCarthy swore up and down that there would be no negative effect on the business.

Ron Sharp, an accounting major at the nearby university, had been a short-order cook on the night shift for five months prior to McCarthy's arrival. Conscientious and ambitious, Sharp enjoyed a fine work record, and even his new boss recognized Ron's superiority over the other cooks. One day Purvis saw Sharp at the post office and asked how things were going. Purvis was stunned to hear about the cutbacks and employee dissatisfaction. Reluctant to undercut his new manager, Purvis said to himself, "I can't understand what went wrong. I wonder what I should do now."

Source: Adapted from Bernard A. Deitzer and Karl A. Schillif, *Contemporary Incidents in Management* (Columbus, OH: Grid, Inc., 1977), pp. 167–168.

QUESTIONS

1. How would you rate the communication climate at the Saddle Creek Deli? How did this climate contribute to the service problems and complaints from customers?

2. How do you think Purvis could improve communications between McCarthy and the employees? Be specific in your recommendations.

3. If you were the manager at the Saddle Creek Deli, how would you improve openness and upward communication?

Chapter 10 Cases

VALENA SCIENTIFIC CORPORATION

Valena Scientific Corporation (VSC) is a large manufacturer of health-care products. The health-care market includes hospitals, clinical laboratories, universities, and industries. Clinical laboratories represent 52 percent of VSC's sales. Laboratories are located in hospitals and diagnostic centers where blood tests and urine analyses are performed for physicians. Equipment sold to laboratories can range from a 50-cent test tube to a $250,000 blood analyzer.

When the industry experienced a move into genetic engineering, companies such as Genentech Corporation and Cetus Scientific Laboratories were created and staffed with university microbiologists. These companies were designed to exploit the commercial potential for gene splicing.

Senior executives at VSC saw the trend developing and decided to create a Biotech Research Program in 2005. Skilled microbiologists were scarce, so the program was staffed with only nine scientists. Three scientists were skilled in gene splicing, three in recombination, and three in fermentation. The specialties reflected the larger departments to which they were assigned. However, they were expected to work as a team on this program. Twenty technicians were also assigned to the program to help the scientists.

Senior management believed that the Biotech Research Program could be self-managed. For the first 18 months of operation, everything went well. Informal leaders emerged among the scientists in gene splicing, recombination, and fermentation. These three informal leaders coordinated the work of the three groups, which tended to stay separate. For example, the work typically started in the gene-splicing group, followed by work in recombination, and then in fermentation. Fermentation was used to breed the bacteria created by the other two groups in sufficient numbers to enable mass production.

During the summer of 2008, the Biotech Research Program was given a special project. Hoffman-LaRoche was developing leukocyte interferon to use as a treatment against cancer. VSC contracted with Hoffman-LaRoche to develop a technique for large-scale interferon production. VSC had only six months to come up with a production technology. Scientists in each of the subgroups remained in their own geographical confines and began immediately to test ideas relevant to their specialty.

In September, the three informal group leaders met to review the team's progress. Alison Chan, the group leader for gene splicing, proudly announced, "Our team has been using an innovative research, one recently developed at my alma mater, MIT. We are excited about the results so far." Rich Bailey, group leader for recombination, leapt from his seat, exclaiming, "This is no time to be experimenting with an untested research program! You should have told us you were going down this path so we could have stopped you sooner. We should all be following the same research path." For the rest of the meeting, the group leaders argued vehemently, defending their positions and refusing to change direction. With the deadline now in jeopardy, Bailey e-mailed his manager, explained the impasse the group leaders had reached, and complained about Chan's arrogance. Managers at VSC decided to appoint a formal leader to the program.

On November 15, a Stanford professor with extensive research experience in recombinant DNA technology was hired. His title was chief biologist for the Biotech Research Program, and all project members reported to him for the duration of the interferon project.

The chief biologist immediately took the nine scientists on a two-day retreat. He assigned them to three tables for discussions, with a member from each subgroup at each table, so they had to talk across their traditional boundaries. He began by discussing their common ground as scientists, and their hopes and vision for this project. After they developed a shared vision, the group turned to scientific issues and, in mixed groups, discussed the ideas that the VSC subgroups had developed. Gradually, one approach seemed to have more likelihood of success than the others. A consensus emerged, and the chief biologist adopted the basic approach that would be taken in the interferon project. Upon their return to VSC, the technicians were brought in and the scientists explained the approach to them. At this point, each subgroup was assigned a set of instructions within the overall research plan. Firm deadlines were established based on group interdependence. Weekly teleconferences were planned and face-to-face meetings with the three group leaders were put on the schedule.

Dramatic changes in the behavior of the scientists were observed after the two-day retreat. Communication among groups became more common. Problems discovered by one group were communicated to other groups so that effort was not expended needlessly. Subgroup leaders coordinated many solutions among themselves. Lunch and coffee gatherings that included several members of the subgroups began to occur. Group leaders and members often had daily discussions and cooperated on research requirements. Enthusiasm for the department and the interferon project was high, and cohesion seemed especially strong.

QUESTIONS

1. Was the research program a group or a team? What about each subgroup? If a team, what type of team was it (functional, cross-functional, self-directed)? Explain.

2. What were the group norms before and after the retreat? How did the interdependence among the subgroups change with the interferon project?

3. What factors account for the change in cohesiveness after the chief biologist took over?

DEVEREAUX-DERING GROUP

Dashing to catch a cab at the corner of Sixth and Vine, the account team was exhilarated. After a quick exchange of high fives, three of the four jumped into the backseat of a cab to return to the Manhattan offices of Devereaux-Dering, a global advertising agency with offices in New York, Hong Kong, and Paris. The team couldn't wait to tell their team leader, Kurt Lansing, that they had won the BMW account that morning. The fourth team member, Brad Fitzgerald, stood apart from the animated group, studying his BlackBerry and then hailing a cab for an afternoon flight out of LaGuardia.

After a two-year slump in sales, Devereaux-Dering needed a big score like the BMW account. To drive new business and land high-profile accounts like this one, the company had hired Kurt Lansing, an MBA from Wharton, with prominent status in the advertising industry. His job was to lead a new business team to study the market, develop strategies, and acquire major accounts. Lansing hand-selected four high achievers for his team that represented each area of the business: Brad Fitzgerald, creative director; Trish Roderick, account services; Adrienne Walsh, production manager; and Tyler Green, brand strategy.

"That was a shocker!" said Roderick as she scooted across the backseat of the cab to make room for her teammates. "The client didn't seem too impressed with our presentation until Fitzgerald presented the last set of slides describing the global campaign. They loved it. I think he single-handedly clinched the deal when he presented the tag line for the Asian market," she said excitedly.

"He's a real whiz, alright," muttered Green. "The eighth wonder of the world." Sighing deeply and losing his earlier exuberance, Green said, "We couldn't have bagged the deal without him, and I know we'll all get credit. But none of us knew he planned to present that last part of the global campaign. I know he was working on that tag line late last night, but there was plenty of time this morning to get team input on it. I hate surprises in front of a client. I felt like a fool, even if we did win the business."

"He's a regular white knight," chuckled Walsh, "riding in at the last minute to save the day. I suppose we should appreciate him, but he's just so irritating. He snapped at me last week for not telling him about a client who was upset about delays in their ad campaign. I reminded him that I had told him about it in our status meeting, but he wasn't listening at the time. He was glued to his precious BlackBerry, as usual. Why have team meetings if he isn't going to participate?"

Roderick was surprised by her teammates' reaction to Fitzgerald. She thought they had been working well together. She was quickly discovering, however, an undercurrent of resentment. This was the first time that she had been exposed to the conflict that was simmering below the surface. No doubt, Fitzgerald did have a strong ego and aggressive personality. A previously successful entrepreneur, Fitzgerald had a track record of success and was very ambitious. However, she did notice that he didn't show respect for differing opinions or invite collaboration on ideas. She wondered if he was placing his own success above the team's. But why complain if the team was sharing the credit and earning fat bonuses along with him? She was content to go with the status quo. "You know," she said, "we're darn lucky to be on his team."

She stared out the cab window at the passing traffic and listened to her two teammates continue to grouse. "I should have known something was up when I walked past his office last night and saw him working with the new copywriter. They must have been hashing out the new tag line," smirked Green. "We are a team, aren't we? The system is bigger than the individual, remember? He doesn't seem too concerned about the welfare of the team—only his own."

"Well, let's all have a heart-to-heart with Mr. McWhiz," said Walsh sarcastically. "I'm sure he'll see things our way. We'll give him a brief overview of Teamwork 101. That will go over great!" As the cab pulled to the curb, they tossed the driver a $20 bill and headed to their offices on the 40th floor. They would all stop to see the team leader, Kurt Lansing, first.

In the meantime, Lansing smiled broadly when he received Fitzgerald's text message that they had won the BMW account. Sinking back in his chair, he marveled at the cohesiveness and success of his team. All that time building a shared vision and building trust was starting to pay off.

QUESTIONS

1. What factors do you think are affecting this team's cohesiveness? Explain.

2. If you were the team leader, what could you do to bring Fitzgerald into the team more and foster better relationships among the team members?

3. As a team member, what would you do? Should the three members of the team confront Fitzgerald with their concerns? Should they inform Kurt Lansing? Explain your answers.

Chapter 11 Cases

NORTHERN INDUSTRIES

Northern Industries asked you, a consultant in organizational change and diversity management, to help them resolve some racial issues that, according to president Jim Fisher, are "festering" in their manufacturing plant in Springfield, Massachusetts. Northern Industries is a family-owned enterprise that manufactures greeting cards and paper and plastic holiday decorations. It employs 125 people full time, including African-Americans and Asians. About 80 percent of the full-time workforce is female. During the peak production months of September and January (to produce orders primarily for Christmas/Hanukah and Mother's Day), the company runs a second shift and adds about 50 part-time workers, most of whom are women and minorities.

All orders are batch runs made to customer specifications. In a period of a week, it is not unusual for 70 different orders to be filled requiring different paper stocks, inks, plastics, and setups. Since these orders vary greatly in size, the company has a long-term policy of giving priority to high-volume customers and processing other orders on a first-come first-served basis. Half a dozen of the company's major customers have been doing business with Northern for more than 20 years, having been signed on by Jim Fisher's father (now retired).

To begin your orientation to the company, Fisher asks his production manager, Walter Beacon, to take you around the plant. Beacon points out the production areas responsible for each of the various steps in the manufacture of a greeting card, from purchasing to printing to quality control and shipping. The plant is clean, but the two large printing rooms, each the workplace for about 25 workers, are quite noisy. You catch snatches of the employees' conversations there, but you cannot figure out what language they are speaking. In the shipping and receiving department you notice that most workers are African-American. Beacon confirms that 8 out of 10 of the workers in that department are African-American males, and that their boss, Adam Wright, is also African-American.

It has been previously arranged that you would attend a meeting of top management in order to get a flavor of the organizational culture. The president introduces you as a diversity consultant and notes that several of his managers have expressed concerns about potential racial problems in the company. He says, "Each of the minority groups sticks together. The African-Americans and Orientals rarely mix. Recently there has been a problem with theft of finished product, especially on the second shift, and we had to fire a Thai worker." Fisher has read a lot lately about "managing diversity" and hopes you will be able to help the company. Several managers nod their heads in agreement.

Fisher then turns his executive team to its daily business. The others present are the general manager, personnel manager (the only woman), sales manager, quality control manager, production manager (Beacon), and the shipping and receiving manager (the only nonwhite manager). Soon an angry debate ensues between the sales and shipping/receiving managers. It seems that orders are not being shipped quickly enough, according to the sales manager, and several complaints have been received from smaller customers about the quality of the product. The shipping/receiving manager argues that he needs more hands to do the job, and that the quality of incoming supplies is lousy. While this debate continues, the other managers are silent and seemingly uncomfortable. Finally one of them attempts to break up the argument with a joke about his wife. Fisher and the other men laugh loudly, and the conversation shifts to other topics.

Source: Copyright 1991 by Rae Andre of Northeastern University. Used with permission.

QUESTIONS

1. What recommendations would you make to Northern's leaders to help them move toward successfully managing diversity issues?

2. If you were the shipping and receiving or personnel manager, how do you think you would feel about your job? Discuss some of the challenges you might face at Northern.

3. Refer to Exhibit 11.6. Based on the information in the case, at what stage of personal diversity awareness do leaders at Northern seem to be? Discuss.

THE TROUBLE WITH BANGLES

Leela Patel was standing by her machine, as she had for eight hours of each working day for the past six years. Leela was happy; she had many friends among the 400 or so women at the food processing plant. Most of them were of Indian origin like herself, although Asian women formed less than a fifth of the female workforce. Leela was a member of a five-woman team that reported to supervisor Bill Evans.

Leela saw Evans approaching now, accompanied by Jamie Watkins, the shop steward. "Hello, Leela; we've come to explain something to you," Evans began. "You must have heard about the accident last month when one of the girls caught a bangle in the machine and cut her wrist. Well, the Safety Committee has decided that no one will be allowed to wear any bangles, engagement rings, earrings, or necklaces at work—only wedding rings, sleepers for pierced ears, and wristwatches will be allowed. So I'm afraid you'll have to remove your bangles." Leela, as was her custom, was wearing three bangles—one steel, one plastic, and one gold. All the married Asian women wore bangles, and many of the English girls had also begun wearing them. Leela explained that she was a Hindu wife and the bangles were important to her religion.

"Don't make a fuss, Leela," Evans said between clenched teeth. "I've already had to shout at Hansa Patel and Mira Desai. Why can't you all be like Meena Shah? She didn't mind taking her bangles off; neither did the English girls." Leela could see that Evans was very angry, so, almost in tears, she removed the bangles. When the two had moved off, however, she replaced the gold bangle and carried on with her work.

Within two or three days, the plant manager, Sam Jones, noticed that all the Asian women were wearing their bangles again—some, in fact, were wearing more than ever before. "I'm staggered by the response that this simple, common-sense restriction on the wearing of jewelry has brought," Jones remarked to the regional race relations employment advisor. "I have had several deputations from the Asian women protesting the ban, not to mention visits by individuals on the instruction of their husbands. In addition, I've just had a letter from something called the Asian Advisory Committee, asking that the ban be lifted until we meet with their representatives. The strength of this discontent has prompted me to talk to you. Jewelry constitutes both a safety and a hygiene hazard on this site, so it must be removed. And I'm afraid if I talk to this Asian Committee, they'll turn out to be a bunch of militants who'll cause all sorts of trouble. At the same time, we can't afford any work stoppages. What do you suggest?"

Several days later, the advisor had arranged for Mr. Singh from the local Council for Community Relations to talk to Jones and other managers. Singh explained that in his opinion there were no obstacles arising from *religious* observance that prevented implementation of the ban on bangles. However, he pointed out, the bangles do have a custom base that is stronger than the English tradition base for wedding rings. "The bangles are a mark not only of marriage but of the esteem in which a wife is held by her husband. The more bangles and the greater their value, the higher her esteem and the greater her social standing. The tradition also has religious overtones, since the wearing of bangles by the wife demonstrates that each recognizes the other as 'worthy' in terms of the fulfillment of their religious obligations. This position is further complicated in that women remove their bangles if they are widowed, and some fear that the removal of the bangles may lead to their husbands' deaths."

Source: Adapted from "Bangles," in Allan R. Cohen, Stephen L. Fink, Herman Gadon, and Robin D. Willits, *Effective Behavior in Organizations: Cases, Concepts, and Student Experiences,* 7th ed. (Burr Ridge, IL: McGraw-Hill Irwin, 2001), pp. 413–414.

QUESTIONS

1. What is your initial reaction to this story? Why do you think you had this reaction?

2. Based on this limited information, how would you rate this organization in terms of developing leadership diversity? Discuss.

3. If you were a top manager at this company, how would you handle this problem?

Chapter 12 Cases

THE UNHEALTHY HOSPITAL

When Bruce Reid was hired as Blake Memorial Hospital's new CEO, the mandate had been clear: Improve the quality of care, and set the financial house in order.

As Reid struggled to finalize his budget for approval at next week's board meeting, his attention kept returning to one issue—the future of six off-site clinics. The clinics had been set up six years earlier to provide primary health care to the community's poorer neighborhoods. Although they provided a valuable service, they also diverted funds away from Blake's in-house services, many of which were underfunded. Cutting hospital personnel and freezing salaries could affect Blake's quality of care, which was already slipping. Eliminating the clinics, on the other hand, would save $256,000 without compromising Blake's internal operations.

However, there would be political consequences. Clara Bryant, the recently appointed commissioner of health services, repeatedly insisted that the clinics were an essential service for the poor. Closing the clinics could also jeopardize Blake's access to city funds. Dr. Winston Lee, chief of surgery, argued forcefully for closing the off-site clinics and having shuttle buses bring patients to the hospital weekly. Dr. Susan Russell, the hospital's director of clinics, was equally vocal about Blake's responsibility to the community, and suggested an entirely new way of delivering health care: "A hospital is not a building," she said, "it's a service. And wherever the service is needed, that is where the hospital should be." In Blake's case, that meant funding *more* clinics. Russell wanted to create a network of neighborhood-based centers for all the surrounding neighborhoods, poor and middle income. Besides improving health care, the network would act as an inpatient referral system for hospital services. Reid considered the proposal: If a clinic network could tap the paying public and generate more inpatient business, it might be worth looking into. Blake's rival hospital, located on the affluent side of town, certainly wasn't doing anything that creative. Reid was concerned, however, that whichever way he decided, he was going to make enemies.

Source: Based on Anthony R. Kovner, "The Case of the Unhealthy Hospital," *Harvard Business Review* (September–October 1991), pp. 12–25.

QUESTIONS

1. What sources of power does Reid have in this situation? Do you believe using legitimate power to implement a decision would have a positive effect at Blake Memorial? Discuss.

2. What influence tactics might you use if you were in Reid's position?

3. Do you see ways in which Reid might use the ideas of coalitional leadership to help resolve this dilemma?

WAITE PHARMACEUTICALS

Amelia Lassiter is chief information officer at Waite Pharmaceuticals, a large California-based company. In an industry where it generally takes $500 million and 10 to 12 years to bring a new drug to market, companies such as Waite are always looking for ways to increase productivity and speed things up. After about eight months on the job, Lassiter suggested to company president James Hsu that Waite implement a new global knowledge-sharing application that promises to cut development time and costs in half. She has done extensive research on knowledge-sharing systems, and has talked closely with an IT director at global powerhouse Novartis, a company on the cutting edge in pharmaceuticals and animal health care, as well as other diverse products. The Novartis director believes the knowledge-sharing system plays an important role in that company's competitiveness.

Hsu presented the idea to the board of directors, and everyone agreed to pursue the project. He has asked Lassiter to investigate firms that could assist Waite's IT department in developing and implementing a global knowledge-sharing application that would be compatible with Waite's existing systems. Hsu explained that he wants to present the information to the board of directors for a decision next month.

Lassiter identified three major firms that she believed could handle the work and took a summary of her findings to Hsu's office, where she was greeted by Lucy Lee, a young, petite, attractive woman who served as a sort of executive assistant to Hsu. Word was that the relationship between Lee and Hsu was totally proper, but besides the value of her good looks, no one in the company could understand why she was working there. Her lack of talent and experience made her a liability more than a help. She was very deferential to Hsu, but condescending to everyone else. Lee was a constant source of irritation and ill will among managers throughout the company, but there was no doubt that the only way to get to Hsu was through Lucy Lee. Lee took the information from Lassiter and promised the president would review it within two days.

The next afternoon, Hsu called Lassiter to his office and asked why Standard Systems, a small local consulting firm, was not being considered as a potential provider. Lassiter was surprised—Standard was known primarily for helping small companies computerize their accounting systems. She was not aware that they had done any work related to knowledge-sharing applications, particularly on a global basis. Upon further investigation into the company, she learned that Standard was owned by an uncle of Lucy Lee's, and things began to fall into place. Fortunately, she also learned that the firm did have some limited experience in more complex applications. She tried to talk privately with Hsu about his reasons for wanting to consider Standard, but Hsu insisted that Lee participate in all his internal meetings. At their most recent meeting, Hsu insisted that Standard be included for possible consideration by the board.

During the next two weeks, representatives from each company met with Hsu, his two top executives, and the IT staff to explain their services and give demonstrations. Lassiter had suggested that the board of directors attend these presentations, but Hsu said they wouldn't have the time and he would need to evaluate everything and make a recommendation to the board. At the end of these meetings, Lassiter prepared a final report evaluating the pros and cons of going with each firm and making her first- and second-choice recommendations. Standard was dead last on her list. Although the firm had some excellent people and a good reputation, it was simply not capable of handling such a large and complex project.

Lassiter offered to present her findings to the board, but again, Hsu declined her offer in the interest of time. "It's best if I present them with a final recommendation; that way, we can move on to other matters without getting bogged down with a lot of questions and discussion. These are busy people." The board meeting was held the following week. Lassiter was shocked when the president returned from the meeting and informed her that the board had decided to go with Standard Systems as the consulting firm for the knowledge-sharing application.

Sources: Based on "Restview Hospital," in Gary Yukl, *Leadership*, 4th ed. (Upper Saddle River, NJ: Prentice Hall, 1998), pp. 203–204; "Did Somebody Say Infrastructure?" in Polly Schneider, "Another Trip to Hell," *CIO* (February 15, 2000), pp. 71–78; and Joe Kay, "Digital Diary," Part I, http://www.forbes.com/asap/2000 (accessed November 19, 2000).

QUESTIONS

1. How would you explain the board's selection of Standard Systems?
2. Discuss the types, sources, and relative amount of power for the three main characters in this story.
3. How might Lassiter have increased her power and influence over this decision? If you were in her position, what would you do now?

Chapter 13 Cases

METROPOLIS POLICE DEPARTMENT

You are in a hotel room watching the evening news as a local reporter interviews people who complain about abuse and mistreatment by police officers. These reports have been occurring in the news media with increasing frequency over the last three years. Some observers believe the problem is the police department's authoritarian style. Police managers encourage paramilitary values and a "them-against-us" attitude. The police orientation has been toward a spit-and-polish force that is efficient and tolerates no foolishness. The city believes that a highly professional, aloof police force is the best way to keep the city under control. Training emphasizes police techniques, the appropriate use of guns, and new technology, but there is no training on dealing with people. Several citizens have won large lawsuits against the police force, and many suits originated with minority groups. Critics believe the police chief is a major part of the problem. He has defended the rough actions of police officers, giving little public credence to complaints of abuse. He resists the community-oriented, people-friendly attitudes of other city departments. The chief has been considered insensitive toward minorities and has been heard to make disparaging public comments about African-Americans, women, and Hispanics.

One vocal critic alleges that police brutality depends on the vision and moral leadership set by the chief of police and lays responsibility for incidents of abuse on the current chief. Another critic believes there is a relationship between his intemperate remarks and the actions of police officers.

The reason you are in Metropolis, watching the news in a hotel room, is that you have been invited to interview for the job of police chief. The mayor and selected council members are preparing to fire the chief and name a replacement. You are thinking about what you would do if you took the job.

QUESTIONS

1. Identify themes that you would like to make a part of your vision for the police department.
2. If you get the job, how will you gain acceptance for your vision? How will you implement changes that will support the new vision and values?
3. Would you relish the challenge of becoming police chief of Metropolis? Why or why not?

THE VISIONARY LEADER

When Frank Coleman first began his job as president of Hi-Tech Aerostructures, most managers and employees felt a surge of hope and excitement. Hi-Tech Aerostructures is a 50-year-old family-owned manufacturing company that produces parts for the aircraft industry. The founder and owner had served as president until his health began to decline, and he felt the need to bring in someone from outside the company to get a fresh perspective. It was certainly needed. Over the past several years, Hi-Tech had just been stumbling along.

Coleman came to the company from a smaller business, but one with excellent credentials as a leader in advanced aircraft technology. He had a vision for transforming Hi-Tech into a world-class manufacturing facility. In addition to implementing cutting-edge technology, the vision included transforming the sleepy, paternalistic culture to a more dynamic, adaptive one and empowering employees to take a more active, responsible role in the organization. After years of just doing the same old thing day after day, vice president David Deacon was delighted with the new president and thrilled when Coleman asked him to head up the transformation project.

Deacon and his colleagues spent hours talking with Coleman, listening to him weave his ideas about the kind of company Hi-Tech could become. He assured the team that the transformation was his highest priority, and he inspired them with stories about the significant impact they were going to have on the company as well as the entire aircraft industry. Together, the group crafted a vision statement that was distributed to all employees and posted all over the building. At lunchtime, the company cafeteria was abuzz with talk about the new vision. And when the young, nattily dressed president himself appeared in the cafeteria, as he did once every few weeks, it was almost as if a rock star had walked in.

At the team's first meeting with Coleman, Deacon presented several different ideas and concepts they had come up with, explaining the advantages of each for ripping Hi-Tech out of the past and slamming it jubilantly into the twenty-first century. Nothing, however, seemed to live up to Coleman's ambitions for the project—he thought all the suggestions were either too conventional or too confusing. After three hours the team left Coleman's office and went back to the drawing board. Everyone was even more fired up after Coleman's closing remarks about the potential to remake the industry and maybe even change the world.

Early the next day, Coleman called Deacon to his office and laid out his own broad ideas for how the project should proceed. "Not bad," thought Deacon, as he took the notes and drawings back to the team. "We can take this broad concept and really put some plans for action into place." The team's work over the next few months was for the most part lively and encouraging. Whenever Coleman would attend the meetings, he would suggest changes in many of their specific plans and goals, but miraculously, the transformation plan began to take shape. The team sent out a final draft to colleagues and outside consultants and the feedback was almost entirely positive.

The plan was delivered to Coleman on a Wednesday morning. When Deacon had still not heard anything by Friday afternoon, he began to worry. He knew Coleman had been busy with a major customer, but the president had indicated his intention to review the plan immediately. Finally, at 6 P.M., Coleman called Deacon to his office. "I'm afraid we just can't run with this," he said, tossing the team's months of hard work on the desk. "It's just . . . well, just not right for this company."

Deacon was stunned. And so was the rest of the team when he reported Coleman's reaction. In addition, word was beginning to get out around the company that all was not smooth with the transformation project. The cafeteria conversations were now more likely to be gripes that nothing was being done to help the company improve. Coleman assured the team, however, that his commitment was still strong; they just needed to take a different approach. Deacon asked that Coleman attend as many meetings as he could to help keep the team on the right track. Nearly a year later, the team waited in anticipation for Coleman's response to the revised proposal.

Coleman called Deacon at home on Friday night. "Let's meet on this project first thing Monday morning," he began. "I think we need to make a few adjustments. Looks like we're more or less headed in the right direction, though." Deacon felt like crying as he hung up the phone. All that time and work. He knew what he could expect on Monday morning. Coleman would lay out his vision and ask the team to start over.

Sources: Based on "The Vision Failed," Case 8.1 in Peter G. Northouse, *Leadership—Theory and Practice,* 2nd ed. (Thousand Oaks, CA: Sage Publications, 2001), pp. 150–151; Joe Kay, "My Year at a Big High Tech Company," *Forbes ASAP* (May 29, 2000), pp. 195–198; "Digital Diary (My Year at a Big High Tech Company)," http://www .forbes.com/asap/2000 (accessed November 19, 2000); and "Digital Diary, Part Two: The Miracle," *Forbes ASAP* (August 21, 2000), pp. 187–190.

QUESTIONS

1. How effective would you rate Coleman as a visionary leader? Discuss.

2. Where would you place Coleman on the chart of types of leaders in Exhibit 13.8? Where would you place Deacon?

3. If you were Deacon, what would you do?

Chapter 14 Cases

LISA BENAVIDES, FOREST INTERNATIONAL

Lisa Benavides has just been hired as the vice president of human resources for Forest International. Previously, the company had only a personnel officer and a benefits specialist, who spent most of their time processing applications and benefit forms and tracking vacation and sick days. However, a new CEO had come to Forest believing that HR could play a key strategic role in the organization, and he had recruited Benavides from a well-known HR consulting firm soon after he took over the top job. The new CEO has lots of ideas about empowerment, shared leadership, and teamwork that he hopes to eventually implement at the company.

Forest International operates in one of the most dangerous industries around. Paper mills, sawmills, and plywood factories are filled with constant noise, giant razor-toothed saw blades, caustic chemicals, and chutes loaded with tons of lumber. Even in this notoriously hazardous industry, Forest's safety record stinks. Within a four-year period, 29 workers had been killed on the job. An average of 9 serious injuries per 100 employees occur each year. In addition, productivity has been declining in recent years, and Forest's competitors are gaining market share. As one of her first major projects, the CEO has asked Benavides for her advice on how to improve the company's safety record and increase productivity.

Based outside Atlanta, Georgia, Forest International has around $11 billion in annual revenues and employs 45,000 people. Many employees' parents and grandparents also worked in Forest's mills and factories. Among many of the workers, missing a finger or two is considered a badge of honor. Taking chances is a way of proving that you're a true *Forest-man* (the term persists even though the company now has a good percentage of female workers). During lunch or break, groups of workers routinely brag about their "close calls" and share stories about parents' or grandparents' dangerous encounters with saw blades or lumber chutes.

It is clear to Benavides that worker attitudes are part of the problem, but she suspects that management attitudes may play a role as well. A production shutdown costs time and money in an industry where profits are slim. Production managers emphasize the importance of keeping the line moving, getting the product out no matter what. Rather than finding a supervisor and asking that the production line be shut down, most line employees take chances on sticking their hands into moving equipment whenever there is a minor problem. As Benavides talks with workers, she learns that most of them believe managers care more about productivity and profits than they do about the well-being of people in the plant.

An accident during the second shift drove home that point. Exhausted from a double shift, a three-man crew stopped a production line to change a belt on a one-ton press. The crew hoisted the press up on a jack, but the jack became unstable. "Bring the press back down," crew leader Jack Taylor yelled. "We have to readjust the jack." A nearby shift supervisor ran over and shouted over the roar of a nearby saw blade, "Get that line back up. We need this load on the dock by midnight." Taylor approached the supervisor to explain that they were worried about the stability of the jack and needed to readjust the press. In response, the supervisor signaled Taylor to stop talking by holding up both hands and mouthing the words, "I don't care." Feeling pressure to meet the deadline, the crew continued to hoist the press on the unstable jack, hoping for the best. Within minutes, the press toppled off the wobbling jack and pinned two men underneath. Both sustained serious injuries.

After air care had taken the two to the hospital, Taylor sat in the break room overwhelmed with guilt and emotion. "I should have known to stop the line and secure that jack. They could have been killed out there. If the supervisors don't start listening to us, somebody's going to lose their life."

The next day, Benavides interviewed Taylor to gather more facts about the accident. Her conversation with Taylor was enlightening. Taylor explained how he had made several suggestions for improving safety on his line, but he had been routinely ignored by management. "They never listen to us; they just expect us to do what we're told," he said. "They don't really care about our safety," he boomed. "They'll do anything to get another shipment out the door."

Sources: Based in part on information in Anne Fisher, "Danger Zone," *Fortune* (September 8, 1997), pp. 165–167; and Robert Galford, "Why Doesn't This HR Department Get Any Respect?" *Harvard Business Review* (March–April 1998), pp. 24–26.

QUESTIONS

1. How would you describe the culture of Forest International as it relates to internal integration and external adaptation?

2. Would you expect that changing the culture at Forest would be easily accomplished now that a new CEO is committed to change? Why or why not?

3. If you were Lisa Benavides, what suggestions would you make to Forest's new CEO?

5 STAR AND AMTECH

5 Star Electronics and Amtech Electronics both manufacture integrated circuits and other electronic parts as subcontractors for large manufacturers. Both 5 Star and Amtech are located in Ohio and often bid on contracts as competitors. As subcontractors, both firms benefited from the electronics boom of the 1990s, and both looked forward to growth and expansion. 5 Star has annual sales of about $100 million and employs 950 people. Amtech has annual sales of $80 million and employs about 800 people. 5 Star typically reports greater net profits than Amtech.

The president of 5 Star, John Tyler, believed that 5 Star was the far superior company. Tyler credited his firm's greater effectiveness to his managers' ability to run a "tight ship." 5 Star had detailed organization charts and job descriptions. Tyler believed that everyone should have clear responsibilities and narrowly defined jobs, which generates efficient performance and high company profits. Employees were generally satisfied with their jobs at 5 Star, although some managers wished for more empowerment opportunities.

Amtech's president, Jim Rawls, did not believe in organization charts. He believed organization charts just put artificial barriers between specialists who should be working together. He encouraged people to communicate face-to-face rather than with written memos. The head of mechanical engineering said, "Jim spends too much time making sure everyone understands what we're doing and listening to suggestions." Rawls was concerned with employee satisfaction and wanted everyone to feel part of the organization. Employees were often rotated among departments so they would be familiar with activities throughout the company. Although Amtech wasn't as profitable as 5 Star, they were able to bring new products on line more quickly, work bugs out of new designs more accurately, and achieve higher quality because of superb employee commitment and collaboration.

It is the end of May, and John Tyler, president of 5 Star, has just announced the acquisition of Amtech Electronics. Both management teams are proud of their cultures and have unflattering opinions of the other's. Each company's customers are rather loyal, and their technologies are compatible, so Tyler believes a combined company will be even more effective, particularly in a time of rapid change in both technology and products.

The Amtech managers resisted the idea of an acquisition, but the 5 Star president is determined to unify the two companies quickly, increase the new firm's marketing position, and revitalize product lines—all by year end.

Sources: Adapted from John F. Veiga, "The Paradoxical Twins: Acme and Omega Electronics," in John F. Veiga and John N. Yanouzas, *The Dynamics of Organization Theory* (St. Paul: West Publishing, 1984), pp. 132–138; and "Alpha and Amtech," Harvard Business School Case 9-488-003, published by the President and Fellows of Harvard College, 1988.

QUESTIONS

1. Using the competing values model in Exhibit 14.3, what type of culture (adaptability, achievement, clan, bureaucratic) would you say is dominant at 5 Star? At Amtech? What is your evidence?

2. Is there a culture gap? Which type of culture do you think is most appropriate for the newly merged company? Why?

3. If you were John Tyler, what techniques would you use to integrate and shape the culture to overcome the culture gap?

Chapter 15 Cases

AMERICAN TOOL & DIE

As the sun rose on a crisp fall morning, Kelly Mueller's Learjet touched down onto a small airstrip outside Tupelo, Mississippi, and taxied toward the hangar, where a festive crowd gathered to await the arrival of Toyota's CEO. This morning, the governor of Mississippi, along with local politicians and business leaders from the automobile industry, would celebrate the construction of a new Toyota plant on a 1,700-acre site in Blue Springs. The new plant would produce 150,000 Highlander sport utility vehicles each year. The energy and enthusiasm of the crowd was palpable. The new plant would give hope to a local community that had been hit hard by the recession.

The purpose of Mueller's visit was to assess new business opportunities for the company she ran for her father, Vince Brofft, CEO of American Tool & Die (AT&D). Mueller had joined the company in 1998 after working for 15 years as an engineer at two U.S. automakers. Then, after seven successful years as chief operations officer at AT&D, this scrappy dynamo convinced her father she was ready to be president. Energetic and tireless, Mueller took over the helm of AT&D, an auto parts manufacturer that sold braking and ignition systems directly to the top three U.S. automakers. With 195 employees, AT&D was located in Farmington Hills, Michigan, among dozens of other automobile parts suppliers in the Upper Midwest. AT&D, established in 1912 by Mueller's great uncle, had a long history in Farmington Hills. Mueller had often talked with employees who would recount stories about their fathers or grandfathers working in the same Farmington Hills plant—the last of the original manufacturing operations in town.

Mueller was in Mississippi to research moving AT&D's plant close to a foreign automaker. The foreign automakers, particularly Honda and Toyota, had been quickly grabbing market share away from the big three automakers, who had severely cut production as the economy worsened. As inventory started stacking up on dealer lots, U.S. automakers curtailed production in order to cope with the sudden drop in demand. Next, they put the squeeze on parts suppliers to lower prices. That's when AT&D leaders started feeling the crunch and watching their financial picture turn grim.

Mueller faced an unprecedented challenge to survive this economic downturn and save her family's company. She pleaded with her father to think creatively and shake up the status quo at AT&D to avoid bankruptcy. Her plan was to forge into new markets and court foreign automakers. This plan would require closing the plant in Michigan and opening one near the new Toyota facilities in Mississippi. Her father adamantly resisted this plan even though he knew she was right. "Dad," a recent text message explained, "we have opportunities here in Mississippi. There's no future in Michigan. We can't sit around waiting for the big three to come back! It's adapt or die!"

Back at the Farmington Hills plant, Brofft pondered his daughter's "adapt or die" theory and considered an alternative to moving the plant to Mississippi—a move that would cause 195 employees to lose their livelihood in a small, close-knit community. Brofft agonized over choices that could dismantle a company that his family had built. He was sickened by the prospect of laying off employees who were like family. As an alternative to moving the plant, Brofft considered ways to stay in Michigan. The only feasible option was to drastically cut payroll costs. To do so, he needed support from the local union.

Brofft called a meeting with the plant manager and union leaders to explain AT&D's dire financial situation. He urged them to make concessions in the employee compensation agreement and explained that these plans would save the company from certain bankruptcy. Assuming he could win their support, Brofft proposed three strategies to the local union reps to keep the company financially afloat: (1) reduce worker wages by 10 percent for one year; (2) mandate a two-week, unpaid furlough at the end of December; and (3) downsize the number of employees by 30 percent. Exasperated, the local union leaders could barely restrain their anger. They were adamantly opposed to all three ideas. Yet probing beyond the fray, Brofft sensed the fear that lurked under the union reps' gruff exterior. He sensed their vulnerability, but could not break through the reactionary bark that protected it. If union leaders would not cooperate, the plant would have to move and everyone in Farmington Hills would suffer.

In the meantime, Mueller held several successful presentations with local Toyota executives while in Mississippi. "I've made progress, Dad," she said in a voice mail. "I can tell it's going to be a long and drawn-out process, but they are very impressed with our product and historical strength. They've agreed to another meeting next month."

Sources: Karen E. Klein, "Survival Advice for Auto Parts Suppliers," *BusinessWeek* (June 16, 2009), http://www.businessweek.com/pri.t/magazine/content/09_62/s0902015954839.htm (accessed November 12, 2009); Amy Barrett, "Auto-Parts Suppliers Brace for Downturn," *BusinessWeek* (February 13, 2009); http://www.businessweek.com/smallbiz/content/jun2009/sb20090616_816915.htm (accessed November 12, 2009); and Toyota, http://www.toyota.com (accessed November 12, 2009).

QUESTIONS

1. Assume you are Vince Brofft and want to lead the change to save the plant. Describe how you would enact the first three stages outlined in Exhibit 15.2.

2. Describe three tactics you would use to overcome union leader resistance.

3. If you were Kelly Mueller, how would you encourage innovative thinking at AT&D? What strategies would you use to encourage others to be more receptive to bold changes?

RIVERSIDE PEDIATRIC ASSOCIATES

Five years ago, doctors Alvero Sanchez and Josh Hudson opened a small pediatrics office in Riverside, California. These longtime friends, who had graduated from medical school together, had finally achieved the dream of starting a pediatrics practice with the vision of providing excellent care to children in their local community. The five doctors, six nurses, and accountant who staffed the office quickly developed a reputation for being caring and conscientious. The staff also partnered with local organizations to serve the underprivileged in the community, providing free flu shots and health clinics at the local YMCA. Sanchez and Hudson were energized and ecstatic that they were living out their dream, managing their small practice in the midst of a community that respected them.

Their dream started to unravel, however, as the practice began growing at an unwieldy pace. The population of nearby Hispanic communities was burgeoning, and so was the number of patients coming to Riverside. Although Sanchez and Hudson had always dreamed of a large, profitable practice, they realized they were not prepared for such unprecedented growth. The number of new patients was skyrocketing, and the staff at Riverside was unprepared to handle the influx. Waiting rooms were packed, the staff was becoming short tempered, and communication among staff was breaking down. Internal systems—like the electronic medical records systems—were overloaded, and patient health records were getting lost. Patient scheduling was chaotic, causing long waits for many people. The systems and procedures that once provided a firm underpinning for the small practice could no longer sustain the rapid patient growth.

Frustration mounted as the founding doctors spent more of their time managing the growing business and less time on patient care. They realized their original vision of providing excellent pediatric care in a comforting environment was fading fast. Most importantly, they were growing dissatisfied with their work. Instead of diagnosing illnesses and building relationships with patients, they were spending more time overseeing expansion and growth of their practice: interviewing and hiring additional doctors and nurses; supervising construction of the office expansion; and training new staff on office procedures. Their primary reason for opening a practice seemed like a long-forgotten memory.

Under the growing pressure, staff morale began to buckle. Heated arguments and short tempers among the staff were becoming commonplace. One stellar nurse had resigned, feeling powerless and disenfranchised by the conditions in the office. Another had been fired after arguing with a frazzled parent. Even Sanchez and Hudson were growing frustrated and unhappy in their work. Secluded for a quick lunch in the break room, Hudson confided in Sanchez. "There was a time," he said, "when we found meaning in our work. I felt most alive and fulfilled when we were just starting out. Now, we're just scrambling to keep pace with the change, but we're falling behind and drifting away from what's important—excellent care for our patients."

Their lunch was interrupted by a knock at the door and some unexpected news from their accountant. The quarterly financial reports painted a grim picture, she told them. The recent pattern of decreasing revenue and escalating costs was continuing in this quarter. A financial crisis was beginning to brew, impacting both cash flow and profitability. The accountant explained that quick action would need to be taken to improve the practice's financial health. "We have three problems" she explained, "and those are declining reimbursement from insurance companies, delinquent payments from patients, and rising costs of medical supplies and lab work." She paused and then added, "It doesn't help that our billing software is archaic. It simply can't manage the size of this practice."

Sanchez tore a page from his prescription pad, flipped it over, and scratched out the following: *To survive, Riverside Pediatric Associates must (1) improve service to patients and family; (2) improve respect and collaborative communication among the staff; (3) save money; (4) collect fees from patients in a timely manner; and (5) encourage innovation and creativity from our staff to solve routine problems.* He slid this list across the table to Hudson, asking, "How do we make this happen?"

Source: Based on Caroline Carter et al., "An Appreciative Inquiry Approach to Practice Improvement and Transformative Change in Health Care Settings," *Q Manage Health Care* 16, no. 3 (© 2007 Wolters Kluwer Health; Lippincott Williams and Wilkins), pp. 194–204.

QUESTIONS

1. Assume you are Sanchez or Hudson and plan to implement immediate organizational change within the practice. Where would you start? What steps would you take?

2. The accountant recommended that Sanchez and Hudson consider using appreciative inquiry (AI) to facilitate positive change within the practice. How would you implement the four steps of AI? Be specific. What kinds of things would you expect to arise during the Discover and Dream steps of AI?

3. Sanchez and Hudson are caught between being physicians and being leaders of their practice. How do you suggest they resolve this dilemma? What leadership qualities will Sanchez and Hudson need to display in order to lead positive change in their practice?

Chapter 1 References

1. Ram Charan, "What DuPont Did Right," *BusinessWeek* (January 19, 2009), p. 36, excerpted from Ram Charan, *Leadership in the Era of Economic Uncertainty: The New Rules for Getting the Right Things Done in Difficult Times* (New York: McGraw-Hill, 2008).

2. David Rothkopf, "Somebody Take Control. (Anybody. Really. Please.); Where Are All the Leaders?" *The Washington Post* (March 29, 2009), p. B1.

3. Carol Hymowitz, "CEOs Must Work Hard to Maintain Faith in the Corner Office" (In the Lead column), *The Wall Street Journal* (July 9, 2002), p. B1.

4. Alex Altman, "Chesley B. Sullenberger III, *Time* (January 16, 2009), http://205.188.238.109/time/nation/article/0,8599,1872247,00 .html (accessed March 11, 2009); and "A Mav Man: Chesley Sullenberger," *MavTV*, http://www.mavtv.com/wordpress/?p=2566 (accessed March 11, 2009).

5. Warren Bennis and Burt Nanus, *Leaders: The Strategies for Taking Charge* (New York: Harper & Row, 1985), p. 4; and James MacGregor Burns, *Leadership* (New York: Harper & Row, 1978), p. 2.

6. J. Meindl, S. Ehrlich, and J. Dukerich, "The Romance of Leadership," *Administrative Science Quarterly* 30 (1985), pp. 78–102.

7. Rakesh Khurana, "The Curse of the Superstar CEO," *Harvard Business Review* (September 2002), pp. 60–66.

8. Jennifer Reingold, "Bob Nardelli Is Watching," *Fast Company* (December 2005), pp. 76–83; and Brian Grow, with D. Foust, E. Thornton, R. Farzad, J. McGregor, S. Zegel, and E. Javers, "Out at Home Depot," *BusinessWeek* (January 15, 2007), pp. 56–62.

9. Bill George, "Truly Authentic Leadership" (Special Report: America's Best Leaders), *U.S. News & World Report* (October 30, 2006), pp. 52–53.

10. Khurana, "The Curse of the Superstar CEO"; Joseph A. Raelin, "The Myth of Charismatic Leaders," *Training and Development* (March 2003), p. 46; and Betsy Morris, "The New Rules," *Fortune* (July 24, 2006), pp. 70–87.

11. Joseph C. Rost, *Leadership for the Twenty-First Century* (Westport, CT: Praeger, 1993), p. 102; and Joseph C. Rost and Richard A. Barker, "Leadership Education in Colleges: Toward a 21st Century Paradigm," *The Journal of Leadership Studies* 7, no. 1 (2000), pp. 3–12.

12. Peter B. Smith and Mark F. Peterson, *Leadership, Organizations, and Culture: An Event Management Model* (London: Sage Publications, 1988), p. 14.

13. Robert E. Kelley, "In Praise of Followers," *Harvard Business Review* (November–December 1988), pp. 142–148.

14. George, "Truly Authentic Leadership."

15. Reported in Margaret Wheatley, "Leadership Lessons from the Real World," *Leader to Leader* (Summer 2006), pp. 16–20.

16. Nicholas D. Kristof, "It Takes a School, Not Missiles," *The New York Times* (July 13, 2008), p. WK14; Kevin Fedarki. "He Fights Terror with Books," *Parade Magazine* (April 6, 2003), pp. 4–6; Richard Halicks, "Schools for Pakistan and Afghanistan: Moving Mountains," *The Atlanta Journal-Constitution* (April 16, 2006), p. F1; and Alice Maggin, "ABC News, World News with Charles Gibson, Person of the Week: Greg Mortenson" (March 27, 2009), https://www.ikat. org/2009/03/27/abc-mar-27-09/ (accessed April 15, 2009). Mortenson's story is told in Greg Mortenson and David Oliver Relin, *Three Cups of Tea; One Man's Mission to Fight Terrorism and Build Nations . . . One School at a Time* (New York: Penguin, 2006). The book was not reviewed by most major newspapers at the time it was published, but it became a publishing sensation propelled by word-of-mouth and spent more than 74 weeks on the paperback best-seller list.

17. Scott R. Schmedel, "Making a Difference," *The Wall Street Journal* (August 21, 2006), pp. R5, R12.

18. Center for Creative Leadership survey reported in Andre Martin, "What Is Effective Leadership Today? A New Study Finds Collaboration Prized over Heroics," *Chief Executive* (July–August 2006), p. 24.

19. The discussion of these transformations is based in part on Fahri Karakas, "The Twenty-First Century Leader: Social Artist, Spiritual Visionary, and Cultural Innovator," *Global Business and Organizational Excellence* (March/April 2007), pp. 44–50; Daniel C. Kielson, "Leadership: Creating a New Reality," *The Journal of Leadership Studies* 3, no. 4 (1996), pp. 104–116; and Mark A. Abramson, "Leadership for the Future: New Behaviors, New Roles, and New Attitudes," *The Public Manager* (Spring 1997). See also Frances Hesselbein, Marshall Goldsmith, and Richard Beckhard, eds., *The Leader of the Future: New Visions, Strategies, and Practices for the Next Era* (San Francisco: Jossey-Bass, 1996).

20. Matthew Karnitschnig, Carrick Mollenkamp, and Dan Fitzpatrick, "Bank of America Eyes Merrill," *The Wall Street Journal* (September 15, 2008), p. A1; and Carrick Mollenkamp and Mark Whitehouse, "Old-School Banks Emerge Atop New World of Finance," *The Wall Street Journal* (September 16, 2008), pp. A1, A10.

21. Neil King, Jr., and Sharon Terlep, "GM Collapses into Government's Arms," *The Wall Street Journal* (June 2, 2009), p. A1.

22. Marvin J. Cetron and Owen Davies, "The Dragon vs. the Tiger," *The Futurist* (July–August 2006), p. 38ff; Bill Powell, "It's China's World (We Just Live In It)," *Fortune* (October 26, 2009), pp. 86–92; and Alyssa Abkowitz, "China Buys the World," *Fortune* (October 26, 2009), pp. 94–96

23. Jack and Suzy Welch, "How to Seize the Storm," *BusinessWeek* (October 13, 2008), p. 108.

24. Greg Ip, "Mind over Matter—Disappearing Acts: The Rapid Rise and Fall of the Intangible Asset," *The Wall Street Journal* (April 4, 2002), pp. A1, A6.

25 Charles Handy, *The Age of Paradox* (Boston: Harvard Business School Press, 1994), pp. 146–147; and Geoff Colvin, "Leader Machines," *Fortune* (October 1, 2007), pp. 98–106.

26 Richard L. Daft, *Organization Theory and Design,* 6th ed. (Cincinnati, OH: South-Western College Publishing, 1998), p. 523.

27 Cyrus F. Friedheim, Jr., *The Trillion-Dollar Enterprise: How the Alliance Revolution Will Transform Global Business* (Reading, MA: Perseus Books, 1999).

28 Silla Brush, "A Vote of No Confidence" (Special Report: America's Best Leaders), *U.S. News & World Report* (October 30, 2006), p. 56.

29 Patricia Sellers, "The New Breed," *Fortune* (November 18, 2002), pp. 66–76.

30 "Not Her Father's Chief Executive" (an interview with Marilyn Carlson Nelson), *U.S. News & World Report* (October 30, 3006), pp. 64–65.

31 "*Maersk Alabama* Crew Recalls Pirate Attack," *USA Today* (April 16, 2009), http://www.usatoday.com/news/nation/2009-04-16-pirates_N.htm (accessed April 30, 2009).

32 See James Collins, *Good to Great: Why Some Companies Make the Leap. . . and Others Don't* (New York: HarperCollins, 2001); Charles A. O'Reilly III and Jeffrey Pfeffer, *Hidden Value: How Great Companies Achieve Extraordinary Results with Ordinary People* (Boston, MA: Harvard Business School Press, 2000); Rakesh Khurana, *Searching for a Corporate Savior: The Irrational Quest for Charismatic CEOs* (Princeton University Press, 2002); Joseph Badaracco, *Leading Quietly* (Boston, MA: Harvard Business School Press, 2002); Jason Jennings, *Think Big, Act Small: How America's Best Performing Companies Keep the Startup Spirit Alive* (New York: Portfolio/Penguin, 2005); Ryan Underwood, "The CEO Next Door," *Fast Company* (September 2005), pp. 64–66; and Linda Tischler, "The CEO's New Clothes," *Fast Company* (September 2005), pp. 27–28,

33 Jim Collins, "Level 5 Leadership: The Triumph of Humility and Fierce Resolve," *Harvard Business Review* (January 2001), pp. 67–76; Collins, "Good to Great," *Fast Company* (October 2001), pp. 90–104; Edward Prewitt, "The Utility of Humility," *CIO* (December 1, 2002), pp. 104–110; A. J. Vogl, "Onward and Upward" (an interview with Jim Collins), *Across the Board* (September–October 2001), pp. 29–34; and Jerry Useem, "Conquering Vertical Limits," *Fortune* (February 19, 2001), pp. 84–96.

34 Jena McGregor, "Game Plan: First Find the Leaders," *BusinessWeek* (August 21, 2006), pp. 102–103.

35 James Lardner, "In Praise of the Anonymous CEO," *Business 2.0* (September 2002), pp. 104–108; and Nanette Byrnes with J. A. Byrne, C. Edwards, L. Lee, S. Holmes, and J. Muller, "The Good CEO," *BusinessWeek* (September 23, 2002), pp. 80–88.

36 Jackie Calmes and Louise Story, "AIG Bonus Outcry Builds; Troubled Insurance Giant Gave Out More Millions Last Week," *Pittsburgh Post Gazette* (March 18, 2009), p. A1.

37 Quoted in David Gergen, "How Business Can Stand Tall Again," *Fortune* (May 11, 2009), p. 25.

38 Gary Yukl and Richard Lepsinger, "Why Integrating the Leading and Managing Roles Is Essential for Organizational Effectiveness," *Organizational Dynamics* 34, no. 4 (2005), pp. 361–375.

39 This section is based largely on John P. Kotter, *A Force for Change: How Leadership Differs from Management* (New York: The Free Press, 1990), pp. 3–18; and John P. Kotter, "What Leaders Really Do," *Harvard Business Review* (December 2001), pp. 3–11.

40 *Leadership, A Forum Issues Special Report* (Boston, MA: The Forum Corporation, 1990), p. 13.

41 See Geoff Colvin, "The 100 Best Companies to Work For, 2006," *Fortune* (January 23, 2006), pp. 71–74; "2004 Special Report: The 100 Best Companies to Work For," *Fortune* (January 12, 2004), pp. 56–80; and Kevin E. Joyce, "Lessons for Employers from *Fortune's* 100 Best," *Business Horizons* (March–April 2003), pp. 77–84.

42 John P. Kotter, quoted in Thomas A. Stewart, "Why Leadership Matters," *Fortune* (March 2, 1998), pp. 71–82.

43 Warren Bennis, *Why Leaders Can't Lead* (San Francisco: Jossey-Bass, 1989).

44 Abraham Zaleznik, "Managers and Leaders: Are They Different?" *Harvard Business Review* (March–April 1992), pp. 126–135; David Rooke and William R. Torbert, "7 Transformations of Leadership," *Harvard Business Review* (April 2005), pp. 67–76; and Rooke and Torbert, *Action Inquiry: The Secret of Timely and Transforming Leadership* (San Francisco: Berrett-Koehler, 2004).

45 Joyce Routson, "Risk Taking Is Necessary, Says Dimon of JPMorgan Chase," *Stanford GSB News* (January 2009), http://www.gsb.stanford.edu/news/headlines/Dimon09.html (accessed March 29, 2009); Christian Schmidt, "JPMorgan Chase CEO Jamie Dimon Speaks at Spangler Auditorium," *The Harbus* (December 3, 2007), http://media.www.harbus.org/media/storage/paper343/news/2007/12/03/News/Jpmorgan.Chase.Ceo.Jamie.Dimon.Speaks.At.Spangler.Auditorium-3126137.shtml (accessed March 29, 2009); Marc Gunther, "Jamie Dimon, Telling It Like It Is," *MarkGunther.com* (December 22, 2008), http:www.marcgunther.com/?p=456 (accessed March 29, 2009); and Shawn Tully, "Jamie Dimon's Swat Team," *Fortune* (September 15, 2008), pp. 64–78.

46 Routson, "Risk Taking Is Necessary."

47 Susan R. Komives, Nance Lucas, Timothy R. McMahon, *Exploring Leadership: For College Students Who Want to Make a Difference* (San Francisco: Jossey-Bass Publishers, 1998), p. 38.

48 Based on Komives, et al., *Exploring Leadership;* and Shann R. Ferch and Matthew M. Mitchell, "Intentional Forgiveness in Relational Leadership: A Technique for Enhancing Effective Leadership," *The Journal of Leadership Studies* 7, no. 4 (2001), pp. 70–83.

49 Craig L. Pearce, "The Future of Leadership: Combining Vertical and Shared Leadership to Transform Knowledge Work," *Academy of Management Executive* 18, no. 1 (2004), pp. 47–57.

50 Morgan W. McCall, Jr., and Michael M. Lombardo, "Off the Track: Why and How Successful Executives Get Derailed" (Technical Report No. 21), (Greensboro, NC: Center for Creative Leadership, January 1983); and Carol Hymowitz, "Five Main Reasons Why Managers Fail," *The Wall Street Journal* (May 2, 1988).

51 Carol Hymowitz, "In the Lead: As Managers Climb, They Have to Learn How to Act the Parts," *The Wall Street Journal* (November 14, 2005), p. B1.

52 Ram Charan and Geoffrey Colvin, "Why CEOs Fail," *Fortune* (June 21, 1999), pp. 68–78.

53 Tricia Bisoux, "What Makes Leaders Great," *BizEd* (September October 2005), pp. 40–45.

54 Russell Palmer, "Can Leadership Be Learned?" *Business Today* (Fall 1989), pp. 100–102.

55 "No Holds Barred" (an interview with Kenneth Chenault), sidebar in Colvin, "Leader Machines."

Chapter 2 References

1 "IHOP's CEO Has a Lot on Her Plate," Fortune (March 31, 2003), p. 143; and "Preparing a Franchisee Business Plan; Julie Stewart of IHOP: Making the Partnership Work," *Franchising.com* (February 15, 2004), http://www.franchising.com/articles/66 (accessed March 16, 2009).

2 Deborah Ancona, Thomas W. Malone, Wanda J. Orlikowski, and Peter M. Senge, "In Praise of the Incomplete Leader," *Harvard Business Review* (February 2007), pp. 92–100.

3 Center for Creative Leadership survey results, reported in "The Demise of the Heroic Leader," *Leader to Leader* (Fall 2006), pp. 55–56.

4 Marcus Buckingham and Donald O. Clifton, *Now, Discover Your Strengths* (New York: The Free Press, 2001); and Chuck Martin, with Peg Dawson and Richard Guare, *Smarts: Are We Hardwired for Success?* (New York: AMACOM, 2007).

5 Buckingham and Clifton, *Now, Discover Your Strengths,* p. 12.

6 G. A. Yukl, *Leadership in Organizations* (Upper Saddle River, NJ: Prentice Hall, 1981); and S. C. Kohs and K. W. Irle, "Prophesying Army Promotion," *Journal of Applied Psychology* 4 (1920), pp. 73–87.

7 Yukl, *Leadership in Organizations*, p. 254.

8 R. M. Stogdill, "Personal Factors Associated with Leadership: A Survey of the Literature," *Journal of Psychology* 25 (1948), pp. 35–71.

9 R. M. Stogdill, *Handbook of Leadership: A Survey of the Literature* (New York: The Free Press, 1974); and Bernard M. Bass, *Bass & Stogdill's Handbook of Leadership: Theory, Research, and Managerial Applications*, 3rd ed. (New York: The Free Press, 1990).

10 S. A. Kirkpatrick and E. A. Locke, "Leadership: Do Traits Matter?" *The Academy of Management Executive* 5, no. 2 (1991), pp. 48–60.

11 R. G. Lord, C. L. DeVader, and G. M. Alliger, "A Meta-Analysis of the Relation Between Personality Traits and Leadership Perceptions: An Application of Validity Generalization Procedures," *Journal of Applied Psychology* 71 (1986), pp. 402–410.

12 Study reported in "From the Front Lines: How Does Leadership Personality Affect Performance?" *Leader to Leader* (Winter 2007), pp. 56–57; and Bradley R. Agle, Nandu J. Nagarajan, Jeffrey A. Sonnenfeld, and Dhinu Srinivasan, "Does CEO Charisma Matter? An Empirical Analysis of the Relationships among Organizational Performance, Environmental Uncertainty, and Top Management Team Perceptions of CEO Charisma," *Academy of Management Journal* 49, no. 1 (2006), pp. 161–174.

13 Edwin Locke and Associates, *The Essence of Leadership* (New York: Lexington Books, 1991).

14 A summary of various studies and surveys is reported in Del Jones, "Optimism Puts Rose-Colored Tint in Glasses of Top Execs," *USA Today* (December 15, 2005).

15 Marcus Buckingham, quoted in Jones, "Optimism Puts Rose-Colored Tint in Glasses of Top Execs."

16 Judy Battista, "A Coaching Success. Secret to Steelers Coach Tomlin's Success: Take Notes," *The New York Times* (January 26, 2009), p. D1.

17 Shelley A. Kirkpatrick and Edwin A. Locke, "Leadership: Do Traits Matter?" *Academy of Management Executive* 5, no. 2 (1991), pp. 48–60.

18 Larry Neumeister and Tom Hays, "Madoff Sent to Jail as Furious Victims Applaud," *Yahoo News* (March 12, 2009), http://news.yahoo.com/s/ap/20090312/ap_on_bi_ge/madoff_scandal (accessed March 13, 2009); and Julie Creswell and Landon Thomas, Jr., "The Talented Mr. Madoff," *The New York Times* (January 25, 2009), p. BU1.

19 James M. Kouzes and Barry Z. Posner, *Credibility: How Leaders Gain and Lose It, Why People Demand It* (San Francisco: Jossey-Bass, 1993), p. 14.

20 Kirkpatrick and Locke, "Leadership: Do Traits Matter?"

21 Henny Sender and Monica Langley, "Buyout Mogul: How Blackstone's Chief Became $7 Billion Man," *The Wall Street Journal* (June 13, 2007), p. A1.

22 Christine Seib, "Blackstone Drops Payout as It Tumbles into the Red," *The Times* (February 28, 2009), p. 54; and Philip Delves, "So Crabby over the Loss of Wealth," *The Evening Standard* (March 12, 2009), p. 39.

23 Geoffrey Colvin, "The Bionic Manager," *Fortune* (September 19, 2005), pp. 88-100.

24 "Towards a More Perfect Match: Building Successful Leaders by Effectively Aligning People and Roles," Hay Group Working Paper, 2004.

25 K. Lewin, "Field Theory and Experiment in Social Psychology: Concepts and Methods," *American Journal of Sociology* 44 (1939), pp. 868–896; K. Lewin and R. Lippett, "An Experimental Approach to the Study of Autocracy and Democracy: A Preliminary Note," *Sociometry* 1 (1938), pp. 292–300; and K. Lewin, R. Lippett, and R. K. White, "Patterns of Aggressive Behavior in Experimentally Created Social Climates," *Journal of Social Psychology* 10 (1939), pp. 271–301.

26 R. Tannenbaum and W. H. Schmidt, "How to Choose a Leadership Pattern," *Harvard Business Review* 36 (1958), pp. 95–101.

27 F. A. Heller and G. A. Yukl, "Participation, Managerial Decision-Making and Situational Variables," *Organizational Behavior and Human Performance* 4 (1969), pp. 227–241.

28 "Jack's Recipe (Management Principles Used by Jack Hartnett, President of D. L. Rogers Corp.)," sidebar in Marc Ballon, "Extreme Managing: Equal Parts Old-Fashioned Dictator and New Age Father Figure, Jack Hartnett Breaks Nearly Every Rule of the Enlightened Manager's Code," Inc. (July 1998), p. 60.

29 Donna Fenn, "The Remote Control CEO," *Inc.* (October 2005), pp. 96–101, 144–146.

30 Ibid.

31 J. K. Hemphill and A. E. Coons, "Development of the Leader Behavior Description Questionnaire," in R. M. Stogdill and A. E. Coons, eds., *Leader Behavior: Its Description and Measurement* (Columbus, OH: Ohio State University, Bureau of Business Research, 1957).

32 P. C. Nystrom, "Managers and the High-High Leader Myth," *Academy of Management Journal* 21 (1978), pp. 325–331; and L. L. Larson, J. G. Hunt and Richard N. Osborn, "The Great High-High Leader Behavior Myth: A Lesson from Occam's Razor," *Academy of Management Journal* 19 (1976), pp. 628–641.

33 Christopher Cooper, "Speed Trap; How a Marine Lost His Command in Race to Baghdad," *The Wall Street Journal* (April 5, 2004), pp. A1, A15.

34 E. W. Skinner, "Relationships Between Leadership Behavior Patterns and Organizational-Situational Variables," *Personnel Psychology* 22 (1969), pp. 489-494; and E. A. Fleishman and E. F. Harris, "Patterns of Leadership Behavior Related to Employee Grievances and Turnover," *Personnel Psychology* 15 (1962), pp. 43–56.

35 A. W. Halpin and B. J. Winer, "A Factorial Study of the Leader Behavior Descriptions," in R. M. Stogdill and A. E. Coons, eds., *Leader Behavior: Its Descriptions and Measurement* (Columbus, OH: Ohio State University, Bureau of Business Research, 1957); and J. K. Hemphill, "Leadership Behavior Associated with the Administrative Reputations of College Departments," *Journal of Educational Psychology* 46 (1955), pp. 385–401.

36 R. Likert, "From Production- and Employee-Centeredness to Systems 1-4," *Journal of Management* 5 (1979), pp. 147–156.

37 J. Taylor and D. Bowers, *The Survey of Organizations: A Machine Scored Standardized Questionnaire Instrument* (Ann Arbor, MI: Institute for Social Research, University of Michigan, 1972).

38 D. G. Bowers and S. E. Seashore, "Predicting Organizational Effectiveness with a Four-Factor Theory of Leadership," *Administrative Science Quarterly* 11 (1966), pp. 238–263.

39 Bowers and Seashore, "Predicting Organizational Effectiveness with a Four-Factor Theory of Leadership."

40 Robert Blake and Jane S. Mouton, *The Managerial Grid III* (Houston: Gulf Publishing Company, 1985).

41 Jo Napolitano, "No, She Doesn't Breathe Fire," *The New York Times* (September 1, 2002), Section 3, p. 2; and Adrienne Carter, "Lighting a Fire under Campbell," *BusinessWeek* (December 4, 2005), pp. 96–101.

42 Gary Yukl, Angela Gordon, and Tom Taber, "A Hierarchical Taxonomy of Leadership Behavior: Integrating a Half Century of Behavior Research," *Journal of Leadership and Organizational Studies* 9, no. 1 (2002), pp. 15–32.

43 Stephanie Desmon, "Schools Chief an Executive, Not an Educator," *The Palm Beach Post* (December 26, 1999), pp. 1A, 22A.

44 Francis J. Yammarino and Fred Dansereau, "Individualized Leadership," *Journal of Leadership and Organizational Studies* 9, no. 1 (2002), pp. 90–99.

45 This discussion is based on Fred Dansereau, "A Dyadic Approach to Leadership: Creating and Nurturing This Approach Under Fire," *Leadership Quarterly* 6, no. 4 (1995), pp. 479–490; and George B. Graen and Mary Uhl-Bien, "Relationship-Based Approach to Leadership: Development of Leader–Member Exchange (LMX) Theory of Leadership over 25 Years: Applying a Multi-Level Multi-Domain Approach," *Leadership Quarterly* 6, no. 2 (1995), pp. 219–247.

46 See A. J. Kinicki and R. P. Vecchio, "Influences on the Quality of Supervisor-Subordinate Relations: The Role of Time Pressure,

Organizational Commitment, and Locus of Control," *Journal of Organizational Behavior* (January 1994), pp. 75–82; R. C. Liden, S. J. Wayne, and D. Stilwell, "A Longitudinal Study on the Early Development of Leader–Member Exchanges," *Journal of Applied Psychology* (August 1993), pp. 662-674; Yammarino and Dansereau, "Individualized Leadership"; and Jean-François Manzoni and Jean-Louis Barsoux, "The Set-Up-to-Fail Syndrome," *Harvard Business Review* (March–April 1998), pp. 101–113.

47 W. E. McClane, "Implications of Member Role Differentiation: Analysis of a Key Concept in the LMX Model of Leadership," *Group and Organization Studies* 16 (1991), pp. 102-113; and Gary Yukl, *Leadership in Organizations,* 2nd ed. (Upper Saddle River, NJ: Prentice Hall, 1989).

48 Manzoni and Barsoux, "The Set-Up-to-Fail Syndrome."

49 Donald F. Kuratko and Richard M. Hodgetts, *Entrepreneurship: A Contemporary Approach,* 4th ed. (Fort Worth, TX: Dryden Press, 1998), p. 30.

50 Steve Stecklow, "StubHub's Ticket to Ride," *The Wall Street Journal* (January 17, 2006).

51 Kristina L. Guo, "Core Competencies of the Entrepreneurial Leader in Health Care Organizations," *Health Care Manager*

28 (January–March 2009), pp. 19–29; and Gary A. Knight, "Cross-Cultural Reliability and Validity of a Scale to Measure Firm Entrepreneurial Orientation," *Journal of Business Venturing* 12 (1997), pp. 213–225.

52 This discussion is based on Ron Garonzik, Geoff Nethersell, and Scott Spreier, "Navigating Through the New Leadership Landscape," *Leader to Leader* (Winter 2006), pp. 30–39; "Towards a More Perfect Match: Building Successful Leaders by Effectively Aligning People and Roles," Hay Group Working Paper (2004); and "Making Sure the 'Suit' Fits," Hay Group Research Brief (2004). Available from Hay Group, The McClelland Center, 116 Huntington Avenue, Boston, MA, 02116, or at http://www .haygroup.com.

53 Reprinted with permission from Gary Yukl, *Leadership in Organizations,* 4th ed. (Upper Saddle River, NJ: Prentice Hall, 1998), pp. 66–67.

54 Based in part on "The Take Over," Incident 52 in Bernard A. Deitzer and Karl A. Shilliff, *Contemporary Management Incidents* (Columbus, OH: Grid, Inc., 1977), pp. 161–162; and "Choosing a New Director of Research," Case 2.1 in Peter G. Northouse, *Leadership Theory and Practice*, 2nd ed. (Thousand Oaks, CA: Sage Publications, 2001), pp. 25–26.

Chapter 3 References

1 John Markoff, "Competing as Software Goes to Web," *The New York Times* (June 5, 2007), pp. C1, C5.

2 Gary Yukl, Angela Gordon, and Tom Taber, "A Hierarchical Taxonomy of Leadership Behavior: Integrating a Half Century of Behavior Research," *Journal of Leadership and Organization Studies* 9, no. 1 (2002), pp. 15–32.

3 Fred E. Fiedler, "Assumed Similarity Measures as Predictors of Team Effectiveness," *Journal of Abnormal and Social Psychology* 49 (1954), pp. 381–388; F. E. Fiedler, *Leader Attitudes and Group Effectiveness* (Urbana, IL: University of Illinois Press, 1958); and F. E. Fiedler, *A Theory of Leadership Effectiveness* (New York: McGraw-Hill, 1967).

4 Reported in George Anders, "Theory & Practice: Tough CEOs Often Most Successful, a Study Finds," *The Wall Street Journal* (November 19, 2007), p. B3.

5 Adam Lashinsky, "Mark Hurd's Moment," *Fortune* (March 16, 2009), pp. 90–100; Jon Fortt, "Mark Hurd, Superstar," *Fortune* (June 9, 2008), pp. 35–40; and "Memo To: Mark Hurd," *BusinessWeek* (April 11, 2005), p. 38.

6 M. J. Strube and J. E. Garcia, "A Meta-Analytic Investigation of Fiedler's Contingency Model of Leadership Effectiveness," *Psychological Bulletin* 90 (1981), pp. 307–321; and L. H. Peters, D. D. Hartke, and J. T. Pohlmann, "Fiedler's Contingency Theory of Leadership: An Application of the Meta-Analysis Procedures of Schmidt and Hunter," *Psychological Bulletin* 97 (1985), pp. 274–285.

7 R. Singh, "Leadership Style and Reward Allocation: Does Least Preferred Coworker Scale Measure Tasks and Relation Orientation?" *Organizational Behavior and Human Performance* 27 (1983), pp. 178–197; D. Hosking, "A Critical Evaluation of Fiedler's Contingency Hypotheses," *Progress in Applied Psychology* 1 (1981), pp. 103–154; Gary Yukl, "Leader LPC Scores: Attitude Dimensions and Behavioral Correlates," *Journal of Social Psychology* 80 (1970), pp. 207–212; G. Graen, K. M. Alvares, J. B. Orris, and J. A. Martella, "Contingency Model of Leadership Effectiveness: Antecedent and Evidential Results," *Psychological Bulletin* 74 (1970), pp. 285–296; and R. P. Vecchio, "Assessing the Validity of Fiedler's Contingency Model of Leadership Effectiveness: A Closer Look at Strube and Garcia," *Psychological Bulletin* 93 (1983), pp. 404–408.

8 J. K. Kennedy, Jr., "Middle LPC Leaders and the Contingency Model of Leadership Effectiveness," *Organizational Behavior and*

Human Performance 30 (1982), pp. 1–14; and S. C. Shiflett, "The Contingency Model of Leadership Effectiveness: Some Implications of Its Statistical and Methodological Properties," *Behavioral Science* 18, no. 6 (1973), pp. 429–440.

9 Roya Ayman, M. M. Chemers, and F. Fiedler, "The Contingency Model of Leadership Effectiveness: Its Levels of Analysis," *Leadership Quarterly* 6, no. 2 (1995), pp. 147–167.

10 Paul Hersey and Kenneth H. Blanchard, *Management of Organizational Behavior: Utilizing Human Resources,* 4th ed. (Upper Saddle River, NJ: Prentice Hall, 1982).

11 Jonathan Kaufman, "A McDonald's Owner Becomes a Role Model for Black Teenagers," *The Wall Street Journal* (August 23, 1995), pp. A1, A6.

12 Carol Hymowitz, "New Face at Facebook Hopes to Map Out a Road to Growth," *The Wall Street Journal* (April 14, 2008), p. B1.

13 Cheryl Dahle, "Xtreme Teams," *Fast Company* (November 1999), pp. 310–326.

14 Carol Hymowitz, "Managers Find Ways to Get Generations to Close Culture Gap" (In the Lead column), *The Wall Street Journal* (July 9, 2007), p. B1.

15 Carole McGraw, "Teaching Teenagers? Think, Do, Learn," *Education Digest* (February 1998), pp. 44–47.

16 M. G. Evans, "The Effects of Supervisory Behavior on the Path–Goal Relationship," *Organizational Behavior and Human Performance* 5 (1970), pp. 277–298; M. G. Evans, "Leadership and Motivation: A Core Concept," *Academy of Management Journal* 13 (1970), pp. 91–102; and B. S. Georgopoulos, G. M. Mahoney, and N. W. Jones, "A Path–Goal Approach to Productivity," *Journal of Applied Psychology* 41 (1957), pp. 345–353.

17 Robert J. House, "A Path–Goal Theory of Leadership Effectiveness," *Administrative Science Quarterly* 16 (1971), pp. 321–338.

18 M. G. Evans, "Leadership," in S. Kerr, ed., *Organizational Behavior* (Columbus, OH: Grid, 1974), pp. 230–233.

19 Robert J. House and Terrence R. Mitchell, "Path–Goal Theory of Leadership," *Journal of Contemporary Business* (Autumn 1974), pp. 81–97.

20 Dyan Machan, "We're Not Authoritarian Goons," *Forbes* (October 24, 1994), pp. 264–268.

21 Timothy Aeppel, "Personnel Disorders Sap a Factory Owner of His Early Idealism," *The Wall Street Journal* (January 14, 1998), pp. A1–A14.

22 Charles Greene, "Questions of Causation in the Path–Goal Theory of Leadership," *Academy of Management Journal* 22 (March 1979), pp. 22–41; and C. A. Schriesheim and Mary Ann von Glinow, "The Path–Goal Theory of Leadership: A Theoretical and Empirical Analysis," *Academy of Management Journal* 20 (1977), pp. 398–405.

23 V. H. Vroom and Arthur G. Jago, *The New Leadership: Managing Participation in Organizations* (Upper Saddle River, NJ: Prentice Hall, 1988).

24 The following discussion is based heavily on Victor H. Vroom, "Leadership and the Decision-Making Process," *Organizational Dynamics* 28, no. 4 (Spring 2000), pp. 82–94.

25 R. H. G. Field, "A Test of the Vroom–Yetton Normative Model of Leadership," *Journal of Applied Psychology* (October 1982), pp. 523–532; and R. H. G. Field, "A Critique of the Vroom–Yetton Contingency Model of Leadership Behavior," *Academy of Management Review* 4 (1979), pp. 249–251.

26 Vroom, "Leadership and the Decision-Making Process"; Jennifer T. Ettling and Arthur G. Jago, "Participation Under Conditions of Conflict: More on the Validity of the Vroom–Yetton Model," *Journal of Management Studies* 25 (1988), pp. 73–83; Madeline E. Heilman, Harvey A. Hornstein, Jack H. Cage, and Judith K. Herschlag, "Reactions to Prescribed Leader Behavior as a Function of Role Perspective: The Case of the Vroom–Yetton Model," *Journal of Applied Psychology* (February 1984), pp. 50–60; and Arthur G. Jago and Victor H. Vroom, "Some Differences in the Incidence and Evaluation of Participative Leader

Behavior," *Journal of Applied Psychology* (December 1982), pp. 776–783.

27 Based on a decision problem presented in Victor H. Vroom, "Leadership and the Decision-Making Process," *Organizational Dynamics* 28, no. 4 (Spring, 2000), pp. 82–94.

28 S. Kerr and J. M. Jermier, "Substitutes for Leadership: Their Meaning and Measurement," *Organizational Behavior and Human Performance* 22 (1978), pp. 375–403; and Jon P. Howell and Peter W. Dorfman, "Leadership and Substitutes for Leadership Among Professional and Nonprofessional Workers," *Journal of Applied Behavioral Science* 22 (1986), pp. 29–46.

29 J. P. Howell, D. E. Bowen, P. W. Doreman, S. Kerr, and P. M. Podsakoff, "Substitutes for Leadership: Effective Alternatives to Ineffective Leadership," *Organizational Dynamics* (Summer 1990), pp. 21–38.

30 Ibid.

31 P. M. Podsakoff, S. B. MacKenzie, and W. H. Bommer, "Transformational Leader Behaviors and Substitutes for Leadership as Determinants of Employee Satisfaction, Commitment, Trust, and Organizational Behaviors," *Journal of Management* 22, no. 2 (1996), pp. 259–298.

32 Howell et al., "Substitutes for Leadership."

33 Reprinted with permission from Gary Yukl, *Leadership in Organizations*, 7th ed. (Upper Saddle River, NJ: Prentice Hall, 2010), pp. 119–120.

34 Based on David Hornestay, "Double Vision," *Government Executive* (April 2000), pp. 41–44.

Chapter 4 References

1 Susan Berfield, "Walk 100 Miles in My Shoes," *BusinessWeek* (June 26, 2006), p. 80.

2 J. M. Digman, "Personality Structure: Emergence of the Five-Factor Model," *Annual Review of Psychology* 41 (1990), pp. 417–440; M. R. Barrick and M. K. Mount, "Autonomy as a Moderator of the Relationships Between the Big Five Personality Dimensions and Job Performance," *Journal of Applied Psychology* (February 1993), pp. 111–118; J. S. Wiggins and A. L. Pincus, "Personality: Structure and Assessment," *Annual Review of Psychology* 43 (1992), pp. 473–504; and Carl Zimmer, "Looking for Personality in Animals, of All People," *The New York Times* (March 1, 2005), p. F1.

3 Del Jones, "Not All Successful CEOs Are Extroverts," *USA Today* (June 6, 2006), p. B1.

4 Anthony J. Mayo and Nitin Nohria, "Double-Edged Sword," *People Management* (October 27, 2005), pp. 36–38; Carol Hymowitz, "Rewarding Competitors over Collaborators No Longer Makes Sense" (In the Lead column), *The Wall Street Journal* (February 13, 2006), p. B1; and Joseph Nocera, "In Business, Tough Guys Finish Last," *The New York Times* (June 18, 2005), p. C1.

5 Adam Bryant, "Lessons Learned at Goldman," (an interview with Lloyd C. Blankfein), *The New York Times* (September 13, 2009), p. BU2; and Diane Brady, "Charm Offensive," *BusinessWeek* (June 26, 2006), pp. 76–80.

6 Tim Sanders, *The Likeability Factor: How to Boost Your L-Factor and Achieve the Life of Your Dreams* (New York: Crown, 2005).

7 Arthur Lubow, "'It's Going to Be Big,'" *Inc.* (March 2009), pp. 52–57.

8 Richard Siklos, "Bob Iger Rocks Disney," *Fortune* (January 19, 2009), pp. 80–86; and Ronald Grover, "How Bob Iger Unchained Disney," *BusinessWeek* (February 5, 2007), pp. 74–79.

9 James B. Hunt, "Travel Experience in the Formation of Leadership: John Quincy Adams, Frederick Douglass, and Jane Addams," *The Journal of Leadership Studies* 7, no. 1 (2000), pp. 92–106.

10 R. T. Hogan, G. J. Curphy, and J. Hogan, "What We Know About Leadership: Effectiveness and Personality," *American Psychologist* 49, no. 6 (1994), pp. 493–504.

11 Randolph E. Schmid, "Psychologists Rate What Helps Make a President Great," *Johnson City Press* (August 6, 2000), p. 10; and "Personality and the Presidency" segment on *NBC News* with John Siegenthaler, Jr., August 5, 2000.

12 Jack and Suzy Welch, "Release Your Inner Extrovert," *BusinessWeek* (December 8, 2008), p. 92.

13 Reported in Jeffrey Kluger, "Why Bosses Tend to Be Blowhards" *Time* (March 2, 2009), p. 48.

14 P. E. Spector, "Behavior in Organizations as a Function of Employee's Locus of Control," *Psychological Bulletin* (May 1982), pp. 482–497; and H. M. Lefcourt, "Durability and Impact of the Locus of Control Construct," *Psychological Bulletin* 112 (1992), pp. 411–414.

15 Ellen McGirt, "Boy Wonder," *Fast Company* (April 2009), pp. 58–65, 96–97.

16 Spector, "Behavior in Organizations as a Function of Employee's Locus of Control"; Lefcourt, "Durability and Impact of the Locus of Control Construct"; and J. B. Miner, *Industrial-Organizational Psychology* (New York: McGraw-Hill, 1992), p. 151.

17 T. W. Adorno, E. Frenkel-Brunswick, D. J. Levinson, and R. N. Sanford, *The Authoritarian Personality* (New York: Harper & Row, 1950).

18 E. C. Ravlin and B. M. Meglino, "Effects of Values on Perception and Decision Making: A Study of Alternative Work Value Measures," *Journal of Applied Psychology* 72 (1987), pp. 666–673.

19 Robert C. Benfari, *Understanding and Changing Your Management Style* (San Francisco: Jossey-Bass, 1999), p. 172.

20 Milton Rokeach, *The Nature of Human Values* (New York: The Free Press, 1973); and M. Rokeach, *Understanding Human Values* (New York: The Free Press, 1979).

21 Carol Hymowitz, "For Many Executives, Leadership Lessons Started with Mom" (In the Lead column), *The Wall Street Journal* (May 16, 2000), p. B1.

22 Lynne Jeter, "Early Lessons Helped Form Leadership Skills," *The Mississippi Business Journal* (March 13, 2006), p. 23.

23 Based on G. W. England and R. Lee, "The Relationship Between Managerial Values and Managerial Success in the United States, Japan, India, and Australia," *Journal of Applied Psychology* 59 (1974), pp. 411–419.

24 Christopher Goodwin, "Shucks, We Just Can't Help Making Billions," *Sunday Times* (September 7, 2008), p. 6; Jon Fine, "Can Craigslist Stay Oddball?" *BusinessWeek* (May 19, 2008), p. 75ff; and "Dealbook: Craigslist Meets the Capitalists," *The New York Times* (December 8, 2006), http://dealbook.blogs.nytimes.com/2006/12/08/craigslist-meets-the-capitalists (accessed December 11, 2006).

25 Katharina Bart, "Leading the News: UBS Job Cuts to Grow Amid Record Losses," *The Wall Street Journal Europe* (February 11, 2009), p. 3; and "No Good Deed; The Fed's Unappreciated Bailout of a Miscreant Swiss Bank," *The Washington Post* (March 7, 2009), p. A12.

26 S. J. Breckler, "Empirical Validation of Affect, Behavior, and Cognition as Distinct Components of Attitudes," *Journal of Personality and Social Psychology* (May 1984), pp. 1191–1205; and J. M. Olson and M. P. Zanna, "Attitudes and Attitude Change," *Annual Review of Psychology* 44 (1993), pp. 117–154.

27 Parker J. Palmer, *Leading from Within: Reflections on Spirituality and Leadership* (Indianapolis: Indiana Office for Campus Ministries, 1990); and Diane Chapman Walsh, "Cultivating Inner Sources for Leadership," in Frances Hesselbein, Marshall Goldsmith, and Richard Beckhard, eds., *The Organization of the Future* (San Francisco: Jossey-Bass, 1997), pp. 295–302.

28 Based on Richard L. Hughes, Robert C. Ginnett, and Gordon J. Curphy, *Leadership: Enhancing the Lessons of Experience* (Boston: Irwin McGraw-Hill, 1999), pp. 182–184.

29 Douglas McGregor, *The Human Side of Enterprise* (New York: McGraw-Hill, 1960).

30 J. Hall and S. M. Donnell, "Managerial Achievement: The Personal Side of Behavioral Theory," *Human Relations* 32 (1979), pp. 77–101.

31 Andrea Coombes, "Managers Rate Themselves High But Workers Prove Tough Critics," *The Wall Street Journal* (September 26, 2006), p. B8; and Jaclyne Badal, "Surveying the Field: Cracking the Glass Ceiling" (sidebar in Theory & Practice column), *The Wall Street Journal* (June 19, 2006), p. B3.

32 H. H. Kelley, "Attribution in Social Interaction," in E. Jones et al., eds., *Attribution: Perceiving the Causes of Behavior* (Morristown, NJ: General Learning Press, 1972).

33 Kevin Kelly, "Branching Out," *FSB* (December 2005-January 2006), p. 39.

34 Dorothy Leonard and Susaan Straus, "Putting Your Company's Whole Brain to Work," *Harvard Business Review* (July-August 1997), pp. 111–121.

35 Henry Mintzberg, "Planning on the Left Side and Managing on the Right," *Harvard Business Review* (July-August 1976), pp. 49–57; Richard Restak, "The Hemispheres of the Brain Have Minds of Their Own," *The New York Times* (January 25, 1976); and Robert Ornstein, *The Psychology of Consciousness* (San Francisco: W. H. Freeman, 1975).

36 This discussion is based on Ned Herrmann, *The Whole Brain Business Book* (New York: McGraw-Hill, 1996).

37 Herrmann, *The Whole Brain Business Book*, p. 103.

38 Herrmann, *The Whole Brain Business Book*, p. 179.

39 Jeff Bailey, "The Education of an Educated CEO," *Inc.* (December 2008), pp. 100–106.

40 Carl Jung, *Psychological Types* (London: Routledge and Kegan Paul, 1923).

41 Otto Kroeger and Janet M. Thuesen, *Type Talk* (New York: Delacorte Press, 1988); Kroeger and Thuesen, *Type Talk at Work* (New York: Dell, 1992); "Conference Proceedings," The Myers-Briggs Type Indicator and Leadership: An International Research Conference, January 12–14, 1994; and S. K. Hirsch, *MBTI™ Team Member's Guide* (Palo Alto, CA: Consulting Psychologists Press, 1992).

42 Reported in Lisa Takeuchi Cullen, "SATS for J-O-B-S," *Time* (April 3, 2006), p. 89.

43 Coeli Carr, "Redesigning the Management Psyche," *The New York Times* (Business Section), (May 26, 2002), p. 14.

44 Based on Mary H. McCaulley, "Research on the MBTI™ and Leadership: Taking the Critical First Step," Keynote Address, The Myers-Briggs Type Indicator and Leadership: An International Research Conference, January 12–14, 1994.

45 These techniques are based on Jamie Walters and Sarah Fenson, "Building Rapport with Different Personalities," *Inc.com* (March 2000), http://www.inc.com/articles/2000/03/17713.html; Tim Millett, "Learning to Work with Different Personality Types," http://ezinearticles.com/?Learning-To-Work-With-Different-Personality-Types&id=725606; and Carol Ritberter, "Understanding Personality: The Secret to Managing People," http://www.dreammanifesto.com/understanding-personality-the-secret-of-managing-people.html (accessed April 17, 2008).

Chapter 5 References

1 Thomas E. Ricks, "Charmed Forces: Army's 'Baby Generals' Take a Crash Course in Sensitivity Training," *The Wall Street Journal* (January 19, 1998), p. A1.

2 Warren Bennis, quoted in Tricia Bisoux, "What Makes Great Leaders," *BizEd* (September–October 2005), pp. 40–45.

3 Robert B. French, "The Teacher as Container of Anxiety: Psychoanalysis and the Role of Teacher," *Journal of Management Education* 21, no. 4 (November 1997), pp. 483–495.

4 This basic idea is found in a number of sources, among them: Jack Hawley, *Reawakening the Spirit in Work* (San Francisco: Berrett-Koehler, 1993); Aristotle, *The Nicomachean Ethics*, trans. by the Brothers of the English Dominican Province, rev. by Daniel J. Sullivan (Chicago: Encyclopedia Britannica, 1952); Alasdair MacIntyre, *After Virtue: A Study in Moral Theory* (Notre Dame, IN: University of Notre Dame Press, 1984); and Stephen Covey, *The Seven Habits of Highly Effective People: Powerful Lessons in Personal Change* (New York: Fireside Books/Simon & Schuster, 1990).

5 Vanessa Urch Druskat and Anthony T. Pescosolido, "The Content of Effective Teamwork Mental Models in Self-Managing Teams: Ownership, Learning, and Heedful Interrelating," *Human Relations* 55, no. 3 (2002), pp. 283–314; and Peter M. Senge, *The Fifth Discipline: The Art and Practice of the Learning Organization* (New York: Doubleday, 1990).

6 Druskat and Pescosolido, "The Content of Effective Teamwork Mental Models."

7 Adam Lashinsky, "Chaos by Design," *Fortune* (October 2, 2006), pp. 86–98.

8 The following discussion is based partly on Robert C. Benfari, *Understanding and Changing Your Management Style* (San Francisco: Jossey-Bass, 1999), pp. 66–93.

9 George Packer, *The Assassins' Gate: America in Iraq* (New York: Farrar, Straus & Giroux, 2005).

10 Micheline Maynard, "The Steady Optimist Who Oversaw G. M.'s Decline," *The New York Times* (March 30, 2009), http://www.nytimes.com/2009/03/30/business/30wagoner.html?emc=etal (accessed March 31, 2009); Bill Vlasic, "Abrupt Transition for G.M. with Wagoner's Dismissal," *International Herald Tribune* (April 2, 2009), p. 19; John D. Stoll, "Shake-Up at GM: Wagoner, with Knack for Survival, Hits Dead End," *The Wall Street Journal Asia*

(March 31, 2009), p. 15; Alex Taylor III, "GM and Me," *Fortune* (December 8, 2008), pp. 92–100; Bill Vlasic, "A G. M. Vow to Get Leaner Now Includes Its Top Ranks," *The New York Times* (July 11, 2009), p. B1; and Jeremy Smerd, "Outsider Thinking for GM HR," *Workforce Management* (August 17, 2009), p. 1.

11 Vlasic, "Abrupt Transition for G.M"; Bill Vlasic, "G. M. Chairman Vows to Defend Market Share," *The New York Times* (August 5, 2009), p. B1; and David Hendricks, "Whitacre Pitches 1st GM Ad As If He Had Written It," *San Antonio Express-News* (September 19, 2009), p. C1.

12 Anthony J. Mayo and Nitin Nohria, *In Their Time: The Greatest Business Leaders of the 20th Century* (Boston: Harvard Business School Press, 2005).

13 Geoffrey Colvin, "The Most Valuable Quality in a Manager," *Fortune* (December 29, 1997), pp. 279–280; and Marlene Piturro, "Mindshift," *Management Review* (May 1999), pp. 46–51.

14 Jeff D. Opdyke, "Decremental? Fitting Word for Ugly Times," *The Wall Street Journal* (March 2, 2009), p. C1.

15 Geoffrey Colvin, "Managing in Chaos," *Fortune* (October 2, 2006), pp. 76–82.

16 Gary Hamel, "Why . . . It's Better to Question Answers Than to Answer Questions," *Across the Board* (November–December 2000), pp. 42–46; and Jane C. Linder and Susan Cantrell, "It's All in the Mind (set)," *Across the Board* (May–June 2002), pp. 39–42.

17 Reported in Sharon Begley, "People Believe a 'Fact' That Fits Their Views, Even If It's Clearly False" (Science Journal column), *The Wall Street Journal* (February 4, 2005), p. A8.

18 Anil K. Gupta and Vijay Govindarajan, "Cultivating a Global Mindset," *Academy of Management Executive* 16, no. 1 (2002), pp. 116–126.

19 Hamel, "Why . . . It's Better to Question Answers Than to Answer Questions"; and Colvin, "Managing in Chaos."

20 Daniel Levinthal and Claus Rerup, "Crossing an Apparent Chasm: Bridging Mindful and Less-Mindful Perspectives on Organizational Learning," *Organization Science* 17, no. 4 (August 2006), pp. 502–513; and Ellen Langer and John Sviokla, "An Evaluation of Charisma from the Mindfulness Perspective," unpublished manuscript, Harvard University. Part of this discussion is also drawn from Richard L. Daft and Robert H. Lengel, *Fusion Leadership: Unlocking the Subtle Forces That Change People and Organizations* (San Francisco: Berrett-Koehler, 1998).

21 T. K. Das, "Educating Tomorrow's Managers: The Role of Critical Thinking," *The International Journal of Organizational Analysis* 2, no. 4 (October 1994), pp. 333–360.

22 Carol Hymowitz, "Building a Board That's Independent, Strong, and Effective" (In the Lead column), *The Wall Street Journal* (November 19, 2002), p. B1.

23 James R. Hagerty, "Directors Are Faulted at Home Loan Banks," *The Wall Street Journal* (May 23–24, 2009), p. A3.

24 Bernard M. Bass, *Leadership and Performance Beyond Expectations* (New York: The Free Press, 1985); and B. M. Bass, *New Paradigm Leadership: An Inquiry into Transformational Leadership* (Alexandria, VA: U.S. Army Research Institute for the Behavioral and Social Sciences, 1996).

25 Leslie Wexner, quoted in Rebecca Quick, "A Makeover That Began at the Top," *The Wall Street Journal* (May 25, 2000), pp. B1, B4.

26 The Pike Syndrome has been discussed in multiple sources.

27 Jeanne Whalen, "Theory & Practice: Chance Turns a Teacher into a CEO—Religion Lecturer Leaves Academic Path and Learns to Run a Biotech Start-Up," *The Wall Street Journal* (October 17, 2005), p. B4.

28 Chris Argyris, *Flawed Advice and the Management Trap* (New York: Oxford University Press, 2000); and Eileen C. Shapiro, "Managing in the Cappuccino Economy" (review of *Flawed Advice*), *Harvard Business Review* (March–April 2000), pp. 177–183.

29 Rajat Gupta, quoted in *Fast Company* (September 1999), p. 120.

30 This section is based on Peter M. Senge, *The Fifth Discipline: The Art and Practice of the Learning Organization* (New York: Doubleday, 1990); John D. Sterman, "Systems Dynamics Modeling: Tools for Learning in a Complex World," *California Management Review* 43, no. 4 (Summer, 2001), pp. 8–25; and Ron Zemke, "Systems Thinking," *Training* (February 2001), pp. 40–46.

31 These examples are cited in Sterman, "Systems Dynamics Modeling."

32 Peter M. Senge, Charlotte Roberts, Richard B. Ross, Bryan J. Smith, and Art Kleiner, *The Fifth Discipline Fieldbook* (New York: Currency/Doubleday, 1994), p. 87.

33 Senge, *The Fifth Discipline.*

34 Timothy A. Judge, Amy E. Colbert, and Remus Ilies, "Intelligence and Leadership: A Quantitative Review and Test of Theoretical Propositions," *Journal of Applied Psychology* (June 2004), pp. 542–552.

35 Daniel Goleman, *Emotional Intelligence: Why It Can Matter More Than IQ* (New York: Bantam Books, 1995); John D. Mayer and David Caruso, "The Effective Leader: Understanding and Applying Emotional Intelligence," *Ivey Business Journal* (November–December 2002); Pamela Kruger, "A Leader's Journey," *Fast Company* (June 1999), pp. 116–129; and Hendrie Weisinger, *Emotional Intelligence at Work* (San Francisco: Jossey-Bass, 1998).

36 Based on Goleman, *Emotional Intelligence;* Goleman, "Leadership That Gets Results," *Harvard Business Review* (March–April 2000), pp. 79–90; J. D. Mayer, D. R. Caruso, and P. Salovey, "Emotional Intelligence Meets Traditional Standards for an Intelligence," *Intelligence* 27, no. 4 (1999), pp. 266–298; Neal M. Ashkanasy and Catherine S. Daus, "Emotion in the Workplace: The New Challenge for Managers," *Academy of Management Executive* 16, no.1 (2002), pp. 76–86; and Weisinger, *Emotional Intelligence at Work.*

37 Studies reported in Stephen Xavier, "Are You at the Top of Your Game? Checklist for Effective Leaders," *Journal of Business Strategy* 26, no. 3 (2005), pp. 35–42.

38 This section is based largely on Goleman, *Emotional Intelligence: Why It Can Matter More Than IQ,* pp. 289–290.

39 Jerry Krueger and Emily Killham, "At Work, Feeling Good Matters," *Gallup Management Journal* (December 8, 2005).

40 Goleman, "Leadership That Gets Results"; and Richard E. Boyatzis and Daniel Goleman, *The Emotional Competence Inventory— University Edition* (Boston, MA: The Hay Group, 2001).

41 Dave Marcum, Steve Smith, and Mahan Khalsa, "The Marshmallow Conundrum," *Across the Board* (March–April 2004), pp. 26–30.

42 Weisinger, *Emotional Intelligence at Work.*

43 Alan Farnham, "Are You Smart Enough to Keep Your Job?" *Fortune* (January 15, 1996), pp. 34–47.

44 Peter J. Frost, "Handling the Hurt: A Critical Skill for Leaders," *Ivey Management Journal* (January–February 2004).

45 Rolf W. Habbel, "The Human[e] Factor: Nurturing a Leadership Culture," *Strategy & Business* 26 (First Quarter 2002), pp. 83–89.

46 Marilyn Adams, "Straightened Up and Flying Right," *USA Today* (February 26, 2007), http://www.usatoday.com (accessed February 26, 2007); and Diane Brady, "Being Mean Is So Last Millennium," *BusinessWeek* (January 15, 2007), p. 61.

47 Research study results reported in Goleman, "Leadership That Gets Results."

48 Michael Sokolove, "Follow Me," *The New York Times Magazine* (February 2006), p. 96.

49 Diane Coutu, "Leadership Lessons from Abraham Lincoln," *Harvard Business Review* (April 2009), pp. 43–47.

50 Xavier, "Are You at the Top of Your Game?"

51 Jeff Bailey, "Outsize Personality Tries to Create a Regional Airline to Match," *The New York Times* (January 19, 2007), p. C1.

52 E. Hatfield, J. T. Cacioppo, and R. L. Rapson, *Emotional Contagion* (New York: Cambridge University Press, 1994).

53 Study by Daniel Goleman, co-chairman of The Consortium for Research on Emotional Intelligence in Organizations, reported in Diann Daniel, "Soft Skills for CIOs and Aspiring CIOs: Four Ways to Boost Your Emotional Intelligence," *CIO* (June 25, 2007), http://www.cio.com (accessed October 18, 2007).

54 Daniel, "Soft Skills for CIOs."

55 P. J. Jordan, N. M. Ashkanasy, C. E. J. Härtel, and G. S. Hooper, "Workgroup Emotional Intelligence: Scale Development and Relationship to Team Process Effectiveness and Goal Focus," *Human Resource Management Review* 12, no. 2 (Summer 2002), pp. 195–214.

56 This discussion is based on Vanessa Urch Druskat and Steven B. Wolf, "Building the Emotional Intelligence of Groups," *Harvard Business Review* (March 2001), pp. 81–90.

57 Daniel Goleman, Richard Boyatzis, and Annie McKee, "The Emotional Reality of Teams," *Journal of Organizational Excellence* (Spring 2002), pp. 55–65.

58 This discussion is based in part on Kathleen D. Ryan and Daniel K. Oestreich, *Driving Fear out of the Workplace: How to Overcome the Invisible Barriers to Quality, Productivity, and Innovation* (San Francisco: Jossey-Bass, 1991); and Scott A. Snook, "Love and Fear and the Modern Boss," *Harvard Business Review* (January 2008), pp. 16–17.

59 S. Lyubomirsky, L. King, and E. Diener, "The Benefits of Frequent Positive Affect: Does Happiness Lead to Success?" *Psychological Bulletin* 131, no. 6 (2005), pp. 803–855; R. Cropanzano and T. A. Wright, "When a 'Happy' Worker Is Really a 'Productive' Worker: A Review and Further Refinement of the Happy-Productive Worker Theory," *Consulting Psychology Journal: Practice and Research* 53, no. 3 (2001), pp. 182–199; and S. G. Barsade and D. E. Gibson, "Why Does Affect Matter in Organizations?" *Academy of Management Perspectives* 21, no. 1 (2007), pp. 36–59.

60 Carol Hymowitz, "Business Is Personal, So Managers Need to Harness Emotions" (In the Lead column), *The Wall Street Journal* (November 13, 2006), p. B1.

61 David E. Dorsey, "Escape from the Red Zone," *Fast Company* (April/May 1997), pp. 116–127.

62 This section is based on Ryan and Oestreich, *Driving Fear out of the Workplace;* and Therese R. Welter, "Reducing Employee Fear:

Get Workers and Managers to Speak Their Minds," *Small Business Report* (April 1991), pp. 15–18.

63 Ryan and Oestreich, *Driving Fear out of the Workplace*, p. 43.

64 Donald G. Zauderer, "Integrity: An Essential Executive Quality," *Business Forum* (Fall 1992), pp. 12–16.

65 Kristy J. O'Hara, "Role Player," *Smart Business Akron/Canton* (March 2009), p. 14.

66 Hawley, *Reawakening the Spirit at Work*, p. 55; and Rodney Ferris, "How Organizational Love Can Improve Leadership," *Organizational Dynamics* 16, no. 4 (Spring 1988), pp. 40–52.

67 Barbara Moses, "It's All About Passion," *Across the Board* (May–June 2001), pp. 55–58.

68 Joseph Campbell with Bill Moyers, *The Power of Myth* (New York: Doubleday, 1988).

69 Covey, *The Seven Habits of Highly Effective People*, p. 80.

70 Gregg Zoroya, "Coping After a Hero Dies Saving You in Iraq," *USA Today* (September 20, 2007), p. A1; "Marine to Receive Medal of Honor for Iraq Heroism," http://www.cnn.com/2006/US/11/10/medal .honor (accessed April 8, 2009); and "Army Sgt. James Witkowski," *Military Times: Honor the Fallen,* http://www.militarycity.com/valor/ 1220880.html (accessed April 8, 2009).

71 Zoroya, "Coping After a Hero Dies Saving You."

72 Hyler Bracey, Jack Rosenblum, Aubrey Sanford, and Roy Trueblood, *Managing from the Heart* (New York: Dell Publishing, 1993), p. 192.

73 Madan Birla with Cecilia Miller Marshall, *Balanced Life and Leadership Excellence* (Memphis, TN: The Balance Group, 1997), pp. 76–77.

74 Ferris, "How Organizational Love Can Improve Leadership."

Chapter 6 References

1 Bill George, "The Courage to Say 'No' to Wall Street" (segment in "America's Best Leaders"), *U.S. News & World Report* (December 1–December 8, 2008), pp. 34–51. This example is based on George, "The Courage to Say 'No' to Wall Street"; Andrew Davidson, "Xerox Saviour in the Spotlight," *Sunday Times* (June 1, 2008), p. 6; and "Anne Mulcahy Becomes the First Woman CEO to Receive *Chief Executive* Magazine's 'CEO of the Year' Award," *PR Newswire* (June 3, 2008).

2 George, "The Courage to Say 'No' to Wall Street."

3 Alan Schwartz, quoted in Roger Parloff, "Wall Street: It's Payback Time," *Fortune* (January 19, 2009), pp. 56–69.

4 Quoted in Betsy Morris, "The Accidental CEO," *Fortune* (June 23, 2003), pp. 58–67.

5 John Chase, "Delay Requested for Indictment; 3 More Months Sought in Case Against Governor," *The Chicago Tribune* (January 1, 2009), p. 4; Glenn R. Simpson and David Crawford, "How Two Scandals Might Overlap; German Investigators Look for Links Between Siemens, Russian Telecom Minister," *The Wall Street Journal* (February 16, 2007), p. A3; Alistair MacDonald and Stephen Fidler, "School for Scandal," *The Wall Street Journal* (May 16–17, 2009), p. W1; Christopher Graveline, "The Unlearned Lessons of Abu Ghraib," *The Washington Post* (October 19, 2006), p. A29; and Rebecca Leung, "Torture, Cover-Up at Gitmo?" *CBSNews.com,* http://www.cbsnews.com/stories/2005/04/28/60minutes/main691602 .shtml (accessed May 26, 2009).

6 Marist College Institute for Public Opinion and Knights of Columbus survey, results reported in Kevin Turner, "Corporate Execs: Nobody Trusts Us; U.S. Lacks Confidence in Business Ethics, Poll Says," *Florida Times Union* (February 27, 2009), p. A1.

7 Ronald W. Clement, "Just How Unethical Is American Business?" *Business Horizons* 49 (2006), pp. 313–327.

8 Roger Parloff, "Wall Street: It's Payback Time," *Fortune* (January 19, 2009), pp. 56–69.

9 Gary R. Weaver, Linda Klebe Treviño, and Bradley Agle, "'Somebody I Look Up To': Ethical Role Models in Organizations," *Organizational Dynamics* 34, no. 4 (2005), pp. 313–330.

10 Chuck Salter, paraphrasing Bill George, former CEO of Medtronic, in "Mr. Inside Speaks Out," *Fast Company* (September 2004), pp. 92–93.

11 David Wessel, "Venal Sins: Why the Bad Guys of the Boardroom Emerged en Masse," *The Wall Street Journal* (June 20, 2002), pp. A1, A6.

12 Simon Romero and Seth Schiesel, "Hubris and the Fall of a Telecommunications Empire," *The New York Times* (March 3, 2004), p. C1.

13 Wessel, "Venal Sins."

14 Michiko Kakutani, "The Tsunami That Buried a Wall Street Giant," *The New York Times* (March 10, 2009), p. C4.

15 Jamie Dimon, "America's Traditional Strengths Will Win Out," *Fortune* (May 4, 2009), p. 66.

16 This section is based on Donald G. Zauderer, "Integrity: An Essential Executive Quality," *Business Forum* (Fall, 1992), pp. 12–16.

17 James Bandler with Doris Burke, "What Cuomo Wants from Wall Street," *Fortune* (December 8, 2008), pp. 103–110; Valerie Bauerlein and Ruth Simon, "WaMu Board Shields Executives' Bonuses," *The Wall Street Journal* (March 5, 2008), p. A3; and Nick Mathiason, "Big Players Fall Amid the Profits of Doom: Some Lost Out, Others Dodged Bullets, Norway Did Well—and Junkets Went On," *The Observer* (October 12, 2008), p. 8.

18 Patricia Wallington, "Honestly?!" *CIO* (March 15, 2003), pp. 41–42.

19 Carly Fiorina, "Corporate Leadership and the Crisis," *The Wall Street Journal* (December 12, 2008), p. A19.

20 Al Gini, "Moral Leadership and Business Ethics," *The Journal of Leadership Studies* 4, no. 4 (Fall 1997), pp. 64–81.

21 Henry Ford, Sr., quoted by Thomas Donaldson, *Corporations and Morality* (Upper Saddle River, NJ: Prentice Hall, 1982), p. 57.

22 Michael E. Brown and Linda K. Treviño, "Ethical Leadership: A Review and Future Directions," *The Leadership Quarterly* 17 (2006), pp. 595–616; Darin W. White and Emily Lean, "The Impact of Perceived Leader Integrity on Subordinates in a Work Team Environment," *Journal of Business Ethics* 81 (2008), pp. 767–778; Gary R. Weaver, Linda K. Treviño, and Bradley Agle, "'Somebody I

Look Up To': Ethical Role Models in Organizations," *Organizational Dynamics* 34, no. 4 (2005), pp. 313–330; and Joseph L. Badaracco, Jr., and Allen P. Webb, "Business Ethics: A View from the Trenches," *California Management Review* 37, no. 2 (Winter 1995), pp. 8–28.

23 J. Lynn Lynsford, "Piloting Boeing's New Course," *The Wall Street Journal* (June 13, 2006), pp. B1, B3; and Kathryn Kranhold, "U.S. Firms Raise Ethics Focus," *The Wall Street Journal* (November 28, 2005), p. B4.

24 Joseph Weber, "The New Ethics Enforcers," *BusinessWeek* (February 13, 2006), pp. 76–77.

25 Jere Longman, "Alabama Fires Coach for Off-Field Indiscretions," *The New York Times* (May 4, 2003), Section 8, 1.

26 Bill George, "The Master Gives It Back" and "Truly Authentic Leadership" segments in "Special Report: America's Best Leaders," *U.S. News & World Report* (October 30, 2006), pp. 50–87; and David Segal, "In Letter, Buffett Accepts Blame and Faults Others," *The New York Times* (March 1, 2009), p. A16.

27 Curtis C. Verschoor and Elizabeth A. Murphy, "The Financial Performance of Large U.S. Firms and Those with Global Prominence: How Do the Best Corporate Citizens Rate?" *Business and Society Review* 107, no. 3 (Fall 2002), pp. 371–381.

28 Phred Dvorak, "Finding the Best Measure of 'Corporate Citizenship,'" *The Wall Street Journal* (July 2, 2007), p. B3.

29 Donald G. Zauderer, "Integrity: An Essential Executive Quality," *Business Forum* (Fall 1992), pp. 12–16.

30 James M. Kouzes and Barry Z. Posner, *Credibility: How Leaders Gain and Lose It, Why People Demand It* (San Francisco: Jossey-Bass, 1993), p. 255.

31 Viktor E. Frankl, *Man's Search for Meaning* (New York: Pocket Books, 1959), p. 104.

32 Lawrence Kohlberg, "Moral Stages and Moralization: The Cognitive Developmental Approach," in Thomas Likona, ed., *Moral Development and Behavior: Theory, Research, and Social Issues* (Austin, TX: Holt, Rinehart and Winston, 1976), pp. 31–53; Linda K. Treviño, Gary R. Weaver, and Scott J. Reynolds, "Behavioral Ethics in Organizations: A Review," *Journal of Management* 32, no. 6 (December 2006), pp. 951–990; Jill W. Graham, "Leadership, Moral Development, and Citizenship Behavior," *Business Ethics Quarterly* 5, no. 1 (January 1995), pp. 43–54; James Weber, "Exploring the Relationship Between Personal Values and Moral Reasoning," *Human Relations* 46, no. 4 (April 1993), pp. 435–463; and Duane M. Covrig, "The Organizational Context of Moral Dilemmas: The Role of Moral Leadership in Administration in Making and Breaking Dilemmas," *The Journal of Leadership Studies* 7, no. 1 (2000), pp. 40–59.

33 Tom Morris, *If Aristotle Ran General Motors* (New York: Henry Holt, 1997).

34 J. R. Rest, D. Narvaez, M. J. Bebeau, and S. J. Thoma, *Postconventional Moral Thinking: A Neo-Kohlbergian Approach* (Mahwah, NJ: Lawrence Erlbaum, 1999).

35 James Weber, "Exploring the Relationship Between Personal Values and Moral Reasoning," *Human Relations* 46, no. 4 (April 1993), pp. 435–463.

36 White and Lean, "The Impact of Perceived Leader Integrity on Subordinates in a Work Team Environment"; Peter Block, "Reassigning Responsibility," *Sky* (February 1994), pp. 26–31; and David P. McCaffrey, Sue R. Faerman, and David W. Hart, "The Appeal and Difficulty of Participative Systems," *Organization Science* 6, no. 6 (November–December 1995), pp. 603–627.

37 Block, "Reassigning Responsibility."

38 This discussion of stewardship is based on Peter Block, *Stewardship: Choosing Service over Self-Interest* (San Francisco: Berrett-Koehler, 1993), pp. 29–31; Block, "Reassigning Responsibility"; and Morela Hernandez, "Promoting Stewardship Behavior in Organizations: A Leadership Model," *Journal of Business Ethics* 80, no. 1 (June 2008), pp. 121–128.

39 Lawrence G. Foster, *Robert Wood Johnson—The Gentleman Rebel* (Lemont, PA: Lillian Press, 1999); and John Cunniff, "Businessman's Honesty, Integrity Lesson for Today," *Johnson City Press* (May 28, 2000).

40 Sen Sendjaya and James C. Sarros, "Servant Leadership: Its Origin, Development, and Application in Organizations," *Journal of Leadership and Organizational Studies* 9, no. 2 (2002), pp. 57–64.

41 Leigh Buchanan, "In Praise of Selflessness; Why the Best Leaders Are Servants," *Inc.* (May 2007), pp. 33–35; Micheline Maynard, "The Corner Deli That Dared to Break Out of the Neighborhood," *The New York Times* (May 3, 2007), p. C1; and Bo Burlingham, "The Coolest Small Company in America," *Inc.* (January 2003), pp. 65–74.

42 Robert Townsend, "Leader at Work," *Across the Board* (January 2001), pp. 13–14.

43 Corey Dade, "Changing Pilots; After Delta's Recovery, New Turbulence Stirs," *The Wall Street Journal* (October 4, 2007), p. A1; and Claudia Deutsch, "Volunteering Abroad to Climb at I.B.M.," *The New York Times* (March 26, 2008), p. C4.

44 Sendjaya and Sarros, "Servant Leadership: Its Origin, Development, and Application in Organizations." Examples include B. M. Bass, "The Future of Leadership in Learning Organizations," *The Journal of Leadership Studies* 7, no. 3 (2000), pp. 18–40; I. H. Buchen, "Servant Leadership: A Model for Future Faculty and Future Institutions," *The Journal of Leadership Studies* 5, no. 1 (1998), p. 125; Y. Choi and R. R. Mai-Dalton, "On the Leadership Function of Self-Sacrifice," *Leadership Quarterly* 9, no. 4 (1998), pp. 475–501; and R. F. Russel, "The Role of Values in Servant Leadership," *Leadership and Organizational Development Journal* 22, no. 2 (2001), pp. 76–83.

45 Robert K. Greenleaf, *Servant Leadership: A Journey into the Nature of Legitimate Power and Greatness* (Mahwah, NJ: Paulist Press, 1977), p. 7.

46 The following is based on Greenleaf, *Servant Leadership;* Walter Kiechel III, "The Leader as Servant," *Fortune* (May 4, 1992), pp. 121–122; and Mary Sue Polleys, "One University's Response to the Anti-Leadership Vaccine: Developing Servant Leaders," *The Journal of Leadership Studies* 8, no. 3 (2002), pp. 117–130.

47 C. William Pollard, "The Leader Who Serves," in Frances Hesselbein, Marshall Goldsmith, and Richard Beckhard, eds., *The Leader of the Future* (San Francisco: Jossey-Bass, 1996), pp. 241–248; and C. W. Pollard, "The Leader Who Serves," *Strategy and Leadership* (September–October 1997), pp. 49–51.

48 John McCain, "In Search of Courage," *Fast Company* (September 2004), pp. 53–56.

49 Richard L. Daft and Robert H. Lengel, *Fusion Leadership: Unlocking the Subtle Forces That Change People and Organizations* (San Francisco: Berrett-Koehler, 1998).

50 McCain, "In Search of Courage."

51 Reported in Nando Pelusi, "The Right Way to Rock the Boat," *Psychology Today* (May–June 2006), pp. 60–61.

52 Jeffrey Zaslow, "Kids on the Bus: The Overlooked Role of Teenagers in the Civil-Rights Era," *The Wall Street Journal* (November 11, 2005), p. D1.

53 Walter Kirn, "The Age of Neo-Remorse," *The New York Times Magazine* (January 25, 2009), pp. 9–10; Christian Plumb and Dan Wilchins, "Lehman CEO Fuld's Hubris Contributed to Meltdown," *Reuters.com*, http://www.reuters.com (accessed March 28, 2009); and "Former Lehman Brothers CEO Subpoenaed," *CNNMoney.com*, http://www.cnnmoney.com (accessed March 28, 2009).

54 Jim Michaels, "Behind Success in Ramadi an Army Colonel's Gamble Pays Off in Iraq," *USA Today* (May 1, 2007), p. A1; and Greg Jaffe, "Midlevel Officers Show Enterprise, Helping U.S. Reduce Violence in Iraq," *The Wall Street Journal* (December 29, 2007), p. A1.

55 Jaffe, "Midlevel Officers Show Enterprise."

56 Reported in Nido R. Qubein, *Stairway to Success: The Complete Blueprint for Personal and Professional Achievement* (New York: John Wiley & Sons, 1997).

57 Michael Luo, "Revisiting a Social Experiment, and the Fear That Goes with It," *The New York Times* (September 14, 2004), Section B, p. 1.

58 Jerry B. Harvey, *The Abilene Paradox and Other Meditations on Management* (Lexington, MA: Lexington Books, 1988), pp. 13–15.

59 Kathleen K. Reardon, "Courage as a Skill," *Harvard Business Review* (January 2007), pp. 58–64.

60 A. J. Vogl, "Risky Work" (an interview with Max DuPree), *Across the Board* (July/August 1993), pp. 27–31.

61 William H. Peace, "The Hard Work of Being a Soft Manager," *Harvard Business Review* (November–December 1991), pp. 40–47.

62 Janet P. Near and Marcia P. Miceli, "Effective Whistle-Blowing," *Academy of Management Review* 20, no. 3 (1995), pp. 679–708.

63 Martin Fackler, "Loyalty No Longer Blind for Salarymen in Japan; Whistle-Blowers a Sign of Changing Times," *International Herald Tribune* (June 7, 2008), p. 1.

64 Jayne O'Donnell, "Some Whistle-Blowers Don't Want Lost Jobs," *USA Today* (August 1, 2005), p. B2.

65 Kerry Kennedy Cuomo, "'Courage Begins with One Voice,'" *Parade Magazine* (September 24, 2000), pp. 6–8.

66 Joseph Rebello, "Radical Ways of Its CEO Are a Boon to Bank," *The Wall Street Journal* (March 20, 1995), p. B1.

67 James M. Kouzes and Barry Z. Posner, *The Leadership Challenge: How to Get Extraordinary Things Done in Organizations* (San Francisco: Jossey-Bass, 1988).

68 Linda Tischler, "The Trials of ImClone," *Fast Company* (September 2004), pp. 88–89.

69 Michael Warshaw, ed., "Great Comebacks," *Success* (July/August 1995), pp. 33–46.

70 Ira Cheleff, *The Courageous Follower: Standing Up to and for Our Leaders* (San Francisco: Berrett-Koehler, 1995).

71 This section is based on Reardon "Courage as a Skill."

72 Example reported in Reardon, "Courage as a Skill."

Chapter 7 References

1   Irvin D. Yalom, with Ben Yalom, "Mad About Me," *Inc.* (December 1998), pp. 37–38.

2   Story told in Robert McGarvey, "And You Thought Your Boss Was Bad," *American Way* (May 1, 2006), pp. 69–74.

3   Barbara Kellerman, "Pecking Orders; Why Some Lead and Others Follow," *The Conference Board Review* (March–April 2008), pp. 49–51.

4   Robert E. Kelley, "In Praise of Followers," *Harvard Business Review* (November/December 1988), pp. 142–148.

5   Bernard M. Bass, *Bass & Stogdill's Handbook of Leadership,* 3rd ed. (New York: The Free Press, 1990).

6   Ira Cheleff, *The Courageous Follower: Standing Up To and For Our Leaders* (San Francisco: Berrett-Koehler, 1995).

7   Ira Cheleff, "Learn the Art of Followership," *Government Executive* (February 1997), p. 51.

8   Reported in Del Jones, "What Do These 3 Photos Have in Common? They Show Leaders and Their Followers, Winning Combos," *USA Today* (December 10, 2003), p. 1B.

9   Keith H. Hammonds, "You Can't Lead Without Making Sacrifices," *Fast Company* (June 2001), pp. 106–116.

10 Robert E. Kelley, *The Power of Followership* (New York: Doubleday, 1992).

11 Ibid., p. 101.

12 Ibid., pp. 111–112.

13 Ibid., pp. 117–118.

14 Based on an incident reported in "Ask Inc.," *Inc.* (March 2007), pp. 81–82.

15 Kelley, *The Power of Followership,* p. 123.

16 Melanie Trottman, "Baggers Get the Sack, But Dawn Marshall Still Excels as One," *The Wall Street Journal* (May 2, 2003), pp. A1, A6.

17 David N. Berg, "Resurrecting the Muse: Followership in Organizations," presented at the 1996 International Society for the Psychoanalytic Study of Organizations (ISPSO) Symposium, New York, NY, June 14–16, 1996.

18 Cheleff, *The Courageous Follower: Standing Up To and For Our Leaders.*

19 Jones, "What Do These 3 Photos Have in Common?"

20 Major (General Staff) Dr. Ulrich F. Zwygart, "How Much Obedience Does an Officer Need? Beck, Tresckow, and Stauffenberg—Examples of Integrity and Moral Courage for Today's Officer," Combat Studies Institute; U.S. Army Command and General Staff College, Fort Leavenworth, Kansas, http://www. cgsc.army.mil/carl/resources/csi/Zwygart/zwygart.asp (accessed March 29, 2007).

21 "Open Mouth, Open Career" (sidebar) in Michael Warshaw, "Open Mouth, Close Career?" *Fast Company* (December 1998), p. 240.

22 Merle MacIsaac, "Born Again Basket Case," *Canadian Business* (May 1993), pp. 38–44.

23 Nick Wingfield, "Apple's No. 2 Has Low Profile, High Impact," *The Wall Street Journal* (October 16, 2006), pp. B1, B9; and Yukari Iwatani Kane and Joann S. Lublin, "Absent Jobs, Cook Emerges as Key to Apple's Core," *The Wall Street Journal* (June 23, 2009), p. B1

24 Greg Jaffe, "The Two-Star Rebel; For Gen. Batiste, a Tour in Iraq Turned a Loyal Soldier into Rumsfeld's Most Unexpected Critic," *The Wall Street Journal* (May 13, 2006), p. A1.

25 Stephen R. Covey, *The Seven Habits of Highly Effective People: Powerful Lessons in Personal Change* (New York: Simon & Schuster, 1989).

26 This discussion of the seven habits is based on Covey, *The Seven Habits of Highly Effective People;* and Don Hellriegel, John W. Slocum, Jr., and Richard Woodman, *Organizational Behavior,* 8th ed. (Cincinnati, OH: South-Western College Publishing, 1998), pp. 350–352.

27 Stephen R. Covey, *The Seven Habits of Highly Effective People* (New York: Fireside/Simon & Schuster, 1990), p. 72.

28 Jia Lynn Yang and Jerry Useem, "Cross-Train Your Brain," *Fortune* (October 30, 2006), pp. 135–136.

29 These are based on Larry Bossidy, "What Your Leader Expects of You," *Harvard Business Review* (April 2007), pp. 58–65; and Peter F. Drucker, "Drucker on Management: Managing the Boss," *The Wall Street Journal* (August 1, 1986).

30 Bossidy. "What Your Leader Expects of You."

31 David K. Hurst, "How to Manage Your Boss," *Strategy+Business,* no. 28 (Third Quarter 2002), pp. 99–103; Joseph L. Badaracco, Jr., *Leading Quietly: An Unorthodox Guide to Doing the Right Thing* (Boston: Harvard Business School Press, 2002); and Michael Useem, *Leading Up: How to Lead Your Boss So You Both Win* (New York: Crown Business, 2001).

32 Len Schlesinger, "It Doesn't Take a Wizard to Build a Better Boss," *Fast Company* (June/July 1996), pp. 102–107.

33 Hurst, "How to Manage Your Boss."

34 Judith Sills, "When You're Smarter Than Your Boss," *Psychology Today* (May–June 2006), pp. 58–59; Sarah Kershaw, "My Other Family Is the Office," *The New York Times* (December 4, 2008), p. E1; and Frank Pittman, "How to Manage Mom and Dad," *Psychology Today* (November/December 1994), pp. 44–74.

35 Kelley, "In Praise of Followers."

36 Chaleff, *The Courageous Follower: Standing Up To and For Our Leaders;* and John J. Gabarro and John P. Kotter, "Managing Your Boss," *Harvard Business Review,* "Best of HBR" (January 2005), pp. 92–99.

37 Christopher Hegarty, *How to Manage Your Boss* (New York: Ballantine, 1985), p. 147.

38 Ibid.

39 Chaleff, *The Courageous Follower: Standing Up To and For Our Leaders.*

40 Peter B. Smith and Mark F. Peterson, *Leadership, Organizations and Culture* (London: Sage Publications, 1988), pp. 144–145.

41 Pittman, "How to Manage Mom and Dad."

42 Hegarty, *How to Manage Your Boss.*

43 Pittman, "How to Manage Mom and Dad."

44 Berg, "Resurrecting the Muse."

45 James M. Kouzes and Barry Z. Posner, *Credibility: How Leaders Gain and Lose It, Why People Demand It* (San Francisco: Jossey-Bass, 1993).

46 This section is based largely on Bossidy, "What Your Leader Expects of You."

47 See Gary P. Latham and Edwin A. Locke, "Enhancing the Benefits and Overcoming the Pitfalls of Goal Setting," *Organizational Dynamics* 35, no. 4 (2006), pp. 332–338; Edwin A. Locke and Gary P. Latham, "Building a Practically Useful Theory of Goal Setting and Task Motivation: A 35-Year Odyssey," *The American Psychologist* 57, no. 9 (September 2002), p. 705ff; Gary P. Latham and Edwin A. Locke, "Self-Regulation Through Goal Setting," *Organizational Behavior and Human Decision Processes* 50, no. 2 (1991), pp. 212–247; G. P. Latham and G. H. Seijts, "The Effects of Proximal and Distal Goals on Performance of a Moderately Complex Task," *Journal of Organizational Behavior* 20, no. 4 (1999), pp. 421–428; P. C. Early, T. Connolly, and G. Ekegren, "Goals, Strategy Development, and Task Performance: Some Limits on the Efficacy of Goal Setting," *Journal of Applied Psychology* 74 (1989), pp. 24–33; and E. A. Locke, "Toward a Theory of Task Motivation and Incentives," *Organizational Behavior and Human Performance* 3 (1968), pp. 157–189.

48 McKinsey & Company's *War for Talent 2000 Survey,* reported in E. Michaels, H. Handfield-Jones, and B. Axelrod, *The War for Talent* (Boston: Harvard Business School Press, 2001), p. 100.

49 Jay M. Jackman and Myra H. Strober, "Fear of Feedback," *Harvard Business Review* (April 2003), pp. 101–108; and Bossidy, "What Your Leader Expects of You."

50 John C. Kunich and Richard I. Lester, "Leadership and the Art of Feedback: Feeding the Hands That Back Us," *The Journal of Leadership Studies* 3, no. 4 (1996), pp. 3–22.

51 Based on Mark D. Cannon and Robert Witherspoon, "Actionable Feedback: Unlocking the Power of Learning and Performance Improvement," *Academy of Management Executive* 19, no. 2 (2005), pp. 120–134.

52 Quoted in Jared Sandberg, "Avoiding Conflicts, The Too-Nice Boss Makes Matters Worse," *The Wall Street Journal* (February 26, 2008), p. B1.

53 Sandberg, "Avoiding Conflicts."

54 Based on "Closing Gaps and Improving Performance: The Basics of Coaching," excerpt, originally published as Chapter 4 of *Performance Management: Measure and Improve the Effectiveness of Your Employees* (Boston: MA: Harvard Business School Press, 2006).

55 Betsy Morris, "Dynamic Duo," *Fortune* (October 15, 2007), pp. 78–86.

56 Patrick Sweeney, "Developing Leadership Potential Through Coaching," *Chief Learning Officer* (March 2009), p. 22ff.

57 This table and the discussion are based on Andrea D. Ellinger and Robert P. Bostrom, "An Examination of Managers' Beliefs About Their Roles as Facilitators of Learning," *Management Learning* 33, no. 2 (2002), pp. 147–179.

58 This section on coaching is based on "Closing Gaps and Improving Performance;" and "What Coaching Is All About: Its Place in Management," excerpt, originally published as Chapter 1 of *Coaching and Mentoring: How to Develop Top Talent and Achieve Stronger Performance* (Boston, MA: Harvard Business School Press, 2004).

59 Michael M. Grant, "Spot Coaching: Develop Leaders Along the Way," *Leadership Excellence* (February 2009), p. 17.

60 "The Business Leader as Development Coach," *PDI Portfolio* (Winter 1996), p. 6; and Personnel Decisions International, http://www.personneldecisions.com (accessed).

Chapter 8 References

1 Phred Dvorak, "Hotelier Finds Happiness Keeps Staff Checked In; Focus on Morale Boosts Joie de Vivre's Grades from Workers, Guests," *The Wall Street Journal* (December 17, 2007), p. B3.

2 Michael West and Malcolm Patterson, "Profitable Personnel," *People Management* (January 8, 1998), pp. 28–31; Richard M. Steers and Lyman W. Porter, eds. *Motivation and Work Behavior*, 3rd ed. (New York: McGraw-Hill, 1983); Don Hellriegel, John W. Slocum, Jr., and Richard W. Woodman, *Organizational Behavior*, 7th ed. (St. Paul, MN: West Publishing Co., 1995), p. 170; and Jerry L. Gray and Frederick A. Starke, *Organizational Behavior: Concepts and Applications*, 4th ed. (New York: Macmillan, 1988), pp. 104–105.

3 Linda Grant, "Happy Workers, High Returns," *Fortune* (January 12, 1998), p. 81; Elizabeth J. Hawk and Garrett J. Sheridan, "The Right Staff," *Management Review* (June 1999), pp. 43–48; and West and Patterson, "Profitable Personnel."

4 Anne Fisher, "Why Passion Pays," *FSB* (September 2002), p. 58; and Curt Coffman and Gabriel Gonzalez-Molina, *Follow This Path: How the World's Greatest Organizations Drive Growth by Unleashing Human Potential* (New York: Warner Books, 2002).

5 Richard M. Steers, Lyman W. Porter, and Gregory A. Bigley, *Motivation and Leadership at Work*, 6th ed. (New York: McGraw-Hill, 1996), pp. 496–498.

6 Steven Bergals, "When Money Talks, People Walk," *Inc.* (May 1996), pp. 25–26.

7 Cynthia Bertucci Kaye, as told to Malika Zouhali-Worrall, "Reviving Incentive," *FSB* (February 2009), pp. 51–52.

8 Robert Levering and Milton Moskowitz, "100 Best Companies to Work For: The Rankings," *Fortune* (February 4, 2008), pp. 75–94.

9 Robert Levering and Milton Moskowitz, "100 Best Companies to Work For: And the Winners Are...," *Fortune* (February 2, 2009), pp. 67–78.

10 Martha Lagace, "Oprah: A Case Study Comes Alive" (Lessons from the Classroom), *HBS Working Knowledge* (February 20, 2006), Harvard Business School, http://hbswk.hbs.edu/item/5214.html (accessed April 2, 2007).

11 Rosabeth Moss Kanter, "How to Fire Up Employees Without Cash or Prizes," *Business 2.0* (June 2002), pp. 134–152.

12 Daniel Roth, "Trading Places," *Fortune* (January 23, 2006), pp. 120–128.

13 Abraham F. Maslow, "A Theory of Human Motivation," *Psychological Review* 50 (1943), pp. 370–396.

14 Frederick Herzberg, "One More Time: How Do You Motivate Employees?" *Harvard Business Review* (January–February 1968), pp. 53–62.

15 Hashi Syedain, "Topped with Satisfaction," *People Management* (July 12, 2007), http://www.peoplemanagement.co.uk/pm/articles/2007/07/toppedwithsatisfaction.htm (accessed May 8, 2009); and http://www.pizzaexpress.com (accessed May 8, 2009).

16 David C. McClelland, *Human Motivation* (Glenview, IL: Scott, Foresman, 1985).

17 John Brant, "What One Man Can Do," *Inc.* (September 2005), pp. 145–153.

18 David C. McClelland, "The Two Faces of Power," in D. A. Colb, I. M. Rubin, and J. M. McIntyre, eds., *Organizational Psychology* (Upper Saddle River, NJ: Prentice Hall, 1971), pp. 73–86.

19 Alfie Kohn, "Why Incentive Plans Cannot Work," *Harvard Business Review* (September–October 1993), pp. 54–63; A. J. Vogl, "Carrots, Sticks, and Self-Deception" (an interview with Alfie Kohn), *Across the Board* (January 1994), pp. 39–44; and Alfie Kohn, "Challenging Behaviorist Dogma: Myths About Money and Motivation," *Compensation & Benefits Review* (March–April 1998), pp. 27, 33–37.

20 H. Richlin, *Modern Behaviorism* (San Francisco: Freeman, 1970); B. F. Skinner, *Science and Human Behavior* (New York: Macmillan, 1953); Alexander D. Stajkovic and Fred Luthans, "A Meta-Analysis of the Effects of Organizational Behavior Modification on Task Performance 1975–1995," *Academy of Management Journal* (October 1997), pp. 1122–1149; and F. Luthans and R. Kreitner, *Organizational Behavior Modification and Beyond,* 2nd ed. (Glenview, IL: Scott Foresman, 1985).

21 Alexander D. Stajkovic and Fred Luthans, "A Meta-Analysis of the Effects of Organizational Behavior Modification on Task Performance, 1975–1995," *Academy of Management Journal* (October 1997), pp. 1122–1149; and Fred Luthans and Alexander D. Stajkovic, "Reinforce for Performance: The Need to Go Beyond Pay and Even Rewards," *Academy of Management Executive* 13, no. 2 (1999), pp. 49–57.

22 Daryl W. Wiesman, "The Effects of Performance Feedback and Social Recognition on Up-Selling at Fast-Food Restaurants," *Journal of Organizational Behavior Management* 26, no. 4 (2006), p. 1.

23 Reported in Charlotte Garvey, "Meaningful Tokens of Appreciation," *HR Magazine* (August 2004), pp. 101–105.

24 Amy Sutherland, "What Shamu Taught Me About a Happy Marriage," *The New York Times* (June 25, 2006), http://www.nytimes.com/2006/06/25/fashion/25love.html?ex=1175659200&en=4c3d257c4d16e70d&ei=5070 (accessed April 2, 2007).

25 Jaclyn Badal, "New Incentives for Workers Combine Cash, Fun" (Theory & Practice column), *The Wall Street Journal* (June 19, 2006), p. B3.

26 Luthans and Kreitner, *Organizational Behavior Modification and Beyond;* L. M. Saari and G. P. Latham, "Employee Reaction to Continuous and Variable Ratio Reinforcement Schedules Involving a Monetary Incentive," *Journal of Applied Psychology* 67 (1982), pp. 506–508; and R. D. Pritchard, J. Hollenback, and P. J. DeLeo, "The Effects of Continuous and Partial Schedules of Reinforcement on Effort, Performance, and Satisfaction," *Organizational Behavior and Human Performance* 25 (1980), pp. 336–353.

27 Victor H. Vroom, *Work and Motivation* (New York: John Wiley & Sons, 1969); B. S. Gorgopoulos, G. M. Mahoney, and N. Jones, "A Path-Goal Approach to Productivity," *Journal of Applied Psychology* 41 (1957), pp. 345–353; and E. E. Lawler III, *Pay and Organizational Effectiveness: A Psychological View* (New York: McGraw-Hill, 1981).

28 Richard M. Daft and Richard M. Steers, *Organizations: A Micro/Macro Approach* (Glenview, IL: Scott, Foresman, 1986).

29 Simona Covel, "Small Business Link: Companies Win as Workers Lose Pounds; Incentive-Based Wellness Programs Give Employees Rewards—With a Payoff of Lower Health-Care Costs," *The Wall Street Journal* (July 10, 2008), p. B6.

30 J. Stacy Adams, "Injustice in Social Exchange," in L. Berkowitz, ed., *Advances in Experimental Social Psychology,* 2nd ed. (New York: Academic Press, 1965); and J. Stacy Adams, "Toward an Understanding of Inequity," *Journal of Abnormal and Social Psychology* (November 1963), pp. 422–436.

31 John Peterman, "The Rise and Fall of the J. Peterman Company," *Harvard Business Review* (September–October, 1999), pp. 59–66.

32 Timothy Aeppel, "Pay Scales Divide Factory Floor," *The Wall Street Journal* (April 9, 2008), p. B4.

33 Amy Joyce, "The Bonus Question; Some Managers Still Strive to Reward Merit," *The Washington Post* (November 13, 2005), p. F6.

34 Survey results from WorldatWork and Hewitt Associates, reported in Karen Kroll, "Benefits: Paying for Performance," *Inc.* (November 2004), p. 46; and Kathy Chu, "Firms Report Lackluster Results from Pay-for-Performance Plans," *The Wall Street Journal* (June 15, 2004), p. D2.

35 Nina Gupta and Jason D. Shaw, "Let the Evidence Speak: Financial Incentives *Are* Effective!!" *Compensation & Benefits Review* (March/April 1998), pp. 26, 28–32.

36 Vogl, "Carrots, Sticks, and Self-Deception," 40; Alfie Kohn, "Incentives Can Be Bad for Business," *Inc.,* (January 1998), pp. 93–94; and Kohn, "Challenging Behaviorist Dogma."

37 Richard M. Steers, Lyman W. Porter, and Gregory A. Bigley, *Motivation and Leadership at Work,* 6th ed. (New York: McGraw-Hill, 1996), p. 512.

38 Steers, Porter, and Bigley, *Motivation and Leadership at Work,* p. 517; and Vogl, "Carrots, Sticks, and Self-Deception," p. 40.

39 Reported in Jared Sandberg, "For Many Employees, a Dream Job Is One That Isn't a Nightmare," *The Wall Street Journal* (April 15, 2008), p. B1.

40 William D. Hitt, *The Leader-Manager: Guidelines for Action* (Columbus, OH: Battelle Press, 1988), p. 153.

41 Steers, Porter, and Bigley, *Motivation and Leadership at Work,* pp. 520–525.

42 Vogl, "Carrots, Sticks, and Self-Deception," p. 43.

43 Alan S. Blinder, "Crazy Compensation and the Crisis," *The Wall Street Journal* (May 28, 2009), p. A15.

44 Liam Pleven and Susanne Craig, "Deal Fees Under Fire Amid Mortgage Crisis; Guaranteed Rewards of Bankers, Middlemen Are in the Spotlight," *The Wall Street Journal* (January 17, 2008), p. A1; Phred Dvorak, "Companies Seek Shareholder Input on Pay Practices," *The Wall Street Journal* (April 6, 2009), p. B4; and Carol Hymowitz, "Pay Gap Fuels Worker Woes," *The Wall Street Journal* (April 28, 2008), p. B8.

45 Blinder, "Crazy Compensation and the Crisis."

46 James M. Kouzes and Barry Z. Posner, *The Leadership Challenge* (San Francisco: Jossey-Bass), p. 153.

47 Kouzes and Posner, *The Leadership Challenge,* p. 282.

48 Edwin P. Hollander and Lynn R. Offerman, "Power and Leadership in Organizations," *American Psychology* 45 (February 1990), pp. 179–189.

49 Jay A. Conger and Rabindra N. Kanungo, "The Empowerment Process: Integrating Theory and Practice," *Academy of Management Review* 13 (1988), pp. 471–482.

50 David P. McCaffrey, Sue R. Faerman, and David W. Hart, "The Appeal and Difficulties of Participative Systems," *Organization Science* 6, no. 6 (November–December 1995), pp. 603–627.

51 Robert C. Ford and Myron D. Fottler, "Empowerment: A Matter of Degree," *Academy of Management Executive* 9 (1995), pp. 21–31.

52 Dennis Cauchon, "The Little Company That Could," *USA Today* (October 9, 2005).

53 McCaffrey, Faerman and Hart, "The Appeal and Difficulties of Participative Systems"; and David E. Bowen and Edward E. Lawler III, "Empowering Service Employees," *Sloan Management Review* (Summer 1995), pp. 73–84.

54 Bowen and Lawler, "Empowering Service Employees."

55 William C. Taylor, "These Workers Act Like Owners (Because They Are)," *The New York Times* (May 21, 2006), Section 3, p. 5.

56 Gretchen Spreitzer, "Social Structural Characteristics of Psychological Empowerment," *Academy of Management Journal* 39, no. 2 (April 1996), pp. 483–504.

57 Russ Forrester, "Empowerment: Rejuvenating a Potent Idea," *Academy of Management Executive* 14, no. 3 (2000), pp. 67–80.

58 Glenn L. Dalton, "The Collective Stretch," *Management Review* (December 1998), pp. 54–59.

59 Bradley L. Kirkman and Benson Rosen, "Powering Up Teams," *Organizational Dynamics* (Winter 2000), pp. 48–66; and Gretchen M. Spreitzer, "Psychological Empowerment in the Workplace: Dimensions, Measurement, and Validation," *Academy of Management Journal* 38, no. 5 (October 1995), p. 1442.

60 Spreitzer, "Social Structural Characteristics of Psychological Empowerment."

61 Roy C. Herrenkohl, G. Thomas Judson, and Judith A. Heffner, "Defining and Measuring Employee Empowerment," *The Journal of Applied Behavioral Science* 35, no. 3 (September 1999), pp. 373–389.

62 Simona Covel, "Small Business Link: How to Get Workers to Think and Act Like Owners—Employee-Owned Firm Van Meter Industrial Prospered After Its Employees Were Persuaded to Take Their Company Stock Seriously," *The Wall Street Journal* (February 7, 2008), p. B6; and Hymowitz, "Pay Gap Fuels Worker Woes."

63 Ford and Fottler, "Empowerment: A Matter of Degree."

64 Lawrence Fisher, "Ricardo Semler Won't Take Control," *Strategy + Business* (Winter 2005), pp. 78–88; and Ricardo Semler, "How

We Went Digital Without a Strategy," *Harvard Business Review* (September–October 2000), pp. 51–58.

65 Curt Coffman and Gabriel Gonzalez-Molina, *Follow This Path: How the World's Greatest Organizations Drive Growth by Unleashing Human Potential* (New York: Warner Books, 2002), as reported in Anne Fisher, "Why Passion Pays," *FSB* (September 2002), p. 58; Rodd Wagner and James K. Harter, "The Third Element of Great Managing; Mom Was Right: You're One of a Kind," *Gallup Management Journal* (June 14, 2007); and Gerard H. Seijts and Dan Crim, "What Engages Employees the Most, or The Ten C's of Employee Engagement," *Ivey Business Journal* (March–April 2006).

66 Barbara Rose, "Zappos Pays to Weed Out Uncommitted Workers," *Chicago Tribune* (June 16, 2008), p. 2.

67 This definition is based on Mercer Human Resource Consulting's Employee Engagement Model, as described in Paul Sanchez and Dan McCauley, "Measuring and Managing Engagement in a Cross-Cultural Workforce: New Insights for Global Companies," *Global Business and Organizational Excellence* (November–December 2006), pp. 41–50; and Seijts and Crim, "What Engages Employees the Most."

68 This discussion is based on Marcus Buckingham and Curt Coffman, *First, Break All the Rules: What the World's Greatest Managers Do Differently* (New York: Simon & Schuster, 1999); Tony Schwartz, "The Greatest Sources of Satisfaction in the Workplace Are Internal and Emotional," *Fast Company* (November 2000), pp. 398–402; and Theresa M. Welbourne, "Employee Engagement: Beyond the Fad and into the Executive Suite," *Leader to Leader* (Spring 2007), pp. 45–51.

69 Wagner and Harter, "The Third Element of Great Managing."

70 Buckingham and Coffman, *First, Break All the Rules.*

71 Coffman and Gonzalez-Molina, *Follow This Path.*

72 Reported in "Many Employees Would Fire Their Boss," Gallup Organization news release, http://gmj.gallup.com/content/28867/Many-Employees-Would-Fire-Their-Boss.aspx (accessed May 11, 2009); and Leigh Woosley, "Rules of Disengagement: Gallup Poll Shows That More Than Half of Workers Are 'Checked Out,'" *Knight Ridder Tribune Business News* (June 11, 2006), p. 1.

73 Jennifer Robison, "This HCA Hospital's Healthy Turnaround," *Gallup Management Journal* (January 13, 2005); and "Medical Center of Plano Named 'Best Places to Work' by the Dallas Business Journal," Medical Center of Plano news release, http://www.medicalcenterofplano.com/CPM/Best%20Places%20to%20Work.doc (accessed May 11, 2009).

74 Taylor, "These Workers Act Like Owners."

75 Michael J. Gaudioso, "How a Successful Gainsharing Program Arose from an Old One's Ashes at Bell Atlantic (Now Verizon) Directory Graphics," *Journal of Organizational Excellence* (Winter 2000), pp. 11–18.

76 Hawk and Sheridan, "The Right Staff."

77 Dalton, "The Collective Stretch."

78 Studies reported in Sarah E. Needleman, "Study Suggests Employers to Shift Bulk of Pay Raises to Top Performers" *The Wall Street Journal* (August 14, 2008), p. D2; and Christopher Caggiano, "The Right Way to Pay," *Inc.* (November 2002), pp. 84–92.

79 Aaron Lucchetti, "Morgan Stanley Boosts Salaries as Its Bonuses Are Limited," *The Wall Street Journal* (May 23–24, 2009), p. B1.

80 Hymowitz, "Pay Gap Fuels Worker Woes."

81 Dalton, "The Collective Stretch."

Chapter 9 References

1 Geoff Colvin and Jessica Shambora, "J&J: Secrets of Success," *Fortune* (May 4, 2009), pp. 116–121.

2 Sonia Alleyne, "Accept No Substitutes," *Black Enterprise* (September 2008), pp. 90–94.

3 "Harris Interactive; A Record Number of Americans, 88%, Say the Reputation of Corporate America is 'Not Good' or 'Terrible,'" *Drug Week* (May 15, 2009).

4 These examples were reported in Mina Kimes, "How Can I Get Candid Feedback from My Employees?" *Fortune* (April 13, 2009), p. 24.

5 Studies from The Elliot Leadership Institute, reported in Louise van der Does and Stephen J. Caldeira, "Effective Leaders Champion Communication Skills," *Nation's Restaurant News* (March 27, 2006), p. 20; and Dennis Tourish, "Critical Upward Communication: Ten Commandments for Improving Strategy and Decision Making," *Long Range Planning* 38 (2005), pp. 485–503.

6 Bernard M. Bass, *Bass & Stogdill's Handbook of Leadership*, 3rd ed. (New York: The Free Press, 1990).

7 Henry Mintzberg, *The Nature of Managerial Work* (New York: Harper & Row, 1973).

8 Mary Young and James E. Post, "Managing to Communicate, Communicating to Manage: How Leading Companies Communicate with Employees," *Organizational Dynamics* (Summer 1993), pp. 31–43; and Warren Bennis and Burt Nanus, *Leaders: The Strategies for Taking Charge* (New York: Harper & Row, 1985).

9 Colin Mitchell, "Selling the Brand Inside," *Harvard Business Review* (January 2002), pp. 99–105.

10 Phillip G. Clampitt, Laurey Berk, and M. Lee Williams, "Leaders as Strategic Communicators," *Ivey Business Journal* (May–June 2002), pp. 51–55.

11 Ian Wylie, "Can Philips Learn to Walk the Talk?" *Fast Company* (January 2003), pp. 44–45.

12 Gary Hamel, "Killer Strategies That Make Shareholders Rich," *Fortune* (June 23, 1997), pp. 70–84.

13 John Luthy, "New Keys to Employee Performance and Productivity," *Public Management* (March 1998), pp. 4–8.

14 Alex Taylor III, "Fixing Up Ford," *Fortune* (May 25, 2009), pp. 44–51.

15 This discussion is based on "The Power of Questions" (Practical Wisdom column), *Leadership: The Journal of the Leader to Leader Institute* (Spring 2005), pp. 59–60; and Quinn Spitzer and Ron Evans, "The New Business Leader: Socrates with a Baton," *Strategy & Leadership* (September–October 1997), pp. 32–38.

16 Ibid.

17 Sterling Newberry, "Difficult Communications: Going Beyond 'I' Statements," *Mediate.com* (January 2003), http://www.mediate.com/articles/redwing9.cfm (accessed July 6, 2009).

18 Reported in Spitzer and Evans, The New Business Leader: "Socrates with a Baton."

19 C. Glenn Pearce, "Doing Something About Your Listening Ability," *Supervisory Management* (March 1989), pp. 29–34; and Tom Peters, "Learning to Listen," *Hyatt Magazine* (Spring 1988), pp. 16–21.

20 Gerald M. Goldhaber, *Organizational Communication*, 4th ed. (Dubuque, IA: Wm. C. Brown, 1980), p. 189.

21 Peters, "Learning to Listen."

22 Amy C. Edmondson and Diana McLain Smith, "Too Hot to Handle? How to Manage Relationship Conflict," *California Management Review* 49, no. 1 (Fall 2006), pp. 6–28.

23 "Desk Rage Rising," *Office Solutions* (January 2009), p. 9; Steve Albrecht, "Mass Murders at Home and at Work," *The San Diego Union-Tribune* (April 12, 2009), p. F4; and Carol Hymowitz, "Bosses Have to Learn How to Confront Troubled Employees," *The Wall Street Journal* (April 23, 2007), p. B1.

24 David Bohm, *On Dialogue* (Ojai, CA: David Bohm Seminars, 1989).

25 Bill Isaacs, *Dialogue and the Art of Thinking Together* (New York: Doubleday, 1999); and "The Art of Dialogue," column in Paul

Roberts, "Live! From Your Office! It's . . ." *Fast Company* (October, 1999), pp. 151–170.

26 Based on Glenna Gerard and Linda Teurfs, "Dialogue and Organizational Transformation," in Kazimierz Gozdz, ed., *Community Building: Renewing Spirit and Learning in Business* (Pleasanton, CA: New Leaders Press, 1995).

27 Scott Kirsner, "Want to Grow? Hire a Shrink!" *Fast Company* (December–January 1998), pp. 68, 70.

28 This discussion is based on Joseph Luft and Harry Ingham, "The Johari Window, A Graphic Model of Interpersonal Awareness," *Proceedings of the Western Training Laboratory in Group Development*, UCLA, 1955; Mike Clayton, "Super Models," *Training Journal* (May 2008), p. 67; Alan Chapman, "Johari Window," http://www.businessballs.com/johariwindowmodel.htm (accessed May 18, 2009); Duen Hsi Yen, "Johari Window," http://www.noogenesis.com/game_theory/johari/johari_window.html (accessed May 18, 2009); and Joseph Luft, *Of Human Interaction* (Palo Alto, CA: National Press, 1969).

29 Erin White, "Theory & Practice: Art of Persuasion Becomes Key; Managers Sharpen Their Skills as Line of Authority Blurs," *The Wall Street Journal* (May 19, 2008), p. B5.

30 This section is based on Jay A. Conger, "The Necessary Art of Persuasion," *Harvard Business Review* (May–June 1998), pp. 84–95.

31 Darren Dahl, "Trust Me: You're Gonna Love This; Getting Employees to Embrace New Technology," *Inc.* (November 2008), p. 41.

32 John Guaspari, "A Shining Example," *Across the Board* (May–June 2002), pp. 67–68.

33 Elizabeth Weiss Green, "The Power of Persuasion," *US News & World Report* (August 7, 2006), pp. 60, 62.

34 J. C. McCroskey and V. P. Richmond, "The Impact of Communication Apprehension on Individuals in Organizations, *Communication Quarterly*, 27 (1979), pp. 55–61.

35 J. C. McCroskey, "The Communication Apprehension Perspective," in J. C. McCroskey and J. A. Daly, eds., *Avoiding Communication: Shyness, Reticence, and Communication Apprehension* (London: Sage Publications, 1984), pp. 13–38.

36 Robert H. Lengel and Richard L. Daft, "The Selection of Communication Media as an Executive Skill," *Academy of Management Executive* 2 (August 1988), pp. 225–232; and Richard L. Daft and Robert Lengel, "Organizational Information Requirements, Media Richness and Structural Design," *Managerial Science* 32 (May 1986), pp. 554–572.

37 Ford S. Worthy, "How CEOs Manage Their Time," *Fortune* (January 18, 1988), pp. 88–97.

38 John R. Carlson and Robert W. Zmud, "Channel Expansion Theory and the Experiential Nature of Media Richness Perceptions," *Academy of Management Journal* 42, no. 2 (1999), pp. 153–170; and R. Rice and G. Love, "Electronic Emotion," *Communication Research* 14 (1987), pp. 85–108.

39 Ronald E. Rice, "Task Analyzability, Use of New Media, and Effectiveness: A Multi-Site Exploration of Media Richness," *Organizational Science* 3, no. 4 (November 1994), pp. 502–527.

40 Richard L. Daft, Robert H. Lengel, and Linda Klebe Treviño, "Message Equivocality, Media Selection and Manager Performance: Implications for Information Systems," *MIS Quarterly* 11 (1987), pp. 355–368.

41 Laura Raines, "Going Forward After Layoffs: Leaders Need to Reassure Employees, Share Vision of Company's Future," *The Atlanta Journal-Constitution* (April 26, 2009), p. G1.

42 Daniel Nasaw, "Instant Messages Are Popping Up All Over," *The Wall Street Journal* (June 12, 2003), p. B4.

43 Stanley Holmes, "Into the Wild Blog Yonder," *BusinessWeek* (May 22, 2006), pp. 84, 86.

44 Anne Fisher, "Readers Weigh In on Rudeness and Speechmaking" (Ask Annie column), *Fortune* (January 10, 2000), p. 194.

45 Edward M. Hallowell, "The Human Moment at Work," *Harvard Business Review* (January–February 1999), pp. 58–66; and Andrea

C. Poe, "Don't Touch That 'Send' Button!" *HR Magazine* (July 2003), pp. 74–80.

46 Hallowell, "The Human Moment at Work."

47 Hallowell, "The Human Moment at Work"; Deborah L. Duarte and Nancy Tennant Snyder, *Mastering Virtual Teams: Strategies, Tools, and Techniques That Succeed* (San Francisco: Jossey-Bass, 2000).

48 Hallowell, "The Human Moment."

49 Carlson and Zmud, "Channel Expansion Theory and the Experiential Nature of Media Richness Perceptions."

50 Mary Lynn Pulley and Jane Hilberry, *Get Smart! How E-Mail Can Make or Break Your Career and Your Organization* (Colorado Springs, CO: Get Smart! Publishing, 2007).

51 Albert Mehrabian, *Silent Messages* (Belmont, CA: Wadsworth, 1971); and Albert Mehrabian, "Communicating Without Words," *Psychology Today* (September 1968), pp. 53–55.

52 Jane Webster and Linda Klebe Treviño, "Rational and Social Theories as Complementary Explanations of Communication Media Choices: Two Policy Capturing Studies," *Academy of Management Journal* (December 1995), pp. 1544–1572.

53 Mac Fulfer, "Nonverbal Communication: How to Read What's Plain as the Nose . . . or Eyelid . . . or Chin . . . on Their Faces," *Journal of Organizational Excellence* (Spring, 2001), pp. 19–27.

54 Dana Mattioli, "Layoff Sign: Boss's Cold Shoulder," *The Wall Street Journal* (October 23, 2008), p. D6.

55 Linda Klebe Treviño, Laura Pincus Hartman, and Michael Brown, "Moral Person and Moral Manager: How Executives Develop a Reputation for Ethical Leadership," *California Management Review* 42, no. 4 (Summer 2000), pp. 128–142.

56 I. Thomas Sheppard, "Silent Signals," *Supervisory Management* (March 1986), pp. 31–33; and Martha E. Mangelsdorf, "Business Insight (A Special Report); Executive Briefing: The Power of Nonverbal Communication" (an interview with Alex Pentland), *The Wall Street Journal* (October 20, 2008), p. R2.

57 Thomas H. Peters and Robert J. Waterman, Jr., *In Search of Excellence* (New York: Harper & Row, 1982); and Tom Peters and Nancy Austin, *A Passion for Excellence: The Leadership Difference* (New York: Random House, 1985).

58 Jeffrey M. O'Brien, "Zappos Knows How to Kick It," *Fortune* (February 2, 2009), pp. 54–60.

59 Philip Rucker, "The Pork Lobbyists, Ready to Reassure; Flu Prompts Daily Damage Control," *The Washington Post* (May 4, 2009), p. A1.

60 This section is based on Leslie Wayne and Leslie Kaufman, "Leadership, Put to a New Test," *The New York Times* (September 16, 2001), Section 3, pp. 1, 4; Jerry Useem, "What It Takes," *Fortune* (November 12, 2001), pp. 126–132; Andy Bowen, "Crisis Procedures That Stand the Test of Time," *Public Relations Tactics* (August 2001), p. 16; and Matthew Boyle, "Nothing Really Matters," *Fortune* (October 15, 2001), pp. 261–264.

61 Useem, "What It Takes."

62 Stephen Bernhut, "Leadership, with Michael Useem" (Leader's Edge interview), *Ivey Business Journal* (January–February 2002), pp. 42–43.

63 Misty Harris, "Maple Leaf Winning the Battle to Bring Consumers Back; Survey Finds Consumer Confidence Returning," *The Vancouver Sun* (January 23, 2009), p. D3.

64 Scott Kirsner, "A Public Relations Pro Tells Bankers It's Time to Eat Crow," *Boston Globe* (February 16, 2009), p. B5; and Barb Iverson, "Viewpoint: Banks, for Your Own Good, Fill the Silence," *American Banker* (October 17, 2008), p. 12.

65 Ian I. Mitroff, "Crisis Leadership," *Executive Excellence* (August 2001), p. 19.

66 Allison Fass, "Duking It Out," *Forbes* (June 9, 2003), pp. 74–76; and John A. Fortunato, "Restoring a Reputation: The Duke University Lacrosse Scandal," *Public Relations Review* 34 (2008), pp. 116–123.

67 Kriengsak Niratpattanasai, "Developing Vision for an Organization," *The Bangkok Post* (February 11, 2008), p. 1.

Chapter 10 References

1   John Paul Newport, "Golf Journal: Team USA's Management Victory," *The Wall Street Journal* (September 27, 2008), p. W9.

2   Lee G. Bolman and Terrence E. Deal, "What Makes a Team Work?" *Organizational Dynamics* (August 1992), pp. 34–44.

3   Linda I. Glassop, "The Organizational Benefit of Teams," *Human Relations* 55, no. 2 (2002), pp. 225–249; and J. D. Osburn, L. Moran, E. Musselwhite, and J. H. Zenger, *Self-Directed Work Teams: The New American Challenge* (Homewood, IL: Business One Irwin, 1990).

4   Carl E. Larson and Frank M. J. LaFasto, *Team Work* (Newbury Park, CA: Sage Publications, 1989); and C. P. Aldefer, "Group and Intergroup Relations," in J. R. Hackman and J. S. Suttle, eds., *Improving Life at Work* (Santa Monica, CA: Goodyear, 1977).

5   Geoffrey Colvin, "Why Dream Teams Fail," *Fortune* (June 12, 2006), pp. 87–92.

6   Study by G. Clotaire Rapaille, reported in Karen Bernowski, "What Makes American Teams Tick?" *Quality Progress* 28, no. 1 (January 1995), pp. 39–42.

7   Robert Albanese and David D. Van Fleet, "Rational Behavior in Groups: The Free-Riding Tendency," *Academy of Management Review* 10 (1985), pp. 244–255.

8   Reported in Matt Vella, "White Collar Workers Shoulder Together—Like It or Not" (Inside Innovation section: InData), *BusinessWeek* (April 28, 2008), p. 58.

9   See David H. Freedman, "The Idiocy of Crowds" (What's Next column), *Inc.* (September 2006), pp. 61–62.

10 "Why Some Teams Succeed (and So Many Don't)," *Harvard Management Update* (October 2006), pp. 3–4.

11 Patrick Lencioni, *The Five Dysfunctions of a Team* (New York: John Wiley & Sons, 2002).

12 Gervase R. Bushe and Graeme H. Coetzer, "Group Development and Team Effectiveness: Using Cognitive Representations to Measure Group Development and Predict Task Performance and Group Viability," *The Journal of Applied Behavioral Science* 43, no. 2 (June 2007), pp. 184–212; Kenneth G. Koehler, "Effective Team Management," *Small Business Report* (July 19, 1989), pp. 14–16; Connie J. G. Gersick, "Time and Transition in Work Teams: Toward a New Model of Group Development," *Academy of Management Journal* 31 (1988), pp. 9–41; and John Beck and Neil Yeager, "Moving Beyond Myths," *Training & Development* (March 1996), pp. 51–55.

13 Bruce W. Tuckman, "Developmental Sequence in Small Groups," *Psychological Bulletin* 63 (1965), pp. 384–399; and B. W. Tuckman and M. A. Jensen, "Stages of Small Group Development Revisited," *Group and Organizational Studies* 2 (1977), pp. 419–427.

14 Brian Hindo, "The Empire Strikes at Silos," *BusinessWeek* (August 20–27, 2007), pp. 63–65.

15 Margaret Frazier, "Flu Prep," *The Wall Street Journal* (March 25–26, 2006), p. A8.

16 Laurianne McLaughlin, "Project Collaboration: How One Company Got a Diverse Team on the Same Page," *CIO* (August 13, 2007), http://www.cio.com/article/130300/Project_Collaboration_How_One_Company_Got_A_Diverse_Team_on_the_Same_Page?contentId=130300&slug=& (accessed August 20, 2008).

17 Pierre van Amelsvoort and Jos Benders, "Team Time: A Model for Developing Self-Directed Work Teams," *International Journal of Operations and Production Management* 16, no. 2 (1996), pp. 159–170.

18 Heleen van Mierlo, Christel G. Rutte, Michiel A. J. Kompier, and Hans A.C.M. Doorewaard, "Self-Managing Teamwork and Psychological Well-Being: Review of a Multilevel Research Domain," *Group & Organization Management* 30, no. 2 (2005), pp. 211–235.

19 Jeanne M. Wilson, Jill George, and Richard S. Wellins, with William C. Byham, *Leadership Trapeze: Strategies for Leadership in Team-Based Organizations* (San Francisco: Jossey-Bass, 1994).

20 Patricia Booth, "Embracing the Team Concept," *Canadian Business Review* (Autumn 1994), pp. 10–13.

21 Gary Hamel, "Break Free," *Fortune* (October 1, 2007), pp. 119–126, excerpted from Gary Hamel, *The Future of Management* (Boston: Harvard Business School Press, 2007).

22 Erin White, "How a Company Made Everyone a Team Player," *The Wall Street Journal* (August 13, 2007), p. B1.

23 Kenneth Labich, "Elite Teams Get the Job Done," *Fortune* (February 19, 1996), pp. 90–99.

24 Ruth Wageman, "Critical Success Factors for Creating Superb Self-Managing Teams," *Organizational Dynamics* (Summer 1997), pp. 49–61.

25 Reported in Jia Lynn Yang, "The Power of Number 4.6," part of a special series, "Secrets of Greatness: Teamwork," *Fortune* (June 12, 2006), p. 122.

26 Martin Hoegl, "Smaller Teams—Better Teamwork: How to Keep Project Teams Small," *Business Horizons* 48 (2005), pp. 209–214.

27 Reported in "Vive La Difference," (box) in Julie Connelly, "All Together Now," *Gallup Management Journal* (Spring 2002), pp. 13–18.

28 Reported in Vella, "White Collar Workers Shoulder Together."

29 For research findings on group size, see M. E. Shaw, *Group Dynamics,* 3rd ed. (New York: McGraw-Hill, 1981); G. Manners, "Another Look at Group Size, Group Problem-Solving and Member Consensus," *Academy of Management Journal* 18 (1975), pp. 715–724; and Albert V. Carron and Kevin S. Spink, "The Group Size–Cohesion Relationship in Minimal Groups," *Small Group Research* 26, no. 1 (February 1995), pp. 86–105.

30 Warren E. Watson, Kamalesh Kumar, and Larry K. Michaelsen, "Cultural Diversity's Impact on Interaction Process and Performance: Comparing Homogeneous and Diverse Task Groups," *Academy of Management Journal* 36 (1993), pp. 590–602; Gail Robinson and Kathleen Dechant, "Building a Business Case for Diversity," *Academy of Management Executive* 11, no. 3 (1997), pp. 21–31; R. A. Guzzo and G. P. Shea, "Group Performance and Intergroup Relations in Organizations," in M. D. Dunnette and L. M. Hough, eds., *Handbook of Industrial & Organizational Psychology,* 2nd ed., vol. 3 (Palo Alto, CA: Consulting Psychologists Press, 1992), pp. 288–290; and David A. Thomas and Robin J. Ely, "Making Differences Matter: A New Paradigm for Managing Diversity," *Harvard Business Review* (September–October 1996), pp. 79–90.

31 Andrew Sobel, "The Beatles Principles," *Strategy + Business* 42 (Spring 2006), pp. 32–35.

32 Kathleen M. Eisenhardt, Jean L. Kahwajy, and L. J. Bourgeois III, "Conflict and Strategic Choice: How Top Management Teams Disagree," *California Management Review* 39, no. 2 (Winter 1997), pp. 42–62.

33 Dee Gill, "Dealing with Diversity," *Inc.* (November 2005), pp. 37–40.

34 Linda A. Hill, "A Note for Analyzing Work Groups," Harvard Business Online (August 28, 1995; revised April 3, 1998), Product # 9-496-026, ordered at http://www.hbsp.harvard.edu.

35 Stanley M. Gully, Dennis J. Devine, and David J. Whitney, "A Meta-Analysis of Cohesion and Performance: Effects of Level of Analysis and Task Interdependence," *Small Group Research* 26, no. 4 (November 1995), pp. 497–520.

36 James Thompson, *Organizations in Action* (New York: McGraw-Hill, 1967).

37 Peter F. Drucker, *Managing in a Time of Great Change* (New York: Truman Talley Books/Dutton, 1995), p. 98.

38 Ibid.

39 Thomas A. Stewart, "The Great Conundrum—You vs. the Team," *Fortune* (November 25, 1996), pp. 165–166.

40 Chuck Salter, "Ford's Escape Route," *Fast Company* (October 2004), pp. 106–110.

41 Bernard Simon, "Ford Aims to Build on Escape Hybrid's Success," *National Post* (January 26, 2005), p. FP-10; and Amy Wilson, "Ford Escape Hybrid: OK, but It's No Prius," *Automotive News* (March 13, 2006), p. 6.

42 Robert C. Liden, Sandy J. Wayne, and Lisa Bradway, "Connections Make the Difference," *HR Magazine* (February 1996), p. 73.

43 Dexter Dunphy and Ben Bryant, "Teams: Panaceas or Prescriptions for Improved Performance," *Human Relations* 49, no. 5 (1996), pp. 677–699; Susan G. Cohen, Gerald E. Ledford, and Gretchen M. Spreitzer, "A Predictive Model of Self-Managing Work Team Effectiveness," *Human Relations* 49, no. 5 (1996), pp. 643–676; Martin Hoegl and Hans Georg Gemuenden, "Teamwork Quality and the Success of Innovative Projects: A Theoretical Concept and Empirical Evidence," *Organization Science* 12, no. 4 (July–August 2001), pp. 435–449; Ruth Wageman, J. Richard Hackman, and Erin Lehman, "Team Diagnostic Survey: Development of an Instrument," *The Journal of Applied Behavioral Science* 41, no. 4 (December 2005), pp. 373–398; and Hill, "A Note for Analyzing Work Groups."

44 Carron and Spink, "The Group Size–Cohesion Relationship in Minimal Groups."

45 Harold J. Leavitt and Jean Lipman-Blumen, "Hot Groups," *Harvard Business Review* (July–August 1995), pp. 109–116.

46 Dorwin Cartwright and Alvin Zander, *Group Dynamics: Research and Theory,* 3rd ed. (New York: Harper & Row, 1968); Eliot Aronson, *The Social Animal* (San Francisco: W. H. Freeman, 1976); and Thomas Li-Ping Tang and Amy Beth Crofford, "Self-Managing Work Teams," *Employment Relations Today* (Winter 1995/96), pp. 29–39.

47 Tang and Crofford, "Self-Managing Work Teams."

48 Gully, Devine, and Whitney, "A Meta-Analysis of Cohesion and Performance: Effects of Level of Analysis and Task Interdependence."

49 Stanley E. Seashore, *Group Cohesiveness in the Industrial Work Group* (Ann Arbor, MI: Institute for Social Research, 1954).

50 Based on Robert A. Baron, *Behavior in Organizations,* 2nd ed. (Boston: Allyn & Bacon, 1986); Don Hellriegel, John W. Slocum, Jr., and Richard W. Woodman, *Organizational Behavior,* 8th ed. (Cincinnati: South-Western, 1998), p. 244; and Gary A. Yukl, *Leadership in Organizations,* 4th ed. (Upper Saddle River, NJ: Prentice Hall, 1998), pp. 384–387.

51 Lynda Gratton and Tamara J. Erickson, "Ways to Build Collaborative Teams," *Harvard Business Review* (November 2007), pp. 101–109.

52 Studies reported in Amy Edmondson, Richard Bohmer, and Gary Pisano, "Speeding Up Team Learning," *Harvard Business Review* (October 2001), pp. 125–132; and Scott Thurm, "Teamwork Raises Everyone's Game—Having Everyone Bond Benefits Companies More Than Promoting Stars" (Theory & Practice column), *The Wall Street Journal* (November 7, 2005), p. B8.

53 The following discussion is based on Mark Sanborn, *Team Built: Making Teamwork Pay* (New York: MasterMedia Limited, 1992); Wilson et al., *Leadership Trapeze;* J. Richard Hackman and R. E. Walton, "Leading Groups in Organizations," in P. S. Goodman and Associates, eds., *Designing Effective Work Groups* (San Fransisco: Jossey-Bass, 1986); and Bolman and Deal, "What Makes a Team Work?"

54 J. Richard Hackman, *Leading Teams: Setting the Stage for Great Performances* (Boston, MA: Harvard Business School Press, 2002), p. 62.

55 J. Richard Hackman, "Group Influences on Individuals," in M. Dunnette, ed., *Handbook of Industrial and Organizational Psychology* (Chicago: Rand McNally, 1976).

56 Simon Taggar and Robert Ellis, "The Role of Leaders in Shaping Formal Team Norms," *The Leadership Quarterly* 18 (2007), pp. 105–120.

57 Patrick J. Sauer, "Tough Guys," *Fast Company* (October 2007), pp. 56–57.

58 This section is based on Stephen D. Reicher, Michael J. Platow, and S. Alexander Haslam, "The New Psychology of Leadership," *Scientific American Mind* (August–September 2007), pp. 23–29.

59 Edmondson, Bohmer, and Pisano, "Speeding Up Team Learning."

60 Eric Matson, "Congratulations, You're Promoted. (Now What?)," *Fast Company* (June–July 1997), pp. 116–130.

61 Dan Schulman, as told to Patricia R. Olsen, "Teamwork's Rewards," *The New York Times* (February 24, 2008), p. BU17.

62 C. Shawn Burke, Kevin C. Stagl, Cameron Klein, Gerald F. Goodwin, Eduardo Salas, and Stanley M. Halpin, "What Type of Leadership Behaviors Are Functional in Teams? A Meta-Analysis," *The Leadership Quarterly* 17 (2006), pp. 288–307; Greg L. Stewart, "A Meta-Analytic Review of Relationships Between Team Design Features and Team Performance," *Journal of Management* 32, no. 1 (February 2006), pp. 29–54; and Abhishek Srivastava, Kathryn M. Bartol, and Edwin A. Locke, "Empowering Leadership in Management Teams: Effects on Knowledge Sharing, Efficacy, and Performance," *Academy of Management Journal* 49, no. 6 (December 2006), pp. 1239–1251.

63 Bradford W. Bell and Steve W. J. Kozlowski, "A Typology of Virtual Teams: Implications for Effective Leadership," *Group & Organization Management* 27, no. 1 (March 2002), pp. 14–49.

64 The discussion of virtual teams is based on Anthony M. Townsend, Samuel M. DeMarie, and Anthony R. Hendrickson, "Virtual Teams: Technology and the Workplace of the Future," *Academy of Management Executive* 12, no. 3 (August 1998), pp. 17–29; Deborah L. Duarte and Nancy Tennant Snyder, *Mastering Virtual Teams* (San Francisco: Jossey-Bass, 1999); and Jessica Lipnack and Jeffrey Stamps, "Virtual Teams: The New Way to Work," *Strategy & Leadership* (January–February 1999), pp. 14–18.

65 Carla Joinson, "Managing Virtual Teams," *HR Magazine* (June 2002), pp. 69–73.

66 Stacie A. Furst, Martha Reeves, Benson Rosen, and Richard S. Blackburn, "Managing the Life Cycle of Virtual Teams," *Academy of Management Executive* 18, no. 2 (2004), pp. 6–20; R. E. Potter and P. A. Balthazard, "Understanding Human Interaction and Performance in the Virtual Team," *Journal of Information Technology Theory and Application* 4 (2002), pp. 1–23; and Kenneth W. Kerber and Anthony F. Buono, "Leadership Challenges in Global Virtual Teams: Lessons from the Field," *SAM Advanced Management Journal* (Autumn 2004), pp. 4–10.

67 The discussion of these challenges is based on Bradford S. Bell and Steve W. J. Kozlowski, "A Typology of Virtual Teams: Implications for Effective Leadership," *Group & Organization Management* 27, no. 1 (March 2002), pp. 14–49; Lipnack and Stamps, "Virtual Teams: The New Way to Work"; Joinson, "Managing Virtual Teams"; and Jon R. Katzenbach and Douglas K. Smith, "The Discipline of Virtual Teams," *Leader to Leader* (Fall 2001), pp. 16–25.

68 This discussion of virtual team leadership skills is based on Arvind Malhotra, Ann Majchrzak, and Benson Rosen, "Leading Virtual Teams," *Academy of Management Perspectives* 21, no. 1 (February 2007), pp. 60–69; Penelope Sue Greenberg, Ralph H. Greenberg, and Yvonne Lederer Antonucci, "Creating and Sustaining Trust in Virtual Teams," *Business Horizons* 50 (2007), pp. 325–333; Elizabeth Garone, "Bonding with Remote Workers Valuable Asset," *The Wall Street Journal* (May 11, 2008), p. H1; Benson Rosen, Stacie Furst, and Richard Blackburn, "Overcoming Barriers to Knowledge Sharing in Virtual Teams," *Organizational Dynamics* 36, no. 3 (2007), pp. 259–273; and Bradley L. Kirkman, Benson Rosen, Cristina B. Gibson, Paul E. Tesluk, and Simon O. McPherson, "Five Challenges to Virtual Team Success: Lessons from Sabre, Inc.," *Academy of Management Executive* 16, no. 3 (August 2002), pp. 67–79.

69 Terri L. Griffith and Margaret A. Neale, "Information Processing in Traditional, Hybrid, and Virtual Teams: From Nascent Knowledge to Transactive Memory," *Research in Organizational Behavior* 23 (2001), pp. 379–421.

70 Charlene Marmer Solomon, "Building Teams Across Borders," *Workforce* (November 1998), pp. 12–17.

71 Ron Young, "The Wide-Awake Club," *People Management* (February 5, 1998), pp. 46–49.

72 Ann Majchrzak, Arvind Malhotra, Jeffrey Stamps, and Jessica Lipnack, "Can Absence Make a Team Grow Stronger?" *Harvard Business Review* 82, no. 5 (May 2004), p. 131.

73 Lynda Gratton, "Working Together... When Apart," *The Wall Street Journal* (June 18, 2007), p. R1; and Kirkman et al., "Five Challenges to Virtual Team Success."

74 Pete Engardio, "A Guide for Multinationals: One of the Greatest Challenges for a Multinational Is Learning How to Build a Productive Global Team," *BusinessWeek* (August 20, 2007), pp. 48–51; and Lynda Gratton, "Working Together...When Apart."

75 Mary O'Hara-Devereaux and Robert Johansen, *Globalwork: Bridging Distance, Culture, and Time* (San Francisco: Jossey-Bass, 1994); Charles C. Snow, Scott A. Snell, Sue Canney Davison, and Donald C. Hambrick, "Use Transnational Teams to Globalize Your Company," *Organizational Dynamics* 24, no. 4 (Spring 1996), pp. 50–67; Vijay Govindarajan and Anil K. Gupta, "Building an Effective Global Business Team," *MIT Sloan Management Review* (Summer, 2001), pp. 63–71; and Edward F. McDonough III, Kenneth B. Kahn, and Gloria Barczak, "An Investigation of the Use of Global, Virtual, and Colocated New Product Development Teams," *The Journal of Product Innovation Management* 18 (2001), pp. 110–120.

76 Phred Dvorak, "Theory & Practice: How Teams Can Work Well Together from Far Apart," *The Wall Street Journal* (September 17, 2007), p. B4.

77 Jane Pickard, "Control Freaks Need Not Apply," *People Management* (February 5, 1998), p. 49.

78 McDonough et al., "An Investigation of the Use of Global, Virtual, and Colocated New Product Development Teams."

79 Richard Pastore, "Global Team Management: It's a Small World After All," *CIO* (January 23, 2008), http://www.cio.com/article/174750/Global_Team_Management_It_s_a_Small_World_After_All (accessed May 20, 2008).

80 This section is based on Govindarajan and Gupta, "Building an Effective Global Business Team"; and Marshall Goldsmith, "Crossing the Cultural Chasm; Keeping Communication Clear and Consistent with Team Members from Other Countries Isn't Easy, Says Author Maya Hu-Chan," *BusinessWeek Online* (May 30, 2007), http://www.businessweek.com/careers/content/may2007/ca20070530_521679.htm (accessed August 24, 2007).

81 Anil K. Gupta and Vijay Govindarajan, "Converting Global Presence into Global Competitive Advantage," *Academy of Management Executive* 15, no. 2 (May 2001), pp. 45–56; and Nadine Heintz, "In Spanish, It's *Un Equipo*; In English, It's a Team; Either Way, It's Tough to Build," *Inc.* (April 2008), pp. 41–42.

82 Benson Rosen, Stacie Furst, and Richard Blackburn, "Overcoming Barriers to Knowledge Sharing in Virtual Teams," *Organizational Dynamics* 36, no. 3 (2007), pp. 259–273.

83 Govindarajan and Gupta, "Building an Effective Global Business Team."

84 Carol Saunders, Craig Van Slyke, and Douglas R. Vogel, "My Time or Yours? Managing Time Visions in Global Virtual Teams," *Academy of Management Executive* 18, no. 1 (2004), pp. 19–31.

85 Govindarajan and Gupta, "Building an Effective Global Business Team."

86 Heintz, "In Spanish, It's *Un Equipo*."

87 Sylvia Odenwald, "Global Work Teams," *Training & Development* (February 1996), pp. 54–57; and Debby Young, "Team Heat," *CIO*, Section 1 (September 1, 1998), pp. 43–51.

88 Yuhyung Shin, "Conflict Resolution in Virtual Teams," *Organizational Dynamics* 34, no. 4 (2005), pp. 331–345.

89 Debra L. Shapiro, Stacie A. Furst, Gretchen M. Spreitzer, and Mary Ann Von Glinow, "Transnational Teams in the Electronic Age: Are Team Identity and High Performance at Risk?" *Journal of Organizational Behavior* 23 (2002), pp. 455–467.

90 Koehler, "Effective Team Management"; and Dean Tjosvold, "Making Conflict Productive," *Personnel Administrator* 29 (June 1984), p. 121.

91 Karen A. Jehn and Elizabeth A. Mannix, "The Dynamic Nature of Conflict: A Longitudinal Study of Intragroup Conflict and Group Performance," *Academy of Management Journal* 44, no. 2 (2001), pp. 238–251.

92 Richard Pérez-Peña, "For Publisher in Los Angeles, Cuts and Worse," *The New York Times* (February 19, 2008), p. A1; R. Pérez-Peña, "Los Angeles Editor Ousted After Resisting Job Cuts," *The New York Times* (January 21, 2008), p. A15; and Emily Steel, "Why Los Angeles Times Can't Keep an Editor," *The Wall Street Journal* (January 22, 2008), p. B1.

93 Michael Oneal and Phil Rosenthal, "Tribune Company Files for Bankruptcy Protection," *The Chicago Tribune* (December 10, 2008), http://www.chicagotribune.com/business/chi-081208tribune-bankruptcy,0,3718621.story (accessed December 11, 2008); and Andrew Ross Sorkin, "Dealbook—Workers Pay for Debacle at Tribune," *The New York Times* (December 8, 2008), http://www.nytimes.com/2008/12/09/business/media/09sorkin.html?ex=1244437200&en=7dc24b443741d025&ei=5087&excamp=GGDBlosangelestimesbankruptcy&WT.srch=1&WT.mc_ev=click&WT.mc_id=DB-S-E-GG-NA-S-los_angeles_times_bankruptcy (accessed December 9, 2008).

94 This discussion is based on K. W. Thomas, "Towards Multidimensional Values in Teaching: The Example of Conflict Behaviors," *Academy of Management Review* 2 (1977), p. 487.

95 Mitzi M. Montoya-Weiss, Anne P. Massey, and Michael Song, "Getting It Together: Temporal Coordination and Conflict Management in Global Virtual Teams," *Academy of Management Journal* 44, no. 6 (2001), pp. 1251–1262.

96 "The Negotiation Process: The Difference Between Integrative and Distributive Negotiation," La Piana Associates Inc., accessed from http://www.lapiana.org/resources/tips/negotiations.

97 Rob Walker, "Take It or Leave It: The Only Guide to Negotiating You Will Ever Need," *Inc.* (August 2003), pp. 75–82.

98 Jennifer Gill, "Squelching Office Conflicts," *Inc.* (November 2005), pp. 40–41.

Chapter 11 References

1 Cari Tuna, "Initiative Moves Women Up Corporate Ladder" (Theory & Practice column), *The Wall Street Journal* (October 20, 2008), p. B4.

2 Susan Berfield, "Bridging the Generation Gap," *BusinessWeek* (September 17, 2007), pp. 60–61.

3 Chad Terhune, "Pepsi, Vowing Diversity Isn't Just Image Polish, Seeks Inclusive Culture" (In the Lead column), *The Wall Street Journal* (April 19, 2005), p. B.1.

4 "Diversity in the New Millennium," *Working Woman* (September 2000), special advertising section.

5 This story is based on the experience of Glenn D. Capel, the only black financial advisor in a Merrill Lynch office in Greensboro, North Carolina, reported in Patrick McGeehan, "Blacks Speak of Isolation, But Merrill Says It's Trying to Change," *The New York Times* (July 14, 2006), p. C1.

6 Marilyn Loden and Judy B. Rosener, *Workforce America!* (Homewood, IL: Business One Irwin, 1991); and Marilyn Loden, *Implementing Diversity* (Homewood, IL: Irwin, 1996).

7 Anthony Oshiotse and Richard O'Leary, "Corning Creates an Inclusive Culture to Drive Technology Innovation and Performance," *Global Business and Organizational Excellence* 26, no. 3 (March–April 2007), pp. 7–21.

8 Frances J. Milliken and Luis I. Martins, "Searching for Common Threads: Understanding the Multiple Effects of Diversity in Organizational Groups," *Academy of Management Review* 21, no. 2 (1996), pp. 402–433.

9 C. Keen, "Human Resource Management Issues in the '90s," *Vital Speeches* 56, no. 24 (1990), pp. 752–754.

10 U.S. Census Bureau figures reported in Russ Wiles, "Businesses Encourage Employees to Learn Spanish," *USA Today* (December 7, 2008), http://www.usatoday.com/money/workplace/2007-12-08-spanish_n.htm?loc=interstitialskip (accessed March 17, 2008).

11 C. J. Prince, "Doing Diversity: The Question Isn't Why to Do It—But How. Here Are a Few Savvy Strategies That Really Work," *Chief Executive* (April 2005), p. 46; and Richard W. Judy and Carol D'Amico, *Workforce 2020: Work and Workers in the 21st Century* (Indianapolis, IN: Hudson Institute, 1997).

12 Edward Iwata, "Companies Find Gold Inside Melting Pot; Diverse Staff Helps Business Run Smoothly Across Borders," *USA Today* (July 9, 2007), p. B1.

13 Louise Story, "Seeking Leaders, U.S. Companies Think Globally," *The New York Times* (December 12, 2007), p. A1; Justin Martin, "The Global CEO: Overseas Experience Is Becoming a Must on Top Executives' Resumes," *Chief Executive* (January–February 2004), p. 24; and G. Pascal Zachary, "Mighty Is the Mongrel," *Fast Company* (July 2000), pp. 270–284.

14 "Britain Recruiters Seek Female Spies," *USA Today* (July 12, 2008), http://www.usatoday.com/news/world/2008-07-12-spy_N.htm (accessed June 5, 2009).

15 Ibid.

16 Orlando C. Richard, "Racial Diversity, Business Strategy, and Firm Performance: A Resource-Based View," *Academy of Management Journal* 43, no. 2 (2000), pp. 164–177.

17 Susan Caminiti, "The Diversity Factor," *Fortune* (October 19, 2007), pp. 95–105.

18 "Diversity Proves to Be Important to Allstate," *The Sacramento Observer* (November 10–November 16, 2005), p. 31; Louisa Wah, "Diversity at Allstate: A Competitive Weapon," *Management Review* (July–August 1999), pp. 24–30; "Allstate Top Company for Diversity; Best Company for African Americans," *Business Wire* (April 18, 2006), p. 1; and information on the company available at http://www.allstate.com.

19 Survey results reported in "Diversity Initiatives Shown to Be Critical to Job Seekers," *The New York Times Magazine* (September 14, 2003), p. 100, part of a special advertisement, "Diversity Works."

20 Universum USA Survey, results reported in "Walking the Walk," *MBA Jungle* (March 2008), pp. 40–41.

21 Thomas E. Poulin, "The Other Diversity," *PA Times, American Society for Public Administration* (March 2009), p. 8; and Clayton H. Osborne and Vincent M. Cramer, "Fueling High Performance Through Diversity," *Chief Learning Officer* (November 2005), p. 22.

22 Geoffrey Colvin, "The 50 Best Companies for Asians, Blacks, and Hispanics," *Fortune* (July 19, 1999), pp. 53–58.

23 Taylor H. Cox, *Cultural Diversity in Organizations* (San Francisco: Berrett-Koehler, 1994).

24 G. Haight, "Managing Diversity," *Across the Board* 27, no. 3 (1990), pp. 22–29.

25 Atul Gawande, "Manning the Hospital Barricades: Why Do Groups—Even Groups of Doctors—Hate Each Other?" *Slate* (June 26, 1998), http://www.slate.com/it/2677/ (accessed April 4, 2009).

26 Norma Carr-Ruffino, *Managing Diversity: People Skills for a Multicultural Workplace* (Tucson, AZ: Thomson Executive Press, 1996), p. 92; and Judy Rosener, *America's Competitive Secret: Women Managers* (New York: Oxford University Press, 1995), pp. 33–34.

27 Susan Webber, "Fit vs. Fitness," *The Conference Board Review* (July–August 2007), pp. 19–25.

28 Roger Parloff, "The War over Unconscious Bias," *Fortune* (October 15, 2007), pp. 90–102.

29 Marianne Bertrand, "Racial Bias in Hiring: Are Emily and Brendan More Employable Than Lakisha and Jamal?" *Capital Ideas* (February 2005), pp. 7–9; and Marianne Bertrand and Sendhil Mullainathan, *Are Emily and Greg More Employable Than Lakisha and Jamal?* (National Bureau of Economic Research Report), as reported in L. A. Johnson, "What's in a Name: When Emily Gets the Job over Lakisha," *The Tennessean* (January 4, 2004), p. 14A.

30 Reported in Michael Orey, "White Men Can't Help It," *BusinessWeek* (May 15, 2006), pp. 54, 57.

31 Johnson, "What's in a Name: When Emily Gets the Job over Lakisha."

32 Roy Harris, "The Illusion of Inclusion," *CFO* (May 2001), pp. 42–50.

33 Jennifer L. Knight, Michelle R. Hebl, Jessica B. Foster, and Laura M. Mannix, "Out of Role? Out of Luck: The Influence of Race and Leadership Status on Performance Appraisals," *The Journal of Leadership and Organizational Studies* 9, no. 3 (2003), pp. 85–93.

34 Ann Morrison, *The New Leaders: Guidelines on Leadership Diversity in America* (San Francisco: Jossey-Bass, 1992), p. 37.

35 Studies reported in Lisa Belkin, "The Feminine Critique," *The New York Times* (November 1, 2007), p. G1; Erin White, "Advice for Women on Developing a Leadership Style," *The Wall Street Journal* (August 28, 2007), p. B5; and Carol Hymowitz, "Looking at Clinton, Seeing Themselves—Executive Women Identify with the Scrutiny She's Facing" (In the Lead column), *The Wall Street Journal* (November 12, 2007), p. B1.

36 Debra E. Meyerson and Joyce K. Fletcher, "A Modest Manifesto for Shattering the Glass Ceiling," *Harvard Business Review* (January–February 2000), pp. 127–136; Julie Amparano Lopez, "Study Says Women Face Glass Walls as Well as Glass Ceiling," *The Wall Street Journal* (March 3, 1992), pp. B1, B2; and Joann S. Lublin, "Women at Top Still Are Distant from CEO Jobs," *The Wall Street Journal* (February 28, 1996), pp. B1, B8.

37 Catalyst survey results reported in Jason Forsythe, "Winning with Diversity," special advertising supplement to *The New York Times Magazine* (March 28, 2004), pp. 65–72.

38 Patricia Sellers, "*Fortune* 500 CEOs: Women on the Rise," *Fortune .cnn.com* (April 21, 2009), http://postcards.blogs.fortune.cnn .com/2009/04/20/fortune-500-ceos-women-on-the-rise (accessed June 3, 2009); "African American CEOs of *Fortune* 500 Companies," *BlackEntrepreneurProfile.com*, http://www.blackentrepreneur-profile.com/fortune-500-ceos (accessed June 3, 2009); and "First Black Woman to Head *Fortune* 500 Company," *The Louisiana Weekly* (June 1, 2009), http://www.louisianaweekly.com/news. php?viewStory=1384 (accessed June 3, 2009).

39 Barbara Reinhold, "Smashing Glass Ceilings: Why Women *Still* Find It Tough to Advance to the Executive Suite," *Journal of Organizational Excellence* (Summer 2005), pp. 43–55; Jory Des Jardins, "I Am Woman (I Think)," *Fast Company* (May 2005), pp. 25–26; Lisa Belkin, "The Opt-Out Revolution," *The New York Times Magazine* (October 26, 2003), pp. 43–47, 58; and Meyerson and Fletcher, "A Modest Manifesto for Shattering the Glass Ceiling."

40 Anat Arkin, "Hidden Talents," *People Management* (July 14, 2006).

41 Sarah Plass, "Wage Gaps for Women Frustrating Germany," *The New York Times* (September 3, 2008), p. C1.

42 Ginny Parker Woods, "Japan's Diversity Problem," *The Wall Street Journal* (October 24, 2005), pp. B1, B4.

43 Sylvia Ann Hewlett and Carolyn Buck Luce, "Off-Ramps and On-Ramps; Keeping Talented Women on the Road to Success," *Harvard Business Review* (March 2005), pp. 43–54.

44 Sheila Wellington, Marcia Brumit Kropf, and Paulette R. Gerkovich, "What's Holding Women Back?" *Harvard Business Review* (June 2003), pp. 18–19.

45 The Leader's Edge/Executive Women Research 2002 survey, reported in "Why Women Leave," *Executive Female* (Summer 2003), p. 4.

46 Reinhold, "Smashing Glass Ceilings"; Des Jardins, "I Am Woman (I Think)"; and Alice H. Eagly and Linda L. Carli, "The Female Leadership Advantage: An Evaluation of the Evidence," *The Leadership Quarterly* 14 (2003), pp. 807–834.

47 Claudia H. Deutsch, "Behind the Exodus of Executive Women: Boredom," *USA Today* (May 2, 2005).

48 Statistics from the National Urban League, reported in E. M. Sicoli, "Closing the Economic Gap," *Fortune* (February 18, 2008), pp. S1–S12, also available at http://www.fortune.com/adsections.

49 U.S. Department of Labor, *Futurework: Trends and Challenges for Work in the 21st Century* (September 1999), available at http:// www.dol.gov/oasam/programs/history/herman/reports/futurework/ report.htm; "A Team Effort to Help Native Americans," *Making a Difference* segment, *NBC Nightly News with Brian Williams*,

http://today.msnbc.com (accessed on August 16, 2009); and "Generational Gains in Postsecondary Education Appear to Have Stalled, a New ACE Report Finds," press release from The American Council on Education (October 9, 2008), http://www.acenet.org (accessed on August 16, 2009).

50 "Diversity: Developing Tomorrow's Leadership Today," *BusinessWeek* (December 20, 1999), special advertising section.

51 E. M. Sicoli, "Closing the Economic Gap," *Fortune* (February 18, 2008), pp. S1–S12, also available at http://www.fortune.com/adsections; Paula Fagerberg, "Ernst & Young: Strong, Flexible Leadership and the Freedom to Create Your Own Space," *The Black Collegian Online,* http://www.black-collegian.com/issues/1stsem06/diversity_employers/universum_ernst_young.htm (accessed on October 6, 2009); and Elissa Silverman, "Accounting Firms Seek to Diversify Image," *The Washington Post* (June 29, 2005), p. D-04.

52 Rosener, *America's Competitive Secret: Women Managers;* Judy B. Rosener, "Ways Women Lead," *Harvard Business Review* (November–December 1990), pp. 119–125; Sally Helgesen, *The Female Advantage: Women's Ways of Leadership* (New York: Currency/Doubleday, 1990); Joline Godfrey, "Been There, Doing That," *Inc.* (March 1996), pp. 21–22; Chris Lee, "The Feminization of Management," *Training* (November 1994), pp. 25–31; and Bernard M. Bass and Bruce J. Avolio, "Shatter the Glass Ceiling: Women May Make Better Managers," *Human Resource Management* 33, no. 4 (Winter 1994), pp. 549–560.

53 Reported in Tamar Lewin, "The New Gender Divide: At Colleges, Women Are Leaving Men in the Dust," *The New York Times* (July 9, 2006), Section 1, p. 1; and Mary Beth Marklein, "College Gender Gap Widens: 57% Are Women," *USA Today* (October 20, 2005), p. A1.

54 Lewin, "At Colleges, Women Are Leaving Men in the Dust"; and Jon Swartz, "Women Break to Front of Tech," *USA Today* (July 10, 2008), http://www.usatoday.com/money/companies/management/2008-07-10-women-ceos_N.htm (accessed July 11, 2008).

55 Michelle Conlin, "The New Gender Gap," *BusinessWeek* (May 26, 2003), pp. 74–82.

56 Quoted in Conlin, "The New Gender Gap."

57 Kathryn M. Bartol, David C. Martin, and Julie A. Kromkowski, "Leadership and the Glass Ceiling: Gender and Ethnic Group Influences on Leader Behaviors at Middle and Executive Managerial Levels," *The Journal of Leadership and Organizational Studies* 9, no. 3 (2003), pp. 8–19; Bernard M. Bass and Bruce J. Avolio, "Shatter the Glass Ceiling: Women May Make Better Managers," *Human Resource Management* 33, no. 4 (Winter 1994), pp. 549–560; and Rochelle Sharpe, "As Leaders, Women Rule," *BusinessWeek* (November 20, 2002), pp. 75–84.

58 Bass and Avolio, "Shatter the Glass Ceiling."

59 Cynthia Carroll, "Why Different Is Better," *Newsweek* (January 29, 2007), p. E4.

60 Catalyst study and other studies reported in Avivah Wittenberg-Cox and Alison Maitland, "Financial Diversity: Why Women in Business Became the Solution, Not the Problem; Numbers of Top Female Executives Are Falling Yet Evidence Suggests They May Hold the Key to Corporate Success," *The Guardian* (February 5, 2008), p. 23; and Dwight D. Frink, Robert K. Robinson, Brian Reithel, Michelle M. Arthur, Anthony P. Ammeter, Gerald R. Ferris, David M. Kaplan, and Hubert S. Morrisette, "Gender Demography and Organization Performance: A Two-Study Investigation with Convergence," *Group & Organization Management* 28, no. 1 (March 2003), pp. 127–147.

61 The study on competitiveness was reported in Hal R. Varian, "The Difference Between Men and Women, Revisited: It's About Competition," *The New York Times* (March 9, 2006), p. C3. For recent reviews and analyses of the research on gender differences in leadership, see Nicole Z. Stelter, "Gender Differences in Leadership: Current Social Issues and Future Organizational Implications," *The Journal of Leadership Studies* 8, no. 4 (2002), pp. 88–99; and Alice H. Eagly, Mary C. Johannesen-Schmidt, and Marloes L. van Engen, "Transformational, Transactional, and Laissez-Faire Leadership Styles: A Meta-Analysis Comparing Women and Men," *Psychological Bulletin* 129, no. 4 (July 2003), p. 569ff.

62 Lena Williams, "A Silk Blouse on the Assembly Line? (Yes, the Boss's)," *The New York Times* (February 5, 1995), Business Section, p. 7.

63 Based on Rosener, *America's Competitive Secret,* pp. 129–135.

64 Susan Carey, "More Women Take Flight in Airline Operations," *The Wall Street Journal* (August 14, 2007), p. B1; and Ann Therese Palmer, "Teacher Learns All About Airline; United VP Began as Reservations Clerk, Rose Through Ranks," *Chicago Tribune* (December 24, 2006), p. 3.

65 Susan J. Wells, "A Female Executive Is Hard to Find," *HR Magazine* (June 2001), pp. 40–49; and Helgesen, *The Female Advantage.*

66 M. Fine, F. Johnson, and M. S. Ryan, "Cultural Diversity in the Workforce," *Public Personnel Management* 19 (1990), pp. 305–319; and Dawn Hill, "Women Leaders Doing It Their Way," *New Woman* (January 1994), p. 78.

67 "Muslim Leader: 150 Workers Fired over Prayer Dispute in Nebraska," *USA Today* (September 19, 2009), http://www.usatoday.com/news/religion/2008-09-19-muslim-prayer-business_N.htm (accessed September 20, 2008).

68 Kevin Maguire, "Harriet Harman's Equality Bill Signposts the Route to a Better Britain," *Mirror.co.uk* (April 29, 2009), http://www.mirror.co.uk/news/columnists/maguire/2009/04/29/harriet-harman-s-equality-bill-points-to-the-route-for-a-better-britain-115875-21316506 (accessed June 5, 2009).

69 Helen Bloom, "Can the United States Export Diversity?" *Across the Board* (March/April 2002), pp. 47–51.

70 "Molding Global Leaders," *Fortune* (October 11, 1999), p. 270.

71 Geert Hofstede, "The Interaction Between National and Organizational Value Systems," *Journal of Management Studies* 22 (1985), pp. 347–357; and Hofstede, "The Cultural Relativity of the Quality of Life Concept," *Academy of Management Review* 9 (1984), pp. 389–398.

72 Debby Young, "Team Heat," *CIO* (September 1, 1998), Section 1, pp. 43–51.

73 Geert Hofstede, "Cultural Constraints in Management Theories," excerpted in Dorothy Marcic and Sheila M. Puffer, *Management International: Cases, Exercises, and Readings* (St. Paul, MN: West Publishing, 1994), p. 24.

74 The discussion of cultural intelligence is based on P. Christopher Earley and Elaine Mosakowski, "Cultural Intelligence," *Harvard Business Review* (October 2004), p. 139; Ilan Alon and James M. Higgins, "Global Leadership Success Through Emotional and Cultural Intelligence," *Business Horizons* 48 (2005), pp. 501–512; P. C. Earley and Soon Ang, *Cultural Intelligence: Individual Actions Across Cultures* (Stanford, CA: Stanford Business Books, 2003); and David C. Thomas and Kerr Inkson, *Cultural Intelligence: People Skills for Global Business* (San Francisco: Berrett-Koehler, 2004).

75 These components are from Earley and Mosakowski, "Cultural Intelligence."

76 Ken Powell, "Move Beyond Your Comfort Zone," *Fortune* (May 4, 2009), p. 48.

77 Karl Moore, "Great Global Managers," *Across the Board* (May–June 2003), pp. 40–43.

78 Alison M. Konrad, Roger Kashlak, Izumi Yoshioka, Robert Waryszak, and Nina Toren, "What Do Managers *Like* to Do?" *Group & Organization Management* 26, no. 4 (December 2001), pp. 401–433.

79 Reported in Jeanne Brett, Kristin Behfar, and Mary C. Kern, "Managing Multicultural Teams," *Harvard Business Review* (November 2006), pp. 84–91.

80 Harry C. Triandis, "The Contingency Model in Cross-Cultural Perspective," in Martin M. Chemers and Roya Ayman, eds., *Leadership Theory and Research: Perspectives and Directions* (San Diego, CA: Academic Press, Inc., 1993), pp. 167–188; and Peter B. Smith and Mark F. Peterson, *Leadership, Organizations, and Culture: An Event Management Model* (London: Sage Publications, 1988).

81 Renee Blank and Sandra Slipp, "The White Male: An Endangered Species?" *Management Review* (September 1994), pp. 27–32; and Sharon Nelton, "Nurturing Diversity," *Nation's Business* (June 1995), pp. 25–27.

82 Based on M. Bennett, "A Developmental Approach to Training for Intercultural Sensitivity," *International Journal of Intercultural Relations* 10 (1986), pp. 179–196.

83 Sue Shellenbarger, "Employers Step Up Efforts to Lure Stay-at-Home Mothers Back to Work," *The Wall Street Journal* (February 9, 2006), p. D1; and Susan Caminiti, "Moving Up the Ranks," *Fortune* (June 25, 2007), pp. S1–S9, also available at http://www.fortune.com/sections.

84 J. Black and M. Mendenhall, "Cross-Cultural Training Effectiveness: A Review and a Theoretical Framework for Future Research," *Academy of Management Review* 15 (1990), pp. 113–136.

85 Laura Egodigwe, "Back to Class," *The Wall Street Journal* (November 14, 2005), p. R4.

86 Lee Smith, "Closing the Gap," *Fortune* (November 14, 2005), pp. 211–218.

87 Martin M. Chemers and Roya Ayman, *Leadership Theory and Research: Perspectives and Directions* (San Diego, CA: Academic Press, 1993), p. 209.

88 Susan J. Wells, "Smoothing the Way," *HR Magazine* (June 2001), pp. 52–58.

89 Irwin Speizer, "Diversity on the Menu," *Workforce Management* (November 2004), p. 41ff; Daniel Valentine, "King Award Given to Denny's Executive," *Capital* (January 15, 2006), p. D1; Jim Adamson, "How Denny's Went from Icon of Racism to Diversity Award Winner," *Journal of Organizational Excellence* (Winter 2000), pp. 55–68; Sonia Alleyne and Nicole Marie Richardson, "The 40 Best Companies for Diversity," *Black Enterprise* (July 2006), p. 100ff; and "Denny's Diversity Speaks," http://www.dennysdiversity.com (accessed on October 6, 2009).

Chapter 12 References

1 Jennifer Reingold, "The Unsinkable Mellody Hobson," *Fortune* (October 27, 2008), pp. 148–157.

2 The terms *transactional* and *transformational leadership* are from James MacGregor Burns, *Leadership* (New York: Harper & Row, 1978); and Bernard M. Bass, "Leadership: Good, Better, Best," *Organizational Dynamics* 13 (Winter 1985), pp. 26–40.

3 This discussion is based on Bernard M. Bass, "Theory of Transformational Leadership Redux," *Leadership Quarterly* 6, no. 4 (1995), pp. 463–478; Noel M. Tichy and Mary Anne Devanna, *The Transformational Leader* (New York: John Wiley & Sons, 1986); and Badrinarayan Shankar Pawar and Kenneth K. Eastman, "The Nature and Implications of Contextual Influences on Transformational Leadership: A Conceptual Examination," *Academy of Management Review* 22, no. 1 (1997), pp. 80–109.

4 See Taly Dvir, Dov Eden, Bruce J. Avolio, and Boas Shamir, "Impact of Transformational Leadership on Follower Development and Performance: A Field Experiment," *Academy of Management Journal* 45, no. 4 (2002), pp. 735–744; Ronald F. Piccola and Jason A. Colquitt, "Transformational Leadership and Job Behaviors: The Mediating Role of Core Job Characteristics," *Academy of Management Journal* 49, no. 2 (2006), pp. 327–340; and Jens Rowold and Kathrin Heinitz, "Transformational and Charismatic Leadership: Assessing the Convergent, Divergent, and Criterion Validity of the MLQ and CKS," *The Leadership Quarterly* 18 (2007), pp. 121–133.

5 Based on Bernard M. Bass, "Theory of Transformational Leadership Redux," *Leadership Quarterly* 6, no. 4 (Winter 1995), pp. 463–478; "From Transactional to Transformational Leadership: Learning to Share the Vision," *Organizational Dynamics* 18, no. 3 (Winter 1990), pp. 19–31; Francis J. Yammarino, William D. Spangler, and Bernard M. Bass, "Transformational Leadership and Performance: A Longitudinal Investigation," *Leadership Quarterly* 4, no. 1 (Spring 1993), pp. 81–102; and B. M. Bass, "Current Developments in Transformational Leadership," *The Psychologist-Manager Journal* 3, no. 1 (1999), pp. 5–21.

6 Noel M. Tichy and Mary Anne Devanna, *The Transformational Leader* (New York: John Wiley & Sons, 1986), pp. 265–266.

7 Manfred F. R. Kets De Vries, "Charisma in Action: The Transformational Abilities of Virgin's Richard Branson and ABB's Percy Barnevik," *Organizational Dynamics* (Winter 1998), pp. 7–21.

8 Katherine J. Klein and Robert J. House, "On Fire: Charismatic Leadership and Levels of Analysis," *Leadership Quarterly* 6, no. 2 (1995), pp. 183–198.

9 Gretel C. Kovach, "Moderate Muslim Voice Falls Silent: Charismatic Young Leader Leaves Egypt as His Popular Sermons Come Under Government Scrutiny," *The Christian Science Monitor* (November 26, 2002), p. 6.

10 Rakesh Khurana, "The Curse of the Superstar CEO," *Harvard Business Review* (September 2002), pp. 60–66.

11 Jerry Porras, Steward Emery, and Mark Thompson, "The Cause Has Charisma," *Leader to Leader* (Winter 2007), pp. 26–31.

12 Keith H. Hammonds, "You Can't Lead Without Making Sacrifices," *Fast Company,* (June 2001), pp. 106–116.

13 Jay A. Conger, Rabindra N. Kanungo, and Associates, *Charismatic Leadership: The Elusive Factor in Organizational Effectiveness* (San Francisco: Jossey-Bass, 1988); Robert J. House and Jane M. Howell, "Personality and Charismatic Leadership," *Leadership Quarterly* 3, no. 2 (1992), pp. 81–108; Klein and House, "On Fire: Charismatic Leadership and Levels of Analysis"; Harold B. Jones, "Magic, Meaning, and Leadership: Weber's Model and the Empirical Literature," *Human Relations* 54, no. 6 (June 2001), pp. 753–771; and Boas Shamir, Michael B. Arthur, and Robert J. House, "The Rhetoric of Charismatic Leadership: A Theoretical Extension, A Case Study, and Implications for Future Research," *Leadership Quarterly* 5, no. 1 (1994), pp. 25–42.

14 The following discussion is based primarily on Conger et al., *Charismatic Leadership.*

15 This discussion is based on Stephen Friedman and James K. Sebenius, "Organizational Transformation: The Quiet Role of Coalitional Leadership," *Ivey Business Journal* (January–February 2009), p. 1; Gerald R. Ferris, Darren C. Treadway, Pamela L. Perrewé, Robyn L. Brouer, Ceasar Douglas, and Sean Lux, "Political Skill in Organizations," *Journal of Management* (June 2007), pp. 290–320; Vadim Liberman, "Mario Moussa Wants You to Win Your Next Argument" (Questioning Authority column), *Conference Board Review* (November–December 2007), pp. 25–26; Samuel B. Bacharach, "Politically Proactive," *Fast Company* (May 2005), p. 93; and Lauren Keller Johnson, "Debriefing Jay Conger: Exerting Influence Without Authority," *Harvard Management Update* (December 2003), pp. 3–4.

16 Friedman and Sebenius, "Organizational Transformation: The Quiet Role of Coalitional Leadership."

17 Meridith Levinson, "The Art of the Schmooze," *CIO* (April 15, 2002), pp. 99–104.

18 Cari Tuna, "Repairing an Agency's Credibility," *The Wall Street Journal* (March 23, 2009), p. B6.

19 These data are adapted from materials supplied by ExperiencePoint Inc., in conjunction with the Global Tech simulation, 2007.

20 Friedman and Sebenius, "Organizational Transformation."

21 James MacGregor Burns, *Leadership* (New York: Harper & Row, 1978).

22 Robert A. Dahl, "The Concept of Power," *Behavioral Science* 2 (1957), pp. 201–215.

23 W. Graham Astley and Paramijit S. Pachdeva, "Structural Sources of Intraorganizational Power: A Theoretical Synthesis," *Academy of Management Review* 9 (1984), pp. 104–113; and Abraham Kaplan, "Power in Perspective," in Robert L. Kahn and Elise Boulding, eds., *Power and Conflict in Organizations* (London: Tavistock, 1964), pp. 11–32.

24 Gerald R. Salancik and Jeffrey Pfeffer, "The Bases and Use of Power in Organizational Decision Making: The Case of the University," *Administrative Science Quarterly* 19 (1974), pp. 453–473.

25 Earle Hitchner, "The Power to Get Things Done," *National Productivity Review* 12 (Winter 1992/93), pp. 117–122.

26 John R. P. French, Jr., and Bertram Raven, "The Bases of Social Power," in D. Cartwright and A. F. Zander, eds., *Group Dynamics* (Evanston, IL: Row Peterson, 1960), pp. 607–623.

27 Reported in Liberman, "Mario Moussa Wants You to Win Your Next Argument."

28 Anna Mulrine, "Harnessing the Brute Force of Soft Power," *US News & World Report* (December 1–December 8, 2008), p. 47.

29 Wesley Clark, "The Potency of Persuasion," *Fortune* (November 12, 2007), p. 48.

30 Jeffrey Pfeffer, *Power in Organizations* (Marshfield, MA: Pitman Publishing, 1981).

31 Steve Moore, "Not Bad for a Hippie Dropout," *Management Today* (March 2009), p. 27; Connie Guglielmo, "What Makes Steve Jobs Run?" *National Post* (May 17, 2008), p. FW-8; and "Editorial: Apple—and U.S.—Need Steve Jobs," *McClatchy-Tribune Business News* (January 18, 2009).

32 Gary A. Yukl and T. Taber, "The Effective Use of Managerial Power," *Personnel* (March–April 1983), pp. 37–44.

33 Jeffrey Pfeffer, *Managing with Power: Politics and Influence in Organizations* (Boston: Harvard University Press, 1992); Gerald R. Salancik and Jeffrey Pfeffer, "Who Gets Power—and How They Hold onto It: A Strategic Contingency Model of Power," *Organizational Dynamics* (Winter 1977), pp. 3–21; Pfeffer, *Power in Organizations*; and Carol Stoak Saunders, "The Strategic Contingencies Theory of Power: Multiple Perspectives," *Journal of Management Studies* 27 (1990), pp. 1–18.

34 R. E. Emerson, "Power-Dependence Relations," *American Sociological Review* 27 (1962), pp. 31–41.

35 Carol Hymowitz, "Managers Are Starting to Gain More Clout over Their Employees" (In the Lead column), *The Wall Street Journal* (January 30, 2001), p. B1.

36 Henry Mintzberg, *Power In and Around Organizations* (Upper Saddle River, NJ: Prentice Hall, 1963).

37 Jared Sandberg, "How Office Tyrants in Critical Positions Get Others to Grovel," *The Wall Street Journal* (August 21, 2007), p. B1.

38 Erik W. Larson and Jonathan B. King, "The Systemic Distortion of Information: An Ongoing Challenge to Management," *Organizational Dynamics* 24, no. 3 (Winter 1996), pp. 49–61; and Thomas H. Davenport, Robert G. Eccles, and Lawrence Prusak, "Information Politics," *Sloan Management Review* (Fall 1992), pp. 53–65.

39 John Hechinger, "Financial Aid Directors Received Payments from Preferred Lender; Student Loan Xpress Puts Three Managers on Leave Amid Multiple Inquiries," *The Wall Street Journal* (April 10, 2007), p. A3; and James Bandler with Doris Burke, "What Cuomo Wants from Wall Street," *Fortune* (December 8, 2008), pp. 103–110.

40 Pfeffer, *Power in Organizations*, p. 70.

41 Gerald R. Ferris, Darren C. Treadway, Robert W. Kolodinsky, Wayne A. Hochwarter, Charles J. Kacmar, Ceasar Douglas, and Dwight D. Frink, "Development and Validation of the Political Skill Inventory," *Journal of Management* 31, no. 1 (February 2005), pp. 126–152.

42 See Amy J. Hillman and Michael A. Hitt, "Corporate Political Strategy Formulation: A Model of Approach, Participation, and Strategy Decisions," *Academy of Management Review* 24, no. 4 (1999), pp. 825–842, for a recent examination of organizational approaches to political action.

43 Stephen Labaton and Jackie Calmes, "Administration Aims to Oversee Derivatives; Complex Financial Instruments Helped Cause Financial Crisis," *Houston Chronicle* (May 14, 2009), p. 1.

44 Jeffrey Pfeffer, *Managing with Power: Politics and Influence in Organizations* (Boston, MA: Harvard Business School Press, 1992); Amos Drory and Tsilia Romm, "The Definition of Organizational Politics: A Review," *Human Relations* 43 (1990), pp. 1133–1154; Donald J. Vredenburgh and John G. Maurer, "A Process Framework of Organizational Politics," *Human Relations* 37 (1984), pp. 47–66; and Lafe Low, "It's Politics, as Usual," *CIO* (April 1, 2004), pp. 87–90.

45 This section is based on Lee G. Bolman and Terrence E. Deal, *Reframing Organizations: Artistry, Choice, and Leadership* (San Francisco: Jossey-Bass, 1991); and L. G. Bolman and T. E. Deal, "Leadership and Management Effectiveness: A Multi-Frame, Multi-Sector Analysis," *Human Resource Management* 30, no. 4 (Winter 1991), pp. 509–534.

46 John R. Carlson, Dawn S. Carlson, and Lori L. Wadsworth, "The Relationship Between Individual Power Moves and Group Agreement Type: An Examination and Model," *SAM Advanced Management Journal* (Autumn 2000), pp. 44–51.

47 D. Kipnis, S. M. Schmidt, C. Swaffin-Smith, and I. Wilkinson, "Patterns of Managerial Influence: Shotgun Managers, Tacticians, and Bystanders," *Organizational Dynamics* (Winter 1984), pp. 58–67.

48 Ibid.; and Pfeffer, *Managing with Power*, Chapter 13.

49 This discussion is based partly on Robert B. Cialdini, "Harnessing the Science of Persuasion," *Harvard Business Review* (October 2001), pp. 72–79.

50 Judith Tingley, *The Power of Indirect Influence* (New York: AMACOM, 2001), as reported by Martha Craumer, "When the Direct Approach Backfires, Try Indirect Influence," *Harvard Management Communication Letter* (June 2001), pp. 3–4.

51 Robert B. Cialdini, *Influence: Science and Practice,* 4th ed. (Boston, MA: Allyn & Bacon, 2001); R. B. Cialdini, "Harnessing the Science of Persuasion," *Harvard Business Review* (October 2001), pp. 72–79; Allan R. Cohen and David L. Bradford, "The Influence Model: Using Reciprocity and Exchange to Get What You Need," *Journal of Organizational Excellence* (Winter 2005), pp. 57–80; and Jared Sandberg, "People Can't Resist Doing a Big Favor—Or Asking for One" (Cubicle Culture column), *The Wall Street Journal* (December 18, 2007), p. B1.

52 Raymond Hernandez and David W. Chen, "Keeping Lawmakers Happy Through Gifts to Pet Charities," *The New York Times* (October 19, 2008), p. A1.

53 Cialdini, "Harnessing the Science of Persuasion."

54 Cohen and Bradford, "The Influence Model."

55 Pfeffer, *Power in Organizations,* p. 70.

56 V. Dallas Merrell, *Huddling: The Informal Way to Management Success* (New York: AMACON, 1979).

57 Ceasar Douglas and Anthony P. Ammeter, "An Examination of Leader Political Skill and Its Effect on Ratings of Leader Effectiveness," *Leadership Quarterly* 15 (2004), pp. 537–550.

58 Mark DeCambre, "Bair Breaks Rank—FDIC Chief Challenges Geithner, Treasury Plan, " *The New York Post* (March 20, 2009), p. 39; Alan Zibel, "FDIC Chairman Sheila Bair Finds Friends in Obama Administration," *The Ledger* (February 9, 2009); Joanna Chung, "Bair Lobbies for Stronger Position," *Financial Times* (June 12, 2009), p. 6; and Michael Crittenden, "Top Women to Watch," *The Wall Street Journal Europe* (November 10, 2008), p. 18.

59 Richard L. Daft, *Organization Theory and Design*, 6th ed. (Cincinnati, OH: South-Western, 1998), Chapter 12.

60 Cialdini, "Harnessing the Science of Persuasion."

61 Robert B. Cialdini, *Influence: Science and Practice,* 4th ed. (Boston: Pearson, Allyn & Bacon, 2000).

62 Steven R. Weisman, "How Battles at Bank Ended 'Second Chance' at a Career," *The New York Times* (May 18, 2007), p. A14.

63 Quoted in Allan R. Cohen, Stephen L. Fink, Herman Gadon, and Robin D. Willits, *Effective Behavior in Organizations,* 7th ed. (New York: McGraw-Hill Irwin, 2001), p. 254.

64 Robert J. House and Jane M. Howell, "Personality and Charismatic Leadership," *Leadership Quarterly* 3, no. 2 (1992), pp. 81–108; and Jennifer O'Connor, Michael D. Mumford, Timothy C. Clifton, Theodore L. Gessner, and Mary Shane Connelly, "Charismatic Leaders and Destructiveness: An Historiometric Study," *Leadership Quarterly* 6, no. 4 (1995), pp. 529–555.

65 For a discussion of personalized and socialized power, see David C. McClelland, *Power: The Inner Experience* (New York: Irvington, 1975).

66 "Stop the Politics," *Forbes ASAP* (April 3, 2000), p. 126.

Chapter 13 References

1 Sharda Prashad, "The Value Chain," *Canadian Business* (February 17–March 2, 2009), pp. 65–69.

2 Keith H. Hammonds, "The Monroe Doctrine," *Fast Company* (October 1999), pp. 230–236.

3 R. Duane Ireland and Michael A. Hitt, "Achieving and Maintaining Strategic Competitiveness in the 21st Century: The Role of Strategic Leadership," *Academy of Management Executive* 13, no. 1 (1999), pp. 43–57; M. Davids, "Where Style Meets Substance," *Journal of Business Strategy* 16, no. 1 (1995), pp. 48–60; and R. P. White, P. Hodgson, and S. Crainer, *The Future of Leadership* (London: Pitman Publishing, 1997).

4 Ireland and Hitt, "Achieving and Maintaining Strategic Competitiveness."

5 Louisa Wah, "The Dear Cost of 'Scut Work,'" *Management Review* (June 1999), pp. 27–31.

6 Gary Hamel and C. K. Prahalad, "Seeing the Future First," *Fortune* (September 5, 1994), pp. 64–70.

7 Ray Maghroori and Eric Rolland, "Strategic Leadership: The Art of Balancing Organizational Mission with Policy, Procedures, and External Environment," *The Journal of Leadership Studies,* no. 2 (1997), pp. 62–81.

8 Pieter Klaas Jagersma, "Aspiration and Leadership," *Journal of Business Strategy* 28, no. 1 (2007), pp. 45–52.

9 James C. Collins and Jerry I. Porras, "Building Your Company's Vision," *Harvard Business Review* (September–October 1996), pp. 65–77.

10 R. J. Baum, E. A. Locke, and S. Kirkpatrick, "A Longitudinal Study of the Relations of Vision and Vision Communication to Venture Growth in Entrepreneurial Firms," *Journal of Applied Psychology* 83 (1998), pp. 43–54; studies reported in Anthony Bell, "Using Vision to Shape the Future," *Leader to Leader* (Summer 2007), pp. 17–21; and Prashad, "The Value Chain."

11 Robert S. Kaplan, "What to Ask the Person in the Mirror," *Harvard Business Review* (January 2007), pp. 86–95.

12 Roger Thurow, "Different Recipe; To Tackle Hunger, a Food Bank Tries Training Chefs," *The Wall Street Journal* (November 28, 2006), pp. A1, A13; and "Joseph Weber, "Waging War on Hunger," *BusinessWeek* (May 16, 2005), pp. 94, 96.

13 Andrea Kilpatrick and Les Silverman, "The Power of Vision," *Strategy & Leadership* 33, no. 2 (2005), pp. 24–26.

14 Andrew Douglas, John O. Burtis, and L. Kristine Pond-Burtis, "Myth and Leadership Vision: Rhetorical Manifestation of Cultural Force," *The Journal of Leadership Studies* 7, no. 4 (2001), pp. 55–69.

15 This section is based on Burt Nanus, *Visionary Leadership* (San Francisco: Jossey-Bass, 1992), pp. 16–18; and Richard L. Daft and Robert H. Lengel, *Fusion Leadership: Unlocking the Subtle Forces That Change People and Organizations* (San Francisco: Berrett-Koehler, 1998).

16 Alan Deutschman, "Can Google Stay Google?" *Fast Company* (August 2005), pp. 62–68.

17 Oren Harari, "Looking Beyond the Vision Thing," *Management Review* (June 1997), pp. 26–29; and William D. Hitt, *The Leader-Manager: Guidelines for Action* (Columbus, OH: Battelle Press, 1988), p. 54.

18 Nancy Chambers, "The Really Long View," *Management Review* (January 1998), pp. 11–15; and Arie de Geus, "The Living Company," *Harvard Business Review* (March–April 1997), pp. 51–59.

19 Study reported in Edward Prewitt, "Watch What You Say," *CIO* (November 1, 2005), p. 26.

20 Nanus, *Visionary Leadership,* p. 16.

21 Collins and Porras, "Building Your Company's Vision," p. 74.

22 Roger E. Herman and Joyce L. Gioia, "Making Work Meaningful: Secrets of the Future-Focused Corporation," *The Futurist* (December 1998), pp. 24–26.

23 "What I Know Now," an interview with Michael L. Eskew by Paul B. Brown, *Fast Company* (November 2008), p. 108.

24 James M. Kouzes and Barry Z. Posner, *The Leadership Challenge: How to Get Extraordinary Things Done in Organizations* (San Francisco: Jossey-Bass, 1988), p. 98.

25 Dean Foust, "The BW 50: The Best Performers of 2008," *BusinessWeek* (April 7, 2008), pp. 51–73.

26 Marshall Sashkin, "The Visionary Leader," in Jay Conger and Rabindra N. Kanungo, eds., *Charismatic Leadership: The Elusive Factor in Organizational Effectiveness* (San Francisco: Jossey-Bass, 1988), pp. 122–160.

27 James C. Collins and Jerry I. Porras, "Organizational Vision and Visionary Organizations," *California Management Review* (Fall 1991), pp. 30–52.

28 Anthony Bell, "Using Vision to Shape the Future," *Leader to Leader* (Summer 2007), pp. 17–21.

29 Nanus, *Visionary Leadership,* p. 26; John W. Gardner, "Leadership and the Future," *The Futurist* (May–June 1990), pp. 9–12; and Warren Bennis and Burt Nanus, *Leaders: The Strategies for Taking Charge* (New York: Harper & Row, 1985), p. 93.

30 Gardner, "Leadership and the Future."

31 William F. Powers, segment in Polly LaBarre, ed., "What's New, What's Not" (Unit of One), *Fast Company* (January 1999), p. 73.

32 Danielle Sacks, "Inspiration Junkies," *Fast Company* (November 2005), pp. 95–97; and http://www.roadtripnation.com/aboutus.php (accessed June 25, 2009).

33 Peter M. Senge, *The Fifth Discipline: The Art and Practice of the Learning Organization* (New York: Doubleday/Currency, 1990), pp. 205–225.

34 Quoted in Senge, *The Fifth Discipline,* p. 218.

35 Joe Jaworski, quoted in Alan M. Webber, "Destiny and the Job of the Leader," *Fast Company* (June–July 1996), pp. 40, 42.

36 Susan Ellingwood, "On a Mission," *Gallup Management Journal* (Winter 2001), pp. 6–7.

37 Bill George, "The Company's Mission Is the Message," *strategy+business* 33 (Winter 2003), pp. 13–14; and Jim Collins and Jerry Porras, *Built to Last: Successful Habits of Visionary Companies* (New York: HarperBusiness, 1994).

38 Ellingwood, "On a Mission."

39 Collins and Porras, "Building Your Company's Vision."

40 Art Kleiner, George Roth, and Nina Kruschwitz, "Should a Company Have a Noble Purpose?" *The Conference Board Review* (January–February 2001).

41 This discussion is based on Nikos Mourkogiannis, "The Realist's Guide to Moral Purpose," *strategy+business* 41 (Winter 2005), pp. 42–53; and Nikos Mourkogiannis, "Purpose: The Starting Point of Great Leadership," *Leader to Leader* (Spring 2007), pp. 26–32.

42 Deutschman, "Can Google Stay Google?"

43 Bill Breen, "The Seoul of Design," *Fast Company* (December 2005), pp. 90–99; and Peter Lewis, "A Perpetual Crisis Machine," *Fortune* (September 19, 2005), pp. 58–76.

44 Mourkogiannis, "Purpose: The Starting Point of Great Leadership."

45 Steve Lohr, "Apple, a Success at Stores, Bets Big on Fifth Avenue," *The New York Times* (May 19, 2006), p. C1; and Michael V. Copeland, "The Apple Ecosystem," *Fortune* (November 23, 2009), pp. 102–109.

46 Bill Vlasic, "Honda Stays True to Efficient Driving," *The New York Times* (August 26, 2008), p. C1.

47 Mourkogiannis, "The Realist's Guide to Moral Purpose."

48 Ibid.

49 John E. Prescott, "Environments as Moderators of the Relationship Between Strategy and Performance," *Academy of Management Journal* 29 (1986), pp. 329–346.

50 C. Chet Miller and Laura B. Cardinal, "Strategic Planning and Firm Performance: A Synthesis of More Than Two Decades of Research," *Academy of Management Journal* 37, no. 6 (1994), pp. 1649–1665.

51 Sydney Finkelstein and Donald C. Hambrick, *Strategic Leadership: Top Executives and Their Effect on Organizations* (St. Paul, MN: West Publishing, 1996), p. 23.

52 Ireland and Hitt, "Achieving and Maintaining Strategic Competitiveness."

53 Christopher Hoenig, "True Grit," *CIO* (May 1, 2002), pp. 50–52.

54 Personal story heard at Farmer's Restaurant in Tenants Harbor, Maine.

55 Rafael Gerena-Morales, "How a Harlem Hospital Healed Itself," *The Wall Street Journal* (June 22, 2006), pp. B1, B5.

56 Gregory M. Bounds, Gregory H. Dobbins, and Oscar S. Fowler, *Management: A Total Quality Perspective* (Cincinnati, OH: South-Western, 1995), p. 244; and Michael Treacy, "You Need a Value Discipline—But Which One?" *Fortune* (April 17, 1995), p. 195.

57 "Not by Bread Alone" (an interview with Ron Shaich by Corey Hajim), *Fortune* (July 10, 2006), p. 126.

58 L. J. Bourgeois III and David R. Brodwin, "Strategic Implementation: Five Approaches to an Elusive Phenomenon," *Strategic Management Journal* 5 (1984), pp. 241–264; Anil K. Gupta and V. Govindarajan, "Business Unit Strategy, Managerial Characteristics, and Business Unit Effectiveness at Strategy Implementation," *Academy of Management Journal* (1984), pp. 25–41; and Michael K. Allio, "A Short Practical Guide to Implementing Strategy," *Journal of Business Strategy* 26, no. 4 (2005), pp. 12–21.

59 2004 *Economist* survey, reported in Allio, "A Short, Practical Guide to Implementing Strategy."

60 M. Corboy and D. O'Corrbui, "The Seven Deadly Sins of Strategy," *Management Accounting* 77, no. 10 (1999), pp. 29–33.

61 Wendy R. Boswell, John B. Bingham, and Alexander J. S. Colvin, "Aligning Employees Through 'Line of Sight,'" *Business Horizons* 49 (2006), pp. 499–509.

62 Ibid.

63 W. Robert Guffey and Brian J. Nienhaus, "Determinants of Employee Support for the Strategic Plan," *SAM Advanced Management Journal* (Spring 2002), pp. 23–30.

64 Michael Powell, "Suit Accuses Wells Fargo of Steering Blacks to Subprime Mortgages," *The New York Times* (June 7, 2009), p. A16.

65 Jennifer Reingold, "Home Depot's Total Rehab," *Fortune* (September 29, 2008), pp. 159–166.

66 Bruce Horovitz, "Payless Is Determined to Put a Fashionably Shod Foot Forward," *USA Today* (July 28, 2006), p. B1.

67 Thanks to Russell Guinn for the story on which this example is based.

68 Based on Gregory A. Patterson, "Land's End Kicks Out Modern New Managers, Rejecting a Makeover," *The Wall Street Journal* (April 3, 1995), pp. A1, A6.

69 Micheline Maynard, "With Eye on Profits, G. M. Began Missing on Innovation," *The New York Times* (December 6, 2008), p. B1; and John D. Stoll, Kevin Helliker, and Neal E. Boudette, "A Saga of Decline and Denial," *The Wall Street Journal* (June 2, 2009), p. A1. The quote is from Maynard.

70 Ibid.

71 Quoted in Pat McHenry Sullivan, "Finding Visions for Work and Life," *Spirit at Work* (April 1997), p. 3.

72 Jill M. Strange and Michael D. Mumford, "The Origins of Vision: Effects of Reflection, Models, and Analysis," *The Leadership Quarterly* 16 (2005), pp. 121–148.

73 Oren Harari, "Catapult Your Strategy Over Conventional Wisdom," *Management Review* (October 1997), pp. 21–24.

Chapter 14 References

1 Max Chafkin, "Everybody Loves Zappos," *Inc.* (May 2009), pp. 66–73; Jeffrey M. O'Brien, "Zappos Knows How to Kick It," *Fortune* (February 2, 2009), pp. 54–60; and "Jena McGregor, "Zappos' Secret: It's an Open Book," *BusinessWeek* (March 23–30, 2009), p. 62.

2 Jeremy Kahn, "What Makes a Company Great?" *Fortune* (October 26, 1998), p. 218; James C. Collins and Jerry I. Porras, *Built to Last: Successful Habits of Visionary Companies* (New York: HarperBusiness, 1994); and James C. Collins, "Change Is Good—But First Know What Should Never Change," *Fortune* (May 29, 1995), p. 141.

3 T. E. Deal and A. A. Kennedy, *The New Corporate Cultures: Revitalizing the Workforce After Downsizing, Mergers, and Reengineering* (New York: Basic Books, 2000).

4 Yoash Wiener, "Forms of Value Systems: A Focus on Organizational Effectiveness and Culture Change and Maintenance," *Academy of Management Review* 13 (1988), pp. 534–545; V. Lynne Meek, "Organizational Culture: Origins and Weaknesses," *Organization Studies* 9 (1988), pp. 453–473; and John J. Sherwood, "Creating Work Cultures with Competitive Advantage," *Organizational Dynamics* (Winter 1988), pp. 5–27.

5 Geoff Colvin, "The Defiant One," *Fortune* (April 30, 2007), pp. 86–92.

6 W. Jack Duncan, "Organizational Culture: Getting a 'Fix' on an Elusive Concept," *Academy of Management Executive* 3 (1989), pp. 229–236; Linda Smircich, "Concepts of Culture and Organizational Analysis," *Administrative Science Quarterly* 28 (1983), pp. 339–358; and Andrew D. Brown and Ken Starkey, "The Effect of Organizational Culture on Communication and Information," *Journal of Management Studies* 31, no. 6 (November 1994), pp. 807–828.

7 Edgar H. Schein, "Organizational Culture," *American Psychologist* 45, no. 2 (February 1990), pp. 109–119.

8 This discussion of the levels of culture is based on Edgar H. Schein, *Organizational Culture and Leadership*, 2nd ed. (San Francisco: Jossey-Bass, 1992), pp. 3–27.

9 Chris Blackhurst, "Sir Stuart Hampson," *Management Today* (July 2005), pp. 48–53.

10 John P. Kotter and James L. Heskett, *Corporate Culture and Performance* (New York: The Free Press, 1992), p. 6.

11 Peter B. Scott-Morgan, "Barriers to a High-Performance Business," *Management Review* (July 1993), pp. 37–41.

12 Arthur Ciancutti and Thomas Steding, "Trust Fund," *Business 2.0* (June 13, 2000), pp. 105–117.

13 Ellen McGirt, "Revolution in San Jose," *Fast Company* (January 2009), pp. 88–94, 134–136.

14 Bernard Arogyaswamy and Charles M. Byles, "Organizational Culture: Internal and External Fits," *Journal of Management* 13 (1987), pp. 647–659.

15 William D. Cohan, *House of Cards: A Tale of Hubris and Wretched Excess on Wall Street* (New York: Doubleday 2009); Chuck Leddy, "When Wall Street Bet the House," *Boston Globe* (March 28, 2009), p. G8; and Robin Sidel and Kate Kelly, "Bear Stearns a Year Later: From Fabled to Forgotten—Bear's Name, and Culture, Fade Away After J.P. Morgan's Fire-Sale Deal," *The Wall Street Journal* (March 14, 2009), p. B1.

16 Kotter and Heskett, *Corporate Culture and Performance*.

17 Paul Ingrassia, "How GM Lost Its Way," *The Wall Street Journal* (June 2, 2009), p. A21; and Micheline Maynard, "Chrysler Is Set, and New Task Is Fixing G.M.; U.S. Takes On the Insular G.M. Culture," *The New York Times* (June 11, 2009), p. A1.

18 Ralph H. Kilmann, Mary J. Saxton, Roy Serpa, and Associates, *Gaining Control of the Corporate Culture* (San Francisco: Jossey-Bass, 1985).

19 Larry Mallak, "Understanding and Changing Your Organization's Culture," *Industrial Management* (March–April 2001), pp. 18–24.

20 Claudia H. Deutsche, "Paper Jam at FedEx Kinko's," *The New York Times* (May 5, 2007), p. C1.

21 Reported in Chip Jarnagan and John W. Slocum, Jr., "Creating Corporate Cultures Through Mythopoetic Leadership," *Organizational Dynamics* 36, no. 3 (2007), pp. 288–302.

22 Jennifer A. Chatman and Sandra Eunyoung Cha, "Leading by Leveraging Culture," *California Management Review* 45, no. 4 (Summer 2003), pp. 20–34; and Jeff Rosenthal and Mary Ann Masarech, "High-Performance Cultures: How Values Can Drive Business Results," *Journal of Organizational Excellence* (Spring 2003), pp. 3–18.

23 Abby Ghobadian and Nicholas O'Regan, "The Link Between Culture, Strategy and Performance in Manufacturing SMEs," *Journal of General Management* 28, no. 1 (Autumn, 2002), pp. 16–34; G. G. Gordon and N. DiTomaso, "Predicting Corporate Performance from Organisational Culture," *Journal of Management Studies* 29, no. 6 (1992), pp. 783–798; and G. A. Marcoulides and R. H. Heck, "Organizational Culture and Performance: Proposing and Testing a Model," *Organization Science* 4 (1993), pp. 209–225.

24 John P. Kotter and John Heskett, *Corporate Culture and Performance* (New York: The Free Press, 1992).

25 Micah R. Kee, "Corporate Culture Makes a Fiscal Difference," *Industrial Management* (November–December 2003), pp. 16–20.

26 Tressie Wright Muldrow, Timothy Buckley, and Brigitte W. Schay, "Creating High-Performance Organizations in the Public Sector," *Human Resource Management* 41, no. 3 (Fall 2002), pp. 341–354.

27 Reggie Van Lee, Lisa Fabish, and Nancy McGaw, "The Value of Corporate Values: A Booz Allen Hamilton/Aspen Institute Survey," *strategy+business* 39 (Summer 2005), pp. 52–65.

28 McGirt, "Revolution in San Jose."

29 Rosenthal and Masarech, "High-Performance Cultures"; Patrick M. Lencioni, "Make Your Values Mean Something," *Harvard Business Review* (July 2002), pp. 113–117; and Thomas J. Peters and Robert H. Waterman, Jr., *In Search of Excellence* (New York: Warner, 1988).

30 Andrew Wahl, "Culture Shock," *Canadian Business* (October 10–23, 2005), pp. 115–116; and Calvin Leung, Michelle Magnan, and Andrew Wahl, "People Power," *Canadian Business* (October 10–23, 2005), pp. 125–126.

31 Harrison M. Trice and Janice M. Beyer, "Studying Organizational Culture Through Rites and Ceremonials," *Academy of Management Review* 9 (1984), pp. 653–669.

32 Alan Farnham, "Mary Kay's Lessons in Leadership," *Fortune* (September 20, 1993), pp. 68–77.

33 Jarnagan and Slocum, "Creating Cultures Through Mythopoetic Leadership."

34 Joan O'C. Hamilton, "Why Rivals Are Quaking as Nordstrom Heads East," *BusinessWeek* (June 15, 1987), pp. 99–100.

35 Joann S. Lublin, "Theory & Practice: Keeping Clients by Keeping Workers; Unique Efforts to Encourage Employee Loyalty Pay Off for U.K. Ad Shop Mother," *The Wall Street Journal* (November 20, 2006), p. B3.

36 Ian D. Colville and Anthony J. Murphy, "Leadership as the Enabler of Strategizing and Organizing," *Long Range Planning* 39 (2006), pp. 663–677.

37 Betsy Morris, "The Best Place to Work Now (100 Best Companies to Work For, 2006)," *Fortune* (January 23, 2006), pp. 79–86.

38 D. C. Feldman, "The Multiple Socialization of Organization Members," *Academy of Management Review* 6 (1981), pp. 309–318; J. Van Maanen, "Breaking In: Socialization to Work," in R. Dubin, ed., *Handbook of Work, Organization, and Society* (Chicago: Rand-McNally, 1976), p. 67; and Blake E. Ashforth and Alan M. Saks, "Socialization Tactics: Longitudinal Effects on Newcomer Adjustment," *Academy of Management Journal* 39, no. 1 (February 1996), pp. 149–178.

39 Debra L. Nelson and James Campbell Quick, *Organizational Behavior*, 5th ed. (Cincinnati, OH: South-Western, 2006), p. 544.

40 Helena D. C. Thomas and Neil Anderson, "Changes in Newcomers' Psychological Contracts During Organizational Socialization: A Study of Recruits Entering the British Army," *Journal of Organizational Behavior* 19, no. 1 (1998), pp. 745–767.

41 Ashforth and Saks, "Socialization Tactics."

42 Deanne N. Den Hartog, Jaap J. Van Muijen, and Paul L. Koopman, "Linking Transformational Leadership and Organizational Culture," *The Journal of Leadership Studies* 3, no. 4 (1996), pp. 68–83; and Schein, "Organizational Culture."

43 Aili McConnon, "Lessons from a Skinflint CEO," *BusinessWeek* (October 6, 2008), pp. 54–55.

44 Bill Munck, "Changing a Culture of Face Time," *Harvard Business Review* (November 2001), pp. 125–131.

45 Ram Charan and Jerry Useem, "Why Companies Fail," *Fortune* (May 27, 2002), pp. 50–62.

46 Jennifer A. Chatman and Karen A. Jehn, "Assessing the Relationship Between Industry Characteristics and Organizational Culture: How Different Can You Be?" *Academy of Management Journal* 37, no. 3 (1994), pp. 522–553.

47 James R. Detert, Roger G. Schroeder, and John J. Mauriel, "A Framework for Linking Culture and Improvement Initiatives in Organizations," *Academy of Management Review* 25, no. 4 (2000), pp. 850–863.

48 Paul McDonald and Jeffrey Gandz, "Getting Value from Shared Values," *Organizational Dynamics* 21, no. 3 (Winter 1992), pp. 64–76; and Daniel R. Denison and Aneil K. Mishra, "Toward a Theory of Organizational Culture and Effectiveness," *Organization Science* 6, no. 2 (March–April 1995), pp. 204–223.

49 Sara Kehaulani Goo, "Building a 'Googley' Workforce; Corporate Culture Breeds Innovation," *The Washington Post* (October 21, 2006), p. D1; Adam Lashinsky, "Chaos by Design," *Fortune* (October 2, 2006), p. 86; and Adam Lashinsky, "Search and Enjoy," part of "The 100 Best Companies to Work For, 2007," *Fortune* (January 22, 2007), pp. 70–82.

50 Elizabeth Montalbano, "Growing Pains for Google", *Computerworld* (October 20, 2008), pp. 28–31; Adam Lashinsky, "Where Does Google Go Next?" *Fortune* (May 26, 2008), pp. 104–110; and Jessica E. Vascellaro and Scott Morrison, "Google Gears Down for Tougher Times," *The Wall Street Journal* (December 3, 2008), pp. A1, A13.

51 Robert Hooijberg and Frank Petrock, "On Cultural Change: Using the Competing Values Framework to Help Leaders Execute a Transformational Strategy," *Human Resource Management* 32, no. 1 (1993), pp. 29–50.

52 Michelle Conlin, "Netflix: Flex to the Max," *BusinessWeek* (September 24, 2007), pp. 72–74.

53 Stacy Perman, "The Secret Sauce at In-N-Out Burger" (excerpt from *In-N-Out Burger: A Behind-the-Counter Look at the Fast-Food Chain That Breaks All the Rules*), *BusinessWeek* (April 20, 2009), pp. 68–69.

54 Carey Quan Jelernter, "Safeco: Success Depends Partly on Fitting the Mold," *Seattle Times* (June 5, 1986), p. D8.

55 Gordon F. Shea, *Practical Ethics* (New York: American Management Association, 1988); and Linda Klebe Treviño, "Ethical Decision Making in Organizations: A Person-Situation Interactionist Model," *Academy of Management Review* 11 (1986), pp. 601–617.

56 Dawn-Marie Driscoll, "Don't Confuse Legal and Ethical Standards," *Business Ethics* (July/August 1996), p. 44.

57 Brian Griffiths, "Markets Can't Be Improved by Rules, Only by Personal Example," *The Times* (April 9, 2009), p. 30.

58 Ibid.

59 Leslie Wayne, "A Promise to Be Ethical in an Era of Temptation," *The New York Times* (May 30, 2009), p. B1; and Kelley Holland, "Is It Time to Retrain B-Schools?" *The New York Times* (March 15, 2009, p. BU1.

60 Quoted in Steven P. Feldman, "Moral Business Cultures: The Keys to Creating and Maintaining Them," *Organizational Dynamics* 36, no. 2 (2007), pp. 156–170.

61 Alison Boyd, "Employee Traps—Corruption in the Workplace," *Management Review* (September 1997), p. 9.

62 Robert J. House, Andre Delbecq, and Toon W. Taris, "Values-Based Leadership: An Integrated Theory and an Empirical Test" (Working Paper).

63 Noel M. Tichy and Warren G. Bennis, "Managing the Tough Call; Great Leaders Know When Their Values Are on the Line," *Inc.* (November 2007), pp. 36–38.

64 Lawrence Kohlberg, "Moral Stages and Moralization: The Cognitive-Developmental Approach," in T. Likona, ed., *Moral Development and Behavior: Theory, Research, and Social Issues* (New York: Holt, Rinehart & Winston, 1976), pp. 31–53; and Jill W. Graham, "Leadership, Moral Development, and Citizenship Behavior," *Business Ethics Quarterly* 5, no. 1 (January 1995), pp. 43–54.

65 Kathy Whitmire, "Leading Through Shared Values," *Leader to Leader* (Summer 2005), pp. 48–54.

66 Laura Reave, "Spiritual Values and Practices Related to Leadership Effectiveness," *The Leadership Quarterly* 16 (2005), pp. 655–687.

67 Neela Banerjee, "At Bosses' Invitation, Chaplains Come Into Workplace and Onto Payroll," *The New York Times* (December 4, 2006), p. A16.

68 R. A. Giacalone and C. L. Jurkiewicz, "Toward a Science of Workplace Spirituality," in R. A. Giacalone and C. L. Jurkiewicz, eds., *Handbook of Workplace Spirituality and Organizational Performance* (New York: M. E. Sharp, 2003), pp. 3–28; K. Krahnke, R. A. Giacalone, and C. L. Jurkiewicz, "Point-Counterpoint: Measuring Workplace Spirituality," *Journal of Organizational Change Management* 16, no. 4 (2003), pp. 396–405; Louis W. Fry, "Toward a Theory of Ethical and Spiritual Well-Being, and Corporate Social Responsibility Through Spiritual Leadership," in R. A. Giacalone, ed., *Positive Psychology in Business Ethics and Corporate Responsibility* (Greenwich, CT: Information Age Publishing, 2005), pp. 47–83; and I. I. Mitroff and E. A. Denton, *A Spiritual Audit of Corporate America* (San Francisco: Jossey-Bass, 1999).

69 Louis W. Fry, "Toward a Theory of Spiritual Leadership," *The Leadership Quarterly* 14 (2003), pp. 693–727.

70 Ibid.

71 Stephanie Armour, "CEO Helps People Keep Their Homes; That's CitiMortgage Chief's Personal Goal," *USA Today* (April 27, 2009), p. B4; Ruth Simon, "Citi to Allow Jobless to Pay Less on Mortgages for a Time," *The Wall Street Journal Europe* (March 4, 2009), p. 17; and Sanjiv Das, "Viewpoint: Early Intervention Can Stem Foreclosures," *American Banker* (December 10, 2008), p. 11.

72 Fry, "Toward a Theory of Spiritual Leadership."

Chapter 15 References

1 Reported in Graham Bowley and Louise Story, "Crisis Reshaping Wall Street as Stars Begin to Scatter," *The New York Times* (April 12, 2009), p. A1.

2 Maria Bartiromo, "Vikram Pandit of Citi: Man on a Tightrope," *BusinessWeek* (June 22, 2009), p. 12; "Citigroup Shakes Up Management with New CFO and Banking Chief," *National Post* (July 10, 2009), p. FP10; and Paul Davis, "Allison Chews On, Chews Out Banks," *American Banker* (January 14, 2009), p. 1.

3 Bowley and Story, "Crisis Reshaping Wall Street."

4 Steve Lohr, "How Crisis Shapes the Corporate Model," *The New York Times* (March 29, 2009), p. BU4.

5 Marlene Piturro, "The Transformation Officer," *Management Review* (February 2000), pp. 21–25.

6 Greg Jaffe, "Next Chapter; As Iraq War Rages, Army Re-Examines Lessons of Vietnam," *The Wall Street Journal* (March 20, 2006), p. A1.

7 Alain Vas, "Top Management Skills in a Context of Endemic Organizational Change: The Case of Belgacom," *Journal of General Management* 27, no. 1 (Autumn 2001), pp. 71–89.

8 Judy Oppenheimer, "A Top Cop Who Gets It," *More* (June 2009), pp. 86–91, 144.

9 The following discussion is based heavily on John P. Kotter, *Leading Change* (Boston: Harvard Business School Press, 1996), pp. 20–25; and "Leading Change: Why Transformation Efforts Fail," *Harvard Business Review* (March–April 1995), pp. 59–67.

10 Paul Ingrassia, "GM Gets a Second Chance," *The Wall Street Journal Europe* (July 10, 2009), p. 13; and "Ford to Seek Same No-Strike Vow from UAW as GM and Chrysler Obtained," *National Post* (June 18, 2009), p. FP3.

11 Patrick Lencioni, "Find a Rallying Cry," *Leader to Leader* (Summer 2006), pp. 41–44.

12 Patrick Flanagan, "The ABCs of Changing Corporate Culture," *Management Review* (July 1995), pp. 57–61.

13 Richard Gibson, "A New Recipe," *The Wall Street Journal* (July 13, 2009), p. R5; Wendy Lee, "New Owner Wants to Restore Shoney's Chain to 'Glory Days,'" *The Tennessean* online edition (November 18, 2007), http://www.tennessean.com (accessed July 15, 2009); and Jack Hayes, "Industry Waits to See if Davoudpour Can Work His Turnaround Magic at Shoney's" *Nation's Restaurant News* (January 22, 2007), p. 38.

14 Chuck Salter, "On the Road Again," *Fast Company* (January 2002), pp. 50–58.

15 Anna Muoio, "Mint Condition," *Fast Company* (December 1999), pp. 330–348.

16 John P. Kotter, *The Heart of Change: Real-Life Stories of How People Change Their Organizations* (Boston, MA: Harvard Business School Press, 2002), pp. 143–159.

17 Ibid.

18 David L. Cooperrider and Shuresh Srivastva, "Appreciative Inquiry in Organizational Life," in R. Woodman and W. Pasmore, eds., *Research in Organizational Change and Development*, Vol. 1 (Greenwich, CT: JAI Press, 1987); and D. Cooperrider and D. Whitney, *Appreciative Inquiry: A Positive Revolution in Change* (San Francisco, CA: Berrett-Koehler, 2005).

19 Quoted in Dave Kovaleski, "Appreciating Appreciative Inquiry," *Corporate Meetings & Incentives* (August 2008), pp. 10–11.

20 This discussion draws from Sarah Lewis, Jonathan Passmore, and Stefan Cantore, "Using Appreciative Inquiry in Sales Team Development," *Industrial and Commercial Training* 40, no. 4 (2008), pp. 175–180; Steven J. Skinner and Scott W. Kelley, "Transforming Sales Through Appreciative Inquiry," *Psychology & Marketing* 23, no 2 (February 2006), pp. 77–93; and Gabriella Giglio, Silvia Michalcova, and Chris Yates, "Instilling a Culture of Winning at American Express," *Organization Development Journal* 25, no. 4 (Winter 2007), pp. 33–37.

21 See http://appreciativeinquiry.case.edu/practice/bibAiStories.cfm (accessed July 16, 2009) for examples of the uses of appreciative inquiry.

22 Frank Barrett, Dave Nystorm, Paul Tripp, and Mark Zipsie, "Highpoint Leadership Stories," The Leadership Summit; Bold and Enlightened Naval Leaders at Every Level: Forging an Empowered Culture of Excellence, http://appreciativeinquiry.case.edu/uploads/HighpointStories.pdf (accessed July 16, 2009).

23 Debra Meyerson, *Tempered Radicals: How People Use Difference to Inspire Change at Work* (Boston: Harvard Business School Press, 2001).

24 William B. Locander and David L. Luechauer, "Leader as Inquirer: Change Your Approach to Inquiry," *Marketing Management* (September–October 2007), pp. 46–49; Skinner and Kelley, "Transforming Sales Organizations Through Appreciative Inquiry."

25 Thomas J. Griffin, "In the Eye of the Beholder: Interview with Jim 'Gus' Gustafson," *Appreciative Leadership Interviews* (The Taos Institute), http://www.taosinstitute.com/resources/gustafson.html (accessed July 16, 2009); and "Getting to Know . . . Gus Gustafson,

CCL Donor and Alumnus," *Making a Difference: A Report on Activities and Impact from the Center for Creative Leadership*, (Greensboro, NC: Center for Creative Leadership, January 2009), http://www.ccl.org/leadership/pdf/news/newsletters/mad0109.pdf (accessed July 16, 2009).

26. Stanley S. Gryskiewicz, "Cashing In on Creativity at Work," *Psychology Today* (September–October 2000), pp. 63–66.

27. Reena Jana, "Do Ideas Cost Too Much?" part of the section, "Inside Innovation: The 25 Most Innovative Companies," *BusinessWeek* (April 20, 2009), pp. 45–48.

28. Dorothy A. Leonard and Walter C. Swap, *When Sparks Fly: Igniting Creativity in Groups* (Boston: Harvard Business School Press, 1999), pp. 6–8.

29. The elements of creative organizations come from Alan G. Robinson and Sam Stern, *Corporate Creativity: How Innovation and Improvement Actually Happen* (San Francisco: Berrett-Koehler, 1997).

30. Sherry Eng, "Hatching Schemes," *The Industry Standard* (November 27–December 4, 2000), pp. 174–175.

31. Reena Jana, "Brickhouse: Yahoo's Hot Little Incubator," Innovation & Design section, *BusinessWeek* (November 26, 2007), p. 14.

32. Alan Deutschman, "The Fabric of Creativity," *Fast Company* (December 2004), p. 54.

33. Robinson and Stern, *Corporate Creativity,* p. 14.

34. Gail Dutton, "Enhancing Creativity," *Management Review* (November 1996), pp. 44–46.

35. Robert D. Hof, "How Google Fuels Its Idea Factory," *BusinessWeek* (May 12, 2008), p. 54; and "Inside Innovation: The 25 Most Innovative Companies," *BusinessWeek* (April 20, 2009), pp. 45–48.

36. Reported in Teresa M. Amabile and Mukti Khaire, "Creativity and the Role of the Leader," *Harvard Business Review* (October 2008), pp. 100–109.

37. Robert D. Austin, Lee Devin, and Erin Sullivan, "Oops! Accidents Lead to Innovations. So, How Do You Create More Accidents?" *The Wall Street Journal* (July 7, 2008), p. R6.

38. Examples from Phred Dvorak, "Businesses Take a Page from Design Firms; Sloan-Kettering Taps Industry for Innovative Ideas on Management," *The Wall Street Journal* (November 10, 2008), p. B4.

39. Henry Chesbrough, "The Era of Open Innovation," *MIT Sloan Management Review* (Spring 2003), pp. 35–41; Amy Muller and Liisa Välikangas, "Extending the Boundary of Corporate Innovation," *Strategy & Leadership* 30, no. 3 (2002), pp. 4–9; Navi Radjou, "Networked Innovation Drives Profits," *Industrial Management* (January–February 2005), pp. 14–21; Darrell Rigby and Barbara Bilodeau, "The Bain 2005 Management Tool Survey," *Strategy & Leadership* 33, no. 4 (2005), pp. 4–12; Ian Mount, "The Return of the Lone Inventor," *FSB (Fortune Small Business)* (March 2005), p. 18; Jena McGregor, M. Arndt, R. Berner, I. Rowley, K. Hall, G. Edmondson, S. Hamm, M. Ihlwan, and A. Reinhardt, "The World's Most Innovative Companies," *BusinessWeek* (April 24, 2006), pp. 62ff; and Henry Chesbrough, "The Logic of Open Innovation: Managing Intellectual Property," *California Management Review* 45, no. 3 (Spring 2003), pp. 33–58.

40. Simona Covel, "My Brain, Your Brawn; Big Companies Are on the Prowl for Small Businesses That Will Hand Over Their Best Ideas," *The Wall Street Journal* (October 13, 2008), p. R12; and Jacques Bughin, Michael Chui, and Brad Johnson, "The Next Step in Open Innovation," *The McKinsey Quarterly* (June 2008), http://www.mckinseyquarterly.com (accessed July 15, 2009).

41. Gary P. Pisano and Roberto Verganti, "Which Kind of Collaboration Is Right For You?" *Harvard Business Review* (December 2008), pp. 78–86.

42. Rob Cross, Andrew Hargadon, Salvatore Parise, and Robert J. Thomas, "Business Insight (A Special Report); Together We Innovate: How Can Companies Come Up with New Ideas? By Getting Employees Working with One Another," *The Wall Street Journal* (September 15, 2007), p. R6.

43. John Bessant, Kathrin Möslein, and Bettina Von Stamm, "Business Insight (A Special Report): In Search of Innovation," *The Wall Street Journal* (June 22, 2009), p. R4.

44. These tips are based on Leigh Thompson, "Improving the Creativity of Organizational Work Groups," *Academy of Management Executive* 17 (2003), pp. 96–109; and Bruce Nussbaum, "The Power of Design," *BusinessWeek* (May 17, 2004), pp. 86–94.

45. David Kirkpatrick, "Throw It at the Wall and See if It Sticks," *Fortune* (December 12, 2005), pp. 142–150.

46. Jared Sandberg, "Brainstorming Works Best if People Scramble for Ideas on Their Own," *The Wall Street Journal* (January 13, 2006), p. B1.

47. Reena Jana, "Real Life Imitates *Real World*," *BusinessWeek* (March 23–30, 2009), p. 42.

48. R. B. Gallupe, W. H. Cooper, M. L. Grise, and L. M. Bastianutti, "Blocking Electronic Brainstorms," *Journal of Applied Psychology* 79 (1994), pp. 77–86; R. B. Gallupe and W. H. Cooper, "Brainstorming Electronically," *Sloan Management Review* (Fall 1993), pp. 27–36; and Alison Stein Wellner, "A Perfect Brainstorm," *Inc.* (October 2003), pp. 31–35.

49. Burt Helm, "Wal-Mart, Please Don't Leave Me," *BusinessWeek* (October 9, 2006), pp. 84–89.

50. Wellner, "A Perfect Brainstorm"; Gallupe and Cooper, "Brainstorming Electronically."

51. Helm, "Wal-Mart, Please Don't Leave Me"; and GSD&M Idea City, http://www.ideacity.com (accessed July 20, 2009).

52. Edward DeBono, *Serious Creativity: Using the Power of Lateral Thinking to Create New Ideas* (New York: HarperBusiness, 1992).

53. Dave Waller, "The Gospel According to Edward DeBono," *Management Today* (August 2007), http://www.managementtoday.co.uk (accessed July 27, 2009).

54. Francine Russo, "The Hidden Secrets of the Creative Mind," *Time* (January 16, 2006), pp. 89–90.

55. Ronald T. Kadish, "Mix People Up," *Harvard Business Review* (August 2002), pp. 39–49.

56. Carol Glover and Steve Smethurst, "Creative License," *People Management* (March 20, 2003), pp. 31–34; Michael Michalko, *Thinkertoys*, 2nd ed., (Berkeley, CA: Ten Speed Press, 2006); and Joseph Weber, "Keeping the Whimsy Coming," *BusinessWeek* (December 5, 2005), pp. 54–55.

57. Derm Barrett, *The Paradox Process: Creative Business Solutions…Where You Least Expect to Find Them* (New York: American Management Association, 1997).

58. R. Donald Gamache and Robert Lawrence Kuhn, *The Creativity Infusion: How Managers Can Start and Sustain Creativity and Innovation* (New York: Harper & Row, 1989); Alison Stein Wellner, "Cleaning Up," *Inc.* (October 2003), p. 35; and Roger von Oech, *A Kick in the Seat of the Pants* (New York: Harper & Row, 1986).

59. Alison Stein Wellner, "Creative Control; Even Bosses Need Time to Dream," *Inc.* (July 2007), pp. 40–42.

60. Richard A. Lovett, "Jog Your Brain," *Psychology Today* (May/June 2006), pp. 55–56; and Mary Carmichael, "Stronger, Faster, Smarter," *Newsweek* (March 26, 2007), pp. 38–46.

61. This word challenge and the answers given for it later in the chapter are from Will Shortz, "RD Challenge," *Readers Digest* (March 2004), p. 204; and Sarnoff A. Mednick, "The Associative Basis of the Creative Process," *Psychological Review* 69, no. 3 (1962), pp. 220–232.

62. This question and the answer given later are from Tahl Raz, "How Would You Design Bill Gates' Bathroom?" *Inc.* (May, 2003), p. 35.

63. These match puzzles are from Michael Michalko, *Thinkertoys,* 2nd ed. (Berkeley, CA: Ten Speed Press, 2006).

64. Based on Paul Stebel, "Why Do Employees Resist Change?" *Harvard Business Review* (May–June 1996), pp. 86–92.

65. Michael A. Roberto and Lynne C. Levesque, "The Art of Making Changes Stick," *MIT Sloan Management Review* (Summer 2005), pp. 53–60.

66 Shaul Fox and Yair Amichai-Hamburger, "The Power of Emotional Appeals in Promoting Organizational Change Programs," *Academy of Management Executive* 15, no. 4 (2001), pp. 84–95.

67 Peter Richardson and D. Keith Denton, "Communicating Change," *Human Resource Management* 35, no. 2 (Summer 1996), pp. 203–216.

68 Dan S. Cohen, "Why Change Is an Affair of the Heart," *CIO* (December 1, 2005), pp. 48–52.

69 T. J. Larkin and Sandar Larkin, "Reaching and Changing Frontline Employees," *Harvard Business Review* (May–June 1996), pp. 95–104; and Rob Muller, "Training for Change," *Canadian Business Review* (Spring 1995), pp. 16–19.

70 Phillip H. Mirvis, Amy L. Sales, and Edward J. Hackett, "The Implementation and Adoption of New Technology in Organizations: The Impact of Work, People, and Culture," *Human Resource Management* 30 (Spring 1991), pp. 113–139.

71 Dean Foust with Gerry Khermouch, "Repairing the Coke Machine," *BusinessWeek* (March 19, 2001), pp. 86–88.

72 Mark Jepperson, "Focused Journey of Change," *Industrial Management* (July–August 2005), pp. 8–13.

73 Reported in Catherine Rampell, with Jack Healy, "Layoffs Spread to More Sectors of the Economy," *The New York Times* (January 27, 2009), p. A1.

74 James R. Morris, Wayne F. Cascio, and Clifford E. Young, "Downsizing After All These Years: Questions and Answers About Who Did It, How Many Did It, and Who Benefited from It," *Organizational Dynamics* (Winter 1999), pp. 78–86; William McKinley, Carol M. Sanchez, and Allen G. Schick, "Organizational Downsizing: Constraining, Cloning, Learning," *Academy of Management Executive* 9, no. 3 (1995), pp. 32–42; Stephen Doerflein and James Atsaides, "Corporate Psychology: Making Downsizing Work," *Electrical World* (September–October 1999), pp. 41–43; and Brett C. Luthans and Steven M. Sommer, "The Impact of Downsizing on Workplace Attitudes," *Group and Organization Management* 2, no. 1 (1999), pp. 46–70.

75 Kathleen Madigan, "More Firms Cut Pay to Save Jobs," *The Wall Street Journal* (June 9, 2009), p. A4; Steven Greenhouse, "Out of Work, Part Time," *The New York Times* (June 16, 2009), p. B1; and Laura Petrecca, "More Companies Turn to Furloughs to Save Money, Jobs," *USA Today* (March 5, 2009), p. B1.

76 Kate O'Sullivan, "Plan B: For Both Altruistic and Business Reasons, Some Companies Are Seeking Alternatives to Layoffs," *CFO* (February 2009), p. 51.

77 McKinley, Sanchez, and Schick, "Organizational Downsizing."

78 K. S. Cameron, S. J. Freeman, and A. K. Mishra, "Downsizing and Redesigning Organizations," in G. P. Huber and W. H. Glick, eds., *Organizational Change and Redesign* (New York: Oxford University Press, 1993), pp. 19–63.

79 These techniques are based on Bob Nelson, "The Care of the Un-Downsized," *Training & Development* (April 1997), pp. 40–43; Shari Caudron, "Teach Downsizing Survivors How to Thrive," *Personnel Journal,* (January 1996), p. 38ff; Joel Brockner, "Managing the Effects of Layoffs on Survivors," *California Management Review* (Winter 1992), pp. 9–28; Kim S. Cameron, "Strategies for Successful Organizational Downsizing," *Human Resource Management* 33, no. 2 (Summer 1994), pp. 189–211; and Kate O'Sullivan, "How to Talk About Layoffs." *CFO* (February 2009), pp. 44–51.

80 O'Sullivan, "How to Talk About Layoffs."

NAME INDEX

INDEX OF ORGANIZATIONS

SUBJECT INDEX